TAXATION OF PARTNERSHIPS AND LIMITED LIABILITY COMPANIES TAXED AS PARTNERSHIPS

(2016–Pub.3245)

TAXATION OF PARTNERSHIPS AND LIMITED LIABILITY COMPANIES TAXED AS PARTNERSHIPS

J. Martin Burke
Professor of Law Emeritus
University of Montana
School of Law

Michael K. Friel
Professor of Law and Director
Graduate Tax Program
University of Florida
Levin College of Law

CAROLINA ACADEMIC PRESS
Durham, North Carolina

Copyright © 2016
Carolina Academic Press, LLC
All Rights Reserved

Casebook ISBN: 978-1-4224-1708-9
Library of Congress Control Number: 2016944370

Carolina Academic Press, LLC
700 Kent Street
Durham, NC 27701
Telephone (919) 489-7486
Fax (919) 493-5668
www.caplaw.com

Printed in the United States of America

Dedication

To Jackie and Jonathan — MKF

To my Mother and Father — JMB

Preface

Partnerships have long been a popular choice for taxpayers to carry on business and investment activities. But a 1988 ruling by the Internal Revenue Service that a limited liability company could be taxed as a partnership — which led to the enactment of limited liability statutes in every state — and the 1997 adoption by the Treasury of the so-called "Check-the-Box" regulations — which permitted most unincorporated entities with more than one member to elect to be taxed as a partnership — brought about a dramatic increase in the number of business entities taxed as partnerships. As a result, the study of Subchapter K of the Internal Revenue Code addressing the taxation of partners and partnerships has taken on increased importance. Law students who envision themselves in business, real estate or estate planning practices, as well as those who aspire to pursue careers focused specifically on tax planning, must have a firm understanding of not only the state laws related to partnerships and limited liability companies, but also the applicable federal laws governing their taxation.

We have designed this book to introduce law students to the fundamental principles, Internal Revenue Code and Regulations provisions, cases and administrative rulings governing taxation pursuant to Subchapter K. Following an introductory chapter, this casebook contains 20 chapters tracking, from formation to liquidation, the life of a partnership or a limited liability company taxed as a partnership. Each of these 20 chapters begins with a set of problems followed by an assignment to applicable materials, including Code and Regulation provisions, case law and administrative rulings. Each chapter also includes an Overview, which, while not an exhaustive analysis of the chapter topic, will provide a perspective and a foundation for your study of the Code and Regulation provisions as well as case law and administrative material pertinent to the chapter topic. We urge you to begin each chapter by reviewing the problems, reading the chapter Overview and studying the assigned materials. You should then return to the problem set and complete each problem.

Because every area of the tax law has its own vocabulary, each of these 20 chapters contains a vocabulary section of significant terms and phrases introduced in the chapter. In addition, each chapter provides a list of measurable learning objectives. Both the vocabulary section and the list of learning objectives are intended as self-assessment tools. After completing the assignment in each chapter, you should test your knowledge of the chapter by defining in your own words each term listed in the vocabulary section and by assessing your understanding of the materials through use of the learning objectives.

We welcome you now to the start of a challenging and most rewarding journey into the world of Subchapter K and the study of partnership taxation.

Acknowledgments

We gratefully acknowledge the excellent work of our long-time editor, Elisabeth Ebben, previously of LexisNexis and now with Carolina Academic Press. We deeply appreciate her attention to detail, thoughtful questions and suggestions, collaborative spirit, patience and encouragement.

Table of Contents

Chapter 1   **INTRODUCTION TO PARTNERSHIP TAXATION** 1

A.	Definition of "Partnership" and "Partner" for Subchapter K Purposes	2
B.	Choice of Entity: An Overview of Partnership Classification and its Benefits	3
1.	General and Limited Partnerships and Limited Liability Companies	3
2.	Tax Benefits of Partnership Classification	5
a.	Number of owners, character of owners, and classes of equity interests.	5
b.	Nonrecognition of gain and loss on contributions of property.	5
c.	Single level of tax.	5
d.	Deductibility of losses.	6
e.	Rates of tax.	7
f.	Tax treatment of nonliquidating distributions.	8
g.	Liquidating distributions.	9
C.	Classification of Unincorporated Business Entities: The Check-the-Box Regulations	9
1.	History	9
2.	Current Law: Classification Under the Check-the-Box Regulations	14

Chapter 2   **NONRECOGNITION OF GAIN OR LOSS ON CONTRIBUTION OF PROPERTY TO A PARTNERSHIP** 17

I.	PROBLEMS	17
II.	VOCABULARY	18
III.	OBJECTIVES	18
IV.	OVERVIEW	19
A.	Nonrecognition in General	19
B.	A Partner's Outside Basis: Preservation of the Contributing Partner's Gain or Loss	20
C.	The Partnership's Inside Basis: Preservation of Gain and Loss at Partnership Level	21
D.	Scope of Nonrecognition under § 721	24
1.	Section 721 and Section 1245 Property	24
2.	Section 721 and Section 453B	25
E.	Property	25
F.	Holding Periods	26
G.	Character of Gain or Loss on Disposition of Contributed Property	27
H.	Conclusion	29

Table of Contents

        United States v. Stafford 30

Chapter 3   **CONTRIBUTION OF ENCUMBERED PROPERTY** 37

I.   PROBLEMS 37
II.   VOCABULARY 38
III.   OBJECTIVES 38
IV.   OVERVIEW 39
   A.   General Principles Regarding Debt Related to the Acquisition or Disposition of Property 39
   B.   Contributed Property Encumbered by Recourse Debt 41
      1.   Allocation of Recourse Liabilities 43
      2.   Treatment of Nonrecourse Liabilities 49
   C.   Contributed Property Encumbered by Nonrecourse Liability Not in Excess of Basis 49
   D.   Contributed Property Encumbered by Nonrecourse Liabilities in Excess of Basis 51
   E.   Treatment of Accounts Payable 52
   F.   Matters for Future Consideration 53

Chapter 4   **CONTRIBUTION OF SERVICES IN EXCHANGE FOR PARTNERSHIP INTERESTS** 55

I.   PROBLEMS 55
II.   VOCABULARY 57
III.   OBJECTIVES 57
IV.   OVERVIEW 57
   A.   Capital Interest for Services 59
   B.   Profits Interest for Services 64
   C.   The 2005 Proposed Regulations Relating to Compensatory Transfers of Partnership Interests 66
   D.   Conclusion 71
        Diamond v. Commissioner 72
        McDougal v. Commissioner 77

Chapter 5   **THE PARTNERSHIP BALANCE SHEET AND PARTNERS' CAPITAL ACCOUNTS** 83

I.   PROBLEMS 83
II.   VOCABULARY 84
III.   OBJECTIVES 84
IV.   OVERVIEW 85
   A.   The Partnership Balance Sheet 85

Table of Contents

B.	Impact of Partnership Operations and Transactions on the Balance Sheet	88
C.	Capital Accounts and Service Partners	97
D.	Conclusion	102

Chapter 6	**THE PARTNERSHIP TAXABLE YEAR; EXPENSES OF PARTNERSHIP FORMATION**	**103**
I.	PROBLEMS	103
II.	VOCABULARY	104
III.	OBJECTIVES	104
IV.	OVERVIEW	104
A.	The Partnership Taxable Year	104
1.	The Partnership as an Entity for Tax Computation Purposes	104
2.	Year in Which Partnership Income Is Includible by Partners; Taxable Year of a Partnership	106
B.	Partnership Formation Expenses: § 709	113
1.	Organizational Expenses	113
2.	Syndication Expenses	114

Chapter 7	**THE PASS-THROUGH OF INCOME, GAIN, LOSS, DEDUCTION, AND CREDIT**	**115**
I.	PROBLEMS	115
II.	VOCABULARY	116
III.	OBJECTIVES	116
IV.	OVERVIEW	116
A.	Distributive Share	117
B.	Accounting for a Partner's Distributive Share	120
C.	Impact of Income/Deduction Pass-Through on a Partner's Basis	125
D.	Impact of Pass-through of Income, Gain, Loss, and Deduction on Capital Accounts	129
E.	Conclusion	131

Chapter 8	**THE § 704(d) LIMITATION ON THE DEDUCTION OF PASSED-THROUGH LOSSES**	**135**
I.	PROBLEMS	135
II.	VOCABULARY	136
III.	OBJECTIVES	136
IV.	OVERVIEW	136
A.	Determination of Adjusted Outside Basis for Purposes of Applying § 704(d)	137
B.	Treatment of Losses in Excess of the § 704(d) Limitation	138

Table of Contents

C.	Allocation of Loss Limitation among Losses of Different Character	139
D.	Impact of § 704(d) on Capital Accounts	139
E.	Who Benefits from the Carryover of a Disallowed Loss?	140

NOTE ON THE AT-RISK RULES AND THE PASSIVE ACTIVITY LOSS RULES 143

Chapter 9   ALLOCATION OF PARTNERSHIP INCOME AND DEDUCTIONS: § 704(b) 149

I.	PROBLEMS	149
II.	VOCABULARY	151
III.	OBJECTIVES	152
IV.	OVERVIEW	152
A.	Pre-1976 History	153
B.	The 1976 Reform Act: Codification of the "Substantial Economic Effect" Test	154
C.	The § 704(b) Regulations	156
1.	The Substantial Economic Effect Test	157
a.	The Economic Effect Test.	157
i.	The Primary Test for Economic Effect.	158
ii.	The Alternative Test for Economic Effect.	163
iii.	The Economic Equivalence Test.	166
b.	The Substantiality Test.	167
i.	Shifting Allocations.	167
ii.	Transitory Allocations.	170
iii.	Allocations with After-Tax Economic Consequences.	172
2.	The Partner's-Interest-in-the-Partnership Test	175
D.	Conclusion	179
	Orrisch v. Commissioner	179
	Revenue Ruling 99-43	183

NOTE ON PARTNERSHIP INTERESTS CREATED BY GIFT 189

Chapter 10   CONTRIBUTED PROPERTY: § 704(c)(1)(A) ALLOCATIONS 193

I.	PROBLEMS	193
II.	VOCABULARY	195
III.	OBJECTIVES	195
IV.	OVERVIEW	196
A.	Pre-1984 Law	196
B.	Current Law: The Enactment of § 704(c)(1)(A)	200
C.	Current Law: "Generally Reasonable" Allocation Methods	202
1.	The Traditional Method	203
a.	Allocation of Gain or Loss on Sale of Nondepreciable § 704(c)	

Table of Contents

		Property. ... 204
	b.	Allocation of Depreciation Deductions with Respect to Depreciable § 704(c) Property. ... 207
	c.	Allocation of Gain or Loss on the Sale of Depreciable Property. ... 211
2.		Traditional Method with Curative Allocations ... 212
3.		Remedial Allocations Method ... 215
D.		Special Rule When Contributed Property Has Built-In Loss ... 219
E.		Exception for "Small Disparities" ... 224
F.		Revaluation of Property: the "Booking-up" and "Booking-down" of Capital Accounts and the Application of § 704(c) ... 224
G.		Conclusion ... 227

Chapter 11   ALLOCATION OF NONRECOURSE DEDUCTIONS .. 229

I.	PROBLEMS ... 229
II.	VOCABULARY ... 231
III.	OBJECTIVES ... 231
IV.	OVERVIEW ... 231
A.	Introduction ... 231
B.	Allocation of Nonrecourse Deductions: Introduction to the Safe Harbor Rules ... 234
C.	Allocation of Nonrecourse Deductions: Definitions and Basic Principles ... 236
1.	Nonrecourse Deductions ... 236
2.	Partnership Minimum Gain ... 236
3.	Increase in Partnership Minimum Gain ... 237
4.	Partnership Minimum Gain as a Measure of Nonrecourse Deductions ... 239
5.	Decrease in Partnership Minimum Gain ... 240
6.	Partner's Share of Partnership Minimum Gain ... 240
7.	Partner's Share of Partnership Minimum Gain Treated as Capital Account Deficit Restoration Obligations ... 242
8.	Partner's Share of the Net Decrease in Partnership Minimum Gain .. 245
D.	The Safe Harbor Requirements ... 246
1.	The Minimum Gain Chargeback Requirement ... 246
2.	The Reasonable Consistency Requirement ... 247
	Commissioner v. Tufts ... 249

Chapter 12   ALLOCATION OF RECOURSE AND NONRECOURSE LIABILITIES ... 259

I.	PROBLEMS ... 259
II.	VOCABULARY ... 261

Table of Contents

III.	OBJECTIVES	261
IV.	OVERVIEW	262
A.	History	263
B.	Definition of Liability	265
C.	Allocation of Recourse Liabilities	266
D.	Allocation of Nonrecourse Liabilities	274
	Revenue Ruling 95-41	281

Chapter 13   TRANSACTIONS BETWEEN PARTNERS AND PARTNERSHIPS 285

I.	PROBLEMS	285
II.	VOCABULARY	286
III.	OBJECTIVES	287
IV.	OVERVIEW	287
A.	Tax Treatment of Partner/Partnership Transactions Prior to the Internal Revenue Code of 1954	288
B.	Tax Treatment of Partner/Partnership Transactions: § 707(a)(1) and (c)	291
1.	When Does a Partner Act in Her Capacity as a Partner?	292
2.	Transactions Engaged in by a Partner in a Nonpartner Capacity — § 707(a)(1)	294
3.	Guaranteed Payments	295
a.	Tax consequences of guaranteed payments.	295
b.	Payment.	296
c.	"Determined without reference to the income of the partnership."	296
d.	Capitalization of guaranteed payment.	297
e.	Application of § 707(c) to a fixed amount guaranteed payment.	298
f.	Application of § 707(c) to "minimum amount guaranteed payments."	299
g.	Transfer of partnership property other than cash in satisfaction of a guaranteed payment.	301
4.	Distributive Share — Partner Acting in Her Capacity as Partner and Payments Determined with Reference to Partnership Income	301
D.	Conclusion	302
	Revenue Ruling 81-301	302
	Revenue Ruling 69-180	304

Chapter 14   PARTNERSHIP DISTRIBUTIONS 307

PART A:	Partnership Distributions — General Rules	307
I.	PROBLEMS	307
II.	VOCABULARY	309

Table of Contents

III.		OBJECTIVES	309
IV.		OVERVIEW	309
	A.	Nonliquidating Distributions	311
	1.	The Nonrecognition Rule of § 731	311
	2.	Related Rules Applicable to Nonliquidating Distributions	313
	a.	Basis of Distributed Property — The General Rule of § 732	313
	b.	Impact on Distributee's Outside Basis — § 733	315
	c.	Impact on Capital Accounts — Reg. § 1.704-1(b)(2)(iv)(b)(5)	316
	d.	Holding Period of Distributed Property — §§ 735 and 1223	316
	e.	Character of Gain or Loss on Subsequent Sale of Distributed Property — § 735	316
	f.	Recognition of Gain on Distributions of Money — §§ 731 and 741	318
	3.	Distributions of Encumbered Assets — § 752	320
	4.	The § 732(a)(2) Limitation and the § 732(c) Allocation of Outside Basis Among Distributed Property	322
	B.	Liquidating Distributions	326
	1.	Recognition of Loss	327
	2.	Potential Increase or Decrease in Basis of Assets (Other than Unrealized Receivables and Inventory) Distributed in Liquidation of the Partners' Interests	329
	C.	Other Provisions Related to Liquidating Distributions	332
		Revenue Ruling 79-205	332
		Revenue Ruling 94-4	335
	PART B:	Distribution of Marketable Securities	337
I.		PROBLEMS	337
II.		VOCABULARY	337
III.		OBJECTIVES	338
IV.		OVERVIEW	338

Chapter 15   INSIDE BASIS ADJUSTMENTS UNDER § 734   343

I.		PROBLEMS	343
II.		VOCABULARY	344
III.		OBJECTIVES	344
IV.		OVERVIEW	345
	A.	Basis Disparities Created by Certain Partnership Distributions	345
	B.	The § 754 Election and the § 734(b) Adjustment	349
	C.	Application of § 734(b) to Examples (1)–(4) in Part A	353
	D.	Additional Examples of § 734(b) Adjustments	357
	E.	The Mandatory Basis Adjustment of § 734(d): The Substantial Basis

Table of Contents

	Reduction Rule	359
F.	The Partnership Anti-Abuse Rules	361

Chapter 16   DISPROPORTIONATE DISTRIBUTIONS: § 751(b) 363

I.	PROBLEMS	363
II.	VOCABULARY	364
III.	OBJECTIVES	364
IV.	OVERVIEW	364
A.	The Purpose of § 751(b)	365
B.	Application of § 751(b)	367
C.	Limitations and Exceptions	378
D.	§ 751(b) — An Imperfect Remedy	379
E.	The Proposed § 751(b) Regulations	380
	Revenue Ruling 84-102	386

Chapter 17   DISTRIBUTIONS TERMINATING A RETIRING PARTNER'S INTEREST 389

I.	PROBLEMS	389
II.	VOCABULARY	390
III.	OBJECTIVES	390
IV.	OVERVIEW	391
A.	Section 736 Classification	392
B.	Tax Significance of § 736 Classification of Payments to a Retiring Partner	392
1.	Section 736(a) Payments — Guaranteed Payments	393
2.	Section 736(a) payments — Distributive Share	393
3.	Section 736(b) Payments — Distributions	393
4.	Application of § 751(b)	394
5.	Section 736(b) payments — Impact on Partnership	394
C.	The 1993 Amendments to § 736 and § 751(c)	395
D.	Application of § 736 under Current Law	398
E.	Liquidating a Partner's Interest by a Series of Distributions	402
F.	Conclusion	407
	Commissioner v. Jackson Investment Company	408

Chapter 18   DISGUISED PAYMENTS FOR SERVICES AND DISGUISED SALES OF PROPERTY 411

I.	PROBLEMS	411
II.	VOCABULARY	412
III.	OBJECTIVES	412

Table of Contents

IV.	OVERVIEW	413
A.	Disguised Payments for Services	413
B.	Disguised Sales	417
1.	Definition of Disguised Sale	418
2.	Two-Year Presumption	419
3.	Tax Consequences of a Sale	419
4.	Liabilities	420
5.	Debt-Financed Distribution	423
6.	Guaranteed Payments and Preferred Returns; Cash Flow Distributions; Reimbursement for Preformation Expenses; Partnership-to-Partner Sales	423

Chapter 19   **DISTRIBUTIONS OF § 704(c) PROPERTY AND DISTRIBUTIONS OF PROPERTY TO THE CONTRIBUTING PARTNER** **425**

I.	PROBLEMS	425
II.	VOCABULARY	426
III.	OBJECTIVES	426
IV.	OVERVIEW	427
A.	Mixing Bowl Transactions	427
B.	Distributions of § 704(c) Property	427
C.	Distributions to the Partner Who Contributed § 704(c) Property	430
D.	Application of §§ 704(c)(1)(B) and 737 to the Same Transaction	434

Chapter 20   **TRANSFERS OF PARTNERSHIP INTERESTS** **437**

	PART A:	SALE OR EXCHANGE OF A PARTNERSHIP INTEREST	437
I.	PROBLEMS		437
II.	VOCABULARY		439
III.	OBJECTIVES		439
IV.	OVERVIEW		439
A.	Tax Consequences to the Transferor Partner		440
1.	The Entity vs. Aggregate Approach to Partnership Taxation		440
a.	Entity approach.		440
b.	Aggregate approach.		441
2.	Application of Section 751(a): General Rules		442
3.	Special Look-through Rules with Respect to Capital Gain		444
B.	Tax Consequences to the Transferee		445
1.	In General		445
2.	§ 754 and the Basis Adjustment under § 743		447
a.	The § 754 Election.		447
b.	The § 743(b) adjustments to basis.		447

Table of Contents

	c.	§ 755 — Allocation of § 743(b) Adjustments.	449
	d.	The Section 743(b) Adjustment to Basis when a Partnership Holds Section 704(c) Property.	451
	e.	The Section 743 Adjustment to Basis when Liabilities Encumber Partnership Property.	452
	3.	Special Basis to Transferee — § 732(d)	453
C.		Conclusion	454
		Ledoux v. Commissioner	455

PART B: THE VARYING INTERESTS RULE ... 463
I. PROBLEMS ... 463
II. VOCABULARY ... 464
III. OBJECTIVES ... 464
IV. OVERVIEW ... 464
   A. Varying Interests: The General Rule ... 465
   B. Allocating Distributive Shares ... 465
   C. Exceptions to the Varying Interest Allocation Rules ... 468
   D. Extraordinary Items ... 468
   E. The Ten-Step Allocation Process ... 469
   F. Allocable Cash Basis Items ... 471

PART C: THE DEATH OF A PARTNER ... 473
I. PROBLEMS ... 473
II. VOCABULARY ... 474
III. OBJECTIVES ... 474
IV. OVERVIEW ... 474
   A. Closing of Partnership Taxable Year ... 475
   B. Basis, Income in Respect of a Decedent, and their Interaction ... 475
   C. Inside Basis Adjustments ... 478

PART D: TERMINATION OF A PARTNERSHIP ... 479
I. PROBLEMS ... 479
II. VOCABULARY ... 480
III. OBJECTIVES ... 480
IV. OVERVIEW ... 480
   A. Cessation of Business ... 481
   B. Termination Consequences Under § 708(b)(1)(A) ... 481
   C. Sale or Exchange of 50-Percent of Interests within 12 Months ... 481
   D. Consequences of Termination under § 708(b)(1)(B) ... 482
NOTE ON MERGERS AND DIVISIONS OF PARTNERSHIPS. ... 483

Table of Contents

Chapter 21	**THE ANTI-ABUSE REGULATIONS**	**489**
I.	PROBLEMS	489
II.	VOCABULARY	489
III.	OBJECTIVES	490
IV.	OVERVIEW	490

Table of Cases. TC-1
Table of Statutes. TS-1

Chapter 1

INTRODUCTION TO PARTNERSHIP TAXATION

As its title indicates, this casebook focuses on the taxation of business entities treated as partnerships for purposes of Subchapter K of the Internal Revenue Code (§§ 701-777) (hereinafter "partnerships") and the owners (hereinafter "partners") of those entities. The casebook tracks the life of a partnership from its formation to its liquidation. It addresses a broad range of tax issues that arise throughout the partnership's life, including the classification of business entities as partnerships and the tax consequences of partnership operations and the various transactions that occur between partners and their partnerships or third parties. It examines contributions made by partners to the partnership; the allocation of partnership income, gain, loss, deductions, and credits among the partners; liquidating and nonliquidating distributions made to partners; the sale of partnership interests; the retirement or death of a partner; and the liquidation of the partnership itself.

In the world of federal tax law, 1954 was a watershed year. It is the year Congress enacted the Internal Revenue Code of 1954, replacing the Internal Revenue Code of 1939. As part of its 1954 Code revision effort, Congress enacted "the first comprehensive statutory treatment of partners and partnerships in the history of the income tax laws." Underscoring the importance of its work in this regard, the House Ways and Means Committee noted:

> The existing tax treatment of partners and partnerships is among the most confused in the entire income tax field. The present statutory provisions are wholly inadequate. The published regulations, rulings, and court decisions are incomplete and frequently contradictory. As a result, partners today cannot form, operate, or dissolve a partnership with any assurance as to tax consequences.
>
> The confusion is particularly unfortunate in view of the great number of business enterprises and ventures carried on in partnership form. It should also be noted that the partnership form of organization is much more commonly employed by small businesses and in farming operations than the corporate form. [H. Rep. No. 1337, p. 65, 83 Cong. 2nd Sess., P.L. 83-591(1954).]

The Committee's assessment of the status of federal tax law related to partners and partnerships prior 1954 was accurate. While the Internal Revenue Code of 1939 specifically provided that partnerships were not taxable entities but rather pass-through entities, it provided no specific guidance regarding the tax treatment of partners or partnerships with respect to basic matters such as contributions to partnerships, liquidating or nonliquidating distributions by partnerships, the transfer of partnership interests by sale or on a partner's death, the determination of a partnership's taxable year, transactions between partners and their partnerships, and payments made to a retiring partner or a deceased partner's estate or heirs.[1] In enacting what is today Subchapter K of the Internal Revenue Code, Congress in 1954 addressed each of these and other important matters, while providing a much fuller development of the relatively few partnership provisions contained in the 1939 Code. Although Congress has amended some of the 1954 provisions and added additional provisions to Subchapter K, the provisions it enacted in 1954 continue to provide most of the basic rules regarding the tax treatment of partners and partnerships.

As will become clear, the provisions of Subchapter K and the regulations interpreting those provisions treat partnerships for certain purposes as entities separate from their partners much as a corporation is an entity separate from its shareholders. Thus, for example, a partnership has its own taxable year. § 706(b)(1). For other purposes, however, Subchapter K and the regulations ignore the partnership entity and treat a partnership as simply an aggregate of its partners or members akin to a group of sole proprietors, each of whom has a separate interest in partnership assets and operations. Thus, for example, Subchapter K provides that a partnership is not a taxable entity, but rather one in which the income, gain, loss, deductions, and credits simply pass through the partnership to the partners or members to be reported by them on their respective tax returns. §§ 701, 702.

A. Definition of "Partnership" and "Partner" for Subchapter K Purposes

The provisions of Subchapter K specifically apply to "partnerships" and "partners." Section 7701(a)(2) provides that, for purposes of Title 26 of the United States Code (and thus, for purposes of Subchapter K), a "partnership" includes "a syndicate, group, pool, joint venture, or other unincorporated organization through or by means of which any business, financial operation or venture is carried on, and which is not . . . a corporation or a trust or estate."[2] The term "partner" means "a member of a partnership." See Reg. § 1.761-1(a) and (b). A partner can be an individual, a corporation, another partnership, or any other legal entity. Regulation § 301.7701-2(c)(1) makes clear that, to be treated as a partnership for purposes of Subchapter K, an organization must have at least two members.

What is apparent from the above definition of "partnership" for purposes of the Internal Revenue Code is that, even though an entity is not organized as a

---

[1] The partnership provisions of the 1939 Code were contained in Supplement F of Subchapter C of that Code. In 1953, immediately prior to the enactment of the Internal Revenue Code of 1954, Supplement F, titled "Partnerships" consisted of 10 provisions headed as follows: Section 181 — Partnership Not Taxable; Section 182 — Tax of Partners (this provision in cursory fashion addressed the pass-through of income and deductions to partners); Section 183 — Computation of Partnership Income; Section 184 — Credits against Net Income; Section 186 Taxes of Foreign Countries and Possessions of United States; Section 187 — Partnership Returns; Section 188 — Different Taxable Years of Partner and Partnership; Section 189 — Net Operating Losses; Section 190 — Allowance of Amortization Deduction; and Section 191 — Family Partnerships.

[2] This definition mirrors the definition of "partnership" that § 761(a) provides for purposes of Subtitle A of the Code.

partnership under state law, it can still be classified as a "partnership" for purposes of the federal tax law. Furthermore, while entities organized as partnerships under state law will have at least one partner (a general partner) who is liable for the obligations of the partnership, the above definition of "partnership" does not require that any member of an entity classified as a "partnership" for federal tax purposes be liable for the obligations of that entity. Thus, for example, an entity organized as a limited liability company under state law and classified as a partnership for federal tax purposes provides limited liability to *all* and not just some of its members.

B. Choice of Entity: An Overview of Partnership Classification and its Benefits

Owners organizing a business must determine the appropriate legal structure for their business. Should the business be organized as a partnership, a limited liability company, a Subchapter C or Subchapter S corporation, or a sole proprietorship? The choice of entity is one of the most common matters for which business owners seek legal counsel. That choice will affect the liability exposure of owners in conducting their business; the tax treatment of the income and losses generated by the business; the ability of the business to borrow money and attract investors; the tax implications of the owners' contributions to the business and distributions to the owners from the business; and the ease with which a business can be liquidated, sold, or otherwise transferred. In advising their business clients regarding choice of entity, lawyers must therefore take into account a host of both tax and nontax considerations. As a result, a basic understanding of state law authorizing specific business structures and the federal and state tax laws governing business organizations is critical to the effective representation of business clients.

1. General and Limited Partnerships and Limited Liability Companies

Small businesses and professionals have commonly structured their business organizations as partnerships under applicable state laws to take advantage of the flexibility afforded by partnerships and the benefits of partnership taxation discussed below. Historically, every partnership was a general partnership. In general partnerships, all partners are jointly and severally liable for partnership debts, they assume the liability for partnership losses, and they share in management responsibilities. Limited partnerships evolved under state law to address the desire of partnerships to attract investors who were averse to assuming the unlimited liability and management responsibilities of general partners. Under state laws, every limited partnership has one or more general partners and at least one limited partner. General partners of limited partnerships share management responsibilities and liability for the partnership's obligations.[3] By contrast, the limited partners, have no liability for partnership obligations beyond their initial capital contributions to the partnership or capital contributions

---

[3] A partner of a limited partnership, however, could be a corporation and thus limited general liability could be achieved for virtually all of the partners.

they may have specifically agreed to make in the future. By definition, limited partners do not participate in management. Indeed, were a limited partner to participate in management, that partner would lose the benefit of limited liability.

In 1977, another important business entity structure — the limited liability company — appeared on the scene. Wyoming enacted the first limited liability company act. The emergence of the limited liability company can be traced to the desire of business owners for an entity that would be taxed as a partnership under Subchapter K and, like a corporation, would provide limited liability to each of its owners, while at the same time enabling some or all of its owners to participate in management of the entity.[4] Depending on state law, a limited liability company, unlike a partnership, can have a single individual as its owner. In 1988, the Internal Revenue Service, applying the then-existing business classification regulations, concluded that a limited liability company created under the Wyoming act was not an association and would be taxed as a partnership. Rev. Rul. 88-76, 1988-2 C.B. 360. That ruling spurred the enactment of limited liability company legislation nationwide. As a result, between 1977 and 2006, every state and the District of Columbia had enacted legislation authorizing limited liability companies. Today, with the exception of single-member limited liability companies that are disregarded as business entities *for federal tax purposes*, a limited liability company can choose to be taxed as a partnership or a corporation.

In the legislative history to the 1954 Act creating Subchapter K, the House Ways and Means Committee stated: "In establishing a broad pattern applicable to partnerships generally, the principal objectives have been simplicity, flexibility, and equity as between partners." H. Rep. No. 1337, p. 65, 83 Cong. 2nd Sess., P.L. 83-591(1954). It is fair to say that Congress and the Treasury have not realized the objective of simplicity. By any measure, partnership taxation is one of the most complex areas of federal taxation. While challenging, mastering the fundamentals of partnership taxation is worth the effort for law students planning to engage in business practices. The importance of a basic understanding of partnership taxation is underscored by the large and ever-increasing number of entities filing as partnerships, the huge number of partners represented in those filings, and the net income generated by partnerships. According to the Internal Revenue Service's Statistics of Income Bulletin (Fall 2015), partnerships filed almost 3.5 million information returns for 2013. More than 27 million partners were represented in the 2013 returns, 10 million more than the number of partners in 2003. And total partnership net income in 2013 — about $770 billion — is more than twice the partnership net income 10 years earlier. The total assets held by entities taxed as partnerships in 2013 exceeds $24 trillion. Indicative of the prominence of limited liability companies, a majority of the entities filing partnership returns are organized as limited liability companies under state laws.

---

[4] State law typically provides that limited liability companies are managed by their members unless otherwise provided in the LLC operating agreement. This dimension of limited liability companies, combined with the fact that all members of the LLC have limited liability, distinguish LLCs from limited partnerships.

B. CHOICE OF ENTITY: OVERVIEW OF PARTNERSHIP CLASSIFICATION 5

2. Tax Benefits of Partnership Classification

The benefits of being treated as a partnership for tax purposes accounts in large part for the organization of businesses as partnerships or limited liability companies under state law rather than as corporations. The tax treatment accorded business entities taxed as partnerships and their partners/members differs significantly from that applicable to corporations and their shareholders. The following overview of some of the tax benefits associated with organizing a business entity as a partnership subject to Subchapter K as opposed to a corporation taxed under either Subchapter C [hereinafter "a C corporation"] or Subchapter S of the Internal Revenue Code [hereinafter an "S corporation"] provides a partial list of factors attorneys consider in advising their business clients regarding choice of entity, and also previews topics discussed in detail in this casebook.

a. Number of owners, character of owners, and classes of equity interests.

No limit exists on the number and character of partners who own a partnership and the partnership can have different classes of equity interests, e.g., general partners and limited partners. While the same is true of C corporations, it is not true of S corporations. An S corporations cannot have more than 100 shareholders, there are significant limitations on the persons who can own S corporation stock and on the types of corporations that are eligible for Subchapter S treatment, and S corporations can have only one class of stock. § 1361(b)(1) and (2).

b. Nonrecognition of gain and loss on contributions of property.

As a general rule, neither gain nor loss is recognized on the contribution of property to a partnership, either on formation or during the partnership's life. § 721. The same is true of C or S corporations. §§ 351; 1371(a). To qualify for nonrecognition of corporate contributions, however, contributing shareholders must satisfy a control requirement. §§ 351(a) and 368(c). No control requirement exists with regard to the nonrecognition rule applicable to partnerships.

c. Single level of tax.

As noted above, Subchapter K, consistent with the treatment of a partnership as an aggregate of partners rather than a separate entity, treats partnerships as pass-through entities, i.e., partnerships are not subject to tax at the entity level. § 701. Rather, items of partnership income, gain, loss, deduction and credit are passed through to the partners and taken into account by them in computing their taxable income. The income of a partnership is thus subject to tax only once.[5] While

---

[5] To ensure that a partner is not taxed twice on income the partner was required to report, a partner's basis in the partnership interest ("outside basis") is adjusted upward in the amount of the income the partner was required to report. § 705(a)(1)(A). Likewise, to ensure that a partner does not reap the benefit of a double deduction for partnership deductions and losses passed through to that partner, a

the same is generally true of S corporations,[6] partnerships provide much greater flexibility than S corporations with respect to the allocation of items of income, gain, deduction, loss, and credit. Pursuant to the pass-through provisions of Subchapter K, each partner takes into account a "distributive share" of these items. See §§ 702-704. A partner's "distributive share" is generally determined by the partnership agreement. § 704(a). Partners thus can determine how specific items of partnership income, gain, loss, deduction, or credit will be allocated.[7] For example, the partners could agree that all depreciation deductions on a commercial building owned by the partnership will be allocated to one partner. S corporations have no such flexibility. Rather, the S corporation's income, gain, loss, deduction or credits must be allocated pro rata among the outstanding corporate shares on a daily basis. § 1366(a), (c). Thus, for example, if an S shareholder owns 10 percent of the outstanding shares of the S corporation, then ten percent of each item of income, gain, loss, deduction or credit will be allocated to that shareholder.

Unlike partnerships (or S corporations), C corporations are taxed as entities separate from their shareholders. The C corporation thus is subject to income tax on its earnings. See § 11. In addition, when the after-tax earnings of a C corporation are distributed to shareholders in the form of dividends, Section 61(a)(7) requires shareholders to include these dividends in gross income. See § 316. As a result, the earnings of a C corporation are subject to double tax.

d. Deductibility of losses.

As noted, if the partnership generates a loss during the year, that loss will pass through to the partners and will reduce their taxable income. As will be discussed in Chapter 8, a partner's deduction for partnership loss is limited to a partner's adjusted basis in the partnership interest (outside basis) with any disallowed loss being carried forward to the next year. Importantly, a partner's outside basis includes the partner's share of partnership debt, thus enabling a partner to deduct currently potentially large amounts of loss.[8] By contrast, an S shareholder's pro rata share of corporate losses is only deductible to the extent of the shareholder's basis in her stock and any indebtedness the corporation has to her. § 1366(d)(1). Thus, unlike partners, shareholders of S corporations cannot include in their basis a share of corporate debt to parties other than the S corporation shareholder.

While deductions and losses of a C corporation reduce the corporation's taxable income, they are not passed through to the shareholders. The difference between partnerships and corporations with regard to the deductibility of losses is particu-

---

partner's outside basis is adjusted downward by the amount of any deductions or losses passed through to that partner. § 705(a)(2). Subchapter S provides similar basis adjustment rules for S shareholders. § 1367(a)(1)(A) and (B), and (2)(B) and (C).

[6] § 1363(a). S corporations, however, can be subject to tax if they were previously C corporations. See §§ 1374 and 1375.

[7] § 704(b) and the regulations thereunder provide that allocations made by the partnership agreement will only be respected if the partner to whom an allocation is made receives the economic benefit or bears the economic burden associated with an allocation and the allocation satisfies a substantiality test discussed in detail in Chapter 9.

[8] The allocation of partnership liabilities among partners is examined in detail in Chapter 12.

larly important if a business anticipates large losses in the early years of its existence. Under those circumstances, the owners may determine that, at least initially, organizing the entity as one that will be taxed as a partnership is preferable to organizing the entity as a corporation. The pass-through of partnership losses, the allocation of partnership liabilities, and the limitations with regard to the availability of those losses to reduce a taxpayer's income are discussed in detail in later chapters.

e. Rates of tax.

Because the income of partnerships and S corporations is not taxable at the entity level but rather is allocated among the partners and shareholders to be taken into account in their respective tax returns, the difference between corporate income tax rates and individual rates becomes a significant factor in determining whether to operate a business as a corporation or a pass-through entity like a partnership or S corporation.

As a separate taxable entity, a C corporation is subject to tax on its taxable income. The tax rates for corporations are set forth in § 11, providing for a modest amount of a corporation's taxable income to be taxed at rates of 15 or 25%. A C corporation's taxable income in excess of $75,000, however, is taxed at a flat rate of either 34 or 35%. Depending on the amount of its taxable income, the C corporation may lose any benefit from the 15% and 25% brackets and, in effect, be subject to a flat tax of 35% on all of its taxable income. Furthermore, a C Corporation, unlike an individual, receives no preferential rate for net capital gain. § 1201. Thus, a C corporation may be subject to a maximum tax of 35% on its net capital gains, whereas an individual who is a partner or a shareholder in an S corporation is generally subject to maximum tax of 15% unless the individual is a "high income" taxpayer in which case the maximum tax on net capital gain is 20%.[9] As noted above, the earnings of a C corporation are subject to tax at both the entity level and the shareholder level. The impact of this double taxation, however, has been eased somewhat given that dividends are generally taxed as net capital gain and thus accorded preferential rates. § 1(h)(1), (11).

By contrast to the corporate rates, individual income tax rates range from 10% to 39.6%. Instead of four brackets as in the case of corporations, there are seven individual income tax brackets. In 2016, a single individual only begins paying the top rate of 39.6% on taxable income in excess of $415,050. Rev. Proc. 2015-53, 2015-44 I.R.B. 615. Furthermore, as noted above, individuals have the benefit of preferential rates on net capital gain.

---

[9] A "high income" taxpayer is one whose ordinary income is taxed at a marginal tax rate of 39.6%, the highest individual rate. See § 1(h)(1)(C) and (D).

f. Tax treatment of nonliquidating distributions.[10]

Subchapter K in large part treats a partnership as an aggregate of owners rather than as a separate entity like a corporation. As a result, it is not surprising that nonrecognition is generally the standard with regard to both liquidating and nonliquidating distributions from partnerships.[11] For example, nonliquidating distributions of cash will generally only result in the recognition of income (gain) by a distributee/partner to the extent that the partner receives cash in an amount greater than the partner's outside basis. § 731(a)(1). As a general rule, nonliquidating distributions of cash will not cause recognition of loss. § 731(a)(2). Similarly, a nonliquidating distribution of appreciated or of loss property[12] will generally not result in the recognition of gain or loss by either the partnership or the partner and the distributee partner will typically take a transferred basis in the property received, thus preserving either the gain or loss inherent in the asset.[13]

By contrast, distributions of property from a corporation can result in the recognition of income or gain. While an S corporation's distributions of cash to its shareholders will be treated in a manner comparable to cash distributions from a partnership,[14] a distribution of appreciated property by an S corporation will result in the recognition of gain and the distributee will take a fair market value basis in the asset distributed. §§ 1371(a), 311(b) and 301(d). Consistent with the double tax regime of Subchapter C, a distribution of cash or other property to shareholders of a C corporation that has earnings and profits will result in dividend treatment, i.e., the shareholders will have gross income in the amount of dividends received.[15] § 316. Furthermore, if a C corporation distributes an appreciated asset to a shareholder, the gain inherent in that asset will be recognized by the distributing corporation just as though the corporation had first sold the asset and then distributed the sale proceeds to its shareholders. § 311(b)(1). The distributee/shareholder will take a fair market value basis in the property distributed. § 301(d). Thus, distributing appreciated property from either a C or S corporation will result in the recognition of gain. While no loss is recognized by either a C corporation or an S corporation on the distribution of loss property to a shareholder, the shareholder receiving the loss property from either a C or S corporation takes a fair market value basis in the property. The loss thus disappears rather than being preserved in the distributed property's basis, as is the case with partnership distributions of loss property.

---

[10] Nonliquidating distributions are those distributions other than distributions that liquidate either an owner's interest or the entire entity. See Chapter 14. Both liquidating and nonliquidating distributions are taxed pursuant to special rules that this casebook addresses in detail.

[11] There are, however, some exceptions to the general nonrecognition rule. See, e.g., §§ 704(c)(1)(B), 737, and 751(b).

[12] Loss property is property having a fair market value that is less than its adjusted basis.

[13] §§ 731(a)(1) and (2), (b) and 732(a)(1). Exceptions discussed in later chapters apply to distributions treated as sales or exchanges of property.

[14] § 1368(b). This statement assumes that the S Corporation has no C corporation history.

[15] §§ 61(a)(7) and 316. See, however, § 243, which provides a special deduction if the shareholder is another corporation.

g. Liquidating distributions.

Consistent with the nonrecognition regime of Subchapter K, on the liquidation of a partner's interest (either as part of the overall liquidation of a partnership or otherwise), a partner recognizes gain only to the extent that any money received exceeds the partner's basis in her partnership interest (outside basis).[16] A partner does not recognize loss on the liquidation of a partner's interest unless the partner receives only cash and/or certain other limited types of property.[17] A partner takes an aggregate basis in the assets distributed to him in liquidation of his interest in the amount of his outside basis reduced by any money received on the liquidation. § 732(b). Pursuant to § 732(c), that aggregate basis is allocated among the various assets (other than cash) received by the partner.

By contrast, gain or loss will be recognized by both C and S shareholders on the complete liquidation of a C or S corporation. The gain or loss recognized is the difference between the amount realized by the shareholder for her stock and the adjusted basis the shareholder had in her stock. §§ 331(a) and 1371. Liquidating distributions will be treated as exchanges and thus will not be treated as dividends to shareholders. §§ 331(b) and 1371. A shareholder will take a fair market value basis in any property received by the shareholder in a complete liquidation. §§ 334(a) and 1371. Gain and loss is also generally recognized by the C or S corporation on the distribution in complete liquidation of the corporation. In the case of an S corporation, any gain or loss recognized by the corporation on the liquidation is passed through to the shareholders.

C. Classification of Unincorporated Business Entities: The Check-the-Box Regulations

1. History

Because so many federal tax rules depend on the tax status of a taxpayer, classifying an unincorporated business organization as a partnership, a corporation — either a Subchapter C or Subchapter S corporation — or a "disregarded entity" (e.g., a single member limited liability company) has significant tax implications. As noted above, were an unincorporated business organization to be classified as a C corporation, the income of the organization would potentially be subject to double taxation. In addition, the organization's taxable income would, in many cases, be subject to what is essentially a flat rate of tax and be denied the benefit of the preferential rates accorded long-term capital gains. By contrast, if an unincorporated business organization were to be classified as either a partnership or a Subchapter S corporation, the organization itself would not be taxable (with minor exceptions for S corporations that have a C history). Rather, the organization's items of income and deduction would be passed through to the S corporation shareholders or, in the case of organizations classified as partnerships, to the partners (or members in the case of a limited liability company). Because the

---

[16] § 731(a)(1). There are exceptions, however, to this general rule. *See, e.g.*, § 751(b).

[17] § 731(a)(2). Again, there are exceptions to this general rule. *See, e.g.*, § 751(b).

character of income and deductions is preserved with respect to pass-through entities like partnerships and S corporations, preferential rates on the entity's long-term capital gain are applicable. If the organization is classified as a disregarded entity for federal tax purposes, it will be taxed as if it were a sole proprietorship. In sum, because of the significant tax consequences associated with the classification of an unincorporated business organization, owners of such a business have historically employed attorneys — often at considerable cost — to structure the unincorporated business in a manner that will ensure the desired classification for federal tax purposes.

The Internal Revenue Code provides important definitions of both partnership and corporations for federal tax purposes. As noted above, under § 7701(a)(2), a partnership includes unincorporated organizations through or by means of which any business, financial operation or venture is carried on and which is not a trust or estate or corporation. Section 7701(a)(3) defines the term "corporation" to include associations. Thus, an unincorporated business organization classified as an association for federal tax purposes would be taxed as a corporation and not as a partnership.

Until 1997, the classification of an unincorporated business as an association for federal tax purposes depended on what was known as the "corporate resemblance test," i.e., is the organization or entity more like a corporation than, for example, a partnership? This "corporate resemblance" test was articulated by the U.S. Supreme Court in its decision in *Morrissey v. Commissioner*, 296 U.S. 344, 357 (1935), which noted "The [statutory] inclusion of associations with corporations implies resemblance; but it is resemblance and not identity. The resemblance points to features distinguishing associations from partnerships as well as from ordinary trusts."

At issue in *Morissey* was the proper classification of a particular trust, i.e., should the trust be treated as an association for federal tax purposes and, as a result, taxed as a corporation or should it be treated as a traditional trust and taxed accordingly? The Court described the trust in question as follows:

> The trust was created for the development of a tract of land through the construction and operation of golf courses, club houses, etc. and the conduct of incidental businesses, with broad powers for the purchase, operation and sale of properties. Provision was made for the issue of shares of beneficial interests, with described rights and priorities. There were to be preferred shares of the value of $100 each and common shares of no par value. Thus those who took beneficial interests became shareholders in the common undertaking to be conducted for their profit according to the terms of the arrangement. They were not the less associated in that undertaking because the arrangement vested the management and control in the trustees. And the contemplated development of the tract of land held at the outset, even if other properties were not acquired, involved what was essentially a business enterprise. The arrangement provided for *centralized control, continuity [of life]*, and *limited liability*, and the analogy to corporate organization was carried still further by the provision for the issue of *transferable certificates*. [296 U.S. at 360] [Emphasis added.]

C. CLASSIFICATION OF UNINCORPORATED BUSINESS ENTITIES

Addressing the classification question, the *Morissey* Court first noted that "[t]he term [association as used in the statute] embraces associations as they may exist at common law. . . .While the use of corporate forms may furnish persuasive evidence of the existence of an association, the absence of particular forms, or of the usual terminology of corporations, cannot be regarded as decisive. . . . " The Court then applied the "resemblance test" focusing on the characteristics of the trust that made its classification as an association for federal tax purposes appropriate:

> What, then, are the salient features of a trust — when created and maintained as a medium for the carrying on of a business enterprise and sharing its gains — which may be regarded as making it analogous to a corporate organization? A corporation, as an entity, holds the title to the property embarked in the corporate undertaking. Trustees, as a continuing body with provision for succession, may afford a corresponding advantage during the existence of the trust. Corporate organization furnishes the opportunity for a centralized management through representatives of the members of the corporation. The designation of trustees, who are charged with the conduct of an enterprise — who act "in much the same manner as directors" — may provide a similar scheme, with corresponding effectiveness. Whether the trustees are named in the trust instrument with power to select successors, so as to constitute a self-perpetuating body, or are selected by, or with the advice of, those beneficially interested in the undertaking, centralization of management analogous to that of corporate activities may be achieved. An enterprise carried on by means of a trust may be secure from termination or interruption by the death of owners of beneficial interests and in this respect their interests are distinguished from those of partners and are akin to the interests of members of a corporation. And the trust type of organization facilitates, as does corporate organization, the transfer of beneficial interests without affecting the continuity of the enterprise, and also the introduction of large numbers of participants. The trust method also permits the limitation of the personal liability of participants to the property embarked in the undertaking . . . [W]e think that these attributes make the trust sufficiently analogous to corporate organization to justify the conclusion that Congress intended that the income of the enterprise should be taxed in the same manner as that of corporations. [296 U.S. at 359–60.]

The significance of the *Morissey* resemblance test cannot be overstated. For example, the *Morissey* resemblance test afforded the possibility that an unincorporated organization, e.g., a group medical practice that, under state law, could not operate as a corporation, could nonetheless be classified for federal tax purposes as an association and thus treated as a corporation for federal tax purposes. In *United States v. Kintner*, 216 F.2d 418 (9th Cir. 1954) a group of doctors (working together as the Western Montana Clinic in Missoula, Montana), sought to take advantage of the favorable pension arrangements available under federal tax law only to corporations. To that end, the doctors terminated their partnership and created an unincorporated association endowing it with the attributes of a corporation. The pension plan created by the organization's articles of association could qualify for exemption under federal income tax law only if the association were treated as a corporation for federal tax purposes. Dr. Kintner and his wife, the taxpayers, did not include in their gross income their share of amounts of association income that the association had set aside as a reserve nor did they include amounts that had been paid into the pension plan on behalf of Dr. Kintner. Were the association to be treated as a partnership for federal tax purposes, the taxpayers would have been required to include both amounts in their income. The Service challenged the taxpayer's position arguing that, because Montana law did not authorize a corporation to practice medicine, the association could not be treated as a corporation for federal tax purposes. The Ninth Circuit rejected the Service's position and, applying the *Morissey* resemblance test, determined the association had the characteristics of a corporation and would be treated for federal tax purposes as a corporation.

The Treasury subsequently promulgated regulations (repealed in 1997) that incorporated the *Morissey* resemblance test. Specifically, with respect to unincorporated business organizations, these regulations (sometimes known as the *Kintner* regulations) identified six basic characteristics of a corporation: (1) associates, (2) an objective to carry on business and divide the gains therefrom, (3) continuity of life, (4) centralization of management, (5) liability for corporate debts limited to corporate property, and (6) free transferability of interests. Because the existence of associates and an objective to carry on business and divide the gains therefrom are generally common to both corporations and partnerships, the regulations provided the determination of whether an unincorporated organization would be treated for federal tax purposes as a partnership or as an association taxable as a corporation depended on the existence or lack of existence of the other four factors, i.e., centralization of management, continuity of life, free transferability of interests, and limited liability. Equal weight was to be accorded to each of the four characteristics. If an unincorporated organization possessed at least three of these four characteristics, the organization would be treated as a corporation. If it possessed less than three of the characteristics, the organization would be taxable as a partnership.

The regulation's "resemblance test" as described above had a decidedly strong bias favoring non-corporation classification for most unincorporated organizations. In effect, the regulations were biased in favor of partnership classification. Over time, the impetus for organizations to seek corporate classification was negated with the passage of state laws recognizing professional service corporations and with the elimination of pension and profit-sharing differences between corporate entities and partnerships. Ironically, classification as a partnership became particularly desirable during the 1970s and 1980s when tax shelter activity flourished. During that period, the limited partnership emerged as the entity of choice for tax shelters, affording limited liability for the limited partner investors while providing those investors the benefit of passed-through losses. The pro-partnership bias of the regulations thus worked against the Service's efforts to classify these partnerships as associations taxable as corporations.

As noted above, in the late 1970s states began to recognize hybrid structures, e.g., limited liability companies. While these new hybrid structures had characteristics of corporations, e.g., limited liability, taxpayers utilizing these structures sought the benefits of the partnership tax rules which, as noted previously, provided a single level of tax rather than the double taxation associated with Subchapter C corporations. The partnership tax rules also allowed greater operational flexibility than rules governing Subchapter S corporations. In a landmark ruling, the Service in Rev. Rul. 88-76, 1988-2 C.B. 360, applied the *Kintner* regulations and concluded that a 25-person limited liability company formed to acquire, own and operate improved real property and organized under the Wyoming Limited Liability Company Act (hereinafter Wyoming's Act) would be classified as a partnership and not a corporation for federal tax purposes. According to that ruling, while the limited liability company had the centralized management and limited liability characteristics of corporations, it lacked the continuity of life and free transferability of interests of corporations. Thus, the organization satisfied only two of the four key characteristics of corporations.

Revenue Ruling 88-76 set the stage for the enactment of limited liability company legislation in every state and the District of Columbia. Given the *Kintner* regulations, the flexibility provided by limited liability company laws in effect afforded organizers the choice of whether the limited liability company would be classified as an association or a partnership for federal tax purposes. A premium was thus placed on securing the advice of knowledgeable practitioners.

The limited liability company discussed in Rev. Rul. 88-76 and the result reached by the Service in that ruling underscored developments occurring in the business organization arena during the 1980s and 1990s. The Service in Notice 95-14, 1995-1 C.B. 297, accurately described those developments and their consequences as follows:

> [M]any states recently have revised their statutes to provide that partnerships and other unincorporated organizations may possess characteristics that have traditionally been associated with corporations, thereby narrowing considerably the traditional distinctions between corporations and partnerships. For example, some partnership statutes have been modified to provide that no partner is unconditionally liable for all of the debts of the partnership. Similarly, almost all states have enacted statutes allowing the formation of limited liability companies. These entities are designed to provide liability protection to all members and to otherwise resemble corporations, while generally qualifying as partnerships for federal tax purposes.
>
> One consequence of the narrowing of the differences under local law between corporations and partnerships is that taxpayers can achieve partnership tax classification for a non-publicly traded organization that, in all meaningful respects, is virtually indistinguishable from a corporation. Taxpayers and the Service, however, continue to expend considerable resources in determining the proper classification of domestic unincorporated business organizations. For example, since the issuance of Rev. Rul. 88-76, the Service has issued seventeen revenue rulings analyzing individual state limited liability company statutes, and has issued several revenue procedures and numerous letter rulings relating to classification of various unincorporated organizations under the classification regulations. In addition, small unincorporated organizations may not have sufficient

resources and expertise to apply the current classification regulations to achieve the tax classification they desire.

2. Current Law: Classification Under the Check-the-Box Regulations

As a result of the developments noted above, Treasury concluded the "*Kintner* regulations" were inadequate and resulted in unnecessary expense. It therefore took steps to address the issues by replacing the *Kintner* regulations with what have become known as the "check-the-box regulations." As the Sixth Circuit noted in *Littriello v. United States*, 484 F.3d 372, 376 (6th Cir. 2007):

> [T]he IRS undertook to replace the *Kintner* regulations with a more practical scheme, consistent with existing tax statutes and with a new provision in § 7704 treating publicly traded entities as corporations, regardless of their structure or status under state law. As to the unincorporated business associations not covered by § 7704, including the newly emerging hybrid entities [e.g., limited liability companies and limited liability partnerships], the IRS proposed to allow an election by the taxpayer to be treated as a corporation or, in the absence of such an election, to be "disregarded," i.e., deemed a partnership (for entities with multiple members) or a sole proprietorship (for those with a single member). After a period for notice and comment, the new regulations were issued and became effective on January 1, 1997, implementing the definitional provisions of § 7701(a)(2) and (3). The regulations were particularly helpful with regard to the tax status of the new hybrids, because the hybrid entities were not, and still are not, explicitly covered by the definitions set out in § 7701. What was avoided by the resulting "check-the-box" provisions was the necessity of forcing those hybrids to jump through the *Kintner* regulation "hoops" in order to achieve a desired — and perfectly legal — classification for federal tax purposes.

The check-the-box regulations address only those organizations treated under federal tax law as entities separate from their owners. As the preamble to the regulations indicates, "the first step in the classification process is to determine whether there is a separate entity for federal tax purposes." 61 F.R. 66584–66593 (December 18, 1996). Whether an organization is treated as a separate entity under state law is irrelevant. Reg. § 301.7701-1(a)(1). According to the regulations, a joint venture or other contractual arrangement may create a "separate entity for federal tax purposes" if its participants carry on a trade, business, financial operation or venture and divide the profits therefrom. Reg. § 301.7701-1(a)(2). By contrast, a joint undertaking merely to share expenses or the co-ownership of property that is maintained, kept in repair, and rented or leased does not constitute a separate entity for federal tax purposes. *Cf.* § 761(f). Again, it makes no difference whether under state law that joint undertaking would be treated as a separate entity. The regulations provide certain organizations having a single owner, e.g., a single-member LLC, can choose to be recognized or disregarded as entities separate from their owners. Reg. § 301.7701-1(a)(4).

C. CLASSIFICATION OF UNINCORPORATED BUSINESS ENTITIES

Assuming an organization qualifies as a separate entity, the next step under the check-the-box regulations is to determine whether the entity is a "business entity." The check-the-box regulations classify so-called "business entities" as either (a) corporations or (b) partnerships for federal tax purposes. A "business entity" is an "entity" (other than a limited category of trusts under Reg. § 301.7701-4) recognized for federal tax purposes. Reg. § 301.7701–2(a). Reg. § 301.7701-2(b) defines the term "corporation" for federal tax purposes. That regulation provides that the term "corporation" includes "a business entity organized under a Federal or State statute, or under a statute of a federally recognized Indian tribe [describing or referring] to the entity as incorporated or as a corporation, body corporate, or body." Reg. § 301.7701-2(b)(1). Thus, if Alex, Burt, and Cal form ABC Inc., under the business corporation laws of Delaware, ABC, Inc., will automatically be treated as a corporation for federal tax purposes. ABC, Inc., cannot elect to be taxed as a partnership. Reg. § 301.7701-1(b) lists other associations or business entities, e.g., insurance companies and business entities in certain foreign jurisdictions, that will also automatically be classified as corporations for federal tax purposes. Reg. § 301.7701-2(b)(3)-(8). That same regulation indicates that the term "corporation" will include those noncorporate business entities that are treated as associations under Reg. § 301.7701-3 discussed below. Reg. § 301.7701-2(b)(2).[18]

By contrast to the automatic corporate classification rule of Reg. § 301.7701-2(b)(1) noted above, Reg. § 301.7701-3(a) provides that any noncorporate business entity (referred to as an "eligible entity") with at least two members can elect to be classified as either an association (and thus a corporation under Reg. 301.7701-1(b)(2)) or a partnership; an eligible entity with a single owner can elect to be classified as an association [and thus taxed as a corporation] or to be disregarded as an entity separate from its owner. A default rule provides that, if no election is made with respect to a domestic eligible entity, the entity will be treated as a partnership if it has two or more members or will be disregarded as an entity separate from its owner if it only has a single owner. Reg. § 301.7701-3(b). As noted in the preamble to the regulations, these default rules are intended to match taxpayers' expectations by providing "most eligible entities with the classification they would choose without requiring them to file an election." 61 F.R. 66584–66593 (December 18, 1996).

The eligible entity may affirmatively elect to be classified under the rules noted above on Form 8832 Entity Classification Election. The election must be signed by (1) each member of the entity or (2) any officer, manager, or member of the entity authorized to make the election who represents, under penalties of perjury, to having such authorization. Reg. § 301.7701-3(c)(2)(i). The election is effective on the date specified by the entity on the form or on the date the form is filed if the entity does not specify an effective date on the form. The eligible entity, however, cannot specify an effective date that is more than 75 days prior to the date on which the election is filed and cannot be more than 12 months after the date in which the election is filed. Reg. § 301.7701-3(c)(1)(iii).

Consider the following examples:

---

[18] Certain publicly traded partnerships are treated as corporations pursuant to § 7703.

Example 1: Alex, Bert, and Cal create a heating and air conditioning business they will operate as Cool/Heat Enterprises. Cool/Heat is a limited liability company formed under the limited liability company laws of Montana. Alex, Bert, and Cal will share all of the profits and losses of Cool/Heat equally. Cool/Heat is a business entity. Because Cool/Heat is not a corporation under Reg. § 301.7701-2(b)(1), (3), (4), (5), (6), (7) or (8), it is an "eligible entity" and can elect to be classified under federal tax law as either a partnership or as an association (and thus a corporation under Reg. 301.7701-1(b)(2)). Cool/Heat can either affirmatively select its classification by filing Form 8832 or it can rely on the default rule and will be classified as a partnership.

Example 2: Assume Alex alone creates Cool/Heat and organizes his business as a single-member limited liability company under Montana's limited liability company laws. Pursuant to Reg. 301.7701-3(a), Cool/Heat, as an eligible entity, has a choice to be classified as an association (and thus be taxed as a corporation) or disregarded as an entity for federal tax purposes. Cool/Heat can make an affirmative election by filing Form 8832 or, in default of filing Form 8832, will be disregarded as an entity for federal tax purposes. In the latter case, Cool/Heat would be treated for tax purposes as a sole proprietorship.

The check-the-box regulations thus create an affirmatively elective regime for determining the tax status of a business organization that is an "eligible entity." By comparison to the period during which the *Kintner* regulations governed the classification of business organizations, achieving the desired classification of unincorporated business organizations is simpler and much cheaper given the check-the-box regulations. Nonetheless, the business planner must have a firm understanding of the both the tax and nontax distinctions between corporations and partnership. In the chapters that follow, you will examine the structure and detail of the Code as it relates to the business organizations classified as partnerships.

Chapter 2

NONRECOGNITION OF GAIN OR LOSS ON CONTRIBUTION OF PROPERTY TO A PARTNERSHIP

I. PROBLEMS

1. Dave, Ellen, and Fred form the DEF general partnership by contributing the following properties in exchange for equal one-third interests in the partnership:

    Dave contributes: (1) Greenacre, land he had held as an investment for several years, which has a value of $100,000 and an adjusted basis of $40,000; (2) Whiteacre, land he had held as an investment for several years, which has a value of $60,000 and an adjusted basis of $90,000; and (3) an installment obligation he received on the sale of Blueacre, land he had held as an investment for several years prior to selling it; the obligation has a face amount and value of $40,000 and an adjusted basis of $10,000. (The partnership will hold Greenacre and Whiteacre for sale to customers in the ordinary course of partnership business.)

    Ellen contributes items from her business as a sole proprietor: (1) accounts receivable acquired earlier this year, which have a value of $50,000 and an adjusted basis of zero; (2) inventory items acquired earlier this year, which have a value of $75,000 and an adjusted basis of $30,000; and (3) equipment held for two years, which has a value of $75,000, an adjusted basis of $40,000, and is subject to § 1245 recapture in the amount of $25,000. (The partnership will not hold the inventory items for sale to customers, but will hold them for appreciation and eventual sale in bulk.)

    Fred contributes: (1) $150,000 in cash; and (2) a binding letter of commitment from a lender to finance the cost of construction of a partnership building on very favorable terms; the letter has a value of $50,000 and an adjusted basis of zero.

    (a) Is any gain or loss recognized by any of the partners or by the partnership upon the transfer of property in exchange for partnership interests?

    (b) What is each partner's adjusted basis and holding period in his or her partnership interest?

    (c) What is the partnership's adjusted basis and holding period in each of the partnership's assets?

(d) What will be the amount and character of the partnership's gain or loss on the sale 13 months from now of (1) Greenacre for $110,000; (2) Whiteacre for $30,000; and (3) the inventory items for $100,000 in a bulk sale. (Note: This question does not ask to whom the partnership gain or loss on the sales may be allocated. Section 704(c) governs the allocation of tax items, e.g., gain and loss, associated with contributed property and will be addressed in detail in Chapter 10.)

Assignment:

Complete the problems.

Read: Internal Revenue Code: §§ 721, 722, 723, 724, 1223(1), (2), 1245 (b)(3).
Treasury Regulations: §§ 1.453-9(c)(2); 1.721-1(a); 1.722-1; 1.723-1; 1.1223-3(b)(1);

Materials: Overview
United States v. Stafford

II. VOCABULARY

outside basis
inside basis
realization
nonrecognition
property
section 1245 property
installment obligation
inventory
unrealized receivables
split holding period
substituted basis property

III. OBJECTIVES

1. To determine what gain or loss, if any, is recognized by a partner on a contribution of property to a partnership.

2. To determine what gain or loss, if any, is recognized to a partnership on a contribution of property by a partner to the partnership.

3. To determine a partner's adjusted basis and holding period for the partnership interest.

4. To determine the partnership's adjusted basis and holding period in property contributed to the partnership.

IV. OVERVIEW

A. Nonrecognition in General

Abbey and Ross recently created Land Yacht Storage, LLC (hereinafter the LLC) to which each of them contributed a five-acre tract of land. Abbey's land has a fair market value of $200,000; Abbey's adjusted basis in the land is $20,000. Ross's land likewise has a fair market value of $200,000; Ross has a $225,000 adjusted basis in this land. Both Abbey and Ross had held their respective tracts of land for investment for a number of years. In exchange for their contributions, Abbey and Ross each received an equal interest in the limited liability company (LLC) which will be taxed as a partnership under Subchapter K.

Consider the parties' circumstances before and after the creation of the LLC. Abbey and Ross each held fee simple title to their land prior to the creation of the LLC. Afterward, they each owned a 50% interest in the LLC which, in turn, held the title to the two tracts of land. In other words, Abbey and Ross have exchanged tangible property (land) for intangible property (their membership interest in the LLC). Based on your prior study of individual income tax, you might assume the exchange of land for a membership interest in the LLC constituted a realization event potentially triggering gain to Abbey and loss to Ross under § 1001. After all, we generally think of income or loss being "realized" when a taxpayer "exchanges property for other property differing materially either in kind or extent." Reg. § 1.1001-1(a). In other words, for tax purposes, an exchange is typically equivalent to cashing in one's investment in the property exchanged — an event clearly considered a realization event. Certainly, one could argue a realization event occurred when, as a result of their transfers, Abbey and Ross shifted title to their land to the LLC and, in exchange, received an interest in an entity that owned both tracts of land.

Typically, if a realization event has occurred, gain or loss is recognized. § 1001(c). Of course, an argument could be made that neither Abbey nor Ross has closed out his or her investment in the tract of land each transferred to the partnership. Viewed from that standpoint, it would be inappropriate to treat the exchange as a realization event causing the recognition of gain or loss. Prior to the enactment of the Internal Revenue Code of 1954, and in the absence of any Code provision specifically addressing contributions to partnerships, the courts adopted this nonrecognition analysis. For example, in *Archbald v. Commissioner*, 27 B.T.A. 837 (1933), *aff'd*, 70 F.2d 720 (2d Cir. 1934), the court, rejecting the Service's position that a contribution of appreciated assets to a partnership resulted in the recognition of gain, stated:

> That the contribution of individual property to a newly organized partnership operates to shift its title from the individual and to change the nature of interest is clear. . . . but it does not follow that such change is itself the realization of gain or loss. . . . On the contrary, the investment is now more fettered than before, as it is bound with others in the joint enterprise. Although a transformation in title has occurred, there has been no exchange of property for other and different property, but only a further venturing of the old investment in a new project with the hope of added

income in the future. . . . [T]he new partnership interest may not be separately disposed of without destroying the partnership . . .

As discussed in Chapter 1, Congress in 1954 addressed comprehensively for the first time the tax treatment of partners and partnerships. With regard to the specific issue raised with respect to our Abbey/Ross hypothetical, Congress enacted § 721, a nonrecognition provision specific to partnerships and their partners.

---

§ 721. Nonrecognition of Gain or Loss on Contribution

(a) **General rule**. — No gain or loss shall be recognized to a partnership or to any of its partners in the case of a contribution of property to the partnership in exchange for an interest in the partnership.

According to the legislative history of the 1954 Act, the enactment of the nonrecognition rule of § 721 represented merely a codification of existing case law. The legislative history notes: "This [nonrecognition] rule is to apply both in the case of contribution to a partnership in the process of formation, and in the case of contribution to a partnership which is already formed and operating." As a result of § 721, the contribution of property to a partnership in exchange for a partnership interest is generally pain free; it is a nonrecognition event like moving money from one pocket to the other. See *Peracchi v. Commissioner*, 143 F.3d 487 (9th Cir. 1998) (addressing comparable nonrecognition rules related to corporate formation).

Applying § 721 to the creation of the LLC, Abbey would recognize no gain and Ross no loss when they exchanged their tracts of land for membership interests in the LLC. Likewise, the LLC would recognize no gain or loss as a result of the exchange.

B. A Partner's Outside Basis: Preservation of the Contributing Partner's Gain or Loss

Nonrecognition provisions merely defer gain or loss rather than permanently excluding gain or disallowing loss. The unrecognized gain or loss is preserved through the basis mechanism. For example, if Abbey and Ross had simply exchanged with one another their respective five-acre tracts of land instead of forming the LLC, neither Abbey's gain nor Ross' loss would be recognized under the like-kind exchange rules of § 1031 (assuming all requirements of that provision were satisfied). Abbey and Ross would simply take the same basis in the land each received from the other as she or he had in the land each relinquished in the exchange. § 1031(d). Section 722 similarly provides that the basis of a partnership interest (commonly referred to as a partner's outside basis) acquired in exchange for a contribution of *property*, including money, to the partnership will be the amount of the money contributed plus the adjusted basis to the contributing partner of any other property contributed.

> **§ 722. Basis of Contributing Partner's Interest**
>
> The basis of an interest in a partnership acquired by a contribution of property, including money, to the partnership shall be the amount of such money and the adjusted basis of such property to the contributing partner at the time of the contribution increased by the amount (if any) of gain recognized under section 721(b) to the contributing partner at such time.

Applying this provision to our hypothetical, Abbey will have a $20,000 basis (outside basis) in her membership interest in the LLC while Ross will have $225,000 outside basis. Notice that, consistent with nonrecognition standards, Abbey's basis in her membership interest preserves the $180,000 gain that inhered in (or was built into) the land she contributed. Were Abbey to sell her LLC interest for $200,000, she would recognize that $180,000 of gain. Likewise, Ross' basis in his LLC membership interest preserves the $25,000 of loss that inhered in the land he contributed. Were Ross to sell his interest in the LLC for $200,000, he would recognize $25,000 of loss.[1]

It may be worth digressing for a moment to consider the basis Abbey and Ross would have taken in their LLC interests if § 721 did not exist and the exchange of their property for interest in the LLC were to be treated as a *taxable exchange*. In that case, Abbey would recognize $180,000 gain on the exchange and, pursuant to the rule of *Philadelphia Park Amusement Co. v. U.S.*, 126 F. Supp. 184 (Ct. Cl. 1954), i.e., "the cost basis of the property received in a *taxable exchange* is the fair market value of the property received in the exchange," Abbey's basis in her LLC interest would be $200,000. Similarly, Ross would recognize $25,000 of loss on the exchange of his land for an interest in the LLC and, under *Philadelphia Park*, would take a $200,000 basis in the $200,000 LLC interest he received in the exchange.[2] This brief digression should make clear the relationship between gain/loss recognition or nonrecognition and a partner's outside basis.

C. The Partnership's Inside Basis: Preservation of Gain and Loss at Partnership Level

Apart from determining the basis Abbey and Ross take in their LLC interests, another basis question must be addressed: what basis will the LLC have in the land contributed by Abbey and Ross. The importance of that question should be apparent to you. Among other reasons, we need to know the basis the LLC will have in each tract of land (commonly referred to as the partnership's inside basis)

---

[1] § 165(c)(1).

[2] These outside bases results, of course, make sense because Abbey will have recognized all of the gain that inhered in the land she contributed and Ross will have recognized all of the loss inherent in the land he contributed. Thus, there is no unrecognized gain or loss to be preserved in the basis of the membership interest each receives in the LLC. *See* Reg. § 1.61-2(d)(2).

so we can determine the tax consequences, if any, were the LLC to sell or exchange one or both tracts.[3]

Before considering the Code provisions addressing the basis (inside basis) the LLC will have in the land contributed by Abbey and Ross, let's digress to consider one possible answer to this basis issue, *albeit an incorrect answer*, i.e., the LLC will have a fair market value basis in each tract of land. In other words, what if we were to apply § 722 as we are required to do in determining Abbey's and Ross's outside bases, but simultaneously applied the *Philadelphia Park* rule in determining the basis the LLC took in the land it received from Abbey and Ross? Were this the answer, the LLC would have a $200,000 basis in each tract of land it received. The problem, of course, is that the exchange in our hypothetical was not a taxable exchange — the nonrecognition rule of § 721 makes that point clearly. Application of the *Philadelphia Park* standard to determine the LLC's inside basis in the tracts of land would open the door for abuse. For example, if the LLC has a $200,000 basis in land contributed by Abbey, it could immediately sell that land for $200,000 and no gain would be recognized. You might be tempted to conclude that result is acceptable because, as noted above, Abbey's basis in her LLC interest preserves the $180,000 of gain that inhered in the land when she contributed it. But Abbey likely won't be selling her interest in the LLC any time soon and, in the meanwhile, will have succeeded in converting her appreciated land into cash (through the LLC) without the recognition of any gain. Giving a partnership (or as in our example, an LLC) a fair market value basis in the properties contributed to it, would thus facilitate tax avoidance, e.g., taxpayers planning to sell appreciated property could inappropriately defer the gain by simply transferring the property first to a partnership or LLC taxed as a partnership and then directing the entity to make the sale.[4]

Long before the 1954 Internal Revenue Code was adopted, Congress prevented the above abuse by enacting a statute that provided a partnership's basis (its inside basis) in contributed property would be "the same as it would be in the hands of the transferor, increased in the amount of gain . . . recognized to the transferor upon such transfer . . . " In 1954, Congress added § 723 corresponding to this earlier Code provision.

---

§ 723. Basis of Property Contributed to Partnership

The basis of property contributed to a partnership by a partner shall be the adjusted basis of such property to the contributing partner at the time of the contribution increased by the amount (if any) of gain recognized

---

[3] If, instead of land, Abbey and Ross had contributed properties that, unlike the land, would be depreciable by the LLC, it would be necessary to know the LLC's basis in the properties so that we could compute allowable depreciation deductions. (If a contributing partner had been depreciating the property, the partnership would continue to depreciate property using same schedule as the contributing partner. § 168(i)(7); Prop. Treas. Reg. 1.168-4(d)(5).)

[4] Depending on the facts, such an abusive strategy might be successfully attacked using the step transaction or sham transaction doctrines.

> under section 721(b) to the contributing partner at such time.

Applying § 723 to the facts of our hypothetical, the LLC will have a $20,000 basis in the land contributed by Abbey and a $225,000 basis in the land contributed by Ross. At this point, you may be puzzled! It appears that, as a result of §§ 722 and 723, the built-in gain on Abbey's land and the built-in loss on Ross's land has been doubled, i.e., Abbey has a $20,000 basis in her LLC interest worth $200,000 and the LLC has a $20,000 basis in Abbey's land worth $200,000 and, likewise, Ross has a $225,000 basis in his LLC interest worth $200,000 and the LLC has a $225,000 basis in Ross' land worth $200,000. But sometimes things aren't as they appear to be. As you will learn later in this course, if the LLC were to sell the land contributed by Abbey for $200,000, the $180,000 of gain that would be recognized would not be taxable to the LLC because, as § 701 makes clear, partnerships and LLCs taxed as partnerships are not subject to tax. Rather, pursuant to § 704(c)(1)(A), addressed in Chapter 10, the $180,000 of gain recognized on the sale will be allocated to Abbey and included by her in her gross income. Consistent with tax cost basis notions,[5] Abbey's outside basis, as a result, would be increased by $180,000 to $200,000. § 705(a)(1)(A). If Abbey were then to sell her LLC interest for its fair market value of $200,000, she would report no gain (i.e., her amount realized of $200,000 would be completely offset by her $200,000 outside basis). See § 731(a)(1). In other words, although § 721 allowed Abbey to defer the $180,000 of gain inherent in the land she contributed to the LLC, she must recognize that gain when the LLC disposes of that land for $200,000 in a taxable transaction. Having recognized the gain, her outside basis is adjusted to prevent the double taxation you might otherwise have assumed would occur.[6]

The example above and footnote 6 demonstrate that there is no doubling of the gains and/or losses inherent in properties contributed to a partnership. Instead, there is ultimately only a single level of tax. This is one of the many ways in which the tax consequences of contributions to partnerships differ from the tax treatment associated with the contribution of properties to Subchapter C corporations.[7]

---

[5] In this regard, you might recall that, in your basic tax course, you studied situations where, for example, a taxpayer, as compensation for services rendered, received property other than cash. Because the taxpayer was required to include the value of the property received in her gross income, the taxpayer was entitled to take a basis in that property equal to the amount included in gross income. See Reg. § 1.61-2(d)(2)(i). That same concept applies in the partnership context as has been demonstrated above.

[6] Similarly, if the LLC were to sell the land contributed by Ross for $200,000, the LLC would recognize a $25,000 loss that would be allocated to Ross. § 704(c)(1)(A). As a result of this allocation, Ross's outside basis will be adjusted downward to reflect his recovery of $25,000 of his unrecovered cost by way of the loss deduction allocated to him. § 705(c)(2)(A). (Recall from your basic tax course that when, for example, a taxpayer is allowed a loss deduction under § 165(c)(2) for damage to business property, the taxpayer is required to reduce her basis in that property to reflect the recovery of part of its cost. § 1016(a)(1).)

[7] If Abbey and Ross had contributed their respective parcels of land to a Subchapter C corporation, they would have taken the same basis in the stock they received in the exchange as they did when they exchanged their land for an interest in the LLC. § 358(a)(1). Similarly, the corporation would have taken the same basis as the LLC did in the land contributed by Abbey and Ross. § 362(a). Unlike the results in our example under Subchapter K, however, if the corporation sold the land, it would be taxable on the gain or loss — thus the gain or loss would be doubled for tax purposes. See § 11.

D. Scope of Nonrecognition under § 721

As noted above, in enacting § 721 and the related basis provisions of §§ 722 and 723, Congress intended to codify the long-standing practice of enabling taxpayers to transfer *properties* (but not *services*) to partnerships without recognition of either gain or loss. In subsequent chapters, you will learn that, in general, Congress provided nonrecognition treatment for both liquidating and nonliquidating distributions. Congress thus created a nonrecognition regime making it possible for taxpayers to transfer properties to partnerships and for partnerships to transfer properties to partners without the recognition of gain or loss.

1. Section 721 and Section 1245 Property

With respect to the formation of a partnership, the strength of this nonrecognition regime is reflected in a number of Code and regulation provisions. You will recall from your basic income tax course that § 1245 recaptures as ordinary income what might be thought of as excess depreciation deductions claimed with respect to Section 1245 property[8] upon disposal of that property.[9] At first glance, the scope of § 1245 is striking. Section 1245 recapture may result whenever Section 1245 property is "disposed of" whether by sale, exchange, involuntary conversion or "other disposition." Moreover, if § 1245(a)(1) characterizes gain as ordinary income, the gain is recognized — and § 1245 applies — "notwithstanding any other provision of this subtitle." Is gain recognized pursuant to § 1245(a) if a taxpayer contributes appreciated Section 1245 property to a partnership? In other words, will § 1245 trump § 721? If it did, the congressional purpose of allowing taxpayers to form partnerships without recognizing gain (or loss) on the transfer of properties to those entities would be significantly frustrated. After all, it is not uncommon for taxpayers forming partnerships to contribute Section 1245 property to the new entity.

In general, no gain is recognized pursuant to § 1245 when a taxpayer contributes Section 1245 property to a partnership. Read § 1245(b)(3) carefully and note the reference therein to § 721. Because, as a general rule, under § 721 no gain will be

---

[8] § 1245 property is generally personal property that is or has been property of a character subject to the allowance of depreciation provided in § 167. § 1245(a)(3)(A).

[9] For example, assume a taxpayer paid $1,000,000 for depreciable equipment for use in her business and was allowed $300,000 in depreciation deductions before she sold the equipment for $800,000. As a result of the depreciation deduction allowed, the taxpayer's adjusted basis in the equipment at the time of the sale was $700,000, resulting in gain recognized of $100,000 on the sale. § 1001. The $100,000 of gain recognized can be understood as reflecting excess depreciation allowed (i.e., the taxpayer claimed $300,000 in depreciation deductions prior to the sale and yet, economically, the equipment depreciated only $200,000 as indicated by the $800,000 sale price). Conceptually you would expect the gain to be characterized as ordinary income, i.e., it would merely make up for the ordinary income that was offset by the $100,000 of excess depreciation deductions. You will recall, however, that depreciable equipment is normally characterized as Section 1231(b) property (review § 1231(b)) and the gain from the sale of Section 1231(b) property would typically be characterized as long-term capital gain subject to a top tax rate of 20%. Congress enacted § 1245 to negate this result. Section 1245 will trump § 1231 and characterize as ordinary income all $100,000 of the gain taxpayer recognizes as ordinary income. *See* Reg. § 1.1245-6(a).

recognized by a transferor on a transfer of property to a partnership, § 1245(a)(1) will not apply to the transfer. Thus, § 721 trumps the general rule of § 1245. Does this mean the § 1245 taint just disappears? That result would simply be too good to be true! Through the definitions of "Section 1245 property" (§ 1245(a)(3)) and "recomputed basis," (§ 1245(a)(2)(A)), § 1245 preserves the "recapture potential" in the hands of the transferee partnership. (Note that § 1250 recapture is likewise postponed by § 721. § 1250(d)(3).)

2. Section 721 and Section 453B

The installment method of accounting is generally available to a taxpayer who sells property and will receive at least one payment following the year of the sale. § 453 (b). Under the installment method, the taxpayer is allowed to spread the gain on a sale — and the tax liability that gain generates — over the period the taxpayer receives payments. § 453(c). In general, when a taxpayer disposes of an installment obligation, the tax deferral authorized by § 453 ends. § 453B(a). If a taxpayer contributes an installment note to a partnership in exchange for a partnership interest, does § 453B require the taxpayer to recognize gain in the amount of the difference between the value of the interest received and the adjusted basis of the installment note? Section 453B is silent on this issue. Regulation §§ 1.721-1(a) and 1.453-9(c)(2), however, say "No." As in the case of the relationship between §§ 721 and 1245 discussed above, the nonrecognition rule of § 721 prevails. No gain will be recognized. Instead, the gain inherent in the installment obligation will be recognized by the partnership under the installment method. Pursuant to § 704(c)(1)(A) (addressed in detail in Chapter 10), the gain recognized by the partnership will, in turn, be allocated to the contributing partner. In other words, for tax purposes, it's just as though the obligation were never contributed to the LLC and the taxpayer directly received all of the payments under the installment obligation.

E. Property

Section 721 only applies to contributions of *property* to a partnership. While § 721 makes no reference to contributions of services, Reg. § 1.721-1(b)(1) provides that a partner contributing services in exchange for a capital interest in a partnership must include in gross income the value of that partnership interest.[10] Chapter 4 addresses the tax consequences associated with the exchange of services for an interest in a partnership.

The term "property" as used in § 721 has been interpreted broadly to encompass both tangible property, e.g., the land or equipment in our prior examples, and intangible property, e.g., installment obligations, and accounts receivable. *United States v. Stafford*, included in the materials, suggests the breadth accorded the term "property" and provides a helpful discussion of how the courts and the Service have utilized the interpretation of "property" under the

---

[10] Section 351(a) in Subchapter C likewise provides nonrecognition treatment to contributions of *property* to corporations in exchange for stock. Unlike § 721, § 351 clarifies that stock issued for *services* will not be considered stock issued in return for property and, as a result, will not be subject to the nonrecognition rule of § 351(a). § 351(d)

nonrecognition rule of § 351 to inform their interpretation of "property" under § 721.

F. Holding Periods

Recall that § 1(h) accords preferential rates only to long-term capital gains (or, more specifically, net capital gains). Under § 1222(3), a long-term capital gain is a gain from the sale or exchange of a capital asset *held for more than one year*. So "long-term" means more than one year. The sale or exchange of a partnership interest will generally be treated as a sale or exchange of a capital asset. § 741. As a result, a taxpayer's holding period in a partnership interest could be significant. Likewise, the holding period a partnership has in its assets, including the assets contributed to it, is also important. Section 1223 excerpted below addresses the holding period of property, including partnership interests.

---

§ 1223. Holding Period of Property

For purposes of this subtitle —

(1) In determining the period for which the taxpayer has held property received in an exchange, there shall be included the period for which he held the property exchanged, if, under this chapter, the property has, for the purpose of determining gain or loss from a sale or exchange, the same basis in whole or in part in his hands as the property exchanged and, in the case of such exchanges after March 1, 1954, the property exchanged at the time of such exchange was a capital asset as defined in section 1221 or property described in section 1231 . . .

(2) In determining the period for which the taxpayer has held property however acquired there shall be included the period for which such property was held by any other person, if under this chapter such property has, for the purpose of determining gain or loss from a sale or exchange, the same basis in whole or in part in his hands as it would have in the hands of such other person.

Pursuant to § 1223(1), the taxpayer's holding period in the property received in an exchange will include the holding period of the property relinquished so long as that property was a capital asset or a § 1231 asset and the taxpayer has the same basis in the property received as the taxpayer had in the property relinquished. For example, in the problem considered at the outset of this Overview, Abbey and Ross both contributed tracts of land they had held long-term in exchange for their interests in the LLC. Applying § 1221(1), Abbey and Ross would each have a long-term holding period in their LLC interest because the land they relinquished in the exchange constituted a capital asset, i.e., it was real property held for investment, and the basis they each took in their LLC interest was the same as the basis they had in the land contributed. In other words, the holding period they had in the land is "tacked" to the holding period of their LLC interest. If, by contrast, Abbey and Ross had contributed business inventory rather than the land, regardless of how long they might have held the inventory, they would not be entitled to tack the holding period of the inventory to the holding period of their LLC interest. In this latter case, their holding period would commence at the time of their contribution to the LLC. The same would be true of cash contributions. See Rev. Rul. 66-7, 1966-1 C.B. 188. See also Reg. § 1.1223-3(f) Ex. 1 (holding period attributable to cash contribution begins on the day after contribution).

At this point, you might well ask what holding period a taxpayer would take in an LLC or partnership interest if the taxpayer, for example, contributed both inventory and a capital asset (or § 1231 asset) to the partnership. Believe it or not, the taxpayer would take a split holding period in her LLC or partnership interest! Assume Abbey had contributed $100,000 of cash and land (held long-term) with a fair market value of $100,000 and an adjusted basis of $10,000 in exchange for her one-half interest in the Land Yacht Storage, LLC. Under § 722, Abbey would have a $110,000 basis in her LLC interest and, under § 1223(1), that interest would have a split holding period — one-half of her interest (attributable to the cash) would have a holding period that commenced at the time of Abbey's contribution (of the cash); the other half of her interest (attributable to the land) would have a long-term holding period. If Abbey were to sell her LLC interest for $200,000 one month later when the partnership's only assets were the $100,000 of cash, $100,000 of land Abbey had contributed, and the $200,000 of land Ross had contributed, Abbey would have $90,000 of gain, one-half of which would be treated as short-term capital gain and the other half of which would be treated as long-term capital gain. *See* Reg. § 1.1223-3(f) Ex. 1. Treasury has provided elaborate regulations addressing the determination of split holding periods for partnership and LLC interests. Reg. § 1.1223-3.[11]

Section 1223(2) applies in determining the holding period a partnership has in property contributed to it in exchange for a partnership interest. As applied to partnerships, that provision, in effect, provides the holding period of the partnership will include the holding period the contributing partner had in the property since the partnership, pursuant to § 723, has the same basis in the property the contributing partner had. Thus, in our Abbey/Ross example where the partners had held for many years the land they contributed to the LLC, the LLC will have a long-term holding period in each tract of land, i.e., the LLC will tack the holding period Abbey and Ross had in their respective tracts of land.

G. Character of Gain or Loss on Disposition of Contributed Property

Assume a situation in which a sole proprietor of a retail farm implement business takes from inventory a tractor and contributes the tractor, together with other property, to a newly formed LLC that will engage in a farming business and will be taxed as a partnership. Assume the taxpayer's basis in the inventory were $50,000 and the tractor had a fair market value of $100,000. As discussed above, the LLC will take a $50,000 basis in the tractor (§ 723) and will have a holding period

---

[11] Apart from Ex. 1 of the regulations noted above, the other examples provided by that regulation implicate aspects of Subchapter K addressed in later chapters.

in the tractor that includes the holding period of the taxpayer (§ 1223(2)). Note that, if the taxpayer had sold the tractor in the course of his farm implement business for $100,000 rather than contributing it to the LLC, the taxpayer would have had $50,000 of *ordinary income* because the tractor constituted inventory in the hands of the taxpayer and was thus neither a capital asset nor a § 1231(b) asset.[12] By contrast, the LLC will use the tractor in its business. As a result, the tractor will be a depreciable asset (§§ 167 and 168). Assume the partnership holds the tractor for more than one year and then sells the tractor for $100,000. If we disregard any depreciation claimed by the partnership and therefore assume the partnership's adjusted basis continued to be $50,000, the partnership would recognize $50,000 of gain. How should that gain be characterized? Under general tax rules, we would treat the gain as § 1231 gain and, as a result, the partnership gain could potentially be characterized as long-term capital gain. § 1231(a)(1). Of course, since the LLC is not a taxable entity, that gain would be allocated under § 704(c)(1)(A) (see Chapter 10) to our taxpayer. Think about what has happened — it appears that by contributing the inventory to an LLC, the taxpayer has succeeded in converting what would otherwise be $50,000 of ordinary income (if the taxpayer had sold the tractor instead of contributing it to the LLC) into long-term capital gain.

Congress in 1984 added § 724 to prevent the use of partnerships to convert ordinary income into capital gain and to address other related matters. Consider the following helpful passage from the legislative history of § 724:

> Congress was concerned that, under some circumstances, a taxpayer could alter the character of gain or loss under prior law merely by contributing property to a new or existing partnership. In particular, the conversion of capital losses to ordinary losses by contributing securities to a dealer partnership allowed a taxpayer to receive the benefits of capital gain taxation on appreciated securities (by selling them individually) while deducting ordinary losses on the sale of securities which had declined in value (by having the dealer partnership sell them and allocate the resulting loss to the taxpayer). Congress believed that these potential abuses should be prevented by preserving the pre-contribution character of contributed (or substituted basis) property in appropriate cases.

The Joint Committee on Taxation, in the General Explanation of the Revenue Provisions of the Tax Reform Act of 1984, at page 235, provided the following explanation of § 724 (we have supplemented the congressional interpretation with our own bracketed comments):

> Under [new § 724], if a partnership disposes of property which was inventory property in the hands of the partner immediately before its contribution [as in our tractor hypothetical above], any gain or loss recognized by the partnership on the disposition of the property for a period of 5 years after the date of the contribution is treated as ordinary

---

[12] This assumes that, at the time of the sale, the taxpayer's basis continued to be $50,000. Because the tractor was inventory, the taxpayer would not have been allowed any depreciation deductions that would have required a downward adjustment in the taxpayer's basis. *See* Reg. § 1.167(a)-2.

income or loss. [**Authors' note:** *Thus, if the tractor is "old and cold", i.e., has been held by the partnership for more than five years, the inventory "taint" would no longer apply. Obviously, under these circumstances, there is no game-playing — the taxpayer is not attempting to convert ordinary income to capital gain by contributing the property to the LLC.*] Gain or loss on a disposition of unrealized receivables contributed by a partner is treated as ordinary income or loss regardless of the date of disposition. [**Authors' note:** *"Unrealized receivables" is a term of art defined in § 751(c). For now, you should think of "unrealized receivables" as generally being the accounts receivable of a cash method taxpayer. Thus, if our farm implement dealer/taxpayer in the above hypothetical also contributed to the LLC certain accounts receivable that the dealer/taxpayer had never included in income, the LLC would recognize ordinary income whenever it collected on the accounts receivable. In other words, the ordinary income inherent in the dealer/taxpayer's accounts receivable will result in ordinary income when the accounts are finally paid.*] Section 724(c) further provides that built-in losses on capital assets retain their character as capital losses for a period of five years after the date of contribution, but only to the extent of pre-contribution unrealized losses. [**Authors' note:** *For example, assume a taxpayer contributed a tract of land held for investment to a partnership in exchange for a partnership interest. Assume the land had a fair market value of $100,000 and an adjusted basis of $150,000. (Thus, the land had a built-in capital loss of $50,000.) The partnership will have a $150,000 basis in the land. § 723. Assume the partnership holds the land as inventory. If, within the five-year period subsequent to the contribution, the partnership sold the land for $100,000, all $50,000 of loss would be characterized under § 724(c) as capital loss notwithstanding the fact the land is inventory. If, however, the LLC were to sell the land during that five-year period for $80,000, § 724(c) would treat only $50,000 of the $70,000 of loss as a capital loss with the remaining $20,000 of loss being treated as an ordinary loss.*]

H. Conclusion

As a general rule, gain or loss is not recognized on the contribution of property to partnerships. § 721. Congress has gone to great lengths in Subchapter K and related provisions to enable taxpayers to transfer property to a newly created partnership without paying a tax toll.[13] As is true in other nonrecognition contexts, the unrecognized gain or loss is preserved through the basis mechanism. Thus, as discussed in this Overview, the basis (outside basis) a contributing partner takes in a partnership interest received in exchange for property will preserve any unrecognized gain or loss built-in to that property (§ 722) and the partnership will have a basis (inside basis) in the property contributed equal to the adjusted basis the contributing partner had in the property. Do not assume, however, that gain will never be recognized on the contribution of property to a partnership. As you

---

[13] The same is true with respect to the formation of a Subchapter C or Subchapter S corporation. *See* §§ 351 and 1371.

will discover in the next chapter, under certain circumstances the contribution of encumbered property may result in gain recognition to a contributing partner. Likewise, as suggested in this Overview and as discussed in detail in Chapter 4, the contribution of services to a partnership in exchange for a partnership interest is not within the scope of the nonrecognition rule of § 721. We urge you to study the provisions addressed in this Overview carefully as they set the foundation for the topics discussed in subsequent chapters.

UNITED STATES v. STAFFORD
727 F.2d 1043 (11th Cir. 1984)

ANDERSON, CIRCUIT JUDGE:

[This] refund action involves the Staffords' 1969 tax return, in which they did not account for their receipt of a limited partnership interest valued at $100,000. The taxpayers argue that the partnership share qualified for nonrecognition treatment under I.R.C. § 721(a) because it was received in "exchange" for "property" they contributed to the partnership. The district court held that nonrecognition was not available because the taxpayers' contribution of a letter of intent to the partnership did not meet the exchange and property requirements of the statute. We conclude that the district court applied an improper legal standard and under the proper legal test several issues should have been decided in favor of the taxpayers. . . . We therefore reverse and remand.

I. HISTORY OF THE CASE

Throughout the 1960s, DeNean Stafford worked as a real estate developer, often in projects involving hotel property. At least two of Stafford's projects had used financing from the Life Insurance Company of Georgia ("LOG"). The business relationship between Stafford and LOG had taken various forms depending on the project. The hotel development involved in the present case, however, was somewhat unique.

In the early 1960s, LOG acquired property in Atlanta and constructed its corporate headquarters. LOG also owned the land adjacent to the headquarters, which at the time was undeveloped. LOG officials, in particular Mr. H. Talmadge Dobbs, who was then an executive vice president and member of the finance committee, approached Stafford and began negotiations for construction of a hotel complex on the unused land. In February of 1967, the LOG finance committee officially authorized continued discussions with Stafford on the hotel development.

Negotiations between Stafford and LOG led to a July 2, 1968, letter from Mr. Dobbs to Stafford, setting forth the numerous points of agreement as of that date and additional details in need of future resolution. In particular, the letter promised 6¾% interest on the loan financing for the hotel and it specified lease terms; both the interest rate and lease terms were very favorable to Stafford given then existing market conditions. Mr. Dobbs sent additional correspondence to Stafford on July 3,

1968, indicating that the favorable conditions described in the July 2 letter would be open for Stafford's consideration for a period of 60 days.

Under the terms of the July 2 letter, Stafford or his designee were to provide 25% equity for the hotel development. With letter in hand, Stafford contacted attorneys and business acquaintances and investigated the formation of a limited partnership to provide that equity share. On August 30, 1968, he responded to the LOG letter of July 2, accepting the general terms set forth in the letter and proposing further negotiation on additional details.

On October 30, 1968, Mr. A.F. Irby, a business associate of Stafford's, contacted potential investors with a draft of a limited partnership agreement and details regarding the proposed development. The letter stated:

> You will note in this file that Mr. Stafford is delivering the lease, which is highly economic, the construction loan and the permanent financing to the partners for what amounts to $100,000 of additional participation. The cost in the open market of procuring these three items would be in excess of $250,000 ***
>
> The Life of Georgia will supply all of the construction funds but will require that $2,000,000 of equity be invested prior to their own advancement of construction monies.
>
> When you consider the fact that this is a very favorable tax arrangement, that the permanent loan is for 30 years at an interest of 6¾% and that the cost of the development is at least $1,500,000 less than it would be under ordinary circumstances this would appear to be an excellent deal.

In January of 1969, Stafford and a number of investors formed Center Investments, Ltd., a Georgia limited partnership, to pursue the development. Stafford was designated the sole general partner. He purchased two $100,000 shares and received a third limited partnership share for contributing to the partnership the letter of intent and the agreement with LOG contained therein. In all, the partnership sold 20 units for $100,000 each, which together with the unit Stafford received for his capital contribution made a total of 21 units. Some eighteen months later, the partnership voted to amend the partnership agreement to provide Stafford a salary for his duties as general manager.

By mid-1970 the necessary capital had been raised and plans for the hotel development were set and approved. LOG and Center Investments executed formal lease and loan documents. The hotel project had expanded to a 550 room facility. This expansion, and unforeseen construction problems, had escalated the cost to over $9,000,000. LOG increased the amount of its loan to $7,127,500, but it substantially abided by the terms set forth in the July 2, 1968, letter to DeNean Stafford. LOG maintained the 6¾% interest rate on the first $5,000,000 it loaned to Center Investments. (The remaining $2,127,500 was financed at 9¾% interest, the market rate in 1970). LOG and Center Investments also followed the formula set forth in the July 2 letter as the method for calculating lease payments. These terms had become even more favorable to Center Investments than when first proposed, owing to changed market conditions.

On their 1969 joint federal tax return, the Staffords did not report as income their receipt of the third partnership share. The Commissioner audited that return and determined that the Staffords should have treated the partnership share as compensation for services that Stafford rendered to the partnership in negotiating and developing the investment. The Commissioner thus concluded that the nonrecognition principles of § 721 did not apply to the third partnership share and assessed a deficiency of $64,000 plus interest. The Staffords paid the assessment and filed a claim for a refund.

. . . The district court, after considering cross-motions for summary judgment, granted summary judgment in favor of the government. *Stafford v. United States*, 552 F. Supp. 311 (M.D. Ga. 1982). The taxpayers appealed to this court.

. . . We must determine the proper tax characterization of the third partnership interest Stafford received . . .

III. EXCHANGE AND PROPERTY REQUIREMENTS

To qualify for nonrecognition treatment on the receipt of a partnership share, the partner must establish that he made a contribution of "property" in "exchange" for that share. I.R.C. § 721(a). Contrary to the district court's holding that the exchange and property requirements were not met, we conclude that these issues should have been decided in the taxpayers' favor.

A. *The Exchange Requirement*

1. Generally

The district court held that Stafford's contribution of the letter of intent to the limited partnership was not an "exchange" for purposes of § 721. The court defined exchange as "a mutual or reciprocal transfer of one thing for another" and suggested that each side to the transaction must have a choice as to whether or not they desire the transfer. . . . Because transfer of the letter of intent to the partnership was part of the partnership agreement as drafted by the taxpayers' attorneys, the court found that the limited partners never had a choice as to whether or not the transfer would take place.

The district court's opinion on this element lacks support in the language and principles of § 721. The regulations under § 721 specify that each partner "is entitled to be repaid his contributions of money or other property to the partnership (at the value placed upon such property by the partnership at the time of the contribution) whether made at the formation of the partnership or subsequent thereto." Treas. Reg. § 1.721-1(b)(1). That Stafford's contribution of the letter of intent was part of the partnership agreement at formation in no way undermines his argument that the contribution was part of an exchange with the partnership under § 721.

Furthermore, the purpose of § 721 is to facilitate the flow of property from individuals to partnerships that will use the property productively. By analogy, § 351 of the Internal Revenue Code allows nonrecognition for individuals transferring property to corporations. Indeed, post-transfer control of the transferee corporation by the contributing shareholder is a prerequisite to tax-free treatment under § 351. We therefore reject the district court's assumption that individual members of the transferee limited partnership must agree to the transfer before an exchange can occur under § 721.

For purposes of determining the meaning of the terms "property" and "exchange" under § 721(a), noted commentators have made frequent reference to judicial and administrative decisions under § 351. *See* W. McKee, W. Nelson & R. Whitmire, *Federal Taxation of Partnerships and Partners* para. 4.01[1] (1977) (hereinafter "Taxation of Partnerships"). Finding the provisions and rationale of §§ 351 and 721 closely analogous, we also will frequently refer to cases decided under § 351 while discussing the issues in the present case.

The district court opinion focused on the lack of agreement between Stafford and the limited partners. Viewed properly, the exchange that took place was between Stafford and the partnership, not the limited partners as individuals. The assignment of January 21, 1969 tends to establish that such an exchange occurred. Stafford contributed the letter of intent and other items; the partnership issued the third share to Stafford. Again, that this exchange occurred at the formation of the partnership and without a formal partnership vote does not alter our conclusion that an exchange took place.

B. *The Property Requirement*

The district court alternatively held that Stafford had not received his third partnership share as the result of a contribution of "property." The court correctly stated that "the key to the benefit of nonrecognition afforded by I.R.C. § 721(a) is that *property must be exchanged for an interest in the partnership.*" The district court then stated as its test for property under § 721:

> After having carefully considered the arguments of counsel in conjunction with the opinion of the court of appeals, it is the opinion of the court that both *value* and *enforceability* are necessary to a conclusion that a document is "property" for purposes of § 721.

Finding as a matter of law that the letter of intent was not enforceable, the court concluded that it was not property and the taxpayers were not eligible for nonrecognition under § 721.

We agree with the district court's conclusion that the letter of intent was not enforceable. Under Georgia law an agreement becomes enforceable when there is a meeting of the parties' minds "at the same time, upon the same subject matter, and in the same sense." In the present case, the July 2 letter of intent and Stafford's subsequent acceptance on August 30 did reflect an agreement on many essential terms; in particular, the parties were in agreement on the interest rate for the loan and the formula for calculating lease terms. However, the July 2, 1968, letter of intent acknowledged that "there were many details to be worked out" and stated only that "we [LOG] would like to continue our negotiations along the following general lines." The July 3 letter from LOG may have converted the proposal to negotiate to a firm proposal of major terms, but Stafford's response again made the execution of final lease and loan agreements expressly "subject to further negotiations" on several items. "Where it is evident from a written instrument, that the parties contemplated that it was incomplete, and that a binding agreement would be made subsequently, there is no agreement." . . .

The agreement in the present case unambiguously contemplated resolution of additional items before execution of the final contract. "An agreement to reach an agreement is a contradiction in terms and imposes no obligations on the parties thereto," . . . ; as such, the agreement between Stafford and LOG embodied in the letter of intent and acceptance letter was unenforceable. Stafford's contention that the parties intended to carry through with the terms of agreement set forth in the letter of intent is unavailing. Where, as here, the parties' written documents clearly and definitely make final agreement subject to mutually satisfactory future negotiations, we must decide as a matter of Georgia law that "the parties did not intend the letter agreement to be a binding, enforceable contract." . . .

Nevertheless, notwithstanding its lack of legal enforceability, we still must determine whether the letter of intent was "property" within the meaning of § 721. The previous panel opinion stated that "enforceability of any agreement evidenced by the letter of intent, while perhaps not dispositive of the question, is important and material." We agree. An enforceable contract would perhaps be assured of property status; but the absence of enforceability does not necessarily preclude a finding that a document, substantially committing the parties to the major terms of a development project, is property.

Several nonenforceable obligations may rise to the level of property for purposes of § 721 or § 351. Unpatented know-how, which results from services and is not enforceable, nevertheless can be deemed property. (. . . citing Rev. Rul. 64-56, 1964-1 (Part 1) C.B. 133 (the term property under § 351 includes unpatented secret processes and formulas); Rev. Rul. 71-564, 1971-2 C.B. 179 (transfer of exclusive right to use trade secret is property under § 351)).

The instant transfer of the letter of intent outlining the major terms of a proposed loan and lease agreement to which both parties felt morally bound is closely analogous to a transfer of goodwill, which, although clearly unenforceable, nevertheless has been treated as property. . . .

> If goodwill is associated with a going business that is transferred to a partnership, there should be no question about the applicability of § 721. Furthermore, even if goodwill is associated with an individual who will remain active in the transferred business, an effective contribution of goodwill may be made. [Quoting from TAXATION OF PARTNERSHIPS]

. . . citing Rev. Rul. 70-45, 1970-1 C.B. 17 (for the proposition that a professional person realizes capital gain on partial sale of goodwill to newly admitted partners); *See also* Rev. Rul. 79-288, 1979-2 C.B. 139 (transfer of trade name and goodwill to newly formed foreign corporation is transfer of property for purposes of § 351); Rev. Rul. 70-45, 1970-1 C.B. 17 (goodwill of a one-man personal service business can be capital asset; whether it is an anticipatory assignment of income or a transfer of goodwill is a question of fact).

Thus, we conclude that the district court's requirement of legal enforceability as an absolute prerequisite to finding property status under § 721 was improper.

For purposes of our discussion as to whether the instant letter of intent is "property," we will assume *arguendo* that the factfinder on remand determines that the letter had value. Under the appropriate legal standard and under the circumstances peculiar to this case, we conclude that the letter of intent encompassed a sufficient bundle of rights to constitute "property" within the meaning of § 721.

Although the Internal Revenue Code does not define property for purposes of § 721 or § 351, the courts have given the term rather broad application. . . . In *Hempt Bros., Inc. v. United States*, 354 F. Supp. 1172, 1175 (M.D. Pa. 1973) . . . , the court stated "that the term [property for purposes of § 351] encompasses whatever may be transferred."

The transfer of a taxpayer's full interest in a venture further supports a conclusion that the transferred item was property. *Cf.* Rev. Rul. 64-56, 1964-1 C.B. 133, 137 (evaluating the transfer of technical knowhow from a United States corporation to a newly organized foreign corporation and stating that "the transfer of all substantial rights and property of the kind hereinbefore specified [technical knowhow] will be treated as a transfer of property for purposes of § 351 of the code"). . . .

As noted in the previous panel opinion, a taxpayer can create property by his provision of personal services. . . .

Finally, we have held that legal enforceability of the rights asserted as property is important, but not dispositive.

In the present case, the letter of intent of July 2 played a unique role. LOG officials have testified that it is the only commitment of this type the company has ever issued and that the letter was part of what they viewed to be a special project. Because the hotel was adjacent to LOG headquarters, officials of the company were willing to provide both construction financing, a permanent mortgage, and a lease for land and airspace, all at terms very favorable to the developer. When Stafford and LOG had reached agreement on these terms, the company offered the letter of intent because "this was a very peculiar transaction and I think because the way it developed, and the way the negotiations went on, this was a proper instrument to put the intent of the parties into something that would be — that we could rely on."

Although not enforceable in a strict legal sense, the written documents — i.e., the terms of the July 2 letter, together with the July 3 letter limiting availability of those terms to acceptance within 60 days, and Stafford's August 30 letter of acceptance wherein he agreed to the essential terms of the letter of intent, including the interest on the loan and the lease terms — represented an agreement on the major terms that was quite firm in the view of the parties. Both of the principals have testified that they felt bound by the terms of the letter. . . . Two years subsequent to the letter, when market conditions made those terms very favorable to the partnership, the parties substantially adhered to the terms stated in the letter of intent. The letter clearly was transferable. The letter itself evidenced a commitment to Stafford "or his designee." The principals have testified that from the outset they anticipated Stafford would transfer the letter to an investment group formed to develop the hotel. LOG officials attended meetings of the prospective partners and were aware that the letter would be transferred. Again, we note that even though Stafford transferred the letter to the partnership, LOG officials were willing to abide by the terms of the letter in subsequent dealing. If property "encompasses whatever may be transferred," then the letter of intent meets this test. In addition, the letter of intent that Stafford transferred to the partnership embodied his entire interest in the hotel development venture; he held nothing back.

A conclusion that the letter of intent is "property" under the instant circumstances comports with the purpose of § 721. Stafford exerted personal efforts on his own behalf in negotiating with LOG. When LOG and Stafford exchanged the letter of intent and acceptance in 1968, the government had not suggested that Stafford recognized taxable income. He could have completed the project as a sole proprietor without recognition of income based on his receipt of the letter. The purpose of §§ 721 and 351 is to permit the taxpayer to change his individual business into partnership or corporate form; the Code is designed to prevent the mere change in form from precipitating taxation. In keeping with this purpose, we can discern no reason to exclude Stafford's transfer of the letter of intent from the protective characterization as "property."

Stafford through his business reputation and work efforts was able to negotiate a very promising development project with LOG. He obtained from LOG officials a written document, morally, if not legally, committing LOG to the major terms of a proposed loan and lease. The transferability of the letter is undisputed and Stafford transferred his full interest in the project to the partnership. We conclude that the letter encompassed a sufficient bundle of rights and obligations to be deemed property for purposes of § 721.

For the foregoing reasons, we have concluded that Stafford's transfer of the letter of intent to the partnership met both the "exchange" and "property" requirements of § 721.

Chapter 3

CONTRIBUTION OF ENCUMBERED PROPERTY

I. PROBLEMS

1. Alex, Cathy, and Erin form the ACE Partnership, a general partnership, in which Alex, Cathy, and Erin will share profits and losses equally. Alex and Cathy each contribute $80,000 of cash and Erin contributes land with a fair market value of $200,000 and an adjusted basis of $60,000. (Erin held the land for investment for many years.) Erin's land is encumbered by a recourse liability of $120,000, which the partnership assumes.

   (a) How much gain, if any, must Erin recognize as a result of the partnership's assumption of the recourse liability encumbering the land she contributed? What bases will Alex, Erin, and Cathy have in their partnership interests?

   (b) How would your answers to (a) change if the land Erin contributed had a fair market value of $180,000 and Erin also contributed $20,000 of cash? (Assume again Erin's land is encumbered by a $120,000 recourse liability that the partnership assumes.)

   (c) How would your answers to questions (a) and (b) change, if at all, if the $120,000 liability encumbering Erin's land were nonrecourse and the partnership took the land subject to that liability?

   (d) How would your answers to questions (a), (b), and (c) change if Erin's adjusted basis in the land she contributed to the partnership were $90,000?

2. Allan and Barbara form the AB general partnership in which they are equal partners. The partnership and the partners use the cash method of accounting. As detailed in the table below, Allan contributes cash as well as land he held for investment purposes; and Barbara contributes some securities she held for investment and the inventory and accounts receivable of a small cash-method business she operated. The partnership assumes the $50,000 of accounts payable of Barbara's business. Assume the land and securities contributed by Allan and Barbara have been held for more than one year. The table below shows the assets each partner contributed, the contributing partner's adjusted bases in the assets, and the assets' fair market values.

Partner	Asset Contributed	Adjusted Basis	Fair Market Value
Allan	Cash	$50,000	$50,000
	Land	$175,000	$150,000
Barbara	Inventory	$30,000	$75,000
	Accounts Receivable	$0	$100,000
	Securities	$10,000	$75,000

Note: As indicated above, the partnership will also assume $50,000 of accounts payable from Barbara's business. Assume the accounts payable will be deductible when the partnership pays them.

(a) Will either partner recognize any gain or loss on the contribution of his or her property to the partnership?

(b) What is each partner's outside basis immediately following the exchange?

(c) When the partnership collects the accounts receivable contributed by Barbara, how much income, if any, must she report? What impact will the partnership's collection of the accounts receivable and payment of the accounts payable have on Barbara's outside basis?

Assignment for Chapter 3:

Complete the Problems above.

Read: Internal Revenue Code: §§ 704(c)(1)(A), 705, 721, 722, 723, 731(a)(1), 733, 752(a)–(c).
Treasury Regulations: §§ 1.722-1; 1.752-1(a)(1) and (2), (b), (c), (d)(1), (e), (f), and (g) Ex. 1; § 1.752-2(a) and (b); § 1.752-3(a); § 1.1001-2(a);
Materials: Overview

II. VOCABULARY

recourse liability
nonrecourse liability
economic risk of loss
constructive liquidation
minimum § 704(c) gain

III. OBJECTIVES

1. To identify a recourse liability.
2. To identify a nonrecourse liability.
3. To identify who bears the economic risk of loss with respect to a recourse liability.
4. To explain in general how recourse liabilities encumbering contributed property are allocated between or among the partners.

5. To determine the minimum § 704(c) gain, if any, with respect to property encumbered by a nonrecourse liability.

6. To explain in general how nonrecourse liabilities encumbering contributed property are allocated between or among the partners.

7. To recall that a decrease in a partner's share of liabilities is treated as a distribution of money to that partner.

8. To recall that an increase in a partner's share of liabilities is treated as a contribution of money to the partnership by that partner.

9. To compute the outside basis of a partner in view of the allocation of either recourse or nonrecourse liabilities encumbering property contributed to a partnership.

IV. OVERVIEW

A. General Principles Regarding Debt Related to the Acquisition or Disposition of Property

Driving through the "wilds" of Montana, one of your authors spotted on the road in front of a ranch a mailbox on the side of which was printed "Robert Z. Smith and Last National Bank." The owner of the ranch, apart from having a good sense of humor, also understood that, while his name might be on the title to the ranch, a bank — undoubtedly holding a mortgage on the ranch — also had a significant interest in the ranch as well. And so it is with much of the real estate and other properties contributed to partnerships and LLCs; the properties are often encumbered with liabilities. In your basic income tax course, you considered the impact of debt on basis and on amount realized. Let's take a moment to review three key principles regarding the tax implications of debt related to the acquisition or disposition of property.

Principle One: When a taxpayer borrows money to acquire property, the taxpayer has no income upon receipt of the borrowed funds because the taxpayer incurs an obligation to repay the loan at some future date. As a corollary, when the taxpayer repays the loan, the taxpayer is not entitled to a deduction (disregarding any interest the taxpayer might have paid).

Principle Two: When a taxpayer acquires property using borrowed funds, the taxpayer's basis in the property is nonetheless the cost of the property regardless of whether the funds were borrowed on recourse or nonrecourse basis. § 1012. See *Crane v. Commissioner*, 331 U.S. 1 (1947). In effect, because the taxpayer has an obligation to repay the loan and presumably will repay the loan in full, the loan is treated as part of the taxpayer's cost of the property. *Commissioner v. Tufts*, 461 U.S. 300 (1982). Those who incur either recourse or nonrecourse liability in acquiring property are thus given advance credit in basis for satisfying that liability in full. For example, if Julie purchases a tract of unimproved land from Paul for $500,000 and borrows $400,000 of the purchase price from a bank (or for that matter from Paul or anyone else), Julie will have a basis of $500,000 in the land. The same would be true if, instead of land, Julie had purchased a piece of equipment for $500,000 using $400,000 of borrowed funds.

The basis of property, of course, plays a significant role in the determination of the tax consequences associated with the use and/or disposition of the property. For example, if the property is depreciable, e.g., facilities or equipment used in a taxpayer's trade or business, depreciation deductions allowed to the taxpayer/owner are computed with reference to the taxpayer's basis in the property. § 168(b); Reg. § 1.167(g)-1. If a taxpayer suffers an uninsured loss with respect to property, a loss deduction is allowed only to the extent of the taxpayer's adjusted basis in the property. § 165(b). A taxpayer's adjusted basis is likewise critical in determining the gain or loss, if any, the taxpayer realizes on a sale or other disposition of property, i.e., gain realized is the excess of the amount realized over the taxpayer's adjusted basis in the property while loss realized is the excess of taxpayer's adjusted basis over the amount realized. § 1001(a).

Principle Three: When a taxpayer sells or otherwise disposes of encumbered property in a taxable transaction, the associated extinguishment of the taxpayer's liability for repayment of the debt encumbering the property is accounted for in the computation of the taxpayer's amount realized, i.e., the taxpayer's amount realized will include not only the cash and fair market value of other property received by the taxpayer, but also the amount of liability assumed or taken subject to by the buyer or other party to the transaction. Reg. § 1.1001-2(a). It makes no difference whether the liability is recourse or nonrecourse. See *Commissioner v. Tufts, supra*. In other words, liability relief is typically treated as the equivalent of money received.[1]

Let's consider an example demonstrating the application of each of these three principles. Assume Lisa purchased Whiteacre for $300,000, borrowing $200,000 of the purchase price from a local bank to which she gave a mortgage on Whiteacre. Applying Principle One *supra*, the loan proceeds would not constitute income to Lisa. Applying Principle Two, Lisa's basis in Whiteacre would be $300,000, i.e., the cost of the land. Five years later, when the balance she owed on the mortgage was $150,000, Lisa sold Whiteacre to Elisabeth for $500,000. Elisabeth agreed to pay Lisa $350,000 in cash and to assume the $150,000 balance Lisa owed on the mortgage encumbering Whiteacre. Applying Principle Three, Lisa's amount realized would be $500,000, i.e., the $350,000 of cash received plus the liability relief of $150,000. Lisa's adjusted basis in Whiteacre would continue to be $300,000 (assuming nothing had occurred that would require Lisa to adjust her basis in Whiteacre). Lisa would thus realize and recognize gain of $200,000. It would make no difference in the above example whether the purchase money mortgage were recourse or nonrecourse.

---

[1] Some Code provisions specifically state as much, e.g., the last sentence of § 1031(d) provides that, for purposes of the like kind exchange provisions, where a taxpayer's liability is assumed by another as part of the consideration for an exchange, "such assumption shall be considered as money received by the taxpayer on the exchange."

B. Contributed Property Encumbered by Recourse Debt

Through the operation of §§ 752, 721, 722, 731 and 733, Subchapter K incorporates the three principles noted above. Let's consider the application of those Code provisions first in the context of a contribution to a partnership of property encumbered by a recourse liability that the partnership assumes.

> **Fact Pattern #1:** Julie purchased Greenacre (a tract of raw land Julie will hold for investment) from Chris for $500,000 using $100,000 of her savings and borrowing the other $400,000 of the purchase price from a bank to which Julie gave a mortgage on Greenacre. Five years later, when Greenacre had a fair market value of $750,000 and Julie still owed the bank $300,000, Julie and Nicole decided to form a general partnership in which they would be equal partners. Julie contributed Greenacre and Nicole contributed Blackacre to the partnership. Assume Nicole had an adjusted basis of $200,000 in Blackacre, which she had held for investment for five years and which had a fair market value of $450,000. The partnership agreed to assume the $300,000 recourse liability encumbering Greenacre. Thus, Julie and Nicole each contributed net value of $450,000 to the partnership.

Note that Julie has actually received two types of consideration in exchange for her contribution of Greenacre to the partnership, i.e., she received a 50% interest worth $450,000 in the Julie/Nicole partnership and was also relieved of the liability encumbering Greenacre. Because liability relief is typically treated as cash, you might speculate that, as a result of the exchange, Julie would recognize some or all of the $250,000 of gain inherent in Greenacre.

Arguably, Julie's situation could be analogized to a like kind exchange in which a taxpayer relinquishing appreciated property is required to recognize any realized gain to the extent the taxpayer, as part of the consideration for the exchange, has been relieved of a liability [§ 1031(b) and 1031(d)(last sentence)]. While that analogy certainly has merit, you might question whether it would be consonant with the nonrecognition treatment Congress intended to confer under § 721. After all, as noted above, real estate and other business properties contributed to partnerships are often encumbered by liabilities. If, as a general rule, a contributing partner were required to recognize gain on the contribution of encumbered appreciated assets to the partnership, the congressional purpose of allowing taxpayers the benefit of nonrecognition on the transfer of property to a partnership would be thwarted. As a result, Congress and the Treasury have taken a lenient approach to the assumption of liabilities by a partnership, i.e., except in limited circumstances, no gain will be recognized.[2]

Using Julie's contribution of Greenacre for illustrative purposes, let's consider the relevant Code and Regulation provisions that accomplish the congressional goal of nonrecognition. First, consider § 752 (a) and (b):

---

[2] The term "assumption" encompasses both a partnership's assumption of recourse liabilities encumbering contributed property and a partnership's receipt of property subject to nonrecourse liabilities. See, e.g., Reg. § 1.752-1(e)

> ## § 752. Treatment of Certain Liabilities
>
> **(a) Increase in partner's liabilities.** Any increase in a partner's share of the liabilities of a partnership, or any increase in a partner's individual liabilities by reason of the assumption by such partner of partnership liabilities, shall be considered as a *contribution of money by such partner to the partnership*. [Emphasis added.]
>
> **(b) Decrease in partner's liabilities.** Any decrease in a partner's share of the liabilities of a partnership, or any decrease in a partner's individual liabilities by reason of the assumption by the partnership of such individual liabilities, shall be considered as a *distribution of money to the partner by the partnership*. [Emphasis added.]

Consistent with our above discussion, liability relief is treated under § 752(b) as money received. More specifically, § 752(b) states that liability relief (i.e., a decrease in a partner's share of liabilities) will be deemed to constitute a *distribution of money to the partner by the partnership*. What are the tax consequences, if any, associated with a partnership's distribution of money to a partner?" The answer to that question is provided by § 731(a):

> ## § 731. Extent of recognition of gain or loss on distribution.
>
> **(a) Partners.** In the case of a distribution by a partnership to a partner
>
> (1) gain shall not be recognized to such partner, except to the extent that any money distributed exceeds the adjusted basis of such partner's interest in the partnership immediately before the distribution, and
>
> (2) loss shall not be recognized to such partner, except that upon a distribution in liquidation of a partner's interest in the partnership . . .

Applying § 731 to our example, Julie would recognize gain only to the extent that any money deemed distributed to her exceeded her adjusted basis in her partnership interest *immediately before the distribution*. How much money is deemed distributed to Julie? According to § 752(b), Julie is deemed to have received money in the amount of any decrease in her share of liabilities. Prior to contributing Greenacre to the partnership, Julie was liable for all $300,000 of the recourse debt encumbering Greenacre. When Julie transferred Greenacre to the partnership, the partnership assumed that liability, i.e., the partnership became economically responsible for the mortgage encumbering Greenacre.[3] Thus, Julie's individual

---

[3] A person contributing encumbered property to a partnership could, of course, agree to remain personally liable on the debt encumbering the property. In that case, there would be no net decrease in

liabilities decreased by $300,000. However, just as Julie, as a general partner, has an interest in each asset held by the partnership (i.e., Greenacre and Blackacre), she also has a share of the recourse liabilities of the partnership. Thus, while the partnership's assumption of the recourse liability encumbering Greenacre reduced Julie's individual liabilities by $300,000, at the same time she, in effect, assumed a share of the partnership's recourse liabilities in her capacity as general partner. What is that share?

1. Allocation of Recourse Liabilities

With regard to recourse liabilities (see definition under Reg. § 1.752-1(a)(1)), the regulations interpreting § 752 provide "a partner's share of a recourse liability equals the portion of that liability, if any, for which the partner . . . bears the economic risk of loss." Reg. § 1.752-2(a). (Chapter 12 examines in detail the § 752 regulations.) Suffice it to say that, in determining the extent to which a partner bears the economic risk of loss, the regulations assume a disaster scenario (termed a "constructive liquidation" by Reg. § 1.752-2(b)(1)) in which the assets of the partnership essentially become worthless, all partnership liabilities are payable in full, the partnership disposes of its assets in a taxable transaction for no consideration, and the partnership liquidates. Were such a disaster to occur, upon the liquidation of their partnership, Julie and Nicole, as general partners, would be economically responsible under state law for the $300,000 in recourse liabilities encumbering Greenacre. See Reg. § 1.752-2(b)(3)(iii); Uniform Partnership Act (1997) § 306(a). Because they are equal partners, Julie and Nicole would each be responsible for $150,000 of the debt. (See detailed analysis in Chapter 12.) In other words, they would each bear the economic risk of loss for $150,000 of the debt. [Note that Reg. § 1.752-2(b)(6) assumes that Julie and Nicole will each pay that part of the debt for which they bear the economic risk of loss; it makes no difference what their actual net worth is.]

Thus, although Julie was relieved of $300,000 of her individual liability when the partnership assumed the debt encumbering Greenacre, Julie, as a general partner, at the same time took on (bore) the economic risk of loss for $150,000 of the partnership's recourse debt. Julie, therefore, has experienced a *net decrease of $150,000* in her share of liabilities. Reg. § 1.752-1(f). See also Reg. § 1.752-1(g) Example 1.

As a result of this net decrease in liabilities, Julie is deemed to have received a distribution of $150,000 in cash from the partnership. § 752(b). Pursuant to § 731(a)(1), Julie will only recognize gain on this deemed cash distribution to the extent her basis in her partnership basis (outside basis) is less than $150,000. As you will recall from Chapter 2, Julie has an outside basis equal to the adjusted basis she had in the property she contributed to the partnership. Julie's outside basis is thus

---

that person's share of liabilities and thus no deemed distribution of money from the partnership to that partner. See Reg. § 1.752-1(g) Ex. 1. Were Julie to agree to remain personally liable for the $300,000 of debt encumbering the land she contributed, she, in effect, would be contributing $750,000 to the partnership and would expect a larger partnership interest than Nicole, who is contributing only $450,000 worth of property. In other words, the deal between Julie and Nicole would necessarily be changed.

$500,000, i.e., the same as the adjusted basis she had in Greenacre. Because the $150,000 of cash deemed distributed by the partnership to Julie under § 752(b) is less than Julie's outside basis, Julie will recognize no gain under § 731(a)(1). Thus, as a result of the operation of §§ 752 and 731, Julie has the benefit of nonrecognition consistent with the congressional purpose noted above.[4]

As demonstrated above, § 731(a)(1) in effect provides that, to the extent a partner receives (or is deemed to receive) a cash distribution from a partnership, the distribution will first be deemed a recovery of the partner's unrecovered investment (i.e., adjusted basis) in the partnership.[5] As a corollary to this basis recovery, Julie's outside basis must be adjusted downward to reflect her $150,000 recovery of investment. Consider the following excerpt from Reg. § 1.722-1:

Reg. § 1.722-1   Basis of contributing partner's interest.

. . . If the contributed property is subject to indebtedness or if the liabilities of the partner are assumed by the partnership, the basis of the contributing partner's interest shall be reduced by the portion of the indebtedness assumed by the other partners, since *the partnership's assumption of his indebtedness is treated as a distribution of money* to the partner. Conversely, the assumption by the other partners of a portion of the contributor's indebtedness is treated as a contribution of money by them. [Emphasis added.]

Applying this regulation, Julie's basis in her partnership interest will be adjusted downward from $500,000 to $350,000. As you know from your study of Chapter 2, Julie's outside basis must preserve the $250,000 gain that inhered in the land that Julie contributed to the partnership. Let's check to see if the $350,000 outside basis we computed above will satisfy that requirement. Assume Julie were to sell her interest in the partnership when the partnership's only assets were Greenacre and

---

[4] Note in this example that Julie incurred the liability in acquiring Greenacre five years before she contributed Greenacre to the partnership. Clearly, Julie's encumbering of Greenacre with a mortgage was not done in an effort to take unfair advantage of the nonrecognition regime of Subchapter K. In other words, there was no "game playing" by Julie. The nonrecognition treatment afforded Julie in this example, however, would not seem to be appropriate if Julie had owned Greenacre free and clear of any encumbrances and then, on the eve of contributing it to the partnership, Julie had borrowed $300,000 from a bank and gave the bank a first mortgage on Greenacre. Congress agreed and enacted § 707(a)(2)(B), which treats such an arrangement as a "disguised sale." We will provide an overview of this anti-abuse rule in Chapter 18. Section 707(a)(2)(B) is consistent with other anti-abuse rules related to debt, e.g., § 357(b) and Reg. § 15a. 453-1(b)(2)(iv).

[5] Compare this result with that associated with liabilities assumed or taken subject to by a purchaser in the context of an installment sale. Recall that under the installment method, a part of each payment is treated as a return of capital (recovery of basis) and part is gain. Note that Reg. § 15a.453-1(b)(3)(i) provides: "[f]or purposes of determining the amount of payment received in the taxable year, the amount of qualifying indebtedness assumed or taken subject to by the person acquiring the property shall be included only to the extent that it exceeds the basis of the property . . . " In effect, this regulation enables a seller under the installment method to avoid reporting any gain as a result of the assumption by the purchaser of the seller's liabilities to the extent that those liabilities don't exceed the seller's basis in the property sold.

Blackacre and both properties had the same fair market value as they did at the time of their contribution. [In other words, assume the partnership holds $1,200,000 worth of land (Greenacre worth $750,000 and Blackacre worth $450,000) and has indebtedness of $300,000 (the amount of debt encumbering Greenacre).] The purchaser of Julie's partnership interest would presumably pay Julie $450,000 in cash, i.e., the value of Julie's interest, and would assume Julie's share of the partnership's liability, i.e., $150,000. (See discussion of Principle Three above regarding the impact of liabilities on amount realized.) Thus, Julie's amount realized would be $600,000. Because her adjusted basis in her partnership interest is $350,000, her gain would be $250,000 — exactly what it should be.

Apart from Reg. § 1.722-1, however, § 733 would require the same reduction of Julie's outside basis to account for the deemed distribution of $150,000 of cash to her by the partnership.[6] Note the language of § 733:

---

§ 733. Basis of distributee partner's interest

In the case of a distribution by a partnership to a partner other than in liquidation of a partner's interest, the adjusted basis to such partner of his interest in the partnership shall be reduced (*but not below zero*) [Emphasis added.] by —

(1) the amount of any money distributed to such partner and . . .

Note also that, pursuant to § 723, the partnership will take the same basis in Greenacre that Julie had "*at the time of the contribution*," i.e., $500,000. If the partnership were to sell Greenacre for its fair market value of $750,000 with the purchaser paying the partnership $450,000 in cash and assuming the $300,000 recourse liability encumbering the land, the partnership would have an amount realized of $750,000 which, in view of the partnership's $500,000 adjusted basis in Greenacre, would result in $250,000 of gain. As discussed in Chapter 2, this is the correct result — before Julie transferred Greenacre to the partnership, $250,000 of gain inhered in that tract of land. Under §§ 722 and 723, that $250,000 of potential gain should be preserved in Julie's basis in her partnership interest (and it is) and in the partnership's basis in Greenacre (and it is). In addition, the partnership will have a holding period in Greenacre that includes Julie's holding period in Greenacre. (In other words, there is tacking of Julie's holding period.) § 1223(2).

The above analysis of Fact Pattern 1 demonstrates Congress' effort to ensure a person contributing property to a partnership will generally have the benefit of nonrecognition treatment. There are limits, however, to nonrecognition when a partnership assumes a liability encumbering contributed property and the contrib-

---

[6] Reg. § 1.722-1 dates from 1960. While the excerpt from Reg. § 1.722-1 printed in this Overview states the correct rule, the examples that follow in that regulation do not reflect the more recent regulations interpreting and applying § 752. Because the reduction in outside basis caused by a net decrease in a partner's share of liabilities is attributable to a deemed cash *distribution* from the partnership to the partner, § 733 is the appropriate authority to cite for this reduction of outside basis.

uting partner experiences a net decrease in her share of liabilities that exceeds her basis in her partnership interest. To demonstrate this limitation, consider the following fact pattern:

Fact Pattern 2: Julie purchased Greenacre from Chris for $100,000, using her savings to make the purchase. Assume over the next 15 years Greenacre appreciated in value to $500,000 and Julie borrowed $400,000 from a local bank on a recourse basis, giving the bank a mortgage on this tract of land. (Assume Julie used the $400,000 in loan proceeds to acquire other investment assets unrelated to Greenacre.) Subsequently, when the amount Julie owed on the mortgage was $300,000 and Greenacre was worth $750,000, Julie and Nicole formed a general partnership with Julie contributing Greenacre (in which she continued to have a $100,000 adjusted basis) and Nicole again contributing Blackacre (worth $450,000 and having a $200,000 adjusted basis). The partnership assumed the $300,000 of recourse liability encumbering Greenacre and Julie and Nicole were equal general partners.

As in the analysis of Fact Pattern #1, Julie has experienced a net decrease in liabilities of $150,000 and, pursuant to § 752(b), will be deemed to have received a cash distribution from the partnership equal to $150,000. The deemed cash distribution of $150,000 exceeds Julie's adjusted basis in her partnership interest immediately before the distribution ($100,000 under § 722) by $50,000. Applying § 731(a)(1), Julie will recognize $50,000 in gain. Note the last sentence of § 731(a) provides that "any gain . . . recognized under this subsection shall be considered as gain . . . from the *sale or exchange* of the partnership interest of the distributee partner." Because § 741 generally treats the sale of a partnership interest as the sale of a capital asset, Julie will be treated as recognizing $50,000 of long-term capital gain.[7]

Having recognized $50,000 of gain, what will Julie's outside basis be? Recall that Julie initially had a $100,000 outside basis, i.e., the same as the adjusted basis she had in Greenacre at the time of contribution. With the decrease in her liability share, Julie is deemed to have received a $150,000 distribution in cash from the partnership. Does that mean she has a negative $50,000 basis in her partnership interest? The answer is "No." By requiring Julie to report $50,000 of gain, § 731 in effect prevents a negative basis result.[8] Section 733 (reprinted above) confirms that, as a result of the deemed distribution of $150,000, Julie's basis will not be negative. Section 733 specifically provides that a distribution cannot reduce a partner's basis below zero. Julie's outside basis should be and is $0 as a result of the deemed distribution: she began with a $100,000 basis in her partnership interest (mirroring

---

[7] Julie has a long-term holding period for her partnership interest because of the tacking rule of § 1223(1).

[8] Under comparable circumstances involving contributions to a corporation, the Ninth Circuit recognized that Subchapter C likewise was designed to avoid negative basis. As the Ninth Circuit noted: ". . . skeptics say that negative basis, like Bigfoot, doesn't exist. . . . Basis normally operates as a cost recovery system: Depreciation deductions reduce basis, and when basis hits zero, the property cannot be depreciated farther. At a more basic level, it seems incongruous to attribute negative value to a figure that normally represents one's investment in an asset." *Peracchi v. Commissioner*, 143 F.3d 487, 491 (1998).

her basis in the property she contributed) but had to recognize $50,000 of gain which in turn should increase her basis to $150,000 (tax cost basis); she must then reduce her basis by the $150,000 of cash deemed distributed to her by the partnership. Again, we can check the accuracy of this result. When Julie contributed Greenacre to the partnership, $650,000 of gain inhered in the land, i.e., Greenacre had an appraised fair market value of $750,000 and Julie's adjusted basis was $100,000. Because pursuant to §§ 752(b) and 731(a)(1), Julie recognized $50,000 of that gain, her outside basis should preserve the remaining $600,000 of unrecognized gain. Does the $0 basis preserve that much gain? The answer is "Yes." As discussed in the prior example, if Julie were to sell her partnership interest in the partnership, she would have an amount realized of $600,000, i.e., $450,000 for her equity interest and liability relief of $150,000. Because of her $0 basis, she would have $600,000 of gain. Thus, the $0 basis is the correct basis.

What basis will the partnership have in Greenacre in Fact Pattern 2? As in Fact Pattern 1, § 723 provides that the partnership will take a basis equal to the basis Julie had in Greenacre "*at the time of the contribution*," i.e., $100,000.[9] As a result, the partnership's basis in Greenacre preserves the $650,000 of gain that inhered in Greenacre at the time of its contribution to the partnership.[10]

As demonstrated in the above example and as tested in Problem 1 at the outset of this Chapter, the contribution of property encumbered by recourse debt will only trigger gain recognition to the extent that the deemed cash distribution resulting from the net decrease in the contributing partner's share of recourse liabilities exceeds that partner's *entire* outside basis in her partnership interest. If, for example, Julie had contributed $50,000 of cash in addition to the land (and, to keep contributions even, Nicole had also contributed $50,000 of cash in addition to her contribution of Blackacre), Julie would have avoided any gain recognition because she would have had a $150,000 outside basis ($100,000 from the contribution of Greenacre and $50,000 from the cash contribution) and thus the deemed cash distribution of $150,000 would have been completely absorbed by her basis.

To complete the analysis of Fact Patterns 1 and 2, let us consider the tax consequences to Nicole who, in both Fact Patterns, contributed Blackacre worth $450,000 and having a $200,000 adjusted basis to Nicole. In exchange, Nicole in both Fact Patterns 1 and 2 received a one-half interest in the Julie/Nicole partnership

---

[9] Note that § 723 would require that any gain recognized by a contributing partner under § 721(b) also be added to the partnership's basis. Section 721(b), however, is inapplicable here because this Julie/Nicole partnership would not constitute an "investment company (within the meaning of § 351) if the partnership were incorporated." *See* § 351(e) and Reg. § 1.351-1(c).

[10] At this point, you may concerned that because Julie has been forced to report $50,000 of the $600,000 gain inherent in Greenacre as a result of the application of §§ 752(b) and 731, the partnership should have a basis in Greenacre that preserves $600,000 of gain much as Julie's outside basis of $0 preserves $600,000 of gain. To accomplish that, the partnership's basis in Greenacre (the inside basis) would have to be $150,000 and not the $100,000 indicated in our analysis. Does that mean that our analysis is incorrect? "No!" Under these circumstances there will be a lack of coherence between the gain preserved in Julie's outside basis and the partnership's basis in Greenacre. As will be discussed in Chapter 15, this lack of coherence will be remedied when the partnership is liquidated or could be remedied immediately if there were a § 754 election in effect.

but, like Julie, also assumed the economic risk for one-half of the recourse liabilities of the partnership. Based on your study of §§ 721 and 723, you could confidently conclude the following: (a) Nicole would recognize none of the $200,000 in gain realized on the transfer — § 721; and (2) the partnership would take a $200,000 basis in Blackacre — § 723.

What basis will Nicole have in her partnership interest? Obviously, pursuant to § 722, Nicole's outside basis will include the $200,000 adjusted basis she had in Blackacre. Shouldn't her outside basis also reflect the fact that she has assumed one-half of the partnership's $300,000 in recourse liabilities associated with Greenacre? Certainly, as noted above, that assumption of liability is part of the deal she made in acquiring her interest as a 50% general partner in the Julie/Nicole partnership. Consistent with Principle Two, discussed at the outset of this Overview, because Nicole has in effect assumed part of the partnership's liability, she should be given advance credit in basis for paying that share of the liability. That is precisely the result reached when §§ 722 and 752(a) are applied.

Note that § 752(a) [reprinted above] will treat Nicole as having *contributed* to the partnership *money in an amount equal to the increase in her liabilities*. Prior to the formation of the Julie/Nicole partnership, Nicole had no liability. As a result of the creation of this partnership, Nicole is allocated $150,000 of the partnership's $300,000 in recourse liability. Nicole has thus experienced an increase of $150,000 in liabilities and therefore will be deemed to have contributed $150,000 of cash to the partnership. Under § 722, Nicole's basis in her partnership interest will therefore be the combination of the $200,000 basis she had in Blackacre and the $150,000 of cash she is deemed to have contributed.

To check whether this resulting $350,000 of outside basis for Nicole is accurate, consider a situation in which Nicole sold her partnership interest. Assume, at the time of that sale, the partnership's only assets were Greenacre (worth $750,000 but encumbered by $300,000 in recourse liability) and Blackacre (worth $450,000). The purchaser presumably would pay Nicole $450,000 in cash for her interest and assume Nicole's $150,000 share of partnership liabilities. Nicole would thus have an amount realized of $600,000. In view of her $350,000 basis in her partnership interest, Nicole should recognize $250,000 of gain. Our calculation of Nicole's outside basis is therefore proven correct since that $350,000 of basis preserves the $250,000 of gain that inhered in Blackacre when Nicole contributed it to the partnership.[11]

This concludes our examination of the tax consequences of the contribution to a partnership of property encumbered by *recourse liabilities*. It should be clear to you that Code and Regulations have ensured nonrecognition insofar as possible. Thus, even in Fact Pattern #2 involving recourse liabilities in excess of Julie's basis in Greenacre, only $50,000 of the potential $600,000 gain was recognized by Julie; the remaining gain was deferred as a result of the application of §§ 721, 722, 731, and 752(b). Chapter 12 will address in detail the allocation of recourse liabilities.

---

[11] It is also worth noting that the character of the gain resulting from Nicole's sale of her partnership interest would be long-term capital gain because Nicole's holding period in her partnership interest would include the period during which she held Blackacre (a capital asset in her hands). § 1223(1).

2. Treatment of Nonrecourse Liabilities

Unlike a recourse liability, *a nonrecourse liability of a partnership is one for which no partner bears the economic risk of loss.* Reg. § 1.752-1(a)(2). Despite the nonrecourse nature of a liability, the tax law still assumes, as in the case of a recourse debt, that debtors will pay their debts in full. See *Commissioner v. Tufts, supra,* and *Crane v. Commissioner*, 331 U.S. 1 (1947).

As a practical matter, if a partnership nonrecourse debt is going to be paid, it will be paid from the profits generated by the entity. Given this source of repayment of nonrecourse loans and the congressional purpose of ensuring nonrecognition of gain on the contribution of property to a partnership, the regulations interpreting § 752 go to considerable lengths to allocate nonrecourse debts encumbering contributed property to the contributing partner, thus minimizing any decrease in that partner's share of liabilities. In so doing, Treasury has succeeded in reducing the amount of money deemed distributed by the partnership to the contributing partner and, in turn, negated gain recognition on the contribution of property encumbered by nonrecourse liability in excess of basis.

We will examine the complex nonrecourse liability sharing rules in more detail in Chapter 12. Let's assume for now there are only two nonrecourse liability sharing rules, both of which address nonrecourse liabilities encumbering contributed property:

> **Nonrecourse Rule 1:** A nonrecourse liability encumbering property contributed to a partnership will be allocated to the contributing partner in an amount equal to the amount, if any, by which the nonrecourse liability exceeds the property's adjusted basis. [We will refer to this gain as "the minimum § 704(c) gain."] Reg. § 1.752-3(a)(2).
>
> **Nonrecourse Rule 2:** Any nonrecourse liabilities encumbering contributed property that are not allocated pursuant to Rule 1 will generally be allocated "in accordance with the partner's share of partnership profits." Reg. § 1.752-3(a)(3) (first sentence).

Because Nonrecourse Rule 1 will only be applicable in situations in which the nonrecourse liability encumbering property exceeds a contributing partner's adjusted basis in the property, we will discuss that rule after first considering Nonrecourse Rule 2, which is the general rule for allocating nonrecourse liabilities.

C. Contributed Property Encumbered by Nonrecourse Liability Not in Excess of Basis

As noted previously, if they are paid, a partnership's nonrecourse debts will be paid from the profits of the partnership. Thus, not surprisingly, because no partner or member bears the economic risk of loss for them, nonrecourse liabilities encumbering contributed property will generally be allocated by reference to each partner's interest in partnership profits. While Regulation § 1.752-3(a)(3) provides that the determination of profit shares is based on all facts and circumstances, it nonetheless gives partners and members of LLCs taxed as partnerships considerable freedom in determining profit shares for purposes of allocating nonrecourse liabilities. Specifically, it allows the partners/members to specify in their agreement what interest each partner/member has in partnership profits for purpose of allocating the nonrecourse liabilities.

Consider the following Fact Pattern based on Fact Pattern 1 above.

Fact Pattern 3: Assume the facts of Fact Pattern #1 except that Julie borrowed the $400,000 from the local bank on a nonrecourse basis and the partnership took Greenacre subject to the nonrecourse liability. Assume also that the partnership agreement provides that, for all purposes including § 752 purposes, Julie and Nicole will share partnership profits equally.

At the outset of our analysis, it might be well to note that Nonrecourse Rule 1 above regarding the allocation of nonrecourse liabilities would not be applicable because the nonrecourse liability encumbering Greenacre does not exceed Julie's $500,000 adjusted basis in Greenacre. Therefore, all $300,000 of the nonrecourse liability would be allocated under Nonrecourse Rule 2. Because the partnership agreement provides that, for purposes of allocating nonrecourse liabilities, the members' profit shares are equal, the $300,000 liability encumbering Greenacre will be allocated equally to Julie and Nicole. Thus, Julie, who was relieved of $300,000 of liabilities when she transferred Greenacre to the partnership subject to the liability, will be allocated $150,000 of the partnership's $300,000 in nonrecourse liability. Julie thus has a *net decrease* in liabilities of $150,000 and will therefore be deemed to have received a distribution of $150,000 in cash from the partnership. Under § 731, this deemed cash distribution will result in gain recognition to Julie only if it exceeds her outside basis determined immediately before the deemed distribution. Here it does not. Julie's outside basis immediately before the distribution is $500,000. § 722. Thus, because the deemed cash distribution of $150,000 is less than Julie's outside basis, Julie does not recognize any gain under § 731(a)(1) on the deemed distribution. Applying § 733, Julie's outside basis must be reduced by the $150,000 deemed distribution of money. She therefore has an outside basis of $350,000. Note that this result is exactly the same as the basis result reached for Julie in Fact Pattern 1. Just as in the case of the rules related to recourse liabilities, the rules for nonrecourse liabilities serve to further the nonrecognition purposes of Congress.

To complete the analysis of the contributions creating the Julie/Nicole Partnership, it should be noted that, as in Fact Pattern 1, Nicole will recognize no gain when she contributes Blackacre to the partnership. § 721. Because she will be allocated $150,000 of the nonrecourse liability, Nicole will be deemed to have contributed that amount of cash to the partnership. § 752 and Reg. § 1.752-3(a)(3). She will therefore have an outside basis equal to $350,000, i.e., $200,000 from the contribution of Blackacre and $150,000 from the deemed contribution of $150,000 of cash. § 722. Similarly, the partnership will have the same bases in Greenacre and Blackacre that the partnership had in Fact Pattern 1, i.e., the partnership will have a $500,000 basis in Greenacre and a $200,000 basis in Blackacre. § 723.

D. Contributed Property Encumbered by Nonrecourse Liabilities in Excess of Basis

Now, let's consider a situation in which the property contributed is encumbered by nonrecourse liability in excess of the property's adjusted basis.

> **Fact Pattern 4:** Assume the facts of Fact Pattern #2, except the $400,000 bank loan was a nonrecourse loan and the partnership took Greenacre subject to that nonrecourse liability. Assume also that the partnership agreement provides that, for all purposes including § 752 purposes, Julie and Nicole will share partnership profits equally.

Nonrecourse Rule 1 requires the nonrecourse liability first be allocated to a contributing partner to the extent the nonrecourse liability exceeds the contributing partner's adjusted basis in the encumbered property, i.e., to the extent there is "§ 704(c) minimum gain." This rule reflects an application of *Commissioner v. Tufts, supra*, and is intended to promote the congressional purpose that, in general, gain or loss should not be recognized on the contribution of property to a partnership. As briefly noted in Chapter 2 and discussed in detail in Chapter 10, pursuant to § 704(c)(1)(A), if a person contributes an appreciated asset to a partnership, the gain inherent in that property will be allocated to the person contributing the property when the partnership finally recognizes that gain.[12] In other words, § 704(c)(1)(A) prevents the shifting of gain inherent in contributed property to other partners. Of course, there is no way of knowing when a partnership will recognize the gain inherent in contributed property, nor can one know how much gain there will be when the partnership finally disposes of the property in a taxable transaction. *Commissioner v. Tufts* teaches, however, that when property is transferred in a taxable transaction subject to a nonrecourse liability, the transferor will have an amount realized *at least equal to the nonrecourse indebtedness encumbering the property*. See also Reg. § 1.1001-2(a)(1). As a result, even if the transferor received no consideration other than relief from the nonrecourse liability, the transferor would recognize gain.

In Fact Pattern 4 above, Julie contributed Greenacre to the Julie/Nicole Partnership subject to the $300,000 in nonrecourse liability. Under § 723, the partnership would take a basis in Greenacre equal to the $100,000 basis Julie had in that property. As a result of the *Tufts* analysis discussed above, there is "minimum 704(c) gain" of $200,000 inherent in Greenacre, i.e., if the partnership were to dispose of Greenacre in a taxable transaction *for no consideration other than relief from the nonrecourse indebtedness encumbering the property*, the partnership would recognize $200,000 of gain. Pursuant to § 704(c)(1)(A), that gain would be allocable to Julie. Because that is so, Nonrecourse Rule 1 requires that $200,000 of the $300,000 in nonrecourse liability be allocated to Julie. That leaves $100,000 of the liability to be allocated in accordance with Nonrecourse Rule 2, i.e., pursuant to the members' profit shares. Because Julie and Nicole have equal profit shares, the remaining $100,000 of nonrecourse liability will be allocated equally between them — $50,000 to Julie and $50,000 to Nicole. Thus, when the dust settles after the application of these two nonrecourse liability sharing rules, $250,000 of the

---

[12] Section 704(c)(1)(A) is discussed in detail in Chapter 10.

partnership's nonrecourse liability will have been allocated to Julie and $50,000 of the liability to Nicole. Applying § 752(b), Julie will be deemed to have received a $50,000 cash distribution from the Partnership because she has experienced a net decrease in liabilities of $50,000 (i.e., her liabilities decreased by $300,000 when she contributed Greenacre to the partnership and her liabilities increased by $250,000 as a result of the operation of the two nonrecourse liability sharing rules as explained above). Julie's outside basis immediately before this deemed distribution was $100,000. Because the deemed $50,000 cash distribution does not exceed this $100,000 basis, no gain will be recognized to Julie under § 731(a)(1). Applying § 733, Julie's outside basis will be reduced to $50,000 as a result of the $50,000 deemed cash distribution.[13]

In sum, as demonstrated by our analysis of Fact Patterns 3 and 4, the two rules for allocating nonrecourse liabilities effectively promote the nonrecognition purpose of Congress by assigning a large enough share of nonrecourse liabilities to the contributing partner to negate the recognition of gain under §§ 752(b) and 731(a). Thus, note that, while a contribution of property encumbered by recourse liabilities substantially in excess of basis can result in gain recognition (see Fact Pattern 2 above), the contribution of property encumbered by nonrecourse liabilities in excess of basis will not result in gain recognition (see Fact Pattern 4).

E. Treatment of Accounts Payable

A taxpayer who owns and operates a business as a sole proprietor may enter into a partnership with another person in an effort to expand the business. It will not be uncommon in these circumstances for the taxpayer/business owner to contribute to the partnership his entire business, including the business's accounts receivable and accounts payable. Should the accounts payable be regarded as liabilities and thus trigger the application of §§ 752 and 731 discussed above? Consider the following Fact Pattern:

> **Fact Pattern 5:** Julie, a cash method taxpayer, owns an interior design business that she operates out of a leased space in a shopping mall. Desiring to expand the business, Julie approaches Nicole and proposes that the two of them form a general partnership with Julie contributing her business's accounts receivable (fair market value $300,000 and a basis of $0) and the partnership agreeing to assume the business's accounts payable of $100,000. Assume Nicole contributes $200,000 of cash. Julie and Nicole will be equal partners.

If the accounts payable were considered recourse liabilities, Julie would be deemed under § 752(b) to have received a $50,000 cash distribution from the partnership, i.e., Julie would have a net decrease of liabilities of $50,000 — her share of liabilities decreased by $100,000 when the partnership assumed the accounts payable and increased by $50,000 as a result of her equal share of the partnership.

---

[13] The allocation of $50,000 of the nonrecourse liability to Nicole results in Nicole's share of liabilities being increased by that amount. As a result, pursuant to § 752(a), Nicole will be deemed to have contributed $50,000 of cash to the partnership. In turn, her outside basis will be increased by $50,000 to $250,000. § 722.

This deemed cash distribution would result in gain recognition of $50,000 under § 731(a)(1) because Julie's basis in the partnership immediately before the distribution would be $0 (i.e., the same as the basis she had in the accounts receivable she contributed to the partnership).

As the above analysis indicates, if accounts payable of a cash method taxpayer are treated as liabilities, the congressional purpose of providing nonrecognition on the formation of partnerships would be seriously undercut. In the context of Subchapter C addressing the taxation of corporations and their shareholders, Congress has, in effect, provided that, when a cash method shareholder transfers accounts payable to a corporation, the accounts payable will not be treated as liabilities. § 357(c)(3)(A). Considering that under § 704(c)(1)(A) and (c)(3), Julie would be allocated (a) the $100,000 deduction the partnership would have when it satisfied the accounts payable it had assumed from Julie and (b) the $300,000 of gross income the partnership would recognize when it collected the accounts receivable contributed by Julie, there is no reason to treat the accounts payable as liabilities. When Congress amended 704(c) in 1984, the legislative history specifically noted: "[The Conference Committee] intends that, similar to the amendments recently made to § 357(c). . . . these accrued but unpaid items (i.e., accounts payable of cash method taxpayers) should not be treated as partnership liabilities for purposes of § 752."[14]

Thus, in the example above, Julie's accounts payable will not be treated as liabilities. Julie will not recognize any gain on the formation of the partnership and will have a $0 basis in her partnership interest. The partnership, of course, would take a $0 basis in both the accounts receivable and the accounts payable. § 723. Assume that, shortly after the partnership is formed, the partnership collects the $300,000 in accounts receivable and pays the $100,000 in accounts payable. Under § 704(c)(1)(A), Julie will be required to report $300,000 of income, which will increase her outside basis to $300,000. § 705(a)(1). Under § 704(c)(3), she will also be allowed the $100,000 deduction associated with the payment of the accounts payable and that deduction will reduce her outside basis to $200,000. § 705(a)(2). Nicole, of course, would have a § 722 basis in her partnership interest reflecting the $200,000 of cash she contributed to the partnership.

F. Matters for Future Consideration

As this Overview has discussed, Congress and the Treasury have gone to considerable lengths to ensure, insofar as possible, nonrecognition on the contribution of encumbered properties to a partnership taxed as a partnership. Chapter 12 will discuss in much greater detail the regulations under § 752 addressing the allocation of recourse and nonrecourse liabilities. Apart from liabilities that are associated with properties contributed to partnerships, there are liabilities that a partnership will incur in its own operation. The allocation of those liabilities will also be considered in Chapter 12, as will the tax implications of the payment of liabilities. In Chapter 8, we will discuss § 704(d), which provides that a

---

[14] Conf. Rep. 98-861, P.L. 98-369, 98th Cong. 2d Sess., pp. 856–57. Section 108(e)(2) similarly provides that "no income shall be realized from the discharge of indebtedness to the extent that payment of the liability would have given rise to a deduction."

partner may not deduct losses in excess of the partner's outside basis. Chapter 8 will thus highlight the important relationship between a partner's share of liabilities and outside basis.

Chapter 4

CONTRIBUTION OF SERVICES IN EXCHANGE FOR PARTNERSHIP INTERESTS

I. PROBLEMS

1. In Year 1, Amy, Ben, and Carla form ABC, a limited liability company that will provide real estate management services to clients. ABC will be taxed as a partnership. Amy and Ben each contribute $100,000 to ABC, and Carla agrees to supervise the managerial services provided by ABC in Year 1. Amy and Ben will each have a 40% interest in ABC's capital and profits. Carla will have a 20% interest in ABC's capital and profits. Assume Carla's interest is vested and transferable. What are the tax consequences on the formation of ABC?

2. Assume the facts of Problem 1, except that Carla received her interest in ABC for agreeing to supervise the managerial services during Years 1 through 4. What are the tax consequences on the formation of ABC?

3. Assume the facts of Problem 2, except that Carla's interest in ABC is nontransferable and will be forfeited if she ceases to supervise the managerial services before the end of Year 4.

    (a) What are the tax consequences on the formation of ABC?

    (b) What are the tax consequences at the end of Year 4 if Carla performs the required services and her interest in ABC is worth $100,000 at that time?

    (c) What are the tax consequences in Year 2 if ABC's net operating income that year is $50,000?

    (d) Do your answers to questions (a), (b) and (c) change if Carla makes a timely § 83 election?

4. In Year 1, Dora acquired Bluesprings, a tract of land used for camping and fishing, for $75,000. Dora immediately hired Frank and paid him a salary for managing the camping and fishing business activities at Bluesprings. The business was successful enough that, at the beginning of Year 4, when Bluesprings was worth $120,000, Dora, Ellen and Frank decided to form a general partnership to further develop Bluesprings. Simultaneously with the formation of the partnership, Dora transferred a one-third interest in Bluesprings to Frank as a reward for his excellent management in the prior three years. Dora contributed her two-thirds interest in Bluesprings for a 40% interest in the partnership; Ellen contributed $80,000 in cash for a 40% interest in the partnership; and Frank contributed his one-third

interest in Bluesprings for a 20% interest in the partnership. What are the tax consequences on the formation of the partnership?

5. Assume the facts of Problem 4, except that in Year 1 Dora and Ellen formed a general partnership to which Dora contributed Bluesprings (with a value and adjusted basis of $75,000) for a 50% partnership interest and Ellen contributed $75,000 in cash for her 50% interest. At the beginning of Year 4, when the partnership's sole asset was Bluesprings, with a value of $200,000 and an adjusted basis of $75,000, Dora and Ellen, as a reward to Frank for his excellent management of the property over the prior three years, reduced their partnership interests to 40% each and admitted Frank as a partner with a 20% interest in the capital and profits of the partnership. What are the tax consequences on the admission of Frank as a partner? In answering this question, contrast the differing results reached under a *McDougal*/sale of assets analysis and the "deemed cash analysis" of Prop. Reg. § 1.721-1(b)(2).

6. Assume in Year 1 Larry and Mark form the LM Partnership, by each contributing $60,000 cash. LM provides real estate management services. In Year 3, when LM's assets consist of $200,000 in cash, Norm is admitted as a partner with a 20% profits-only interest, in return for his agreement to supervise LM's managerial services on an ongoing basis. Applying Prop. Reg. § 1.83-3(l), what are the tax consequences on Norm's admission as an LM partner?

7. Assume the facts of Problem 6, except that LM in Year 1 purchased Greenacre with the cash contributions from Larry and Mark. When Norm is admitted as a profits-only partner in Year 3, Greenacre (which is LM's only asset) is worth $200,000 and has an adjusted basis of $120,000. What are the tax consequences of Norm's admission as an LM partner?

8. Does your answer to Problem 7 change if in Years 1 and 2 Larry and Mark had owned Greenacre as tenants in common (each half interest worth $100,000, with an adjusted basis of $60,000)? Assume during those two years, Norm was employed by Larry and Mark to maintain Greenacre, and at the beginning of Year 3 the LM Partnership was formed with Larry and Mark contributing their half interests in Greenacre to the partnership, and with Norm agreeing, in return for a 20% profits-only interest, to provide management services to LM. Would it affect your answer if Norm sold his profits-only interest 18 months after receiving it?

Assignment for Chapter 4:

Complete the problems.

Read: Internal Revenue Code §§ 83(a)–(c), (h); 721
        Treasury Regulations §§ 1.83-3(e), -6(b); 1.721-1(b)(1), (2);; 1.722-1.
        Proposed Treasury Regulations: §§ 1.83-3(e), (l); 1.721-1(b); 1.761–1(b).

        Materials: Overview
                    Diamond v. Commissioner
                    McDougal v. Commissioner

II. VOCABULARY

capital interest (or capital and profits interest)
profits interest (or profits-only interest)
property transferred in connection with performance of services
forfeitable interest
substantially nonvested
nontransferable
compensatory partnership interest
liquidation value
deemed sale of assets theory
deemed cash analysis

III. OBJECTIVES

1. To explain the difference between a profits (or profits-only) interest and a capital (or capital and profits) interest.

2. To determine the tax consequences to a partner on the receipt of a capital interest in a partnership in exchange for services.

3. To determine the tax consequences to a partnership on the transfer to a partner of a capital interest in the partnership in exchange for services.

4. To determine the tax consequences to a partner on the receipt of a profits-only interest in a partnership in exchange for services.

5. To determine the tax consequences to a partnership on the transfer to a partner of a profits-only interest in the partnership in exchange for services.

IV. OVERVIEW

Introduction: As discussed in Chapter 2, § 721 provides nonrecognition treatment on the contribution of *property* to a partnership in exchange for a partnership interest. Based solely on the language of § 721, one would likely conclude § 721 nonrecognition does not extend to the receipt of a partnership interest in exchange for services. No Code provision, however, confirms that conclusion.[1] Instead, one must look to the following regulation interpreting § 721:

Reg. § 1.721-1 Nonrecognition of Gain or Loss on Contribution

(b)(1) . . . Normally, under local law, each partner is entitled to be repaid his contribution of money or other property to the partnership (at the value placed upon such property by the partnership at the time of the contribution) whether made at the formation of the partnership or subse-

---

[1] Contrast Subchapter C (taxation of corporations and shareholders), which, while providing for nonrecognition on the transfer of *property* to a corporation in exchange for stock (§ 351(a)), specifically states in § 351(d)(1) that stock issued for services will not be considered issued in exchange for property.

quent thereto. To the extent that any of the partners gives up any part of his right to be repaid his contributions (*as distinguished from a share in partnership profits*) in favor of another partner as compensation for services . . . section 721 does not apply. The transfer of such a partnership interest [*a capital interest*] transferred to a partner as compensation for services constitutes income to the partner undersection 61. The amount of such income is the fair market value of the interest in capital so transferred, either at the time the transfer is made for past services, or at the time the services have been rendered where the transfer is conditioned on the completion of the transferee's future services. The time when such income is realized depends on all the facts and circumstances, including any substantial restrictions or conditions on the compensated partner's right to withdraw or otherwise dispose of such [capital] interest. [Emphasis added.]

Pursuant to the above regulation (promulgated in 1960), the receipt of a capital interest in a partnership in exchange for services constitutes gross income under § 61. With the enactment in 1969 of § 83 (addressing the tax consequences of property transferred in connection with the performance of services), Treasury in 1971 issued a proposed regulation (never finalized and since withdrawn) specifying that § 83 rather than § 61 would apply to the receipt of a partnership capital interest in exchange for services. The 1971 proposed regulation substituted the following language for the last three sentences of the existing regulation above:

The transfer of such a partnership interest [a capital interest] transferred to a partner as compensation [for services] constitutes income to the partner as follows:

(i) If the partnership interest is transferred after June 30, 1969 . . . then the transfer of such **interest in partnership capital** shall be treated as a transfer of property to which section 83 and the regulations thereunder apply. [Emphasis added.]

The highlighted language in both the existing regulation and the 1971 proposed regulation indicate that those provisions are applicable to the transfer of an interest in partnership capital [*a "capital interest"*] in exchange for services. The quoted regulations do not apply to a "profits interest" in a partnership. What is a "capital interest"? What is a "profits interest"? The Service provided the following definitions in Rev. Proc. 93-27, 1993-2 C.B. 343.

A capital interest is an interest that would give the holder a share of the proceeds if the partnership's assets were sold at fair market value and then the proceeds were distributed in complete liquidation of the partnership. This determination generally is made at the time of receipt of the partnership interest.

A profits interest is a partnership interest other than a capital interest.

Section 83 specifically addresses the tax consequences associated with the transfer of property by one person to another in connection with the performance of services. A capital interest in a partnership is "property" for purposes of § 83. See *Schulman v. Commissioner*, 93 T.C. 623 (1989); *Kenroy, Inc. v. Commissioner*, T.C.

Memo 1984-232. As will be discussed briefly below, proposed regulations issued by Treasury in 2005 apply § 83 to all partnership interests without distinguishing between capital interests and profits interests.[2]

---

§ 83 Property Transferred in Connection with Performance of Services.

(a) General rule. If, in connection with the performance of services, property is transferred to any person other than the person for whom such services are performed, the excess of —

(1) the fair market value of such property . . . at the first time the rights of the person having the beneficial interest in such property are transferable or are not subject to a substantial risk of forfeiture, whichever occurs earlier, over

(2) the amount (if any) paid for such property, shall be included in the gross income of the person who performed such services in the first taxable year in which the rights of the person having the beneficial interest in such property are transferable or are not subject to a substantial risk of forfeiture, whichever is applicable. . . .

. . .

(h) Deduction by employer. In the case of a transfer of property to which this section applies . . . , there shall be allowed as a deduction under section 162, to the person for whom were performed the services in connection with which such property was transferred, an amount equal to the amount included under subsection (a) . . . in the gross income of the person who performed such services. Such deduction shall be allowed for the taxable year of such person in which or with which ends the taxable year in which such amount is included in the gross income of the person who performed such services.

A. Capital Interest for Services

Let's first consider the tax treatment of a capital interest in a partnership received in exchange for services. In this regard, consider the following examples applying § 83:

Example 1: Transfer of Capital Interest in Exchange for Services upon Formation of the Partnership. Ron, who lives in Beverly Hills, collects classic cars that he rents for use in motion pictures, advertising campaigns, etc. In 2012, Ron, at the urging of Dan, who had managed Ron's rental business for many years, purchased at auction a car Dan recognized as a rare 1955 Porsche 356 Speedster. Ron paid only $15,000 for the car, which

---

[2] The proposed amendment to Reg. § 1.83-3(e) provides that "[a]ccordingly, property includes a partnership interest." Prop. Reg. § 1.83-3(e).

was in poor physical and mechanical condition. Dan, a classic car enthusiast himself, knew a Porsche mechanic who could completely restore the car. Dan was convinced that, given the nature of the vehicle, he could rent the restored Porsche at a premium price to studios and other businesses so as to ensure Ron recovery of all of his costs within a 30–36 month period. Ron promised Dan that, if Dan managed the rental of the Porsche in a manner that returned to Ron his costs in acquiring and restoring the vehicle within 36 months following the car's restoration, he would give Dan a one-half interest in the Porsche. In January 2013, the restoration of the car was completed and the car was placed in service. Just as he anticipated, Dan was successful in renting the vehicle to movie studios and other businesses at premium rates. By January 2016, Ron had earned $50,000 net rental income, enough to completely cover the $50,000 he had invested in the car (the $50,000 included the $15,000 purchase price of the vehicle, costs of replacement parts, and compensation paid to the mechanic who restored the vehicle). Consistent with his arrangement with Dan, Ron, in January 2016, transferred a one-half interest in the car to Dan. Simultaneously, Ron and Dan created an LLC (taxed as a partnership) to which each transferred his one-half interest in the Porsche in exchange for a 50% interest in the LLC. The Porsche's appraised fair market value at the time was $150,000. Assume Ron had been allowed $20,000 of depreciation on the Porsche and thus had an adjusted basis in the vehicle of $30,000. (Note that Ron has not only recovered the $50,000 cash he invested in the vehicle, he has also had the benefit of $20,000 of depreciation deductions.)

Dan's tax consequences. The receipt of the one-half interest in the Porsche clearly constitutes compensation to Dan for his management services. Dan's interest is not subject to a substantial risk of forfeiture (§ 83(c)(1)) and is transferable (§ 83(c)(2)). As a result, under § 83 (and also under § 61), Dan would have ordinary income of $75,000 and would take a tax cost basis of $75,000, his one-half interest in the Porsche. When Dan contributed his interest in the Porsche to the LLC in exchange for a 50% LLC interest worth $75,000, Dan would have no gain and would take a $75,000 basis in the LLC interest he received. §§ 721 and 722. The LLC would take a § 723 basis of $75,000 in one-half interest contributed by Dan.

Ron's tax consequences. Pursuant to § 162, Ron will be allowed a business deduction for the half-interest in the Porsche he gave to Dan. Ron will claim the deduction for the year in which he transfers the interest to Dan and Dan includes in gross income the $75,000 value of the interest. § 83(h). At the same time, because Ron is using an appreciated asset to pay Dan compensation for his management services, Ron will recognize $60,000 gain, i.e., the amount of the difference between the $75,000 value of the interest given to Dan and Ron's $15,000 adjusted basis in that interest (i.e., one-half of the $30,000 adjusted basis he had in the Porsche). See *McDougal v. Commissioner*, included in the materials.[3] Because the

---

[3] *See also* United States v. Davis, 370 U.S. 65 (1962) and Kenan v. Commissioner, 114 F.2d 217 (2d Cir. 1940) (note the *McDougal* court's reliance upon both *Davis* and *Kenan*).

Porsche is Section 1245 property, $10,000 of Ron's recognized gain will be characterized as ordinary income with the remaining $50,000 of gain characterized as § 1231 gain.[4] When Ron contributes his remaining half-interest in the Porsche to the LLC, Ron will recognize no gain (§ 721) and will take a $15,000 basis in his 50% interest in the LLC. (§ 722). The LLC will have a $15,000 basis in the one-half interest in the Porsche contributed by Ron. § 723. Thus, the LLC's total basis in the Porsche would be $90,000 (i.e., $75,000 in the half-interest contributed by Dan plus $15,000 in the half-interest contributed by Ron).

Review *McDougal* in the materials and note how the above analysis of Example 1 mirrors the approach taken by the court. It is important to note that, in *McDougal* and in this example, the partnership (or LLC) was formed *after or simultaneously with the transfer of an interest in property to the service provider* who then transferred that compensatory interest to the partnership (or LLC).

Example 2: Transfer of a Capital Interest in Exchange for Services — Existing Partnership. Assume the facts of Example 1 except that in 2012, after acquiring the Porsche, Ron and his sister, Sharon, formed an LLC to restore the Porsche and rent the restored vehicle to movie studios. Ron contributed the unrestored Porsche and $10,000 in cash and Sharon contributed $25,000 in cash to the new LLC. In exchange for their contributions, Ron and Sharon each received a 50% interest in the LLC.[5] The LLC hired Dan to manage the rental of the Porsche and immediately arranged for the restoration of the vehicle. The total cost of the restoration work was $35,000, thus resulting in a total investment of $50,000 in the Porsche. When the restoration work was completed in 2013, Dan successfully rented it at premium prices. In 2016, Ron and Sharon decided to give Dan a 10% capital interest in the LLC as a bonus for the superb management services he had rendered the LLC. Assume, at the time, the only asset held by the LLC was the Porsche.[6] As a result of this transfer, Ron and Sharon's interests in the LLC were each reduced to 45%. As in Example 1, assume that the Porsche had a fair market value at the time of $150,000 and an adjusted basis to the LLC of $30,000.[7]

---

[4] Ron's $30,000 adjusted basis reflected $20,000 in depreciation deduction allowed. Thus, Ron's recomputed basis in the Porsche was $50,000. Therefore, his recomputed basis in the half-interest he gave to Dan was $25,000. Ron's adjusted basis in that one-half interest given to Dan was $15,000 (i.e., one-half of Ron's $30,000 adjusted basis in the Porsche). Therefore, pursuant to § 1245(a), Ron would have $10,000 of ordinary income (i.e., the recomputed basis of $25,000 less Ron's $15,000 adjusted basis in the one-half interest given to Dan).

[5] Ron and Sharon would each have a $25,000 basis in their LLC interest, i.e., Sharon has contributed $25,000 to the LLC and Ron has contributed $10,000 plus the vehicle with a value and adjusted basis of $15,000. § 722.

[6] In other words, we assume for simplicity's sake that prior to the transfer of the interest to Dan, all profits had been distributed. As described in Chapter 7, profits and losses of the LLC and distributions made by the LLC will be reflected in Ron's and Sharon's outside bases.

[7] The assumed adjusted basis of $30,000 reflects (1) the $15,000 purchase price of the unrestored Porsche; plus (2) the restoration costs of $35,000 capitalized and added to basis of the car, with the resulting total of $50,000 reduced by depreciation deductions, assumed for the sake of convenience to be $20,000, the same amount as in Example 1.

The McDougal Analysis. First, let's consider the consequences to Dan, the LLC, Ron, and Sharon if we apply the *McDougal* analysis as in Example 1. Pursuant to that analysis (sometimes called the "sale-of-assets analysis"), the LLC would be deemed to have transferred a 10% undivided interest in the Porsche to Dan as compensation for his past management services and Dan would be deemed to have immediately transferred that undivided interest back to the LLC in exchange for a 10% interest in that entity. As a result, Dan would have $15,000 of ordinary income on receipt of the 10% undivided interest in the Porsche (§ 83(a) and Reg. § 1.721-1(b)(2) (which would treat the 10% interest as a guaranteed payment under § 707(c) and thus ordinary income to Dan)), and would have a tax cost basis of $15,000 in that interest. § 1012. Dan would then be deemed to recontribute the interest to the LLC and would have a $15,000 basis in his membership interest. § 722. The LLC would take a $15,000 basis (§ 723) in that undivided 10% interest in the Porsche that, when combined with the LLC's adjusted basis in the other 90% of the Porsche ($27,000),[8] the LLC would have a total adjusted basis of $42,000 in the Porsche.

Under the *McDougal* or "sale of assets" theory, the LLC would be entitled to a deduction of $15,000 under § 83(h) and § 162 for the compensation paid to Dan for his past services. Because the LLC is not a taxable entity, the deduction would pass through to the members and, in this case, would be allocated to Ron and Sharon.[9] (Allocations of income, gain, loss, and deduction are addressed in Chapter 9.)

In addition, under the *McDougal*/sale-of-assets theory, one might conclude the LLC "should be treated as satisfying its compensation obligation with a fractional interest in each asset of the partnership. Under this "deemed sale of assets theory, the [LLC] would recognize gain . . . equal to the excess of the fair market value of [a 10% interest in the Porsche] deemed transferred to [Dan] over the [LLC's] adjusted basis in that [10% interest]."[10] Under this theory, the LLC should recognize the $12,000 gain inherent in the 10% undivided interest in the Porsche transferred to Dan. (The 10% undivided interest has a fair market value of $15,000 and an adjusted basis of $3,000, thus resulting in $12,000 of gain recognition under a *McDougal* analysis.) This gain should be allocated to Ron and Sharon in equal shares.[11]

As noted above, however, *McDougal* concerned a transfer to a service provider that occurred before (or simultaneous with) the creation of a partnership. In Example 2, the LLC is already in existence when the transfer occurs. Should the

---

[8] The adjusted basis of the Porsche was assumed to be $30,000. Thus, the basis of a 90% undivided interest in the Porsche would be $27,000. The adjusted basis the LLC had in the 10% interest it transferred to Dan would have been $3,000.

[9] An amendment should be made to the LLC agreement specifically allocating this deduction equally to Sharon and Ron.

[10] Preamble to 2005 Proposed Regulations on the Contribution of Services to a Partnership.

[11] An amendment should be made to the LLC agreement specifically allocating this gain equally to Sharon and Ron.

McDougal/sale-of-assets analysis be applied to an existing partnership? Under these circumstances, some "commentators believe that a partnership [or LLC as in our example] should not recognize gain or loss on the transfer of a compensatory partnership interest. They argue, among other things, that the transfer of such an interest is not properly treated as a realization event for the partnership because no property owned by the partnership has changed hands. They also argue that taxing a partnership on the transfer of such an interest would result in inappropriate gain acceleration, would be difficult to administer, and would cause economically similar transactions to be taxed differently."[12] In effect, these commentators, in urging nonrecognition, could be thought of as advocating an approach whereby, in this example, the LLC is viewed as distributing cash instead of an interest in the Porsche to Dan, and Dan, in turn, contributed the cash back to the LLC in exchange for his LLC interest. Obviously, the distribution of cash from the LLC for Dan's services would trigger income to Dan but would not trigger any gain to the LLC. The 2005 proposed regulations discussed below, in effect, adopt this nonrecognition approach. As noted in the preamble to the proposed regulations, "partnerships are not taxed on the transfer or substantial vesting of a compensatory partnership interest." Apart from these 2005 proposed regulations, no clear authority exists regarding which approach, i.e., the deemed sale-of-assets analysis of *McDougal* or the nonrecognition approach (or deemed cash analysis), as set forth in this paragraph, should be applied. If the latter approach is applied, the LLC would not be required to recognize the $12,000 of gain inherent in the compensatory LLC interest transferred to Dan.[13]

Example 3: Transfer of Forfeitable Capital Interest in Exchange for Services — Existing Partnership. Assume the same facts as Example 2, except Ron and Sharon in 2012 transferred to Dan a 10% capital and profits interest in the LLC conditioned, however, on Dan continuing to manage the rental of the Porsche until January 2016. (The total value of the LLC at the time was $50,000.) If, for any reason, Dan failed to perform the management services, his interest would be forfeited. Furthermore, Dan's interest was nontransferable (within the meaning of § 83). Assume that Dan performs the required management services and, in 2016, his interest is no longer subject to the restrictions indicated. Assume in January 2016 that the Porsche had a fair market value of $150,000 and was the only asset held by the LLC. Assume also that the LLC had been allowed $20,000 in depreciation deductions and had a $30,000 adjusted basis in the Porsche.

Tax consequences to Dan. Because Dan's interest is "substantially nonvested" (subject to a substantial risk of forfeiture and not transferable within the meaning of § 83 — see Reg. § 1.83-3(b)), Dan would not recognize any gross income upon the receipt of his interest in the LLC. Instead, he would have gross income in 2016. (Furthermore, during this interim period, Sharon and Ron would be deemed the owners of Dan's

---

[12] Preamble to 2005 Proposed Regulations on the Contribution of Services to a Partnership.

[13] Under this theory, the gain that inhered in the interest transferred to Dan would ultimately be taxed to Ron and Sharon under § 704(c)(1)(A) principles (discussed in detail in Chapter 10) when the Porsche was sold or otherwise disposed of in a taxable transaction.

interest. Reg. § 1.83-1(a); see also Prop. Reg. § 1.761-1(b).) In 2016, Dan's 10% capital and profits interest would be worth $15,000 (i.e., 10% of the $150,000). Under § 83(a), Dan would thus have $15,000 of ordinary income. Using a *McDougal*/sale-of-assets analysis, Dan will be deemed to have received a one-tenth interest in the Porsche, which he then contributes to the LLC. Because he will have reported $15,000 of ordinary income on the receipt of the interest, he will take a § 722 basis of $15,000 in his LLC interest.

Tax consequences to the LLC. Pursuant to § 83(h), the LLC will be entitled to a $15,000 deduction in 2016 when Dan reports the $15,000 of compensation income. This deduction should be allocated to Sharon and Ron. As in Example 2, we would have to also consider the potential recognition of gain on the transfer of the compensatory LLC interest. Again, under a *McDougal*/deemed sale-of-assets analysis, the LLC would recognize gain in the amount of the difference between the fair market value of the interest transferred (here $15,000) and the LLC's adjusted basis in that interest ($3,000). Thus, the LLC would recognize $12,000 of gain, which is allocable to Sharon and Ron. If the nonrecognition theory of the 2005 proposed regulations, discussed below, is followed, the LLC would not recognize the $12,000 of gain and thus Sharon and Ron would have no gain allocated to them.

One final point to be made with regard to Example 3 is the possibility of a § 83(b) election. In effect, § 83(b) affords a taxpayer like Dan the opportunity to report the value of the LLC interest immediately upon its receipt, even though the interest is not substantially vested. Were Dan to elect under § 83(b), he would recognize $5,000 of ordinary income immediately (i.e., his LLC interest would have a value of 10% of the $50,000 total value of the LLC) and he would have a $5,000 basis in his interest. The LLC would be entitled to a deduction of $5,000 at that time. § 83(h). In 2016, when the risk of forfeiture ended and Dan's interest became transferable within the meaning of § 83, Dan would not be required to report any additional income. Were Dan to sell his interest at that time for its presumed value of $15,000, he would recognize $10,000 of gain (amount realized of $15,000 less the $5,000 adjusted basis of his LLC interest).[14] Note how, in this example, a § 83(b) election effectively limits the amount of ordinary income by measuring the compensation element at the time of the receipt of the interest.[15]

B. Profits Interest for Services

In Example 2, Dan received a capital interest in an existing LLC. As a result, he had immediate income because his LLC interest was not subject to a substantial risk of forfeiture and was transferable within the meaning of § 83(c)(2). Consider the following example in which Dan does not receive a capital interest, but receives

---

[14] Dan's gain would presumably be capital gain. § 741.

[15] Apart from the immediate recognition of income, a downside of a § 83(b) election is the denial of a deduction in the event the property should subsequently be forfeited. § 83(b)(1).

only a 10% profits interest (commonly referred to as a profits-only interest) in the LLC.

Example 4: Transfer of Profits-Only Interest in Exchange for Services — Existing Partnership. Assume the same facts as in Example 2, except that, instead of Ron and Sharon giving Dan a capital and profits interest for his management services, they gave him a profits-only interest of 10%, i.e., Dan would only be entitled to receive 10% of any profits subsequently generated by the LLC. Dan has clearly received a property interest that is not subject to any risk of forfeiture and is transferable. Under § 83 and general tax principles, one might conclude that Dan must include in his gross income the value of the profits-only interest upon its receipt. But what is the value of that interest? Conceptually, one could argue that the profits-only interest has no value on the theory that, if the LLC liquidated immediately upon the transfer of the interest to Dan, Dan would receive nothing. Under this theory, Dan would not report income until profits were actually realized by the LLC and Dan would then include in gross income his allocable share of those profits. By contrast, one could argue Dan's right to a 10% share of the LLC's future profits has a present value and Dan should be taxed immediately on that present value. A couple of problems presented by this latter theory are: (1) the present value of future profits is conjectural; and (2) a double taxation problem would be presented were Dan to be taxed immediately upon receipt of the profits interest and then subsequently taxed on his allocable share of profits actually realized by the LLC.

In addition to the problems with respect to Dan's tax treatment, a number of issues are raised regarding the tax consequences to the LLC. If Dan is deemed to have gross income upon receipt of the profits-only interest, should we assume the LLC had anticipated its profits and used those anticipated profits to compensate Dan? If so, shouldn't the LLC have income immediately?[16] Likewise, if Dan is required to include the value of the profits-only interest in income upon receipt, shouldn't the LLC be entitled to a deduction at the same time? See § 83(h).

Given the speculative value of profits-only interests, it is not surprising that practitioners long assumed that the receipt of a profits-only interest in a partnership did not result in gross income to the recipient, give rise to a deduction by the partnership, or trigger any gain at the partnership level. *Diamond v. Commissioner*, included in the materials, however, muddied the waters. The court in *Diamond* concluded that the receipt of a purported profits-only interest on the formation of the partnership resulted in immediate taxation.

Subsequent to *Diamond*, the relatively few cases addressing profits-only interests have focused primarily on either (1) whether the interest in question was truly a profits-only interest rather than a capital interest; or (2) whether the interest, if

---

[16] Consider *Stranahan's Estate v. Commissioner*, 472 F.2d 867 (6th Cir. 1973) where a taxpayer sold a stream of anticipated stock dividends to his son for a lump sum payment and was deemed to have gain characterized as ordinary income equal to the difference between the amount paid by the son and the taxpayer's zero basis in the anticipated dividends.

indeed a profits-only interest, was susceptible of valuation.[17] Some courts also struggled with whether profits-only interests constituted property for purposes of § 83.[18] The Service mercifully relieved the considerable anxiety generated by *Diamond* and its progeny by issuing Rev. Proc. 93-27, 1993-2 C.B. 343, in which the Service ruled that it would not treat as a taxable event (for either the partner or the partnership) the receipt of a profits interest for services to or for the benefit of a partnership in a partner capacity or in anticipation of being a partner. The Revenue Procedure, however, did not apply in certain situations, including: (1) where the profits interest relates to a substantially certain and predictable stream of income from partnership assets, such as income from high-quality debt securities or a high-quality net lease; (2) where the partner disposes of the profits interest within two years of receipt; or (3) where the profits interest is a limited partnership interest in a § 7704(b) "publicly traded partnership." Why would the Service identify these three situations as exceptions to the general rule that receipt of a profits interest is not a taxable event?[19]

C. The 2005 Proposed Regulations Relating to Compensatory Transfers of Partnership Interests

In 2005, Treasury issued proposed regulations regarding the contribution of services to a partnership in exchange for a "compensatory partnership interest."[20] Simply stated, a "compensatory partnership interest" is any interest in the partnership, including a capital interest or a profits-only interest, which is transferred to a person in connection with the performance of services for the partnership. The 2005 proposed regulations address a host of issues associated with the transfer and receipt of a "compensatory partnership interest," including application of §83 as well as the application of § 721. The following excerpt from the preamble to these proposed regulations provides a helpful overview:

Valuation of Compensatory Partnership Interests.

---

[17] *See* St. John v. United States, 1983 U.S. Dist. LEXIS 11635 (Nov. 16, 1983); Campbell v. Commissioner, 943 F.2d 815 (8th Cir. 1991), *rev'g* T.C. Memo 1990-162; Vestal v. United States, 498 F.2d 487 (8th Cir. 1974); Mark IV Pictures, Inc. v. Commissioner, T.C. Memo 1990-571, *aff'd*, 969 F.2d 669 (8th Cir. 1992).

[18] *See* St. John v. United States, 1983 U.S. Dist. LEXIS 11635 (Nov. 16, 1983); Campbell v. Commissioner, 943 F.2d 815 (8th Cir. 1991), *rev'g* T.C. Memo 1990-162.

[19] The Service clarified Revenue Procedure 93-27 in Rev. Proc. 2001-43, 2001-2 C.B. 191, noting that whether an interest granted to a service provider is a profits interest will be tested at the time the interest is granted, even if at the time the interest is substantially nonvested within the meaning of Reg. § 1.83-3(b). Accordingly, the Service will not treat the grant of the interest or the event that causes the interest to become substantially vested as a taxable event for the partner or the partnership. Thus, taxpayers need not file an election under § 83(b). For purposes of Revenue Procedure 93-27, if the profits interest is not substantially vested, the service provider will be deemed to have received the interest on the date of the grant so long as the service provider is treated as the owner of the partnership interest from the date of the grant and thus begins reporting an allocable share of the partnership tax items, e.g., income, gain, loss, deduction. Furthermore, neither the partnership nor any of the partners may deduct any amount (as wages, compensation, or otherwise) for the fair market value of the interest upon the grant of the interest or when the interest becomes substantially vested.

[20] These proposed regulations apply only to those interests that are transferred on or after the date final regulations are published in the Federal Register.

Section 83 generally provides that the recipient of property transferred in connection with the performance of services recognizes income equal to the fair market value of the property, disregarding lapse restrictions. . . . However, some authorities have concluded that, under the particular facts and circumstances of the case, a partnership profits interest had only a speculative value or that the fair market value of the partnership interest should be determined by reference to the liquidation value of that interest.

The Treasury Department and the IRS have determined that, provided certain requirements are satisfied, it is appropriate to allow partnerships and service providers to value partnership interests based on *liquidation value*. This approach ensures consistency in the treatment of partnership profits interests and partnership capital interests . . .[21]

[**Authors' note:** Reg. § 1.83-3(l) refers to the special election to use the liquidation value for purposes of determining the fair market value as creating a safe harbor. In Notice 2005-43. 2005-1 C.B. 1221 (issued at the same time as the proposed regulations), the Service set forth a proposed revenue procedure which when finalized will obsolete Rev. Proc. 93-27 and 2001-43 noted above. The proposed revenue procedure specifically provides that the liquidation value safe harbor of Prop. Reg. § 1.83-3(l) will apply only to so-called "safe harbor partnership interests." A "safe harbor partnership interest" is defined by the proposed revenue procedure as a partnership interest ... transferred to a service provider ... in connection with services provided to the partnership (either before or after the formation of the partnership), provided that the interest is not (a) related to a substantially certain and predictable stream of income from partnership assets, such as income from high-quality debt securities or a high-quality net lease, (b) transferred in anticipation of a subsequent disposition, or (c) an interest in a publicly traded partnership within the meaning of § 7704(b)." (Note how the proposed revenue procedure borrows from Rev. Proc. 93-27 discussed above.)

"Liquidation value," as used in the proposed regulations, refers to "the amount of cash a holder of the interest would receive if, immediately after the transfer of the interest, the partnership sold all of its assets (including goodwill, going concern value, and any other intangibles associated with the partnership's operations for their fair market value and then liquidated." Under those circumstances, the recipient of a profits-only interest would not receive anything if the partnership were to sell its assets and liquidate immediately after the profits-only interest were transferred to that person. Thus, the

---

[21] Proposed Reg. § 1.83-3(l) creates a "safe harbor" allowing the use of liquidation value if certain conditions are satisfied. The conditions essentially relate to provisions in the partnership agreement whereby the partnership is authorized and directed to elect the safe harbor, and the partnership and all partners are bound by the election of the liquidation value safe harbor. If the partnership agreement fails to contain the necessary provision, each partner in a partnership transferring an interest in connection with the performance of services must execute a document containing comparable provisions. Prop. Reg. § 1.83-3(l)(1), (ii), (iii).

profits-only interest would have a value of $0 for § 83 purposes. By contrast, the recipient of a 10% capital interest, for example, would be entitled to an amount equal to 10% of the net cash proceeds resulting from this hypothetical liquidation sale. Thus, for example, if the liquidation value of a partnership were $1,000,000, the transfer of a 10% capital and profits interest in the partnership in connection with the performance of services would result in the service provider having § 83 income [ordinary income] equal to $100,000.]

Application of Section 721 to Partnership on Transfer

There is a dispute among commentators as to whether a partnership should recognize gain or loss on the transfer of a compensatory partnership interest. Some commentators believe that, on the transfer of such an interest, the partnership should be treated as satisfying its compensation obligation with a fractional interest in each asset of the partnership. Under this *McDougal*/deemed sale of assets theory, the partnership would recognize gain or loss equal to the excess of the fair market value of each partial asset deemed transferred to the service provider over the partnership's adjusted basis in that partial asset. Other commentators believe that a partnership should not recognize gain or loss on the transfer of a compensatory partnership interest. They argue, among other things, that the transfer of such an interest is not properly treated as a realization event for the partnership because no property owned by the partnership has changed hands. They also argue that taxing a partnership on the transfer of such an interest would result in inappropriate gain acceleration, would be difficult to administer, and would cause economically similar transactions to be taxed differently.

Generally, when appreciated property is used to pay an obligation, gain on the property is recognized. . . . [T]he Treasury Department and IRS believe that partnerships should not be required to recognize gain on the transfer of a compensatory partnership interest. Such a rule is more consistent with the policies underlying section 721 — to deter recognition of gain and loss when persons join together to conduct a business — than would be a rule requiring the partnership to recognize on the transfer of these types of interests. Therefore, the proposed regulations provide that partnerships are not taxed on the transfer or substantial vesting of a compensatory partnership interest. Under § 1.704-1(b)(4)(i) (reverse section 704(c) principles), the historic partners generally will be required to recognize any income or loss attributable to the partnership's assets as those assets are sold, depreciated, or amortized.

The rule providing for nonrecognition of gain or loss does not apply to the transfer or substantial vesting of an interest in an eligible entity, as defined in § 301.7701-3(a) of the Procedure and Administration Regulations, that becomes a partnership under § 301.7701-3(f)(2) as a result of the transfer or substantial vesting of the interest. See

McDougal v. Commissioner, 62 T.C. 720 (1974) (holding that the service recipient recognized gain on the transfer of a one-half interest in appreciated property to the service provider, immediately prior to the contribution by the service recipient and the service provider of their respective interests in the property to a newly formed partnership.)

Proposed Regulation § 1.721-1.
Nonrecognition of Gain or Loss on Contribution.

(b)(1) Except as otherwise provided in this section or § 1.721-2, section 721 does not apply to the transfer of a partnership interest in connection with the performance of services or in satisfaction of an obligation. The transfer of a partnership interest to a person in connection with the performance of services constitutes a transfer of property to which section 83 and the regulations thereunder apply . . .

(2) Except as provided in section 83(h) and 1.83-6(c), no gain or loss shall be recognized by a partnership upon –

   (i) The transfer or substantial vesting of a ***compensatory partnership interest***; . . .

(3) For purposes of this section, a ***compensatory partnership interest*** is an interest in the transferring partnership that is transferred in connection with the performance of services for that partnership (either before or after the formation of the partnership) . . .

(4) To the extent that a partnership interest is —

   (i) Transferred to a partner in connection with the performance of services rendered to the partnership, it is a *guaranteed payment* for services under section 707(c);

   (ii) Transferred in connection with the performance of services rendered to a partner, it is not deductible by the partnership, but is deductible only by such partner to the extent allowable under Chapter 1 of the Code.

In view of these proposed regulations and the preamble excerpt above, let us reconsider each of the four examples discussed above.

Application of 2005 Proposed Regulations to Example 1: The analysis and the results in Example 1 will be identical under the Proposed Regulations. Note that Treasury, in the above preamble, specifically provides that the non-recognition rule of the Prop. Reg. § 1.721-1(b) does not apply to a situation like that presented in Example 1 where Dan receives a one-half interest in the Porsche from Ron and Dan, and Ron immediately created an LLC to which they contributed their respective interests in the Porsche.

Application of 2005 Proposed Regulations to Example 2: As discussed in the analysis of Example 2, § 83 will apply and, assuming that the safe harbor of the proposed § 83 regulations is elected, Dan's income will equal the amount of cash Dan would be deemed to have received if the LLC, immediately after the transfer to Dan, had sold all of its assets for cash and distributed that cash in liquidation of the LLC. On the facts of Example 2, the liquidation sale proceeds would be $150,000 and thus Dan, who has a 10% capital interest, would be entitled to receive $15,000 in cash. When he receives the 10% capital interest, Dan's income will be $15,000 reportable immediately because his interest is vested. In turn, the LLC will be entitled to a $15,000 deduction for the compensation deemed paid to Dan. Dan will be treated as though he contributed $15,000 cash to the LLC and will, as a result, have a $15,000 basis in his LLC interest. As noted above, the *McDougal*/deemed sale-of-assets analysis is rejected by the Proposed Regulations. Given Prop. Reg. § 1.721-1(b), the LLC will not recognize any gain when it gives Dan the compensatory LLC interest. Again, it is just as though the LLC had distributed $15,000 in cash to Dan for his services. Were that the case, the LLC would obviously have no gain.

Application of 2005 Proposed Regulations to Example 3: The results to Dan will be the same, i.e., under § 83 he will report $15,000 of ordinary income in 2016. In effect, he will be treated as having received $15,000 of cash compensation in 2016. In turn, he will have a $15,000 basis in his LLC interest just as though he had contributed $15,000 cash to the LLC. The LLC will be entitled to a $15,000 deduction in 2016 just as in Example 3. Under Prop. Reg. § 1.721-1(b), the LLC will not recognize any gain when Dan's compensatory LLC interest vests. Again, the LLC will be treated as if it had merely distributed $15,000 in cash to Dan for his services.

Application of Proposed Regulations to Example 4: Under the proposed regulations, the profits-only interest Dan receives is a "compensatory partnership interest." Assuming the LLC elects to use the safe harbor of the proposed § 83 regulations, Dan's profits-only interest — which is a vested interest — will be valued at $0 pursuant to the liquidation value method discussed above. Dan would thus include nothing in income upon receipt of the profits interest and would take a $0 basis in that interest. Consistent with this analysis, the LLC would have no deduction and would recognize no gain as a result of the transfer of the profits-only interest to Dan.[22]

---

[22] As discussed above, under § 83, if a compensatory interest in a partnership is transferred in connection with the performance of services and the interest is not substantially vested, i.e., is nontransferable or is subject to a substantial risk of forfeiture, inclusion (if any) by the recipient of the interest and, in turn, deduction (if any) by the transferor will be deferred until the interest is substantially vested unless a § 83(b) election is made. If no § 83(b) election is made, the service partner is not treated as a partner until the interest is substantially vested. The proposed regulations adopt these

In sum, the 2005 proposed regulations are beneficial in a number of respects, including:

1. The proposed regulations provide for nonrecognition of gain or loss at the partnership/LLC level upon the transfer of a compensatory partnership/LLC interest (either a capital interest or a profits-only interest) in connection with the performance of services. This nonrecognition result is consistent with the nonrecognition regime you have studied in prior chapters.

2. The liquidation value safe harbor ensures that the profits-only interest will be valued at zero, thus eliminating many uncertainties that have existed in this area since the *Diamond* decision discussed above. But a word of caution is in order: By their own terms, the proposed regulations do not apply to the situation where the transfer of property creates the partnership, as in *McDougal*. In such a case, if the interest received is a profits-only interest, the inapplicability of the proposed regulations suggests the need to consider *Diamond* and the Service's revenue procedures to determine whether the receipt of the interest may be taxable.

3. The proposed regulations clarify that § 83 controls the determination of the value of the compensatory partnership/LLC interest and the timing of the inclusion by the recipient and deduction by the transferor.

D. Conclusion

As the above discussion indicates, determining the tax consequences of an exchange of services for a capital interest or a profits-only interest in a partnership can be complex. Those consequences depend on whether the service partner receives an interest in an existing partnership or on the formation of the partnership. In either case, Section 83 must be applied in determining the timing of income and deductions associated with the transfer of the partnership interest. The transfer of a profits-only interest raises numerous issues that the 2005 proposed regulations address. In the next chapter, you will examine the creation and maintenance of a service partner's capital accounts. This chapter provides an important foundation for your understanding of the capital accounts of service partners.

---

§ 83 rules. In this respect, the proposed regulations differ from Revenue Procedure 2001-43 discussed above, which provides that, if a partnership profits interest is transferred in connection with the performance of services, the holder of the profits interest may be treated as a partner even if no § 83 (b) election is made, provided certain conditions are met. As noted above, Rev. Proc. 93-27 and Rev. Proc. 2001-43 will be obsoleted when the proposed regulations are finalized. Notice 2005-43, 2005-1 C.B. 1221.

DIAMOND v. COMMISSIONER
492 F.2d 286 (7th Cir. 1974)

FAIRCHILD, CIRCUIT JUDGE.

This is an appeal from a decision of the Tax Court upholding the Commissioner's assessment of deficiencies against Sol and Muriel Diamond for the years 1961 and 1962. The deficiencies for each year were consolidated for trial, but are essentially unrelated. The Tax Court concluded that Diamond realized ordinary income on the *receipt of a right to a share of profit or loss* to be derived from a real estate venture (the 1962 partnership case) . . .

The 1962 Partnership Case.

During 1961, Diamond was a mortgage broker. Philip Kargman had acquired for $25,000 the buyer's rights in a contract for the sale of an office building. Kargman asked Diamond to obtain a mortgage loan for the full $1,100,000 purchase price of the building. Diamond and Kargman agreed that Diamond would receive a 60% share of profit or loss of the venture if he arranged the financing.

Diamond succeeded in obtaining a $1,100,000 mortgage loan from Marshall Savings and Loan. On December 15, 1961 Diamond and Kargman entered into an agreement which provided:

(1) The two were associated as joint venturers for 24 years (the life of the mortgage) unless earlier terminated by agreement or by sale;

(2) Kargman was to advance all cash needed for the purchase beyond the loan proceeds;

(3) Profits and losses would be divided, 40% to Kargman, 60% to Diamond;

(4) In event of sale, proceeds would be devoted first to repayment to Kargman of money supplied by him, and net profits thereafter would be divided 40% to Kargman, 60% to Diamond.

Early in 1962, Kargman and Diamond created an Illinois land trust to hold title to the property. The chief motivation for the land trust arrangement was apparently to insulate Diamond and Kargman from personal liability on the mortgage note.

The purchase proceeded as planned and closing took place on February 18, 1962. Kargman made cash outlays totaling $78,195.33 in connection with the purchase. Thus, under the terms of the agreement, the property would have to appreciate at least $78,195.33 before Diamond would have any equity in it.

Shortly after closing, it was proposed that Diamond would sell his interest and one Liederman would be substituted, except on a 50-50 basis. Liederman persuaded Diamond to sell his interest for $40,000. This sale was effectuated on March 8, 1962 by Diamond assigning his interest to Kargman for $40,000. Kargman in turn then conveyed a similar interest, except for 50-50 sharing, to Liederman for the same amount.

On their 1962 joint return, the Diamonds reported the March 8, 1962 $40,000 sale proceeds as a short term capital gain. This gain was offset by an unrelated short term capital loss. They reported no tax consequences from the February 18 receipt of the interest in the venture. Diamond's position is that his receipt of this type of interest in partnership is not taxable income although received in return for services. He relies on § 721 and Reg. § 1.721-1(b)(1). He further argues that the subsequent sale of this interest produced a capital gain under § 741. The Tax Court held that the receipt of this type of interest in partnership in return for services is not within § 721 and is taxable under § 61 when received. The Tax Court valued the interest at $40,000 as of February 18, as evidenced by the sale for that amount three weeks later, on March 8.

Both the taxpayer and the Tax Court treated the venture as a partnership and purported to apply partnership income tax principles. It has been suggested that the record might have supported findings that there was in truth an employment or other relationship, other than partnership, and produced a similar result, but these findings were not made. See Cowan, *The Diamond Case*, 27 Tax Law Review 161 (1972). It has also been suggested (and argued, alternatively, by the government) that although on the face of the agreement Diamond appeared to receive only a right to share in profit (loss) to be derived, the value of the real estate may well have been substantially greater than the purchase price, so that Diamond may really have had an interest in capital, if the assets were properly valued. This finding was not made. The Tax Court . . . suggested the possibility that Diamond would not in any event be entitled to capital gains treatment of his sale of a right to receive income in the future, but did not decide the question.[23]

Taking matters at face value, taxpayer received, on February 18, an interest in partnership, limited to a right to a share of profit (loss) to be derived. In discussion we shall refer to this interest either as his interest in partnership or a profit-share.

The Tax Court, with clearly adequate support, found that Diamond's interest in partnership had a market value of $40,000 on February 18. Taxpayer's analysis is that under the regulations the receipt of a profit-share February 18, albeit having a market value and being conferred in return for services, was not a taxable event, and that the entire proceeds of the March 8 sale were a capital gain. The Tax Court analysis was that the interest in partnership, albeit limited to a profit-share, was property worth $40,000, and taxpayer's acquisition thereof on February 18 was compensation for services and ordinary income. Assuming that capital gain treatment at sale would have been appropriate, there was no gain because the sale was for the same amount.

There is no statute or regulation which expressly and particularly prescribes the income tax effect, or absence of one, at the moment a partner receives a profit-share in return for services. The Tax Court's holding rests upon the general principle that a valuable property interest received in return for services is compensation, and income. Taxpayer's argument is predicated upon an implication which his counsel, and others, have found in Reg. § 1.721-1(1) (b), but which need not, and the government argues should not, be found there.

---

[23] Because of the decision we reach, it is also unnecessary for us to consider this possibility and we express no conclusions concerning it.

I.R.C. § 721 is entitled "Nonrecognition of gain or loss on contribution," and provides: "No gain or loss shall be recognized to a partnership or to any of its partners in the case of a contribution of property to the partnership in exchange for an interest in the partnership." Only if, by a strained construction, "property" were said to include services, would § 721 say anything about the effect of furnishing services. It clearly deals with a contribution like Kargman's, of property, and prescribes that when he contributed his property, no gain or loss was recognized. It does not, of course, explicitly say that no income accrues to one who renders services and, in return, becomes a partner with a profit-share.

Reg. § 1.721-1 presumably explains and interprets § 721, perhaps to the extent of qualifying or limiting its meaning. Subsection (b) (1), particularly relied on here, reads in part as follows:

> Normally, under local law, each partner is entitled to be repaid his contributions of money or other property to the partnership (at the value placed upon such property by the partnership at the time of the contribution) whether made at the formation of the partnership or subsequent thereto. To the extent that any of the partners gives up any part of his right to be repaid his contributions (as distinguished from a share in partnership profits) in favor of another partner as compensation for services (or in satisfaction of an obligation), section 721 does not apply. The value of an interest in such partnership capital so transferred to a partner as compensation for services constitutes income to the partner under section 61 . . .

The quoted portion of the regulation may well be read, like § 721, as being directly addressed only to the consequences of a contribution of money or other property. It asserts that when a partner making such contributions transfers to another some part of the contributing partner's right to be repaid, in order to compensate the other for services or to satisfy an obligation to the other, § 721 does not apply, there is recognition of gain or loss to the contributing partner, and there is income to the partner who receives, as compensation for services, part of the right to be repaid.

The regulation does not specify that if a partner contributing property agrees that, in return for services, another shall be a partner with a profit-share only, the value of the profit-share is not income to the recipient. An implication to that effect, such as is relied on by taxpayer, would have to rest on the proposition that the regulation was meant to be all inclusive as to when gain or loss would be recognized or income would exist as a consequence of the contribution of property to a partnership and disposition of the partnership interests. It would have to appear, in order to sustain such implication, that the existence of income by reason of a creation of a profit-share, immediately having a determinable market value, in favor of a partner would be inconsistent with the result specified in the regulation.

We do not find this implication in our own reading of the regulation. It becomes necessary to consider the substantial consensus of commentators in favor of the principle claimed to be implied and to look to judicial interpretation, legislative history, administrative interpretation, and policy considerations to determine whether the implication is justified.

The Commentators: There is a startling degree of unanimity that the conferral of a profit-share as compensation for services is not income at the time of the conferral, although little by way of explanation of why this should be so, or analysis of statute or regulation to show that it is prescribed.

One of the most unequivocal statements, with an explanation in terms of practicality or policy, was made by Arthur Willis in a text:

> However obliquely the proposition is stated in the regulations, it is clear that a partner who receives only an interest in future profits of the partnership as compensation for services is not required to report the receipt of his partnership interest as taxable income. The rationale is twofold. In the first place, the present value of a right to participate in future profits is usually too conjectural to be subject to valuation. In the second place, the service partner is taxable on his distributive share of partnership income as it is realized by the partnership. If he were taxed on the present value of the right to receive his share of future partnership income, either he would be taxed twice, or the value of his right to participate in partnership income must be amortized over some period of time.[24]

Judicial Interpretation: Except for one statement by the Tax Court no decision cited by the parties or found by us appears squarely to reach the question, either on principle in the absence of the regulations, or by application of the regulations. In a footnote in *Herman M. Hale*, 1965 T.C. Memo 274, 24 T.C.M. 1497, 1502 (1965) the Tax Court said: "Under the regulations, the mere receipt of a partnership interest in future profits does not create any tax liability. Sec. 1.721-1(b), Income Tax Regs." There was no explanation of how this conclusion was derived from the regulations.

Legislative History: The legislative history is equivocal. An advisory group appointed in 1956 to review the regulations evidently felt concern about whether the provision of Reg. § 1.721-1 that the value of an interest in capital transferred to a partner in compensation for services constitutes income had a statutory basis in the light of § 721 providing that there shall be no recognition of gain or loss in the case of a contribution of property. The group proposed enactment of a new section to provide such basis, and legislation introduced into the 86th Congress in 1959 incorporated this recommendation. The bill, H.R. 9662, would have created a new § 770 providing specifically for the taxation of a person receiving an interest in partnership capital in exchange for the performance of services for the partnership. However, neither proposed § 770 nor anything else in H.R. 9662 dealt with the receipt merely of a profit-share. The lack of concern over an income tax impact when only a profit-share was conferred might imply an opinion that such conferring of a profit-share would not be taxable under any circumstances, or might imply an opinion that it would be income or not under § 61 depending upon whether it had a determinable market value or not.

Several statements in the course of the hearings and committee reports

---

[24] WILLIS ON PARTNERSHIP TAXATION 84–85 (1971). *See* Cowan, *The Diamond Case*, 27 TAX LAW REVIEW 181 n. 56 (1972).

paralleled the first parenthetical phrase in Reg. § 1.721-1(b) and were to the effect that the provision did not apply where a person received only a profit-share. There was, however, at least one specific statement by the chairman of the advisory group (Mr. Willis) that if the service partner "were to receive merely an interest in future profits in exchange for his services, he would have no immediate taxable gain because he would be taxed on his share of income as it was earned."[25] H.R. 9662 passed the House of Representatives, and was favorably reported to the Senate by its finance committee, but never came to a vote in the Senate. Even had the bill become law, it would not have dealt expressly with the problem at hand.

Administrative Interpretation: We are unaware of instances in which the Commissioner has asserted delinquencies where a taxpayer who received a profit-share with determinable market value in return for services failed to report the value as income, or has otherwise acted consistently with the Tax Court decision in *Diamond*. Although the consensus referred to earlier appears to exist, the Commissioner has not by regulation or otherwise acted affirmatively to reject it, and in a sense might be said to have agreed by silence.

Consideration of partnership principles or practices: There must be wide variation in the degree to which a profit-share created in favor of a partner who has or will render service has determinable market value at the moment of creation. Surely in many if not the typical situations it will have only speculative value, if any.

In the present case, taxpayer's services had all been rendered, and the prospect of earnings from the real estate under Kargman's management was evidently very good. The profit-share had determinable market value.

If the present decision be sound, then the question will always arise, whenever a profit-share is created or augmented, whether it has a market value capable of determination. Will the existence of this question be unduly burdensome on those who choose to do business under the partnership form?

Each partner determines his income tax by taking into account his distributive share of the taxable income of the partnership. 26 U.S.C. § 702. Taxpayer's position here is that he was entitled to defer income taxation on the compensation for his services except as partnership earnings were realized. If a partner is taxed on the determinable market value of a profit-share at the time it is created in his favor, and is also taxed on his full share of earnings as realized, there will arguably be double taxation, avoidable by permitting him to amortize the value which was originally treated as income. Does the absence of a recognized procedure for amortization militate against the treatment of the creation of the profit-share as income?

Do the disadvantages of treating the creation of the profit-share as income in those instances where it has a determinable market value at that time outweigh the desirability of imposing a tax at the time the taxpayer has received an interest with determinable market value as compensation for services?

We think, of course, that the resolution of these practical questions makes clearly desirable the promulgation of appropriate regulations, to achieve a degree of

---

[25] *See* Hearings on Advisory Group Recommendations on Subchapters C, J, and K of the Internal Revenue Code before the House Comm. on Ways and Means, 86th Cong., 1st Sess. 53 (1959).

certainty. But in the absence of regulation, we think it sound policy to defer to the expertise of the Commissioner and the Judges of the Tax Court, and to sustain their decision that the receipt of a profit-share with determinable market value is income . . .

The [judgment] of the Tax Court in . . . the 1962 partnership case [is] . . . affirmed.

MCDOUGAL v. COMMISSIONER
62 T.C. 720 (1974)

FAY, JUDGE.

OPINION

. . . .

F.C. and Frankie McDougal are husband and wife, as are Gilbert and Jackie McClanahan. Each couple filed joint Federal income tax returns for the years 1968 and 1969 with the district director of internal revenue in Austin, Tex. . . .

[F.C. McDougal (hereinafter McDougal) and his wife, Frankie] maintained farms at Lamesa, Tex., where they were engaged in the business of breeding and racing horses. Gilbert McClanahan [hereinafter McClanahan] was a licensed public horse trainer who rendered his services to various horse owners for a standard fee. He had numbered the McDougals among his clientele since 1965.

On February 21, 1965, a horse of exceptional pedigree, Iron Card, had been foaled at the Anthony Ranch in Florida. Title to Iron Card was acquired in January of 1967 by one Frank Ratliff, Jr., who in turn transferred title to himself, M.H. Ratliff, and John V. Burnett (Burnett). The Ratliffs and Burnett entered Iron Card in several races as a 2-year-old; and although the horse enjoyed some success in these contests, it soon became evident that he was suffering from a condition diagnosed by a veterinarian as a protein allergy.

When, due to a dispute among themselves, the Ratliffs and Burnett decided to sell Iron Card for whatever price he could attract, McClanahan (who had trained the horse for the Ratliffs and Burnett) advised the McDougals to make the purchase. He made this recommendation because, despite the veterinarian's prognosis to the contrary, McClanahan believed that by the use of home remedy Iron Card could be restored to full racing vigor. Furthermore, McClanahan felt that as Iron Card's allergy was not genetic and as his pedigree was impressive, he would be valuable in the future as a stud even if further attempts to race him proved unsuccessful.

The McDougals purchased Iron Card for $10,000 on January 1, 1968. At the time of the purchase McDougal promised that if McClanahan trained and attended to Iron Card, a half interest in the horse would be his once the McDougals had recovered the costs and expenses of acquisition. This promise was not made in lieu of payment of the standard trainer's fee; for from January 1, 1968, until the date of the transfer, McClanahan was paid $2,910 as compensation for services rendered as Iron Card's trainer.

McClanahan's home remedy proved so effective in relieving Iron Card of his allergy that the horse began to race with success, and his reputation consequently grew to such proportion that he attracted a succession of offers to purchase, one of which reached $60,000. The McDougals decided, however, to keep the horse and by October 4, 1968, had recovered out of their winnings the costs of acquiring him. It was therefore on that date that they transferred a half interest in the horse to McClanahan in accordance with the promise which McDougal had made to the trainer. A document entitled "Bill of Sale," wherein the transfer was described as a gift, was executed on the following day.

Iron Card continued to race well until very late in 1968 when, without warning and for an unascertained cause, he developed a condition called "hot ankle" which effectively terminated his racing career. From 1970 onward he was used exclusively for breeding purposes. That his value as a stud was no less than his value as a racehorse is attested to by the fact that in September of 1970 petitioners were offered $75,000 for him; but after considering the offer, the McDougals and McClanahan decided to refuse it, preferring to exploit Iron Card's earning potential as a stud to their own profit.

On November 1, 1968, petitioners had concluded a partnership agreement by parol to effectuate their design of racing the horse for as long as that proved feasible and of offering him out as a stud thereafter. Profits were to be shared equally by the McDougals and the McClanahans, while losses were to be allocated to the McDougals alone.

. . . .

> [Note: the McDougals, on an amended return filed in April of 1970, claimed to have transferred the half interest in Iron Card to McClanahan as compensation for services rendered and thus to be entitled to a $30,000 business expense deduction, computed by reference to the last offer to purchase Iron Card received prior to October 4, 1968. Furthermore, the McDougals acknowledged that they had recognized a gain on the transfer of the half interest in Iron Card to McClanahan. By charging the entire depreciation deduction they had claimed with respect to Iron Card (for the period January 1, 1968 through October 4, 1968) against the portion of their unadjusted cost basis allocable to the half interest in Iron Card which they retained, the McDougals computed this gain to be $25,000 (i.e., the $30,000 value transferred to McClanahan less $5,000, i.e., one-half of the purchase price of Iron Card) and characterized their gain as a long-term capital gain under § 1231(a).]

ULTIMATE FINDINGS OF FACT

The transfer of October 4, 1968, gave rise to a joint venture to which the McDougals are deemed to have contributed Iron Card and in which they are deemed to have granted McClanahan an interest in the capital and profits thereof, equal to their own, as compensation for his having trained Iron Card . . .

OPINION

Respondent contends that the McDougals did not recognize a $25,000 gain on the transaction of October 4, 1968, and that they were not entitled to claim a $30,000 business expense deduction by reason thereof. He further contends that were Iron Card to be contributed to a partnership or joint venture under the circumstances obtaining in the instant case, its basis in Iron Card at the time of contribution would have been limited by the McDougals' cost basis in the horse, as adjusted. Respondent justifies these contentions by arguing that the transfer of October 4, 1968, constituted a gift.

In the alternative, respondent has urged us to find that at some point in time no later than the transfer of October 4, 1968, McDougal and McClanahan entered into a partnership or joint venture to which the McDougals contributed Iron Card and McClanahan contributed services. Respondent contends that such a finding would require our holding that the McDougals did not recognize a gain on the transfer of October 4, 1968, by reason of section 721, and that under section 723 the joint venture's basis in Iron Card at the time of the contribution was equal to the McDougals' adjusted basis in the horse as of that time.

We dismiss at the outset respondent's contention that the transfer of October 4, 1968, constituted a gift, and we are undeterred in so doing by the fact that petitioners originally characterized the transfer as a gift, *Bogardus v. Commissioner*, 302 U.S. 34 (1937). A gift has been defined as a transfer motivated by detached and disinterested generosity, *Commissioner v. Duberstein*, 363 U.S. 278 (1960). The presence of such motivation is belied in this instance by two factors. The relationship of the parties concerned was essentially of a business nature, and the transfer itself was made conditional upon the outcome of an enterprise which McDougal had undertaken at McClanahan's suggestion and in reliance upon McClanahan's ability to render it profitable. These factors instead bespeak the presence of an arm's-length transaction.

With respect to respondent's alternative contention, we note firstly that the law provides no rule easy of application for making a determination as to whether a partnership or joint venture has been formed but rather directs our attention to a congeries of factors relevant to the issue, of which none is conclusive. . . .

A joint venture is deemed to arise when two or more persons agree, expressly or impliedly, to enter actively upon a specific business enterprise, the purpose of which is the pursuit of profit; the ownership of whose productive assets and of the profits generated by them is shared; the parties to which all bear the burden of any loss; and the management of which is not confined to a single participant. . . .

While in the case at bar the risk of loss was to be borne by the McDougals alone, all the other elements of a joint venture were present once the transfer of October 4, 1968, had been effected. Accordingly, we hold that the aforesaid transfer constituted the formation of a joint venture to which the McDougals contributed capital in the form of the horse, Iron Card, and in which they granted McClanahan an interest equal to their own in capital and profits as compensation for his having trained Iron Card. We further hold that the agreement formally entered into on November 1, 1968, and reduced to writing in April of 1970, constituted a continuation of the original joint venture under section 708(b)(2)(A). Furthermore, that McClanahan continued to receive a fee for serving as Iron Card's trainer after October 4, 1968, in no way militates against the soundness of this holding. See sec. 707(c), and sec. 1.707-1(c), example 1, Income Tax Regs. However, this holding does not result in the tax consequences which respondent has contended would follow from it. See sec. 1.721-1(b)(1), Income Tax Regs.

When on the formation of a joint venture a party contributing appreciated assets satisfies an obligation by granting his obligee a capital interest in the venture, he is deemed first to have transferred to the obligee an undivided interest in the assets contributed, equal in value to the amount of the obligation so satisfied. He and the obligee are deemed thereafter and in concert to have contributed those assets to the joint venture.

The contributing obligor will recognize gain on the transaction to the extent that the value of the undivided interest which he is deemed to have transferred exceeds his basis therein. The obligee is considered to have realized an amount equal to the fair market value of the interest which he receives in the venture and will recognize income depending upon the character of the obligation satisfied.[26] The joint venture's basis in the assets will be determined under section 723 in accordance with the foregoing assumptions. Accordingly, we hold that the transaction under consideration constituted an exchange in which the McDougals realized $30,000, *United States v. Davis*, 370 U.S. 65 (1962); *Kenan v. Commissioner*, 114 F. 2d 217 (C.A. 2, 1940), affirming 40 B.T.A. 824 (1939).

In determining the basis offset to which the McDougals are entitled with respect to the transfer of October 4, 1968, we note the following: that the McDougals had an unadjusted cost basis in Iron Card of $ 10,000; that they had claimed $1,390 in depreciation on the entire horse for the period January 1 to October 31, 1968; and that after an agreement of partnership was concluded on November 1, 1968, depreciation on Iron Card was deducted by the partnership exclusively.

Section 704(c) [prior to its amendment] allows partners and joint venturers some freedom in determining who is to claim the deductions for depreciation on contributed property. As is permissible under the statute, petitioners clearly intended the depreciation to be claimed by the common enterprise once it had come into existence, an event which they considered to have occurred on November 1, 1968. Consistent with their intent and with our own holding that a joint venture arose on October 4, 1968, we now further hold that the McDougals were entitled to claim depreciation on Iron Card only until the transfer of October 4, 1968. Thereafter depreciation on Iron Card ought to have been deducted by the joint venture in the computation of its taxable income.

In determining their adjusted basis in the portion of Iron Card on whose disposition they are required to recognize gain, the McDougals charged all the

---

[26] For example, if the obligation arose out of a loan, the obligee will recognize no income by reason of the transaction; if the obligation represents the selling price of a capital asset, he will recognize a capital gain to the extent that the amount he is deemed to have realized exceeds his adjusted basis in the asset; if the obligation represents compensation for services, the transaction will result in ordinary income to the obligee in an amount equal to the value of the interest that he received in the joint venture.

depreciation which they had taken on the horse against their basis in the half in which they retained an interest. This procedure was improper. As in accordance with section 1.167(g)-1, Income Tax Regs., we have allowed the McDougals a depreciation deduction with respect to Iron Card for the period January 1 to October 4, 1968, computed on their entire cost basis in the horse of $10,000; so also do we require that the said deduction be charged against that entire cost basis under section 1016(a)(2)(A).

As the McDougals were in the business of racing horses, any gain recognized by them on the exchange of Iron Card in satisfaction of a debt would be characterized under section 1231(a) provided he had been held by them for the period requisite under section 1231(b) as it applies to livestock acquired before 1970. In that as of October 4, 1968, Iron Card had been used by the McDougals exclusively for racing and not for breeding, we do now hold that they had held him for a period sufficiently long to make section 1231(a) applicable to their gain on the transaction. . . .

The joint venture's basis in Iron Card as of October 4, 1968, must be determined under section 723 in accordance with the principles of law set forth earlier in this opinion. In the half interest in the horse which it is deemed to have received from the McDougals, the joint venture had a basis equal to one-half of the McDougals' adjusted cost basis in Iron Card as of October 4, 1968, i.e., the excess of $5,000 over one-half of the depreciation which the McDougals were entitled to claim on Iron Card for the period January 1 to October 4, 1968. In the half interest which the venture is considered to have received from McClanahan, it can claim to have had a basis equal to the amount which McClanahan is considered to have realized on the transaction, $30,000. The joint venture's deductions for depreciation on Iron Card for the years 1968 and 1969 are to be determined on the basis computed in the above-described manner.

When an interest in a joint venture is transferred as compensation for services rendered, any deduction which may be authorized under section 162(a)(1) by reason of that transfer is properly claimed by the party to whose benefit the services accrued, be that party the venture itself or one or more venturers, sec. 1.721-1(b)(2), Income Tax Regs. Prior to McClanahan's receipt of his interest, a joint venture did not exist under the facts of the case at bar; the McDougals were the sole owners of Iron Card and recipients of his earnings. Therefore, they alone could have benefited from the services rendered by McClanahan prior to October 4, 1968, for which he was compensated by the transaction of that date. Accordingly, we hold that the McDougals are entitled to a business expense deduction of $ 30,000, that amount being the value of the interest which McClanahan received. Respondent has contended that a deduction of $30,000 would be unreasonable in amount in view of the nature of the services for which McClanahan was being compensated. But having found that the transaction under consideration was not a gift but rather was occasioned by a compensation arrangement which was entered upon at arm's length, we must reject this contention. See sec. 1.162-7(b)(2), Income Tax Regs.

. . . .

Decisions will be entered under Rule 155.

Chapter 5

THE PARTNERSHIP BALANCE SHEET AND PARTNERS' CAPITAL ACCOUNTS

I. PROBLEMS

On January 1 of Year 1, Margaret and Evan formed a limited liability company (LLC) to engage in a small engine repair business. Margaret and Evan each own a 50% interest in the LLC, which will be taxed as a partnership. In exchange for their LLC interests, Margaret and Evan contributed the following assets to the LLC:

Margaret's contributions:

Asset	Adjusted Basis	Fair Market Value
Land	$50,000	$100,000
Building	$300,000	$300,000

Assume the building, which was used by Margaret for personal purposes, was encumbered by a $100,000 recourse liability that the LLC will assume.

Evan's contributions:

Asset	Adjusted Basis	Fair Market Value
Cash	$40,000	$40,000
Stock	$20,000	$60,000
Equipment	$0	$200,000*

*Assume the $200,000 of gain inherent in the equipment is all § 1245 gain.

(a) Prepare an opening balance sheet for the LLC reflecting the LLC's adjusted basis in and book value of each of the assets it has received and the outside bases of the two LLC members as well as their capital accounts.

(b) Explain how each of the following *alternative* circumstances would change the balance sheet prepared in (a) above:

(1) In Year 1, the LLC earns and receives $110,000 in revenue and is allowed $30,000 in depreciation deductions with respect to the building and thus has net income of $80,000. It makes no distributions during the year.

(2) In Year 1, the LLC sells for $60,000 the stock contributed by Evan. It makes no distributions during the year. How would the balance sheet

change if the LLC sold the stock for $80,000?

(3) The LLC sells the stock in Year 1 for $60,000 and immediately distributes $20,000 of the proceeds to Margaret and $20,000 to Evan.

(4) The LLC in Year 1 borrows $50,000 from a local bank on a nonrecourse basis.

(5) Assume the facts of (1) above and that the LLC also sold the stock in Year 1 for $60,000 and paid the recourse liability in full. On the first day of Year 2, the LLC gives Aaron a 10% capital and profits interest in the LLC for his commitment to serve as manager of the LLC's repair business. Assume (unrealistically) the interest given to Aaron is not subject to a substantial risk of forfeiture and is transferable within the meaning of § 83. Disregard any depreciation deductions that might be available for Year 2. Apply the proposed regulations under §§ 721 and 83 as discussed in Chapter 4.

(6) Same as (5) except Aaron receives a 10% profits-only interest in the LLC. Use the liquidation method of Prop. Reg. § 1.83-3(l) in valuing Aaron's interest.

Assignment for Chapter 5:

Complete the above Problem.

Read: Internal Revenue Code: §§ 61(a)(13), 721, 722, 723, 752(a), 704(c)(1)(A).
Treasury Regulations: § 1.704-1(b)(2)(iv)(b), (c), (d)(1), (e), (f), and (h)(1). Prop. Reg. §§ 1.83-3(l); and 1.721-1(b)(1). Skim Prop. Reg. § 1.704-1(b)(2)(iv)(f).

Materials: Overview

II. VOCABULARY

balance sheet
capital account
book value
booking-up or booking-down of capital accounts

III. OBJECTIVES

1. To create a balance sheet upon the formation of a partnership reflecting the property contributions of each partner as well as the partnership's inside basis in each asset and each partner's outside basis.

2. To reflect in the balance sheet liabilities encumbering contributed property as well as liabilities incurred by the partnership.

3. To explain the adjustments that are made to a partnership balance sheet to reflect allocations to partners of income, gains, and losses recognized by the partnership.

4. To explain generally how built-in gains and losses when recognized are reflected in the outside basis and capital accounts of the contributing

partner.

5. To explain generally how distributions affect the outside bases and capital accounts of the partners.

6. To explain how a partnership balance sheet is affected by the admission of a service partner who receives either a capital and profits interest or a profit-only interest in the partnership.

7. To identify circumstances when capital accounts may be booked-up or booked-down to reflect revaluation of partnership property.

IV. OVERVIEW

As will become apparent in later chapters of this casebook, the proper maintenance of partners' capital accounts plays a significant role in the operation of Subchapter K. Capital accounts reflect the book value of a partner's equity in the partnership. As illustrated below, the partnership balance sheet provides a snapshot of the partnership at a given point during its existence. Contributions to the partnership, allocation of partnership profits and losses, partnership assumption of liabilities and borrowing, and partnership distributions all affect the partnership balance sheet. This chapter will address the creation and use of partnership balance sheets and the maintenance of partner capital accounts.

A. The Partnership Balance Sheet

What is a balance sheet? Essentially, it is an accounting document that provides an overview of the financial condition of the partnership at a given point in time. A partnership's balance sheet is based on the following equation:

$$\text{Assets} = \text{Liabilties} + \text{Equity or Net Worth}$$

When a partnership (or LLC taxed as a partnership) is created, the "Asset" side of the opening balance sheet will list each asset contributed and will record that asset's fair market value at the time of contribution. This "opening" value is referred to as the "book value" or the partnership's "historical cost" in acquiring the asset. Consider the following example demonstrating the "Asset" side of the balance sheet.

> **Example 1:** On January 1, Year 1, Jessica and Brandon create the Jessica/Brandon Partnership, a cash method, calendar year general partnership that will conduct a yacht and recreational vehicle storage business. Jessica contributes to the partnership $100,000 in cash and a parcel of land (hereinafter Land A) with a fair market value of $300,000. Brandon contributes to the partnership a parcel of land (hereinafter Land B) worth $400,000. Assume Jessica and Brandon had each held for many years their respective parcels of land. In exchange for their contributions, Jessica and Brandon each receive a 50% interest in partnership capital and profits. By the terms of their partnership agreement, all partnership profits and losses will be divided equally between them and, upon liquidation, the assets of the partnership will likewise be divided equally.

Given these facts, the "Asset" side of the partnership's opening balance sheet will be as follows:

Partnership Assets	Book Value
Cash	$100,000
Land A	$300,000
Land B	$400,000
Total	**$800,000**

The asset side of the opening balance sheet thus reflects the fair market value of Land A and Land B at the time Jessica and Brandon contributed those assets to the partnership. As noted, we refer to this value as the "book value" of Land A and Land B. (In other words, we "booked" the assets at their fair market value at the time Jessica and Brandon contributed the assets to the new partnership.)

Assume we create a balance sheet for the partnership one year later on January 1, Year 2, when the partnership still owns both parcels of land and Land A had increased in value to $400,000 and Land B had fallen in value $350,000. Will this later balance sheet reflect the changed fair market value of these parcels of land? The answer is generally "No." Rather the Year 2 balance sheet would show Land A and Land B as having the same fair market value as shown in the opening balance sheet. In other words, the balance sheet would continue to show the "book value" of those two assets. By so doing, the need for an annual appraisal of each asset of the partnership is negated.

Let us now consider the "Liabilities and Partners' Equity" side of the balance sheet. (In later balance sheets, we will refer to this side of the balance sheet as either "Liabilities and Partners' Capital" or simply "Partners' Capital.") This side of the balance sheet will include the sum of any liabilities assumed or taken subject to by the partnership and any initial borrowing by the partnership. In addition, this side of the balance sheet will record the equity or net worth of the partnership as well as each partner's share of the partnership equity or net worth. A partnership's equity or net worth is determined by the following equation:

$$\text{Assets - Liabilities = Equity}$$

A partner's share of partnership equity or net worth is the amount the partner would be entitled to receive if the partnership were liquidated and all of its assets were sold *at their book value*, all of its liabilities were paid, and the net proceeds were distributed. We call this share of equity, the partner's *capital account*.[1] Among other items, a partner's capital account reflects the amount of money a

---

[1] Technically, one might refer to the capital account as computed above as the "book capital account" because it reflects the contributed assets' book values, i.e., the fair market value of the assets at the time of contribution. As discussed in Chapter 9, there are circumstances under which a partnership agreement may, on the occurrence of certain events, provide that the capital accounts of the partners will be "booked-up" or "booked-down" to reflect a revaluation of partnership property (including intangible assets such as goodwill) on the partnership books. Reg. § 1.704-1(b)(2)(iv)(f). For example, partners' capital accounts can be "booked-up" "in connection with a contribution of money or other property (other than a de minimis amount) to the partnership by a new or existing partner as consideration for an interest in the partnership" or in connection with the grant of a partnership interest as consideration for

partner has contributed to a partnership as well as the fair market value of any assets a partner has contributed to the partnership.[2]

Applying the above to the Jessica/Brandon Partnership, the "Liabilities and Equity side" of the partnership's opening balance sheet would show no liabilities. The partnership's equity or net worth would be $800,000. Jessica's capital account will be equal to the $100,000 cash she contributed plus the fair market value of Land A ($300,000) or $400,000. Brandon's capital account will likewise equal $400,000, i.e., the fair market value of Land B that he contributed to the partnership. (In other words, were the partnership to sell all of its assets at their total book value and immediately liquidate, the partnership would have $800,000 to distribute in liquidation and Jessica and Brandon would each be entitled to receive a liquidating distribution of $400,000.)

Combining the "Asset side" and the "Liabilities and Equity side," the Jessica/Brandon partnership would have an opening balance sheet as follows:

Partnership Assets	Book Value	**Liabilities and Partners' Capital**	Book Value
Cash	$100,000	**Liabilities:** None	
Land A	$300,000	**Capital Accounts:**	
Land B	$400,000	Jessica	$400,000
		Brandon	$400,000
Total	**$800,000**		**$800,000**

Note the "balance sheet" balances! Also note that, because we are again using book values in determining liquidation proceeds, Jessica's and Brandon's capital accounts are shown at their book value. As noted above, if, during the year following the creation of the Jessica/Brandon Partnership, Land A increased in value to $400,000 and Land B decreased in value to $350,000, the "Asset side" of the balance sheet would not change. Likewise, the "Liabilities and Equity side" of the balance sheet would not change. Jessica's and Brandon's capital accounts would remain at $400,000 each, i.e., they would not reflect the increased value of land A and the decreased value of land B.

In Chapter 2, you learned that, under the nonrecognition regime of §§ 721, 722 and 723, neither Jessica nor Brandon would recognize gain or loss on the contribution of the parcels of land to the partnership in exchange for their 50% interest in the partnership. Likewise, the partnership would recognize no gain or loss on the exchange. Instead, the gain or loss would be preserved through the basis rules of § 722 and 723. Jessica and Brandon will each take a basis (outside basis) in their partnership interest equal to the adjusted basis they had in the assets contributed to the partnership; the partnership will have a basis (inside

---

services "by a new partner acting in a partner capacity or in anticipation of being a partner." Reg. § 1.704-1(b)(2)(iv)(f)(5)(i) and (iii).

[2] Reg. § 1.704-1(b)(2)(iv)(b)(1) and (2).

basis) in the contributed assets equal to the adjusted basis Jessica and Brandon had in those assets.

The partnership's inside basis in each asset and each partner's outside basis are obviously important for tax purposes. Let us, therefore, add a tax dimension to our balance sheet by reflecting the inside or adjusted bases of the partnership's assets and Jessica's and Brandon's outside bases. Assume for this purpose that Jessica had an adjusted basis of $100,000 in Land A. Thus, Land A, which has a fair market value of $300,000, had a built-in gain of $200,000 when it was contributed by Jessica. As a result of § 721, none of that built-in gain will be recognized, but instead will be preserved in the § 723 basis the partnership takes in Land A. Pursuant to § 722, Jessica's outside basis will be $200,000, i.e., the combination of the $100,000 basis she had in Land A and the $100,000 basis she had in the $100,000 of cash she contributed to the partnership.[3] Assume Brandon had an adjusted basis of $450,000 in parcel of Land B, which had a fair market value of $400,000. Under § 721, the $50,000 of built-in loss will not be recognized by Brandon when he contributes Land B to the partnership. Rather, that loss will be preserved in the § 723 basis of $450,000 the partnership takes in Land B and, pursuant to § 722, in the $450,000 outside basis Brandon will have. With the addition of this inside and outside basis[4] information, the partnership's balance sheet will be as follows:

Partnership Assets	Inside Basis	Book Value	**Liabilities and Partners' Capital**	Outside Basis	Book Value
Cash	$100,000	$100,000	Liabilities: None		
Land A	$100,000	$300,000	Capital Accounts		
Land B	$450,000	$400,000	Jessica	$200,000	$400,000
			Brandon	$450,000	$400,000
Total	$650,000	$800,000		$650,000	$800,000

B. Impact of Partnership Operations and Transactions on the Balance Sheet

---

Reg. § 1.704-1(b)(2)(iv)(b). Basic Rules [for Maintaining a Partner's Capital Accounts]

Except as otherwise provided in this paragraph (b)(2)(iv), the partners'

---

[3] Jessica's partnership interest is worth $400,000 and thus the outside basis preserves the $200,000 of gain that inhered in Land A (built-in gain) and was not recognized when Jessica contributed the land to the partnership.

[4] There is also what is known as a "tax capital account" that reflects the adjusted tax bases the partners have in their partnership interest *without adjustment for any share of partnership liabilities*. There is thus a close relationship between a partner's tax capital account and his or her outside basis. Unless otherwise indicated, we will be using outside basis and not tax capital accounts in the balance sheets shown in this casebook.

capital accounts will be considered to be determined and maintained in accordance with the rules of this paragraph (b)(2)(iv) if, and only if, each partner's capital account is *increased by* (1) the amount of money contributed by him to the partnership, (2) the fair market value of property contributed by him to the partnership (net of liabilities that the partnership is considered to assume or take subject to), and (3) allocations to him of partnership income and gain (or items thereof) . . . ; and is **decreased by** (4) the amount of money distributed to him by the partnership, (5) the fair market value of property distributed to him by the partnership (net of liabilities that such partner is considered to assume or take subject to), (6) allocations to him of expenditures described in § 705(b)(2)(B), and (7) allocations of partnership loss and deduction (or item thereof) . . .

Having addressed the creation of an opening balance sheet upon the formation of a partnership, let us now consider the impact of partnership operations and transactions on the partnership balance sheet, including each partner's capital account.

1. Impact of Partnership Borrowing. For a variety of reasons, a partnership may borrow funds. As demonstrated in the following example, borrowing will affect both sides of the partnership balance sheet.

Example 2: Assume the facts of Example 1. In July, Year 1, the Jessica/Brandon Partnership borrows $500,000 from Last National Bank with Jessica and Brandon both guaranteeing the promissory note the partnership gave to the Bank. The partnership immediately used the $500,000 in loan proceeds plus $50,000 of its own cash to purchase a large storage facility. What are the tax consequences, if any, of these developments and how will these developments be reflected in the partnership's balance sheet?

The partnership, of course, has no income as a result of the receipt of the $500,000 it receives in loan proceeds as it must repay the loan. In addition, the partnership is not entitled to a deduction when it utilizes the $550,000 to purchase the storage facility. Instead, the partnership must capitalize that $550,000 expenditure. § 263(a). In turn, the partnership will have a basis of $550,000 in the storage facility. § 1012.

Obviously, in using $50,000 of its own funds to acquire the storage facility, the partnership will have reduced the amount of its cash from $100,000 to $50,000. That reduction in cash assets, however, has no impact on Jessica's or Brandon's capital accounts as there is no change in the net worth of the partnership. Likewise, the use of the $50,000 will have no impact on the outside bases of the partners.

Reg. § 1.704-1(b)(2)(iv)(c). Treatment of Liabilities.

. . . [M]oney contributed by a partner to a partnership . . . does not include increases in such partner's share of [partnership] liabilities (see

§ 752(a)).

Similarly, because of the repayment obligation associated with the $500,000 loan, there is no change in the partnership's equity or net worth. As a result, the value of Jessica's and Brandon's shares in partnership equity, i.e., their capital accounts, do not change. Jessica's and Brandon's outside bases, however, are affected by the borrowing. As discussed in Chapter 3, the $500,000 loan would be considered a recourse liability because Jessica and Brandon are ultimately liable for the repayment of the loan under their guarantee agreement with Last National Bank.[5] As equal partners, Jessica and Brandon will each be assumed to have a $250,000 share of the liability. Reg. § 1.752-2(b)(1). Pursuant to § 752(a), Jessica and Brandon will each be deemed to have contributed an additional $250,000 in cash to the partnership and will thus increase their outside bases in the partnership by that amount. § 722. (In other words, Jessica and Brandon are each given advance credit in basis for the additional contribution of $250,000 each is deemed to be making to the partnership.)

In view of the above analysis, the Jessica/Brandon partnership will have the following balance sheet:[6]

Partnership Assets	Inside Basis	Book Value	Liabilities and Partners' Capital	Outside Basis	Book Value
			Liabilities:		$500,000
Cash	$50,000	$50,000			
Land A	$100,000	$300,000	Capital Accounts:		
Land B	$450,000	$400,000	Jessica	$450,000	$400,000
Storage Facility	$550,000	$550,000	Brandon	$700,000	$400,000
Total	$1,150,000	$1,300,000		$1,150,000	$1,300,000

2. Impact of Operating Income and Deductions. As a partnership generates income from its operations and pays or incurs costs (other than costs that must be capitalized), both sides of the partnership's balance sheet will also be impacted. Consider the following example:

Example 3: Assume the facts of Example 2. During Year 1, the Jessica/Brandon Partnership earned and received $100,000 income from its storage business. Assume the partnership made no payments of principal or interest on the loan and made no distributions during Year 1. Assume also that the partnership properly claimed $10,000 in depreciation deductions on the storage facility in Year 1. The partnership thus had $90,000 of net

---

[5] Reg. §§ 1.752-1(a)(1); 1.752-2(b)(3)(i).

[6] Note that, if instead of showing Jessica's and Brandon's outside bases, the balance sheet had shown their tax capital accounts, Jessica's tax capital account would be $200,000 and Brandon's tax capital account would be $450,000, i.e., their tax capital accounts would equal their outside bases less the share of the liability allocated to each.

income. What are the tax consequences to the partnership and its partners and how will the balance sheet account for the income in Year 1?

As will be more fully developed in Chapter 7, a partnership is not a taxable entity. Instead, it is a pass-through entity, i.e., its items of income, gain, loss, deduction, and credit will be allocated to the partners who will report their *distributive shares* on their individual income tax returns.[7] Here, although they have received nothing from the partnership, Jessica and Brandon as 50/50 partners will each report on their individual tax returns a 50% distributive share of the partnership's net income or $45,000. § 61(a)(13).[8] Under § 705, this share of net income that Jessica and Brandon each must report on their individual income tax returns will be accounted for by increasing their outside bases in the partnership.[9] This adjustment in basis simply represents an application of the tax cost basis concept. See, e.g., Reg. § 1.61-2(d)(2)(i).

From a balance sheet standpoint, the $100,000 of income from the storage business, of course, increases the cash held by the partnership. At the same time, the $10,000 in depreciation deductions will be accounted for by reducing the book value and inside basis of the storage facility by the amount of depreciation claimed.[10] There is thus, overall, a $90,000 increase in the book value of the partnership. As equal partners, Jessica and Brandon will each be allocated $45,000 of that increased book value, thus increasing their capital accounts by that amount.[11] Therefore, if, immediately after the end of this first year, the partnership were to sell all of its assets at book value, pay the outstanding $500,000 liability, distribute its assets, and then liquidate, Jessica and Brandon would each receive $445,000. As noted above, Jessica's and Brandon's outside basis will also both be increased by the $45,000 of net income each was allocated for reporting purposes.[12]

As a result of the operating income and deductions, the partnership balance sheet will be as follows:

---

[7] Don't be confused by the term "distributive share." That term does not mean that anything has actually been distributed, but only indicates the share of partnership income, gain, loss, deduction, and credit that a partner must report for tax purposes.

[8] In other words, the net income of the partnership for the year was $90,000, i.e., $100,000 in gross income less the $10,000 depreciation deduction. Jessica and Brandon each were allocated one-half of the $90,000 in net income, or $45,000.

[9] The increased basis will prevent Jessica and Brandon from being taxed a second time on the $45,000 of net income when the partnership finally distributes that income to them.

[10] Reg. § 1.704-1(b)(2)(iv)(g)(3).

[11] Reg. § 1.704-1(b)(2)(iv)(b)(3) and (7).

[12] In Chapters 9 and 10 we will discuss in greater detail the relationship between adjustments to capital accounts and adjustments to the partners' outside bases. We will see that, as a general rule, "tax follows book." Thus, because Jessica and Brandon each shared $45,000 of book gain as a result of the partnership's operations, each also has $45,000 of net income they had to report for tax purposes.

Partnership Assets			Liabilities and Partners' Capital		
	Inside Basis	Book Value		Outside Basis	Book Value
			Liabilities:		$500,000
Cash	$150,000	$150,000			
Land A	$100,000	$300,000	Capital Accounts:		
Land B	$450,000	$400,000	Jessica	$495,000	$445,000
Storage Facility	$540,000	$540,000	Brandon	$745,000	$445,000
Total	$1,240,000	$1,390,000		$1,240,000	$1,390,000

As noted before, even if one or more of the partnership assets had increased or decreased in value during the first year of the partnership's operation, no change would be made to the book value of those assets because appreciation or depreciation would only be recognized when there was a realization event.

3. Impact of Sale of Partnership Asset. A partnership may recognize a book gain or a book loss on the sale of a partnership asset. Likewise, it may recognize a tax gain or loss on the sale. In turn, the partners' outside bases and their capital accounts must be adjusted to reflect the book and tax gains or losses. Consider the following example:

Example 4: Assume the facts of Example 3. Assume also that the Jessica/Brandon Partnership sold Land B for $400,000 on the last day of Year 1. What are the tax consequences, if any, to the partnership and its members as a result of this sale and how will the balance sheet reflect the sale?

As reflected in the balance sheet at the end of Year 1, the book value of Land B was $400,000. Thus, the sale of the Land B for $400,000 would generate no partnership book gain or loss. By contrast, because the partnership had a basis in Land B of $450,000, the sale of Land B for $400,000 results in the partnership realizing and recognizing a $50,000 loss. (Note, this loss will presumably be a § 1231 loss.) In other words, the partnership will recognize the $50,000 of loss that inhered in Land B (the built-in loss) when that property was contributed by Brandon. In Chapter 2, we noted that, under § 704(c)(1)(A) (discussed in Chapter 10), any built-in gain or loss will be allocated to the contributing partner when the gain or loss is recognized. The entire $50,000 of recognized loss, therefore, will be allocated to Brandon and will be reported by him on his individual tax return. To account for this loss, Brandon's outside basis should be reduced by $50,000 to $695,000.

The partnership's balance sheet will reflect the $400,000 increase in cash assets and the transfer of Land B. Will Jessica's and Brandon's capital accounts change as a result of the Land B sale? The answer is "No." With the sale, all that has happened is that the LLC has substituted cash of $400,000 for Land B. The partnership is neither richer nor poorer as a result of the sale; likewise, neither Jessica's nor

Brandon's capital account is changed.[13]

As a result of the sale of Land B and in light of the above analysis, the LLC's balance sheet will now be as follows:

Partnership Assets	Inside Basis	Book Value	Liabilities and Partners' Capital	Outside Basis	Book Value
			Liabilities:		$500,000
Cash	$550,000	$550,000			
Land A	$100,000	$300,000	Capital Accounts:		
Storage Facility	$540,000	$540,000	Jessica	$495,000	$445,000
			Brandon	$695,000	$445,000
Total	$1,190,000	$1,390,000		$1,190,000	$1,390,000

What results if the partnership had sold Land B for less than its book value? Consider the following example.

> **Example 5:** Assume the facts of Example 4 except that the partnership sold Land B for $380,000.

Under these circumstances, the partnership will have a book loss of $20,000 on the sale, i.e., Land B had a book value to the partnership of $400,000 and it sold the land for $380,000. As equal partners, Jessica and Brandon will each have a $10,000 share of the book loss which will reduce their capital account. At the same time, the partnership has a $70,000 tax loss on the sale. As noted in Example 4, $50,000 of that loss, i.e., the $50,000 of built-in loss on Land B when Brandon contributed it to the partnership must be allocated to Brandon pursuant to § 704(c)(1)(A). The remaining $20,000 of tax loss will be allocated in equal shares to Jessica and Brandon consistent with their shares of the book loss (tax follows book). Jessica's $10,000 share of the tax loss will reduce her outside basis from $495,000 to $485,000; Brandon's $60,000 share of the tax loss will reduce his outside basis from $745,000 to $685,000. As a result of the sale, the partnership's cash will be increased by $380,000 to $530,000 (i.e., $150,000 plus $380,000). The balance sheet of the partnership following the sale will thus be as follows:

---

[13] One might wonder why Brandon, who is allocated all $50,000 of the tax loss, doesn't have a corresponding $50,000 reduction in his capital account. The answer is simple. At the time Brandon contributed Land B, that parcel was booked at its fair market value of $400,000 and Brandon was credited in his capital account with only $400,000 and not with the adjusted basis (or unrecovered cost) of 450,000 he had in Land B. In effect, the loss inherent in Land B was already taken into account in Brandon's capital account. *See* Reg. § 1.704-1(b)(2)(iv)(d)(3)(last sentence).

Partnership Assets			Liabilities and Partners' Capital		
	Inside Basis	Book Value		Outside Basis	Book Value
			Liabilities:		$500,000
Cash	$530,000	$530,000			
Land A	$100,000	$300,000	Capital Accounts:		
Storage Facility	$540,000	$540,000	Jessica	$485,000	$435,000
			Brandon	$685,000	$435,000
Total	$1,170,000	$1,370,000		$1,170,000	$1,370,000

4. Impact of Non-liquidating Distributions. Obviously, non-liquidating distributions reduce a partnership's assets and constitute a partial recovery by the partners of their investment. Consider the following example illustrating the impact of non-liquidating distributions on the partnership's balance sheet.

> **Example 6:** Assume the facts of Example 5. Assume also that, immediately following the sale of Land B at the end of Year 1, the Jessica/Brandon Partnership distributed $100,000 in cash to both Jessica and Brandon. What are the tax consequences of this distribution to the partners and how will the balance sheet reflect the distribution?

As discussed in both Chapters 2 and 3, Subchapter K generally provides for nonrecognition upon contribution of properties to a partnership and upon distributions of property from the partnership. The distribution of the cash to Jessica and Brandon, implicates both §§ 731 and 733. Under § 731(a)(1), no gain is recognized by Jessica or Brandon upon the receipt of the $100,000 distribution unless the amount of cash received exceeds their outside basis. In this case, one can glance at the balance sheet in Example 5 above and see that Jessica and Brandon each has an outside basis far in excess of $100,000. Thus, no gain is recognized on the distribution.[14] Consistent with the understanding that the $100,000 Jessica and Brandon each received reflects a recovery of their investment in the partnership, § 733 mandates a reduction in Jessica's and Brandon's outside bases to reflect the cash distribution to them. Thus, Jessica's outside basis will become $ 385,000 and Brandon's outside basis will become $585,000.

Obviously, as a result of the distribution, the partnership's cash assets have been reduced by $200,000 and likewise the net worth of the partnership has been reduced by $200,000. Not surprisingly, the capital account maintenance rules require Jessica and Brandon to each reduce their capital account by the $100,000 distributed to them.[15] Therefore, Jessica's and Brandon's capital accounts are now valued at $335,000 each. Reflecting the distribution, the balance sheet of the partnership will be as follows:

---

[14] Section 731(a)(2) only provides for the recognition of loss in the event of a liquidation. In our example, the distribution is not a liquidating distribution.

[15] Reg. § 1.704-1(b)(2)(iv)(b)(4).

Partnership Assets			Liabilities and Partners' Capital		
	Inside Basis	Book Value		Outside Basis	Book Value
			Liabilities:		$500,000
Cash	$330,000	$330,000			
Land A	$100,000	$300,000	Capital Accounts:		
Storage Facility	$540,000	$540,000	Jessica	$385,000	$335,000
			Brandon	$585,000	$335,000
Total	$970,000	$1,170,000		$970,000	$1,170,000

5. Liquidation. At this point, there is value in considering a situation in which a partnerships sells all of its assets at their book value and then distributes all of its cash in complete liquidation of the partnership. The balance sheet will be adjusted to reflect the impact of the sale of the assets and the repayment of any partnership debt. Consider the following example:

> **Example 7:** Assume the facts of Example 6 and that, early in Year 2, Jessica and Brandon decide to liquidate the partnership in light of an unexpected downturn in the economy of the area. Assume both Land A and the Storage Facility are sold at their book value, which we will assume is also their fair market value at the time of the sale. In addition, assume the partnership earns no income in Year 2, pays no interest on the loan, and (unrealistically) is not entitled to any depreciation on the Storage Facility. Following the sale of its assets, the partnership pays the loan in full and, consistent with the partnership agreement, distributes its remaining cash in equal shares to Jessica and Brandon. What are the tax consequences to the parties and what will the balance sheet of the partnership be immediately before the distribution of the remaining cash to Jessica and Brandon?

The sale of Land A for $300,000 will result in the recognition of $200,000 of gain by the partnership. This gain is exactly the amount of built-in gain associated with Land A when Jessica contributed it to the partnership. Again, as required by § 704(c)(1)(A), all of that gain will be allocated to Jessica. That allocation, in turn, will result in a $200,000 increase in Jessica's outside basis pursuant to § 705(a)(1). Jessica's outside basis will therefore become $585,000, the same as Brandon's outside basis. The sale of Land A will have no effect on Jessica's or Brandon's capital account because Land A was booked at a value of $300,000 when it was contributed and the sale merely replaces the $300,000 of land with $300,000 of cash. In other words, the partnership's net worth or equity has not been increased (or decreased) by the sale of Land A. In turn, Jessica's and Brandon's capital accounts are similarly unaffected by the sale.[16]

---

[16] One might wonder why Jessica, who is required to report $200,000 of tax gain, doesn't have a corresponding increase in her capital account. Again, as in footnote 13, the answer is simple. Upon contributing Land A to the partnership, Jessica was credited in her capital account not only with her unrecovered cost (adjusted basis) in Land A of $100,000, but also with the $200,000 of gain that inhered in Land A, i.e., she was credited with the full fair market value of Land A. Thus, she has already been

The sale of the Storage Facility for its book value of $540,000 results in neither gain nor loss because the partnership's adjusted basis in that facility is also $540,000. As with the sale of Land A, the sale of the Storage Facility does not increase the partnership's net worth, i.e., the $540,000 Storage Facility has simply been replaced with $540,000 of cash.

As a result of the asset sales, the partnership has increased its cash assets from $330,000 to $1,170,000, i.e., $330,000 plus the $300,000 in cash from the sale of Land A and the $540,000 in cash from the sale of the Storage Facility. The partnership now repays the $500,000 loan it had taken out in Year 1. The repayment of the loan will reduce the partnership's cash to $670,000. Under § 752(b), the payment of the liability reduces Jessica's and Brandon's share of partnership liabilities from $250,000 each to $0 and treats each partner as having received a $250,000 cash distribution. In turn, this deemed cash triggers application of both §§ 731 and 733. Under § 731(a)(1), neither Jessica nor Brandon would recognize any gain on the deemed cash distribution because each has an outside basis in excess of $250,000. Pursuant to § 733, Jessica's and Brandon's outside basis of $585,000 must each be reduced by $250,000 to $335,000 to reflect the deemed cash distribution.

In view of this analysis, immediately before the distribution of the partnership's remaining cash, the partnership's balance sheet would be as follows:

Partnership Assets			Liabilities and Partners' Capital		
	Inside Basis	Book Value		Outside Basis	Book Value
Cash	$670,000	$670,000	Liabilities: None		
			Capital Accounts:		
			Jessica	$335,000	$335,000
			Brandon	$335,000	$335,000
Total	$670,000	$670,000		$670,000	$670,000

Consistent with their partnership agreement, the liquidation proceeds of $670,000 will be distributed in equal shares of $335,000 to Jessica and Brandon. Note that the $335,000 distribution to Jessica and Brandon will exactly equal their capital accounts. That result is precisely what we would expect because, as discussed above, Jessica's and Brandon's capital accounts reflect their respective shares of the partnership's net worth or equity.[17] The cash distribution of $335,000 to Jessica will result in the recognition of neither gain nor loss by Jessica because the distribution exactly equals her outside basis. § 731(a). The same is true for Brandon.

Let's check this result. Does it make sense that, upon liquidation of the partnership, Jessica and Brandon would each receive $335,000? The answer is "Yes." The correctness of the $335,000 figure is clear if one considers that Jessica and Brandon each contributed $400,000 in assets to the partnership and each had

---

credited in her capital account with the $200,000 of gain she finally has to report when Land A is sold. *See* Reg. § 1.704-1(b)(2)(iv)(d)(3) (last sentence).

[17] Indeed, as developed in Chapter 9, liquidating distributions in amounts that differed from the partners' capital account balances would raise serious tax issues.

a share of Year 1's operating net income equal to $45,000 for a total of $445,000 of value attributable to each. Jessica and Brandon each were allocated a $10,000 share of the $20,000 book loss in Example 5, thus reducing the value of their interests in the partnership to $435,000. Both also subsequently received a $100,000 cash distribution (Example 6) thus leaving each with $335,000 left to recover. Likewise, it makes sense that Jessica and Brandon would recognize neither gain nor loss on the receipt of a liquidating distribution of $335,000. During the existence of the partnership, both had reported any built-in gain or built-in loss associated with the assets they had contributed to the partnership. (See Examples 5, 6 and 7.) Likewise, they had each reported in income their $45,000 share of the net operating income of the partnership. Thus, no additional tax gain or loss existed.

In addition to illustrating the evolving balance sheet of a hypothetical partnership, the above series of examples have demonstrated some basic points regarding the maintenance of capital accounts (book capital accounts). Note that in Example 1, the initial balance in Jessica's and Brandon's capital accounts equaled the fair market value of the assets each had contributed. Example 2 reflects the fact that, because borrowed funds do not increase the equity or net worth of the partnership, Jessica's and Brandon's capital accounts were not adjusted when the partnership borrowed $500,000 to acquire the Storage Facility. Example 3 demonstrates that capital accounts are adjusted to reflect the allocation to partners of partnership income or loss. Thus, Jessica's and Brandon's capital accounts were each increased by $45,000 to reflect their distributive share of the net income of the partnership. Examples 4, 5, and 7 demonstrate that, when a partnership finally recognizes the built-in gain or built-in loss associated with contributed property, the contributing partner will be allocated that gain or loss for tax purposes but his or her capital account will not be adjusted upward or downward to reflect that allocation.[18] Distributions obviously decrease the net worth or equity of a partnership and, accordingly, Examples 6 and 7 indicate that a partner's capital account must be adjusted downward to reflect amounts distributed to that partner.

C. Capital Accounts and Service Partners

In Chapter 4, we considered the tax consequences of the transfer of a compensatory interest in a partnership in connection with and in consideration for the performance of services. Consider the following examples illustrating the treatment of compensatory partnership interests in a balance sheet, including the capital account of a service partner.

Example 8: Assume the facts of Example 1 above and that, after the Jessica/Brandon Partnership had been in operation for five months, Jessica and Brandon decided to bring on another partner who would manage the day-to-day operations of the partnership business. Therefore, before the partnership borrowed the money to acquire the Storage Facility, the partnership enlisted Jackie to manage the business. In exchange for her agreement to manage the partnership business, the partnership trans-

---

[18] After studying Example 1, the reason for no capital account adjustment should be apparent — the partner or member was already credited in his or her capital account with the fair market value of any property contributed.

ferred to Jackie a 10% capital and profits interest in the partnership. [Assume (unrealistically) that Jackie's interest is not subject to a substantial risk of forfeiture and is transferable.] Assume also that, at the time of the transfer of the interest to Jackie, the fair market values of Land A and B continued to be the same as when those properties were contributed by Jessica and Brandon. Applying Prop. Regs. §§ 1.721-1(b) and 1.83-3(l), what are the tax consequences to the partners and how will the transfer of this compensatory partnership interest affect the balance sheet, including the partners' capital accounts? (Begin your analysis by reviewing the partnership's balance sheet at the end of the analysis in Example 1 above.)

Applying the proposed regulations as discussed in Chapter 4, we would value the compensatory partnership interest given to Jackie by assuming the partnership liquidated immediately after the transfer of the interest to Jackie. See Prop. Reg. § 1.83-3(l). Under this liquidation method,[19] the partnership would be treated as selling all of its assets at their fair market value and then distributing all of its cash to its members in proportion to their respective interests in the partnership. If that happened, the partnership would have a total of $800,000 in cash to distribute (i.e., the $100,000 of cash it had to start with plus the $300,000 sale proceeds of Land A and the $400,000 sale proceeds of Land B). Because Jackie would be entitled to 10% of the liquidation proceeds or $80,000, her capital and profits interest will be deemed to be worth $80,000. When she received the capital and profits interest, Jackie is therefore treated just as if she had received $80,000 in cash from the partnership.[20]

Applying § 83, Jackie will have $80,000 of ordinary income in Year 1. Because she is treated as having immediately recontributed the deemed $80,000 cash liquidation proceeds to the partnership, Jackie will be treated as having a tax cost basis in her partnership interest of $80,000 and having a capital account of $80,000.

With regard to the partnership, the transfer of the compensatory partnership interest to Jackie will not result in the recognition of either gain or loss under Prop. Reg. 1.721-1(b)(1) discussed in Chapter 4.[21] The partnership, however, will be entitled to a deduction of $80,000 under § 83(h). This deduction should be allocated to Jessica and Brandon equally. Under § 705(a)(2), the allocation of $40,000 deduction to both Jessica and Brandon will have the effect of reducing their outside basis by $40,000 each. With the admission of Jackie as a partner, Jessica and Brandon each now has only a 45% interest in the partnership, which continues to have a net worth of $800,000. Thus, Jessica's and Brandon's capital accounts will have a value of $360,000 (i.e., if the partnership immediately liquidated, Jessica and

---

[19] See the Authors' Note in Chapter 4 discussing "liquidation value" under the proposed regulations.

[20] Technically, under the proposed regulations (and under current Reg. § 1.721-1(b)(1), this transfer of $80,000 is treated as a guaranteed payment. We will discuss guaranteed payments in Chapter 13.

[21] Note that, under a *McDougal* analysis, discussed in Chapter 4, some of the gain associated with Land A and some of the loss associated with Land B would be recognized by the partnership. For purposes of this course, we will assume, consistent with the Preamble to the proposed regulations (see discussion in Chapter 4), that the *McDougal* analysis is inapplicable in a case such as this, where the partnership is already in existence when a compensatory transfer of a partnership interest in connection with services occurs.

Brandon would each receive 45% of the $800,000 in liquidation proceeds).[22]

Following the transfer of the capital and profits interest to Jackie, the balance sheet of the partnership will thus be as follows:[23]

Partnership Assets			Liabilities and Partners' Capital		
	Inside Basis	Book Value		Outside Basis	Book Value
Cash	$100,000	$100,000	**Liabilities:** None		
Land A	$100,000	$300,000	**Capital Accounts:**		
Land B	$450,000	$400,000	Jessica	$160,000	$360,000
			Brandon	$410,000	$360,000
			Jackie	$80,000	$80,000
Total	$650,000	$800,000		$650,000	$800,000

Now, let us consider how the transfer of a profits-only interest will be treated from a balance sheet and capital account angle.

> **Example 9:** Assume the facts of Example 8, except that Jackie is given a 10% profits-only interest. In other words, Jackie will be entitled to 10% of all future profits of the partnership but is not entitled to any share of the existing value of the partnership. As in Example 8, assume that Jackie's interest is not subject to a risk of forfeiture and is transferable.

We will assume again that the partnership will value Jackie's interest using the liquidation method of Prop. Reg. § 1.83-3(l) discussed in Chapter 4. Again, under that method, we would determine how much cash would be distributed to Jackie if, immediately after the transfer of the profits-only interest to Jackie, the partnership sold for cash all of its assets at their fair market value and then liquidated by transferring its cash to the partners in proportion to their interests. Under this method, Jackie would receive none of the $800,000 in liquidation proceeds. In other words, her profits-only interest will be worth zero. She will thus have no income under § 83(a); and she will not be treated as having recontributed any cash to the partnership as she was in Example 7. As a result, her basis in her partnership interest is $0. Her capital account will also be zero.

Under Prop. Reg. § 1.721-1(b)(1), the partnership will have no gain or loss on the transfer of the profits-only interest to Jackie. Unlike Example 8, because the interest transferred here is deemed to have no value, the partnership will not be entitled to any deduction on the transfer. Under the liquidation method of valuing capital accounts, Jessica and Brandon would continue to be entitled to the entire

---

[22] As will be discussed in Chapter 10, under § 704(c)(1)(A) principles, the built-in gain inherent in Land A should continue to be attributable to Jessica and the built-in loss inherent in Land B should continue to be allocable to Brandon.

[23] Under Reg.§ 1.704-1(b0(2)(iv)(f)(5)(iii), a partnership may revalue its property on its books and, in turn, adjust capital accounts accordingly upon the grant of a partnership interest in consideration for services. In this example, we have purposely provided that the fair market values of Lands A and B remained the same as they were at the time of contribution, thereby eliminating any need to address revaluation (sometimes referred to as the "booking up" or "booking down" of a partnership's assets and the partners' capital accounts).

$800,000 net worth of the partnership and, thus, their capital accounts would remain at $400,000 each.

Applying the above analysis, the balance sheet of the partnership will be as follows:

Partnership Assets	Inside Basis	Book Value	Liabilities and Partners' Capital	Outside Basis	Book Value
Cash	$100,000	$100,000	**Liabilities:** None		
Land A	$100,000	$300,000	**Capital Accounts:**		
Land B	$450,000	$400,000	Jessica	$200,000	$400,000
			Brandon	$450,000	$400,000
			Jackie	$0	$0
Total	**$650,000**	**$800,000**		**$650,000**	**$800,000**

What are the results if the partnership as described in Example 9 subsequently generates profit? Consider the following example:

Example 10: Assume the facts of Example 9. Assume also that, subsequent to the transfer of the profits-only interest to Jackie, the partnership earns and receives $100,000 in net profit from the operation of its business. The partnership does not distribute the profits. What are the tax consequences to the partners and how will the balance sheet be affected by this profitable operation of the partnership?

Given the pass-through nature of partnerships, the partnership's profits of $100,000 will be allocated to Jessica, Brandon, and Jackie consistent with their distributive share of the profits. § 704(a). Here, Jessica and Brandon each have a 45% share of profits and Jackie has a 10% share. As a result, Jessica and Brandon will each report $45,000 of the profits on their individual tax returns and Jackie will report $10,000 in profits on her return. §§ 61(a)(13) and 702. Because none of the profits are distributed, the outside basis of each partner and each partner's capital account will be increased to account for the distributive share of profits each partner was required to report. § 705(a)(1) and Reg. § 1.704-1(b)(2)(iv)(3). Thus, Jessica's and Brandon's outside bases and capital accounts will be increased by $45,000 and Jackie's outside basis and capital account will increase by $10,000. Having added an additional $100,000 in cash, the partnership now has a net worth that is $100,000 greater than before. That additional net worth is reflected, as noted, in the increases in the partners' capital accounts.

The balance sheet of the partnership now will be as follows:

Partnership Assets			Liabilities and Partners' Capital		
	Inside Basis	Book Value		Outside Basis	Book Value
Cash	$200,000	$200,000	**Liabilities:** None		
Land A	$100,000	$300,000	**Capital Accounts:**		
Land B	$450,000	$400,000	Jessica	$245,000	$445,000
			Brandon	$495,000	$445,000
			Jackie	$10,000	$10,000
Total	$750,000	$900,000		$750,000	$900,000

Examples 9 and 10 demonstrate that, under the liquidation method of the proposed regulations, Jackie's profits-only interest initially has a zero value and, in turn, Jackie's capital account is likewise zero. When the partnership thereafter becomes profitable, Jackie will be allocated a 10% share of the net profit. As a result, to the extent profits are not distributed, Jackie will have an outside basis in her profits-only interest.[24] She will also have a capital account that reflects the undistributed profits to which she would be entitled upon ultimate liquidation of the partnership.

Chapter 4 discussed *McDougall* and noted that the 2005 proposed regulations limit the applicability of *McDougall* to situations where the transfer of an interest to a service provider occurred before or simultaneously with the creation of a partnership. Let us return to Example 1 in Chapter 4 and create the opening balance sheet for the partnership in that example. Recall Ron entered into an arrangement with Dan, whereby Ron would give Dan a one-half interest in a 1955 Porsche if Dan were able to manage the rental of the Porsche in a manner that returned to Ron his costs in acquiring and restoring the vehicle within a 30-month period following the car's restoration. Dan accomplished that goal and Ron transferred a one-half interest in the car to Dan. Simultaneously, Ron and Dan created an LLC to which each transferred his one-half interest in the Porsche in exchange for a 50% interest in the LLC. The Porsche's appraised fair market value at the time was $150,000 and Ron's adjusted basis in the vehicle was $20,000.

As noted in Chapter 4 and consistent with *McDougall*, the transfer of the one-half interest in the vehicle to Dan constituted compensation to Dan for his services. He thus had ordinary income in the amount of $75,000. As a result, Dan took a tax cost basis in his one-half interest in the Porsche of $75,000. When Dan contributed his interest in the Porsche to the LLC in exchange for a 50% LLC interest worth $75,000, Dan had no gain and took a $75,000 basis in the LLC interest he received.

---

[24] This outside basis will ensure that when the profit share that Jackie has already reported in income is finally distributed to her, she will not have to report any additional income. Thus, in Example 10, Jackie would report $10,000 of the partnership's profits. Because she has not received a distribution of those profits, she has a $10,000 basis in her partnership interest and a $10,000 capital account. If the partnership were subsequently to distribute to Jackie the $10,000 of profits, under § 731(a)(1), she would have no income because the cash distributed did not exceed her outside basis. In turn, her outside basis would be reduced to $0 under § 733 and her capital account would be reduced to $0 as well. Reg. § 1.704-1(b)(2)(iv)(b)(4).

§§ 721 and 722. The LLC, in turn, took a § 723 basis of $75,000 in one-half of the Porsche.

Ron was entitled a deduction of $75,000 under § 162 for the compensation he paid to Dan. At the same time, because Ron used an appreciated asset (the one-half interest in the Porsche) to pay Dan compensation for his management services, Ron, pursuant to the *McDougall* analysis, had to recognize $60,000 gain, i.e., the amount of the difference between the $75,000 value of the interest given to Dan and Ron's $15,000 adjusted basis in that interest (i.e., one-half of the $30,000 adjusted basis he had in the Porsche). When Ron contributed his remaining half interest in the Porsche to the LLC, Ron recognized no gain (§ 721) and took a $15,000 basis in his 50% interest in the LLC. (§ 722). The LLC thus had a $15,000 basis in the one-half interest in the Porsche contributed by Ron. § 723. The LLC's total basis in the Porsche was thus $90,000 (i.e., $75,000 in the half contributed by Dan plus $15,000 in the half contributed by Ron).

The opening balance sheet of the LLC would thus be as follows:

	LLC Assets			Liabilities and Members' Capital	
	Inside Basis	Book Value		Outside Basis	Book Value
			Liabilities: None		
Porsche	$90,000	$150,000	Capital Accounts:		
			Ron	$15,000	$75,000
			Dan	$75,000	$75,000
Total	$90,000	$150,000		$90,000	$150,000

D. Conclusion

This Chapter has provided a general overview of the partnership balance sheet and the impact of various transactions on the balance sheet during the life of a partnership. It has also provided an introduction to partner capital accounts and the rules regarding maintenance of capital accounts. While this initial foray into balance sheets and the maintenance of capital accounts may seem daunting, do not despair. Points made in this chapter will be explored in greater depth in subsequent chapters where we will use balance sheets and capital accounts to illustrate the application and significance of provisions of Subchapter K and the regulations interpreting and applying those provisions. Note that, in future balance sheets, we will substitute the abbreviation A/B for Inside Basis and Outside Basis.

Chapter 6

THE PARTNERSHIP TAXABLE YEAR; EXPENSES OF PARTNERSHIP FORMATION

I. PROBLEMS

1. The Lakefront Golf Course, LLC (hereinafter Lakefront), a limited liability company taxed as a partnership, operates a golf course in Southern California. Its revenues are spread evenly throughout the year. Lakefront's ownership structure is as follows: 25 individuals, whose tax year is the calendar year, each own interests of 1% in profits, losses, and capital; ABC Corporation, which reports on the fiscal year ending January 31, owns the remaining 75% of Lakefront. What is the required taxable year for Lakefront?

2. How does the answer to Problem 1 change if the 25 individuals each own 2% of Lakefront, ABC Corporation owns 25%, and the KLM Corporation, which also reports on a fiscal year ending January 31, owns 25% of Lakefront?

3. How does the answer to Problem 2 change if KLM Corporation reports on a fiscal year ending February 28 instead of January 31?

4. May Lakefront have a different taxable year from the required taxable year if the golf course were located in Fairbanks, Alaska, instead of Southern California? Explain.

5. Might Lakefront have a different taxable year than the required taxable year, regardless of its location? Explain.

6. The following expenses were incurred by Lakefront within a reasonable time before it began business and prior to the time for filing its tax return for the year it began business: (1) $5,000 in printing costs of promotional material for soliciting ownership interests in Lakefront; (2) $10,000 in legal fees for preparation and negotiation of the agreement among the Lakefront owners; (3) $7,000 in legal fees for the costs of transferring assets contributed to Lakefront by the owners; (4) $4,000 in state filing fees incurred in forming the limited liability company; (5) $6,000 in accounting fees incurred in connection with the promotional materials; and (6) $15,000 in property taxes paid by Lakefront. What is the total amount Lakefront can deduct on its first return? When will the remainder be deductible?

Assignment for Chapter 6:

Complete the problems.

Read: Internal Revenue Code: §§ 706(a), (b); 709. Skim § 444(a), (b)(1), (3), (4)(c).
Treasury Regulations: §§ 1.706-1(a), (b)(1)-(4); 1-709-1(b)(1), -2(a)-(c).
Materials: Overview

II. VOCABULARY

Required taxable year
Majority interest taxable year
Principal partner
Principal partners taxable year
Least aggregate deferral taxable year
Business purpose taxable year
Organizational expenses
Syndication expenses

III. OBJECTIVES

1. To determine the required taxable year for a partnership.
2. To apply the majority interest taxable year.
3. To apply the principal partners' taxable year.
4. To explain the least deferral taxable year.
5. To explain the business purpose taxable year.
6. To explain when a partnership may elect to have a taxable year other than the required taxable year.
7. To determine the amount of deductible organizational expenses.
8. To distinguish organizational expenses from syndication expenses.

IV. OVERVIEW

A. The Partnership Taxable Year

1. The Partnership as an Entity for Tax Computation Purposes

> **§ 701. Partners, Not Partnership, Subject to Tax**
>
> A partnership as such shall not be subject to the income tax imposed by this chapter. Persons carrying on business as partners shall be liable for income tax only in their separate or individual capacities.

In effect, § 701, the first provision in Subchapter K of the Code, provides that partnership income is subject to a single tax, i.e., the income, gain, loss, deductions and credits of a partnership are passed through to the partners and the partners are liable "in their separate or individual capacities" for the income tax. Thus, the taxation structure of Subchapter K differs substantially from the C corporation tax structure, which involves a double tax, i.e., a tax at both the entity and shareholder levels.[1]

Although § 701 states unequivocally that partnerships are not taxable entities, students, upon their initial review of Subchapter K, are surprised when they read § 703(a), which begins "[t]he *taxable income* of a partnership shall be computed in the same manner as an individual . . . " [Emphasis added.] Read that provision carefully. While the Subchapter K pass-through structure (discussed in detail in the next chapter) reflects the treatment of a partnership as an aggregate of its partners (aggregate approach) rather than a separate entity, § 703, unlike § 701, seems to treat the partnership as an entity for tax purposes. This *entity approach* is also evident in § 703(b) providing that elections affecting the taxable income of a partnership, e.g., § 453(d) or § 1033, be made by the partnership. Similarly, the entity approach is reflected in § 702(b) providing that the character of any item of income, gain, loss, deduction, or credit included in a partner's distributive share (see § 704(b)) be determined at the partnership level and in § 706 providing that a partnership has its own tax year.

If a partnership is not a taxable entity, why should we worry about computing its taxable income or its tax year? As the Supreme Court in *United States v. Basye*, 410 U.S. 441, 448 n.8 (1973) noted, partnerships are entities *"for purposes of calculating and filing informational returns but . . . are conduits through which the taxpaying obligation passes to the individual partners in accord with their distributive shares."* Provisions such as §§ 702(b), 703 and 706, in effect, enable us to determine what is passed through the partnership to be accounted for at the partner level. By treating the partnership as an entity for calculating income, deductions, etc., the Code avoids the confusion and inconsistent treatment that could result if, for example, each partner were allowed to determine whether: (a) a partnership receipt constitutes income and, if so, when and of what character; (b) an expenditure is deductible and if so, when; or (c) an election provided by the Code is to be made.

Demirijian v. Commissioner[2] provides an excellent example of the application of this entity approach to partnerships. In that case, a partnership's sole operating asset, an office building in Newark, New Jersey, was conveyed to the Newark Housing Authority after an involuntary condemnation proceeding. Section 1033 of the Code allows taxpayers to *elect* to defer gain on an involuntary conversion if they reinvest the conversion proceeds within a given period in property "similar or related in service or use" to the property converted. The partnership's two partners each received 50% of the proceeds from the conversion of the office building. Each,

---

[1] With regard to an entity, the pass-through structure of Subchapter K is not the only model employed by the Code to accomplish a single tax. Subchapter J of the Code, addressing the taxation of trusts and estates, utilizes a very different single tax model, i.e., beneficiaries of trusts and estates are taxed on income that is currently distributed to them, while income that is accumulated by the trust or estate is taxed at the entity level. See §§ 651, 652, 661 and 662. Even Subchapter S, while generally employing a pass-through method similar to Subchapter K, provides for an entity-level tax under certain limited circumstances. See, e.g., §§ 1374 and 1375.

[2] 457 F.2d 1 (3d Cir. 1972), *aff'g* 54 T.C. 1691 (1970).

in her individual partner capacity, made a timely acquisition of qualified replacement property and elected under § 1033 to defer her gain. The Service challenged the deferral of gain, contending that§ 703(b) required the partnership and not the individual partners to make the § 1033 election and acquire the replacement property. The Tax Court agreed with the Service and held that the partners recognized gain on the transaction. Affirming the Tax Court, the Third Circuit noted:

> The partnership provisions of the Internal Revenue Code treat a partnership as an aggregate of its members for purposes of taxing profits to the individual members and as an entity for purposes of computing and reporting income. In light of this entity approach to reporting income, Congress included § 703(b) to avoid the possible confusion which might result if each partner were to determine partnership income separately only on his own return for his own purposes. To avoid the possible confusion which could result from separate elections under § 1033, the election must be made by the partnership as an entity, and the failure of the partnership to so act results in the recognition of the gain on the sale of the partnership property.[3]

2. Year in Which Partnership Income Is Includible by Partners; Taxable Year of a Partnership

Consistent with the pass-through nature of partnerships, a partner in computing her taxable income must account for her distributive share of partnership income, gain, loss, deduction, and credit.[4] Consider the timing rule of § 706(a) reprinted below:

---

§ 706(a). Year In Which Partnership Income Is Includible

In computing the taxable income of a partner for a taxable year, the inclusions required by section 702 . . . with respect to a partnership shall be based on the income, gain, loss, deduction, or credit of the partnership for any taxable year of the partnership ending within or with the taxable year of the partner.

Section 706(a) raises an important question: what is the taxable year of a partnership? Before we answer that question, consider the following example demonstrating the application of § 706(a).

Example 1: In August 2013, Lenny and Laurie created an LLC (taxed as a partnership) to operate an ice skating rink. The rink is open only on a

---

[3] 457 F.2d at 6.

[4] *See, e.g.*, § 61(a)(13), providing that a partner, in computing her gross income for her tax year, must include in gross income her distributive share of the partnership gross income. As discussed in detail in the next chapter, the partnership agreement generally determines a partner's distributive share of income, gain, loss, deduction, or credit. § 704(a).

seasonal basis — between October 1 and March 31. Pursuant to their operating agreement, Lenny and Laurie each have a 50% interest in the LLC, entitling them each to a 50% distributive share of all LLC income, gain, loss, deduction and credit. Thirty percent of the LLC's annual income is generated in the two-month period between February 1 and March 31 each year. Assume the LLC is permitted to elect a taxable year (a fiscal year) ending March 31 and that Lenny and Laura are calendar year taxpayers, i.e., their tax years end on December 31. For the LLC's tax year ending March 31, 2016, the LLC, which uses the cash method of accounting, had gross income of $150,000 (all ordinary income) and expenses of $50,000 (all ordinary expenses). Thus, the LLC's taxable income for its tax year ending in 2016 was $100,000.[5] Lenny and Laurie thus each have a distributive share of $50,000 of the LLC's taxable income. When will Lenny and Laurie report the $50,000 share of the LLC taxable income?

Analysis: Note, in computing its $100,000 in taxable income, the LLC took into account all its receipts and expenditures between April 1, 2015 and March 31, 2016. Under § 706(a), Lenny and Laurie will each report their $50,000 share of the LLC taxable income on their tax returns for 2016 which are not due until April 15, 2017.

As illustrated by the above example, tax will not be paid on income earned by the partnership in October, November, and December 2015 until Lenny and Laurie file their 2016 tax returns, which are due April 15, 2017. This deferral of tax results from the LLC having a different tax year (a March 31 fiscal year) from Lenny's and Laurie's tax year (a calendar year). Tax deferral of this nature could not be achieved were the ice skating rink business being conducted by Lenny as a sole proprietorship. In that case, the income he earned in October, November, and December 2015 would have been includible in his tax return for 2015 with the tax due and payable April 15, 2016.

In Example 1, a strong business reason exists for the LLC to have a taxable year different from that of its owners, i.e., March 31 marks the end of the LLC's seasonal business operations and a substantial amount of its annual income is earned in February and March each year. As discussed below, on these facts the LLC would be permitted to use the March 31 fiscal year under current law because it has established a business purpose for using a March 31 fiscal year. Pre-1954, however, partnerships were free to select any tax year they desired *without any showing of a business reason for the tax year selected*. With the enactment of Subchapter K in 1954, however, Congress began limiting this flexibility by requiring *new* partnerships to use the tax year of their principal partners, i.e., partners who had at least a five percent interest in the partnership profits or capital. Pursuant to the 1954 legislation, if a partnership's principal partners had different tax years, the

---

[5] In the next chapter you will learn that § 702 requires that certain items of income, gain, loss, and deduction be separately stated as they pass through to the partners. In this case, we are assuming that neither the gross income items nor the items of expense were required to be separately stated. As a result, the net income (taxable income in this example) of $100,000 passes through in equal shares to Lenny and Laura.

partnership generally was required to use a calendar year as its taxable year.[6] The 1954 legislation provided an important business purpose exception, enabling partnerships to adopt a tax year other than the required tax year if the partnership could establish it had a "natural business year." Unfortunately, Congress provided little guidance regarding this business purpose exception.[7] Somewhat surprisingly, the Service issued Rev. Proc. 72-51, 1972-2 C.B. 832, which relaxed the limitations imposed by the 1954 legislation by permitting the adoption of a taxable year allowing deferral of three months or less without any showing of business purpose.[8]

The Tax Reform Act of 1986 significantly tightened the rules regarding the taxable year of partnerships.[9] Section 706(b) added by that Act required *all* partnerships to use a tax year [hereinafter referred to as the "required taxable year"] that, insofar as possible, conforms to the tax year of the partners. Old partnerships were thus forced to change their taxable year to conform to the new rules; the automatic approval of taxable years resulting in up to three months deferral of income was eliminated. As noted in the legislative history for the 1986 Act: "Where prior law allowed income earned by a partnership . . . to be subjected to Federal income tax in a taxable year later than that in which it was earned, the value of the income earned is understated. This deferral of income was normally available only to certain types of taxpayers, resulting in preferential treatment of certain taxpayers at the overall expenses of others."[10]

Consider the following provision from the current Code:

---

§ 706(b). Taxable Year

(1) Partnership's taxable year.

(A) Partnership treated as taxpayer. The taxable year of a partnership shall be determined as though the partnership were a taxpayer.

(B) Taxable year determined by reference to partners. Except as

---

[6] The 1954 legislation "grandfathered" partnerships created before 1954, permitting them to continue to use the taxable year they had previously adopted even though that taxable year did not conform to that of the partnership's principal partners and thus resulted in significant tax deferral.

[7] Rev. Rul. 60-182, 1960-1 C.B. 264, defined "natural business year" as a year ending at or soon after the close of the partnership's peak period of business. It, however, provided no guidance as to how to determine the "peak" business period. Subsequently, Revenue Procedure 74-33, 1974-2 C.B. 489, indicated the Service would use a facts-and-circumstances test focusing on the type of business the partnership was conducting and the locality of the business.

[8] Revenue Procedure 72-51 held in pertinent part: ". . . [R]equests by partnerships to adopt or change an accounting period differing from that of its principal partners will generally be approved where the request for the adoption or change would result in a deferment of income to the partners of three months or less. Thus, for example, a calendar year partnership will generally be granted permission to change to or adopt a fiscal year ending September 30, even though the partners are on a calendar year."

[9] The 1986 legislation also addressed the taxable year of S corporations and personal service corporations.

[10] General Explanation of the Tax Reform Act of 1986, prepared by the Staff of the Joint Committee on Taxation, pp. 534-535.

> provided in subparagraph (C), a partnership shall not have a taxable year other than —
>
> (i) the *majority interest* taxable year . . .
>
> (ii) if there is no taxable year described in clause (i), the taxable year of all the *principal partners* of the partnership, or
>
> (iii) if there is no taxable year described in clause (i) or (ii), the calendar year unless the Secretary by regulations prescribes another period.
>
> **(C) Business purpose.** A partnership may have a taxable year not described in subparagraph (B) if it establishes, to the satisfaction of the secretary, a *business purpose* therefore. For purposes of this subparagraph, any deferral of income to the partners shall not be treated as a business purpose.

Read the definitions of "majority interest taxable year" and "principal partner" in § 706(b)(3) and (4). But for the business purpose exception of § 706(b)(1)(C), the Lenny/Laurie LLC above would be required to use the calendar year, which is the "majority interest taxable year" because Lenny and Laurie own 100% of the LLC's profits and capital and both partners are calendar year taxpayers. Because individuals are almost always calendar year taxpayers, any partnership in which an individual owns more than 50% of the partnership's profits and capital will generally be required to use the calendar year in computing its taxable income unless the partnership can qualify under the business purpose exception.

Consider the following examples illustrating the application of the various parts of § 706(b)(1)(B).

Example 2: Twenty-five individuals and Linda Vista Corporation create a LLC (taxed as a partnership) in which each of the 25 individuals owns a 3% interest and Linda Vista Corporation owns a 25% interest. The 25 individuals are calendar year taxpayers while Linda Vista Corporation, a Subchapter C corporation, is a fiscal year taxpayer with a January 31 year-end. Assuming the LLC cannot establish a business purpose within the meaning of § 706(b)(1)(C), what taxable year would the LLC be required to use under § 706(b)(1)?

Analysis: In the aggregate, the 25 individuals own 75% of the LLC. Because they own more than 50% of the profits and capital and all have the same taxable year (i.e., a calendar year), the calendar year constitutes the majority interest taxable year and will therefore be the required tax year of the LLC.

Example 3: Assume the same facts as Example 2 except the 25 individuals each own only a 2% interest in the LLC, Linda Vista Corporation owns a 46% interest, and Bellevue Corporation, a Subchapter C corporation, owns a 4% interest. Assuming the LLC cannot establish a business purpose within the meaning of § 706(b)(1)(C), what taxable year would the LLC be required to use under § 706(b)(1)?

Analysis: First, we would consider whether there is a majority interest taxable year. There is not. In the aggregate, the 25 individuals do not own *more than 50%* of the profits and capital of the LLC; they own exactly 50%. Obviously, neither Linda Vista Corporation nor Bellevue Corporation owns more than 50% of the profits and capital of the LLC. With regard to § 706(b)(1)(B)(ii), only Linda Vista Corporation qualifies as a "principal partner" because it is the only LLC member who has an interest of 5% or more in the LLC's profits and capital. As a result, the LLC will have a required taxable year that is a January 31 fiscal year. Note, a January 31 fiscal year will provide significant tax deferral to the 25 individual owners of the LLC. For example, if we assumed the LLC was formed on February 1, 2015, the individual partners would report their shares of the LLC's taxable income for the LLC's tax year ending on January 31, 2016 on their 2016 individual income tax returns due on April 15, 2017. Thus, the tax on their shares of the income earned between February 1, 2015 and December 31, 2015 would not be due until April 15, 2017.

Example 4: Assume Laurie and Linda Vista Corporation created a partnership in which the two partners each had a 50% interest in the partnership's capital and profits. Assume Laurie is a calendar year taxpayer and Linda Vista, a Subchapter C corporation, uses a March 31 fiscal year. Assuming the LLC cannot establish a business purpose within the meaning of § 706(b)(1)(C), what taxable year would the LLC be required to use under § 706(b)(1)?

Analysis: Note, there is no majority interest taxable year; Laurie and Linda Vista Corporation have different taxable years and neither owns more than 50% of the profits and capital of the partnership. Both Laurie and Linda Vista Corporation, however, are "principal partners." Because Laurie and Linda Vista Corporation have different taxable years, § 706(b)(1)(B)(ii) is inapplicable and we must consider the application of § 706(b)(1)(B)(iii). Section 706(b)(1)(B)(iii) represents a default rule, i.e., where there is no majority interest taxable year and the taxable years of the principal partners are not the same, the calendar year is mandated unless the Secretary of the Treasury has provided otherwise by regulation. The Secretary has so provided in Reg. § 1.706-1(b)(3). That regulation provides that the taxable year resulting in the least aggregate deferral of income will be the taxable year of the partnership. Regulation § 1.706-1(b)(3) underscores the congressional intent to reduce or negate deferral of tax. In general, the regulation requires in this example that one compare the deferral if the partnership used a calendar year to the deferral if the partnership used a March 31 year. If the calendar year were used, Laurie would have no deferral because she is a calendar year taxpayer. By contrast, Linda Vista Corporation would experience a three-month deferral, i.e., for its taxable year ending March 31, 2016, Linda Vista Corporation would only report its share of partnership income through December 31, 2015; its share of partnership income for the period January 1, 2016–March

31, 2016 would not be reported until it filed its income tax return for its tax year ending March 31, 2017. (See § 706(a) and the discussion of that provision above.) If, instead, the partnership used a March 31 fiscal year, Linda Vista Corporation would have no deferral. By contrast, Laurie would have nine months' deferral, i.e., for her calendar year ending December 31, 2016, Laurie would report her share of partnership income through March 31, 2016; her share of income for the period April 1, 2016 through December 31, 2016 would not be reported until she filed her income tax return for 2016, due on April 15, 2017. (See § 706(a) and the discussion of that provision above.) Comparing the two possible tax years, if the calendar year is used by the partnership, there is deferral of a 50% share of the partnership income (i.e., Linda Vista's share) for 3 months; if a March 31 fiscal year is used, there is deferral of a 50% share of partnership income (i.e., Laurie's share) for 9 months. Obviously, the calendar year produces the lesser deferral and, under § 706(b)(1)(B)(iii) and Reg. § 1.706-1(b)(3) will be the required taxable year of the partnership. Apart from this simple example, the complex calculations required by the regulation are beyond the scope of this casebook.

As noted above, § 706(b)(1)(C) provides that a taxable year other than the required taxable year may be used if a partnership establishes to the satisfaction of the Secretary of the Treasury a business purpose for having a different taxable year.[11] Thus, Congress in the 1986 Act continued the post-1954 practice of allowing a partnership to adopt a taxable year that did not conform to the taxable year of its owners if a business purpose were established. The Act's legislative history specifically endorses a mechanical test for determining a partnership's natural business year — the so-called "25-percent test."[12] Under this test:

(a) A computation is made of the partnership's gross receipts from sales and services for the most recent 12-month period ending before the filing of the request and with the last month of the requested fiscal year. This amount is divided into the amount of gross receipts from sales and services for the last two months of this 12-month period.

(b) The same computation as in (a) above is made for the two 12-month periods immediately preceding the 12-month period described in (a).

(c) If each of the results for each of the three years described in (a) and (b) equals or exceeds 25 percent, the requested fiscal year is the taxpayer's natural business year.[13]

Although the partnership fails to satisfy the mechanical 25% test, it may still qualify for a taxable year other than the required taxable year if, based on all the facts and circumstances, it can establish a valid business purpose for the proposed

---

[11] The 1986 legislation permitted an existing partnership to continue to use its existing taxable year if it had received a ruling finding the partnership's taxable year met the business purpose standard.

[12] *See* Rev. Proc. 2006–46, 2006–2 C.B. 859 § 5.07.

[13] If the partnership doesn't have sufficient history to satisfy the mechanical test, it will have to rely on the facts-and-circumstances test to establish its business purpose.

taxable year.[14] According to the Conference Report for the 1986 Tax Reform Act, the following nontax factors are ordinarily not sufficient to establish a business purpose: "(1) the use of a particular year for regulatory or financial accounting purpose; (2) the hiring patterns of a particular business — for example, the fact that a firm typically hires staff during certain times of the year; (3) the use of a particular year for administrative purposes, such as the admission or retirement of partners . . . , promotion of staff, and compensation or retirement arrangements with staff, partners . . . and [4] the fact that a particular business involves the use of price lists, a model year, or other items that change on an annual basis."[15]

Example 1 above presents facts supporting the use of a March 31 fiscal year as the natural business year for the Lenny/Laurie LLC, i.e., the LLC's only business is a seasonal business operated from October 1 through March 31 and the partnership earns more than 25% of its gross income in the last two months of the proposed fiscal year.

As noted above, Congress in 1986 required existing partnerships to adopt the taxable year required by § 706(b)(1)(B) unless they could establish a business purpose. This change in the law meant that many existing partnerships whose tax years had been grandfathered under the 1954 legislation or that had a taxable year permitted pursuant to Revenue Procedure 72-51 (allowing deferral of income up to three months) were required to adopt a new taxable year in conformance with the 1986 legislation. Bowing to the pressure of lobbyists, Congress in 1987 added § 444 authorizing a partnership to elect a taxable year other than the required taxable year as long as the income deferral period of the taxable year elected does not exceed the shorter of three months or the deferral period of the taxable year being changed. § 444(b)(1) and (2). For example, assume Benjamin and Megan, calendar year taxpayers, form an LLC on January 1, 2016. Under § 706(b)(b)(1)(B), the LLC's required taxable year would be the calendar year (the majority interest taxable year). Even if the LLC has no business purpose for any other taxable year, the LLC could elect under § 444 to use a September 30 fiscal year,[16] thereby allowing a three-month tax deferral. [For example, Benjamin and Megan would each report their share of the LLC's taxable income for the period January 1–September 30, 2015 on their tax returns for 2015. Their share of the LLC's taxable income for the period October 1–December 31, 2015 would be reported on their 2016 tax return due April 15, 2017. They will have thus deferred reporting their share of three months of income earned in 2015 for a full year.]

The election under § 444, however, comes with a price, i.e., the partnership must make required payments to the government under § 7519 approximating the value of any taxes deferred as a result of the election. While the detail of § 444 and the annual calculations of the required § 7519 payments are beyond the scope of this

---

[14] The partnership seeking to use a taxable year other than the required taxable year must obtain approval of the Commissioner of the Internal Revenue Service under § 442. Reg. § 1.441-1(c)(2).

[15] H.R. Rep. No. 99-841 (Conf. Rep.), 99th Cong., 2d Sess, II-318-19 (1986), 1986-3 (Vol. 4) C.B. 319. *See* Rev. Rul. 87-57, 1987-2 C.B. 117 for examples of circumstances that qualify or fail to qualify under the business purpose exception.

[16] Under § 444, the LLC could also elect either an October 31 fiscal year (affording two months' deferral) or a November 30 fiscal year (affording one month's deferral).

casebook, you should nonetheless be aware that § 444 affords the possibility of avoiding the use of a required taxable year even though a partnership lacks a business purpose justifying the avoidance.

B. Partnership Formation Expenses: § 709

Section 709(a) denies the partnership or any partner a deduction for partnership organizational or syndication expenses. This stricture, however, is relieved as to organizational expenses in § 709(b), described below, but not as to syndication expenses.

1. Organizational Expenses

Under § 709(b)(1), a partnership may elect to deduct its organizational expenses in the year it begins business to the extent of the lesser of: (1) its organizational expenses, or (2) $5,000, reduced (but not below zero) by the amount such expenses exceed $50,000. A partnership is deemed to have made the election unless it affirmatively elects out. Reg. § 1.709-1(b)(2). Any organizational expenses in excess of the limit are amortizable ratably over 180 months (15 years) beginning with the month the partnership begins business. (The date a partnership begins business is a "question of fact . . . in light of all the circumstances. . . . Ordinarily, a partnership begins business when it starts the business operations for which it was organized." Reg. § 1.709-2(c).)

For example, if the ABC Partnership makes a § 709(b)(1) election and its organizational expenses are $5,000 or less, all the expenses may be fully deducted in the year ABC begins business. If the expenses are $55,000 or more, the entire amount will be deducted ratably (amortized) over 180 months. If the expenses are more than $5,000 but less than $55,000, a maximum of $5,000 may be deducted under the "lesser of" test (the currently deductible amount will be less than $5,000 if the organizational expenses exceed $50,000), with the balance ratably deducted (amortized) over 180 months. The deduction and ratable amortization, however, are allowed only if an election is made. In the absence of an election, organizational expenses are nondeductible under the general rule of § 709(a), i.e., they cannot be deducted or amortized. An election to amortize is made by attaching a statement to that effect, with expenses listed, to the partnership return for the year it begins business. The election, once made, is irrevocable.

If the electing partnership liquidates before the close of the 180-month amortization period, any deferred organizational expenses not previously allowed as a deduction may be deducted to the extent allowable under § 165. § 709(b)(2). Even upon liquidation, however, a partnership that did not make a § 709(b)(1) election is not entitled to deduct the capitalized organizational expenses. Rev. Rul. 87-111, 1987-2 C.B. 160. Nonetheless, a partner's share of such capitalized expenses may give rise upon liquidation to a larger capital loss or a reduced capital gain to the partner "to the extent that the adjusted basis of [the partner's] partnership interest [would have been reduced by the partner's] share of the Section 165 loss if the deduction were permitted. . . . " Rev. Rul. 87-111.

Organizational expenses for purposes of § 709 are capital expenditures incident to the creation of the partnership that would be amortizable over the life of the partnership if it had an ascertainable life. § 709(b)(3). Examples of such expenses include filing fees and legal and accounting fees for services incident to the organization of a partnership, e.g., negotiation and preparation of a partnership agreement. Reg. § 1.709-2(a). Specifically excluded as organizational expenses are the expenses of acquiring or transferring assets to the partnership, expenses connected with admitting or removing partners other than at initial organization, expenses of contracts connected with operation of the partnership business, and syndication expenses. Qualifying expenses must be incurred no earlier than a "reasonable time" before the partnership begins business and no later than the date for filing the partnership return (without extensions). In general, organizational expenses are those incurred "for creation of the partnership and not for operation or starting operation of the trade or business. . . . [T]he expense must be for an item normally expected to benefit the partnership throughout the entire life of the partnership." Reg. § 1.709-2(a).

2. Syndication Expenses

Syndication expenses cannot be deducted. § 709(a). There is no current deduction/amortization election as there is for organizational expenses under § 709(b)(1). Syndication expenses are those that promote the sale of partnership interests and are "connected with the issuing and marketing" of those interests. § 709(a); Reg. § 1.709-2(b). The regulations give as examples of such expenses brokerage fees; registration fees; legal fees for securities advice, and advice on the adequacy of tax disclosures in promotional material; accounting fees in connection with offering materials; and printing costs of promotional material. All syndication expenses must be capitalized and cannot be amortized or otherwise deducted. Reg. § 1.709-2(b); Rev. Rul. 85-32, 1985-1 C.B. 186. In this respect, syndication expenses are like organizational expenses the partnership has not elected to amortize. As nondeductible expenses chargeable to capital accounts, a partner's share of such expenses does not reduce the partner's basis in her partnership interest. See § 705(a)(2). Accordingly, upon liquidation of her interest, the partner's basis is correspondingly greater than it would have been had the expense been deductible; as a result, the partner's gain on liquidation is correspondingly less, or a loss on liquidation correspondingly greater.

Chapter 7

THE PASS-THROUGH OF INCOME, GAIN, LOSS, DEDUCTION, AND CREDIT

I. PROBLEMS

1. Brian and Jennifer are partners in a general partnership operating a marina and boat storage business on a large freshwater lake in the Northwest. Their only contributions to the partnership have been in cash. Based on her cash contributions to the partnership, Jennifer has a 60% interest in the capital and profits of the partnership while Brian has a 40% interest. Consistent with their partnership interests, Jennifer has a 60% distributive share and Brian a 40% share of all items of partnership income, gain, loss, deduction, and credit. At the beginning of Year 5 of the partnership, Brian's outside basis is $400,000 and Jennifer's outside basis is $600,000. Assume their capital accounts at the beginning of Year 5 equal their outside bases. In Year 5, the partnership has the following tax significant items:

   $200,000 in income from services they provide as part of their operation of the marina;

   $50,000 in rental income from the storage of boats;;

   $60,000 in salary expense;

   $30,000 of depreciation on equipment and facilities;

   $15,000 of gain on the sale of equipment used in their business (all of the gain is § 1245 gain);

   $40,000 of § 1231 gain from the sale of land used in the business;

   $15,000 of § 1231 loss from the theft of a boat;

   $6,000 in qualified dividend income as defined in § 1(h)(11)(B);

   $10,000 in long-term capital loss from the sale of IBM stock;

   $5,000 short-term capital loss from the sale of Microsoft stock;

   $1,000 charitable contribution to a § 501(c)(3) environmental organization; and

   $2,000 in political contributions.

   (a) Identify the "variable effect" items that must be separately stated in computing the taxable income of the partnership.

   (b) Compute the taxable income of the partnership exclusive of items requiring separate statement under § 702(a).

(c) Compute the outside basis of each partner at the end of Year 5 assuming no distributions have been made to partners during Year 5.

(d) Compute the capital account of each partner at the end of Year 5.

Assignment for Chapter 7:

Complete the problems.

Read: Internal Revenue Code: §§ 61(a)(13), 63(c)(6)(D), 701, 702, 703, 704(a) and (b), 705 and 733.
Treasury Regulations: §§ 1.701-1, 1.702-1(a)(1)–(5), (7), (8), and (9), (b) and (c)(1); 1.702-2; 1.703-1; 1.704-1(b)(2)(iv)(a) and (b); 1.705–1(a). Skim § 1.704-1(b)(3)(i) and (ii).
Materials: Overview
Schedule K-1 (Form 1065)

II. VOCABULARY

pass-through entity
distributive share
partners' interest in the partnership
aggregate approach to the taxation of partnerships
entity approach to the taxation of partnerships
variable effect items

III. OBJECTIVES

1. To recall that a partnership is not a taxable entity and to explain the pass-through nature of partnerships.

2. To calculate the taxable income of a partnership pursuant to § 703.

3. To explain why certain items of income or loss must be separately stated in computing a partnership's taxable income.

4. To identify items that must be separately stated pursuant to § 702 and the regulations thereunder.

5. To recall a partner must report her distributive share of separately stated items of income and loss as well as her distributive share of the partnership's taxable income or loss exclusive of the separately stated items.

6. To compute the outside basis of a partner taking into account a partner's distributive share of partnership income, gain, loss, deduction, and credit.

7. To explain the impact of the pass-through of a partnership's income and loss on the capital accounts of the partners.

IV. OVERVIEW

Chapter 6 addressed § 706(a) specifying the timing of inclusion of a partner's share of partnership taxable income and § 706(b) providing rules for establishing the taxable year of the partnership. Chapter 6 noted that Congress employed an *entity approach* to partnerships in enacting § 703(b) authorizing the partnership to make most elections pertinent to the computation of the taxable income derived from a partnership. This chapter will address each partner's distributive share of the income, gains, losses, deductions, and credits of a partnership, how that share is reported, and the impact of a partner's distributive share on the partner's outside basis and capital account. While the Code provisions addressed in Chapter 6 emphasized the entity approach to the taxation of partners and partnership, the provisions addressed in this chapter largely reflect the *aggregate approach*.

A. Distributive Share

Sections 701 and 702(a) establish the pass-through nature of partnerships. These provisions exemplify the aggregate approach to the taxation of partnerships, i.e., the partnership is not taxed but, instead, the partnership's income, gain, loss, deduction, and credit (hereinafter referred to as the partnership's tax items) are allocated to the partners in accord with each partner's *distributive share* and are taken into account by the partners in determining their income tax for the year.[1] *See, e.g.,* § 61(a)(13). The fact a partner is allocated a distributive share of the partnership's tax items for the year, however, does not mean the partner will actually receive a partnership distribution during the year. Often, for example, a profitable partnership will choose to retain and reinvest the profits it generates during the year rather than distribute the profits to its partners. Nonetheless, the partners must report for tax purposes their distributive share of the partnership's profits.

How is the "distributive share" of each partner determined? Consider the following excerpt from § 704:

---

§ 704 Partner's distributive share

(a) Effect of partnership agreement. A partner's distributive share of income, gain, loss, deduction or credit shall, except as otherwise provided in this chapter, *be determined by the partnership agreement.*

(b) Determination of distributive share. A partner's distributive share of income, gain, loss, deduction, or credit (or item thereof) shall be determined in accordance with the partner's interest in the partnership (determined by taking into account all the facts and circumstances), if —

(1) the partnership agreement does not provide as to the partner's distributive share of income, gain, loss deduction, or credit (or item thereof) or

(2) the allocation to a partner under the agreement of income, gain, loss deduction or credit (or item thereof does not have substantial economic effect.

---

[1] A partner's share of those partnership tax items is referred to as the partner's "distributive share."

As § 704(a) indicates, the "distributive share" of each partner is generally determined by reference to the partnership agreement, i.e., how the partners have agreed among themselves to allocate the partnership's tax items. The Code thus accords partners considerable flexibility in allocating partnership tax items. If the partnership agreement fails to provide for a partner's distributive share of partnership tax items, § 704(b)(1) provides the partner's distributive share will be determined in accord with the partner's interest in the partnership. As will be discussed in detail in Chapter 9, the regulations interpreting and applying § 704(b)(1) provide the determination of a partner's interest in the partnership will be made by considering factors such as: (a) the relative contributions of the partners to the entity and (b) the rights of the partners to non-liquidating and liquidating distributions.[2] For example, assume two individuals form a general partnership with each partner contributing the same amount of cash. The partners expect to share equally in all partnership distributions. The partnership agreement, however, is silent with regard to the allocation of partnership tax items. Under these circumstances and consistent with the regulations, we would conclude that each partner has a 50% interest in the partnership and therefore all partnership tax items should be allocated equally between the two partners.

Despite the apparent flexibility accorded partners in determining their distributive shares of partnership tax items, that flexibility is not unlimited. After all, the tax law generally prohibits the assignment of income and losses and, apart from Subchapter K, the Code goes to considerable lengths to prevent avoidance of tax. It would be strange indeed were Subchapter K to allow partnerships to disregard assignment of income and other tax avoidance rules. It does not! Thus, for example, notwithstanding allocations made in a partnership agreement, when a partnership recognizes the built-in gain or loss associated with an item of contributed property, § 704(c)(1)(A) (discussed in detail in Chapter 10), allocates the built-in gain or loss to the contributing partner.

> **Example:** Kevin and Dan form a partnership with Kevin contributing publicly traded stock with a fair market value of $50,000 and an adjusted basis of $20,000 and Dan contributing $50,000 in cash. The partnership agreement specifically provides that all tax items will be allocated equally between Kevin and Dan. Within six months of its creation, the partnership sells the stock contributed by Kevin for $50,000.
>
> **Analysis:** Pursuant to § 704(c)(1)(A) and the regulations thereunder, the $30,000 of tax gain recognized by the partnership on the sale of the stock contributed by Kevin will all be allocated to Kevin. It makes no difference that the partnership agreement provides for an equal allocation of partnership tax items.

In addition to the special rules of § 704(c)(1)(A) regarding the allocation of built-in gains and losses, § 704(b)(2) (noted above and discussed in detail in Chapter 9) specifically provides a partnership agreement's allocation of an item of income, gain, loss, deduction or credit (often referred to as "a special allocation") will be respected only if the allocation has "substantial economic effect," i.e., the allocation

---

[2] Reg. § 1.704-1(b)(3)(i) and (ii).

must reflect the *economic* deal between and among the partners and satisfy certain other requirements discussed in detail in Chapter 9. If it does not, the specifically allocated tax item will be reallocated between or among the partners in accord with each partner's interest in the partnership (just as though the partnership agreement were silent with respect to the distributive share of that tax item).

Example: Assume Jack and Jill each contributes $100,000 in cash to form a partnership. Their partnership agreement specifies that they will divide all partnership profits equally but, *for tax reporting purposes only*, they will allocate all partnership net income to Jack who, in his business activities apart from the partnership, generates significant tax losses that would completely offset the partnership's net income allocated to him. Jill, meanwhile, is in a high tax bracket and, while expecting to receive liquidating and nonliquidating distributions exactly equal to those Jack receives, would prefer to report as little income as possible from the partnership.

Analysis: In this example, the partnership agreement specifies the distributive share, i.e., it provides that all of the profits or net income of the partnership will be allocated to Jack *for tax reporting purposes only*. This allocation of tax items, however, does not comport with the economic arrangement of the parties, i.e., Jack and Jill are each entitled ultimately to receive one-half of the profits or net income and liquidating distributions of this partnership. The tax avoidance game being played by the parties in this example should be apparent. Jack is willing to have the partnership's net income allocated to him for tax reporting purposes because he can offset that income with the losses he generates in his other business activities. In the end, Jack isn't harmed by the allocation, Jill benefits from not reporting any partnership income, and the only loser is the federal fisc. Under these circumstances, the allocation of the net income to Jack for tax purposes only will not be deemed to have "substantial economic effect" and will not be respected. Instead, the profits will be allocated for tax reporting purposes consistent with each partner's interest in the partnership. Here, Jack and Jill are equal partners who are ultimately entitled to equal shares of all partnership distributions, including liquidating distributions. As a result, they each have a 50% interest in the partnership and therefore 50% of the net income will be taxable to Jack and 50% taxable to Jill.

For now, you should simply be aware that §§ 704(b)(2) and 704(c)(1)(A) are intended to protect the integrity of our income tax system by preventing "game playing" or tax avoidance by partnerships when it comes to the allocation of tax items generated by the partnership. As noted, we will defer the detailed study of § 704(b)(2) and the "substantial economic effect" test until Chapter 9 where we will also consider in depth the partner's-interest-in-the-partnership test of § 704(b)(1); we will defer the detailed study of § 704(c)(1)(A) until Chapter 10. For purposes of this chapter, we will assume the partnership properties had no built-in gain or loss upon contribution. We will also assume the partnership agreement specifies a distributive share arrangement that matches the economic arrangement of the partners, i.e., the partners' distributive share of all partnership tax items will be proportionate to their contributions of capital to the partnership and their share of liquidation proceeds.

B. Accounting for a Partner's Distributive Share

Assume, on January 1, 2016, Jackie and Jonathan each contributed $250,000 to create a calendar-year partnership in which each will have a 50% interest in the capital and profits. The partnership agreement specifically provides that, for tax reporting purposes, Jackie and Jonathan will be allocated equal shares of the partnership's items of income, gain, loss, deduction, and credit. [In other words, they will have equal distributive shares.] Assume in 2016 the partnership made no distributions and its expenses exactly equaled its income. Thus, Jackie's and Jonathan's outside basis and capital accounts at the end of 2016 were each $250,000. For 2017, the second year of its operation, the partnership made no distributions to the partners and had the following items of income and deduction:

$120,000 of ordinary income from business operations;

$40,000 of ordinary business expenses (wages, supplies, rent, and depreciation);

$10,000 in cash contributions made to a local museum qualifying as a public charity under § 501(c)(3);

$20,000 of short-term capital loss from the sale of stock the partnership had purchased; and

$30,000 of § 1231 loss resulting from the theft of a truck owned and used by the partnership in its business.

How should Jackie and Jonathan report their distributive shares of the partnership's tax items? Should they simply compute the taxable income or loss of the partnership as if the partnership were a taxable entity (like a Subchapter C corporation) and divide the resulting taxable income or loss between themselves? Were this *entity approach* to be the standard, the final character of the § 1231 theft loss would be determined by engaging in the § 1231 hotchpot analysis at the partnership level.[3] Likewise, one would apply at the partnership level the § 1211(b) limitation on the deduction of capital losses and the § 170(b) limitation on the deduction for charitable contributions. Alternatively, should we employ an *aggregate approach* and pass through to each partner a share of each tax item that the partner, in computing her income tax, would combine with her income, gain, loss, deductions, and credits from other sources? As a result of this aggregate approach, for example, the tax effect of each partner's share of the partnership's $30,000 theft loss (a § 1231 loss) may vary because of the different tax circumstances of the partners.

---

[3] If that were done, we would conclude on the facts presented in the hypothetical that the $30,000 theft loss would be characterized as an ordinary loss. Specifically, § 1231(a)(4)(C) creates the preliminary hotchpot (or firepot as it is sometimes known) and provides that, if the § 1231 losses included in this hotchpot exceed the § 1231 gains in the hotchpot, all of the losses and gains in the hotchpot will be characterized outside of § 1231 and thus will be ordinary. In our hypothetical, the theft loss is the only § 1231 item that would be assigned to the preliminary hotchpot and therefore necessarily would be characterized outside of § 1231 as an ordinary loss.

Example: Assume in 2017 Jackie, apart from her $15,000 share of the partnership's § 1231 loss, has no other § 1231 gains or losses. By contrast, assume Jonathan, in addition to his $15,000 share of the partnership's § 1231 loss, has $16,000 in § 1231 gain resulting from fire insurance proceeds he received as a result of the destruction of property he uses in a business he operates as a sole proprietor. Under these circumstances, Jackie's $15,000 share of the partnership's § 1231 loss would be characterized as an ordinary loss in her hands while Jonathan's $15,000 share of the partnership's § 1231 loss would be characterized as a long-term capital loss.[4]

If an aggregate approach rather than an entity approach is used, Jackie's and Jonathan's shares of the partnership's charitable contribution and their share of the short-term capital loss will, like their shares of the § 1231 loss, have different tax consequences to each depending on their tax profiles.[5]

As the following excerpt from § 702 makes clear, Congress determined the aggregate approach should be used and, as a result, each partner must report separately her distributive share of tax items like the § 1231 loss, the charitable contribution, and the short-term capital loss in our example, which may have varying tax consequences depending on a partner's tax profile.[6]

---

§ 702. Income and credits of partner

(a) **General Rule.** In determining his income tax, each partner shall take into account separately his *distributive share* of the partnership's —

(1) gain and losses from sales or exchanges of capital assets held for not more than 1 year,

(2) gain and losses from sales or exchanges of capital assets held for

---

[4] With respect to Jonathan, the preliminary hotchpot rule of § 1231(a)(4)(C) would not be applicable because Jonathan's $16,000 in § 1231 gain from the receipt of fire insurance proceeds exceeds his $15,000 share of the partnership's § 1231 theft loss. Instead, the general characterization rule of § 1231(a)(1) would apply. Under that rule (the principal or primary hotchpot rule), because Jonathan's § 1231 gain of $16,000 from the fire insurance proceeds exceeds his $15,000 share of the partnership's § 1231 theft loss, his gain would be characterized long-term capital gain and his share of the theft loss would be characterized as long-term capital loss.

[5] For example, Jackie and Jonathan would each have a $10,000 share of the partnership's short-term capital loss. If Jackie had at least $7,000 of capital gain from transactions outside the partnership, e.g., sale of stock from her personal portfolio of stock, she would be entitled to deduct the full $10,000 share of the partnership's short-term capital loss that was passed through to her. By contrast, if Jonathan had no capital gains, he could only deduct $3,000 of the $10,000 share of partnership short-term capital loss that passed through to him. He would carry over the $7,000 balance to the following year. §§ 1211(b) and 1212.

[6] Working together, §§ 702(a) and (b) (identifying variable effect items that must be separately stated and the character of items constituting a partner's distributive share) and 703(a)(1) (requiring the partnership in computing its taxable income to separately state those items listed in § 702(a)), provide the mechanism that preserves the character of variable effect items as they pass through the partnership to the partners.

more than 1 year,

(3) gains and losses from sales or exchanges of property described in section 1231 . . .

(4) charitable contributions (as defined in section 170(c)),

(5) dividends with respect to which section 1(h)(11) . . . applies,

(6) taxes, described in section 901, paid or accrued to foreign countries and to possessions of the United States,

(7) other items of income, gain, loss, deduction, or credit to the extent provided by regulations prescribed by the Secretary, and

(8) taxable income or loss, exclusive of items requiring separate computation under other paragraphs of this subsection.

(b) Character of items constituting distributive share. The character of any item of income, gain, loss, deduction, or credit included in a partner's distributive share under paragraphs (1) through (7) of subsection (a) shall be determined as if such items were realized directly from the source from which realized by the partnership, or incurred in the same manner as incurred by the partnership.

Consistent with the aggregate approach to partnership taxation, § 702(a) requires a partner, in determining her taxable income, to take into account her distributive share of the partnership tax items listed in that Code provision or in the Treasury regulations interpreting it. Regulation § 1.702-1(a)(8)(ii) confirms that, as a result of the aggregate approach employed in § 702, a separate accounting must be made for those items for which the tax consequence will vary depending on the tax circumstances of the partner. These items are often referred to in the literature as "variable effect" items. That regulation states:

> Each partner must also take into account separately the partner's distributive share of any partnership item which, if separately taken into account by a partner, would result in an income tax liability for that partner, or for any other person, different from that which would result if that partner did not take the item into account separately.

Review Reg. § 1.702-1(a)(8) and note the range of items identified therein as variable effect items.[7] Applying § 702 and the regulations thereunder to the Jackie/Jonathan partnership, Jackie and Jonathan, in determining their taxable

---

[7] Note also that § 702(b) provides that the characterization of those items specified in § 702(a)(1)-(7) will be determined as though the partner realized the item directly from the source from which it was realized by the partnership or incurred it in the same manner as the partnership. For example, if the Jackie/Jonathan partnership realized a $30,000 loss as a result of a theft of a truck used in its business, each partner's share of that theft loss would be treated as though the partner had realized it as a result of the theft of a truck used in his or her individual business. Just as the theft loss would be a § 1231 theft loss to the partnership, Jackie's and Jonathan's $15,000 distributive shares of that loss would each be a § 1231 theft loss to be characterized as a long-term capital loss or an ordinary loss depending upon the outcome of the application of § 1231 at their individual levels.

income, will take into account separately their distributive shares of the partnership's short-term capital loss (§ 702(a)(1)), § 1231 theft loss (§ 702(a)(3)), and charitable contribution (§ 702(a)(4)).

What about Jackie's and Jonathan's distributive shares of the partnership's $120,000 in ordinary business income and $40,000 in ordinary business expenses? Must these items be separately stated? The answer is "No." The reason should be apparent, i.e., ordinary business income and ordinary business expenses (wages, rents, supplies, etc.), unlike capital gains and losses, § 1231 gains and losses, charitable contributions etc., are not subject to special limitations or characterization rules that may result in them having a variable tax effect depending on the tax profiles of the partners. In other words, the tax impact of these items on Jackie and Jonathan will be no different whether they are separately stated or not.

Apart from separately stating their distributive shares of the partnership's short-term capital loss, § 1231 loss, and charitable contribution in determining their income tax, Jackie and Jonathan must each report their distributive share of the partnership's *taxable income or loss exclusive of those items requiring separate computation under § 702(a)(1)–(7)*. § 702(a)(8). Section 703(a) addresses the computation of a partnership's taxable income as follows:

---

§ 703. Partnership computations.

(a) Income and deductions. — The taxable income of a partnership shall be computed in the same manner as in the case of an individual except that —

(1) *the items described in section 702(a) shall be separately stated*, and

(2) the following deductions shall not be allowed to the partnership:

(A) the deductions for personal exemptions provided in section 151,

(B) the deduction for taxes provided in section 164(a) with respect to taxes, described in section 901, paid or accrued to foreign countries and to possessions of the United States,

(C) the deduction for charitable contributions provided in section 170,

(D) the net operating loss deduction provided in section 172.

(E) the additional itemized deductions for individuals provided in part VII of subchapter B (sec. 211 and following), and

(F) the deduction for depletion under section 611 with respect to oil and gas wells.

Note how § 703(a)(1) works in tandem with § 702(a) by requiring the partnership to separately state those items described in § 702 (a)(1)–(7) (the variable effect items). [See Schedule K-1 in the materials that the partnership must provide each partner and that demonstrates this separate accounting for variable effect items.] As discussed above, § 702(a) requires each partner to take into account his or her distributive share of these items and also requires each partner to account for his or her distributive share of the partnership's taxable income or loss as computed without these variable effect items.[8]

For purposes of computing a partnership's taxable income, § 703(a)(2) disallows a number of deductions. Thus, § 703(a)(2)(A) appropriately provides the partnership shall not claim a deduction for the personal exemption under § 151; the partners will claim that deduction, when allowable, on their own tax returns. Likewise § 703(a)(2)(D) appropriately denies a partnership the § 172 deduction for net operating losses because the losses that would normally comprise the net operating losses have already been passed through to the partners, who will each compute their own net operating loss. See Reg. § 1.702-2. Section 703(a)(2)(E) denies a partnership a deduction for the additional itemized deductions accorded individuals under §§ 211 *et seq.*; these are deductions we would not expect a partnership to have and, if they did, they should be separately stated as they would have variable effect.[9] Section 703(a)(2)(B), (C), and (F) lists a number of deductions that are also not allowed in computing the partnership's taxable income, including the § 170 charitable contribution deduction.[10] These deductions, although disallowed in computing taxable income under § 703, will nonetheless be deductible by the partners as they are tax items that must be separately accounted for as variable effect items.[11]

Applying § 703(a), let's compute the taxable income of the Jackie/Jonathan partnership with an eye toward § 702(a)(8) and its requirement that Jackie and Jonathan each report their share of taxable income exclusive of those items identified in § 702(a)(1)–(7). Here, apart from the charitable contribution deduction that § 703 specifically disallows in computing taxable income,[12] the only other

---

[8] Note that Reg. § 1.703-1(a)(1)(i) and(ii) define "taxable income" and "loss" for purposes of § 702(a)(8): taxable income means the amount by which the total of not-separately-stated items of partnership gross income exceeds the total of the not-separately-stated items of deduction allowed to the partnership. Correspondingly, the term "loss" means the amount by which total of all of the not-separately-stated items of deduction allowed to the partnership exceeds the total of not-separately-stated items of partnership gross income.

[9] Reg. § 1.702-1(a)(8)(i).

[10] Note that § 63(c)(6)(D) specifically provides that a partnership is not eligible for the standard deduction. Again, this makes sense because the partners will either itemize their deductions or, in lieu of itemization, will claim the standard deduction.

[11] Thus, for example, while § 703(a)(2)(C) specifically provides that the partnership may not claim a § 170 charitable contribution deduction in computing its taxable income, § 702(a)(4) specifically requires that each partner report his or her distributive share of charitable contributions. In this regard, note also § 703(a)(2)(B) (denying the partnerships a deduction for taxes paid or accrued to foreign countries) and § 702(a)(6) requiring partners to report their distributive share of such taxes.

[12] Because § 703(a)(2)(C) denies the partnership a deduction for charitable contributions, we are not listing the partnership's charitable contributions among those items that must be separately stated. The fact is, however, that § 702(a)(4) specifically requires partners to report their distributive shares of a partnership's charitable contributions because charitable contributions are a variable effect item. Congress thus may appropriately be accused of a little overkill in specifying in § 703(a)(2)(C) that the partnership, in computing its taxable income, is not allowed a charitable deduction under § 170.

variable effect items that must be separately accounted for are the $20,000 in short-term capital losses and the § 1231 theft loss of $15,000. Excluding the charitable contribution and these two other variable effect items, the partnership's taxable income is therefore $80,000, determined as follows:

Ordinary business income	$120,000
Ordinary business expenses	($40,000)
Taxable income (exclusive of separately stated items)	**$80,000**

Thus, under § 702(a)(8), Jackie and Jonathan will each report $40,000, i.e., their 50% share of the $80,000 of taxable income of the partnership (exclusive of the separately stated items).

In summary, when the "dust settles," Jackie and Jonathan, in computing their taxable income for 2017, will each report the following items:

$10,000 of short-term capital loss from the sale of stock (§ 702(a)(2));

$15,000 of § 1231 theft loss (702(a)(3));

$5,000 of charitable contribution to a public charity (the museum) (§ 702(a)(4)); and

$40,000 share of the partnership's taxable income exclusive of separately stated items. (§ 702(a)(8)).

C. Impact of Income/Deduction Pass-Through on a Partner's Basis

We have considered above the operation of the single-level tax regime of Subchapter K and studied how the partnership operates as a kind of conduit with each partner reporting his or her distributive share of the partnership's tax items. We now turn our attention to the impact of this pass-through regime on the partner's outside basis in the partnership. In doing so, recall *the fact that a partner is required to report her distributive share of the partnership's tax items doesn't mean the partner has actually received any distribution.*

Consistent with tax cost basis notions, when a partner includes her distributive share of partnership income and gain or reports a distributive share of deduction or loss, the reporting of these tax items should be reflected by appropriate adjustments to the basis the partner has in her partnership interest. For example, to the extent a partner has reported her share of partnership income for the year but has received no distribution from the partnership, the partner's outside basis should be increased by the amount of income reported. Failure to do so would ultimately result in the partner, in effect, being taxed again on the same income when it was finally distributed. Similarly, to the extent that a partner has been allocated partnership losses, including capital losses and § 1231 losses, the partner's outside basis should be decreased by the amount of those losses. Failure to do so would, in effect, ultimately result in the partner claiming the loss a second time. Consider the following examples, which demonstrate these points:

Example 1: Assume in 2016 Abigail contributed $100 in cash for her interest in a partnership. Her initial outside basis was thus $100. § 722. Assume Abigail's distributive share of partnership income (all rental income) for 2016 was $20. The partnership distributed nothing to Abigail in 2016. Under § 61(a)(13) and § 702(a), Abigail would nevertheless be required to report the $20 distributive share of rental income as part of her gross income for the 2016. Now assume that, at the beginning of 2017, the partnership liquidates and Abigail receives $120 in cash in complete liquidation of her partnership interest. If Abigail's outside basis were not adjusted upward by $20 to $120 to reflect the $20 distributive share of income allocated to her in 2016, Abigail would be required to report $20 of income (gain) upon the liquidation of the partnership, i.e., if her outside basis remained $100 and she received a liquidating distribution of $120, she would have $20 of income (gain). § 731(a)(1). In other words, Abigail would be taxed twice on the $20 share of partnership rental income, i.e., she would have been taxed on the $20 share in 2016 and would be taxed on it again when the partnership liquidated in 2017. That result makes no sense. To prevent double taxation, we need to adjust Abigail's outside basis upward to reflect the $20 of partnership income she reported in 2016. Then, when the partnership liquidates and distributes $120 to Abigail, her adjusted outside basis of $120 will completely offset the distribution and Abigail will have no additional income.

Example 2: Assume the same facts as Example 1, except in 2016 the partnership experienced a loss instead of having any net income. Abigail's distributive share of the loss was $20. Abigail will be entitled to deduct this loss on her individual income tax return. See § 704(d). Assume at the beginning of 2017, the partnership liquidated and distributed to Abigail $80 in cash in complete liquidation of her partnership interest. If Abigail's outside basis has not been adjusted downward to $80 to reflect the $20 distributive share of loss in 2016, Abigail would have a $20 loss when she receives a liquidating distribution in 2017 of $80. § 731(a)(2). In other words, she would have deducted the $20 loss twice. That result makes no sense. To prevent the double counting of loss, we need to adjust Abigail's outside basis downward to reflect the $20 of loss she was allocated in 2016. Then, when the partnership liquidates and distributes $80 to Abigail, she will have neither gain nor loss on the liquidating distribution because she will have received an amount exactly equal to the adjusted basis she had in her partnership interest.

Congress enacted § 705 addressing the ongoing adjustment to outside basis to reflect the impact on partners of the conduit or pass-through approach of Subchapter K. As the above examples illustrate, determination of outside basis is critical when a partnership liquidates. As will be discussed in subsequent chapters of this casebook, determination of outside basis is critical in a number of other contexts, e.g., application of § 704(d), which prevents a partner from deducting losses in excess of the partner's outside basis; computation of the basis in property other than cash distributed to a partner (§ 702); determination of gain, if any, when the entity makes non-liquidating distributions of cash to a partner (§ 731(a)); and the gain or loss on the sale or other taxable disposition of a partnership interest (§ 741).[13] Consider the following excerpt from § 705:

> **§ 705. Determination of basis of partner's interest.**
>
> (a)   **General rule.** — The adjusted basis of a partner's interest in a partnership shall . . . be the basis of such interest determined under section 722 (relating to contributions to a partnership) . . .
>
> (1) increased by the sum of his distributive share for the taxable year and prior taxable years of —
>
> (A) taxable income of the partnership as determined under section 703(a),
>
> (B) income of the partnership exempt from tax under this title, and
>
> . . .
>
> (2) decreased (but not below zero) by distributions by the partnership as provided in section 733 and by the sum of his distributive share for the taxable year and prior taxable years of —
>
> (A) losses of the partnership, and
>
> (B) expenditures of the partnership not deductible in computing its taxable income and not properly chargeable to capital account; and
>
> . . .

This provision can best be understood by considering its application to the Jackie and Jonathan partnership discussed above. Recall that Jackie and Jonathan created the partnership in 2016 by contributing $250,000 cash each to the partnership in exchange for a 50% partnership interest. Thus, under § 722, each had an initial $250,000 outside basis in the partnership; each also had a $250,000 capital account. Reg. § 1.704–1(b)(2)(iv)(b)(1). Note that the partner's initial outside basis is the starting point for § 705, which then directs, in § 705(a)(1)(A) and (B), that Jackie's and Jonathan's outside bases be increased by their distributive share of both the taxable income of the partnership (e.g., ordinary business profits as well as separately stated items of income such as capital gains or § 1231 gains) and tax-exempt income (interest on tax-free government bonds). In our example, the partnership had no net business profits in 2016 and made no distributions in that year. Thus, Jackie's and Jonathan's outside bases as well as their capital accounts remained the same. In 2017, the partnership had net business profits, i.e., net ordinary income of $80,000. (This is the partnership's taxable income exclusive of the separately stated items.) That amount would be allocated equally — $40,000 to

---

[13] Reg. § 1.705-1(a)(1) provides: "A partner is required to determine the adjusted basis of his interest in a partnership only when necessary for the determination of his tax liability. . . . The determination of the *adjusted basis* of a partnership interest is ordinarily made as of the end of a partnership taxable year." (Emphasis added.)

Jackie and $40,000 to Jonathan — increasing each of their outside bases to $290,000.

Although the Jackie/Jonathan partnership has no tax exempt income, let's consider § 705(a)(1)(B), which provides that a partner's outside basis is increased by his distributive share of any tax exempt income of the partnership. Why should a partner's outside basis be increased by his distributive share of tax exempt income? The answer is straightforward. If the partnership had tax exempt income for the year, although it would not include it in computing its taxable income, the partnership would nonetheless be worth more as a result of that income. To ensure the tax exempt income is never taxed to the partners, it is important that their distributive shares of that income be added to their outside basis, thus ensuring that, upon distribution, the tax exempt income will not result in recognition of income (gain) by the distributee partner under § 731(a)(1). In this regard, return to Example 1 above regarding Abigail and assume her $20 distributive share of partnership income was comprised entirely of tax exempt income. As Example 1 demonstrates, if an upward adjustment is not made to Abigail's outside basis, Abigail will be taxed on the income. That result, of course, would make no sense because the income is tax exempt.

Section 705(a)(2) appropriately requires us to decrease the outside basis by any distributions made by the partnership to a partner. We will examine distributions in considerable detail in later chapters of this casebook. Suffice for now to note that, to the extent a partner receives a distribution, the partner has recovered part of her cost and must reflect that recovery by a reduction in her outside basis. See also § 733.

Much as § 705(a)(1)(A) and (B) adjust upward a partner's outside basis to reflect the partner's distributive share of taxable and tax exempt income, § 705(a)(2)(A) and (B) require a downward adjustment of outside basis to reflect a partner's distributive share of losses of the partnership (including capital losses)[14] as well expenditures (other than capital expenditures) which are not deductible in computing a partnership's taxable income or loss. Apart from the separately stated items, the Jackie/Jonathan Partnership did not experience a loss (rather it had $80,000 of taxable income determined exclusive of the separately stated items). But each partner has a distributive share of separately stated items of loss, i.e., Jackie and Jonathan are each allocated $10,000 of short-term capital loss from the sale of stock, $5,000 of the partnership's charitable contributions, and $15,000 of § 1231 theft loss. Thus, they will each adjust their outside basis downward by $30,000.

Section 705(a)(2)(B) also requires a downward adjustment for expenditures that are non-deductible by the partnership (e.g., political contributions) *other than capital expenditures*. This adjustment makes sense because these expenditures reduce the value of the partnership. Were the partners' outside bases not reduced by their distributive share of such expenditures, they would ultimately, in effect, be allowed a loss deduction. Return to Example 2 above involving Abigail and assume the partnership had no income or loss during the year but did make a political contribution, $20 of which was allocable to Abigail. If Abigail's outside basis is not adjusted downward by $20, upon liquidation of the partnership she would be

---

[14] Reg. § 1.705-1(a)(3).

entitled to claim a $20 loss pursuant to § 731(a)(2) — in effect, a deduction would be allowed for the political contribution.[15]

Section 705(a)(2)(B) specifically excludes capital expenditures from the downward basis adjustment required by that provision. The reason, again, is simple: a capital expenditure doesn't reduce the value of the partnership but rather merely substitutes one item for another. For example, if the Jackie/Jonathan Partnership used $200,000 of its available cash to acquire some land to be used in its business, the $200,000 purchase price of the land would have to be capitalized (§ 263(a)(1)). The partnership would not be worth any less than it was before the purchase; rather, the partnership would have simply substituted $200,000 of land for $200,000 of cash.

In sum, as a result of the partnership operation in 2017, Jackie's and Jonathan's outside bases will each be $260,000 computed as follows:

	Jackie's Basis		Jonathan's Basis
Initial contribution	$250,000	§ 722	$250,000
Taxable income[16]	$40,000	§ 705(a)(1)(A)	$40,000
Losses (including separately stated deductions/losses)	($10,000 STCL)	§ 705(a)(2)(A)	($10,000 STCL)
	($15,000 § 1231 loss)	§ 705(a)(2)(A)	($15,000 § 1231 loss)
	(5,000 § 170 item)	§ 705(a)(2)(B)	($5,000 § 170 item)
Adjusted Outside Basis	$260,000		$260,000

D. Impact of Pass-through of Income, Gain, Loss, and Deduction on Capital Accounts

As discussed in Chapter 5, a capital account is maintained for each partner and reflects that partner's equity in the partnership, i.e., the amount the partner would be entitled to receive if the partnership were liquidated and all of its assets were sold at their book value, all of its liabilities were paid, and the net proceeds were distributed to the partners. Obviously, as a partnership operates, earns income or suffers losses, the equity of the partnership changes as do the partner's capital accounts.

Chapter 5 described the maintenance of capital accounts. In view of the above discussion regarding the operation of the Subchapter K pass-through of items of income, gain, loss, deduction, and credit, it is worth reviewing certain key aspects of the capital account maintenance rules implicated by the pass-through of a partnership's tax items to partners. Review the following excerpt from the

---

[15] Note that § 705(a)(2)(B) would also apply to charitable contributions because they are not deductible by the partnership (§ 703(a)(2)(C)). (As noted *supra*, however, § 702(a)(4) requires each partner to account separately for his share of charitable contributions as defined in § 170(c)(4). As a result, even though § 703(a)(2)(C) denies a charitable deduction to the partnership, a partner is allowed to deduct her distributive share of the partnership's charitable contributions.)

[16] Computed exclusive of the separately stated items.

regulations addressing the maintenance of capital accounts:

Excerpt from Reg. § 1.704-1(b)(2)(iv) Maintenance of Capital Accounts:

(b)   Basic rules.

. . . [E]ach partner's *capital account is increased by* (1) the amount of money contributed by him to the partnership, (2) the fair market value of property contributed by him to the partnership (net of liabilities . . . [assumed or taken subject to by the partnership]), and *(3) allocations . . . of [partnership] income and gain, including income and gain exempt from tax.* ... and [his capital account] is decreased by (4) the amount of money distributed to him by the partnership, (5) the fair market value of property distributed to him by the partnership (net of liabilities . . . [assumed or taken subject to by the partner]), *(6) allocations to him of expenditures . . . described in § 705(a)(2)(B) [e.g., nondeductible political contributions of the partnership],* and *(7) allocation of partnership loss and deduction* . . . (Emphasis added).

Note that a partner's capital account is increased by allocations of income and gain to the partner. Thus, a partner's capital account will be increased by both her share of income/gain that is taxable as well as tax exempt income. In this regard, the capital account maintenance rules track the ongoing basis adjustments of § 705 discussed above. Similarly, a partner's capital account is decreased by allocations of losses and deductions allocated to the partner and by the partner's share of § 705(a)(2)(B) expenditures, i.e., those expenditures (other than capital expenditures) that are non-deductible. Again, one sees the parallel between the capital account maintenance rules and the § 705 basis adjustment rules discussed above.

Consider the application of the capital account maintenance rules to the Jackie/Jonathan Partnership. As noted above, Jackie's and Jonathan's capital accounts initially were $250,000 each, i.e., the amount of cash each contributed to form the partnership. As a result of the operation of the partnership in 2017, their capital accounts would each be adjusted upward by $40,000 to reflect their shares of the $80,000 of ordinary net business income (taxable income exclusive of separately stated items) and will be adjusted downward by $30,000 to reflect their shares of the $20,000 short-term capital loss, $10,000 charitable contribution, and $30,000 § 1231 theft loss of the partnership. At the end of 2017, Jackie's and Jonathan's capital accounts will be as follows:

	Jackie's Capital Account		Jonathan's Capital Account
Initial contribution	$250,000	Reg. § 1.704-1(b)(2)(iv)(b)(1)	$250,000
Income and gain	$40,000	Reg. § 1.704-1(b)(2)(iv)(b)(3)	$40,000
Loss and deductions	($10,000 STCL)	Reg. § 1.704-1(b)(2)(iv)(b)(7)	($10,000 STCL)
	($15,000 § 1231 loss)	Reg. § 1.704-1(b)(2)(iv)(b)(7)	($7,500 § 1231 loss)
	($5,000 § 170)	Reg. § 1.704-1(b)(2)(iv)(b)(6)	($5,000 § 170)
Capital Account	**$260,000**		**$260,000**

Thus, if the Jackie/Jonathan Partnership were to sell all of its assets at book value and liquidate at the end of 2017, we would expect Jackie and Jonathan to each receive $260,000 in liquidation proceeds, i.e., the amount of the balance that each has in his or her capital account.[17]

E. Conclusion

This chapter has discussed in considerable detail the operation of the basic pass-through rules of Subchapter K with a particular emphasis on §§ 701, 702, 703 and 704. It has also addressed the impact of the pass-through of items of income, gain, loss, and deduction on the outside basis and capital account of a partner pursuant to § 705 and the capital account maintenance rules of Reg. § 1.704-1(b)(2)(iv)(b). This chapter has set the stage for a detailed examination in Chapters 9 and 10 of the special allocation rules of § 704(b) and the § 704(c)(1)(A) allocation rules regarding contributed property with built-in gain and loss.

---

[17] Again, book value is the value at which assets were "booked" by the partnership, i.e., the fair market value at the time the asset was acquired by contribution or purchase. Obviously, during the life of the partnership, each of its assets may increase or decrease in value. Upon a liquidation sale, the partnership may realize more or less than the book value, i.e., the partnership may have a book gain or loss (as well as a tax gain or loss). Any book (and, in turn, tax) gain or loss on such sale will be allocated to the partners in accord with their distributive shares and will serve to increase or decrease, as the case may be, the partner's capital accounts. Reg. § 1.704-1(b)(2)(iv)(3) and (7). Ultimately, the amount distributed to each partner in a liquidating distribution should equal the partner's capital account as adjusted.

Schedule K-1 (Form 1065) 2015

651113

☐ Final K-1 ☐ Amended K-1   OMB No. 1545-0123

Schedule K-1 (Form 1065)
Department of the Treasury
Internal Revenue Service

For calendar year 2015, or tax
year beginning _____, 2015
ending _____, 20 ___

Partner's Share of Income, Deductions, Credits, etc.   ► See back of form and separate instructions.

Part I   Information About the Partnership

A Partnership's employer identification number

B Partnership's name, address, city, state, and ZIP code

C IRS Center where partnership filed return

D ☐ Check if this is a publicly traded partnership (PTP)

Part II   Information About the Partner

E Partner's identifying number

F Partner's name, address, city, state, and ZIP code

G ☐ General partner or LLC member-manager   ☐ Limited partner or other LLC member

H ☐ Domestic partner   ☐ Foreign partner

I1 What type of entity is this partner? _____
I2 If this partner is a retirement plan (IRA/SEP/Keogh/etc.), check here ☐

J Partner's share of profit, loss, and capital (see instructions):

	Beginning	Ending
Profit	%	%
Loss	%	%
Capital	%	%

K Partner's share of liabilities at year end:
Nonrecourse . . . . . . $ _____
Qualified nonrecourse financing . $ _____
Recourse . . . . $ _____

L Partner's capital account analysis:
Beginning capital account . . . $ _____
Capital contributed during the year $ _____
Current year increase (decrease) . $ _____
Withdrawals & distributions . . $ (_____)
Ending capital account . . . $ _____

☐ Tax basis   ☐ GAAP   ☐ Section 704(b) book
☐ Other (explain)

M Did the partner contribute property with a built-in gain or loss?
☐ Yes   ☐ No
If "Yes," attach statement (see instructions)

Part III   Partner's Share of Current Year Income, Deductions, Credits, and Other Items

1	Ordinary business income (loss)		15	Credits
2	Net rental real estate income (loss)			
3	Other net rental income (loss)		16	Foreign transactions
4	Guaranteed payments			
5	Interest income			
6a	Ordinary dividends			
6b	Qualified dividends			
7	Royalties			
8	Net short-term capital gain (loss)			
9a	Net long-term capital gain (loss)		17	Alternative minimum tax (AMT) items
9b	Collectibles (28%) gain (loss)			
9c	Unrecaptured section 1250 gain			
10	Net section 1231 gain (loss)		18	Tax-exempt income and nondeductible expenses
11	Other income (loss)			
			19	Distributions
12	Section 179 deduction			
13	Other deductions		20	Other information
14	Self-employment earnings (loss)			

*See attached statement for additional information.

For IRS Use Only

For Paperwork Reduction Act Notice, see Instructions for Form 1065.   IRS.gov/form1065   Cat. No. 11394R   Schedule K-1 (Form 1065) 2015

IV. OVERVIEW

Schedule K-1 (Form 1065) 2015 — Page 2

This list identifies the codes used on Schedule K-1 for all partners and provides summarized reporting information for partners who file Form 1040. For detailed reporting and filing information, see the separate Partner's Instructions for Schedule K-1 and the instructions for your income tax return.

1. **Ordinary business income (loss).** Determine whether the income (loss) is passive or nonpassive and enter on your return as follows.

	Report on
Passive loss	See the Partner's Instructions
Passive income	Schedule E, line 28, column (g)
Nonpassive loss	Schedule E, line 28, column (h)
Nonpassive income	Schedule E, line 28, column (j)

2. **Net rental real estate income (loss)** — See the Partner's Instructions
3. **Other net rental income (loss)**
   - Net income — Schedule E, line 28, column (g)
   - Net loss — See the Partner's Instructions
4. **Guaranteed payments** — Schedule E, line 28, column (j)
5. **Interest income** — Form 1040, line 8a
6a. **Ordinary dividends** — Form 1040, line 9a
6b. **Qualified dividends** — Form 1040, line 9b
7. **Royalties** — Schedule E, line 4
8. **Net short-term capital gain (loss)** — Schedule D, line 5
9a. **Net long-term capital gain (loss)** — Schedule D, line 12
9b. **Collectibles (28%) gain (loss)** — 28% Rate Gain Worksheet, line 4 (Schedule D instructions)
9c. **Unrecaptured section 1250 gain** — See the Partner's Instructions
10. **Net section 1231 gain (loss)** — See the Partner's Instructions
11. **Other income (loss)**

Code		Report on
A	Other portfolio income (loss)	See the Partner's Instructions
B	Involuntary conversions	See the Partner's Instructions
C	Sec. 1256 contracts & straddles	Form 6781, line 1
D	Mining exploration costs recapture	See Pub. 535
E	Cancellation of debt	Form 1040, line 21 or Form 982
F	Other income (loss)	See the Partner's Instructions

12. **Section 179 deduction** — See the Partner's Instructions
13. **Other deductions**

Code		Report on
A	Cash contributions (50%)	
B	Cash contributions (30%)	
C	Noncash contributions (50%)	
D	Noncash contributions (30%)	See the Partner's Instructions
E	Capital gain property to a 50% organization (30%)	
F	Capital gain property (20%)	
G	Contributions (100%)	
H	Investment interest expense	Form 4952, line 1
I	Deductions—royalty income	Schedule E, line 19
J	Section 59(e)(2) expenditures	See the Partner's Instructions
K	Deductions—portfolio (2% floor)	Schedule A, line 23
L	Deductions—portfolio (other)	Schedule A, line 28
M	Amounts paid for medical insurance	Schedule A, line 1 or Form 1040, line 29
N	Educational assistance benefits	See the Partner's Instructions
O	Dependent care benefits	Form 2441, line 12
P	Preproductive period expenses	See the Partner's Instructions
Q	Commercial revitalization deduction from rental real estate activities	See Form 8582 instructions
R	Pensions and IRAs	See the Partner's Instructions
S	Reforestation expense deduction	See the Partner's Instructions
T	Domestic production activities information	See Form 8903 instructions
U	Qualified production activities income	Form 8903, line 7b
V	Employer's Form W-2 wages	Form 8903, line 17
W	Other deductions	See the Partner's Instructions

14. **Self-employment earnings (loss)**

    Note: If you have a section 179 deduction or any partner-level deductions, see the Partner's Instructions before completing Schedule SE.

Code		Report on
A	Net earnings (loss) from self-employment	Schedule SE, Section A or B
B	Gross farming or fishing income	See the Partner's Instructions
C	Gross non-farm income	See the Partner's Instructions

15. **Credits**

Code		Report on
A	Low-income housing credit (section 42(j)(5)) from pre-2008 buildings	
B	Low-income housing credit (other) from pre-2008 buildings	
C	Low-income housing credit (section 42(j)(5)) from post-2007 buildings	See the Partner's Instructions
D	Low-income housing credit (other) from post-2007 buildings	
E	Qualified rehabilitation expenditures (rental real estate)	
F	Other rental real estate credits	
G	Other rental credits	
H	Undistributed capital gains credit	Form 1040, line 73; check box a
I	Biofuel producer credit	
J	Work opportunity credit	See the Partner's Instructions
K	Disabled access credit	

Code		Report on
L	Empowerment zone employment credit	
M	Credit for increasing research activities	See the Partner's Instructions
N	Credit for employer social security and Medicare taxes	
O	Backup withholding	
P	Other credits	

16. **Foreign transactions**

Code		Report on
A	Name of country or U.S. possession	
B	Gross income from all sources	Form 1116, Part I
C	Gross income sourced at partner level	

    Foreign gross income sourced at partnership level

D	Passive category	
E	General category	Form 1116, Part I
F	Other	

    Deductions allocated and apportioned at partner level

G	Interest expense	Form 1116, Part I
H	Other	Form 1116, Part I

    Deductions allocated and apportioned at partnership level to foreign source income

I	Passive category	
J	General category	Form 1116, Part I
K	Other	

    Other information

L	Total foreign taxes paid	Form 1116, Part II
M	Total foreign taxes accrued	Form 1116, Part II
N	Reduction in taxes available for credit	Form 1116, line 12
O	Foreign trading gross receipts	Form 8873
P	Extraterritorial income exclusion	Form 8873
Q	Other foreign transactions	See the Partner's Instructions

17. **Alternative minimum tax (AMT) items**

Code		Report on
A	Post-1986 depreciation adjustment	
B	Adjusted gain or loss	See the Partner's Instructions and the Instructions for Form 6251
C	Depletion (other than oil & gas)	
D	Oil, gas, & geothermal—gross income	
E	Oil, gas, & geothermal—deductions	
F	Other AMT items	

18. **Tax-exempt income and nondeductible expenses**

Code		Report on
A	Tax-exempt interest income	Form 1040, line 8b
B	Other tax-exempt income	See the Partner's Instructions
C	Nondeductible expenses	See the Partner's Instructions

19. **Distributions**

Code		Report on
A	Cash and marketable securities	
B	Distribution subject to section 737	See the Partner's Instructions
C	Other property	

20. **Other information**

Code		Report on
A	Investment income	Form 4952, line 4a
B	Investment expenses	Form 4952, line 5
C	Fuel tax credit information	Form 4136
D	Qualified rehabilitation expenditures (other than rental real estate)	See the Partner's Instructions
E	Basis of energy property	See the Partner's Instructions
F	Recapture of low-income housing credit (section 42(j)(5))	Form 8611, line 8
G	Recapture of low-income housing credit (other)	Form 8611, line 8
H	Recapture of investment credit	See Form 4255
I	Recapture of other credits	See the Partner's Instructions
J	Look-back interest—completed long-term contracts	See Form 8697
K	Look-back interest—income forecast method	See Form 8866
L	Dispositions of property with section 179 deductions	
M	Recapture of section 179 deduction	
N	Interest expense for corporate partners	
O	Section 453(l)(3) information	
P	Section 453A(c) information	
Q	Section 1260(b) information	
R	Interest allocable to production expenditures	See the Partner's Instructions
S	CCF nonqualified withdrawals	
T	Depletion information—oil and gas	
U	Reserved	
V	Unrelated business taxable income	
W	Precontribution gain (loss)	
X	Section 108(i) information	
Y	Net investment income	
Z	Other information	

Chapter 8

THE § 704(d) LIMITATION ON THE DEDUCTION OF PASSED-THROUGH LOSSES

I. PROBLEMS

Linda is a one-third partner in the LPS Partnership. All partnership income, gains, losses, and liabilities are shared equally among Linda and her two partners. Assume Linda's outside basis at the beginning of Year 1 is $30,000 and the partnership during its first five years has the following results:

1. In Year 1, LPS has $3,000 in long-term capital gains, $6,000 in long-term capital losses, and a § 702(a)(8) operating loss of $60,000.

2. In Year 2, Linda receives a distribution from LPS of $5,000, and LPS has an § 702(a)(8) operating loss (determined without regard to any Year 1 suspended loss) of $30,000.

3. In Year 3, LPS has § 702(a)(8) operating income (determined without regard to any suspended loss from prior years) of $21,000, and LPS incurs a partnership recourse liability of $15,000.

4. In Year 4, LPS pays the partnership recourse liability, and it has long-term capital gain of $12,000, short-term capital loss of $3,000, § 1231 losses of $18,000, and a § 702(a)(8) operating loss of $24,000. (All losses are determined without regard to any suspended losses from prior years.)

5. On January 1, Year 5, Linda transfers her partnership interest to her daughter Diane as a gift. The partnership in Year 5 has short-term capital gain of $3,000, § 1231 gain of $12,000, and § 702(a)(8) operating income of $15,000.

Explain the extent to which any losses in Years 1–4 are suspended by § 704(d). What are the tax consequences to Diane in Year 5?

Assignment for Chapter 8:

Complete the Problems.

Read: Internal Revenue Code: 704(d).
       Treasury Regulations: § 1.704-1(d). Review § 1.704-1(b)(2)(iv)(b).
       Materials: Overview

II. VOCABULARY

suspended losses or losses held in abeyance
carryover of suspended losses
negative basis
negative capital account

III. OBJECTIVES

1. To apply the ordering rule of Reg. § 1.704-1(d)(2) in determining a partner's adjusted basis for purposes of ascertaining the extent to which the partner's distributive share of loss will be allowed.

2. To determine the character and amount of the loss, if any, suspended by the loss limitation rule of § 704(d).

3. To explain the carryover of suspended losses.

4. To identify ways in which partners can increase their outside bases to avoid the suspension of losses or take advantage of loss carryovers.

5. To explain the treatment of loss carryovers on the sale or other disposition of the partnership interest.

6. To explain the impact of the § 704(d) limitation on a partner's capital account.

7. To recognize that a loss not suspended by § 704(d) may nonetheless be suspended by § 465 or § 469.

IV. OVERVIEW

Section 165(b) provides that, if a taxpayer sustains an uncompensated loss with respect to property, the loss is deductible only to the extent of the taxpayer's adjusted basis in the property.[1] In other words, because the loss deduction is a means of recovering one's unrecovered cost, it is logical that one's adjusted basis (or unrecovered cost) in an asset sets a ceiling for the amount of loss deductible with respect to that asset. Conceptually, were a taxpayer's losses in excess of basis deductible, the taxpayer would have a negative basis — a result abhorred by the Code.

§ 704(d). Limitation on Allowance of Losses

A partner's distributive share of partnership loss (including capital loss) shall be allowed only to the extent of the adjusted basis of such partner's interest in the partnership at the end of the partnership year in which such loss occurred. Any excess of such loss over such basis shall be allowed as a deduction at the end of the partnership year in which such excess is repaid

---

[1] *See* § 166(b), which imposes a comparable limitation with regard to bad debts.

> to the partnership.

Consistent with § 165(b), a partner may only deduct her distributive share of losses to the extent of her outside basis. § 704(d). Section 705(a)(2) works in tandem with § 704(d), providing the decrease in a partner's outside basis as a result of partnership losses cannot reduce that basis "below zero."[2]

Section 704(d) raises at least five questions: (1) How is the adjusted basis of a partner's interest in a partnership determined for purposes of applying § 704(d)? (2) How are losses in excess of outside basis treated and are they ever deductible? (3) If § 704(d) applies to limit the deductibility of a partner's share of losses and that share includes losses of different character, which losses are currently deductible and which are suspended and carried over to a subsequent year? (4) How does the limitation on losses affect, if at all, the adjustments made to a partner's capital account? (5) Does a suspended loss pass to transferees of a partnership interest? Let's consider each of these five questions separately.

A. Determination of Adjusted Outside Basis for Purposes of Applying § 704(d)

Under Reg. § 1.704-1(d)(1), a partner's "distributive share of partnership loss will be allowed only to the extent of the adjusted basis (before reduction by current year's losses) of such partner's interest in the partnership at the end of the partnership taxable year in which such loss occurred." According to Reg. § 1.704-1(d)(2), the adjusted basis of a partner's interest shall be determined by first increasing that basis as required by § 705(a)(1) and then decreasing it as required by § 705(a)(2) "except for losses of the taxable year and losses previously disallowed." In other words, Reg. § 1.704-1(d)(2) is an ordering regulation directing a partner to make all other required adjustments to basis before determining the extent to which a partner's distributive share of losses (including capital losses and § 1231 losses) will be deductible.

> **Example 1:** Marcella is a partner in a calendar-year partnership. At the beginning of 2016, Marcella's outside basis in her partnership interest was $15,000. As a result of partnership operations in 2016, Marcella had the following distributive share of the partnership's tax items:
>
> $1,000 in long-term capital gain (§ 702(a)2));
>
> $3,500 in § 1231 losses (§ 702(a)(3));
>
> $2,000 in charitable contributions to a local museum (§ 702(a)(4));
>
> $10,000 in ordinary business losses (§ 702(a)(8)).
>
> **Analysis:** Applying the ordering rule of Reg. § 1.704-1(d)(2), Marcella would first increase her outside basis to $16,000 by adding her $1,000 distributive share of long-term capital gain as required by § 705(a)(1). She would then decrease her basis to $14,000 by subtracting her $2,000

---

[2] At the end of this Overview, we address the § 465 "at risk" rules and the § 469 "passive activity loss" rules and discuss the interaction of § 704(d) with these loss deduction limitation rules.

distributive share of the charitable contribution. Under § 704(d), the resulting $14,000 outside basis represents the ceiling on the partnership losses Marcella can deduct in 2016. Because those losses amount to only $13,500 (i.e., $10,000 in ordinary business losses and $3,500 in § 1231 losses), Marcella is allowed to deduct her entire distributive share of the partnership's losses. As a result, Marcella's outside basis at the end of 2016 will be $500 (i.e., $14,000 less $13,500). § 705(a)(2).

B. Treatment of Losses in Excess of the § 704(d) Limitation

If a partner's distributive share of partnership losses exceeds the § 704(d) loss ceiling, the excess losses are not deductible currently but are held in abeyance (suspended) and are carried forward indefinitely until a partner has sufficient outside basis to use the losses.[3] Consider the following example:

Example 2: Assume the facts of Example 1 except that Marcella's distributive share of § 1231 losses in 2016 is $5,000 instead of $3,500. As a result, Marcella's distributive share of losses totals $15,000 and exceeds her $14,000 loss ceiling by $1,000. Thus, § 704(d) would disallow $1,000 of Marcella's losses, requiring that amount of loss to be held in abeyance and deducted only when and to the extent Marcella's outside basis increased to an amount greater than zero.[4] For example, if during 2017, Marcella's distributive share of the taxable income generated by the partnership were $5,000, Marcella's outside basis would be increased from $0 to $5,000 thus enabling her to deduct the $1,000 of suspended losses held in abeyance. § 705(a)(1)(A) and Reg. § 1.704-1(d)(2). In turn, Marcella's outside basis at the end of 2017 would be $4,000, i.e., the basis would be adjusted upward to reflect her $5,000 share of LLC taxable income (§ 705(a)(1)(A)) and would be adjusted downward to reflect the carryover loss of $1,000 (§ 705(a)(2)). Reg. § 1.704-1(d)(4) Ex. 1 applies the § 704(d) loss limitation and should be read with care.

Apart from increasing her outside basis as a result of income subsequently generated by the partnership, Marcella could also increase her outside basis and thereby be entitled to use the suspended losses if she made an additional contribution to the partnership.[5] In addition, Marcella's outside basis could be increased as a result of a new liability incurred by the partnership, e.g., the partnership could borrow money on either a recourse or nonrecourse basis. But see the Note on the At-Risk Rules and the Passive Activity Loss Rules, *infra*. As discussed in Chapter 3, Marcella's share of that liability, as determined under § 752, would be treated as an additional contribution to the partnership, thus resulting in an increased outside basis. §§ 752(a) and 722. Study Reg. § 1.704-1(d)(4) Ex. 2.

---

[3] Accordingly, on an annual basis, a taxpayer's outside basis must be adjusted to reflect the operation of the partnership for that year.

[4] Note that § 704(d) provides that any excess losses "shall be allowed as a deduction at the end of the partnership year in which such excess is *repaid to the partnership*." [Emphasis added.]

[5] An additional contribution to capital may create problems in terms of the economic sharing arrangement of the partners unless all partners make additional contributions proportional to their interest in the entity.

C. Allocation of Loss Limitation among Losses of Different Character

In Example 2, which losses are suspended? $1,000 of the § 1231 loss? $1,000 of the ordinary business losses? Some combination of the two types of losses? May Marcella decide which losses are suspended? The answer to the last question is "No." A partner is not allowed to choose which losses to deduct currently and which losses to hold in abeyance. Rather the regulations provide for the allocation of the § 704(d) loss limitation. Consider the following excerpt from Reg. § 1.704-1(d)(2):

Reg. § 1.704-1(d)(2)

. . . If the partner's distributive share of the aggregate of items of loss specified in section 702(a)(1, (2), (3) [(7) and (8)] exceeds the basis of the partner's interest computed under the preceding sentence, the limitation on losses under section 704(d) must be allocated to his distributive share of each such loss. This allocation shall be determined by taking the proportion that each loss bears to the total of all such losses. For purposes of the preceding sentence, the total losses for the taxable year shall be the sum of his distributive share of losses for the current year and his losses disallowed and carried forward from prior years.

Applying this regulation to Example 2, Marcella's $5,000 distributive share of the partnership's § 1231 losses represents one-third of her total share of losses. As a result, pursuant to the regulation, one-third of her losses suspended under § 704(d) (i.e., $1,000 of losses) or $333 of the suspended losses are § 1231 losses. Marcella may therefore only deduct $4,667 of the $5,000 of § 1231 losses in 2016. Marcella's ordinary business losses represent 2/3 ($10,000/$15,000) of Marcella's total distributive share of partnership losses. Therefore, 2/3 of the $1,000 of suspended losses or $667 of those losses are ordinary losses. Marcella will thus be allowed to deduct $9,333 of her share of ordinary business losses in 2016. Reg. § 1.704-1(d)(4). Ex. 3 uses a slightly different approach that provides the same result: Without regard to her distributive share of losses, Marcella's outside basis at the end of 2016 is $14,000. Her total distributive share of losses is $15,000. Therefore, $14,000/$15,000 (14/15) of her $10,000 share of ordinary losses or $9,333 is allowed in 2016; 14/15 of her $5,000 share of § 1231 losses or $4,667 is allowed in 2016.

D. Impact of § 704(d) on Capital Accounts

A partner's distributive share of partnership losses reduces the partner's capital account even though § 704(d) prevents the partner from deducting all or part of the losses currently. Furthermore, while § 705 and § 704(d) combine to prevent a negative outside basis, *a capital account can be negative!*[6] Consider again the purpose of capital accounts, i.e., to provide a yardstick measuring the economic

---

[6] The significance of negative capital accounts will be discussed in Chapter 9.

value (using book values) of a partner's interest in a partnership. To the extent a partnership incurs losses, it is only appropriate that each partner's capital accounts be decreased to reflect that partner's distributive share of the losses. Return to Example 2 above, where Marcella's share of § 1231 losses was $5,000 and, as a result, $1,000 of Marcella's losses were held in abeyance. If we assume Marcella's capital account at the beginning of 2016 was $15,000, her capital account at the end of 2016 would be computed as follows:

Capital Account beginning of 2016:	$15,000	
Increased by:		
Long-term capital gain	$1,000	Reg. § 1.704-1(b)(2)(iv)(b)(3)
Decreased by:		
§ 1231 capital loss	($5,000)	Reg. § 1.704-1(b)(2)(iv)(b)(7)
ordinary business loss	($10,000)	Reg. § 1.704-1(b)(2)(iv)(b)(7)
charitable contributions	($2,000)	Reg. § 1.704-1(b)(2)(iv)(b)(6)
Capital Account at the end of 2016:	**($1,000)**	

Note Marcella's capital account at the end of 2016 is negative. Although Marcella's distributive share of losses exceeded her outside basis, that basis could not be decreased below zero. § 705(a)(2). By contrast, her capital account can be decreased below zero and, given the facts of Example 2, would be.

E. Who Benefits from the Carryover of a Disallowed Loss?

As illustrated in the discussion of Example 2, when § 704(d) suspends a passed-through loss, the partner is entitled to utilize the suspended loss in a future year to the extent she then has a positive outside basis. What if, before taking advantage of the suspended loss, the partner disposes of her partnership interest by sale, gift, or otherwise? Does the suspended loss pass to the purchaser, donee, or other transferee? Consider the following examples:

Example 3: Assume the facts of Example 2 where $1,000 of Marcella's distributive share of losses was held in abeyance pursuant to § 704(d). Assume Marcella sold her partnership interest to her son, Sean, on January 1, 2017 for $50,000.[7] (Note that, pursuant to § 1012, Sean's basis in the partnership interest would be $50,000.) Would Marcella's $1,000 in losses that were held in abeyance pass to Sean, enabling him to deduct all $1,000 in 2017?[8] The assignment of income doctrine generally prohibits taxpayers from shifting income, gain, or loss to another taxpayer. Consis-

---

[7] You might question how Marcella's partnership interest could have a $50,000 fair market value considering she has a negative capital account. Recall that capital accounts represent book value. Thus, for example, the partnership's assets may have appreciated in value over time; that appreciation, however, will not be reflected in the partners' capital accounts until it is realized, e.g., through a sale of an appreciated asset, or until capital accounts are revalued. See Reg. § 1.704-1(b)(2)(iv)(f).

[8] Note that, if Marcella sold her partnership interest later in 2017, Marcella would be allocated a share of the partnership's income, gain, loss, or deduction for the portion of the year prior to the sale to Sean. § 706(c) and (d). Any income allocated to Marcella for 2017 would increase her outside basis and thus allow her to deduct some or all of the loss held in abeyance. Any loss held in abeyance that Marcella is unable to deduct in the year of transfer is lost as she will no longer be a partner and thus cannot benefit

tent with this doctrine, Marcella should not be allowed to shift to Sean any loss that was attributable to a period during which she was a partner. The loss belongs to her alone. See *Meinerz v. Commissioner*, T.C. Memo 1983-191.

Example 4: Assume the facts of Example 3 except, instead of selling her partnership interest to Sean, she transferred it to him as a gift on January 1, 2017. Would the $1,000 loss held in abeyance transfer to Sean? Under § 1015, Sean would have a transferred basis (§ 7701(a)(43)) of zero in the partnership interest (worth $50,000) and would tack Marcella's holding period to his own (§ 1223(2)). Sean would also succeed to Marcella's capital account, and, as we will discuss in Chapter 10, would be attributed under § 704(c)(1)(A) any built-in gain or loss attributable to Marcella.[9] In other words, Sean, as the donee, would step into Marcella's shoes. One might argue that § 1015 does not permit the shifting of a donor's accrued loss to a donee and that, therefore, Marcella can't shift the suspended loss to Sean. The counter argument, of course, is that a loss held in abeyance under § 704(d) is different from the loss-shifting barred by § 1015. As a technical matter, the § 1015 bar on loss-shifting is implicated when the fair market value of the gift is less than the donor's adjusted basis. But, by definition, when the donor of a partnership interest has suspended losses, the donor's adjusted basis is zero — that is, the fair market value of the interest exceeds the basis, the reverse of the barred loss-shifting under § 1015. Moreover, as a policy matter, § 1015 permits the donee to take advantage of the donor's accrued, but unrealized, loss to reduce the realization and recognition of gain that accrues during the donee's ownership of the property — in other words, if the property appreciates (becomes "profitable") during the donee's ownership, the donee's gain on disposition is measured by the donor's basis — i.e., the donee makes use of the donor's accrued loss to reduce gain accruing to the donee. Conceptually, the same thing is happening here: the donee of the partnership interest is not claiming a loss; the donee is instead using the donor's suspended loss to reduce the donee's income if the partnership turns profitable. While there is no authority on this point, your authors' position is that the suspended loss should be available to Sean when he has sufficient basis to use it.

The inter-vivos gift analysis above, however, does not apply to a transfer of a partnership interest by devise or inheritance.

Example 5: Assume the facts of Example 4 except that Marcella dies on January 1, 2017, and devises her partnership interest (worth $50,000) to Sean. Will the $1,000 loss held in abeyance transfer to Sean? Unlike the inter-vivos gift situation presented in Example 4 where Sean has a zero basis in the partnership interest under § 1015, Sean in this example would have a § 1014 basis (fair market value at date of Marcella's death) of $50,000 in the interest. No tacking of the holding period would be allowed under

---

from the carryover rule of § 704(d) and Reg. § 1.704-1(b)(1). See *Sennell v. Com.*, 752 F.2d 428 (1985). We will discuss the sale of a partnership interest in Chapter 20.

[9] Sean, in effect, will have the same share of the partnership's inside basis that Marcella had.

§ 1223(2) because Sean does not take Marcella's basis in the interest.[10] Furthermore, as will be discussed in Chapter 20, Sean will have the possibility of a special inside basis with respect to the partnership assets. § 743(b). Again, no authority addresses the precise question raised here. Given the significant difference, however, between the position of a donee and a devisee or heir, we believe the losses held in abeyance under § 704(d) should be terminated at death much as an individual's capital loss carry-overs under § 1212 are terminated at death and do not pass to the individual's heirs or devisees.[11]

---

[10] See, however, § 1223(9), which essentially ensures Sean a long-term holding period.

[11] Rev. Rul. 74-175, 1974-1 C.B. 52. *See also*, Sennett v. Commissioner, 80 T.C. 825 (1983), *aff'd per curiam*, 752 F.2d 428 (9th Cir. 1985).

NOTE ON THE AT-RISK RULES AND THE PASSIVE ACTIVITY LOSS RULES

This Note discusses two additional limitations on the deduction of a partner's losses: the at risk rules of § 465 and the passive activity loss rules of § 469. The § 465 and § 469 limitations are applied — in that order — only to losses not otherwise suspended by § 704(d). See Reg. § 1.469-2T(d)(6).

The At-Risk Rules. The at risk rules, while quite complicated in their detail, essentially prohibit a partner from deducting losses from business and other income-producing activities to the extent those losses exceed the partner's aggregate amount "at risk" — the amount the partner could actually lose — in that activity. § 465(a)(1). The at-risk limitation applies to individuals (as well as to closely held Subchapter C corporations), and thus must be determined and applied at the partner level, rather than the partnership level, based on the partner's amount at risk. § 465(a)(1)(A). For § 465 purposes, a loss is the excess of deductions attributable to an activity over the income from the activity. § 465(d). A loss in an activity that is disallowed by § 465 is carried over to the next year as a deduction allowable to that activity. Assume, for example, that Lisa is a partner in a calendar-year partnership. Assume in Year 1, Lisa's outside basis is zero and her share of partnership losses (i.e., her share of the excess of partnership deductions over partnership income) for that year is $2,000. As discussed in this chapter, § 704(d) would, in effect, disallow the deduction of the $2,000 loss in Year 1. Instead, the deduction would be carried over to Year 2. Because the loss of $2,000 in Year 1 was barred by § 704(d), there would not be an allowable loss for § 465 to disallow, and the at-risk rules would not be applied. Suppose, however, Lisa's outside basis in Year 1 is $5,000. Now the $2,000 loss is not disallowed by § 704(d), and it would be necessary to determine if Lisa's Year 1 amount at risk is at least $2,000.

As previously noted, the § 704(d) rule limiting partnership losses to outside basis is consistent with the principle that a taxpayer's basis in property generally limits the deductions allowable with respect to that property. § 165(b). But because the cost basis of acquired property includes that part of the purchase price financed by nonrecourse debt, a taxpayer's basis may represent borrowing with respect to which the taxpayer has no personal liability. As a result, nonrecourse financing of investments made it attractive for taxpayers to invest in activities that were economically unsound but offered tax deferral opportunities through the nonrecourse financing. The at risk rules of § 465 were enacted to limit the ability of taxpayers — particularly through limited partnerships — to claim the "artificial" deductions that nonrecourse financing made possible. According to the legislative history of § 465, "it was not equitable to allow individual investors to defer tax on income from other sources through losses generated by tax sheltering activities. One of the most significant problems in tax shelters was the use of nonrecourse financing and other risk-limiting devices which enabled investors in those activities to deduct losses from the activities in amounts which exceeded the total investment the investor actually placed at risk in the activity. The Act consequently provides an 'at risk' rule to deal directly with this abuse in tax shelters." Staff of the Joint Committee on Taxation, *General Explanation of the Tax Reform Act of 1976*, 94th Cong. 2d Sess., 1976-3 vol. 2 C.B. 47.

Generally, a partner's initial amount at risk in an activity is the total of the partner's cash contributions to the activity, the adjusted basis of property the partner contributed to the activity, and the portion of amounts borrowed for use in the activity for which the partner has ultimate personal liability. § 465(b). To the extent a partner is protected against loss by nonrecourse financing, stop loss agreements, or similar arrangements, the partner is not considered at risk. § 465(b)(4). Under a special exception applicable only to the activity of holding real property, however, a partner's share of "qualified nonrecourse financing" is taken into account in computing the partner's amount at risk. As the name suggests, qualified nonrecourse financing involves an amount borrowed with respect to which no one is personally liable for repayment. It constitutes qualified nonrecourse financing if the borrowing is with respect to the activity of holding real property, and if the amount is borrowed from a governmental agency (or is government-guaranteed) or from a "qualified person" — generally, someone regularly engaged in lending money, but not the seller or someone who receives a fee from the partner's investment in the property. § 465(b)(6)(B), (D). A partner's share of any qualified nonrecourse financing of the partnership is determined on the basis of the partner's share of such liabilities under § 752. § 465(b)(6)(C).

A partner's initial amount at risk in an activity is adjusted for the partner's share of income and losses from the activity and for withdrawals from the activity. For example, assume Lisa has contributed cash of $2,000 to a partnership; her share of recourse liabilities of the partnership is $3,000; and her share of partnership qualified nonrecourse financing is $5,000. Her initial amount at risk is thus $10,000. (Note that Lisa's outside basis would also be $10,000.) If Lisa's share of partnership losses in Year 1 is $2,000 and if she is distributed $1,000 from the partnership, her amount at risk is reduced by $3,000 down to $7,000 entering Year 2. (Her outside basis would also be reduced to $7,000.)

Suppose in Year 2 Lisa's amount at risk (and her outside basis) are further reduced to $1,000 when the partnership distributes $6,000 to her. If Lisa's share of partnership losses in Year 2 is $2,500, only $1,000 of the losses are allowed, reducing Lisa's amount at risk to zero. The remaining $1,500 of loss is suspended and carried forward indefinitely until Lisa's amount at risk increases to the point that the suspended loss becomes allowable. § 465(a)(2). (Note that § 704(d) would allow Lisa to deduct only $1,000 of the Year 2 losses and would suspend the remaining $1,500 of losses.)

Generally, losses suspended under § 465 will also be allowable when an activity or an interest in an activity is transferred or otherwise disposed of. Gain, if any, recognized on the transfer or other disposition will be taxed as income from the activity, giving rise to an increase in the amount at risk and, in effect, generally enabling the deduction of losses suspended under § 465. See Prop. Reg. § 1.465-66. By way of an example based in part on Prop. Reg. § 1.465-66, assume, at the beginning of Year 5, Lisa's outside basis and at risk amount were both zero. Early in Year 5 the partnership incurs a nonrecourse liability. Because Lisa's share of the nonrecourse liability is $10,000, her outside basis increases to $10,000. Lisa's at risk amount, however, remains zero because the liability does not constitute qualified nonrecourse financing. Assume the partnership realizes a substantial operating loss in Year 5 and Lisa's distributive share of that loss is $7,000. Because Lisa's outside basis exceeds her distributive share of the loss, § 704(d) will not suspend any of the loss and Lisa's outside basis will be reduced to $3,000. Lisa's at risk amount, however, is zero and therefore, pursuant to § 465, all $7,000 of the loss is suspended. On January 1, Year 6, Lisa sells her partnership interest for $11,000. The purchaser pays Lisa $1,000 in cash and takes her interest subject to her $10,000 share of the nonrecourse debt. Lisa's gain on the sale is $8,000 ($11,000 amount realized, less basis of $3,000), and the gain is treated as income from the activity. Assuming Lisa's only deductions from the partnership for Year 6 are the $7,000 carried over from Year 5, there is no Year 6 partnership loss because Year 6 income ($8,000) exceeds Year 6 deductions ($7,000). The $7,000 in deductions are thus allowed in Year 6. Prop. Reg. § 1.465-66(b).

The Passive Activity Loss Rules. Although § 465 restricted the losses a partner could deduct to the amount the partner had at risk in an activity, it did not address the matter of when deductions generated by one activity — albeit deductions with respect to which the partner was at risk — could be used to offset income from other sources. The opportunity continued to exist to offset income from sources such as wages, dividends, and interest with deductions from other activities, including tax shelter activities. The congressional response in 1986 was the enactment of the anti-tax shelter legislation of § 469.

Section 469 essentially requires partners and other covered taxpayers (individuals, estates, trusts, closely held Subchapter C corporations, and personal service corporations) to classify their income, losses, and credits as being generated by "passive activities" or 'nonpassive activities." Passive activity deductions may only offset income from passive activities. § 469(a)(1)(A). Passive activity losses that cannot be used currently under § 469 are carried forward to the next year and treated as passive activity deductions in that year. § 469(b). There is no limit to the carryover of passive activity losses. Generally, suspended losses are allowed in full when the partner disposes of the interest in the passive activity in a taxable transaction. § 469(g)(1).

A passive activity is, in general, any trade or business or rental activity in which the partner does not materially participate. § 469(c)(1), (2). To be material, a partner's participation in the activity must be regular, continuous, and substantial. § 469(h)(1). The temporary regulations under § 469 provide seven alternative ways to satisfy this test: (1) material participation based on participation in the activity in excess of 500 hours during the year; (2) material participation based on participation that constitutes "substantially all" of the participation in the activity; (3) material participation based on participation in excess of 100 hours, where that participation is not less than any other individual's participation; (4) material participation in the current year through material participation in five of the past ten years; (5) material participation in a personal service activity (trades or businesses such as law in which capital is not a material income-producing factor) in the current year based upon material participation in any three prior years; (6) participation in a significant participation activity (that is, a trade or business where the individual participates for more than 100 hours, but not enough to otherwise achieve material participation) and aggregate participation in all significant participation activities exceeds 500 hours; and (7) material participation based on all the facts and circumstances. Temp. Reg. § 1.469-5T(a).

Limited partners are subject to special rules: generally, a limited partner does not materially participate with respect to the limited partnership interest. § 469(h)(2). The temporary regulations provide, however, that a limited partner can materially participate by satisfying one of three material participation tests: the 500-hour test; the five-years-out-of-ten test; or the personal service activity test. Temp. Reg. § 1.469-5T(e)(2). An interest in a limited liability company, however, is not an interest in a limited partnership as a limited partner. *Newell v. Commissioner*, T.C. Memo. 2010-23; *Garnett v. Commissioner*, 132 T.C. 368 (2009). Proposed regulations eliminate the current regulation's focus on limited liability for purposes of determining limited partner status and focus instead on the right to participate in management of the activity. Prop. Reg. § 1.469-5(a)(3).

Although, as noted previously, rental activities are generally passive activities under § 469(c)(2), certain real estate rental activities will not be considered per se passive activities if the taxpayer performs more than 750 hours of service during the year in real property trades or businesses in which she materially participates and those hours are more than half of the personal services the taxpayer performs in all trades or businesses in which she materially participates. § 469(c)(7). (In addition, there is a limited exception of up to $25,000 from § 469 limitations for individuals engaged in rental real estate activity whose adjusted gross income does not exceed $150,000. § 469(i).)

Because material participation is determined activity by activity, defining the scope of an activity is critical; regulations under § 469 provide a facts and circumstances test for determining what constitutes an activity and the scope of a given activity. Reg. § 1.469-4.

The operation of § 469 requires a taxpayer to compute gains and losses from each passive activity, first offsetting losses from an activity against the gains from the activity, then offsetting losses against excess gains from other passive activities, with the result that all losses from passive activities can be deducted from all gains from passive activities. Any excess loss is the "passive activity loss" that cannot be currently deducted but is instead carried forward to be applied against gains from passive activities in future years. The disallowed loss must be apportioned among the various passive activities in which a loss was realized during the year.

A special rule in § 469(e)(1) excludes portfolio income — for example, dividends, interest and royalties — from classification as a passive activity. Thus, portfolio income cannot be used to offset losses from passive activities.

The passive activity loss limitation is applied only after § 704(d) and the at risk rules of § 465. Thus, if a partner's outside basis is zero, the partner's distributive share of losses, if any, for the year will be suspended by § 704(d). Neither § 465 nor § 469 is applied to the already-disallowed loss. If the partner has sufficient outside basis to absorb a loss, but the partner's at risk amount is zero, the partner's outside basis will be reduced by the amount of the loss, but the loss will be suspended by § 465. (See the above example.) In this case, the passive activity loss rules of § 469 are not applied. Section 469 will be applied only to that part of the loss not disallowed by either § 704(d) or § 465.

Assume, for example, that Lisa is a limited partner in a partnership and that her distributive share of losses in Year 1 is $5,000. If she does not satisfy one of the material participation tests for limited partners, her activity in the limited partnership will be a passive activity. Assume Lisa is also a limited partner in a second partnership, and that her share of losses in Year 1 from that partnership is $10,000. Again, if Lisa does not satisfy a material participation test for limited partners, this will also be a passive activity. Assume her outside basis and amount at risk are sufficient with respect to each partnership to absorb the losses. Finally, assume that Lisa's Year 1 portfolio income is $20,000 and that her income from a law practice is $100,000. If Lisa materially participates only in the law practice and not in either of the two partnerships, her passive activity loss will be $15,000. This loss cannot be applied against either her portfolio income or her law practice income, but will instead be carried forward to Year 2, with $5,000 allocated to her interest in the first partnership and $10,000 allocated to her interest in the second partnership. Thus, deductibility in Year 2 will turn on whether Lisa generates sufficient passive activity income to absorb these carried forward losses. If, for example, Lisa's share of Year 2 income of the first partnership — still a passive activity, one assumes — is $20,000, the suspended losses from Year 1 will be fully absorbed and there will be no passive activity loss for Year 2.

When a partner (or other covered taxpayer) disposes of her entire interest in a passive activity in a fully taxable disposition to an unrelated party, any suspended losses, as well as any loss realized on the disposition, are no longer treated as passive activity losses and become deductible as set forth in § 469(g)(1). This rule docs not apply to transfer by gift (§ 469(j)(6)) or to transfers at death (§ 469(g)(2)).

Chapter 9

ALLOCATION OF PARTNERSHIP INCOME AND DEDUCTIONS: § 704(b)

I. PROBLEMS

1. At the beginning of Year 1, Anne and Bob each contribute $750,000 to form a general partnership to engage in the apartment rental business. The partnership uses the cash to purchase an apartment building on leased land for $1,500,000. Assume the building is depreciable at the rate of $100,000 per year over 15 years. (Disregard all conventions.) The partnership agreement provides that all partnership income, gain, loss, and deductions will be shared equally, except that all depreciation deductions will be allocated entirely to Bob. The partnership agreement also provides that: (1) capital accounts will be maintained consistent with Reg. § 1.704-1(b)(2)(iv); (2) liquidating distributions will be made in accordance with positive capital account balances; and (3) each partner will have an unconditional obligation to restore a capital account deficit consistent with Reg. § 1.704-1(b)(2)(ii)(b)(3). Assume partnership income and expenses are equal each year, except for the $100,000 depreciation deduction. The partnership thus has a $100,000 loss each year, all of which is allocated to Bob because of the special allocation noted above.

   (a) Given the partnership agreement and assuming the special allocation of the depreciation deductions satisfies the "substantiality test" of Reg. § 1.704-1(b)(2)(iii):

      (i) What will the partnership's balance sheet (including the partners' outside bases and capital accounts) be at the end of Year 2? At the end of Year 8? At the end of Year 15?

      (ii) What will the partnership's balance sheet (including the partners' outside bases and capital accounts) be if the apartment building is sold for: (i) $1,200,000 at the end of Year 2; or (ii) $700,000 at the end of Year 8; or (iii) $1,500,000 at the end of Year 15? What are the consequences to the partners if the partnership liquidates at the end of each of those years?

   (b) How would your answers to (a)(2) change, if at all, if the partnership contained a so-called "gain chargeback" provision whereby Bob would be allocated any gain recognized on the sale of the apartment building to the extent of the depreciation deductions that had been allocated to him?

2. Assume the facts of Problem 1, except the partnership agreement contains no provision requiring any partner to restore a capital account deficit on liquidation of the partnership. How will the depreciation deductions with respect to the apartment building be allocated?

3. Assume the facts of Problem 2. In addition, assume the partnership agreement contains no provision requiring liquidating distributions to be made in accordance with positive capital account balances. How will the depreciation deductions with respect to the apartment building be allocated?

4. Assume the facts of Problem 1, except that the partnership is a limited partnership, and Bob is the limited partner and thus has no obligation to restore a capital account deficit. Assume the partnership has a "qualified income offset" and satisfies the "alternative test for economic effect" under Reg. § 1.704-1(b)(2)(ii)(d). How will the depreciation deductions with respect to the apartment building be allocated?

5. In Year 1, Don and Ellen each contributed $250,000 to create the DE Partnership, a general partnership. Don and Ellen each has a 50% interest in all items of partnership income and deduction, except as noted below. Assume Don is in the 10% income tax bracket and Ellen is in the 50% income tax bracket. The partnership agreement, consistent with the requirements of the economic effect test of Reg. § 1.704-1(b)(2)(ii)(b), provides that capital accounts will be properly maintained, with liquidating distributions made in accordance with positive capital account balances, and with each partner having an unconditional obligation to restore a capital account deficit. In Year 1, the partnership invests in taxable corporate bonds and tax-exempt municipal bonds. The partnership agreement provides that, for the Year 1 only, the first $50,000 of interest on corporate bonds will be allocated to Don; interest in excess of $50,000 on corporate bonds will be shared equally. The agreement further provides that, for Year 1 only, the first $50,000 of interest on municipal bonds will be allocated to Ellen; interest in excess of $50,000 on municipal bonds will be shared equally.

    (a) Assume the partnership expects to earn and actually does earn in Year 1 $50,000 in interest on both the corporate bonds and the municipal bonds. Do the allocations have substantial economic effect?

    (b) Alternatively, assume the partnership expects to earn and actually does earn in Year 1 $50,000 in interest on the corporate bonds and $30,000 in interest on the municipal bonds. Do the allocations have substantial economic effect?

    (c) Does the answer to (b) change if Don is in the 45% income tax bracket and Ellen is in the 50% income tax bracket?

    (d) If the allocations do not have substantial economic effect, how will the interest on the corporate bonds and the municipal bonds be allocated?

6. Assume the facts of Problem 5, except that the DE Partnership, instead of purchasing corporate and municipal bonds, purchases depreciable machinery for $500,000 for use in its business. Assume the machinery is

depreciable over five years at the rate of $100,000 per year, and that, there is a strong likelihood the partnership will have a net loss of $100,000 per year for Years 1 through 3, will break even for Years 4 through 6, and will generate net taxable income at the rate of $75,000 per year for Years 7 through 10. Assume that is precisely what occurred.

The partnership agreement provides that partnership net loss will be allocated 100% to Ellen until there is partnership net income. Partnership net income will then be allocated 100% to Ellen until Ellen has been allocated net income equal to the net loss previously allocated to her. Thereafter, net income and net loss will be allocated equally to Don and Ellen.

(a) Will the special allocations of partnership net income and loss in Years 1 through 3 be treated as "transitory" and thus without substantial economic effect under Reg. § 1.704–1(b)(2)(iii)(c)?

(b) Does the answer to (a) change if partnership net income of $75,000 per year was expected to begin in Year 4?

(c) Assume the partnership agreement also provides that any gain upon the sale of the machinery will be allocated to Ellen to the extent of prior allocations of net loss not offset by allocations of net income. Throughout the years in which partnership net losses were sustained, it was expected there would be sufficient gain, if the machinery were sold, to offset fully the prior net losses. Do the allocations of net loss have substantial economic effect?

Assignments for Chapter 9:

Complete the Problems

Read: Internal Revenue Code: §§ 704(b) and 704(c)(1)(A).
Treasury Regulations: §§ 1.704-1(b)(2)(ii)(a), (b), (c), (d), (g), and (i); 1.704-1(b)(2)(iii)(a), (b), (c); 1.704-1(b)(2)(iv)(b); 1.704-1(b)(2)(iv)(d)(2); 1.704-1(b)(2)(iv)(g)(3); 1.704-1(b)(3)(i), (ii), (iii); 1.704-1(b)(5) Exs. 1–7.

   Materials: Overview
   Orrisch v. Commissioner
   Revenue Ruling 99-43

II. VOCABULARY

special allocation
substantial economic effect
primary test for economic effect
alternative test for economic effect
economic equivalence test ("dumb but lucky" rule)
partner's interest in the partnership test
tax follows book
capital account maintenance rules
capital account deficit
qualified income offset provision

substantiality test
shifting allocations
transitory allocations
after-tax economic consequences
tax profiles of the partners
the "five-year safe harbor"
the "fair market value equals basis" rule
gain chargeback provision
"bottom line" or § 702(a)(8) income or loss

III. OBJECTIVES

1. To recall that capital accounts must be increased by tax allocations of partnership income and gain and decreased by tax allocations of partnership losses and deductions.

2. To apply the requirements of the primary test for economic effect.

3. To apply the requirements of the alternative test for economic effect.

4. To apply the requirements of the economic equivalence test.

5. To apply the general rule for substantiality of economic effect.

6. To recall and define three types of insubstantial allocations: shifting allocations, transitory allocations, and allocations with insubstantial after-tax economic consequences.

7. To recall the safe harbors of the "five-year rule" and the "fair market value equals adjusted basis rule."

8. To identify factors considered in applying the partner's-interest-in-the-partnership test.

IV. OVERVIEW

As discussed in Chapter 7, partnerships are not taxable entities but, rather, the various tax items of a partnership, e.g., income and deductions, are passed through the partnership to the partners for tax reporting purposes. In this regard, § 702(a) specifically requires partners *in determining their income tax* to take into account their "distributive shares"[1] of the partnership's income, gain, loss, deductions, and credits, including so-called "bottom line" income and loss (see § 702(a)(8).[2] Section 704(a), enacted by Congress in 1954, provides that a partner's "distributive share" of these tax items will generally be determined by the *partnership agreement*. Since its inception, Subchapter K has thus provided partners considerable latitude in determining how the partnership's tax items for a given taxable year will be

---

[1] As noted in Chapter 7, the term "distributive share" does not refer to anything actually distributed to a partner, but rather to the share of the partnership's tax items that each partner must report for income tax purposes.

[2] *See* § 61(a)(13), which defines gross income as including the taxpayer's "distributive share of partnership gross income."

allocated between or among the partners.[3] The latitude accorded partners served to accommodate the wide variety of arrangements made by partners with regard to the division of a partnership's economic profits and losses. As will be discussed in Chapter 10, however, Congress enacted § 704(c)(1)(A) imposing special rules for the allocation of income, gain, loss, and deductions with respect to contributed property that has "built-in" gain or loss (so-called "§ 704(c) property").[4]

A. Pre-1976 History

In granting partnerships flexibility with regard to the allocation of partnership tax items, however, Congress intended the allocation of those items (and thus the determination of a partner's distributive share) to parallel the economic arrangements adopted by the partners in their partnership agreement. Congress was clearly aware of the abuses, e.g., inappropriate shifting of gains or losses, that might otherwise result. As noted in the legislative history to the 1954 Act, Congress limited § 704(a) by enacting *former* § 704(b),[5] which in essence provided that:

> [I]f the principal purpose of any provision in the partnership agreement dealing with a partner's distributive share of a particular item is to avoid or evade the Federal income tax, the partner's distributive share of that item shall be redetermined [in accordance with the partner's interest in the partnership.] For example, if the provisions of a partnership agreement allocate all partnership loss on the sale of depreciable property used in trade or business to one partner. . . . such [provision] may be disregarded if the principal purpose is tax avoidance or evasion.

The 1954 legislative history notes, however, that

> [W]here . . . a provision in a partnership agreement for a special allocation of certain items has *substantial economic effect* and is not merely a device for reducing the taxes of certain partners without actually

---

[3] Section 761(c) defines "partnership agreement" to include the original agreement and "any modifications of the partnership agreement made prior to, or at, the time prescribed by law for the filing of the partnership return for the taxable year . . . " Partnership agreements can be oral or in writing. Reg. § 1.761-1(c). Given the definition of "partnership agreement," it would be possible for partners to agree upon a different allocation of partnership tax items each year.

[4] Regulation § 1.704-1(b)(2)(iv)(d)(3) specifically provides that § 704(c) and Reg. § 1.704-3 "govern the determination of a partner's distributive share of income, gain, loss, and deduction, as computed for tax purposes, with respect to property contributed to a partnership."

[5] As enacted in 1954, Section 704(b) provided:

(b) Distributive share determined by income or loss ratio.

A partner's distributive share of any item of income, gain, loss, deduction, or credit shall be determined in accordance with his distributive share of taxable income or loss of the partnership, as described in *section 702(a)(9)*, for the taxable year, if —

(1) the partnership agreement does not provide as to the partner's distributive share of such item, or

(2) the principal purpose of any provision in the partnership agreement with respect to the partner's distributive share of such item is the avoidance or evasion of any tax imposed by this subtitle.

affecting their share of partnership income, then such a provision will be recognized for tax purposes.[6]

The regulations interpreting the tax avoidance limitation of former § 704(b) specifically identified "substantial economic effect" as a key factor in determining whether a special allocation of a tax item in a partnership agreement would be respected.[7] For example, assume a partnership with two equal partners — Partner A and Partner B — had $100,000 of ordinary income for the year and no expenses. The partnership's economic profit for the year likewise totaled $100,000. Assume also that Partner A had a $100,000 net operating loss carryforward scheduled to expire that same year. Were the partnership agreement to be amended to allocate all of $100,000 of the ordinary income of the partnership to Partner A for that year only, the validity of that special allocation would depend on whether Partner A would ultimately enjoy the *economic benefit* of the $100,000 of ordinary income allocated to him. If no change were made in Partner A's share of the partnership's economic profits for the year, i.e., Partner A and Partner B each were entitled ultimately to receive $50,000 of the $100,000 in economic profits for the year, a court applying former § 704(b)(2) would invalidate the special allocation on the grounds that its primary purpose was tax avoidance. The allocation of the ordinary income to Partner A would be viewed as nothing more than a paper transaction that did not correspond to the economic deal struck by the partners. By contrast, were Partner A's actual share of the partnership's economic profits to be modified for the year so that A would ultimately actually receive all $100,000 of the partnership's profits for that year, the allocation of all $100,000 of ordinary income to that partner would be respected as having substantial economic effect. See *Kresser v. Commissioner*, 54 T.C. 1621 (1970).

While the above hypothetical dealt with a special allocation of income, the analysis regarding special allocations of deductions or losses was comparable, i.e., a judgment must be made whether the economic deal of the partners is such that a partner to whom deductions or losses are specially allocated will actually bear the economic burden corresponding to the deduction or loss. *Orrisch v. Commissioner*, included in the materials, provides an instructive example of how a court applied the "substantial economic effect" test of the regulations under former § 704(b)(2) to invalidate a special allocation of depreciation deductions.

B. The 1976 Reform Act: Codification of the "Substantial Economic Effect" Test

The 1976 Tax Reform Act codified in § 704(b)(2) the "substantial economic effect" test of the regulations promulgated under former § 704(b), requiring that allocations of income, gain, loss, deduction, or credit (or an item thereof) must reflect the *actual* division of income or loss among the partners when viewed from

---

[6] S. Rep. No. 1622, 83d Cong., 2d Sess., p. 379 (1954). Apparently, the Senate Finance Committee added this reference to a special allocation having "substantial economic effect" "to allay fears that a special allocation of income or deductions would be denied effect in every case where the allocation resulted in a reduction in the income tax liabilities of one or more of the partners." *Orrisch v. Commissioner*, 55 T.C. 395, 400–01, (1970), *aff'd per curiam*, in unpublished opinion (9th Cir. 1973).

[7] Former Reg. § 1.704-1(b)(2).

the standpoint of economic, rather than tax, consequences. In amending § 704(b)(2), the 1976 Act likewise made clear that an allocation of bottom line income or loss (see § 702(a)(8)) must also satisfy the substantial economic effect test.[8] Congress accomplished this latter result by including in amended § 704(b)(2) the phrase "income, gain, loss, deduction, or credit (*or item thereof*)." [Emphasis added.] Study current § 704(b) carefully.

---

§ 704(b). Determination of Distributive Share

A partner's distributive share of income, gain, loss, deduction, or credit (or item thereof, shall be determined in accordance with the partner's interest in the partnership (determined by taking into account all facts and circumstances), if —

(1) the partnership agreement does not provide as to the partner's distributive share of income, gain, loss, deduction, or credit (or item thereof), or

(2) the allocation to a partner under the agreement of income, gain, loss, deduction, or credit (or item thereof) does not have substantial economic effect.

The legislative history of the 1976 Act provides the following instructive overview of both the law prior to the 1976 Tax Reform Act and the purpose of Section 704(b) as amended by Congress in the 1976 Act:

Prior Law. A limited (or a general) partnership agreement may allocate income, gain, loss, deduction, or credit (or items thereof) among the partners in a manner that is disproportionate to the capital contributions of the partners. These are sometimes referred to as "*special allocations*" and, with respect to any taxable year, may be made by amendment to the partnership agreement [See Section 761(c) defining "partnership agree-

---

[8] Prior to the 1976 Act, courts had held that the phrase "with respect to the partner's distributive share of such item" contained in former § 704((b)(2) limited the scope of that section to the allocation of items delineated in § 702 and thus § 704(b)(2) did not apply to bottom line allocations. Nonetheless, the courts applied a test to bottom line allocations that reached results similar to those that would have been reached under the tax avoidance test of former § 704(b)(2). Thus, the Tax Court in *Boynton v. Commissioner*, 72 T.C. 1147, 1159 (1979), *aff'd*, 649 F.2d 1168 (5th Cir. 1981), *cert. denied*, 454 U.S. 1146 (1982) held: "in construing the partnership agreement, the formula which [the partners] select for actually dividing profits and apportioning losses among themselves will be determinative of their 'distributive' shares, rather than a different formula arbitrarily included in the agreement which is to be applicable only for the purpose of filing income tax returns, and which is to have no legal consequences in respect of their rights against one another. In short, where one provision of the agreement which purports to characterize as "distributive" a certain division of profits and losses is contradicted by another provision which legally fixes the rights of the partners *inter sese*, it is the latter provision, rather than the former, which establishes the 'distributive' shares of the partners within the meaning of the statute. The overriding principle is sometimes referred to as the doctrine of 'substance over form,' or is alternatively described as the 'economic substance' test."

ment."] at any time up to the initial due date of the partnership tax return for that year. [Emphasis added.]

A special allocation was not recognized under prior law . . . if its principal purpose was to avoid or evade a Federal tax. *In determining whether a special allocation had been made principally for the avoidance of tax, the regulations focused upon whether the special allocation had "substantial economic effect," that is, whether the allocation may actually affect the dollar amount of the partner's share of the total partnership income or loss independently of tax consequences.* The regulations also inquired as to whether there was a business purpose for this special allocation, whether related items from the same source were subject to the same allocation, whether the allocation ignored normal business factors and was made after the amount of the specially allocated item could reasonably be estimated, the duration of the allocation, and the overall tax consequences of the allocation. [Emphasis added]

[***Explanation of 1976 Amendments to Section 704(b)(2)***.] The Act provides that an allocation of overall income or loss [bottom line income or loss currently described in Section 702(a)(8)], or of any item of income, gain, loss, deduction, or credit [currently described in Section 702(a)(1)-(7)] shall be controlled by the partnership agreement if the partner receiving the allocation can demonstrate that [the allocation] has "substantial economic effect," i.e., whether the allocation may actually affect the dollar amount of the partner's share of the total partnership income or loss, independent of tax consequences. . . .

If an allocation made by the partnership is set aside, a partner's share of the income, gain, loss, deduction, or credit (or item thereof) will be determined in accordance with his interests in the partnership.

In determining a "partner's interest in the partnership," all the relevant facts and circumstances are to be taken into account. Among the relevant factors to be taken into account are the interest of the respective partners in profits and losses (if different from that in taxable income or loss), cash flow, and their rights to distributions of capital upon liquidation.

C. The § 704(b) Regulations

Following the amendments to § 704(b) in the 1976 Act, Treasury replaced the regulations interpreting and applying former § 704(b) with new regulations in 1985. These regulations provide three methods whereby an allocation will be respected under § 704(b):

1. the allocation satisfies the *"substantial economic effect"* test as established in the regulations;

2. the allocation is in accordance with the *partner's interest in the partnership* taking into account all facts and circumstances; or

3. the allocation is *deemed* to be in accordance with the partner's interest in the partnership, e.g., Reg. § 1.704-2 (addressing the allocation of

nonrecourse deductions, a topic discussed in detail in Chapter 11).

This Overview will address the first two methods — satisfaction of the "substantial economic effect" test or the "partner's-interest-in-the-partnership test. As will become apparent, these two tests have the same goal: to ensure that the tax allocations contained in partnership agreements are consistent with the partners' economic sharing arrangement as reflected in the capital accounts of the partners. In other words, both methods have as a goal that *tax must follow book*. The third method whereby special allocations will be deemed to be in accordance with a partner's interest in the partnership will be addressed in subsequent chapters.

1. The Substantial Economic Effect Test

As noted above, in codifying the substantial economic effect test, Congress emphasized that, to be respected, a special allocation must "actually affect the dollar amount of the partner's share of the total partnership income or loss, independent of tax consequences." The legislative history noted that a determination in this regard would require an examination of how the allocation was treated in a partner's capital account for *financial purposes* rather than *tax accounting purposes*. To that end, Congress indicated that the partners' capital accounts should be understood to "actually reflect the dollar amounts that the partners would have the right to receive upon the liquidation of the partnership."[9] Having provided that limited guidance, Congress left to Treasury the arduous task of developing regulations detailing the requirements of the substantial economic effect test.

Treasury responded by creating a set of complex regulations that establish a two-part analysis to be applied at the end of the partnership taxable year to which an allocation relates: (1) whether the allocation has economic effect and (2) whether the economic effect is substantial. The two-part test — hereinafter the "economic effect test" and the "substantiality test" — established by the regulations has been deemed a "safe harbor" test, i.e., it purports to be an objective test that will provide certainty to partners regarding the tax consequences of allocations meeting its requirements.

a. The Economic Effect Test.

The economic effect test requires that a partner to whom a tax allocation is made must receive the economic benefit or bear the economic burden corresponding to the tax allocation.[10] In other words, tax allocations will pass the economic effect test only if they reflect the economic sharing arrangement agreed to by the partners.

A tax allocation can satisfy the economic effect test by meeting the requirements of one of three tests, i.e., (1) the primary test for economic effect; (2)

---

[9] Joint Committee on Taxation, General Explanation of the Tax Reform Act of 1976, H.R. 10612, 94th Cong., P.L. 94-455 (1976), pp. 94–95.

[10] Reg. § 1.704-1(b)(2)(ii)(a).

the alternative test for economic effect; or (3) the economic equivalence test. As discussed below, the regulations use the partners' capital accounts as a means of linking tax allocations and the economic benefits and burdens associated with those allocations. Indeed, the capital account maintenance rules and the rules regarding (a) the use of capital accounts in determining the amount of liquidating distributions and (b) the restoration of capital account deficits are the core of the § 704 regulations. These rules are designed to ensure that the allocation of tax items is consistent with the economic arrangement of the partners.

i. The Primary Test for Economic Effect.

A partnership allocation will satisfy the primary test for economic effect if the partnership agreement provides, throughout the full term of the partnership, that:[11]

a. the partners' capital accounts will be determined and maintained in accordance with the capital account maintenance rules of Reg. § 1.704-1(b)(2)(iv);

b. in the event of the liquidation[12] of a partnership or the interest of any partner, liquidating distributions will be made consistent with positive capital account balances; and

c. each partner shall be unconditionally obligated following liquidation of her partnership interest to restore any deficit in her capital account by the end of the taxable year of the liquidation or, if later, within 90 days after such liquidation.

As should be evident from the above summary, the primary test for economic effect is mechanical. If a partnership agreement includes provisions incorporating the three requirements summarized above and, if partners abide by those requirements, the tax allocations made by the partnership agreement will satisfy the primary test for economic effect.

Central to the operation of the primary test for economic effect is the role of capital accounts. As discussed in Chapter 5, a partner's capital account reflects the partner's share of partnership equity, i.e., the amount the partner would be entitled to receive if the partnership were liquidated and all of its assets were sold at their book value, all of its liabilities were paid, and the net proceeds were distributed to the partners. It is important to understand how the capital accounts serve to link tax allocation to economic benefits and burdens. In that regard, Reg. § 1.704-1(b)(2)(iv), addressing the maintenance of capital accounts requires, a partner's capital account to be increased by tax allocations of partnership income and gain to that partner. Likewise, the regulation requires a partner's capital account to be decreased by tax allocations of partnership losses and deductions to the partner. Chapter 5 examined the maintenance of capital accounts and, together with Reg. § 1.704-1(b)(2)(iv), should be carefully reviewed.[13]

---

[11] Reg. § 1.704-1(b)(2)(ii)(b).

[12] Reg. § 1.704-1(b)(2)(ii)(g) defines "liquidation."

[13] Under certain circumstances, the partners' capital accounts may be increased ("booked-up") or

Consider the following example demonstrating the linkage between tax allocations and capital accounts when a partnership agreement satisfies the three requirements of the primary economic benefit test.

Example 1:

> **Basic Facts:** On January 1, Year 1, Ashley and Erik form a general partnership to engage in the office rental business. Ashley and Erik each contribute $500,000 to the partnership and the partnership immediately uses the cash to purchase for $1,000,000 an office building situated on leased land. For the sake of simplicity, assume the office building is depreciable over 10 years on a straight-line basis and disregard any depreciation conventions, e.g., the mid-month convention. The partnership is a cash method, calendar-year partnership. The economic deal of the partners is that, with the exception of depreciation, they will share equally all economic profits and losses. The partnership agreement accordingly allocates all partnership tax items equally, except the depreciation deductions that are allocated in their entirety to Ashley. Assume the partnership agreement includes the three requirements of the primary test for economic effect noted above. Thus, the special allocation of tax depreciation to Ashley will satisfy the primary test for economic effect as Ashley will be expected to bear the economic burden corresponding to the depreciation deductions allowed.

Analysis: The opening balance sheet of the partnership will be as follows:[14]

	Partnership Assets			**Partners' Capital**	
	A/B	**Book**		**A/B**	**Book**
Office bldg	$1,000,000	$1,000,000	Ashley	$500,000	$500,000
			Erik	$500,000	$500,000
Total	$1,000,000	$1,000,000		$1,000,000	$1,000,000

Let us now consider various liquidation scenarios.

> **Liquidation End of Year 1 — Sale of building for $900,000:** Assume the partnership's income and expenses are equal in Year 1 except for the $100,000 depreciation deduction allowed to the partnership. The partnership will thus have a $100,000 loss, all allocable to Ashley pursuant to the special allocation of all depreciation deductions to her. As a result, the balance sheet of the partnership at the end of Year 1 would be as follows:

---

decreased ("booked-down") to reflect the revaluation of the assets of a partnership. Reg. § 1.704-1(b)(2)(iv)(f). The "booking-up" or "booking-down" of partnership assets will be discussed in Chapter 10.

[14] Note that the balance sheet shows the book value of partnership assets and the book value of each partner's capital account. In addition, note that each partner's capital account is credited with the $500,000 contribution the partner made. *See* Reg. § 1.704-1(b)(2)(iv)(b)(1).

	Partnership Assets			Partners' Capital	
	A/B	Book		A/B	Book
Office bldg	$900,000	$900,000[15]	Ashley	$400,000	$500,000
			Erik	$500,000	$400,000
Total	$900,000	$900,000		$900,000	$900,000

As this balance sheet reflects, Ashley's outside basis in her partnership interest is reduced[16] by $100,000 and, consistent with the capital account maintenance rules, her capital account is also reduced by $100,000.[17] Were the partnership to sell the office building at the end of Year 1 for $900,000 and immediately liquidate, the partnership would have no book or tax gain or loss on the sale and, pursuant to the primary test for economic effect, would be required to distribute the $900,000 in sale proceeds consistent with the positive balances in the partner's capital accounts. Thus, Ashley would receive only $400,000 while Erik would receive $500,000. Neither Ashley nor Erik would recognize any gain on the liquidating distributions.[18] This result illustrates that, while Ashley had the benefit of a $100,000 depreciation deduction in Year 1, she also had to bear the economic burden corresponding to the depreciation deduction, i.e., as the building decreased in value to $900,000, Ashley bore the burden of that decrease and received $100,000 less in liquidation proceeds than Erik.

Liquidation End of Year 1 — Sale of Building for $1,050,000: Assume, instead, the partnership had sold the office building at the end of Year 1 for $1,050,000 and immediately liquidated. There would thus be $150,000 of *book gain*[19] as well as $150,000 of tax gain (i.e., amount realized of $1,050,000 less adjusted basis of $900,000 equals $150,000 gain). Because Ashley and Erik are equal partners and have agreed to share economic gains equally, each will be credited with $75,000 of the book gain and, accordingly, will each have a $75,000 distributive share of the tax gain to report. Again, note how tax follows book. Ashley and Erik will adjust their book capital accounts and outside bases accordingly. As a result, immedi-

---

[15] The tax and book depreciation are identical in this case because the partnership purchased the office building. As will be discussed in Chapter 10 addressing contributed property, the tax and book depreciation will differ when depreciable property is contributed to the partnership and the contributing partner has an adjusted basis in the property that differs from the fair market value of the property. See Reg. § 1.704-1(b)(2)(iv)(g)(3).

[16] I.R.C. § 705(a)(2)(A).

[17] Reg. § 1.704-1(b)(2)(iv)(b)(7).

[18] § 731(a)(1).

[19] As a result of the $100,000 in depreciation allowed the partnership in Year 1, the book value of the building was decreased to $900,000. Recall that book value and fair market value may differ. This hypothetical provides a good example of how that can happen — the partnership has been allowed $100,000 in depreciation deduction and yet the building actually appreciated in value by $50,000. The book value is $900,000, reflecting the $100,000 depreciation deduction allowed and yet the fair market value of the building is $1,050,000. Thus, the sale of the building for $1,050,000 produces a book gain of $150,000, matching the tax gain.

ately prior to the liquidating distribution, the partnership's balance sheet would be as follows:

	Partnership Assets			**Partners' Capital**	
	A/B	Book		A/B	Book
Office bldg	$1,050,000	$1,050,000	Ashley	$475,000	$475,000
			Erik	$575,000	$575,000
Total	$1,050,000	$1,050,000		$1,050,000	$1,050,000

As required by the primary test for economic effect, on liquidation, the $1,050,000 would again, be allocated consistent with the positive balances in the partners' capital accounts, i.e., $475,000 to Ashley and $575,000 to Erik. Neither Ashley nor Erik would recognize any gain or loss. Again, note how Ashley, while having the benefit of the depreciation deduction, has also borne the economic burden corresponding to that deduction.[20]

Liquidation End of Year 1 — Sale of Building for $850,000: Similarly, if the partnership had sold the office building at the end of Year 1 for $850,000, there would be a $50,000 book loss and a corresponding $50,000 tax loss. Pursuant to the partnership agreement, both the $50,000 book loss and $50,000 tax loss would be allocated in equal shares to Ashley and Erik. Ashley's capital account would be reduced from $400,000 to $375,000 and Erik's capital account would be reduced from $500,000 to $475,000. The $850,000 in liquidation proceeds would be distributed consistent with those capital account balances. Again, Ashley has clearly borne the economic burden associated with the $100,000 depreciation deduction allocated to her.

Liquidation End of Year 6 — Sale of Building for $400,000: After six years of depreciating the office building, the partnership will have been allowed depreciation deductions totaling $600,000. If we assume the income of the partnership and the expenses of the partnership were equal in each of the six years, except for the $100,000 in depreciation deduction allowed each year, the partnership's balance sheet would be as follows:

---

[20] If, as in *Orrisch v. Commissioner*, included in the materials, Ashley and Erik had agreed upon a gain chargeback whereby Ashley would be allocated any gain on the sale of the office building up to the amount of the depreciation allocated to her, Ashley would have been required to report a total of $125,000 of gain, i.e., $100,000 as a result of the gain chargeback and $25,000 as her share of the remaining $50,000 of gain. Her capital account would likewise have been increased by $125,000 — from $400,000 to $525,000. Erik, by contrast, would have been allocated $25,000 of the book and tax gain and would have increased his capital account from $500,000 to $525,000. The partnership would have distributed the $1,050,000 of liquidation proceeds equally to the two partners, i.e., $525,000 each. Gain chargeback provisions will be considered later in this Overview.

	Partnership Assets			**Partners' Capital**	
	A/B	Book		A/B	Book
Office bldg	$400,000	$400,000[21]	Ashley	$0[22]	($100,000)
			Erik	$500,000	$500,000
Total	$400,000	$400,000		$500,000[23]	$400,000

Were the partnership to sell the office building for $400,000 at the end of Year 1 and immediately liquidate, Ashley would be required to restore the $100,000 deficit in her capital account by contributing an additional $100,000 to the partnership. The additional $100,000 contribution would increase Ashley's outside basis to $100,000 and thus enable her to use the $100,000 depreciation deduction that had been held in abeyance pursuant to § 704(d). In turn, the partnership would use Ashley's additional $100,000 contribution together with the $400,000 of sale proceeds to make a liquidating distribution of $500,000 to Erik — an amount equal to the positive balance in Erik's capital account. Again, Ashley is bearing the burden of the $600,000 in depreciation deductions specially allocated to her, i.e., she contributed a total of $600,000 in cash to the partnership, was allocated $600,000 in depreciation deductions and received $0 upon liquidation of the partnership.

Now consider an example where the partnership agreement fails to satisfy the three requirements of the primary economic test.

Example 2: Assume the same Basic Facts as in Example 1 above except that, although the partnership agreement requires capital accounts to be maintained, it provides that liquidation proceeds will be divided equally.

Analysis: Under these circumstances, the special allocation of the Year 1 depreciation to Ashley will not be respected. The logic of that result is apparent if one assumes the partnership sold the office building for $900,000 at the end of Year 1 and immediately liquidated. At the end of Year 1 the partnership balance sheet would be as follows:

---

[21] The tax and book depreciation are identical in this case because the partnership purchased the office building.

[22] As doscussed in Chapter 8, § 704(d) provides that losses may not be deducted by a partner in an amount greater than the partner's outside basis. Thus, Ashley's outside basis cannot be negative. The $100,000 Year 6 depreciation deduction will have to be held in abeyance by Ashley until such time as she increases her outside basis.

[23] The total outside basis of the partners is greater than the total inside basis of the partnership under these circumstances. If the tax law permitted a negative basis, Ashley would have been allowed to use the Year 6 $100,000 depreciation deduction rather than holding it in abeyance until she had a positive outside basis. If she had been permitted to deduct the Year 6 depreciation allocated to her, her outside basis would have been a negative $100,000, which when combined with Erik's outside basis of $500,000, would have produced a net $400,000 of outside basis, thus matching the $400,000 inside basis of the partnership.

	Partnership Assets			Partners' Capital	
	A/B	Book		A/B	Book
Office bldg	$900,000	$900,000[24]	Ashley	$400,000	$500,000
			Erik	$500,000	$400,000
Total	$900,000	$900,000		$900,000	$900,000

If the partnership were to sell the office building for $900,000 at that time, it would have no gain or loss. Upon liquidation, were it to distribute the $900,000 to the partners in equal shares as required by the partnership agreement, it would be clear that Erik, whose capital account balance is $500,000 but who receives a liquidating distribution of only $450,000, bears the economic burden corresponding to $50,000 of the Year 1 depreciation. As a corollary, it would also be clear that Ashley, whose capital account was only $400,000 but who receives a liquidating distribution of $450,000, bears the economic burden of only $50,000 of the tax depreciation notwithstanding the fact she had the benefit of all $100,000 of the tax depreciation. In other words, tax did not follow book in this example and, as would be expected, the tax allocation flunks the primary test for economic effect.[25] Consistent with § 704(b)(2), the depreciation would have to be allocated in accordance with the partners'-interest-in-the-partnership test. As discussed, *infra*, that test will result in the Year 1 depreciation deduction being divided equally. Review *Orrisch v. Commissioner*, included in the materials, and note how, on facts similar to those in this Example 2, the court, applying the law as it existed pre-1976 Tax Reform Act, reached the same result.

ii. The Alternative Test for Economic Effect.

Considering that limited partners generally intend to limit their obligation to make capital contributions beyond their initial contributions to a partnership, the deficit restoration requirement of the primary test for economic effect would not be satisfied. As a result, special allocations to limited partners could not be respected. To accommodate special tax allocation by limited partnership, while at the same time preserving the requirement that tax follows book, the regulations provide an alternative test for economic effect.

Regulation § 1.704-1(b)(2)(ii)(d) creates that alternative test and requires the following:

1. the first two requirements of the primary test for economic effect (proper maintenance of capital accounts and distribution of liquidation proceeds pursuant to positive capital account balances) be satisfied;

2. the partner to whom a tax allocation is made has no obligation or

---

[24] The tax and book depreciation are again identical in this case because the partnership purchased the office building.

[25] See Reg. § 1.704–1(b)(5) Ex. 1(i). As will be clear from the discussion below, neither the alternative test for economic effect or the economic equivalence test can save this allocation.

only a limited obligation to restore a capital account deficit; and

3. a "qualified income offset" provision be included in the partnership agreement.

As developed *infra*, under the alternative test for economic effect, tax allocations to a partner will be respected as having economic effect so long as the allocations do not create a deficit in the capital account the partner is not obligated to restore.

The "qualified income offset" provision included in the partnership agreement must provide that a partner who unexpectedly receives certain adjustments, allocations, or distributions be allocated items of income and gain so as to eliminate as quickly as possible any capital account deficit the partner has no obligation to restore. Study Reg. § 1.704-1(b)(2)(ii)(d). Note that the regulation specifically provides that any allocation required by the qualified income offset will be deemed to be made in accordance with the partner's interest in the partnership. Although generally a promissory note[26] contributed to a partnership by a partner who is the maker of the note will not increase the partner's capital account,[27] for purposes of the alternative test for economic effect, the partner will be treated as having an obligation to restore a capital account deficit to the extent of the outstanding balance of that note.[28]

The application of the alternative test for economic effect is illustrated by the following examples:

Example 3: In Year 1, Ian and Anna form a limited partnership in which Ian, the general partner, contributes $100,000 in cash and Anna, the limited partner, contributes $400,000 in cash. The partnership immediately purchases a piece of equipment for $500,000. The equipment is depreciable over a 10-year period on a straight-line basis at the rate of $50,000 per year. (Disregard all depreciation conventions.) The partnership agreement requires the partners' capital accounts be maintained consistent with Regulation § 1.704-1(b)(2)(iv) and that liquidation proceeds be distributed in accord with the partners' positive capital account balances. Ian, but not Anna, is unconditionally obligated to restore a capital account deficit. The partnership agreement, however, does contain a qualified income offset provision. The partners agree that all of depreciation deductions on the equipment will be allocated to Anna.

Analysis: Given the failure to include a deficit restoration obligation, the partnership agreement fails to satisfy the primary test for economic effect. The agreement, however, does satisfy the alternative test for economic effect. Assume in every year of the partnership, the income and expenses (other than depreciation deductions) are exactly equal. Assume also that

---

[26] A promissory note for this purpose does not include a promissory note that is readily tradable on an established securities market. Such a note would increase the contributing partner's capital account. Reg. § 1.704-1(b)(2)((iv)(d)(2).

[27] Reg. § 1.704-1(b)(2)(iv)(d)(2).

[28] Reg. § 1.704-1(b)(2)(ii)(c).

the partnership makes no distributions. Following the purchase of the equipment, the balance sheet of the partnership will be as follows:

	Partnership Assets			Partners' Capital	
	A/B	Book		A/B	Book
Equipment	$500,000	$500,000	Anna	$400,000	$400,000
			Ian	$100,000	$100,000
Total	$500,000	$500,000		$500,000	$500,000

Pursuant to the alternative test for economic effect, the allocation of the $50,000 of Year 1 depreciation to Anna will have economic effect as it will not create a deficit in Anna's capital account. The partnership's balance sheet at the end of Year 1 will be as follows:

	Partnership Assets			Partners' Capital	
	A/B	Book		A/B	Book
Equipment	$450,000	$450,000	Anna	$350,000	$350,000
			Ian	$100,000	$100,000
Total	$450,000	$450,000		$450,000	$450,000

For each of the next seven years (i.e., Years 2 - 8), the allocation of the $50,000 depreciation deduction will be respected. The balance sheet at the end of Year 8 will be as follows:

	Partnership Assets			Partners' Capital	
	A/B	Book		A/B	Book
Equipment	$100,000	$100,000	Anna	$0	$0
			Ian	$100,000	$100,000
Total	$100,000	$100,000		$100,000	$100,000

Under the alternative test for economic effect, the allocation of the Year 9 depreciation deduction to Anna will not be respected as it would create a deficit in her capital account for which she has no restoration obligation. As a result, the Year 9 as well as the Year 10 depreciation deductions will have to be allocated in accord with the partner's interest in the partnership. The application of that test is discussed below. Suffice it to say at this point that the depreciation deductions for Years 9 and 10 will be allocated to Ian pursuant to that test.

Example 4: Assume the facts of Example 3 except that, at the beginning of Year 9, there is an unexpected[29] partnership distribution of $25,000 in cash to both Ian and Anna. Assume the partnership in Year 9 had $60,000 of gross income and, disregarding the $50,000 depreciation deduction for the year, had $60,000 of expenses.

---

[29] The regulations have not defined "expected." It is difficult to imagine that a distribution would not be "expected." Nonetheless, we will assume the Year 9 distribution to the partners was unexpected.

Analysis: As a result of the unexpected distribution, a $25,000 deficit is created in Anna's capital account.[30] Because Anna has no deficit restoration obligation, the qualified income offset provision will require the partnership to allocate $25,000 of the partnership's gross income for the year to Anna. This allocation will, as noted above, be deemed to be consistent with the partner's interest in the partnership.[31] As a result of this allocation, the negative balance in Anna's capital account will be eliminated and her capital account would again show a $0 balance.

iii. The Economic Equivalence Test.

Often referred to as the "dumb but lucky" rule, the economic equivalence test is set forth in Regulation § 1.704-1(b)(2)(ii)(i). Under this test, even though the partnership agreement fails to satisfy the primary test for economic effect, an allocation will still be respected as having economic effect if it is established that, were the partnership liquidated at the end of the year to which allocations apply, the economic results would be the same as if the partnership agreement satisfied the three requirements of the primary test for economic effect.

Example 5: Assume Jack contributes $100,000 in cash and Bernadette contributes $200,000 in cash to establish a general partnership. The partnership agreement does not require the maintenance of capital accounts. The agreement allocates one-third of all income, gain, loss, deduction, and credit to Jack and the balance of those items to Bernadette. All liquidating and nonliquidating distributions are likewise to be made one-third to Jack and two-thirds to Bernadette. Assume Jack and Bernadette are liable under state law for one-third and two-thirds respectively of any debts of the partnership.

Analysis: The partnership agreement does not satisfy the primary test for economic effect (or the alternative test for economic effect). Nonetheless, the allocations will have economic effect under the economic equivalence test.[32] If the partnership were to liquidate at the end of any year to which an allocation relates, the economic results to the partners would be the same as if the partnership agreement satisfied all three requirements of the primary test for economic effect. This example suggests the kind of very simple partnership arrangements that exist in many cases. The arrangements are clearly nonabusive and Treasury concluded they should ultimately should not be deprived of qualifying for the use of the "substantial economic effect" safe harbor.

---

[30] A partner's capital account must be reduced by the amount of any distribution. Reg. § 1.704-1(b)(2)(iv)(b)(4).

[31] As a result of this allocation, the partnership, in addition to having a $50,000 depreciation deduction for Year 9 ,will also have a net loss of $25,000 (i.e., $60,000 of expense less the $35,000 remaining gross income). Both the net loss as well as the depreciation deduction of $50,000 will be allocated to Ian.

[32] *See* Reg. § 1.704-1(b)(5) Example 4(ii).

b. The Substantiality Test.

Although an allocation satisfies the economic test, it will not be respected unless it also satisfies the substantiality test. The § 704(b) regulations promulgated in 1985 provide the following general rule: "the economic effect of an allocation is substantial if there is a reasonable possibility that the allocation will affect substantially the dollar amounts to be received by the partners from the partnership, independent of tax consequences."[33] The regulations specifically identify three types of allocations that are "insubstantial." Two of the three types of "insubstantial" allocations, i.e., so-called "shifting" and "transitory" allocations, have no substantial impact on partners' capital accounts when one compares those accounts after the allocations to what those accounts would have been had the partnership agreement not contained the allocations. The third type of "insubstantial" allocations are those that may substantially impact the partners' capital accounts, i.e., which may substantially affect the dollar amounts received by partners, but which, after taking into account the partners' tax profiles, provide favorable *after-tax economic consequences* to the partners as a group when compared to a situation where the partnership agreement does not contain the allocations.[34] We will refer to this type of insubstantial allocation as "allocations with after-tax economic consequences."

As will become clear in the discussion below, the "substantiality" test is far less mechanical than the economic effect test. Indeed, the "substantiality" test can involve subjective judgments. Notwithstanding the subjectivity introduced by the "substantiality test," the overall substantial economic effect test is deemed a safe harbor test, intended to provide certainty regarding tax implications of various partnership allocations.

i. Shifting Allocations.

For an allocation to be characterized as a "shifting allocation," there must be a strong likelihood at the time the allocation becomes part of the partnership agreement that the allocation:

(1) will not result in net increases or decreases in partner capital accounts *in a given year* that differ substantially from the net increases or decreases in those capital accounts that would have occurred *in that year* had the partnership agreement not contained the allocations; and

(2) given the tax profiles[35] of the partners, will reduce the partners' total tax liability in a given year.

The regulations create a rebuttable presumption that the above requirements were met if, at the end of the year, the capital accounts in fact do not differ

---

[33] Reg. § 1.704-1(b)(2)(iii)(a).

[34] Regulation § 1.704-1(b)(2)(iii)(a) provides that "references . . . to a comparison to consequences arising if an allocation . . . were not contained in the partnership agreement mean that the allocation is determined in accordance with the partners' interests in the partnership, . . . disregarding the allocations being tested [under the substantiality test.]"

[35] The tax profiles of partners include "partner tax attributes that are unrelated to the partnership." Reg. § 1.704-1(b)(2)(iii)(b)(2).

substantially from what they would have been had no special allocations been contained in the partnership agreement and the overall tax liability of the partners has been reduced. Reg. § 1.704-1(b)(2)(iii)(b).

Consider the following example:

Example 6: Pat and Laura form a general partnership in which each has a 50% interest in capital and profits. Assume the partnership satisfies the three requirements of the primary test for economic effect. In the current year, assume Pat is in the top individual income tax bracket and Laura has a $100,000 net operating loss carryforward that will expire during the current year. Assume the partnership's accountants project that the partnership will have $100,000 of ordinary income for the year and $50,000 of tax exempt interest. Assume also that, apart from the partnership, Patrick expects to have ordinary income of $40,000 from wages and Laura expects to have $25,000 of net income (all ordinary) from a separate business venture. In view of these projections, the partners amend their partnership agreement at the beginning of the year to provide that all of the tax exempt interest will be allocated to Pat and that the same amount of ordinary income will be allocated to Laura. All other income will be shared equally. The projections of the accountants proved correct — the partnership had exactly $100,000 of ordinary income for the year and $50,000 of tax-exempt income. Assume for the sake of simplicity that the partnership had no expenses during the year. Thus, its total profit for the year amounted to $150,000 and, pursuant to the economic sharing arrangement of the partners, each partner would be entitled to $75,000 of that profit.

Analysis: Begin by comparing the partners' capital accounts at the end of the current year, taking into account the special allocations, with the partners' capital accounts had there been no special allocations and the partners simply shared the ordinary income and tax exempt interest equally. Assume the balance in each of their capital accounts at the beginning of the year was $250,000.

	Pat's Capital Account		Laura's Capital Account	
	With allocation	Without allocation	With allocation	Without allocation
opening balance	$250,000	$250,000	$250,000	$250,000
ordinary income	$25,000	$50,000	$75,000	$50,000
tax exempt interest	$50,000	$25,000	$0	$25,000
closing balance	$325,000	$325,000	$325,000	$325,000

As the above chart indicates, the partners' capital accounts, taking into account the special allocations, are identical to what the capital accounts would have been had the partnership agreement not been amended to include the special allocations. Under either circumstance, each partner's capital account increased by $75,000. See Reg. § 1.704-1(b)(2)(iv)(3). The chart demonstrates that the capital account maintenance rules ensure that tax allocations follow book allocations. Thus, because in this example the partners' economic agreement required the $150,000 of total profit be shared equally, the economic effect test required each partner to be allocated tax items of income or gain totaling $75,000. The character of that $75,000 tax allocation is irrelevant under the economic test.

The second requirement of the shifting allocation test requires a determination of whether, given the partners' tax profiles, a strong likelihood exists that the total tax liability of the partners will be less than they would be if the allocations were not included in the partnership agreement. In this example, that standard should be easily met. Patrick, who is in the highest individual tax bracket, will have only $25,000 of ordinary income to report from the partnership because the other $50,000 of income allocated to him is tax-exempt interest. Had the special allocations not been included in the partnership agreement, Patrick would have reported $50,000 of ordinary income and had $25,000 of tax exempt interest. Clearly, Patrick's tax liability has been decreased. Laura had a $100,000 net operating loss (NOL) carryforward that would expire during the year. That NOL carryforward will completely offset both the $75,000 of partnership ordinary income allocated to her and her anticipated net ordinary income from the separate business venture. She will thus have no tax for the year. Had the allocations not been included in the partnership agreement, she would have been allocated $50,000 of partnership ordinary income and $25,000 of tax exempt interest. Her NOL carryforward would have completely offset both the $50,000 ordinary income from the partnership as well as the $25,000 of net income she expected from her separate business. Again, she would have had no tax for the year and would have wasted $25,000 of the NOL carryforward. In the aggregate, it is clear that the partners' total tax liability for the year would be less than it would have been were no special allocations included in the partnership agreement.

Given the above analysis, the special allocations constitute "shifting allocations" and thus fail the substantial economic effect test. As a result, the allocations will be disregarded and the partnership's ordinary income and tax exempt interest will be allocated in accord with the partners'-interest-in-the-partnership test. As discussed below, that test focuses on the economic sharing arrangement the partners have agreed upon. In this case, they agreed that each would be entitled to an equal share of whatever profits were generated by the partnership in that year. Thus, Patrick and Laura would each report 50% of the ordinary income and have 50% of the tax exempt interest. See Reg. § 1.704-1(b)(5) Ex. 6.

Note that, if the only test for special allocations were the economic effect test, the special allocations included in the partnership agreement in this example would have passed muster even though they resulted in an assignment of income that reduced their overall tax liability — something they could not have done outside of the partnership. The government would have been the only loser.

ii. Transitory Allocations.

Transitory allocations are like shifting allocations except that, rather than occurring in a single year, they occur over two or more years. Thus, the economic effect of partnership allocations will not be substantial if the partnership agreement provides for an allocation (the original allocation) that will be largely offset later by another allocation (the offsetting allocation) and, at the time the allocations become part of the partnership agreement, there is a strong likelihood that:

1. the net increases or decreases in partner capital accounts *for the years to which the allocations relate* will not differ substantially from the increases or decreases in those capital accounts that would have occurred *in those years* had the partnership agreement not contained the allocations; and

2. given the tax profiles of the partners, the partners' total tax liability for the years in which the allocations are taken into account will be reduced as a result of the allocations.[36]

As in the case of shifting allocations, the regulations provide a rebuttable presumption: if, at the end of the year to which the offsetting allocation relates, both results (1) and (2) above occur, "it will be presumed that, at the time the allocation became part of the partnership agreement, there was a strong likelihood that these results would occur."[37]

The following examples illustrates a transitory allocation:

Example 7: Assume a two-person general partnership in which the partners — Partner A and Partner B — have equal interests. Over the next two years, the partnership is expected to generate a total of $100,000 of loss; in its third year, the partnership is expected to generate at least $100,000 of income. Because of business activity outside the partnership, Partner A expects to have an unusually large income for the next two years and thus could use the losses the partnership anticipates in those years. At the same time, Partner B has a substantial net operating loss carryforward and has no use for the partnership losses. The partners amend their partnership agreement to provide that, during the next two years, all partnership losses will be allocated to Partner A (the original allocation) and that, in the third year, Partner A will be allocated income in the amount of the losses allocated to him in the previous two years (the offsetting allocation). Any additional income in that year would be allocated equally between the partners. Assume the partners' projections regarding loss in the next two years and income the third year proved accurate.

Analysis: Given these facts, the allocations would satisfy the requirements for "transitory allocations." After the offsetting allocation of income was taken into account in the third year, the changes in the capital accounts of the partners over the three-year period would match the changes that would have occurred in the capital accounts had the allocations not been

---

[36] Reg. § 1.704-1(b)(2)(iii)(c).

[37] *Id.*

included in the partnership agreement. (Compare Reg. § 1.704-1(b)(5) Ex. 3.) Furthermore, given the tax profiles of Partners A and B, it seems clear that the aggregate tax liability of the partners during the three-year period would be less than it would have been had the special allocations not been included in the partnership agreement. As a result of the allocations, only the government was the loser. Because the economic effect of the allocations is not substantial, the allocations will not be respected. Consequently, the losses and the income during the three-year period would be allocated in accordance with the partners' interests in the partnership. (See the discussion below.)

The transitory allocation rule contains two important safe harbors: (1) the "five year rule" and (2) the "fair market value equals adjusted basis rule."[38]

The "Five-Year Rule." Under the "five-year safe harbor," the original and offsetting allocations will not be insubstantial if, at the time the allocations become part of the partnership agreement, there is a strong likelihood the offsetting allocation(s) will not, in large part, be made within five years after the original allocation(s) is made.[39] Thus, in Example 7, if the partnership was likely to continue to generate loss for a number of years and, as a result, the offsetting income allocation to Partner A was not expected to be made until more than five years after the original loss allocation, the economic effect of the allocations would not be considered insubstantial. This safe harbor reflects the fact that the partners are subjecting themselves to considerable risk if an offsetting allocation is not to be made for a number of years. The risk factor thus justifies the safe harbor.

The "Fair Market Value Equals Adjusted Basis Rule." Pursuant to this safe harbor rule, the adjusted tax basis of partnership property is presumed to be the fair market value of the property, and any adjustments to the tax basis (typically depreciation deductions) are presumed to matched by corresponding changes in the property's fair market value. *This rule is applicable not only for purposes of the "substantiality" test but also for purposes of the alternative test for economic effect and the special rule of the partner's-interest-in-the-partnership test of Regulation § 1.704-1(b)(3)(iii) discussed below.* Thus, for example, if a partnership purchases a commercial building on leased land for $1,000,000 and the building is depreciable over a 10-year period at the rate of $100,000 per year, it will be assumed that the fair market value of the building will decrease by $100,000 per year to reflect the $100,000 in depreciation allowed the partnership annually with respect to the building. In other words, the tax depreciation is deemed to reflect actual economic depreciation. This rule is justified as being consistent with the general capital account maintenance rules and also on the ground that it negates controversies between the Service and partners regarding valuation.

---

[38] *Id.*

[39] See Reg. § 1.704–1(b)(5) Ex. 2. Note how the "five-year rule" is applied on a first-in, first-out basis. Compare Reg. § 1.704–1(b)(5) Ex. 7.

As a result of this safe harbor rule, a so-called gain chargeback often encountered in real estate partnerships will not be deemed insubstantial. Consider the following example:

Example 8: Assume the Basic Facts of Example 1 above. In addition, assume the partnership agreement contained a gain chargeback provision whereby Ashley, upon the taxable disposition of the office building, would first be allocated tax and book gain in an amount of the depreciation deductions allocated to her. Any remaining gain would be allocated to Ashley and Erik equally. In including both the special allocation of depreciation to Ashley and the gain chargeback provision, the partners assumed the building would not suffer any economic depreciation. If anything, they expect the office building would likely appreciate in value over time. Assume the building was sold for $1,200,000 at the end of Year 6 after the partnership had been allowed a total of $600,000 in depreciation, all of which had been allocated to Ashley.

Analysis: The partnership's adjusted basis in the building at the time of the sale and the book value of the building would be $400,000. As a result, the partnership would recognize $800,000 of tax and book gain on the sale. Pursuant to the gain chargeback, the first $600,000 of the tax and book gain would be allocated to Ashley with the remaining $200,000 of gain being divided equally between Ashley and Erik. As a result of the gain chargeback allocation, Ashley's capital account would be the same as what it would have been had the special depreciation allocation not been included in the partnership agreement. While the special allocation of depreciation and the gain chargeback provision could easily be attacked as transitory allocations, they are immune from such an attack thanks to the "fair market value equals adjusted basis rule." See Reg. § 1.704–(b)(5) Ex. 1 (xi).

iii. Allocations with After-Tax Economic Consequences.

The third category of allocations the economic effects of which are not substantial is described in the general rules of Reg. § 1704-1(b)(2)(iii)(a). We characterize these as "allocations with after-tax economic consequences." As discussed above, shifting and transitory allocations do not cause the partners' capital accounts to differ substantially from what they would have been without the allocations. In other words, they don't substantially affect the dollar amounts partners would receive from the partnership upon liquidation. By contrast, "allocations with after-tax consequences" can substantially affect the partners' capital accounts. Specifically, after taking into account the partners' tax profiles, these allocations actually enhance (in present value terms) the after-tax economic consequences of one or more partners when compared to the economic consequences if the allocations were not contained in the partnership agreement. At the same time, there is a strong likelihood that these allocations will not substantially diminish (in present value terms) the after-tax economic consequences of any partner when compared to the economic consequences, were the allocations not contained in the partnership agreement.

The kind of allocations that fall within this category of insubstantial allocations is best understood by considering an example. The following example is based on Example 5 of Reg. § 1.704-1(b)(5). Study that regulation example and then consider the following version of that example.

Example 9: Andy (hereinafter A) and Barb (hereinafter B) form an investment partnership. The partnership owns corporate bonds and tax exempt bonds. Over the next several years, A expects to be in a 35% marginal tax bracket and B expects to be in a 15% marginal tax bracket. There is a strong likelihood that, in each of the next several years, the partnership will realize between $190 and $200 of tax-exempt interest and $190 and $200 of taxable interest each year. (Add all the zeroes you want.)

A and B made equal capital contributions to the partnership and they agree to share equally in gains and losses from the sale of the partnership's investment securities. A and B agree, however, that, rather than share the interest from the different securities equally, they will allocate the tax-exempt interest 90% to A and 10% to B and will distribute cash derived from interest received on the tax-exempt bonds in the same percentages. In addition, they agree to allocate 100% of the partnership's taxable interest to B and to distribute all cash derived from the interest on the corporate bonds to B. Assume the partnership agreement contains the three requirements of the primary test for economic effect. The allocations thus have economic effect.

Analysis: As the following detailed analysis will demonstrate, given the differing marginal tax brackets of the partners, the special allocation of taxable and tax-exempt interest will fail the substantiality test. Let us begin by considering the after-tax economic consequences to the partners assuming the special allocations are not contained in the partnership agreement and assuming an equal division of the interest from both the corporate bonds and the tax exempt bonds.

Without the allocation, A would be allocated between $95 and $100 of the tax-exempt interest and between $95 and $100 of the taxable interest. A is in a 35% bracket. A would therefore have between $33.25 [$95 x .35] and $35 [$100 x .35] of tax. After tax, A would have between $156.75 [assuming $95 each of tax exempt and taxable interest] and $165 [assuming $100 each of tax exempt and taxable interest] for himself.

Without the allocation, B would be allocated between $95 and $100 of the tax-exempt interest and between $95 and $100 of the taxable interest. B is in a 15% bracket. B would therefore have between $14.25 [$95 x .15] and $15 [$100 x .15] of tax. After tax, B would have between $175.75 [assuming $95 each of tax exempt and taxable interest] and $185 [assuming $100 each of tax exempt and taxable interest] for herself.

Without the allocations, the government would thus have collected in the aggregate $47.50 and $50 in tax.

Now, let us compare those results with the after-tax economic consequences to the partners assuming the allocations are contained in the partnership agreement.

With the allocation, A will be allocated between $171 [90% of 190] and $180 [90% of $200] of tax exempt income. A would be allocated $0 of interest from the corporate bonds. A will have no tax. After tax, A will have between $171 and $180 for himself. *Thus, as a result of the special allocations, A's after-tax economic consequences have been enhanced.*

With the allocation, B will be allocated between $19 [10% of $190] and $20 [10% of $200] of tax-exempt interest and between $190 [100% of $190] and $200 [100% of $200] of taxable interest. B is in a 15% bracket and thus will have between $28.50 [$190 x .15] and $30 [$200 x .15] of tax liability. After tax, B will have between $180.50 and $190 for herself. *Thus, as a result of the special allocations, B's after-tax economic consequences have been enhanced.*

With the allocations, the government will collect a total of between $28.50 and $30 in tax.

Under the combination of investment outcomes least favorable to A, the partnership would realize $190 of tax-exempt interest and $200 of taxable interest. This would give A $171 of tax-exempt interest [i.e., 90% of $190] and that amount would represent A's after-tax economic consequence. This is still better than what A would have received had the tax-exempt and taxable interest been allocated equally between the partners. [A would have been entitled to $95 of tax-exempt interest and $100 of taxable interest. A's tax would have been $35 (i.e., $100 x .35). After tax, A would have had $165 for himself.] Under those circumstances, B would be entitled to $19 of the tax-exempt interest and all $200 of the taxable interest. B's tax would be $30 (i.e., $200 x .15). After tax, B would have $189 for herself, an after-tax result that is better than it would have been had the allocations not been contained in the partnership agreement. [Without the allocations, B would have been entitled to $95 of tax-exempt interest and $100 of taxable interest. Her tax would have been $15 (i.e., $100 x .15). After tax, B would have had $180 for herself.]

Under the combination of investment outcomes least favorable to B, the partnership would realize $200 of tax-exempt interest and $190 of taxable interest. This would give A $180 of tax-exempt interest [i.e., 90% of $200] and that amount would represent A's after-tax economic consequence. This is clearly better than what A would have received had the tax exempt and taxable interest been allocated equally between the partners. [A would have been entitled to $100 of tax exempt interest and $95 of taxable interest. His tax would have been $33.25 (i.e., $95 x .35). After tax, A would have had $162.75 for himself.] Under those circumstances, B would be entitled to $20 of the tax exempt interest and all $190 of the taxable interest. B's tax would be $28.5 (i.e., $190 x .15). After tax, B would have $181.50 for herself, an after-tax result that is better than it would have been had the allocations not been contained in the partnership agreement.

[Without the allocations, B would have been entitled to $100 of tax exempt interest and $95 of taxable interest. Her tax would have been $14.25 (i.e., $95 x .15). After tax, B would have had $180.75 for herself.]

Thus, while the allocations specified in the partnership agreement may satisfy the "economic effect" test, they flunk the "substantiality" test because at the time the allocations became part of the partnership agreement, A is expected to enhance his after-tax economic consequences as a result of the allocation and there is a strong likelihood that neither A nor B would diminish his or her economic consequences as a result of the allocation. As a result, the *tax allocations* will not be respected and, for tax purposes, the tax exempt interest and taxable interest will have to be reallocated pursuant to the partners'-interest-in-the-partnership test. *Note only the tax allocations are not respected. The partners are free to allocate their income economically however they choose.*

To understand how the partner's-interest-in-the-partnership test would apply to this example, assume that, in the first tax year in which the allocation described above was in effect, the partnership realized $190 of tax exempt interest and $200 of taxable interest. Pursuant to the partnership agreement, A is entitled to receive $171 (i.e., 90% of the $190 of tax exempt interest) and B is entitled to receive $219 (i.e., 10% of the tax exempt interest or $19 and all $200 of the taxable interest). That is the economic arrangement the partners have established and it will be respected. Therefore A's capital account would be credited with $171 and B's capital account would be credited with $219. But, as noted above, the *tax allocations* of tax-exempt interest and taxable interest will not be respected and the tax items must therefore be reallocated pursuant to the partners'-interest-in-the-partnership test. Because, under the partnership agreement, A is entitled to receive $171 or approximately 42% of the partnership's total investment income of $390 and B is entitled to receive $219 or approximately 58% of the partnership's total investment income, the tax exempt interest and taxable interest for tax purposes will be reallocated 42% to A and 58% to B.[40]

Note: Although A and B are equal partners, the partnership agreement provides A is actually entitled to receive $171 of the total $390 of partnership investment income while B is entitled to receive $219. As the above example illustrates, the regulations prevent A and B from deciding between themselves the tax character of the amounts they are entitled to receive.

2. The Partner's-Interest-in-the-Partnership Test

Section 704(b) generally provides that the partner's interest in the partnership test is applicable if the partnership agreement: (1) fails to address the partners' distributive shares in partnership income, gain, loss, deduction, or credit or (2) the partnership agreement's allocations of partnership income, gain, loss, deduction, or credit (or item thereof) do not have "substantial economic effect." As noted in the 1976 legislative history discussed above, the partner's-interest-in-the-partnership

---

[40] Reg. § 1.704-1(b)(5) Ex. 5(ii).

test is a facts and circumstances test that seeks to ensure each partner's share of partnership tax items, i.e., income, gain, loss, deduction, loss, and credit accurately reflects the *economic arrangement* of the partners. Thus, it is necessary to determine exactly what economic arrangement or economic deal has been agreed upon by the partners. The regulations identify four of the factors that will be considered in determining the partner's interest in the partnership: (a) the partner's relative contributions to the partnership; (b) the interest of the partners in economic profits and losses (if different from that in taxable income or loss), (c) the partners' interests in the cash flow and other nonliquidating distributions, and (d) the rights of the partners to distributions upon liquidation of the partnership.[41]

The regulations provide a special rule for determining a partner's interest in a partnership if the partnership agreement requires that capital accounts be maintained in the manner provided by Reg. § 1.704-1(b)(2)(iv) and liquidating distributions are made in accordance with positive capital account balances. This special rule is illustrated by the following example:

Example: On January 1, Year 1, Gavin and Margaret form a general partnership to which each contributes $100,000 in cash. The partnership immediately uses the money contributed to purchase a $200,000 piece of equipment that will be depreciated on a straight-line basis over a 10-year period at the rate of $20,000 per year.

Thus, after purchasing the equipment at the beginning of Year 1, the partnership's balance sheet would be as follows:

	Partnership Assets			**Partners' Capital**	
	A/B	Book		A/B	Book
Equipment	$200,000	$200,000	Gavin	$100,000	$100,000
			Margaret	$100,000	$100,000
Total	$200,000	$200,000		$200,000	$200,000

Assume the following:

1. The partnership agreement provides that the partnership will maintain its capital accounts in the manner prescribed by Reg. § 1.704-1(b)(2)(iv) and liquidating distributions will be made in a manner consistent with the partners' positive capital account balances. Neither partner is required to restore a deficit in his or her capital account. Thus, the partnership agreement does not satisfy the primary test for economic effect. (Assume the partnership will also not satisfy either the alternative test for economic effect or the economic equivalence test.)

2. The partnership provides all income and losses, with the exception of depreciation deductions, will be allocated equally to Gavin and Margaret.

3. The partnership agreement specially allocates all depreciation deductions to Margaret.

4. Apart from the depreciation deductions, the income and expenses of the

---

[41] Reg. § 1.704-1(b)(3).

partnership are exactly equal each year.

Analysis: Because the special allocation of the depreciation deductions does not satisfy the substantial economic effect test of § 704(b), the allocation will be tested using the partner's-interest-in-the-partnership test. As noted above, when the partnership agreement, as in this case, provides for the maintenance of capital accounts in accordance with the regulations and for distributions of liquidation proceeds in a manner consistent with the positive capital account balances of the partners, a special rule is applied to determine a partner's interest in the partnership. Pursuant to that rule, a comparison is made between:

(a) the manner in which liquidating distributions would be made if all property of the partnership were to be sold at book value and the partnership were liquidated immediately following the end of the taxable year to which the allocation relates; and

(b) the manner in which liquidating distributions would be made if all partnership property were sold at book value and the partnership were liquidated immediately following the end of the prior taxable year.[42]

With that rule in mind, consider the partnership balance sheet at the end of Year 1, taking into account the $20,000 in depreciation on the equipment and the allocation of that depreciation deduction to Margaret:

	Partnership Assets			**Partners' Capital**	
	A/B	Book		A/B	Book
Equipment	$180,000	$180,000	Gavin	$100,000	$100,000
			Margaret	$80,000	$80,000
Total	$180,000	$180,000		$180,000	$180,000

If the partnership were to sell the equipment for its book value at the end of Year 1 and immediately liquidate, Margaret, consistent with the partnership agreement, would be entitled to receive $80,000 while Gavin would receive $100,000. Thus, while Margaret had a $100,000 capital account at the beginning of Year 1 and would have been entitled to receive $100,000 if the partnership had been liquidated immediately after its formation, she is receiving only $80,000 at the end of the year. She has clearly borne the economic burden associated with the $20,000 depreciation deduction allocated to her. Pursuant to the special rule noted above, the allocation of depreciation to Margaret in Year 1 will be respected. Likewise, the allocation of the $20,000 in depreciation deduction to Margaret in Years 2 through 5 will also be respected under the partner's-interest-in-the-partnership test. At the end of Year 5, the partnership balance sheet will be as follows, reflecting the total of $100,000 in depreciation deductions claimed and the allocation of those deductions to Margaret:

---

[42] Reg. § 1.704-1(b)(3)(iii).

	Partnership Assets			Partners' Capital	
Asset	A/B	Book		A/B	Book
Equipment	$100,000	$100,000	Gavin	$100,000	$100,000
			Margaret	$0	$0
Total	$100,000	$100,000		$100,000	$100,000

Given the balance sheet, it should be clear that, were the partnership to sell the equipment for its book value of $100,000 at the end of Year 5, Margaret would receive nothing and Gavin would receive all $100,000. Margaret thus will have borne economically the burden associated with the $100,000 in depreciation allowed the partnership over the first five years of its existence. For that reason, as noted above, the allocation of the $20,000 depreciation deduction to Margaret in Years 1 through 5 accurately reflects Margaret's interest in the partnership.

Now consider the $20,000 Year 6 depreciation deduction that will reduce the adjusted basis and book value of the equipment to $80,000. If the allocation of the deduction to Margaret were respected, Margaret would have a $20,000 deficit in her capital account that she had no obligation to restore. In other words, Margaret does not bear the economic burden associated with the Year 6 depreciation deduction. By contrast, at the end of Year 5, as noted above, Gavin would have been entitled to $100,000 if the partnership had sold the equipment for its book value and immediately liquidated. At the end of Year 6, however, the partnership would only have $80,000 to distribute to Gavin. Thus, it is Gavin who bears the economic burden associated with the Year 6 depreciation deduction. Pursuant to the special rule under Reg. § 1.704-1(b)(3)(iii) for determining a partner's interest in the partnership, the Year 6 allocation to Margaret cannot be respected and Gavin will be entitled to the Year 6 depreciation deduction. As a result, the partnership's balance sheet at the end of Year 6 will be as follows:

	Partnership Assets			Partners' Capital	
	A/B	Book		A/B	Book
Equipment	$80,000	$80,000	Gavin	$80,000	$80,000
			Margaret	$0	$0
Total	$80,000	$80,000		$80,000	$80,000

With the exception of the special rule discussed above, the application of the partner's interest in the partnership test is difficult to apply and does not provide the kind of certainty that partners seek in structuring their arrangements. Thus, not surprisingly, with respect to allocations provided in their partnership agreement, partners have typically sought to meet the requirements of the "substantial economic effect" test of § 704(b)(2). Although complex, the substantial economic effect test, as a safe harbor test, provides partners certainty with regard to the tax treatment of special allocations provided in a partnership agreement.

D. Conclusion

This Overview highlights the complexity of the regulations interpreting and applying § 704(b)(2). As noted at the outset, Congress intended to accord partnerships considerable flexibility in allocating tax items listed in § 702 and the regulations interpreting that section. That flexibility accommodates the wide variety of economic arrangements seen in partnerships and limited liability companies taxed as partnerships. The § 704(b) regulations, however, provide guardrails to ensure that the flexibility granted by § 704(b) is not abused.

ORRISCH v. COMMISSIONER
55 T.C. 395 (1970)

FEATHERSTON, JUDGE.

Respondent determined deficiencies in petitioners' income tax for 1966 and 1967 in the respective amounts of $2,814.19 and $3,018.11. The only issue for decision is whether an amendment to a partnership agreement allocating to petitioners the entire amount of the depreciation deduction allowable on two buildings owned by the partnership was made for the principal purpose of avoidance of tax within the meaning of § 704(b).

FINDINGS OF FACT

Stanley C. Orrisch (hereinafter sometimes referred to as Orrisch) and Gerta E. Orrisch . . . husband and wife . . . filed joint Federal income tax returns for 1966 and 1967.

In May of 1963, Domonick J. and Elaine J. Crisafi (hereinafter the Crisafis) and petitioners [the Orrischs] formed a partnership to purchase and operate two apartment houses. The purchase of each property was financed principally by a secured loan. Petitioners and the Crisafis initially contributed to the partnership cash in the amounts of $26,500 and $12,500, respectively. During 1964 and 1965 petitioners and the Crisafis each contributed additional cash in the amounts of $8,800. Under the partnership agreement, which was not in writing, they agreed to share equally the profits and losses from the venture.

During each of the years 1963, 1964, and 1965, the partnership suffered losses, attributable in part to the acceleration of depreciation — the deduction was computed on the basis of 150 percent of straight-line depreciation.

Petitioners and the Crisafis respectively reported in their individual income tax returns for these years the partnership losses allocated to them.

Petitioners enjoyed substantial amounts of income from several sources [and reported taxable income on their tax returns for 1963, 1964, and 1965. By contrast, the Crisafis realized losses on real property they owned and reported no net taxable income in those same years.]

Early in 1966, petitioners and the Crisafis orally agreed that, for 1966 and subsequent years, the entire amount of the partnership's depreciation deductions would be specially allocated to petitioners, and that the gain or loss from the partnership's business, computed without regard to any deduction for depreciation, would be divided equally. They further agreed that, in the event the partnership property was sold at a gain, the specially allocated depreciation would be "charged back" to petitioner's capital account and petitioners would pay the tax on the gain attributable thereto . . .

OPINION

The only issue presented for decision is whether tax effect can be given the agreement between petitioners and the Crisafis that, beginning with 1966, all the partnership's depreciation deductions were to be allocated to petitioners for their use in computing their individual income tax liabilities. In our view, the answer must be in the negative, and the amounts of each of the partners' deductions for the depreciation of partnership property must be determined in accordance with the ratio used generally in computing their distributive shares of the partnership's profits and losses.

Among the important innovations of the 1954 Code are limited provisions for flexibility in arrangements for the sharing of income, losses, and deductions arising from business activities conducted through partnerships. The authority for special allocations of such items appears in § 704(a), which provides that a partner's share of any item of income, gain, loss, deduction, or credit shall be determined by the partnership agreement. That rule is coupled with a limitation in § 704(b), however, which states that a special allocation of an item will be disregarded if its "principal purpose" is the avoidance or evasion of Federal income tax. . . . In case a special allocation is disregarded, the partner's share of the item is to be determined in accordance with the ratio by which the partners divide the general profits or losses of the partnership. Sec. 1.704-1(b)(2), Income Tax Regs.

The report of the Senate Committee on Finance accompanying the bill finally enacted as the 1954 Code. . . . explained the tax-avoidance restriction prescribed by § 704(b) as follows:

> Subsection (b) . . . provides that if the principal purpose of any provision in the partnership agreement dealing with a partner's distributive share of a particular item is to avoid or evade the Federal income tax, the partner's distributive share of that item shall be redetermined in accordance with his distributive share of partnership income or loss described in section 702(a)(9) [i.e., the ratio used by the partners for dividing general profits or losses].
>
> Where, however, a provision in a partnership agreement for a special allocation of certain items has substantial economic effect and is not merely a device for reducing the taxes of certain partners without actually affecting their shares of partnership income, then such a provision will be recognized for tax purposes.

This reference to "substantial economic effect" did not appear in the House Ways and Means Committee report . . . discussing § 704(b), and was apparently added in by the Senate Finance Committee to allay fears that special allocations of income or deductions would be denied effect in every case where the allocation resulted in a reduction in the income tax liabilities of one or more of the partners. The statement is an affirmation that special allocations are ordinarily to be recognized if they have business validity apart from their tax consequences . . .

In resolving the question whether the principal purpose of a provision in a partnership agreement is the avoidance or evasion of Federal income tax, all the facts and circumstances in relation to the provision must be taken into account. § 1.704-1(b)(2), Income Tax Regs., lists the following as relevant circumstances to be considered:

> Whether the partnership or a partner individually has a business purpose for the allocation; whether the allocation has "substantial economic effect," that is, whether the allocation may actually affect the dollar amount of the partners' shares of the total partnership income or loss independently of tax consequences; whether related items of income, gain, loss, deduction, or credit from the same source are subject to the same allocation; whether the allocation was made without recognition of normal business factors and only after the amount of the specially allocated item could reasonably be estimated; the duration of the allocation; and the overall tax consequences of the allocation. . . .

Applying these standards, we do not think the special allocation of depreciation in the present case can be given effect.

The evidence is persuasive that the special allocation of depreciation was adopted for a tax-avoidance rather than a business purpose. Depreciation was the only item which was adjusted by the parties; both the income from the buildings and the expenses incurred in their operation, maintenance, and repair were allocated to the partners equally. Since the deduction for depreciation does not vary from year to year with the fortunes of the business, the parties obviously knew what the tax effect of the special allocation would be at the time they adopted it. Furthermore, as shown by our Findings, petitioners had large amounts of income which would be offset by the additional deduction for depreciation; the Crisafis, in contrast, had no taxable income from which to subtract the partnership depreciation deductions, and, due to depreciation deductions which they were obtaining with respect to other housing projects, could expect to have no taxable income in the near future. On the other hand, the insulation of the Crisafis from at least part of a potential capital gains tax was an obvious tax advantage. The inference is unmistakably clear that the agreement did not reflect normal business considerations but was designed primarily to minimize the overall tax liabilities of the partners.

Petitioners urge that the special allocation of the depreciation deduction was adopted in order to equalize the capital accounts of the partners, correcting a disparity ($14,000) in the amounts initially contributed to the partnership by them ($26,500) and the Crisafis ($12,500). But the evidence does not support this contention. Under the special allocation agreement, petitioners were to be entitled, in computing their individual income tax liabilities, to deduct the full amount of the depreciation realized on the partnership property. For 1966, as an example, petitioners were allocated a sum ($18,904) equal to the depreciation on the partnership property ($18,412) plus one-half of the net loss computed without regard to depreciation ($492). The other one-half of the net loss was, of course, allocated to the Crisafis. Petitioners' allocation ($18,904) was then applied to reduce their capital account. The depreciation specially allocated to petitioners ($18,412) in 1966 alone exceeded the amount of the disparity in the contributions. Indeed, at the end of 1967, petitioners' capital account showed a deficit of $25,187.11 compared with a positive balance of $405.65 in the Crisafis' account. By the time the partnership's properties are fully depreciated, the amount of the reduction in petitioners' capital account will approximate the remaining basis for the buildings as of the end of 1967. The Crisafis' capital account will be adjusted only for contributions, withdrawals, gain, or loss, without regard to depreciation, and similar adjustments for these factors will also be made in petitioners' capital account. Thus, rather than correcting an imbalance in the capital accounts of the partners, the special allocation of depreciation will create a vastly greater imbalance than existed at the end of 1966. In the light of these facts, we find it incredible that equalization of the capital accounts was the objective of the special allocation.

Petitioners rely primarily on the argument that the allocation has "substantial economic effect" in that it is reflected in the capital accounts of the partners. Referring to the material quoted above from the report of the Senate Committee on Finance, they contend that this alone is sufficient to show that the special allocation served a business rather than a tax-avoidance purpose.

According to the regulations, an allocation has economic effect if it "may actually affect the dollar amount of the partners' shares of the total partnership income or loss independently of tax consequences." The agreement in this case provided not only for the allocation of depreciation to petitioners but also for gain on the sale of the partnership property to be "charged back" to them. The charge back would cause the gain, for tax purposes, to be allocated on the books entirely to petitioners to the extent of the special allocation of depreciation, and their capital account would be correspondingly increased. The remainder of the gain, if any, would be shared equally by the partners. If the gain on the sale were to equal or exceed the depreciation specially allocated to petitioners, the increase in their capital account caused by the charge back would exactly equal the depreciation deductions previously allowed to them and the proceeds of the sale of the property would be divided equally. In such circumstances, the only effect of the allocation would be a trade of tax consequences, i.e., the Crisafis would relinquish a current depreciation deduction in exchange for exoneration from all or part of the capital gains tax when the property is sold, and petitioners would enjoy a larger current depreciation deduction but would assume a larger ultimate capital gains tax liability. Quite clearly, if the property is sold at a gain, the special allocation will affect only the tax liabilities of the partners and will have no other economic effect.

To find any economic effect of the special allocation agreement aside from its tax consequences, we must, therefore, look to see who is to bear the economic burden of the depreciation if the buildings should be sold for a sum less than their original cost. There is not one syllable of evidence bearing directly on this crucial point. We have noted, however, that when the buildings are fully depreciated, petitioners' capital account will have a deficit, or there will be a disparity in the capital accounts, approximately equal to the undepreciated basis of the buildings as of the beginning of 1966. Under normal accounting procedures, if the building were sold at a gain less than the amount of such disparity petitioners would either be required to contribute to the partnership a sum equal to the remaining deficit in their capital account after the gain on the sale had been added back or would be entitled to receive a proportionately smaller share of the partnership assets on liquidation. Based on the record as a whole, we do not think the partners ever agreed to such an arrangement. On dissolution, we think the partners contemplated an equal division of the partnership assets which would be adjusted only for disparities in cash contributions or withdrawals. Certainly there is no evidence to show otherwise. That being true, the special allocation does not "actually affect the dollar amount of the partners' share of the total partnership income or loss independently of tax consequences" within the meaning of the regulation referred to above.

Our interpretation of the partnership agreement is supported by an analysis of a somewhat similar agreement . . . which petitioners made as part of a marital property settlement agreement in 1968. Under this agreement, Orrisch was entitled to deduct all the depreciation for 1968 in computing his income tax liability, and his wife was to deduct none; but on the sale of the property they were to first reimburse Orrisch for "such moneys as he may have advanced," and then divide the balance of the "profits or proceeds" of the sale equally, each party to report one-half of the capital gain or loss on his income tax return. In the 1969 amendment to this agreement the unequal allocation of the depreciation deduction was discontinued, and a provision similar to the partnership "charge back" was added, i.e., while the proceeds of the sale were to be divided equally, only Orrisch's basis was to be reduced by the depreciation allowed for 1968 so that he would pay taxes on a larger portion of the gain realized on the sale. Significantly, in both this agreement and the partnership agreement, as we interpret it, each party's share of the sales proceeds was determined independently from his share of the depreciation deduction.

In the light of all the evidence we have found as an ultimate fact that the "principal purpose" of the special allocation agreement was tax avoidance within the meaning of section 704(b). Accordingly, the deduction for depreciation for 1966 and 1967 must be allocated between the parties in the same manner as other deductions.

Decision will be entered for the respondent.

Revenue Ruling 99-43
1999-2 C.B. 506

ISSUE

Do partnership allocations lack substantiality under § 1.704-1 (b)(2)(iii) of the Income Tax Regulations when the partners amend the partnership agreement to create offsetting special allocations of particular items after the events giving rise to the items have occurred?

FACTS

A and *B*, both individuals, formed a general partnership, *PRS*. *A* and *B* each contributed $1,000 and also agreed that each would be allocated a 50-percent share of all partnership items. The partnership agreement provides that, upon the contribution of additional capital by either partner, *PRS* must revalue the partnership's property and adjust the partners' capital accounts under § 1.704-1 (b) (2) (iv) (i).

PRS borrowed $8,000 from a bank and used the borrowed and contributed funds to purchase nondepreciable property for $10,000. The loan was nonrecourse to A and B and was secured only by the property. No principal payments were due for 6 years, and interest was payable semi-annually at a market rate.

After one year, the fair market value of the property fell from $10,000 to $6,000, but the principal amount of the loan remained $8,000. As part of a workout arrangement among the bank, *PRS*, *A*, and *B*, the bank reduced the principal amount of the loan by $2,000, and *A* contributed an additional $500 to *PRS*. *A*'s capital account was credited with the $500, which *PRS* used to pay currently deductible expenses incurred in connection with the workout. All $500 of the currently deductible workout expenses were allocated to *A*. *B* made no additional contribution of capital. At the time of the workout, *B* was insolvent within the meaning of § 108 (a) of the Internal Revenue Code. *A* and *B* agreed that, after the workout, *A* would have a 60-percent interest and *B* would have a 40-percent interest in the profits and losses of *PRS*.

As a result of the property's decline in value and the workout, *PRS* had two items to allocate between *A* and *B*. First, the agreement to cancel $2,000 of the loan resulted in $2,000 of cancellation of indebtedness income (COD income). Second, *A*'s contribution of $500 to *PRS* was an event that required *PRS*, under the partnership agreement, to revalue partnership property and adjust *A*'s and B's capital accounts. Because of the decline in value of the property, the revaluation resulted in a $4,000 economic loss that must be allocated between *A*'s and *B*'s capital accounts.

Under the terms of the original partnership agreement, *PRS* would have allocated these items equally between *A* and *B*. *A* and *B*, however, amend the partnership agreement (in a timely manner) to make two special allocations. First, *PRS* specially allocates the entire $2,000 of COD income to *B*, an insolvent partner. Second, *PRS* specially allocates the book loss from the revaluation $1,000 to *A* and $3,000 to *B*.

While *A* receives a $1,000 allocation of book loss and *B* receives a $3,000 allocation of book loss, neither of these allocations results in a tax loss to either partner. Rather, the allocations result only in adjustments to *A*'s and *B*'s capital accounts. Thus, the cumulative effect of the special allocations is to reduce each partner's capital account to zero immediately following the allocations despite the fact that *B* is allocated $2,000 of income for tax purposes.

LAW

Section 61(a)(12) provides that gross income includes income from the discharge of indebtedness.

Rev. Rul. 91-31, 1991-1 C.B. 19, holds that a taxpayer realizes COD income when a creditor (who was not the seller of the underlying property) reduces the principal amount of an under-secured nonrecourse debt.

Under § 704(b) and the regulations thereunder, allocations of a partnership's items of income, gain, loss, deduction, or credit provided for in the partnership agreement will be respected if the allocations have substantial economic effect. Allocations that fail to have substantial economic effect will be reallocated according to the partners' interests in the partnership (as defined in § 1.704-1(b)(3)).

Section 1.704-1(b)(2)(iv)(i) provides that a partnership may, upon the occurrence of certain events (including the contribution of money to the partnership by a new or existing partner), increase or decrease the partners' capital accounts to reflect a revaluation of the partnership property.

Section 1.704-1(b)(2)(iv)(g) provides that, to the extent a partnership's property is reflected on the books of the partnership at a book value that differs from the adjusted tax basis, the substantial economic effect requirements apply to the allocations of book items. Section 704 (c) and § 1.704-1 (b) (4) (i) govern the partners' distributive shares of tax items.

Section 1.704-1(b)(2)(i) provides that the determination of whether an allocation of income, gain, loss, or deduction (or item thereof) to a partner has substantial economic effect involves a two-part analysis that is made at the end of the partnership year to which the allocation relates. In order for an allocation to have substantial economic effect, the allocation must have both economic effect (within the meaning of § 1.704-1(b)(2)(ii)) and be substantial (within the meaning of § 1.704-1(b)(2)(iii)).

Section 1.704-1(b)(2)(iii)(a) provides that the economic effect of an allocation (or allocations) is substantial if there is a reasonable possibility that the allocation (or allocations) will substantially affect the dollar amounts to be received by the partners from the partnership independent of the tax consequences. However, the economic effect of an allocation is not substantial if, at the time the allocation becomes part of the partnership agreement, (1) the after-tax economic consequences of at least one partner may, in present value terms, be enhanced compared to the consequences if the allocation (or allocations) were not contained in the partnership agreement, and (2) there is a strong likelihood that the after-tax economic consequences of no partner will, in present value terms, be substantially diminished compared to the consequences if the allocation (or allocations) were not contained in the partnership agreement. In determining the after-tax economic benefit or detriment to a partner, tax consequences that result from the interaction of the allocation with the partner's tax attributes that are unrelated to the partnership will be taken into account.

Section 1.704-1(b)(2)(iii)(b) provides that the economic effect of an allocation (or allocations) in a partnership taxable year is not substantial if the allocations result in shifting tax consequences. Shifting tax consequences result when, at the time the allocation (or allocations) becomes part of the partnership agreement, there is a strong likelihood that (1) the net increases and decreases that will be recorded in the partners' respective capital accounts for the taxable year will not differ substantially from the net increases and decreases that would be recorded in the partners' respective capital accounts for the year if the allocations were not contained in the partnership agreement, and (2) the total tax liability of the partners (for their respective tax years in which the allocations will be taken into account) will be less than if the allocations were not contained in the partnership agreement.

Section 1.704-1(b)(2)(iii)(c) provides that the economic effect of an allocation (or allocations) in a partnership taxable year is not substantial if the allocations are transitory. Allocations are considered transitory if a partnership agreement provides for the possibility that one or more allocations (the "original allocation(s)") will be largely offset by other allocations (the "offsetting allocation(s)"), and, at the time the allocations become part of the partnership agreement, there is a strong likelihood that (1) the net increases and decreases that will be recorded in the partners' capital accounts for the taxable years to which the allocations relate will not differ substantially from the net increases and decreases that would be recorded in such partners' respective capital accounts for such years if the original and offsetting allocation(s) were not contained in the partnership agreement, and (2) the total tax liability of the partners (for their respective tax years in which the allocations will be taken into account) will be less than if the allocations were not contained in the partnership agreement.

Section 761(c) provides that a partnership agreement includes any modifications made prior to, or at, the time prescribed for filing a partnership return (not including extensions) which are agreed to by all partners, or which are adopted in such other manner as may be provided by the partnership agreement.

ANALYSIS

PRS is free to allocate partnership items between *A* and *B* in accordance with the provisions of the partnership agreement if the allocations have substantial economic effect under § 1.704-1(b)(2). To the extent that the minimum gain chargeback rules do not apply, COD income may be allocated in accordance with the rules under § 1.704-1(b)(2). This is true notwithstanding that the COD income arises in connection with the cancellation of a nonrecourse debt.

The economic effect of an allocation is not substantial if, at the time that the allocation becomes part of the partnership agreement, the allocation fails each of two tests. The allocation fails the first test if the after-tax consequences of at least one partner may, in present value terms, be enhanced compared to the consequences if the allocation (or allocations) were not contained in the partnership agreement. The allocation fails the second test if there is a strong likelihood that the after-tax economic consequences of no partner will, in present value terms, be substantially diminished compared to such consequences if the allocation (or allocations) were not contained in the partnership agreement.

A and B amended the PRS partnership agreement to provide for an allocation of the entire $2,000 of the COD income to B. B, an insolvent taxpayer, is eligible to exclude the income under § 108, so it is unlikely that the $2,000 of COD income would increase B's immediate tax liability. Without the special allocation, A, who is not insolvent or otherwise entitled to exclude the COD income under § 108, would pay tax immediately on the $1,000 of COD income allocated under the general ratio for sharing income. A and B also amended the PRS partnership agreement to provide for the special allocation of the book loss resulting from the revaluation. Because the two special allocations offset each other, B will not realize any economic benefit from the $2,000 income allocation, even if the property subsequently appreciates in value.

The economics of PRS are unaffected by the paired special allocations. After the capital accounts of A and B are adjusted to reflect the special allocations, A and B each have a capital account of zero. Economically, the situation of both partners is identical to what it would have been had the special allocations not occurred. In addition, a strong likelihood exists that the total tax liability of A and B will be less than if PRS had allocated 50 percent of the $2,000 of COD income and 50 percent of the $4,000 book loss to each partner. Therefore, the special allocations of COD income and book loss are shifting allocations under § 1.704-1(b)(2)(iii)(b) and lack substantiality. (Alternatively, the allocations could be transitory allocations under § 1.704-1(b)(2)(iii)(c) if the allocations occur during different partnership taxable years).

This conclusion is not altered by the "value equals basis" rule that applies in determining the substantiality of an allocation. See § 1.704-1(b)(2)(iii)(c)(2). Under that rule, the adjusted tax basis (or, if different, the book value) of partnership property will be presumed to be the fair market value of the property. This presumption is appropriate in most cases because, under § 1.704-1(b)(2(iv), property generally will be reflected on the books of the partnership at its fair market value when acquired. Thus, an allocation of gain or loss from the disposition of the property will reflect subsequent changes in the value of the property that generally cannot be predicted.

The substantiality of an allocation, however, is analyzed "at the time the allocation becomes part of the partnership agreement," not the time at which the allocation is first effective. See § 1.704-1(b) (2) (iii) (a). In the situation described above, the provisions of the PRS partnership agreement governing the allocation of gain or loss from the disposition of property are changed at a time that is after the property has been revalued on the books of the partnership, but are effective for a period that begins prior to the revaluation. See § 1.704-1(b)(2)(iv)(f).

Under these facts, the presumption that value equals basis does not apply to validate the allocations. Instead, PRS's allocations of gain or loss must be closely scrutinized in determining the appropriate tax consequences. Cf. § 1.704-1(b)(4)(vi). In this situation, the special allocations of the $2,000 of COD income and $4,000 of book loss will not be respected and, instead, must be allocated in accordance with the A's and B's interests in the partnership under § 1.704-1(b)(3).

Close scrutiny also would be required if the changes were made at a time when the events giving rise to the allocations had not yet occurred but were likely to occur or if, under the original allocation provisions of a partnership agreement, there was a strong likelihood that a disproportionate amount of COD income earned in the future would be allocated to any partner who is insolvent at the time of the allocation and would be offset by an increased allocation of loss or a reduced allocation of income to such partner or partners.

HOLDING

Partnership special allocations lack substantiality when the partners amend the partnership agreement to specially allocate COD income and book items from a related revaluation after the events creating such items have occurred if the overall economic effect of the special allocations on the partners' capital accounts does not differ substantially from the economic effect of the original allocations in the partnership agreement.

NOTE ON PARTNERSHIP INTERESTS CREATED BY GIFT

Partnership interests may be created by gift, as, for example, where a partnership interest is transferred from one family member to another. At one time, it was uncertain whether such so-called family partnerships would be respected as partnerships for federal tax purposes. In *Commissioner v. Culbertson*, however, the Supreme Court rejected the position that a family member needed to contribute "vital services" or "original capital" (as opposed, for example, to capital donated by another family member) to be recognized as a partner. Instead, said the Court, the question was "whether, considering all the facts . . . the parties in good faith and acting with a business purpose intended to join together in the present conduct of the enterprise." *Commissioner v. Culbertson*, 337 U.S. 733, 742 (1949).

Congress enacted the predecessors to §§ 704(e) and 761(b) (second sentence) in 1951, in the aftermath of *Culbertson*, to reinforce both the Court's decision and certain "basic principles" of tax law:

> [This proposed legislation] is intended to harmonize the rules governing interests in the so-called family partnership with those generally applicable to other forms of property or business. Two principles governing attribution of income have long been accepted as basic: (1) income from property is attributable to the owner of the property; (2) income from personal services is attributable to the person rendering the services. There is no reason for applying different principles to partnership income. If an individual makes a bona fide gift of real estate, or of a share of corporate stock, the rent or dividend income is taxable to the donee. . . . [H]owever the owner of a partnership interest may have acquired such interest, the income is taxable to the owner, if he is the real owner. If the ownership is real, it does not matter what motivated the transfer to him or whether the business benefitted from the entrance of a new partner.
>
> Although there is no basis under existing statutes for any different treatment of partnership interests, some decisions in this field have ignored the principle that income from property is to be taxed to the owner of the property. Many court decisions since . . . *Culbertson* have held invalid for tax purposes family partnerships which arose by virtue of a gift of a partnership interest from one family member to another, where the donee performed no vital services for the partnership.
>
> Since legislation is now necessary to make clear the fundamental principle that, where there is a real transfer of ownership, a gift of a family partnership interest is to be respected for tax purposes without regard to the motives which actuated the transfer, it is considered appropriate at the same time to provide specific safeguards — whether or not such safeguards may be inherent in the general rule — against the use of the partnership device to accomplish the deflection of income from the real owner.
>
> Therefore, [the legislation] provides that, in the case of any partnership income created by gift, the allocation of income according to the terms of the partnership agreement shall be controlling for income tax purposes, except where the shares are allocated without proper allowance of reason-

able compensation for services rendered to the partnership by the donor, and except to the extent that the allocation to the donated capital is proportionately greater than that attributable to the donor's capital. [S. Rep. No. 781, 82nd Cong., 1st Sess., reprinted in 1951-2 C.B. 458, 485–86.]

---

§ 704(e). Partnership Interests Created by Gift

(1) Distributive share of donee includible in gross income — In the case of any partnership interest created by gift, the distributive share of the donee under the partnership agreement shall be includible in his gross income, except to the extent that such share is determined without allowance of reasonable compensation for services rendered to the partnership by the donor, and except to the extent that the portion of such share attributable to donated capital is proportionately greater than the share of the donor attributable to the donor's capital . . .

(2) Purchase of interest by member of family — . . . For purposes of this subsection, an interest purchased by one member of a family from another shall be considered to be created by gift from the seller, and the fair market value of the purchased interest shall be considered to be donated capital. The "family" of any individual shall include only his spouse, ancestors, and lineal descendants, and any trusts for the primary benefit of such persons.

---

§ 761(b). Partner—

. . . In the case of a capital interest in a partnership in which capital is a material income-producing factor, whether a person is a partner with respect to such interests shall be determined without regard to whether such interest was derived by gift from any other person.

The provisions of § 704(e) and 761(b) reflect these congressional concerns. Under § 761(b), a person is recognized as a partner if he owns a capital interest in a partnership in which capital is a material income-producing factor without regard to whether the interest was acquired by gift. The regulations (which predate the second sentence of § 761(b)) go into considerable detail with respect to both requirements, i.e., whether the purported owner of the partnership interest is, in fact, an "owner" — see the regulation's "basic tests as to ownership" at Reg. § 1.704-1(e)(2) — and whether capital is a material income-producing factor — see Reg. § 1.704-1(e)(1)(iv). If both requirements are met, then the person is recognized as a partner.

The allocation of income concerns are addressed in § 704(e)(1), providing that the partnership agreement controls as to distributive shares, (1) "except to the extent that such share is determined without allowance of reasonable compensation for services rendered to the partnership by the donor" and (2) also "except to the extent that the portion of such share attributable to donated capital is proportionately greater than the share of the donor attributable to the donor's capital." If either of these "safeguards" is not observed, a reallocation of income is necessary so as to provide the reasonable allowance for donor's services and to attribute income to partnership capital between donor and donee in accordance with their respective interests in such capital. *See* Reg. § 1.704-1(e)(3).

Section 704(e)(1) applies by its terms to partnership interests "created by gift." To counter efforts by family members to disguise gifts as purported purchases, in the hope of avoiding the § 704(e)(1) reallocation rules, § 704(e)(2) provides an interest purchased by one family member from another "shall be considered to be created by gift" and the fair market value of the purchased interest "shall be considered to be donated capital." For this purpose, an individual's family consists of spouse, ancestors, lineal descendants, and trusts for their primary benefit.

Note that § 761(b) applies only to partnerships where capital is a material income-producing factor. Where capital is not a material income-producing factor, i.e., in service partnerships, the *Culbertson* test (acting in good faith and with a business purpose, intending to join together in the present conduct of an enterprise) should be applied to determine whether the purported partner is, in fact, a partner. If so, the reallocation rules of § 704(e)(1) and (2) will apply to these partnership interests created by gift, even where capital is not a material income-producing factor in the partnership.

Finally, note that the substantial economic effect provisions of § 704(b) do not prevail over assignment of income principles addressed by other parts of Subchapter K. In this regard, the § 704(b) regulations explicitly state that an allocation "respected under § 704(b) . . . nevertheless may be reallocated under other provisions, such as . . . section 704(e)(2) [now § 704(e)(1)] . . . (and related assignment of income principles) . . . " Reg. § 1.704-1(b)(1)(iii).

Chapter 10

CONTRIBUTED PROPERTY: § 704(c)(1)(A) ALLOCATIONS

I. PROBLEMS

1. On February 1, Year 1, Patrick and Megan created a general partnership to conduct a used car business. Their partnership is a calendar year partnership. In forming the partnership, Patrick and Megan each contributed $150,000 of cash. In addition, Patrick contributed a tract of raw land with a fair market value of $200,000 and an adjusted basis of $80,000 and Megan contributed publicly traded stock with a fair market value of $ 200,000 and an adjusted basis of $250,000. Patrick and Megan each has a 50% interest in partnership capital and profits. Assume Patrick had held the land for investment for 10 years and Megan had owned the stock for three years.

   (a) Create an opening balance sheet for the partnership.

   (b) Assume in Year 1 the partnership's operating income exactly equaled its operating expenses. Explain the tax consequences to Patrick and Megan if, on December 31, Year 1, the partnership sells the land contributed by Patrick for $200,000 and sells the stock contributed by Megan for $200,000. Assume that, in applying § 704(c)(1)(A), the partnership uses the "Traditional Method" of allocation. In addition, with respect to the sale of the stock, utilize the assigned proposed regulations regarding contributed property with built-in loss. In view of the sale of the land and stock, how will the year-end balance sheet differ from the opening balance sheet?

   (c) How would your answer to (b) change if the partnership sold the land for $220,000 and sold the stock for $180,000?

   (d) How would your answer to (b) change if the partnership in Year 1 sold the stock for $220,000 and did not sell the land?

   (e) How would your answer to (b) change if the partnership in Year 1 sold the land for $180,000 and did not sell the stock?

   (f) How would your answer to (e) change if the partnership used the Remedial Method?

   (g) How would your answer to (e) change if the partnership used the Traditional Method with Curative Allocations and the partnership sold the stock for $220,000 at the same time it sold the land for $180,000?

2. At the beginning of Year 1, Emily and Braedon formed a general partnership to which Emily contributed $150,000 in cash and Braedon contributed a piece of depreciable property with a fair market value of $150,000 and an adjusted basis of $100,000. Assume the property has a remaining recovery period under § 168(i)(7) of five years and will be depreciated by the partnership on a straight-line basis.

   (a) Assuming the partnership elects to use the Traditional Method, how will the partnership allocate the annual depreciation allowable on the property contributed by Braedon? Assume Emily and Braedon each has a 50% interest in partnership capital and profits.

   (b) How will your answer to (a) change if the property's adjusted basis is $50,000 instead of $100,000?

   (c) How would your answer to (b) change if the partnership utilized the Remedial Method, assuming, pursuant to Reg. § 1.704-3(d)(2), the partnership will use a 10-year recovery period and the straight-line method to recover "the amount by which the book basis exceeds the property's adjusted tax basis?"

   (d) How will your answer to (a) change if the property's adjusted basis is $200,000 instead of $100,000, In answering this question, utilize the assigned proposed regulations regarding contributed property with built-in loss.

   (e) Assume the facts of (a). The partnership sells the property contributed by Braedon at the end of Year 2 after claiming depreciation for two years. Explain the tax consequences to Emily and Braedon if the sale price is: (1) $130,000 or (2) $70,000. Create a balance sheet for the partnership immediately before and a balance sheet immediately after the sales. (In doing so, assume the partnership's only property is $150,000 in cash and the piece of depreciable property, and assume that, during the first two years, the partnership's income and expenses, except for depreciation, had been equal.

3. Mike and Martin each contributed $125,000 in forming the M&M Partnership. Each will have a 50% interest in partnership capital and profits. Immediately following its formation, the M&M Partnership used $150,000 of the cash contributed to purchase a tract of land (Tract A) for business use. Assume the partnership agreement satisfies the three requirements for economic effect of Reg. § 1.704-1(b)(2)(ii)(b). Subsequently, the partnership acquired an adjacent tract of land (Tract B) for $100,000. Two years later, the partnership's only assets were Tract A, which then had a value of $250,000 and an adjusted basis of $150,000, and Tract B, which then had a value of $50,000 and an adjusted basis of $100,000. In need of cash, the partnership invited Jackie to join as an equal one-third partner. To acquire her one-third interest, Jackie contributed $150,000 in cash to the partnership. Assume that, pursuant to Reg. § 1.704-1(b)(2)(iv)(f), the partnership revalued its assets in anticipation of Jackie's admission as a partner. Three years later, the partnership decided to relocate its operations and sold Tract A for $400,000 and Tract B for $20,000. Applying the Traditional

Method, explain the tax consequences of the sales to the three partners.

Assignment for Chapter 10:

Complete the above Problems.

Read: Internal Revenue Code: §§ 704(c)(1)(A), (C), 705, and 721–723.
Treasury Regulations: §§ 1.704-1(b)(1)(iv)-(vi); 1.704-1(b)(2)(iv)(b), (d)(1), (3), (e), (f), (g), and (h)(1); 1.704-3(a)(1)–(6), (b), (c)(1)–(4) Exs. 1 and 2, (d)(1)–(7) Exs. 1 and 2, (e)(1), (2). Prop. Reg. § 1.704-3(f)(1)–(3)(ii).
Materials: Overview

II. VOCABULARY

§ 704(c) property
built-in gain
built-in loss
book/tax disparity
ceiling rule
traditional method
traditional method with curative allocations
remedial method
remedial or notional items
booked-up capital accounts
booked-down capital accounts
revaluation of partnership assets
reverse § 704(c) allocations

III. OBJECTIVES

1. To identify property that qualifies as § 704(c) property.

2. To calculate the built-in gain or loss, if any, associated with property contributed to a partnership.

3. To explain the allocation of book and tax gain or loss, if any, on the sale of non-depreciable § 704(c) property using the Traditional Method.

4. To explain the allocation of book and tax gain or loss, if any, on the sale of non-depreciable § 704(c) property using the Traditional Method with Curative Allocations.

5. To explain the allocation of book and tax gain or loss, if any, on the sale of non-depreciable § 704(c) property using the Remedial Method.

6. To explain the allocation of book and tax depreciation using the Traditional Method, the Traditional Method with Curative Allocations, and the Remedial Method.

7. To explain the allocation of book and tax gain or loss on the sale of depreciable § 704(c) property using the Traditional Method, the Traditional Method with Curative Allocations, and the Remedial Method.

8. To identify circumstances under which partners may restate their capital accounts to reflect a revaluation of partnership assets on the partnership books.

9. To explain "reverse § 704(c) allocations" resulting from the contribution of money or property by a new or existing partner in exchange for an interest in the partnership.

IV. OVERVIEW

As discussed in detail in Chapter 2, § 721 provides that neither gain nor loss will be recognized on the contribution of property to a partnership in exchange for a partnership interest. Pursuant to § 722, the contributing partner takes a basis in her partnership interest (her outside basis) equal to the adjusted basis she had in the property contributed. The partnership's basis in the contributed property (the partnership's inside basis) is the adjusted basis the contributing partner had in the property. § 723. As noted in Chapter 5, the contributing partner's capital account reflects the fair market value of the property contributed. Reg. § 1.704-1(b)(2)(iv)(b)(1) and (d)(1). Thus, for capital account purposes, the contributing partner has, in effect, been credited with any gain or loss that inheres in the contributed property.

This chapter addresses a number of important questions raised by the nonrecognition regime of § 721, i.e., with respect to contributed property, who will be allocated the built-in gain or loss if the partnership sells the property, how will depreciation deductions be allocated among the partners if the contributed property is depreciable in the hands of the partnership, and what adjustments, if any, must be made to the contributing partner's capital account and outside basis as a result of the allocation of built-in gain, built-in loss, or depreciation? Section 704(c)(1)(A), enacted as part of the Deficit Reduction Act of 1984, and the regulations interpreting that provision specifically address these allocation questions and will be the focus of this chapter.

A. Pre-1984 Law

To understand the current treatment of allocations with regard to contributed property, it is helpful to review the law prior to the enactment of § 704(c)(1)(A). Prior to the Deficit Reduction Act of 1984, when a person contributed property with built-in gain or built-in loss to a partnership, former § 704(c)(1) and (2)[1] provided two alternatives for the allocation of the gain, loss, or depreciation associated with the contributed property. The alternatives reflected the tension between the aggregate and entity approaches to partnership tax. Pursuant to former § 704(c)(1), *if the partnership agreement so provided*, part or all of the gain, loss, or depreciation with respect to contributed property would be shared among the partners so as to take into account any variation between the adjusted basis of the property at the time of its contribution and its fair market value at that time.[2]

---

[1] Enacted as part of the 1954 Internal Revenue Code, which created Subchapter K of the Code.

[2] Former § 704(c)(1) and former Reg. § 1.704-1(c)(2).

The aggregate approach to partnership taxation appears to dominate here as the contributing partner is viewed as having a continuing interest in the specific property that partner contributed. By contrast, pursuant to former § 704(c)(2), *if the partnership agreement were silent as to treatment of items with respect to contributed property*, the gain, loss, or depreciation would be allocated as if the property had been *purchased* by the partnership.[3] This alternative clearly reflects an entity approach to partnership taxation.

Consider the following examples demonstrating these two pre-1984 alternatives. As you consider these examples, consider the income-shifting potential and timing distortions created by the former § 704(c) rules.

> **Example 1:** On January 1, Year 1, Adam and Eve form the A&E Partnership, a calendar year, general partnership, with Eve contributing $100,000 in cash for her 50% partnership interest and Adam contributing land with a fair market value of $100,000 and an adjusted basis of $60,000 for his 50% partnership interest. (There is thus $40,000 of "built-in" gain in the land.) Adam had held the land for business purposes for a number of years. The partnership agreement specifically allocates built-in gain and loss to the contributing partner and provides that both liquidating and nonliquidating distributions will be made in equal shares to the two partners. Assume the partnership sells the land on December 31, Year 1 for $100,000. Assume also that, in Year 1, the partnership's deductions had exactly equaled its income other than the gain from the land.
>
> **Analysis:** Pursuant to §§ 722 and 1012, Eve would have a $100,000 basis (outside basis) in her partnership interest[4] and an initial capital account equal to $100,000. Reg. § 1.704-1(b)(2)(iv)(b)(1). Adam would take a $60,000 basis (outside basis) in his partnership interest (§ 722) and would also have an initial capital account of $100,000.) Reg. § 1.704-1(b)(2)(iv)(b)(2). Note that, although for tax purposes Adam's unrecovered cost, i.e., adjusted basis, in the land was $60,000, Adam is credited in his capital account with making a $100,000 investment in the partnership. Reg. § 1.704-1(b)(2)(iv)(b)(2) and (d)(1). This book/tax disparity is ultimately at the heart of the § 704(c) rules. For its part, the partnership would take a basis of $60,000 in the land Adam contributed and tack Adam's holding period. §§ 723 and 1223(2).
>
> As a result of the sale, the partnership has neither book gain nor book loss; it has merely substituted $100,000 of cash for the $100,000 of land. Given the absence of any book gain or loss to be shared by the partners, no adjustments are made to Adam's and Eve's capital (book) accounts. As a result, at the end of Year 1, Adam's and Eve's capital accounts would still be $100,000.[5] The partnership, however, would realize and recognize $40,000 of

---

[3] Former § 704(c)(2) and former Reg. § 1.704-1(c)(2).

[4] Her holding period in her partnership interest would commence the day following her purchase of that interest for $100,000. Rev. Rul. 66-7, 1966-1 C.B. 188; see Reg. §1.1223-3(f) Ex. 1.

[5] Although, as indicated in this example, Adam will be required to report $40,000 of tax gain, Adam's capital account would not be increased because Adam's capital account, as noted above, was credited at

tax gain, i.e., an amount of tax gain equal to the "built-in gain" inhering in the property when Adam contributed it. Under former § 704(c)(1), the $40,000 of realized and recognized gain would be allocated to Adam. To reflect this allocation of gain, Adam's outside basis would be increased from $60,000 to 100,000.[6] Were the partnership to liquidate immediately after the sale and the partnership's only assets were $200,000 of cash, i.e., the $100,000 originally contributed by Eve and the $100,000 in sale proceeds from the land, the $200,000 in cash would be distributed in equal shares consistent with the partnership agreement (and with partners' capital account balances). Thus, Adam and Eve would each receive $100,000. Because each has a $100,000 outside basis, neither would recognize any gain or loss on the liquidating distribution. § 731.

Example 2: Assume the same facts as Example 1 except the partnership agreement was silent on the allocation of items with respect to contributed property. As a result, pursuant to former § 704(c)(2), the gain, loss, and depreciation with respect to that property would be allocated as though the property had been *purchased* by the partnership. What are the tax consequences to Adam and Eve as a result of a sale of the land and a subsequent liquidation of the partnership?

Analysis: Unlike the results in Example 1, when the A&E Partnership sells the land, the $40,000 of gain[7] would be allocated equally to Adam and Eve just as though the partnership had purchased the land for $60,000 instead of receiving the land with a $60,000 adjusted basis as a contribution from Adam. Eve's $100,000 outside basis would be increased to $120,000 and Adam's $60,000 outside basis would be increased to $80,000. Again, because there is no book gain or loss, Adam's and Eve's capital accounts — both of which are $100,000 as in Example 1 — would not be adjusted. Were the partnership to be liquidated immediately after the sale of the land, the $200,000 of cash held by the partnership would be distributed $100,000 to Adam and $100,000 to Eve. Because Adam's outside basis was only $80,000, Adam would have $20,000 of gain to report.[8] By contrast, Eve would have a $120,000 outside basis and, as a result, she would recognize a $20,000 loss.[9]

In Example 2, because the partnership agreement was silent regarding allocations, former § 704(c)(2) enabled Adam to shift to Eve $20,000 of the built-in gain on the land he contributed to the partnership. As the example demonstrates, however,

---

the time of the land's contribution with the gain inherent in the land, i.e., although Adam had only a $60,000 adjusted basis in the land, his capital account reflected the $100,000 fair market value of the property.

[6] § 705(a)(1)(A). Adam would have a holding period in his partnership interest that included the period during which he held the land he contributed to the partnership. § 1223(1). Because he had held the land for a number of years, he would have a long-term holding period.

[7] The gain would presumably be § 1231 gain.

[8] § 731(a)(1). This gain would be long-term capital gain. § 741.

[9] § 731(a)(2). Eve's loss would be short-term capital loss because she had not held her partnership interest for more than one year.

this shift is potentially temporary because Adam would have to report $20,000 of gain on the liquidation of the partnership and Eve would be entitled to a $20,000 loss on the facts presented. Unlike the facts presented in Example 2, the liquidation of the partnership, instead of occurring immediately after the sale of the land, could be delayed for years, along with the ultimate recognition of the gain by Adam and the loss by Eve. In addition, however, consider the possibility that a permanent distortion would exist if either Adam or Eve were to die before the liquidation and the application of § 1014 resulted in either a stepped-up or stepped down basis for the decedent's partnership interest.[10] Former § 704(c)(2) thus, in effect, allowed a temporary (or permanent) assignment of income — a result generally prohibited in our tax law as the assignment of income undermines the integrity of our progressive rate structure.

The regulations interpreting former § 704(c)(1) also established what has become known as the "ceiling rule." Specifically, the regulations provided that, if the partnership agreement provided for the allocation of built-in gain or built-in loss or depreciation with respect to contributed property, the total gain, loss, or depreciation that could be allocated to the partners was "limited to a 'ceiling' which cannot exceed the amount of gain or loss realized by the partnership or the depreciation . . . allowable to it."[11] Consider the following example applying this "ceiling rule" of the regulations promulgated under former § 704(c)(1).

> **Example 3:** Assume the facts of Example 1, except the partnership sold the land for $80,000 contributed by Adam and thus realized and recognized only $20,000 of gain. Thus, the partnership, which had booked the land contributed by Adam at $100,000, has suffered a $20,000 book loss that would be allocated in equal shares to Adam and Eve. (Adam's and Eve's capital accounts would therefore each be decreased to $90,000.) In a perfect tax world, it would seem that each partner should be allocated a $10,000 tax loss to account for the $10,000 book loss allocated to each. At the same time, in that perfect world, Adam would be allocated $40,000 of tax gain to account for the $40,000 of gain that was built into the land he contributed to the partnership. (Note that, taking into account the $20,000 of tax loss plus the $40,000 of tax gain, the net amount allocated in this perfect world would be $20,000 of gain, the exact amount of gain that was actually realized and recognized on the sale.) As a result of these allocations, Adam's outside basis would be increased by the $40,000 of gain he was required to

---

[10] Thus, in this example, were Eve to die before the liquidation occurred, the application of § 1014 would result in Eve's partnership interest having a basis of $100,000, i.e., the fair market value of that interest at the date of Eve's death. By contrast, were Adam to die immediately before the liquidation of the partnership, § 1014 would step up the basis of his partnership interest to $100,000 to reflect the fair market value of that interest at the time of Adam's death.

An additional distortion that may exist has to do with character. If, in Example 2, instead of contributing land, Adam had contributed inventory with a value of $100,000 and an adjusted basis of $60,000, the sale of the inventory would have resulted in $40,000 of ordinary income, allocated in equal shares to Adam and Eve. Upon the subsequent liquidation, both Adam and Eve would have short-term capital gain. (Note that, under § 1223(1), Adam could not tack the holding period of the inventory to his partnership interest.) Thus, apart from the timing distortion, a character distortion also is created.

[11] Former Reg. § 1.704-1(c)(2).

report and decreased by the $10,000 loss he was allocated. Thus, Adam's outside basis would be $90,000 (i.e., $60,000 + $40,000 - $10,000 = $90,000). Eve's outside basis would be reduced by the $10,000 of loss allocated to her and her outside basis would thus equal $90,000. Adam's and Eve's capital accounts would each be reduced by their $10,000 share of the book loss resulting from the sale of the land for $20,000 less than the value at which it had been booked. Thus, each would have a $90,000 capital account. If the partnership were to liquidate immediately, Adam and Eve would each receive $90,000 of cash and, because each had a $90,000 adjusted basis in his or her partnership interest, neither would recognize any gain or loss.

But, as noted above, the old regulations interpreting and applying former § 704(c)(1) did not allow for that ideal world. Under those regulations, because the only tax item that existed was the $20,000 gain on the partnership's sale of the land, that $20,000 of gain was all that could be allocated. (In other words, the regulations did not permit the creation, as was the case in our perfect tax world above, of $20,000 of tax loss and $40,000 of tax gain for purposes of making the allocation.) Given the ceiling rule, Adam would be allocated all $20,000 of the actual tax gain recognized on the sale. Adam's outside basis would be increased from $60,000 to $80,000. Eve's basis in her partnership interest would remain at $100,000. Adam's and Eve's capital accounts would, as noted above, be $90,000 because they each experienced $10,000 of book loss. If the partnership were to be liquidated immediately after the sale, Adam and Eve would each receive $90,000 of cash. As a result of the liquidating distribution, Adam would have a $10,000 gain pursuant to § 731(a)(1) and Eve would have a $10,000 loss pursuant to § 731(a)(2).

In Example 3, note that the ceiling rule has the effect of depriving Eve of any immediate tax deduction as a result of her $10,000 share of the book loss realized on the sale of the land. At the same time (and again because of the ceiling rule), Adam, who conceptually should have reported a net gain of $30,000 (i.e., $40,000 of gain to reflect the amount of built-in gain on contribution and a $10,000 loss to reflect the loss on the sale by the partnership) is only required to report $20,000 of net gain. Thus, it is as though Eve has shifted to Adam the $10,000 tax loss she should have been able to claim. Of course, in this example everything is rectified (at least dollar-wise) upon liquidation of the partnership when Eve finally recognizes her $10,000 tax loss and Adam is forced to recognize an additional $10,000 of gain. Again, however, the distortion created by the ceiling rule may not be resolved for many years or ever, if one of the partners were to die before liquidation of the partnership. § 1014.

B. Current Law: The Enactment of § 704(c)(1)(A)

Concerned about the shifting of tax consequences with respect to contributed property illustrated in the above examples, Congress in 1984 amended § 704(c), eliminating former § 704(c)(1) and (2) discussed above and replacing them with current § 704(c)(1)(A). Section 704(c)(1)(A) prevents the transfer of built-in gain or loss from the contributing partner by requiring a partnership to allocate income, gain, loss, and deduction with respect to contributed property to take into account the difference between the property's fair market value and adjusted basis at the time of contribution.[12] In other words, a partnership no longer has the option of treating contributed property as being *purchased* by the partnership.

---

§ 704(c). Contributed Property

(1)(A) Under regulations prescribed by the Secretary income, gain, loss, and deduction with respect to property contributed to the partnership by a partner shall be shared among the partners so as to take account of the variation between the basis of the property to the partnership and its fair market value at the time of contribution.

Note the Code provision directs Treasury to develop the rules regarding the allocation of the income, gain, loss, and deduction with respect to contributed property. It took until 1993 — 10 years following the enactment of § 704(c)(1)(A) — to finalize regulations interpreting and applying that Code provision. By the time the § 704(c)(1)(A) regulations were finalized, the complex regulations governing the § 704(b) substantial economic effect test, discussed in Chapter 9, had also been finalized. The § 704(b) regulations require that tax allocations follow book allocations, i.e., to the extent that a partner is allocated a share of book income, gain, loss, or deduction, the taxpayer should be allocated an equal amount of tax income, gain, loss, or deduction.

With respect to § 704(c) property, however, it would appear that the "tax-follows-book" standard of the § 704(b) regulations could not be readily applied, at least not with respect to tax allocations to the contributing partner. For example, if X contributed property worth $100,000 to a partnership and the property had an adjusted basis of $60,000, a subsequent sale of the property by the partnership for $100,000 would result in no book gain or loss because the book value of the property was also $100,000. Thus, it would appear that no tax gain or loss could be allocated to the partners under the "tax-follows-book" standard. Nonetheless, in this example, $40,000 of tax gain has been recognized on the sale and § 704(c)(1)(A) will allocate that gain to X, the contributing partner. A closer consideration of X's situation, however, will suggest that, in fact, the "tax-follows-book" standard is actually satisfied, albeit on a delayed basis. Because X was credited in his capital account with a $100,000 investment in the partnership even though X's unrecovered cost in the property was only $60,000, the allocation of the $40,000 of gain to X required by § 704(c)(1)(A) could be understood as simply requiring X to report as tax gain the amount of built-in gain X was credited with in his capital account on the contribution of the property. In other words, tax ultimately follows book even with regard to § 704(c) property.

---

[12] As discussed in some detail in Chapter 19, Congress in 2004 added a further limitation with respect to § 704(c) property to prevent the transfer of built-in losses in situations that had not been adequately addressed by § 704(c)(1)(A). See § 704(c)(1)(B).

Under the new regime introduced by the 1984 Act and the 1993 regulations interpreting and applying § 704(c)(1)(A), tax allocations will generally follow book allocations with respect to the noncontributing partner. Thus, a noncontributing partner should be allocated tax items that match the book gains and losses allocated to that partner. The result reached in Example 2 above does not make sense under this regime. Recall in that example, Eve, the noncontributing partner, experienced no book gain but was allocated $20,000 of tax gain.

C. Current Law: "Generally Reasonable" Allocation Methods

While the regulations finalized in 1993 authorize the use of any "reasonable method" of allocation consistent with the purpose of § 704(c), the regulations provide three methods deemed "generally reasonable." Reg. § 1.704-3(a)(1). Those methods are: (a) the Traditional Method; (b) the Traditional Method with Curative Allocations; and (c) the Remedial Method. Merely because the method chosen by the partnership results in lesser aggregate tax liability than another method will not render the method chosen to be "unreasonable." *Id.*

Section 704(c) applies on a property-by-property basis. Thus, the aggregation of the built-in gains or losses on items of contributed property is prohibited in determining whether a difference exists between the fair market value of property a taxpayer contributes and the taxpayer's adjusted basis. Reg. § 1.704-3(a)(2).[13]

In applying § 704(c)(1)(A), one must first determine whether an item of property is "§ 704(c) property." Regulation § 1.704-3(a)(3)(i) defines *"§ 704(c) property" as property that, at the time of contribution, has a book value differing from the contributing partner's adjusted basis in the property.* Book value is equal to the fair market value of the property at the time of its contribution and is adjusted for depreciation and other items affecting the basis of property. *Id.*

A second critical step in applying § 704(c) and the regulations interpreting it is the determination of "built-in gain" and "built-in loss" *at any given time.* Regulation 1.704-3(a)(3)(ii) provides that, at the time of contribution, built-in gain is the difference between the book value of the property and the contributing partner's adjusted basis. *The built-in gain, however, must thereafter be reduced by any decrease in the difference between the property's book value and the property's adjusted basis.* A comparable definition is provided for "built-in loss." Thus, the amount of built-in gain or built-in loss does not necessarily remain static.

> **Example 1:** Dick and Jane form a general (calendar year) partnership in which each has a 50% interest. On January 1, Year 1 Dick contributes $100,000 cash to the partnership and Jane contributes a building with a $100,000 fair market value and a $60,000 adjusted basis. At the time of contribution, the building would have a book value of $100,000 and, as a result, the built-in gain with respect to the building is $40,000. Assume the

---

[13] Special rules, however, permit the aggregation for § 704(c) purposes of certain properties contributed by one partner during the partnership taxable year. Reg. § 1.704-3(e)(2). Thus, for example, all property, other than real property, included in a specific general asset account under § 168 may be aggregated, as may all zero basis property other than real property. *Id.*

partnership will depreciate the building on a straight-line basis over the next 10 years. Thus, the tax depreciation will be 10% of the adjusted basis or $6,000 per year. Reg. § 1.704-1(b)(2)(iv)(g)(3) provides that book depreciation "is the amount that bears the same relationship to the book value of such property as the depreciation computed for tax purposes with respect to the such property . . . bears to the adjusted basis of such property." Thus, the rate of book depreciation, like the rate of tax depreciation, will be 10% or $10,000 per year, i.e., 10% X $100,000 (book value). At the end of Year 1, the partnership will be allowed $6,000 in tax depreciation resulting in the partnership having a $54,000 adjusted basis in the building at the beginning of Year 2. The partnership's corresponding book depreciation of $10,000 for Year 1 results in the building having a book value of $90,000 at the beginning of Year 2. As a result, the built-in gain at the beginning of Year 2 is $36,000, i.e., the difference between the $90,000 book value and the building's adjusted basis of $54,000. As this example illustrates, built-in gain has changed over time, i.e., the built-in gain was $40,000 at the time of contribution of the building to the partnership and decreased to $36,000 as a result of the book and tax depreciation allowed in Year 1. See Reg. § 1.704-3(b)(2) Ex. 1(ii).

Finally, one should determine the allocation method to be used. While generally a different allocation method can be used for each item of contributed property "a single reasonable method" must be consistently used with respect to each item of contributed property. Reg. § 1.704-3(a)(2). What follows is an examination of the three methods the regulations describe as "generally reasonable."

1. The Traditional Method

As emphasized above, tax should generally follow book, For example, were a two-person equal partnership to purchase a tract of land for $200,000 and later sell that land for $300,000, the partnership would realize a $100,000 book gain that would be divided equally between the two partners, i.e., $50,000 of book gain each. In turn, each should be allocated $50,000 of the $100,000 of tax gain.

With regard to § 704(c) property, however, the regulations provide that, under the "Traditional Method," a partnership must allocate gain, loss, or deductions with respect to that property so as to avoid shifting the tax consequences of the built-in gain or built-in loss to the non-contributing partner(s). Reg. § 1.704-3(b)(1). The regulations provide guidance in this regard with respect to (1) situations in which gain or loss is recognized by the partnership on a sale or exchange of the § 704(c) property; and (2) situations in which the § 704(c) property is depreciable. *In both of these situations, however, the regulations impose the "ceiling rule" (discussed above) that existed before the enactment of 704(c)(1)(A) in 1984.* Regulation § 1.704-3(b)(1) specifically provides:

> [T]he total income, gain, loss, or deduction allocated to the partners for a taxable year with respect to a property cannot exceed the total partnership income, gain, loss, or deduction with respect to that property for the taxable year (the ceiling rule).

a. Allocation of Gain or Loss on Sale of Nondepreciable § 704(c) Property.

If the partnership sells or exchanges § 704(c) property, the recognized gain or loss on the property must be allocated, *subject to the ceiling rule*, to the contributing partner to the extent of the built-in gain or built-in loss on the property. Reg. § 1.704-3(b)(1). Pursuant to the regulations, and disregarding § 704(c)(1)(C) (see discussion of proposed regulations, *infra*), one could identify the following steps to be followed in applying the Traditional Method (see Reg. § 1.704-3(b)(2) Ex. 1(iii)):

Step 1: Allocate the book gain or loss, if any, to the partners based on their profit/loss sharing arrangement.

Step 2: Allocate any tax gain recognized on the transaction to the contributing partner to the extent of built-in gain attributable to that partner; allocate any tax loss on the transaction to the contributing partner to the extent of built-in loss attributable to that partner. (Again, the ceiling rule will limit the amount of the tax gain or tax loss that can be allocated.)

Step 3: Allocate any remaining tax gain or tax loss to the partners in the same proportion as the allocation of book gain or loss in Step 1.

Consider the following examples of sales of *nondepreciable* § 704(c) property that has built-in gain. (Part D below addresses the special rule of § 704(c)(1)(C) addressing allocations with respect to property with built-in loss.) In addition to demonstrating the application of § 704(c)(1)(A), these examples, based in part on Reg. § 1.704-3(b)(2) Ex. 1, provide a review of the rules previously studied regarding maintenance of capital accounts and adjustments made to basis to reflect the allocation of tax gains and losses.

Example 2: On January 1, Year 1, Dick and Jane formed a general (calendar year) partnership in which Dick and Jane are equal partners, having agreed to share all partnership items equally and to use the Traditional Method to make § 704(c) allocation. At the time of the partnership's formation, Dick contributed $200,000 cash to the partnership for his partnership interest and Jane contributed land she had held for investment for a number of years. The land had a $200,000 fair market value and a $150,000 adjusted basis. Pursuant to § 721, Jane recognized no gain on the contribution of the land and took a basis in her partnership interest equal to the adjusted basis of the contributed land, i.e., $150,000. § 722. The partnership booked the land at $200,000 and, pursuant to § 723, took a $150,000 basis in the land. The land is § 704(c) property with $50,000 of built-in gain. Reg. § 1.704-3(a)(3)(ii). Assume that, during the first four years of the partnership's existence, partnership income and deductions were equal. During the fifth year of its existence, the partnerships sold the land contributed by Jane for $200,000. Assume the partnership's basis in the land at the time of the sale was still $150,000. Other than the tax gain resulting from the sale, the partnership's income and deductions were equal for the year.

Analysis: The following chart shows the adjusted basis (outside basis)[14] and capital account of each of the partners for the first four years of the partnership's existence:

	Dick		Jane	
	A/B	Book	A/B	Book
Beginning of Partnership	$200,000	$200,000	$150,000	$200,000
Years 1–4 Taxable Income (§ 705)	$0	$0	$0	$0
End of Year 4	$200,000	$200,000	$150,000	$200,000

On the sale of the land for $200,000, the partnership would recognize $50,000 in gain pursuant to § 1001. Because the land had a book value of $200,000, no book gain would be realized on the sale. As a result, Dick's and Jane's capital accounts would remain the same, i.e., $200,000 each.

Under the Traditional Method, the $50,000 of tax gain must be allocated to Jane to the extent of the built-in gain on the land at the time of the sale. The built-in gain at the time of the sale was still $50,000, i.e., the difference between the $200,000 book value of the land at the time of the sale and the partnership's $150,000 adjusted basis in the land at the time of the sale. As a result, the entire $50,000 of tax gain must be allocated to Jane. In other words, because Jane's capital account was credited with $50,000 of built-in gain when she contributed the land to the partnership, it is appropriate to allocate that amount of tax gain to her at the time of the sale. Pursuant to § 705(a)(1)(A), Jane's outside basis would be increased from $150,000 to $200,000 to reflect the $50,000 of gain allocated to her.

By contrast to Jane, one could think of Dick as having purchased for $100,000 a one-half interest in the land Jane contributed to the partnership. Based on that understanding, Dick would have a § 1012 basis of $100,000 in his one-half interest in the land. When the partnership sold the land for $200,000, Dick's share of the amount realized would be $100,000, exactly matching his basis in his one-half share. Thus, he would recognize no gain (or loss).

Assume that, at the beginning of Year 6, the partnership liquidates and pursuant to the partnership agreement the liquidation proceeds are distributed in accordance with capital account balances. On the liquidation, Dick and Jane would each be entitled to receive the liquidation proceeds of $200,000 — exactly the amount of their capital accounts. Applying § 731, neither would report any gain or loss on the liquidating distribution because the amount of the distribution equals their adjusted basis in their partnership interests.

---

[14] Note: Dick's and Jane's capital accounts and adjusted bases will be the same, as the example does not involve liabilities.

Example 3: Assume the facts of Example 2 except the partnership sold the land contributed by Jane for $240,000.

Analysis: On a sale of the land for $240,000, the partnership will recognize a $40,000 book gain and $90,000 of tax gain. As equal partners, Dick and Jane will each have a $20,000 share of the book gain and, as a result, will increase their capital accounts to $220,000. Reg. § 1.704-1(b)(2)(iv)(d)(3). Pursuant to § 704(c)(1)(A) and the Traditional Method, the first $50,000 of tax gain must be allocated to Jane to account for the $50,000 of built-in gain associated with the land. (See Example 1.) This allocation will result in an upward adjustment of $50,000 to Jane's outside basis, giving her an outside basis of $200,000. The remaining $40,000 of tax gain should be allocated to Dick and Jane in the amount of their share of book gain, i.e., tax should follow book with respect to $40,000 of gain. Thus, Dick will have $20,000 of the tax gain and Jane an additional $20,000 of tax gain. Pursuant to § 705(a)(1)(A), Dick's outside basis will be increased by $20,000 to $220,000 and Jane's outside basis will be increased by $70,000 (i.e., $50,000 of built-in gain plus her $20,000 share of the remaining gain) to $220,000. Were the partnership to liquidate at the beginning of Year 6, Dick and Jane would each receive $220,000. Because, as calculated above, the outside basis of each partner is also $220,000, neither would report any gain or loss on the liquidation.

Example 4: Assume the facts of Example 2 except that the partnership sold the land for $190,000.

Analysis: If the partnership sells the land for $190,000, it will recognize $40,000 of tax gain and a $10,000 book loss. The book loss will be allocated equally between Dick and Jane ($5,000 of book loss each) thereby reducing their capital accounts to $195,000. Reg. § 1.704-1(b)(2)(iv)(d)(3). As there was $50,000 of built-in gain associated with the land she contributed, Jane will be allocated all $40,000 of the tax gain on the sale. Although the partnership experienced a book loss on the sale of the land, there is no corresponding tax loss to be allocated. Under the ceiling rule of the Traditional Method, we can't allocate a $5,000 tax loss to both Dick and Jane to match the book loss each suffered. For the same reason, we can't allocate $50,000 of tax gain to Jane to reflect the built-in gain that inhered in the property when she contributed it and that was not recognized because of § 721. As a result, the ceiling rule creates a significant distortion. Jane reports $40,000 of gain and her outside basis is increased to $190,000. There is thus $5,000 of gain that continues to inhere in Jane's partnership interest. She won't recognize that gain until she sells her partnership interest or the partnership liquidates. Because of the ceiling rule, Jane will have $5,000 less gain in Year 5, i.e., she should have reported a net of $45,000 of gain ($50,000 of built-in gain and $5,000 of loss on the sale) but instead is required to report only $40,000 of gain. By contrast, Dick, who has experienced a $5,000 loss, does not get the benefit of a loss deduction. His capital account is reduced to $195,000 while his outside basis remains at $200,000. In other words, the $5,000 loss in the value of his partnership interest is preserved in his basis. Dick will not recognize that loss until he sells his interest or the partnership liquidates. Because he is deprived of a $5,000 loss deduction in Year 5, he will have $5,000 more in taxable income in Year 5. In effect, the ceiling rule has temporarily shifted $5,000 of income from Jane to Dick. If we assume the partnership liquidates at the beginning of Year 6, Dick and Jane will each receive $195,000 in cash. Under § 731(a)(2), Dick, who has a $200,000 outside basis, will recognize a $5,000 loss on the liquidation.[15] By contrast, Jane, who has $190,000 outside basis, will recognize $5,000 of gain.[16] Note that, if either Dick or Jane were to die before liquidation of the partnership, the distortion created by the ceiling rule could be made permanent by the § 1014 stepped-up/stepped-down basis.

b. Allocation of Depreciation Deductions with Respect to Depreciable § 704(c) Property.

The above examples illustrate the application of the Traditional Method with respect to the allocations of gains or losses on sales or taxable exchanges of nondepreciable property. With regard to depreciable property, gains or losses on the sales of such property will be allocated consistent with the general rules noted above, i.e., the recognized gain or loss on the property must be allocated, *subject to the ceiling rule*, to the contributing partners to the extent of the built-in gain or built-in loss on the property at the time of the sale or exchange. A question that must be addressed, however, is how depreciation deductions associated with depreciable § 704(c) property will be allocated.

The sale or exchange rule is inadequate to fully address the income/loss shifting potential associated with built-in gains and losses with respect to depreciable § 704(c) property. To illustrate this, let us assume the facts of Example 1 (involving the Dick and Jane Partnership) above, except that the property Jane contributed was depreciable property that the partnership would depreciate on a straight line basis over a 10-year period. (Thus, the partnership's $150,000 basis would be recovered at the rate of $15,000 per year.) As in Example 1, there was $50,000 of built-in gain attributable to the property at the time of its contribution to the partnership. After 10 years, the partnership would have fully depreciated the property, leaving the partnership with a zero adjusted basis in the property. Furthermore, as discussed below, the book value of the property would likewise be zero at the end of the 10-year period. (Assume the property is worthless at that point.) There would thus be no built-in gain associated with the property, i.e., book value of $0 less adjusted basis of $0 = $0 (see definition of "built-in gain above). If the $150,000 in tax depreciation allowed the partnership over the 10-year period were simply divided equally between Dick and Jane, each would have been allocated $75,000 of depreciation deductions. Under those circumstances, Jane would have avoided accounting during the life of the partnership for the $50,000 of built-in gain attributable to the property she contributed. By contrast, Dick would not have been allowed the depreciation deductions he would have been allowed if he were treated as having purchased for $100,000 a one-half interest in the property,

---

[15] Dick's loss will be characterized as a long-term capital loss. § 741.

[16] § 731(a)(1). Jane's gain will be long-term capital gain. § 741.

i.e., Dick would have been allowed a total of $100,000 of depreciation deductions assuming his one-half interest in the property were depreciated over a 10-year period on a straight-line basis.

To ensure that, insofar as possible (given the ceiling rule), the contributing partner will be accountable for the built-in gain or have the benefit of built-in loss, § 704(c)(1)(A) and the regulations appropriately require built-in gain and loss be taken into account when allocating tax depreciation. To accomplish this, the regulations focus on the noncontributing partner (Dick in the example) to ensure that, insofar as possible, he is allocated a share of depreciation equal to what he would have been entitled had he purchased an interest in the property. To that end, and consistent with the tax-follows-book principle noted above, the regulations provide that the allocations of cost recovery deductions to a noncontributing partner must generally equal the book depreciation allocations to that partner. Reg. § 1.704-3(b)(1). Consider the following examples (based in part on Reg. § 1.704-3(b)(2) Ex. 1), which ignore any depreciation conventions:

>**Example 5:** Assume the facts of Example 2 above except that, instead of contributing land, Jane had contributed a piece of depreciable property worth $200,000 with an adjusted basis of $150,000. Dick's and Jane's outside basis and opening capital accounts will be the same as those in Example 1. Assume the partnership will depreciate the property over 10 years on a straight-line basis. Thus, in this example, the partnership, which has a $150,000 adjusted basis in the depreciable property, would be allowed $15,000 in tax depreciation each year. Pursuant to Reg. § 1.704-1(b)(2)(iv)(g)(3), the partnership's book depreciation each year "is the amount that bears the same relationship to the book value of such property as the depreciation (or cost recovery deduction). . . . computed for tax purposes with respect to such property for such period bears to the adjusted tax basis of such property." Thus, because the tax depreciation each year represents 1/10 or 10% of the partnership's basis in the depreciable property, the book depreciation will also be 10% per year. The partnership's annual book depreciation on the property contributed by Jane will therefore be 10% of $200,000 or $20,000. Because Dick and Jane are equal partners, each will have a $10,000 share of book depreciation. This will reduce each of their capital accounts by $10,000 each year during the depreciation period.
>
>**Analysis:** Under the Traditional Method, in allocating depreciation deductions with respect to the § 704(c) property contributed by Jane, one must take into account the built-in gain of $50,000 associated with the property. The Traditional Method does so by allocating to Dick, the noncontributing partner, an amount of tax depreciation equal to the book depreciation allocated to him. Thus, of the $15,000 of tax depreciation allowed to the partnership each year, $10,000 should be allocated to Dick. [It is just as though Dick had purchased for $100,000 a one-half interest in the depreciable property contributed by Jane. As noted above, that one-half interest depreciated on a straight-line basis over a 10-year period would produce tax depreciation for Dick of $10,000 per year.] Dick's outside basis will thus be reduced by the $10,000 of depreciation deductions allocated to him each

year. After 10 years, Dick's outside basis will have been reduced by a total of $100,000. If we assume that, during the 10-year depreciation period, the partnership's income and expenses (other than depreciation) were exactly equal, Dick's outside basis would be $100,000 (i.e., $200,000 less $100,000 of depreciation = $100,000).

Jane will be allocated the remaining $5,000 of tax depreciation each year. While Dick has a $10,000 deduction annually, Jane has only $5,000. As a result, all other things being equal, Jane will have $5,000 more in taxable income each year than Dick does. Over the 10-year period during which the § 704(c) property will be depreciated, Jane will thus have been allocated a total of $50,000 of tax depreciation by comparison to the $100,000 in depreciation deductions allocated to Dick. Again, all things being equal, she will have $50,000 more taxable income than Dick over the 10-year period. The regulations have thus accounted for the built-in gain of $50,000.[17]

Example 6: Assume the facts of Example 5 except that Jane and, in turn, the partnership, had an adjusted basis in the depreciable property of $90,000. As a result, there was $110,000 of built-in gain on the property. The partnership would be allowed annual tax depreciation of only $9,000 (i.e., $90,000 x 10%) but its book depreciation would still be $20,000 per year. Again, Dick and Jane would share the book depreciation equally.

Analysis: Under the Traditional Method, the tax depreciation would be allocated to Dick up to Dick's share of book depreciation. In a perfect tax world for reasons discussed in Example 4, Dick would be entitled to $10,000 of tax depreciation each year to match the $10,000 of book depreciation he would be allocated annually for 10 years. The ceiling rule, however, renders our tax world something less than perfect. Under that rule, only $9,000 of actual tax depreciation is available to be allocated. All of it will be allocated to Dick. At the end of Year 1, Dick's capital account will have thus been reduced from $200,000 to $190,000 while his outside basis will have been reduced from $200,000 to $191,000. Note the disparity that has now been created between Dick's capital account and Dick's outside basis. That disparity is a function of the fact that while Dick's share of book depreciation was $10,000, the ceiling rule limited the tax depreciation allocated to him to the $9,000 of depreciation actually allowed the partnership. As a result of this disparity, Dick will have $1,000 more in taxable income each year than he otherwise would have had.

By contrast, Jane will not be allocated any tax depreciation during the 10-year depreciation period, even though her share of book depreciation is $10,000 per year. At the end of Year 1, her capital account will have also

---

[17] Note that, after Year 1, the built-in gain is decreased to $45,000, i.e., the book value of the § 704(c) property has been reduced to $180,000 and the adjusted basis has been reduced from $150,000 to $135,000. In Year 2, the built-in gain is decreased to $40,000, i.e., the book value of the property has been reduced to $160,000 and the adjusted basis has been reduced from $135,000 to $120,000. The built-in gain will be reduced annually by $5,000 through Year 10. At the beginning of Year 11, the book value will be zero and the partnership's adjusted basis in the property will likewise be zero. Thus, there will be no built-in gain remaining. Jane will have accounted fully for all the built-in gain.

been reduced to $190,000. Jane's outside basis, however, will remain at $90,000. As in Example 3 above, the ceiling rule creates a distortion. That distortion is best illustrated by considering the results if the partnership were to liquidate at the beginning of Year 11, after the property has been fully depreciated, and by assuming that (a) during the 10-year period the partnership's income and expenses were exactly equal and (b) the § 704(c) property, having been fully depreciated, was worthless. At the end of Year 10, after being allocated $100,000 of book depreciation and $90,000 of tax depreciation, Dick's capital account would be $100,000 and his adjusted basis would be $110,000. Jane's capital account would likewise be $100,000 and Jane's adjusted basis would be $90,000. Dick and Jane would each receive $100,000 in liquidation distributions. Dick would have a $10,000 loss and Jane would have a $10,000 gain.[18] In effect, during the 10-year depreciation period, Dick reported $10,000 more income than he should have and Jane reported $10,000 less income than she should have. The distortion created by the ceiling rule should be evident.

Example 7: Assume the facts of Example 6 except Jane and, in turn, the partnership, had an adjusted basis of $240,000 in the depreciable property. As a result, there was $40,000 of built-in loss on the property. Disregard for now § 704(c)(1)(C). (See discussion and application of proposed regulations, *infra*.) The partnership would be allowed annual tax depreciation of $24,000 (i.e., $240,000 x 10%) but its book depreciation would still be $20,000 per year. Again, Dick and Jane would share the book depreciation equally.

Analysis: Under the Traditional Method, the tax depreciation would be allocated to Dick in an amount equal to Dick's share of book depreciation, i.e., $10,000. Thus, of the $24,000 of tax depreciation allowed to the partnership annually, $10,000 should be allocated to Dick. Dick's outside basis will thus be reduced by the $10,000 of depreciation deductions allocated to him each year. After 10 years, Dick's outside basis will have been reduced by a total of $100,000. If we assume that during that 10-year period the partnership's income and expenses (other than depreciation) were exactly equal, Dick's outside basis would be $100,000 (i.e., $200,000 less $100,000 of depreciation = $100,000).

Jane would be allocated the remaining $14,000 of tax depreciation each year. As a result, all other things being equal, Jane will have $4,000 less in taxable income each year than Dick does. Over the 10-year period during which the § 704(c) property will be depreciated, Jane will thus have been allocated a total of $140,000 of tax depreciation by comparison to the $100,000 in depreciation deductions allocated to Dick. Again, all things being equal, she will have $40,000 less taxable income than Dick over that 10-year period. This allocation of depreciation thus fully accounts for the built-in loss of $40,000.

---

[18] See Reg. § 1.704-3(b)(2) Ex. 1 (ii) and (iv). The $10,000 loss Jane recognized on the liquidation, combined with the fact that she was not allowed $10,000 in depreciation deductions each year to match the $10,000 per year book depreciation allocated to her, in effect results in her accounting for the full $110,000 of built-in gain on the property she contributed to the partnership.

c. Allocation of Gain or Loss on the Sale of Depreciable Property.

If a partner contributed depreciable property to the partnership and, after depreciating the property for a number of years, the partnership sells the property, the computation of built-in gain or built-in loss, if any, at the time of the sale will be critical in allocating any gain or loss on the sale. Again, the contributing partner should be allocated, subject to the ceiling rule, tax gain or tax loss to the extent of remaining built-in gain or built-in loss respectively. Any remaining tax gain or loss should be allocated consistent with the partners' shares of book gain or loss on the sale. Consider the following examples (based in part on Reg. § 1.704-3(b)(2) Ex. 1(iii)), which address depreciable property with built-in gain:[19]

Example 8: Assume the facts of Example 5. Also assume the partnership, at the beginning of Year 6, sells the property contributed by Jane for $110,000.

Analysis: Disregarding any depreciation conventions, the adjusted tax basis of the property at the time of the sale will be $75,000 (i.e., beginning basis of $150,000 less 5 years of tax depreciation ($15,000 X 5=$75,000) and the book value of the property at that time will be $100,000 (i.e., the beginning book value of $200,000 less 5 years of book depreciation ($20,000 x 5 = $100,000). There is thus $25,000 of built-in gain remaining (i.e., book value of $100,000 less adjusted basis of $75,000). The sale of the property by the partnership for $110,000 produces a book gain of $10,000 and a tax gain of $35,000. The book gain of $10,000 will be allocated equally between Dick and Jane — $5,000 each. Accordingly, both Dick's and Jane's capital accounts would be increased by that amount. The tax gain would be allocated to Jane to the extent of the remaining built-in gain which, as noted above, is $25,000. Therefore, $25,000 of the $35,000 in tax gain is allocated to Jane and the remaining $10,000 of tax gain is allocated between the partners in an amount equal to the book gain allocated to them, i.e., $5,000 each.

Example 9 Assume the facts of Example 8 except the partnership sells the property for $90,000.

Analysis: Now the partnership realizes a book loss of $10,000 and a tax gain of $15,000. The book loss will be allocated equally to Dick and Jane — $5,000 each. The tax gain will first be allocated to Jane up to the amount of the remaining built-in gain, i.e., $25,000. Conceptually, Jane should be allocated $25,000 of tax gain and Dick and Jane should each be allocated $5,000 of tax loss to reflect the book loss each has sustained. Because of the ceiling rule, however, Jane can only be allocated $15,000 of tax gain (the total amount of the tax gain on the sale) and neither Dick nor Jane can be allocated any tax loss as there is none.

---

[19] See Part D below, which addresses the special rule of § 704(c)(1)(C) addressing allocations with respect to property with built-in loss.

2. Traditional Method with Curative Allocations

"To correct distortions created by the ceiling rule, a partnership using the traditional method . . . may make *reasonable* curative allocations to reduce or eliminate disparities between book and tax items of noncontributing partners." Reg. § 1.704-3(c)(1). That regulation defines a "curative allocation" as "an allocation of income, gain, loss, or deduction for tax purposes that differs from the partnership's allocation of the corresponding book item." To be reasonable, the partnership agreement must provide for curative allocations and those allocations must "be expected to have substantially the same effect on each partner's tax liability as the tax item limited by the ceiling rule." Consider the following example, based in part on Reg. § 1.704-3(c)(4) Ex. 2, demonstrating the application of the Traditional Method with Curative Allocations.

Example 10: In Year 1, Abbey and Jackson form a partnership. Abbey contributes a piece of depreciable property with a fair market value of $100,000 and an adjusted basis of $80,000, and Jackson contributes a piece of depreciable property with a fair market value of $100,000 and an adjusted basis of $40,000. Abbey and Jackson agree that each will be allocated 50% of all partnership items. Assume the partnership will depreciate both properties on a straight line basis over a 10-year period, i.e., a depreciation rate of 10% per year. (For purposes of this example, disregard any depreciation conventions.) For reasons discussed previously, the rate of book depreciation on partnership assets will likewise be 10% per year. As a result, the annual book depreciation on each property will be $10,000. Abbey and Jackson will thus have a $5,000 share of book depreciation annually with respect to both the property contributed by Abbey and the property contributed by Jackson. With regard to tax depreciation, the partnership will be allowed $8,000 of depreciation annually on to the property contributed by Abbey and $4,000 depreciation annually on the property contributed by Jackson. Assume the partnership will use the Traditional Method with Curative Allocations.

Analysis: Assume initially that Abbey and Jackson agreed to use the Traditional Method to allocate tax depreciation. As discussed previously, under the Traditional Method, tax depreciation is allocated to the noncontributing partner in an amount equal to the book depreciation allocable to that partner, subject to the ceiling rule. Thus, Jackson would be entitled to $5,000 of tax depreciation with respect to the property contributed by Abbey and Abbey would be entitled to the remaining $3,000 of tax depreciation on that property. With respect to the property contributed by Jackson, while Abbey should be entitled to $5,000 of tax depreciation to match her share of book depreciation, as a result of the ceiling rule she would be allocated only $4,000, i.e., the total amount of the tax depreciation on that property. Abbey has thus been allocated $1,000 less tax depreciation than she should have been. Assuming, apart from the tax depreciation, the partnership's expenses and income for Year 1 were exactly equal, Abbey's and Jackson's adjusted bases (outside bases) and capital accounts would be as follows at the end of the first year:

	Abbey		**Jackson**	
	A/B	Book	A/B	Book
Initial Contribution	$80,000	$100,000	$40,000	$100,000
Depreciation (property contributed by Abbey)	($3,000)	($5,000)	($5,000)	($5,000)
Depreciation (property contributed by Jackson)	($4,000)	($5,000)	($0)	($5,000)
End of Year 1	$73,000	$90,000	$35,000	$90,000

At the end of Year 10, assuming that, apart from depreciation deductions, partnership expenses exactly equaled partnership income in each year, the outside basis and capital account of each partner would be as follows:

	Abbey		**Jackson**	
	A/B	Book	A/B	Book
Initial Contribution	$80,000	$100,000	$40,000	$100,000
Depreciation Year 1 (property contributed by Abbey)	($3,000)	($5,000)	($5,000)	($5,000)
Depreciation Yrs 2–10	($27,000)	($45,000)	($45,000)	($45,000)
Depreciation Year 1 (property contributed by Jackson)	($4,000)	($5,000)	($0)	($5,000)
Depreciation Yrs 2–10	($36,000)	($45,000)	($0)	($45,000)
End of Year 10	$10,000	$0	($10,000)[20]	$0

As the above analysis demonstrates, the Traditional Method's ceiling rule creates a disparity between the book and tax amounts allocable to Abbey with respect to the property contributed by Jackson. If, however, at the time Jackson and Abbey contributed the properties to the partnership, they had agreed, as indicated in Example 10, to use the Traditional Method with Curative Allocations, the disparity could be resolved. Using that method, Abbey and Jackson could provide that, rather than Jackson being allocated $5,000 in tax depreciation with respect to the property contributed by Abbey, he would be allocated only $4,000 and Abbey would be allocated $4,000 of the depreciation rather than the $3,000 otherwise allocable to

---

[20] Because § 704(d) would prevent Jackson from claiming deduction in excess of his outside basis, Jackson technically would not have a negative basis of $10,000. Rather, a total of $10,000 of depreciation deductions would be held in abeyance until Jackson had adequate outside basis to use these deductions. *See* Chapter 8.

her. Reg. § 1.704-3(c)(1). Under the Traditional Method, the curative allocation of $1,000 more of tax depreciation to Abbey each year from the property contributed by her is reasonable because it obviously has "substantially the same effect on each partner's tax liability as the tax item limited by the ceiling rule" (i.e., the $1,000 of additional depreciation she should have been allocated each year with respect to the property contributed by Jackson). Reg. § 1.704-3(c)(1)(iii). As a result of the curative allocation, the outside basis and capital account of each partner will be as follows at the end of Year 1:

	Abbey		Jackson	
	A/B	Book	A/B	Book
Initial Contribution	$80,000	$100,000	$40,000	$100,000
Depreciation (property contributed by Abbey)	($4,000)	($5,000)	($4,000)	($5,000)
Depreciation (property contributed by Jackson)	($4,000)	($5,000)	($0)	($5,000)
End of Year 1	$72,000	$90,000	$36,000	$90,000

At the end of Year 10, assuming that, apart from depreciation deductions, partnership expenses exactly equaled partnership income in each year, each partner's outside basis and capital account would be $0 as demonstrated by the following table:

	Abbey		Jackson	
	A/B	Book	A/B	Book
Initial Contribution	$80,000	$100,000	$40,000	$100,000
Depreciation Year 1 (property contributed by Abbey)	($4,000)	($5,000)	($4,000)	($5,000)
Depreciation Yrs 2-10 (property contributed by Abbey)	($36,000)	($45,000)	($36,000)	($45,000)
Depreciation Year 1 (property contributed by Jackson)	($4,000)	($5,000)	($0)	($5,000)
Depreciation Yrs 2-10 (property contributed by Abbey)	($36,000)	($45,000)	($0)	($45,000)
End of Year 10	$0	$0	$0	$0

3. Remedial Allocations Method

The regulations also provide partnerships the option of using the so-called Remedial Method to address the disparity caused by the ceiling rule. Regulation § 1.704-3(d)(1) provides:

> If the ceiling rule causes the book allocation of an item to a noncontributing partner to differ from the tax allocation of the same item to [that] partner, the partnership *creates* a remedial item of income, gain, loss, or deduction equal to the full amount of the difference and allocates it to the noncontributing partner. The partnership simultaneously creates an offsetting remedial item in an identical amount and allocates it to the contributing partner. [Emphasis added]

The remedial items created by the partnership are not taken into account by the partnership in computing its taxable income and do not affect the partnership's adjusted basis in partnership property. Reg. § 1.704-3(d)(4). Likewise these created or "notional items" do not affect the partners' capital accounts. They do, however, "have the same effect as tax items on a partner's tax liability and on the partner's adjusted tax basis (outside basis) in the partnership interest." Reg. § 1.704-3(d)(5).

Consider the following example (using the facts of Example 4 *supra*, and based in part on Reg. § 1.704-3(d)(7) Ex. 2) demonstrating the application of the remedial method with regard to the sale of nondepreciable property contributed to a partnership.

> **Example 11:** On January 1, Year 1, Dick and Jane formed a general (calendar year) partnership in which Dick and Jane are equal partners, having agreed to share all partnership items equally and to use the Traditional Method to make § 704(c)(1)(A) allocation. At the time of the partnership's formation, Dick contributed $200,000 cash to the partnership for his partnership interest, and Jane contributed land she had held for investment for a number of years. The land had a $200,000 fair market value and a $150,000 adjusted basis. Pursuant to § 721, Jane recognized no gain on the contribution of the land and took a basis in her partnership interest equal to the adjusted basis of the contributed land, i.e., $150,000. § 722. The partnership booked the land at $200,000 and, pursuant to § 723, the partnership took a basis in the land of $150,000. The land is § 704(c) property, and at the time of contribution there was $50,000 of built-in gain associated with the land. Reg. § 1.704-3(a)(3)(ii). Assume, at the end of Year 1, the partnership, after using the land in its business for the year, sells the land for $190,000, thereby realizing and recognizing a gain of $40,000 but suffering a book loss of $10,000. The book loss of $10,000 will be shared equally by Dick and Jane, i.e., $5,000 book loss each.
>
> **Analysis:** Conceptually, the following tax allocations should be made: (a) Dick should be allocated a $5,000 tax loss to match the book loss he has sustained; and (b) Jane should be allocated $50,000 of gain to reflect the built-in gain on the land and should also be allocated a $5,000 tax loss to match the book loss allocated to her. (Jane would thus have $45,000 of net tax gain to report).

With regard to the above facts, consider first the allocations that would be made under the Traditional Method, taking into account the ceiling rule. Because there is only a tax gain of $40,000 on the sale of the land, no tax loss could be allocated under that method to either partner, and only the $40,000 of gain could be allocated. All of the $40,000 of gain would be allocated to Jane.

The following table assumes that, except for the gain on the sale of land, the income and expenses of the partnership are exactly the same for the year. The table shows the outside basis and capital account of each partner at the end of Year 1 and illustrates the distortion caused by the ceiling rule.

	Dick		Jane	
	A/B	Book	A/B	Book
Initial Contribution	$200,000	$200,000	$150,000	$200,000
Allocation of Tax Gain on Sale	$0		$40,000	
Book Loss on Sale of Land		($5,000)		($5,000)
End of Year 1	$200,000	$195,000	$190,000	$195,000

As indicated in Example 4, because of the ceiling rule, Dick's book loss is not matched by a tax loss of $5,000 and Jane, instead of being allocated $45,000 of tax gain (i.e., $50,000 of tax gain to reflect the built-in gain on the land and a $5,000 tax loss to match Jane's share of the book loss), is allocated only $40,000 of tax gain.

Had the Dick and Jane partnership adopted the remedial method, the partnership could create a $5,000 tax loss to allocate to Dick so as to match his share of the book loss. In turn, it would create a $5,000 tax gain to offset the $5,000 tax loss and that gain would be allocated to Jane. These notional items would have the same character as the $40,000 of tax gain actually recognized on the sale. Reg. § 1.704-3(d)(3). Because under § 1223(2) the partnership would be deemed to have held the land for more than one year, the land would be § 1231 property and thus the actual recognized gain on the land, as well as the notional items of gain and loss, would be treated as § 1231 items. The following table illustrates the use of the remedial method and the resulting outside bases and capital accounts of the partners at the beginning of Year 2:

IV.   OVERVIEW   217

	Dick		Jane	
	A/B	Book	A/B	Book
Initial Contribution	$200,000	$200,000	$150,000	$200,000
Allocation of Tax Gain on Sale	$0		$40,000	
Book Loss on Sale of Land		($5,000)		($5,000)
Remedial item of Tax Loss	($5,000)			
Remedial item of Tax Gain			$5,000	
End of Year 1	$195,000	$195,000	$195,000	$195,000

With regard to depreciable contributed property, the Remedial Method applies a special rule for determining the book depreciation. Regulation § 1.704-3(d)(2) provides:

> The portion of the partnership's book basis in the property equal to the adjusted tax basis in the property at the time of the contribution is recovered in the same manner as the adjusted tax basis in the property is recovered. . . . The remainder of the partnership's book basis in the property (the amount by which book basis exceeds adjusted tax basis) is recovered using any recovery period and depreciation method. . . . available to the partnership for newly purchased property (of the same type as the contributed property) that is placed in service at the time of contribution.

Consider the following example, based on Reg. § 1.704-3(d)(7) Ex. 1, demonstrating the application of the Remedial Method with respect to the allocation of depreciation deductions:

Example 12: Assume Dick and Jane in Year 1 form an equal partnership, with Dick contributing a piece of depreciable property with a fair market value of $100,000 and an adjusted basis of $40,000 and Jane contributing $100,000 of cash. Under § 723, the partnership will have a $40,000 adjusted basis in the property received from Dick. Assume that Dick's property was 10-year property and that there are only four years left in the recovery period. The partnership will depreciate the property contributed by Dick using the straight-line method over the four remaining years in the recovery period, and thus will be allowed $10,000 in tax depreciation per year. (Note that the book depreciation will be $25,000 per year and will be divided equally — $12,500 to Dick and $12,500 to Jane in each of the four years.)

Analysis: Conceptually, during the four-year recovery period, Jane should be allowed a total of $50,000 of depreciation deductions (i.e., $12,500 in depreciation each year for four years) to match her share of the book depreciation. In effect, it is as though Jane has purchased a one-half interest in the depreciable property Dick contributed). Under the ceiling rule of the Traditional Method, however, there will only be a $10,000 depreciation deduction that can allocated annually (i.e., one-fourth of the $40,000 adjusted basis each year). The entire $10,000 depreciation deduction would be allocated to Jane. The distortion created by the ceiling rule is reflected in the following table showing the allocation of the book and tax depreciation during Years 1–4 of the partnership's existence. (This table assumes that, except for the depreciation deductions, the expenses of the partnership exactly equal the partnership's income.)

	Dick		**Jane**	
	A/B	Book	A/B	Book
Initial Contribution	$40,000	$100,000	$100,000	$100,000
Depreciation Year 1 (property contributed by Dick)	($0)	($12,500)	($10,000)	($12,500)
Depreciation Yrs 2–4	($0)	($37,500)	($30,000)	($37,500)
End of Year 4	$40,000	$50,000	$60,000	$50,000

As the above table indicates, Jane has a potential $10,000 loss built into her partnership interest as a result of the ceiling rule that limited her depreciation deduction to $10,000 per year, instead of the $12,500 deduction to which she should have been entitled. If the partnership had adopted the Remedial Method, the total *book* depreciation allowable with respect to the property, i.e., a total of $100,000 of depreciation equal to the book value of the property, will be recovered through a two-part method. In Part 1, $40,000 of the depreciable property's book value, i.e., an amount equal to the property's adjusted basis, would be recovered over the four-year period at the rate of $10,000 per year. (*See* excerpt from Reg. § 1.704-3(d)(2) above.) In Part 2, the remaining $60,000 of the book value (the excess of the $100,000 book value over the property's adjusted basis of $40,000) would be recovered using any recovery period and depreciation method available to the partnership for newly purchased property of the same type. Let's assume that the straight-line method will be used and the recovery period for this portion of the book value will be 10 years. Thus, this portion of the book value will be recovered at the rate of $6,000 per year.

As a result, under the Remedial Method, during each of the first four years, the total book depreciation will be $16,000, i.e., $10,000 per year from Part 1 and $6,000 per year from Part 2. Because Dick and Jane are equal partners, the $16,000 of annual book depreciation will be allocated $8,000 to each. The tax depreciation in each of those four years will be $10,000. Consistent with the Traditional Method, the annual tax depreciation during these four years will be allocated $8,000 to Jane and $2,000 to Dick. In short, the ceiling rule will not limit the depreciation deductions available to Jane in Years 1–4. By contrast, in Years 5–10, the book depreciation each year will be $6,000, but there will be no tax depreciation to be allocated. As a result, were the ceiling rule applicable, it would create a distortion, i.e., Jane would be allocated $3,000 of book depreciation in each year during the Year 5–10 period, but would not be allowed any tax depreciation.

If, however, the partnership has adopted the Remedial Method, the partnership will create a $3,000 depreciation deduction for the benefit of Jane each year during Years 5–10. In turn, an offsetting notional item of $3,000 of income (of the same character as the income produced by the property) will be created and allocated to Dick in each year during Years 5–10. Assuming that, apart from the depreciation deduction, the partnership's expenses and income during the 10-year period are exactly equal, Dick's and Jane's outside bases and capital accounts will be as follows:

	Dick		**Jane**	
	Tax	Book	Tax	Book
Initial Contribution	$40,000	$100,000	$100,000	$100,000
Book Depreciation Yrs 1–4		($32,000)		($32,000)
Tax Depreciation Yrs 1–4	($8,000)		($32,000)	
Book Depreciation Yrs 5–10		($18,000)	($18,000)	
Remedial tax deduction Yrs 5–10				($18,000)
Remedial income item Yrs 5–10	$18,000			
End of Year 10	$50,000	$50,000	$50,000	$50,000

D. Special Rule When Contributed Property Has Built-In Loss

Given the Traditional Method's ceiling rule, it would be possible for partnerships electing to use the Traditional Method to shift, at least temporarily, the benefit of built-in losses to a noncontributing partner. Consider the following example:

Example 13: In creating the Dick and Jane equal partnership in Year 1, Dick contributes $100,000 in cash and Jane contributes land with a fair market of $100,000 and an adjusted basis of $125,000. Jane's land has a built-in loss of $25,000. While she will have a $100,000 capital account reflecting the fair market value of her land, her outside basis will be $125,000, thus preserving the $25,000 loss inherent in the land she contributed. (Dick's outside basis and capital account will, of course, be $100,000.) Assume the partnership elects to use the Traditional Method. If, at the end of Year 1, the partnership sells the land contributed by Jane for $110,000, the partnership will have a book gain of $10,000, which will be allocated equally between Dick and Jane, i.e., $5,000 each. The partnership, however, will have a tax loss of $15,000, all of which will be allocated to Jane.

Analysis: Conceptually, Dick and Jane should each have been allocated a $5,000 tax gain to match their book gain of $5,000 and Jane should have been allocated a $25,000 loss to match the built-in loss on the land she contributed. Adding these gains and losses together, there would be a net loss of $15,000. The ceiling rule, however, prevents the allocation of gain to Dick and Jane because there is only a tax loss. Assuming that, disregarding the sale of the land, the partnership's income and expenses were equal in Year 1, the outside basis and capital account of each partner would be as follows immediately after the sale:

	Dick		Jane	
	A/B	Book	A/B	Book
Beginning of Partnership	$100,000	$100,000	$125,000	$100,000
Year 1 Taxable Income (§ 705)	$0	$0	$0	$0
Book gain on sale of land		$5,000		$5,000
Tax loss on sale of land			($15,000)	
End of Year 4	$100,000	$105,000	$110,000	$105,000

In situations such as this, where there is built-in loss on the contributed property, the ceiling rule enables the noncontributing partner to avoid tax gain even though the partnership has recognized book gain. Thus, in the above example, Dick has, in effect, taken advantage of the built-in loss on the land Jane contributed; he has avoided reporting $5,000 of gain. At the same time, Jane has not had the benefit of the $20,000 net loss to which she should be entitled, i.e., she should have been entitled to the $25,000 built-in loss less $5,000 gain on the sale or a net loss of $20,000. Instead, Jane was only allowed a $15,000 loss.

To prevent the noncontributing partner from reaping the benefit of a built-in loss in the situation presented in the above example as well as other situations (e.g., the liquidation of the contributing partner's interest before the partnership disposed of the built-in loss property), Congress enacted § 704(c)(1)(C), which provides:

> **§ 704(c). Contributed Property**
>
> (1) In general — Under regulations prescribed by the Secretary —
>
> (C) if any property so contributed has a built-in loss —
>
> (i) such built-in loss shall be taken into account only in determining the amount of items allocated to the contributing partner, and
>
> (ii) except as provided in the regulations, in determining the amount of items allocated to other partners, the basis of the contributed property in the hands of the partnership shall be treated as being equal to its fair market value at the time of contribution.

The Treasury has recently proposed extensive regulations interpreting and applying § 704(c)(1)(C). These regulations refer to a partner who contributes § 704(c) property with a built-in loss, or "section 704(c)(1)(C) property" as "the section 704(c)(1)(C) partner," (Prop. Reg. § 1.704-3(f)(2)(i)), and all other partners as "the non-contributing partners." Prop. Reg. § 1.704-3(f)(1)(ii). Consistent with § 704(c)(1)(C), the proposed regulations provide "the excess of the adjusted basis of the section 704(c)(1)(C) property ... over its fair market value immediately before the contribution will be taken into account only in determining the amount of items allocated to the section 704(c)(1)(C) partner ... that contributed such section 704(c)(1)(C) property .... In determining the amount of items allocated to partners other than the section 704(c)(1)(C) partner, the initial basis of section 704(c)(1)(C) in the hands of the partnership is equal to the property's fair market value at the time of contribution." Prop. Reg. § 1.704-3(f)(1)(i) and (ii).

The proposed regulations provide "the section 704(c)(1)(C) partner" with a special basis adjustment referred to as the "section 704(c)(1)(C) basis adjustment." (This basis adjustment is comparable to the special inside basis adjustment accorded a transferee of a partnership interest pursuant to § 743(b) discussed at lengthy in Chapter 20 Part A.) The "section 704(c)(1)(C) basis adjustment" is equal to "the excess of the adjusted basis of the section 704(c)(1)(C) over its fair market value immediately before the contribution" and "will be taken into account only in determining the amount of items allocated to the section 704(c)(1)(C) partner that contributed such section 704(c)(1)(C) property." Prop. Reg. § 1.704-3(f)(2)(iii).

From an operational angle, the proposed regulations exclude the "section 704(c)(1)(C) basis adjustment" from the partnership's basis of section 704(c)(1)(C) property. Among the operational rules provided at Prop. Reg. § 1.704-3(f)(3)(ii) are the following:

> 1. "[F]or purposes of calculating income, deduction, gain, and loss, the section 704(c)(1)(C) partner will have a special basis for section 704(c)(1)(C) property in which the partner has a section 704(c)(1)(C) basis adjustment. The section 704(c)(1)(C) basis adjustment has no effect on the partnership's computation of any item under section 703."

2. "The partnership first computes its items of income, deduction, gain, or loss at the partnership level under section 703. The partnership then allocates the partnership items among the partners, including the section 704(c)(1)(C) partner, in accordance with section 704, and adjusts the partners' capital accounts accordingly. The partnership then adjusts the section 704(c)(1)(C) partner's distributive share of the items of partnership income, deduction, gain, or loss in accordance with paragraphs (f)(3)(ii)(C) and (D) of this section, to reflect the effects of the section 704(c)(1)(C) partner's section 704(c)(1)(C) basis adjustment.... The adjustments to the section 704(c)(1)(C) partner's distributive shares do not affect the section 704(c)(1)(C) partner's capital account."

3. "The amount of a section 704(c)(1)(C) partner's income, gain, or loss from the sale or exchange of partnership property in which the section 704(c)(1)(C) partner has a section 704(c)(1)(C) basis adjustment is equal to the section 704(c)(1)(C) partner's share of the partnership's gain or loss from the sale of the property ... minus the section 704(c)(1)(C) partner's section 704(c)(1)(C) basis adjustment for the partnership property."

4. "If section 704(c)(1)(C) property is subject to ... depreciation under section 168, or other cost recovery in the hands of the section 704(c)(1)(C) partner, the section 704(c)(1)(C) basis adjustment associated with the property is recovered in accordance with ... section 168(i)(7).... The amount of any section 704(c)(1)(C) basis adjustment that is recovered by the section 704(c)(1)(C) partner in any year is added to the section 704(c)(1)(C) partner's distributive share of the partnership's depreciation ... deductions for the year. The basis adjustment is adjusted under section 1016(a)(2) to reflect the recovery of the section 704(c)(1)(C) basis adjustment."

Applying these proposed regulations to the facts of our example, the partnership would take a basis in the land contributed by Jane (the "section 704(c)(1)(C) property") of $100,000. Jane as the "section 704(c)(1)(C) partner" would have a "section 704(c)(1)(C) basis adjustment" of $25,000. When the partnership sells the land for $110,000, it would realize a book gain of $10,000 and a tax gain of $10,000. The book and tax gain would be divided equally, i.e., $5,000 to Jane and $5,000 to Dick. Dick's adjusted basis would be increased by $5,000 to $105,000 and his capital account would be increased by $5,000 to $105,000. Jane would be allocated $5,000 of tax gain, from which the proposed regulations subtract the $25,000 "section 704(c)(1)(C) basis adjustment," leaving Jane with a $20,000 tax loss. She would thus reduce her outside basis to $105,000 and her capital account would be increased to $105,000 on account of the book gain.

The following chart reflects the impact of the proposed regulations on Dick's and Jane's outside bases and capital accounts:

IV. OVERVIEW

	Dick		Jane	
	A/B	Book	A/B	Book
Beginning of Partnership	$100,000	$100,000	$125,000	$100,000
Year 1 Taxable Income (§ 705)	$0	$0	$0	$0
Book gain on sale of land		$5,000		$5,000
Tax gain deemed to exist by reason of § 704(c)(1)(C)	$5,000		$5,000	
Section 704(c)(1)(C) basis adjustment			($25,000)	
End of Year 1	$105,000	$105,000	$105,000	$105,000

In the case of depreciable "section 704(c)(1)(C) property," the proposed regulations provide the following helpful example of how depreciation would be allocated between the "section 704(c)(1)(C) contributing partner" and the "non-contributing partners." Prop. Reg. § 1.704-3(f)(3)(ii)(D)(2):

> **Example.** A contributes Property, with an adjusted basis of $12,000 and a fair market value of $5,000 on January 1 of the year of contribution, and B contributes $5,000 to PRS, a partnership. Prior to the contribution, A depreciates Property under section 168 over 10 years using the straight-line method and the half-year convention. On the contribution date, Property has 7.5 years remaining in its recovery period. Property is section 704(c)(1)(C) property, and A's section 704(c)(1)(C) basis adjustment is $7,000. PRS's basis in Property is $5,000 (fair market value) and, in accordance with section 168(i)(7), the depreciation is $667 per year ($5,000 divided by 7.5 years), which is shared equally between A and B. A's $7,000 section 704(c)(1)(C) basis adjustment is subject to depreciation of $993 per year in accordance with section 168(i)(7) ($7,000 divided by 7.5 years), which is taken into account by A.

Assume in Example 13 that, instead of contributing land, Jane had contributed depreciable property that she had been depreciating on a straight-line basis. Assume there are 10 years remaining in the recovery period for that property. (Disregard any depreciation conventions.) As noted above, Jane's property is "section 704(c)(1)(C) property" and thus the partnership will take a basis in that property equal to its fair market value of $100,000. In accordance with § 168(i)(7), the partnership will be allowed $10,000 in depreciation each year (i.e., 10% of $100,000) for the ten-year period. Jane, as indicated above, has a $25,000 "section 704(c)(1)(C) basis adjustment," and will be allowed a depreciation deduction of $2,500 per year (i.e., 10% of her $25,000 "section 704(c)(1)(C) basis adjustment") for the ten-year period. Thus, over the ten-year period, Jane will have been allowed a total of $75,000 in depreciation with respect to the "section 704(c)(1)(C) property" and Dick, the "non-contributing partner" will have been allowed $50,000 in depreciation with respect to that property. Through the increased depreciation, Jane has thus recovered the tax loss of $25,000 inherent in the property she contributed. Return to Example 7 and apply § 704(c)(1)(C) and the proposed regulations discussed above.

The proposed regulations are not applicable until on or after the date of publication of the Treasury decision adopting these rules as final regulations in the Federal Register. Prop. Reg. § 1.704-3(g).

E. Exception for "Small Disparities"

Section 704(c)'s purpose is clear — it is intended "to prevent the shifting of tax consequences among partners with respect to precontribution gain or loss." Reg. § 1.704-3(a)(1). In some instances, however, the disparity between the book value of contributed property and the contributing partner's adjusted basis in the property is so small that the partnership may disregard the application of § 704(c) to the property. A "small disparity" is defined by the regulations as one in which the book value of all properties contributed by one partner during the partnership taxable year does not differ from the aggregate adjusted tax basis the contributing partner had in the properties by more than 15% of that aggregate adjusted tax basis and the gross disparity does not exceed $20,000. Reg. § 1.704-3(e)(1)(ii). Under these circumstances, the partnership may disregard the application of § 704(c) to the properties, use a reasonable § 704(c) method, or defer application of § 704(c) until the partnership disposes of the property. Reg. § 1.704-3(e)(1)(i).

F. Revaluation of Property: the "Booking-up" and "Booking-down" of Capital Accounts and the Application of § 704(c)

Pursuant to Reg. § 1.704-1(b)(2)(iv)(f), the partners may agree that, on the occurrence of certain events, the partnership may restate (i.e., "book-up" or "book-down") the partners' capital accounts to reflect a revaluation of the partnership assets on the partnership's books.[21] According to the regulations, the restatement of partners' capital accounts must be "made principally for a substantial non-tax business purpose." Reg. § 1.704-1(b)(2)(iv)(f)(5). The regulations provide a number of examples of situations in which the restatement of capital accounts will be appropriate, e.g., the contribution of money or other property to the partnership in exchange for a partnership interest. Reg. § 1.704-1(b)(2)(iv)(f)(5)(i) The regulations also specify a number requirements for "booking-up" or "booking-down" the

---

[21] Note that the "booking-up" or "booking-down" of the partner's capital accounts and the revaluation of partnership assets on the partnership books pursuant to Reg. § 1.704-1(b)(2)(iv)(f) is not mandatory. See, however, Reg. § 1.704-1(b)(2)(iv)(e)(1) (discussed in Chapter 14) which, on distributions, requires the capital accounts of partners to be adjusted to reflect the unrealized income, gain, loss, and deduction inherent in the distributed partnership property if not previously reflected. (Of course, unrealized gain and loss inherent in contributed property (§ 704(c) property) are reflected in the contributing partner's capital account. Reg. § 1.704-1(b)(2)(iv)(b)(2).) Note also that Prop. Reg. § 1.704-1(b)(2)(iv)(f) will mandate revaluation of partnership assets and correspondingly the restatement of partners' capital accounts in certain situations involving § 751 property. See discussion in Chapter 16.

partners' capital accounts. Reg. § 1.704-1(b)(2)(iv)(f)(1)–(4). Among them is a requirement that adjustments reflect the manner in which the unrealized income, gain, loss, or deduction inherent in the partnership property would be allocated if there were a taxable disposition of the property for its fair market value. Reg. § 1.704-1(b)(2)(iv)(f)(2).

Let's consider a situation in which partners commonly choose to revalue partnership assets and restate their capital accounts pursuant to Reg. § 1.704-1(b)(2)(iv)(f) — the admission of a new partner. Consider the following example:

> Example: Austin, Becky, and Casey each contribute $120,000 in cash to partnership ABC in exchange for a one-third interest. They each share in the profits and losses of ABC in accordance with their one-third interest. Assume the partnership agreement satisfies the three requirements for economic effect of Reg. § 1.704-1(b)(2)(ii)(b). ABC immediately uses $100,000 of the cash to acquire a parcel of land for $100,000. Following the purchase of the land, the partnership balance sheet would be as follows:

	Partnership Assets			Partners' Capital	
	A/B	Book		A/B	Book
Cash	$260,000	$260,000	Austin	$120,000	$120,000
Land	$100,000	$100,000	Becky	$120,000	$120,000
			Casey	$120,000	$120,000
Total:	$360,000	$360,000		$360,000	$360,000

Assume that, at the end of Year 3, ABC continues to hold $260,000 in cash and the land, which then has a fair market value of $220,000 and a $100,000 adjusted basis. (Thus, the total fair market value of the partnership's assets is $480,000 resulting in the interest of each partner having a fair market value of $160,000.)[22] At that point, Austin, Becky, and Casey invite Dan to join the partnership as an equal partner. Dan contributes $160,000 in cash to the partnership for his one-fourth interest. In anticipation of the admission of Dan to the partnership, the partnership booked-up the capital accounts of Austin, Becky, and Casey to reflect a revaluation of the partnership's land. Were the partnership to sell the land for $220,000, it would recognize $120,000, which would be allocated in equal $40,000 shares to the three original partners. Therefore, Reg. § 1.704-1(b)(2)(iv)(f)(2) would require the capital accounts of Austin, Becky, and Casey to be booked-up to $160,000. Dan's capital account, of course, equals the amount of money he contributed, i.e., $160,000. Reg. § 1.704-1(b)(2)(iv)(b)(1). As a result, the partnership's balance sheet after the admission of Dan as a partner will be as follows:

---

[22] Notwithstanding the significant appreciation in the land, absent a decision to restate or "book-up" their capital accounts, the partners' capital accounts would continue to be $120,000.

	Partnership Assets			Partners' Capital	
	A/B	Booked-up Value (FMV)		A/B	Booked-up Value (FMV)
Cash	$420,000	$420,000	Austin	$120,000	$160,000
Land	$100,000	$220,000	Becky	$120,000	$160,000
			Casey	$120,000	$160,000
			Dan	$160,000	$160,000
Total:	$520,000	$640,000		$520,000	$640,000

Compare the two balance sheets above. Note that, following the booking-up of the capital accounts of the original partners, a book/tax disparity is created that is analogous to the book/tax disparity of a partner who contributes property with a built-in gain or loss.[23]

As noted previously, book/tax disparities are the focus of § 704(c), which is applicable to contributed property. Nonetheless, Reg. § 1.704-3(a)(6)(i) provides that the principles of § 704(c) "apply to allocations with respect to property for which differences between book value and adjusted tax basis are created when a partnership revalues partnership property pursuant to Reg. § 1.704-1(b)(2)(iv)(f)." The regulations refer to these allocations as "reverse § 704(c) allocations." In applying the § 704(c) principles to reverse allocations, the partnership is free to use any of the allocation methods discussed in this Overview, e.g., the Traditional Method, used for allocations with respect to contributed property. Reg. § 1.704-3(a)(6).[24] Thus, if, subsequent to Dan's admission, the partnership sold the land for $220,000, the $120,000 of gain recognized would all be allocated to the original partners in equal shares consistent with Reg. § 1.704-3(a)(6)(i).

It is worth noting that the allocation of the gain on the land would be the same under the regulations interpreting and applying § 704(b) discussed in Chapter 9. Specifically, Reg. § 1.704-1(b)(4)(i) provides that, under these circumstances, the separate allocation of the tax gain on the sale of the land cannot have economic effect under Reg. § 1.704-1(b)(2)(ii)(b)(1) and must be governed by § 704(c) principles. Ex. 14(i) of Reg. § 1.704-1(b)(5) illustrates this point.[25]

---

[23] The creation of a book/tax disparity on the restatement of capital accounts of existing partners like Austin, Becky, and Casey is not surprising considering that property (other than cash) commonly gains or loses value over time.

[24] Note that Reg. § 1.704-3(a)(6)(i) provides that a partnership is not required to use the same allocation method for reverse § 704(c) allocations as for contributed property, even if, at the time of revaluation, the property is already subject to § 704(c) and Reg. § 1.704-3(a).

[25] If, on the admission of Dan, the partnership had chosen not to "book-up" the partners' capital accounts to reflect a revaluation of the partnership property on the partnership's books, the same allocation of the $120,000 of gain could be accomplished by way of a special allocation provision added to the partnership agreement when Dan became a partner. Reg. § 1.704-1(b)(5) Ex. 14(iv) on similar facts notes that the special allocation will satisfy the substantial economic effect test of § 704(b). *See* Chapter 9. By contrast, if there had been no "booking-up" pursuant to Reg. § 1.704-1(b)(2)(iv)(f) and no special allocation were made, Dan would be allocated a share of the partnership's $120,000 of book and tax gain. As a result, his capital account would be increased and he would correspondingly have a greater share

Reflecting on situations such as that presented in the above example, one would expect the results reached. Dan, a new partner, paid fair market value for his partnership interest and presumably would not want to be taxed on the gain inherent in the partnership's land at the time he joined the partnership.[26] That gain, when recognized, should be allocated to the three original partners and, as the example indicates, will be.[27]

G. Conclusion

As discussed above, in allocating items of income, gain, loss, and deduction with respect to contributed property, a partnership may choose any "reasonable method that is consistent with the purpose of § 704(c)." This chapter has reviewed the three methods specifically identified as being "generally reasonable" allocation methods. Considering the operation of these three methods, why would a partnership chose one method over another?

---

of liquidation proceeds. Dan would thus have benefited economically from the appreciation of the land occurring prior to his admission as a partner. Under these circumstances, Reg. § 1.704-1(b)(5) Ex. 14(iv) raises the specter of other possible tax consequences resulting from such an allocation and, in that regard, references Reg. § 1.704-1(b)(1)(iii) and (iv).

[26] Were the partnership to be holding loss property at the time of Dan's admission as a partner, the existing partners would not want Dan to share in the loss that then existed.

[27] Assume, however, that, subsequent to Dan's admission to the partnership, the land decreased in value to $190,000 and was sold for that amount. There would be $90,000 of gain recognized by the partnership (i.e., amount realized of $190,000 less $100,000 adjusted basis). There has been a loss of $30,000 in value since Dan became a partner. Pursuant to the traditional allocation method, Dan would be denied a loss deduction because of the ceiling rule. As discussed above, use of the traditional method with curative allocations or the remedial method would resolve the distortion created by the ceiling rule.

Chapter 11

ALLOCATION OF NONRECOURSE DEDUCTIONS

I. PROBLEMS

On January 1, Year 1, Cathy and George created a limited partnership to which Cathy, the general partner, contributed $100,000 and George, the limited partner, contributed $400,000. The partnership immediately purchased an apartment complex on leased land from an unrelated party for $2,000,000 using the $500,000 Cathy and George contributed and borrowing the remaining $1,500,000 on a nonrecourse basis. The nonrecourse borrowing is secured only by a mortgage on the apartment building. Although no principal payments are due on the nonrecourse loan for 20 years, interest on the loan is payable annually. Pursuant to the partnership agreement, only Cathy, the general partner, is required to restore any deficit in her capital account following the liquidation of her interest. The partnership agreement requires that the partners' capital accounts be maintained consistent with Reg. § 1.704-1(b)(2)(iv) and that liquidating distributions be made in accordance with the partners' positive capital account balances. The partnership agreement contains both qualified income offset and minimum gain chargeback provisions. Except as otherwise provided by the qualified income offset and minimum gain chargeback provisions, all partnership items will be allocated 80% to George and 20% to Cathy until the first time the partnership has recognized items of income and gain that exceed the items of loss and deduction it has recognized over it life. All further partnership items will thereafter be allocated equally between Cathy and George. In addition, the partnership agreement provides that all distributions, other than liquidating distributions, will be made 80% to George and 20% to Cathy until a total of $500,000 has been distributed and, thereafter, the distributions will be equal. Assume the apartment building is depreciable over a 20-year period at the rate of $100,000 per year. Assume also that the partnership will pay $80,000 for the lease of the land on which the apartment building is situated. During each of the first 10 years, the partnership will generate rental income of $200,000 and have total operating expenses (maintenance and lease expenses) of $125,000, interest expense of $75,000, and depreciation of $100,000. The partnership thus will realize $100,000 net taxable loss in each of the first 10 years of its existence. The partnership makes no distributions unless otherwise indicated. Assume there is a reasonable likelihood that, over its life, the partnership will realize amounts of income and gain significantly in excess of the amount of losses and deductions (other than nonrecourse deductions) and the equal allocation of excess income and gain will have substantial economic effect.

    (a) Create the partnership's opening balance sheet showing the partners' outside bases and capital accounts. For purposes of this problem, assume that, pursuant to § 752 and the regulations thereunder, the nonrecourse liability will be allocated 80% (or $1,200,000) to George and 20% (or $300,000) to Cathy.

(b) Given the facts presented, what will the outside bases and capital accounts of the partners be at the end of Year 5? How much partnership minimum gain, if any, will there be at the end of Year 5? What is the dollar amount and nature of partnership nonrecourse deductions, if any, for Year 5?

(c) How will your answers to (b) change if the year in question is Year 6? Year 7?

(d) Explain the tax consequences to Cathy and George if, at the beginning of Year 8, the partnership disposes of the apartment building for no consideration other than the full satisfaction of the $1,500,000 nonrecourse liability encumbering the building (and has no other economic activity in Year 8).

(e) What is the partnership minimum gain, if any, at the end of Year 7 if, during that year, Cathy contributes $100,000 to the partnership and George contributes $400,000 and the partnership immediately uses the $500,000 to pay down the nonrecourse indebtedness to $1,000,000? Will Cathy and George be subject to a minimum gain chargeback under those circumstances?

(f) What will the increase in partnership minimum gain, if any, be in Year 7 if the partnership borrows an additional $100,000 on a nonrecourse basis and immediately distributes $20,000 of the loan proceeds to Cathy and $80,000 to George? Assume the additional borrowing is secured only by a second mortgage on the apartment building. Disregard any interest associated with the second mortgage. How will any increase in partnership minimum gain be shared?

(g) Assuming the facts of (f), what are the consequences to Cathy and George if, at the beginning of Year 8, the partnership disposes of the apartment building for no consideration other than the full satisfaction of the $1,600,000 of nonrecourse liability (i.e., the original purchase money loan of $1,500,000 plus the additional $100,000 loan in Year 7)? Assume the partnership has no other economic activity in Year 8.

(h) Given the requirement of Reg.§ 1.704-2(e)(2), what flexibility do Cathy and George have with respect to the allocation of nonrecourse deductions?

Assignment for Chapter 12:

Complete the problems

Read: Internal Revenue Code: §§ 752(a) and (b)
Treasury Regulations: §§ 1.704-1(b)(2)(iv)(a)-(d)(3); 1.704-2(b), (c), (d)(1), (e), (f)(1), (3) and (6), (g)(1) and (2), (h), (j)(1), (2), (m) Ex. 1(i) - (iv) and (3)(i).
Materials: Overview
Commissioner v. Tufts

II. VOCABULARY

nonrecourse debt
nonrecourse deductions
partnership minimum gain
increase in partnership minimum gain
decrease in partnership minimum gain
partner's share of partnership minimum gain
minimum gain chargeback
reasonable consistency requirement

III. OBJECTIVES

1. To explain how *Commissioner v. Tufts* sets the stage for the allocation of nonrecourse deductions under Reg. § 1.704-2(e).

2. To explain each of the four requirements of the safe harbor test for allocation of nonrecourse deductions.

3. To calculate the increase in partnership minimum gain for a given year.

4. To determine each partner's share of partnership minimum gain.

5. To identify the nature of any nonrecourse deductions.

6. To explain the impact of the distribution of the proceeds of nonrecourse borrowing on a partner's share of partnership minimum gain.

7. To calculate the decrease in partnership minimum gain for any given year.

8. To identify situations that result in a decrease in partnership minimum gain.

9. To determine each partner's share of any decrease in partnership minimum gain.

10. To explain the consequences of partner contributions that result in a decrease in partnership minimum gain.

11. To determine, with respect to a given partnership, the range of nonrecourse deductions and allocations that will satisfy the reasonable consistency requirement of the safe harbor provided by Reg. § 1. 704-2(e)(2).

12. To explain the operation of a minimum gain chargeback provision.

IV. OVERVIEW

A. Introduction

As developed in Chapter 9, an allocation to a partner of a deduction or loss will generally be respected only if that partner bears the economic burden associated with the deduction or loss. Consider the following examples.

Example: In Year 1, Dennis and Mary form a general partnership (the Dennis/Mary Partnership), to which each contributes $150,000 of cash. The partnership uses the $300,000 of cash contributed by the partners to purchase a piece of depreciable property for $300,000. Assume the property is depreciable at the rate of 10% or $30,000 per year (and disregard any depreciation conventions) and all depreciation deduction are allocated to Mary. Assume (unrealistically) the partnership's only tax item in Year 1 is the $30,000 depreciation deduction, which happens to match the actual economic decline in the fair market value of the property. Recognizing the unlikelihood of realizing any profit from the property, the partnership sells the property at the end of Year 1 for $270,000 to an unrelated party and immediately liquidates.

Analysis: The allocation of the $30,000 in depreciation deduction to Mary will be respected only if she bears the economic burden if the property actually declines in value by $30,000. Thus, for the depreciation allocation to be respected, the $270,000 in liquidation proceeds would have to be distributed as follows: $150,000 to Dennis and $120,000 to Mary. Assuming the partnership agreement contained the three requirements for economic effect specified in Reg. § 1.704-1(b)(2)(ii)(b) or satisfied the alternative test for economic effect under Reg. § 1.704-1(b)(2)(ii)(d), that is precisely what would occur.[1] Mary's initial capital account of $150,000 would have been reduced to $120,000 as a result of the Year 1 depreciation allocation; Dennis' capital account at the end of Year 1 would be unchanged from the $150,000 capital account he had at the outset.[2] The liquidation proceeds of $270,000 would be distributed consistent with these capital account balances. Mary, who contributed $150,000 in cash to form the partnership, would receive only $120,000 of the partnership's liquidation proceeds while Dennis would receive $150,000, i.e., the amount he had contributed.[3] Given this analysis, it should be apparent that Mary alone bears the economic burden of the $30,000 decline in the property's value.

Example 2: Assume the facts of Example 1 except that Dennis and Mary contributed nothing to the partnership and the partnership financed the purchase of the property using the proceeds of a $300,000 recourse loan. Assume the $300,000 loan is secured by a mortgage on the property and is repayable in a lump sum in Year 11. Assume also the sales agreement required Dennis and Mary to transfer the property to the purchaser free and clear of any encumbrances, i.e., the purchaser did not assume the recourse mortgage.

Analysis: Dennis's and Mary's opening capital accounts would initially be $0 but, as a result of the Year 1 depreciation deduction of $30,000 allocated to Mary, a deficit of $30,000 would be created in her capital account.[4] Again,

---

[1] Even if the partnership agreement did not contain the three requirements for economic effect, the results would also be the same under the partners'-interest-in-the-partnership test of Reg. § 1.704-1(b)(3).

[2] Reg. § 1.704-1(b)(2)(iv)(b). Dennis and Mary would each initially have a $150,000 outside basis reflecting the $150,000 cash contribution each made to the partnership. As a result of the depreciation deduction allocated to her, Mary's outside basis would be reduced to $120,000. § 705(a)(2)(A).

[3] Neither Dennis nor Mary would recognize any gain as a result of the liquidation. See § 731(a)(1).

[4] Dennis and Mary would again initially each have an outside basis of $150,000 reflecting their share

assume as in Example 1 that, by the end of Year 1, the property had declined in value to $270,000, the partnership sold the property for that amount, and immediately liquidated. The allocation to Mary will only be respected if Mary is required to restore the deficit in her capital account, thus enabling the partnership to repay the lender the amount borrowed.[5] Again, if the partnership agreement contained the three requirements for economic effect specified in Reg. § 1.704-1(b)(2)(ii)(b), that is precisely what would occur.[6] In restoration of her capital account deficit, Mary would be obligated to pay $30,000 to the partnership and thus will have borne the economic burden of the depreciation deduction allocated to her.[7]

What is the result if, instead of recourse financing, a partnership acquired property with nonrecourse financing — a common situation encountered in real estate partnerships? Consider the following example:

Example 3: Assume the facts of the Dennis/Mary Partnership in Example 2, except the $300,000 loan is nonrecourse and the partnership sold the property to an unrelated third party (the purchaser) subject to the nonrecourse debt and for no other consideration.

Consider first the fact that, if the property declined in value to $270,000 and the Dennis/Mary Partnership defaulted on the loan, the lender could look only to the property securing the nonrecourse loan for repayment and not to the partners, i.e., the lender could foreclose on the property but would have no further recourse against Dennis, Mary, or the partnership. Thus, the lender alone would bear the economic burden of the property's decline in value.

Under these circumstances, one might reasonably conclude the lender/mortgagee and not the partnership or Mary should be allowed the Year 1 $30,000 depreciation deduction with regard to the property. In other words, we could think of the lender/mortgagee as the owner or co-owner of the property with a basis of $300,000 in its ownership interest. That, however, is not the how the law has evolved.

In *Commissioner v. Tufts*, included in the materials, the Supreme Court affirmed the position the Court had taken in *Crane v. Commissioner*[8] that bona fide nonrecourse indebtedness should be accorded the same treatment as recourse indebtedness. The nonrecourse loan is thus understood as "the mortgagor's investment in the property, and does not constitute a co-investment by the mortgagee." (See footnote 45 of *Tufts, infra*.) As a result, the mortgagee is entitled

---

of the recourse liability. §§ 752(a) and 722. The allocation of recourse liabilities is examined in detail in Chapter 12. As a result of the $30,000 depreciation deduction allocated to her, Mary's outside basis would be reduced to $120,000. § 705(a)(2)(A).

[5] The partnership would repay the lender $300,000 using the $270,000 in sale proceeds and the $30,000 Mary paid to the partnership to restore the deficit in her capital account.

[6] *Id.*

[7] Having paid $30,000 to the partnership, Mary's outside basis would be increased to $150,000. § 722. When the partnership repaid the $300,000 to the lender, Dennis' and Mary's outside bases would each be reduced to zero to reflect the $150,000 decrease in their share of partnership liabilities. §§ 752(b) and 733. Neither Dennis nor Mary would have any gain or loss on the liquidation of the partnership.

[8] 331 U.S. 1 (1947).

to no portion of the basis. In other words, the Dennis/Mary Partnership would be treated as having a $300,000 cost basis in the depreciable property and, pursuant to § 168, would be allowed depreciation deductions computed with reference to that basis. More generally, as a result of *Crane* and *Tufts*, any losses or deductions attributable to nonrecourse financing belong to the mortgagor rather than the mortgagee, even though the latter bears the economic burden associated with such deductions or losses.

While allowing the mortgagor to benefit from the losses or deductions attributable to nonrecourse financing, *Crane* and *Tufts* at the same time impose a tax burden on the mortgagor, i.e., when the mortgagor disposes of the property encumbered by a nonrecourse debt, the mortgagor must include in its amount realized the balance owing on the debt. See Reg. § 1.1001-2(a)(1) and (4)(i). As demonstrated in *Tufts*, this means a mortgagor, who has claimed substantial depreciation deductions attributable to nonrecourse debt and disposes of the property for no consideration other than the satisfaction of that debt, may recognize significant taxable gain. *Crane* and *Tufts* set the stage for an exception to the general rule that partners must bear the economic burden associated with any items of deduction or loss allocated to them. Thus, as further developed in Reg. § 1.704-2, partnerships and their partners, like individuals, are allowed to claim the benefit of losses and deductions attributable to nonrecourse liabilities on the condition that they account for those losses and deductions by including income or gain when the nonrecourse liability is reduced or eliminated.

This chapter will address the regulation exception enabling partnerships to allocate deductions and losses attributable to nonrecourse financing (hereinafter "nonrecourse deductions"). As discussed previously in Chapter 8, a partner's distributive share of partnership losses is only deductible to the extent of the partner's outside basis. § 704(d). Chapter 3 provided an introduction to the allocation of partnership liabilities, noting that, to the extent a partner is allocated recourse or nonrecourse liabilities, the partner is treated as contributing cash to the partnership, thereby increasing the partner's outside basis. As will be discussed in Chapter 12 addressing in detail the allocation of recourse and nonrecourse liabilities, the regulations have carefully linked the allocation of nonrecourse deductions to the allocation of nonrecourse liabilities.

B. Allocation of Nonrecourse Deductions: Introduction to the Safe Harbor Rules

Regulation § 1.704-2(b)(1) provides that, because "nonrecourse deductions" cannot have economic effect, they "must be allocated in accordance with the partners' interest in the partnership." Just as Reg. § 1.704-1 interpreting § 704(b) provides a safe harbor test — the substantial economic effect test, Reg. § 1.704-2, addressing the allocation of nonrecourse deductions, also provides a safe harbor test that "deems allocations of nonrecourse deductions to be in accordance with the partners' interests in the partnership." Reg. § 1.704-2(b). Only if the partnership fails to satisfy the safe harbor test of Reg. § 1.704-2(e) will the partners' distributive shares of nonrecourse deductions be determined under the partners'-interest-in-the-partnership test (the PIP test) of Reg. § 1.704-1(b)(3). As noted in

Chapter 9, Reg. § 1.704-1(b)(3) provides only limited guidance in applying the PIP test. Thus, to ensure certainty regarding the distributive shares of nonrecourse deductions, partnerships will seek to take advantage of the safe harbor provided by Reg. § 1.704-2(e).

The four-pronged safe harbor test. Pursuant to Reg. § 1.704-2(e), allocations of nonrecourse deductions are deemed to be in accordance with the partner's interest in the partnership only if the following four requirements are met:

1. The partnership agreement satisfies the primary test for "economic effect" under Reg. § 1.704-1(b)(2)(ii)(b) (i.e., maintenance of capital accounts and distribution of liquidation proceeds in accord with positive capital account balances, and an unconditional obligation to restore any deficit in a partner's capital account) or satisfies the alternative test for economic effect under Reg. § 1.704-1(b)(2(ii)(d) (qualified income offset rules). See discussion in Chapter 9.

2. The partnership agreement provides for the allocation of nonrecourse deductions in a manner *reasonably consistent* with allocations having substantial economic effect of some other significant item attributable to property securing the nonrecourse liabilities;

3. The partnership agreement contains a *minimum gain chargeback provision* compliant with regulation requirements; and

4. All other material allocations and capital account adjustments are "recognized" (i.e., respected) under Reg. § 1.704-1(b).

Simply stated, the safe harbor, while providing partnerships considerable flexibility in allocating nonrecourse deductions, seeks to ensure that partners benefiting from deductions attributable to nonrecourse liabilities (or, under certain circumstances, receiving distributions of the proceeds of nonrecourse liabilities) will be required to bear any tax liability associated with the nonrecourse liabilities. That result is accomplished through a so-called "minimum gain chargeback." Were the four safe harbor requirements in place in Example 3 above, the partnership's allocation of the $30,000 in depreciation to Mary in Year 1 would be respected and a deficit of $30,000 would be created in Mary's capital account. When the partnership transferred the property at the end of Year 1 to the purchaser subject to the $300,000 nonrecourse liability and for no other consideration, the partnership would recognize $30,000 of gain (i.e., amount realized of $300,000 (pursuant to *Tufts*) less the adjusted basis of $270,000). As will be discussed below, the minimum gain chargeback provision (requirement 3 of the safe harbor), would require that Mary, who had the benefit of the $30,000 of depreciation deductions allocable to the nonrecourse liability, recognize all $30,000 of the gain.

To understand these requirements, as well as the operation of the safe harbor provided by the regulations, however, it is necessary first to define a range of terms as well as explain certain principles employed by the regulations. Part C of this chapter will address those basic definitions and principles. Part D will then analyze the second and third requirements. (The first and fourth requirements of the safe harbor do not involve new matters but rather simply repeat standards and rules discussed in prior chapters.)

C. Allocation of Nonrecourse Deductions: Definitions and Basic Principles

1. Nonrecourse Deductions

In considering the rules governing the allocation of nonrecourse deductions, we begin by defining the term "nonrecourse deductions." That term has been defined as those "losses, deductions, or § 705(a)(2)(B) expenditures (e.g., charitable contributions) attributable to partnership nonrecourse liabilities."[9] The depreciation deductions allowed the partnership in *Commissioner v. Tufts*, included in the materials, are classic "nonrecourse deductions," i.e., the *Tufts* partnership was allowed to claim the depreciation deductions with respect to the apartment building's basis — a basis generated by nonrecourse financing secured by the apartment building.[10] Likewise the $30,000 in depreciation deductions discussed in Example 3 above are nonrecourse deductions. The determination of the amount of nonrecourse deductions in any taxable year of the partnership is explained below.

2. Partnership Minimum Gain

As demonstrated in *Commissioner v. Tufts*, although the partnership did not have to repay the nonrecourse loan used to acquire the apartment building, there was nonetheless a price to be paid for the nonrecourse deductions claimed by the partnership, i.e., to the extent those deductions reduced the partnership's adjusted basis below the balance of the nonrecourse liability encumbering the apartment building, the partnership, upon disposing of the building, had to recognize gain at least equal to the excess of the excess of the nonrecourse liability over the partnership's adjusted basis in the building. The *Tufts* holding is reflected in Reg. § 1.704-2(b)(2) providing that, "to the extent a nonrecourse liability exceeds the adjusted tax basis of the partnership property it encumbers, a disposition of that property will generate gain at least equal to that excess ("partnership minimum gain")." Thus, as noted by the Service, "partnership minimum gain is the spread between the property's basis and the amount of non-recourse debt encumbering the property."[11] Because the concept of partnership gain evolves from the analysis in *Commissioner v. Tufts*, partnership minimum gain is often referred to as *"Tufts* gain." As will become apparent, an understanding of what "partnership minimum gain" is, how it is increased or decreased, and to whom any net increase or decrease in partnership minimum gain is allocated is critical in determining the allocation of nonrecourse deductions and applying the safe harbor noted above. Indeed, the concept of partnership minimum gain and the related concept of minimum gain chargeback comprise the basic core of the regulations addressing the allocation of nonrecourse deductions.

---

[9] Reg. § 1.704-2(b)(1).

[10] It is not uncommon today for nonrecourse liabilities of partnerships and limited liability companies to be merely general obligations of the entity rather than being secured by specific property. In the case of a default, the lender can foreclose on the assets of the partnership or limited liability company but cannot bring a collection action against any of the partners or members. Deductions attributable to such nonrecourse liabilities are also "nonrecourse deductions."

[11] IRS Partnership Audit Technique Guide Chapter 6 (Rev. December 2007).

3. Increase in Partnership Minimum Gain

As reflected in *Tufts* and in Example 3 above, partnership minimum gain is created or increased when a partnership claims depreciation deductions that decrease the partnership's adjusted basis in the property below the balance of the nonrecourse debt secured by the property.[12] Let's examine the creation of a net increase in partnership minimum gain by considering a more complex set of facts than that provided in Example 3 above. (This set of facts will be used throughout the balance of this chapter to illustrate the meaning of various terms and principles and the operation of the safe harbor of the regulations.)

Example 4: On January 1, Year 1, Katie and Matt form a limited partnership with Katie, the general partner, contributing $50,000 in cash and Matt, the limited partner, contributing $150,000 in cash. The partnership is a calendar-year partnership. The partnership agreement requires Katie to restore deficits in her capital account upon liquidation of her interest, but does not impose the same requirement on Matt. The partnership agreement contains a qualified income offset, requires capital accounts to be maintained consistent with the regulations, and requires liquidation proceeds to be distributed in accordance with the partners' positive capital account balances. The partnership agreement also contains a minimum gain chargeback provision. The agreement provides that all items of partnership income, gain, loss, and deduction (including nonrecourse deductions) will be allocated 25% to Katie and 75% to Matt. The partnership immediately purchases a $1,000,000 piece of depreciable property using the $200,000 contributed by Katie and Matt and borrowing the $800,000 balance of the purchase price from an unrelated lender on a nonrecourse basis. (Assume the partnership agreement allocates the nonrecourse liability for § 752 purposes 25% to Katie and 75% to Matt consistent with their shares of the partnership's nonrecourse deductions. The nonrecourse debt is secured by the property and is repayable in a lump sum in Year 11. Assume the property is depreciable at the rate of 10% or $100,000 per year.

Issue: In which years of the 10-year period — Years 1 through 10 — will the partnership experience a net increase in partnership minimum gain?

Analysis: In Year 1, the partnership will claim $100,000 in depreciation deductions, thus reducing the property's adjusted basis to $900,000. If the property were disposed of at the end of Year 1 for no consideration other than relief from the $800,000 nonrecourse liability, there would be no partnership minimum gain for Year 1, i.e., the $800,000 balance owing on the nonrecourse debt is less than the partnership's $900,000 adjusted basis in the property. At the end of Year 2, there would likewise be no partnership minimum gain as the $800,000 balance owing on the nonrecourse debt would exactly equal the partnership's adjusted basis in the property. At the end of Year 3, however, the $800,000 balance owing on the nonrecourse debt would exceed the partnership's $700,000 adjusted basis in the property,

---

[12] Reg. § 1.704-2(b)(2).

thus triggering a net increase of $100,000 in the partnership minimum gain, i.e., at the end of Year 2 partnership minimum gain was $0 and at the end of Year 3 it was $100,000. With each passing year, there will be a *net increase* of $100,000 in partnership minimum gain as a result of the depreciation deductions allowed the partnership with respect to the property.[13] At the end of the 10-year depreciation period, when the principal balance of the nonrecourse indebtedness is still $800,000 and when the partnership's adjusted basis in the property has been reduced to $0, there will be $800,000 of total partnership minimum gain associated with the property.

Partnership minimum gain can also be increased by new nonrecourse borrowing secured by the property.[14]

> **Example 5:** Assume the facts of Example 4. Assume that, as of the beginning of Year 7, the property has appreciated in value to $1,200,000. At that time, the total partnership minimum gain would be $400,000.[15] Given the increased value of the property, the partnership in Year 7 borrows an additional $100,000 on a nonrecourse basis, using the property as security for the loan. (Assume, for § 752 purposes, the partnership agreement also allocates this nonrecourse liability 25% to Katie and 75% to Matt.)
>
> **Issue:** For Year 7, what is the amount of net increase in partnership minimum gain?
>
> **Analysis:** A taxpayer does not realize gain when the taxpayer, using appreciated property as security, borrows on a nonrecourse basis an amount that exceeds the taxpayer's adjusted basis in that property. That result was confirmed in *Woodsam Associates, Inc. v. Commissioner*, 198 F.2d 357 (2d Cir. 1952). Therefore, when the partnership in this example borrows an additional $100,000 on a nonrecourse basis, the partnership will not realize any gain, notwithstanding that the overall nonrecourse debt encumbering the property greatly exceeds the partnership's adjusted basis in the property.
>
> Turning then to the question of partnership minimum gain, at the end of Year 7, after claiming an additional $100,000 of depreciation deductions, the partnership minimum gain will be $600,000, i.e., the $900,000 balance of the nonrecourse indebtedness less the partnership's $300,000 adjusted basis in the property. Recall that, at the end of Year 6, there was only a total of $400,000 of partnership minimum gain. There has thus been a $200,000 net increase in partnership minimum gain in Year 7.[16]

---

[13] Reg. § 1.704-2(d)(1).

[14] *See* Reg. § 1.704-2(b)(2). The partnership minimum gain can also be increased by the conversion of recourse debt to nonrecourse debt. See Reg. § 1.704-2(d)(1) and (g)(3).

[15] The $400,000 partnership minimum gain is the difference between the $800,000 balance of the nonrecourse financing and the partnership's $400,000 adjusted basis (original basis of $1,000,000 less 6 years of depreciation at the rate of $100,000 per year).

[16] Reg. 1.704-2(d)(1).

4. Partnership Minimum Gain as a Measure of Nonrecourse Deductions

Having defined "partnership minimum gain" and determined how it is increased, let us now consider the link between partnership minimum gain and the measurement of nonrecourse deductions for the year. *The amount of nonrecourse deductions for a partnership's taxable year will equal the net increase for that year in partnership minimum gain reduced by the aggregate distributions made during the year of proceeds of nonrecourse liabilities allocable to an increase in partnership minimum gain.*[17] Thus, in the case of the Katie and Matt partnership in Example 4, because no partnership minimum gain exists at the end of either Year 1 or Year 2, there are no nonrecourse deductions for those years.[18] As noted in Example 4, in each of the Years 3-10, however, there is a net increase of $100,000 in partnership minimum gain. As a result, there is $100,000 of nonrecourse deductions in each of those years. Regulation § 1.704-2(c) provides "generally, nonrecourse deductions consist first of depreciation or cost recovery deductions. . . ." See also Reg. § 1.704-2(j)(1)(ii). Thus, the $100,000 in depreciation deductions allowed the partnership in each of the Years 3–10 in Example 4 are nonrecourse deductions.

In Example 5, the net increase in partnership minimum gain in Year 7 was $200,000, thus generating $200,000 of nonrecourse deductions. As in Example 4, $100,000 of those deductions will consist of the depreciation deduction allowed the partnership. The remaining $100,000 of nonrecourse deductions in Year 7 will consist of "a pro rata portion of other partnership losses, deductions and § 705(a)(2)(B) expenditures for the year."[19] Thus, in a situation like that presented in Example 5, the Treasury assumes that the partnership is using the proceeds of the new nonrecourse borrowing to pay for other costs of the partnership business, thereby generating nonrecourse deductions in addition to the nonrecourse deductions consisting of depreciation deductions. For example, if the partnership in Year 7 had only two tax items, $100,000 in depreciation deductions and $100,000 in supply expenses, the deduction for the supply expenses would be treated as a nonrecourse deduction. If there are insufficient "other partnership losses, deductions and § 705(a)(2)(B) expenditures for the year, [any] excess nonrecourse deductions are carried over."[20] In Example 5, if the partnership had distributed the $100,000 of new nonrecourse borrowing to Katie and Matt, the amount of nonrecourse deductions in Year 7 would be only $100,000, consisting solely of the $100,000 in depreciation deductions allowed the partnership that year.[21]

---

[17] Reg. § 1.704-2(c). Note that the reduction for distributions of the proceeds of liabilities allocable to an increase in partnership minimum gain makes sense given that the distribution of the proceeds negates any use of those proceeds to generate deductions.

[18] In other words, the $200,000 of depreciation deductions claimed during Years 1 and 2 were attributable to the partner's equity (the $200,000 Katie and Matt contributed in forming the partnership) and thus not to the nonrecourse financing.

[19] Reg. § 1.704-2(c) and Reg. § 1.704-2(j)(1)(ii).

[20] Reg. § 1.704-2(c) and Reg. § 1.704-2(j)(1)(iii).

[21] Reg. § 1.704-2(c) (first sentence).

5. Decrease in Partnership Minimum Gain

As noted in the regulations, "partnership minimum gain decreases as reductions occur in the amount by which the nonrecourse liability exceeds the adjusted tax basis of the property encumbered by the liability."[22] Decreases in partnership minimum gain occur under a variety of circumstances, one of the most common being the disposition of an asset subject to a nonrecourse liability.[23] Consider the following example.

> **Example 6:** Assume the facts of Example 4. Assume also that, at the beginning of Year 6, the partnership sold the depreciable property for no consideration other than relief from the $800,000 nonrecourse liability encumbering the property. What is the net decrease, if any, in partnership minimum gain?
>
> **Analysis:** As noted in the analysis to Example 4, the partnership would have experienced a $100,000 increase in partnership minimum gain in Year 3 and in each year thereafter during the 10-year cost recovery period. Thus, there would have been a total of $300,000 of partnership minimum gain at the time the partnership sold the property. With the sale, the partnership minimum gain associated with that property is necessarily extinguished as the partnership no longer holds the property. Thus, although the partnership has recognized $300,000 in tax gain on the sale of the property (i.e., amount realized of $800,000 less adjusted basis of $500,000), there is a net decrease of $300,000 in the partnership minimum gain.

A decrease in partnership minimum gain will also occur when the partnership repays a nonrecourse debt. See Reg. § 1.704–2(b)(2). Thus, in Example 6 above, were the partnership, instead of selling the property, to repay the nonrecourse loan at the beginning of Year 6, there would also be a $300,000 decrease in partnership minimum gain.

6. Partner's Share of Partnership Minimum Gain

As noted, partnership minimum gain is the gain that would be realized were the partnership to dispose of the property subject to a nonrecourse liability for no consideration other than the full satisfaction of the nonrecourse liability. That gain (the *Tufts* gain) would, of course, have to be allocated among the partners. The proper allocation of that gain depends on the share a partner has in the partnership minimum gain. Intuitively, we would expect a partner who has benefited from an allocation of nonrecourse deductions (or has received a distribution of the proceeds of nonrecourse borrowing resulting in an increase in partnership minimum gain) should ultimately be allocated gain (or other income) when any *Tufts*-type gain is realized (or, to use the language of the regulations, when there is a decrease in partnership minimum gain). Thus, it is not surprising that, in general, a partner's

---

[22] Reg. § 1.704-2(b)(2).

[23] Were the sale of the apartment building in *Tufts* to be analyzed under the regulations we have today, i.e., Reg. § 1.704-2, and assuming the partnership agreement satisfied the safe harbor requirements of Reg. § 1.704–2(e), the sale would have resulted in a net decrease in partnership minimum gain, triggering application of the minimum gain chargeback discussed *infra*.

share of partnership minimum gain equals the sum of:[24]

(a) nonrecourse deductions allocated to the partner; and

(b) any distributions made to the partner of proceeds of nonrecourse liabilities that resulted in increases in partnership minimum gain.

Consider the following examples:

Example 7: Assume the facts of Example 4. In Year 3, when the partnership experienced a $100,000 net increase in partnership minimum gain, the nonrecourse deductions for the year amounted to $100,000 and consisted exclusively of depreciation. Pursuant to the partnership agreement, Katie would be allocated $25,000 of those deductions and Matt would be allocated $75,000 of the nonrecourse deductions. As a result, Katie's share of partnership minimum gain is $25,000 and Matt's share would be $75,000. In each of the seven years thereafter, there would again be a $100,000 net increase in partnership minimum gain allocated in the same manner as the Year 3 net increase. Thus, by the end of the 10-year cost recovery period, Katie's share of the $800,000 total partnership minimum gain would be $200,000 and Matt's share would be $600,000.

Example 8: Assume the facts of Example 5. Assume the partnership distributed the proceeds of the Year 7 nonrecourse loan $25,000 to Katie and $75,000 to Matt.[25]

Analysis: In Example 5, when the partnership in Year 7 borrowed an additional $100,000 on a nonrecourse basis, it did not distribute the proceeds of that borrowing. Because it was assumed the partnership would use those proceeds in its business, giving rise to partnership deductions, the regulations assumed the amount of nonrecourse deductions included the amount of the borrowing. (See analysis in Example 5.) In this example, however, we assume the partnership distributed the proceeds of the new loan to Katie and Matt. Thus, the new loan would not give rise to nonrecourse deductions although it increased partnership minimum gain. As a result, even though the partnership minimum gain is increased by $200,000 in Year 7, there are only $100,000 of nonrecourse deductions, i.e., the depreciation deduction for the year. To ensure the appropriate allocation of partnership minimum gain, the regulations take into account (1) any distributions to partners of the proceeds of a nonrecourse liability allocable to increases in partnership minimum gain, and (2) the nonrecourse deductions allocated to partners. As a general rule, therefore, Katie's and Matt's share of the $100,000 net increase in partnership minimum gain allocable to the Year 7 nonrecourse liability would match the amount of proceeds distributed to each.[26] Thus, Katie's share of the $200,000 increase

---

[24] From that amount, one must subtract the partner's share of net decreases in partnership minimum gain (as discussed below). Reg. § 1.704-2(g)(1)

[25] Assume the loan proceeds were distributed to Katie and Matt in Year 7. *See* Reg. § 1.704-2(c), which provides the rule for calculating the amount of nonrecourse deductions.

[26] Review Reg. § 1.704-2(h)(1)-(3).

in partnership minimum gain in Year 7 would amount to $50,000 (i.e., $25,000 in nonrecourse loan proceeds and $25,000 in nonrecourse deductions) and Matt's share would be $150,000 (i.e., $75,000 in nonrecourse loan proceeds and $75,000 in nonrecourse deductions).

7. Partner's Share of Partnership Minimum Gain Treated as Capital Account Deficit Restoration Obligations

Considering Matt has no obligation to restore a deficit in his capital account, you are likely questioning how Matt could be allocated nonrecourse deductions as in Example 7 or be distributed the proceeds of a nonrecourse loan as in Example 8. Let's step back and consider the status of Katie's and Matt's initial capital accounts and outside bases as well as the adjustments that would be made to their capital accounts and outside bases in view of the facts provided in Examples 7 and 8. For simplicity's sake, assume the only tax items the partnership has in any year are the depreciation deductions claimed by the partnership. As a result, the partnership will generate a $100,000 loss in each of the years. This loss will be allocated between Katie and Matt using the 25%/75% ratio they agreed upon for sharing profits and losses.

Upon the formation of the partnership on January 1, Year 1, when Katie and Matt each made their cash contributions and the partnership borrowed $800,000 on a nonrecourse basis, Katie's capital account would have been $50,000, reflecting her contribution of $50,000 to the partnership and Matt's capital account would have been $150,000, reflecting his contribution to the partnership. Reg. § 1.704-1(b)(2)(iv)(b)(1).

As noted in Chapter 3, an increase in a partner's share of partnership liabilities is treated as an additional cash contribution to the partnership that increases the partner's outside basis.[27] The $800,000 nonrecourse liability will be allocated $200,000 to Katie and $600,000 to Matt thereby increasing their outside bases by those amounts.[28] As a result, Katie's outside basis will be $250,000, i.e., the sum of the $50,000 in cash she contributed and the $200,000 of nonrecourse liability she is allocated.[29] Matt's outside basis will be $750,000, i.e., the sum of the $150,000 in cash he contributed and the $600,000 of nonrecourse liability he is allocated. The following table shows the initial outside bases (A/B) and capital accounts (Book) of

---

[27] §§ 752(a) and 722.

[28] As will be discussed in Chapter 12, pursuant to Reg. § 1.752-3(a), Katie's and Matt's shares of the nonrecourse liabilities would each equal the sum of their respective shares of partnership minimum gain and their shares of "excess nonrecourse liabilities." Because they share the nonrecourse deductions associated with the initial $800,000 of nonrecourse borrowing (and share the distribution of the proceeds of the $100,000 nonrecourse liability incurred in Year 7) in the same ratio as they share all other profits and losses, the nonrecourse liabilities would be allocated 25% to Katie and 75% to Matt. Note that the relevant examples above assume the partnership agreement provides for that very allocation.

[29] Note, with their bases increased by their respective shares of the nonrecourse liability, both Katie and Matt will have sufficient outside basis to take advantage of their distributive shares of the depreciation deductions (or losses) without being limited by § 704(d). As will be discussed in Chapter 12, the liability allocation rules are designed to produce that result.

Katie and Matt:[30]

	Katie		Matt	
	A/B	Book	A/B	Book
	$250,000	$50,000	$750,000	$150,000

In each of the partnership tax years, the $100,000 depreciation deduction claimed by the partnership will result in a $100,000 loss because the depreciation deductions are the partnership's only tax item in each year. The annual $100,000 loss is allocated 25% to Katie and 75% to Matt, reducing both their outside bases and capital accounts. The following table shows the Year 1 and 2 adjustments to the partners' capital accounts and outside bases resulting from the annual loss of $100,000. The table also notes that, in Years 1 and 2, there is no net increase in partnership minimum gain.

	Katie		Matt		Net increases in Partnership minimum gain	
	A/B	Book	A/B	Book		
Formation[31]	$250,000	$50,000	$750,000	$150,000		
Year 1 loss	($25,000)	($25,000)	($75,000)	($75,000)	Year 1	$0
Year 2 loss	($25,000)	($25,000)	($75,000)	($75,000)	Year 2	$0
Balance	$200,000	$0	$600,000	$0		

In Year 3, the $100,000 in depreciation claimed by the partnership will create partnership minimum gain in the amount of $100,000. Reg. § 1.704-2(b)(2). Thus, there are $100,000 in nonrecourse deductions consisting of the $100,000 depreciation deduction. The $100,000 nonrecourse deduction would be allocated 25% to Katie and 75% to Matt and thus Katie will have a $25,000 share and Matt a $75,000 share of the net increase in partnership minimum gain. The table below tracks the adjustments to the partners' capital accounts and outside bases, as well as the net increases in partnership minimum gain for Years 1–3:

	Katie		Matt		Net increases in Partnership minimum gain	
	A/B	Book	A/B	Book		
Formation[32]	$250,000	$50,000	$750,000	$150,000		
Year 1 loss	($25,000)	($25,000)	($75,000)	($75,000)	Year 1	$0
Year 2 loss	($25,000)	($25,000)	($75,000)	($75,000)	Year 2	$0
Year 3 loss	($25,000)	($25,000)	($75,000)	($75,000)	Year 3	$100,000
Balance	$175,000	$(25,000)	$525,000	($75,000)		

---

[30] We assume that the nonrecourse liability was incurred at the same time as the contribution of cash by Katie and Matt.

[31] Id.

[32] Id.

At the end of Year 3 and in each of the seven years thereafter, the allocation of the partnership's $100,000 annual loss resulting from the depreciation deduction for the year will produce even larger deficits in Katie's and Matt's capital accounts. In each of those years, Katie's and Matt's share of the net increase in partnership minimum gain will be the same as that in Year 3, i.e., $25,000 to Katie and $75,000 to Matt. The $100,000 nonrecourse loan in Year 7 will increase the partnership's minimum gain as noted in Example 5. The distribution of the $100,000 in proceeds of the Year 7 nonrecourse loan will further increase the deficits in their capital accounts and likewise increase their share of partnership minimum gain. (As a result of the nonrecourse loan distribution, Katie's share of the increase in partnership minimum gain triggered by the loan will be $25,000 and Matt's share will be $75,000.) *The Year 7 nonrecourse loan will be allocated to Katie and Matt just as the initial $800,000 nonrecourse loan was allocated — 25% or $25,000 to Katie and 75% or $75,000 to Matt. This in turn will increase their outside bases by those amounts.* Reg. 1.752-3(a). At the end of Year 7, after the allocation of the partnership's $100,000 loss for the year and the distribution to the partners of the $100,000 in proceeds from the new nonrecourse loan, the adjustments to the partners' capital accounts and outside basis and the net increases in the partnership minimum gain for each year will be as follows:

	Katie		**Matt**		**Net increases in Partnership**	
	A/B	Book	A/B	Book	minimum gain	
Formation[33]	$250,000	$50,000	$750,000	$150,000		
Year 1 loss	($25,000)	($25,000)	($75,000)	($75,000)	Year 1	$0
Year 2 loss	($25,000)	($25,000)	($75,000)	($75,000)	Year 2	$0
Year 3 loss	($25,000)	($25,000)	($75,000)	($75,000)	Year 3	$100,000
Year 4 loss	($25,000)	($25,000)	($75,000)	($75,000)	Year 4	$100,000
Year 5 loss	($25,000)	($25,000)	($75,000)	($75,000)	Year 5	$100,000
Year 6 loss	($25,000)	($25,000)	($75,000)	($75,000)	Year 6	$100,000
Year 7 loss	($25,000)	($25,000)	($75,000)	($75,000)	Year 7	$100,000
Year 7 loan allocation	$25,000		$75,000			
Year 7 loan distribution	($25,000)	($25,000)	($75,000)	($75,000)	Year 7[34]	$100,000
Balance	$75,000	($150,000)	$225,000	($450,000)		

As the above tables reflect, after Years 1 and 2, Katie and Matt have deficits in their capital accounts. Matt has no obligation to restore a capital account deficit and thus normally allocations or distributions to Matt that would create a capital account deficit would not be respected or would immediately trigger the requirements of the qualified income offset (i.e., the allocation to Matt of income necessary

---

[33] *Id.*

[34] In Year 7 the total net increase in partnership minimum gain is $200,000 (*See* Example 5). There will, however, be only $100,000 of nonrecourse deductions in that year because there was a distribution of $100,000 of proceeds from a nonrecourse loan allocable to an increase in partnership minimum gain. Reg. § 1.704-2(c).

to eliminate any deficit). That, however, is not the case. *The regulations provide that a partner will be treated as having a deficit restoration obligation to the extent of the partner's share of partnership minimum gain.*[35] Therefore, the allocations of the depreciations deductions in Years 3–10 and the distribution of the proceeds of the nonrecourse loan to Matt in Year 7 will be respected. Upon disposition of the property and repayment of the loan, however, Katie and Matt will, as required by the minimum gain chargeback discussed below, be allocated income or gain in an amount equal to their respective shares of the net decrease in partnership minimum gain. This, in turn, will restore their capital accounts to $0.

8. Partner's Share of the Net Decrease in Partnership Minimum Gain

As discussed *supra*, a partnership has a net decrease in partnership minimum gain during the taxable year when certain events occur, e.g., the taxable disposition of the property encumbered by nonrecourse debt. A decrease in partnership minimum gain generally triggers the allocation of income or gain to a partner to the extent of the partner's share, if any, of the net decrease in partnership minimum gain. In general, a partner's share of the net decrease in partnership minimum gain for a taxable year is determined by multiplying the total net decrease for the year "by the partner's percentage share of the partnership's minimum gain calculated at the end of the immediately preceding year."[36]

> **Example 9:** Assume the facts of Example 4 and that the partnership sells the property at the beginning of Year 7 with the purchaser taking subject to the $800,000 nonrecourse loan and providing no other consideration. At the end of Year 6, the total partnership minimum gain would be $400,000, i.e., $800,000 outstanding balance of nonrecourse liability less $400,000 adjusted basis of the property.[37] The $400,000 of partnership minimum gain had generated a total of $400,000 of nonrecourse deductions (all depreciation deductions) in Years 3–6. Katie was allocated a total of $100,000 or 25% of the nonrecourse deductions and corresponding partnership minimum gain over that four-year period, while Matt was allocated $300,000 or 75% of the nonrecourse deductions and corresponding partnership minimum gain. The sale of the property, of course, extinguishes the nonrecourse liability and results in a $400,000 net decrease in partnership minimum gain. The $400,000 net decrease in partnership minimum gain as a result of the sale in Year 7 will be allocated accordingly — 25% or $100,000 to Katie and 75% or $300,000 to Matt.

---

[35] Reg. § 1.704-2(g)(1) (last two sentences).

[36] Reg. § 1.704-2(g)(2).

[37] The partnership will have claimed a total of $600,000 in depreciation deductions in Years 1–6, thus reducing its adjusted basis in the property to $400,000.

D. The Safe Harbor Requirements

As noted *supra*, the regulations provide a safe harbor consisting of four requirements. Reg. § 1.704-2(e)(2). With regard to the first and fourth requirements of the safe harbor, Chapter 9 addressed at length the substantial economic effect test, including the alternative test for economic effect, as well as the partner's-interest-in-the partnership test. There is thus no need for further elaboration on the first and fourth requirements. This part will address the other two requirements: (1) the requirement of a minimum gain chargeback provision (introduced above) and (2) the so-called "reasonable consistency" requirement.

1. The Minimum Gain Chargeback Requirement

To comply with the safe harbor, once a partnership has generated nonrecourse deductions or has made distributions of the proceeds of nonrecourse liabilities attributable to an increase in partnership minimum gain, the partnership agreement must contain a minimum gain chargeback provision throughout the full term of the partnership. If there is a net decrease in partnership minimum gain during a taxable year, the minimum gain chargeback provision requires, with some exceptions,[38] an allocation of partnership income and gain for that year to each partner equal to that partner's share of the net decrease in partnership minimum gain.[39] [Note, the allocation of items of income and gain could not have substantial economic effect "because the gain merely offsets nonrecourse deductions previously claimed by the partnership."[40] (See discussion of substantial economic effect in Chapter 9).] Therefore, according to the regulations, allocations pursuant to a minimum gain chargeback must be made to the partners who were allocated nonrecourse deductions or who received distributions of proceeds attributable to nonrecourse liabilities allocable to increases in partnership minimum gain.[41] As noted by the Service:

> The general idea behind the *minimum gain chargeback* is that a partner who receives the tax advantages of a deduction for which [the partner] bears no economic risk of loss [i.e., nonrecourse deductions such as depreciation deductions generated by basis created by nonrecourse borrowing] may bear a tax liability in the future due to the allocation of income.

---

[38] Reg. § 1.704-2(f)(2)-(4) provides circumstances under which a partner will not be subject to the minimum gain chargeback requirements. The most common circumstances are two:

(1) the conversion of the nonrecourse debt to recourse debt for which, by definition, one or more partners will bear the economic risk of loss; (To the extent the conversion results in some but not all partners bearing the risk of loss, the partners who do not bear the risk of loss will be subject to the minimum gain chargeback requirement and be allocated income or gain. See Reg. § 1.704-2(f)(2).) and

(2) the contribution by a partner of money to repay the nonrecourse liability or to undertake activity that would increase the adjusted basis of the property. To that extent, the partner has "restored" her share of nonrecourse deductions or distributions of the proceeds of nonrecourse liabilities that increased partnership minimum gain. Reg. § 1.704-2(f)(3).

[39] Reg. § 1.704-2(b)(2) and (f)(1).

[40] Reg. § 1.704-2(b)(2).

[41] *Id.*

This allocation of income is called a "minimum gain chargeback." At the appropriate time, income must be allocated to the partner who received the corresponding *nonrecourse deductions*.[42] (Emphasis added.)

The operation of the minimum gain chargeback is illustrated in the following examples:

Example 10: Assume the facts of Example 4. Assume also that on January 1, Year 6, the partnership sold the property for $900,000. The partnership had an adjusted basis in the property of $500,000[43] and thus recognized $400,000 of gain. The sale of the property resulted in a $300,000 net decrease in partnership minimum gain. Katie has 25% or $75,000 share of that net decrease while Matt has 75% or a $225,000 share. Reg. § 1.704–2(g)(2). Pursuant to the minimum gain chargeback requirement, Katie will have to report $75,000 of the gain and Matt $225,000 of the gain. With regard to the remaining $100,000 of gain, Katie and Matt will allocate that amount in accord with their profit-sharing ratio of 25% to Katie and 75% to Matt (thus $25,000 of gain to Katie and $75,000 of gain to Matt).

2. The Reasonable Consistency Requirement

In establishing the "reasonable consistency" requirement (the second requirement) of the safe harbor test, Treasury sought "to tie the partnership's allocation of non-recourse deductions to other items in the partnership which have substantial economic effect. By doing this, the regulations attempt to establish a rational relationship between the partner's economic interest in the partnership and his or her share of the nonrecourse deductions."[44] Partnerships in which nonrecourse deductions are allocated in the same ratio as all other partnership items of income, gain, loss, and deduction will satisfy the reasonable consistency requirement of the safe harbor. Thus, in Example 4 above, because Katie and Matt agreed to share all profits and losses of the partnership, including nonrecourse deductions in accord with their contributions to the partnership, i.e., 25% to Katie and 75% to Matt, the Katie/Matt Partnership would satisfy the "reasonable consistency" requirement. By contrast, however, the "reasonable consistency" requirement of the safe harbor would surely be violated if Katie and Matt had agreed that all nonrecourse deductions would be allocated to Matt, while all other profits and losses would be allocated consistent with their contributions to the partnership.

Because the safe harbor requires only that allocations of nonrecourse deductions be *reasonably consistent* with other items meeting the substantial economic effect test, it is apparent that Treasury did not intend that the allocation of nonrecourse deductions had to match precisely the allocation of other partnership items. The obvious question therefore arises: What allocation of nonrecourse deductions will satisfy "the reasonable consistency" requirement when a partnership agreement

---

[42] IRS Partnership Audit Technique Guide, Chapter 6 (Rev. December 2007).

[43] The partnership would have claimed a total of $500,000 in depreciation deductions with respect to the property during Years 1–5, thus reducing its adjusted basis in the property to $500,000. We will assume no depreciation for Year 6.

[44] IRS Partnership Audit Technique Guide, Chapter 6 (Rev. December 2007).

provides for the sharing of nonrecourse deductions in a manner differing from the sharing of other partnership profits and losses? Consider the following example, which is a variation of Example 4 above and is based on Reg. § 1.704-2(m) Example 1(ii):

Example 11. On January 1, Year 1, Katie and Matt form a limited partnership with Katie, the general partner, contributing $50,000 in cash and Matt, the limited partner, contributing $150,000 in cash. The partnership is a calendar-year partnership. The partnership immediately purchases a $1,000,000 piece of depreciable property using the $200,000 contributed by Katie and Matt and borrowing the $800,000 balance of the purchase price from an unrelated lender on a nonrecourse basis. The nonrecourse debt is secured by the property and is repayable in a lump sum in Year 11. Assume the property is depreciable at the rate of 10% or $100,000 per year. The partnership agreement: (1) satisfies the first two requirements of the economic effect test of Reg. § 1.704-1(b)(2)(ii)(b); (2) requires Katie as general partner to restore a deficit in her capital account following the liquidation of her interest; (3) contains a qualified income offset (as defined in Reg. § 1.704-1(b)(2)(ii)(d) and (4) otherwise satisfies the alternative test for economic effect; and contains a minimum gain chargeback provision (as defined in Reg. § 1.704-2(f)(1). The partnership agreement provides that, except as otherwise provided by its qualified income offset and minimum gain chargeback provisions, all items of partnership income, gain, loss, and deduction (with the exception of nonrecourse deductions) will be allocated 25% to Katie and 75% to Matt until the first time the partnership has recognized items of income and gain that exceed the items of loss and deduction it has recognized over its life. All further partnership items will be allocated equally between Katie and Matt. Nonrecourse deductions will be allocated 40% to Katie and 60% to Matt. Assume at the time the parties enter into the partnership agreement there is a reasonable likelihood the partnership will realize amounts of income and gain significantly in excess of amounts of loss and deduction (other than nonrecourse deductions) over its life. Will the allocation of the nonrecourse deductions satisfy the reasonable consistency requirement of the safe harbor?

Analysis: In illustrating the application of the reasonable consistency requirement, Reg. § 1.704-2(m) Example 1(ii) suggests the latitude Treasury intended to provide partnerships with respect to this requirement of the nonrecourse deduction safe harbor. The regulation provides a partnership with an income/deduction sharing arrangement comparable to that in our example. In that example, the partnership allocated nonrecourse deductions equally between the general partner and the limited partner. All other partnership items were to be allocated 90 percent to the limited partner and 10% to the general partner until the first time the partnership had recognized items of income and gain exceeding the items of loss and deduction recognized by the partnership over its life; all further deductions were then to be allocated equally between the general and the limited partner. According to the example, "the allocations of nonrecourse deductions 75 percent to the limited partner and 25 percent to the general partner or in any other ratio between 90 percent to the limited partner/10 percent to the general partner and 50 percent to the limited partner/50 percent to the general partner also would satisfy requirement (2) (the reasonably consistent requirement) [of the safe harbor]." Thus, the regulations provide considerable latitude to partnerships with respect to the allocation of nonrecourse deductions.

Given Reg. § 1.704-2(m) Example 1(ii), the allocation in our example of the nonrecourse deductions — 60 percent to the limited partner and 40 percent to the general partner — should satisfy the reasonable consistency requirement of the safe harbor. In fact, any allocation between 75 percent to the Matt/25 percent to Katie and 50 percent to Matt/50 percent to Katie would also the satisfy requirement. Note, however, that a sharing arrangement whereby Matt was allocated 80% of the nonrecourse deductions and Katie was allocated 20% would not meet the reasonable consistency requirement.

E. Conclusion

As discussed above, the allocation to partners of those deductions, e.g., depreciation deductions, attributable to partnership nonrecourse liabilities cannot have economic effect because it is the lender and not the borrower who bears the economic burden associated with the nonrecourse deduction. As a general rule, therefore, the regulations require that nonrecourse deductions be allocated in accordance with the partners' interest in the partnership. The regulations, however, provide an important safe harbor rule whereby the allocation of nonrecourse deductions will be treated as being in accordance with the partners' interest in the partnership. The four-pronged safe harbor test of Reg. § 1.704-2(e), discussed in detail above, provides certainty with regard to the distributive shares of nonrecourse deductions. Based on the analysis of *Commissioner v. Tufts*, included in the materials, the safe harbor allows partners the benefit of losses and deductions attributable to nonrecourse liabilities (and distribution of the proceeds of nonrecourse liabilities to them) on the condition that they account for those losses and deductions allocated to them (or the proceeds of nonrecourse liabilities distributed to them) by including income or gain when the nonrecourse liability is reduced or eliminated (i.e., when there is a decrease in partnership minimum gain).

COMMISSIONER v. TUFTS
United States Supreme Court
461 U.S. 300 (1982)

JUSTICE BLACKMUN delivered the opinion of the Court.

Over 35 years ago, in *Crane v. Commissioner*, 331 U.S. 1 (1947), this Court ruled that a taxpayer, who sold property encumbered by a nonrecourse mortgage (the amount of the mortgage being less than the property's value), must include the unpaid balance of the mortgage in the computation of the amount the taxpayer realized on the sale. The case now before us presents the question whether the same rule applies when the unpaid amount of the nonrecourse mortgage exceeds the fair market value of the property sold.

I

On August 1, 1970, respondent Clark Pelt, a builder, and his wholly owned corporation, respondent Clark, Inc., formed a general partnership. The purpose of the partnership was to construct a 120-unit apartment complex in Duncanville, Tex., a Dallas suburb. Neither Pelt nor Clark, Inc., made any capital contribution to the partnership. Six days later, the partnership entered into a mortgage loan agreement with the Farm & Home Savings Association (F&H). Under the agreement, F&H was committed for a $1,851,500 loan for the complex. In return, the partnership executed a note and a deed of trust in favor of F&H. The partnership obtained the loan on a nonrecourse basis: neither the partnership nor its partners assumed any personal liability for repayment of the loan. Pelt later admitted four friends and relatives, respondents Tufts, Steger, Stephens, and Austin, as general partners. None of them contributed capital upon entering the partnership.

The construction of the complex was completed in August 1971. During 1971, each partner made small capital contributions to the partnership; in 1972, however, only Pelt made a contribution. The total of the partners' capital contributions was $44,212. In each tax year, all partners claimed as income tax deductions their allocable shares of ordinary losses and depreciation. The deductions taken by the partners in 1971 and 1972 totaled $439,972. Due to these contributions and deductions, the partnership's adjusted basis in the property in August 1972 was $1,455,740.

In 1971 and 1972, major employers in the Duncanville area laid off significant numbers of workers. As a result, the partnership's rental income was less than expected, and it was unable to make the payments due on the mortgage. Each partner, on August 28, 1972, sold his partnership interest to an unrelated third party, Fred Bayles. As consideration, Bayles agreed to reimburse each partner's sale expenses up to $250; he also assumed the nonrecourse mortgage.

On the date of transfer, the fair market value of the property did not exceed $1,400,000. Each partner reported the sale on his federal income tax return and indicated that a partnership loss of $55,740 had been sustained. [Note: The loss was the difference between the adjusted basis, $1,455,740, and the fair market value of the property, $1,400,000. On their individual tax returns, the partners did not claim deductions for their respective shares of this loss. In their petitions to the Tax Court, however, the partners did claim the loss.] The Commissioner of Internal Revenue, on audit, determined that the sale resulted in a partnership capital gain of approximately $400,000. His theory was that the partnership had realized the full amount of the nonrecourse obligation.

Relying on *Millar v. Commissioner*, 577 F.2d 212, 215 (CA3), *cert. denied*, 439 U.S. 1046 (1978), the United States Tax Court, in an unreviewed decision, upheld the asserted deficiencies. 70 T.C. 756 (1978). The United States Court of Appeals for the

Fifth Circuit reversed. 651 F.2d 1058 (1981). That court expressly disagreed with the *Millar* analysis, and, in limiting *Crane v. Commissioner, supra*, to its facts, questioned the theoretical underpinnings of the *Crane* decision. We granted certiorari to resolve the conflict. 456 U.S. 960 (1982).

II

Section 752(d) of the Internal Revenue Code . . . specifically provides that liabilities involved in the sale or exchange of a partnership interest are to "be treated in the same manner as liabilities in connection with the sale or exchange of property not associated with partnerships." Section 1001 governs the determination of gains and losses on the disposition of property. Under § 1001(a), the gain or loss from a sale or other disposition of property is defined as the difference between "the amount realized" on the disposition and the property's adjusted basis. Subsection (b) of § 1001 defines "amount realized": "The amount realized from the sale or other disposition of property shall be the sum of any money received plus the fair market value of the property (other than money) received." At issue is the application of the latter provision to the disposition of property encumbered by a nonrecourse mortgage of an amount in excess of the property's fair market value.

A

In *Crane v. Commissioner, supra*, this Court took the first and controlling step toward the resolution of this issue. Beulah B. Crane was the sole beneficiary under the will of her deceased husband. At his death in January 1932, he owned an apartment building that was then mortgaged for an amount which proved to be equal to its fair market value, as determined for federal estate tax purposes. The widow, of course, was not personally liable on the mortgage. She operated the building for nearly seven years, hoping to turn it into a profitable venture; during that period, she claimed income tax deductions for depreciation, property taxes, interest, and operating expenses, but did not make payments upon the mortgage principal. In computing her basis for the depreciation deductions, she included the full amount of the mortgage debt. In November 1938, with her hopes unfulfilled and the mortgagee threatening foreclosure, Mrs. Crane sold the building. The purchaser took the property subject to the mortgage and paid Crane $3,000; of that amount, $500 went for the expenses of the sale.

Crane reported a gain of $2,500 on the transaction. She reasoned that her basis in the property was zero (despite her earlier depreciation deductions based on including the amount of the mortgage) and that the amount she realized from the sale was simply the cash she received. The Commissioner disputed this claim. He asserted that Crane's basis in the property, under [§ 1014] was the property's fair market value at the time of her husband's death, adjusted for depreciation in the interim, and that the amount realized was the net cash received plus the amount of the outstanding mortgage assumed by the purchaser.

In upholding the Commissioner's interpretation of [§ 1014], the Court observed that to regard merely the taxpayer's equity in the property as her basis would lead to depreciation deductions less than the actual physical deterioration of the property, and would require the basis to be recomputed with each payment on the mortgage. . . . The Court rejected Crane's claim that any loss due to depreciation belonged to the mortgagee. The effect of the Court's ruling was that the taxpayer's basis was the value of the property undiminished by the mortgage . . .

The Court next proceeded to determine the amount realized under [§ 1001(b)]. In order to avoid the "absurdity" of Crane's realizing only $2,500 on the sale of property worth over a quarter of a million dollars, the Court treated the amount realized as it had treated basis, that is, by including the outstanding value of the mortgage. To do otherwise would have permitted Crane to recognize a tax loss unconnected with any actual economic loss. The Court refused to construe one section of the Revenue Act so as "to frustrate the Act as a whole." . . .

Crane, however, insisted that the nonrecourse nature of the mortgage required different treatment. The Court, for two reasons, disagreed. First, excluding the nonrecourse debt from the amount realized would result in the same absurdity and frustration of the Code. . . . Second, the Court concluded that Crane obtained an economic benefit from the purchaser's assumption of the mortgage identical to the benefit conferred by the cancellation of personal debt. Because the value of the property in that case exceeded the amount of the mortgage, it was in Crane's economic interest to treat the mortgage as a personal obligation; only by so doing could she realize upon sale the appreciation in her equity represented by the $2,500 boot. The purchaser's assumption of the liability thus resulted in a taxable economic benefit to her, just as if she had been given, in addition to the boot, a sum of cash sufficient to satisfy the mortgage.

In a footnote, pertinent to the present case, the Court observed:

> Obviously, if the value of the property is less than the amount of the mortgage, a mortgagor who is not personally liable cannot realize a benefit equal to the mortgage. Consequently, a different problem might be encountered where a mortgagor abandoned the property or transferred it subject to the mortgage without receiving boot. That is not this case.

Id., at 14, n. 37.

B

This case presents that unresolved issue. We are disinclined to overrule *Crane*, and we conclude that the same rule applies when the unpaid amount of the nonrecourse mortgage exceeds the value of the property transferred. *Crane* ultimately does not rest on its limited theory of economic benefit; instead, we read *Crane* to have approved the Commissioner's decision to treat a nonrecourse mortgage in this context as a true loan. This approval underlies *Crane*'s holdings that the amount of the nonrecourse liability is to be included in calculating both the basis and the amount realized on disposition. That the amount of the loan exceeds the fair market value of the property thus becomes irrelevant.

When a taxpayer receives a loan, he incurs an obligation to repay that loan at some future date. Because of this obligation, the loan proceeds do not qualify as income to the taxpayer. When he fulfills the obligation, the repayment of the loan likewise has no effect on his tax liability.

Another consequence to the taxpayer from this obligation occurs when the taxpayer applies the loan proceeds to the purchase price of property used to secure the loan. Because of the obligation to repay, the taxpayer is entitled to include the amount of the loan in computing his basis in the property; the loan, under § 1012, is part of the taxpayer's cost of the property. Although a different approach might have been taken with respect to a nonrecourse mortgage loan,[45] the Commissioner has chosen to accord it the same treatment he gives to a recourse mortgage loan. The Court approved that choice in *Crane*, and the respondents do not challenge it here. The choice and its resultant benefits to the taxpayer are predicated on the assumption that the mortgage will be repaid in full.

When encumbered property is sold or otherwise disposed of and the purchaser assumes the mortgage, the associated extinguishment of the mortgagor's obligation to repay is accounted for in the computation of the amount realized. . . . Because no difference between recourse and nonrecourse obligations is recognized in calculating basis,[46] *Crane* teaches that the Commissioner may ignore the nonrecourse nature of the obligation in determining the amount realized upon disposition of the encumbered property. He thus may include in the amount realized the amount of the nonrecourse mortgage assumed by the purchaser. The rationale for this treatment is that the original inclusion of the amount of the mortgage in basis rested on the assumption that the mortgagor incurred an obligation to repay. Moreover, this treatment balances the fact that the mortgagor originally received the proceeds of the nonrecourse loan tax-free on the same assumption. Unless the outstanding amount of the mortgage is deemed to be realized, the mortgagor effectively will have received untaxed income at the time the loan was extended and will have received an unwarranted increase in the basis of his property.[47] The

---

[45] The Commissioner might have adopted the theory, implicit in Crane's contentions, that a nonrecourse mortgage is not true debt, but, instead, is a form of joint investment by the mortgagor and the mortgagee. On this approach, nonrecourse debt would be considered a contingent liability, under which the mortgagor's payments on the debt gradually increase his interest in the property while decreasing that of the mortgagee. . . . Because the taxpayer's investment in the property would not include the nonrecourse debt, the taxpayer would not be permitted to include that debt in basis. . . .

We express no view as to whether such an approach would be consistent with the statutory structure and, if so, and *Crane* were not on the books, whether that approach would be preferred over *Crane*'s analysis. We note only that the *Crane* Court's resolution of the basis issue presumed that when property is purchased with proceeds from a nonrecourse mortgage, the purchaser becomes the sole owner of the property. 331 U.S., at 6. Under the *Crane* approach, the mortgagee is entitled to no portion of the basis. *Id.*, at 10, n. 28. The nonrecourse mortgage is part of the mortgagor's investment in the property, and does not constitute a coinvestment by the mortgagee. . . .

[46] The Commissioner's choice in *Crane* "laid the foundation stone of most tax shelters," Bittker, *Tax Shelters, Nonrecourse Debt, and the* Crane *Case*, 33 Tax L. Rev. 277, 283 (1978), by permitting taxpayers who bear no risk to take deductions on depreciable property.

[47] Although the *Crane* rule has some affinity with the tax benefit rule . . . the analysis we adopt is different. Our analysis applies even in the situation in which no deductions are taken. It focuses on the obligation to repay and its subsequent extinguishment, not on the taking and recovery of deductions. *See generally* Note, 82 Colum. L. Rev., at 1526–1529.

Commissioner's interpretation of § 1001(b) in this fashion cannot be said to be unreasonable.

C

The Commissioner in fact has applied this rule even when the fair market value of the property falls below the amount of the nonrecourse obligation. Treas. Reg. § 1.1001-2(b), 26 CFR § 1.1001-2(b) (1982); 9 Rev. Rul. 76-111, 1976-1 Cum. Bull. 214. Because the theory on which the rule is based applies equally in this situation . . . we have no reason, after *Crane*, to question this treatment.[48]

Respondents received a mortgage loan with the concomitant obligation to repay by the year 2012. The only difference between that mortgage and one on which the borrower is personally liable is that the mortgagee's remedy is limited to foreclosing on the securing property. This difference does not alter the nature of the obligation; its only effect is to shift from the borrower to the lender any potential loss caused by devaluation of the property. If the fair market value of the property falls below the amount of the outstanding obligation, the mortgagee's ability to protect its interests is impaired, for the mortgagor is free to abandon the property to the mortgagee and be relieved of his obligation.

This, however, does not erase the fact that the mortgagor received the loan proceeds tax-free and included them in his basis on the understanding that he had

---

[48] Professor Wayne G. Barnett, as *amicus* in the present case, argues that the liability and property portions of the transaction should be accounted for separately. Under his view, there was a transfer of the property for $ 1.4 million, and there was a cancellation of the $ 1.85 million obligation for a payment of $ 1.4 million. The former resulted in a capital loss of $ 50,000, and the latter in the realization of $ 450,000 of ordinary income. Taxation of the ordinary income might be deferred under § 108 by a reduction of respondents' bases in their partnership interests.

Although this indeed could be a justifiable mode of analysis, it has not been adopted by the Commissioner. Nor is there anything to indicate that the Code requires the Commissioner to adopt it . . .

The Commissioner also has chosen not to characterize the transaction as cancellation of indebtedness. We are not presented with and do not decide the contours of the cancellation-of-indebtedness doctrine. We note only that our approach does not fall within certain prior interpretations of that doctrine. In one view, the doctrine rests on the same initial premise as our analysis here — an obligation to repay — but the doctrine relies on a freeing-of-assets theory to attribute ordinary income to the debtor upon cancellation. *See Commissioner v. Jacobson*, 336 U.S. 28, 38–40 (1949); *United States v. Kirby Lumber Co.*, 284 U.S. 1, 3 (1931). According to that view, when nonrecourse debt is forgiven, the debtor's basis in the securing property is reduced by the amount of debt canceled, and realization of income is deferred until the sale of the property. . . . Because that interpretation attributes income only when assets are freed, however, an insolvent debtor realizes income just to the extent his assets exceed his liabilities after the cancellation. *Lakeland Grocery Co. v. Commissioner*, 36 B.T.A. 289, 292 (1937). Similarly, if the nonrecourse indebtedness exceeds the value of the securing property, the taxpayer never realizes the full amount of the obligation canceled because the tax law has not recognized negative basis.

Although the economic benefit prong of *Crane* also relies on a freeing-of-assets theory, that theory is irrelevant to our broader approach. In the context of a sale or disposition of property under § 1001, the extinguishment of the obligation to repay is not ordinary income; instead, the amount of the canceled debt is included in the amount realized, and enters into the computation of gain or loss on the disposition of property. According to *Crane*, this treatment is no different when the obligation is nonrecourse: the basis is not reduced as in the cancellation-of-indebtedness context, and the full value of the outstanding liability is included in the amount realized. Thus, the problem of negative basis is avoided.

an obligation to repay the full amount. See *Woodsam Associates, Inc. v. Commissioner*, 198 F.2d 357, 359 (CA2 1952); Bittker, *supra* n. 7, at 284. When the obligation is canceled, the mortgagor is relieved of his responsibility to repay the sum he originally received and thus realizes value to that extent within the meaning of § 1001(b).From the mortgagor's point of view, when his obligation is assumed by a third party who purchases the encumbered property, it is as if the mortgagor first had been paid with cash borrowed by the third party from the mortgagee on a nonrecourse basis, and then had used the cash to satisfy his obligation to the mortgagee.

Moreover, this approach avoids the absurdity the Court recognized in *Crane*. Because of the remedy accompanying the mortgage in the nonrecourse situation, the depreciation in the fair market value of the property is relevant economically only to the mortgagee, who by lending on a nonrecourse basis remains at risk. To permit the taxpayer to limit his realization to the fair market value of the property would be to recognize a tax loss for which he has suffered no corresponding economic loss.[49] Such a result would be to construe "one section of the Act . . . so as . . . to defeat the intention of another or to frustrate the Act as a whole." 331 U.S., at 13.

In the specific circumstances of *Crane*, the economic benefit theory did support the Commissioner's treatment of the nonrecourse mortgage as a personal obligation. The footnote in *Crane* acknowledged the limitations of that theory when applied to a different set of facts. *Crane* also stands for the broader proposition, however, that a nonrecourse loan should be treated as a true loan. We therefore hold that a taxpayer must account for the proceeds of obligations he has received tax-free and included in basis. Nothing in either § 1001(b) or in the Court's prior decisions requires the Commissioner to permit a taxpayer to treat a sale of encumbered property asymmetrically, by including the proceeds of the nonrecourse obligation in basis but not accounting for the proceeds upon transfer of the encumbered property . . .

III

Relying on the Code's § 752(c) . . . however, respondents argue that Congress has provided for precisely this type of asymmetrical treatment in the sale or disposition of partnership property. Section 752 prescribes the tax treatment of certain partnership transactions and § 752(c) provides that "[for] purposes of this section, a liability to which property is subject shall, to the extent of the fair market

---

[49] In the present case, the Government bore the ultimate loss. The nonrecourse mortgage was extended to respondents only after the planned complex was endorsed for mortgage insurance under §§ 221(b) and (d)(4) of the National Housing Act, 12 U. S. C. §§ 1715*l*(b) and (d)(4) (1976 ed. and Supp. V).After acquiring the complex from respondents, Bayles operated it for a few years, but was unable to make it profitable. In 1974, F&H foreclosed, and the Department of Housing and Urban Development paid off the lender to obtain title. In 1976, the Department sold the complex to another developer for $1,502,000. The sale was financed by the Department's taking back a note for $1,314,800 and a nonrecourse mortgage. To fail to recognize the value of the nonrecourse loan in the amount realized, therefore, would permit respondents to compound the Government's loss by claiming the tax benefits of that loss for themselves.

value of such property, be considered as a liability of the owner of the property." Section 752(c) could be read to apply to a sale or disposition of partnership property, and thus to limit the amount realized to the fair market value of the property transferred. Inconsistent with this interpretation, however, is the language of § 752(d), which specifically mandates that partnership liabilities be treated "in the same manner as liabilities in connection with the sale or exchange of property not associated with partnerships." The apparent conflict of these subsections renders the facial meaning of the statute ambiguous, and therefore we must look to the statute's structure and legislative history.

Subsections (a) and (b) of § 752 prescribe rules for the treatment of liabilities in transactions between a partner and his partnership, and thus for determining the partner's adjusted basis in his partnership interest. Under § 704(d), a partner's distributive share of partnership losses is limited to the adjusted basis of his partnership interest. . . . When partnership liabilities are increased or when a partner takes on the liabilities of the partnership, § 752(a) treats the amount of the increase or the amount assumed as a contribution by the partner to the partnership. This treatment results in an increase in the adjusted basis of the partner's interest and a concomitant increase in the § 704(d) limit on his distributive share of any partnership loss. Conversely, under § 752(b), a decrease in partnership liabilities or the assumption of a partner's liabilities by the partnership has the effect of a distribution, thereby reducing the limit on the partner's distributive share of the partnership's losses. When property encumbered by liabilities is contributed to or distributed from the partnership, § 752(c) prescribes that the liability shall be considered to be assumed by the transferee only to the extent of the property's fair market value. Treas. Reg. § 1.752-1(c). . . .

The legislative history indicates that Congress contemplated this application of § 752(c). Mention of the fair market value limitation occurs only in the context of transactions under subsections (a) and (b).[50] The sole reference to subsection (d) does not discuss the limitation.[51] While the legislative history is certainly not conclusive, it indicates that the fair market value limitation of § 752(c) was directed to transactions between a partner and his partnership.[52] . . .

---

[50] "The transfer of property subject to a liability by a partner to a partnership, or by the partnership to a partner, shall, to the extent of the fair market value of such property, be considered a transfer of the amount of the liability along with the property." H. R. Rep. No. 1337, 83d Cong., 2d Sess., A236 (1954); S. Rep. No. 1622, 83d Cong., 2d Sess., 405 (1954).

[51] "When a partnership interest is sold or exchanged, the general rule for the treatment of the sale or exchange of property subject to liabilities will be applied." H. R. Rep. No. 1337, at A236-A237; S. Rep. No. 1622, at 405. These Reports then set out an example of subsection (d)'s application, which does not indicate whether the debt is recourse or nonrecourse.

[52] The Treasury Regulations support this view. The Regulations interpreting § 752(c) state:

Where property subject to a liability is contributed by a partner to a partnership, or distributed by a partnership to a partner, the amount of the liability, to an extent not exceeding the fair market value of the property at the time of the contribution or distribution, shall be considered as a liability assumed by the transferee. § 1.752-1(c), 26 CFR § 1.752-1(c) (1982).

The Regulations also contain an example applying the fair market limitation to a contribution of encumbered property by a partner to a partnership. *Ibid.* The Regulations interpreting § 752(d) make no mention of the fair market limitation.§ 752-1(d). Both Regulations were issued contemporaneously

By placing a fair market value limitation on liabilities connected with property contributions to and distributions from partnerships under subsections (a) and (b), Congress apparently intended § 752(c) to prevent a partner from inflating the basis of his partnership interest. Otherwise, a partner with no additional capital at risk in the partnership could raise the § 704(d) limit on his distributive share of partnership losses or could reduce his taxable gain upon disposition of his partnership interest. . . . There is no potential for similar abuse in the context of § 752(d) sales of partnership interests to unrelated third parties. In light of the above, we interpret subsection (c) to apply only to § 752(a) and (b) transactions, and not to limit the amount realized in a sale or exchange of a partnership interest under § 752(d).

IV

When a taxpayer sells or disposes of property encumbered by a nonrecourse obligation, the Commissioner properly requires him to include among the assets realized the outstanding amount of the obligation. The fair market value of the property is irrelevant to this calculation. We find this interpretation to be consistent with *Crane v. Commissioner*, 331 U.S. 1 (1947), and to implement the statutory mandate in a reasonable manner.

The judgment of the Court of Appeals is therefore reversed.

---

with the passage of the statute, T. D. 6175, 1956-1 Cum. Bull. 211, and are entitled to deference as an administrative interpretation of the statute. See *Commissioner v. South Texas Lumber Co.*, 333 U.S. 496, 501 (1948).

Chapter 12

ALLOCATION OF RECOURSE AND NONRECOURSE LIABILITIES

I. PROBLEMS

1. David and Nancy create a general partnership with David contributing a tract of land with a fair market value of $500,000. The land, which David had held for investment for a number of years, is encumbered by a liability of $250,000. Nancy contributes cash of $250,000. David and Nancy will be equal partners and will share partnership profits and losses equally. In each of the alternatives below, explain how the $250,000 liability encumbering the land contributed by David will be allocated; calculate the gain, if any, David must recognize; and determine each partner's outside basis.

   (a) At the time he contributed the land, David had an adjusted basis in the land of $400,000. The liability encumbering the land is a recourse liability that the partnership will assume. Assume the partnership agreement satisfies the economic effect test of Reg. § 1.704-1(b)(2)(ii)(b).

   (b) Assume the facts of (a), except David's adjusted basis in the land was $100,000.

   (c) Assume the facts of (a), except the partnership agreement allocated partnership losses 60% to David and 40% to Nancy and this special allocation satisfied the substantial economic effect test of § 704(b).

   (d) How would your answer to (a) change if the liability is nonrecourse and David's adjusted basis in the land was $100,000? Assume the partnership takes the land subject to the nonrecourse liability.

   (e) Assume the facts of (d), except the partnership agreement allocates partnership profits 60% to Nancy and 40% to David and this special allocation satisfies the substantial economic effect test of § 704(b).

2. Quinn and Abby form a general partnership to which each contributes $200,000 in cash. Quinn and Abby agree to share all profits and losses equally. The partnership immediately borrows $600,000 from a local bank on a recourse basis and uses the $600,000 in loan proceeds plus the $400,000 of cash contributed by the partners to construct a commercial building on land that the partnership leases. The bank loan is a general obligation of the partnership, i.e., neither Quinn nor Abby has been relieved from personal liability. Answer the following alternative questions:

(a) How will the recourse liability be allocated and what will Quinn's and Abby's outside bases be? Assume the partnership agreement satisfies the economic effect test of Reg. § 1.704-1(b)(2)(ii)(b).

(b) How would your answer to (a) change, if at all, if the partnership agreement did not contain a requirement that the partners restore any deficit in their capital accounts upon liquidation of the partnership?

(c) How would your answers to (a) change if Quinn had contributed $300,000 in cash and Abby had contributed $100,000 in cash and the partners agreed to share profits and losses in proportion to their contributions, i.e., 75% to Quinn and 25% to Abby? How would your answers change if the partners agreed to share profits and losses equally?

(d) How would your answers to (a) change if the bank required that Abby personally guarantee the loan?

(e) How would your answers to (a) change if the partnership were a limited partnership with Abby as the general partner and Quinn as the limited partner? Assume that, pursuant to the partnership agreement, Quinn has an obligation to restore a deficit in his capital account of up to $100,000 on the liquidation of his partnership interest and the partnership agreement contains a qualified income offset.

3. In Year 1, Rob and Misty form a limited liability company (LLC) that will be taxed as a partnership. Rob and Misty each contribute $500,000 in cash to the LLC. In Year 1, the LLC borrows $1,000,000 on a nonrecourse basis from a local bank and uses the loan proceeds plus $500,000 of the money contributed by Rob and Misty to purchase a commercial building on leased land for $1,500,000. The $1,000,000 loan is secured by a mortgage on the commercial building. No payments (other than interest payable annually) are due on the nonrecourse loan for 15 years. Assume the LLC will depreciate the building over a 15-year period on a straight-line basis and will thus be entitled to claim $100,000 in depreciation each year during the 15-year recovery period. (Disregard any conventions.) Assume also that in each year, apart from the annual depreciation deduction, the LLC's income and expenses are exactly equal. The LLC thus has $100,000 of loss each year (all allocable to depreciation). The LLC's operating agreement:

1. provides that all items of income, gain, loss and deduction will be allocated equally between the LLC's members;

2. satisfies the alternative test for economic effect (Reg. § 1.704-1(b)(ii)(d)); and

3. contains a minimum gain chargeback provision that complies with Reg. § 1.704-2(f).

Given these facts, answer the following questions:

(a) Applying the three-tier analysis of Reg. § 1.752–3(a), how will the $1,000,000 nonrecourse liability be allocated in Year 1? Explain how that allocation will affect Rob's and Misty's outside bases and capital accounts.

(b) How will the $1,000,000 in nonrecourse liability be allocated in Year 6? In Year 7? Explain the impact on Rob's and Misty's outside bases and capital accounts.

(c) What are the results to Rob and Misty if, on the last day of Year 7, the LLC sells the commercial building for no consideration other than relief from the $1,000,000 in nonrecourse liability encumbering the building?

(d) Instead of allocating the LLC's tax items equally, assume the LLC's operating agreement had allocated items of income, gain, loss, and deductions (other than nonrecourse deductions) differently and in a manner satisfying the substantial economic effect test. Assume also that the agreement allocated nonrecourse deductions 75% to Rob and 25% to Misty and that this special allocation satisfied the safe harbor requirements of Reg. § 1.704-2(e). What flexibility could the LLC operating agreement have provided with respect to "excess nonrecourse liabilities"?

Assignment for Chapter 11:

Complete the problems

Read: Internal Revenue Code: §§ 704(c)(1)(A), 704(d), 722, 723, 752.
Treasury Regulations: §§ 1.752-1, 1.752-2(a), (b), (f) Exs 1-4, (h); 1.752-3(a) and (c) Exs. 1 and 2.

Materials: Overview
Revenue Ruling 95-41

II. VOCABULARY

liability
recourse liability
nonrecourse liability
constructive liquidation
partnership minimum gain
excess nonrecourse liabilities
minimum § 704(c) gain

III. OBJECTIVES

1. To define "liability."
2. To identify a recourse liability.
3. To identify a nonrecourse liability.
4. To recall that an increase in a partner's share of partnership liabilities will be treated as a contribution of cash by the partner to the partnership.
5. To recall that a decrease in a partner's share of partnership liabilities will be treated as a distribution of cash to the partner.
6. To explain the elements of a constructive liquidation as envisioned by the regulations addressing the allocation of recourse liabilities.

7. To identify the obligations that will be taken into consideration in determining whether a partner has an obligation to make a payment to any person because a liability becomes due and payable.

8. To apply the recourse liability allocation rules in a given factual situation.

9. To explain the "three-tier" approach used in allocating nonrecourse liabilities.

10. To apply the nonrecourse liability allocation rules in a given factual situation.

11. To explain the flexibility partners have in allocating "excess nonrecourse liabilities."

IV. OVERVIEW

A person who borrows money on either a recourse or nonrecourse basis to acquire property takes a basis in that property reflecting the amount borrowed. For example, if Dennis purchases an apartment building on a leased tract of land for $900,000, paying $300,000 of his own money and borrowing the other $600,000 (on either a recourse or nonrecourse basis) from a third-party lender or from the seller, Dennis's basis in the land will be $900,000. § 1012. *See Crane v. Commissioner,* 331 U.S. 1 (1947) and *Commissioner v. Tufts,* 461 U.S. 300 (1983).[1] By reflecting in basis the debt incurred in acquiring property, our tax system gives credit to the taxpayer for an investment the taxpayer has yet to make.

Assume, instead of Dennis making the purchase in his individual capacity, a partnership in which Dennis owns a one-third interest in capital and profits purchases the apartment building for $900,000, using $300,000 of its cash and a $600,000 loan from a local bank. Section 752(a), reflecting an aggregate approach to partnerships, treats Dennis as though he had individually purchased an interest in the building and had used borrowed money to complete his part of the purchase. Specifically, § 752(a) treats Dennis as having contributed money to the partnership to the extent of his share of the $600,000 of debt incurred by the partnership in acquiring the apartment building.[2]

---

§ 752. Treatment of Certain Liabilities

(a) Increase in partner's liabilities. Any increase in a partner's share of the liabilities of a partnership, or any increase in a partner's individual liabilities by reason of the assumption by such partner of partnership

---

[1] Regarding loan proceeds used to acquire property, the Supreme Court noted in *Tufts*: "Because of the obligation to repay, the taxpayer is entitled to include the amount of the loan in computing his basis in the property; the loan, under Section 1012, is part of the taxpayer's cost of the property. Although a different approach might have been taken with respect to a nonrecourse mortgage loan, the Commissioner has chosen to accord it the same treatment to be given to a recourse mortgage loan." 461 U.S., at 307–08.

[2] By contrast, § 752(b) treats any decrease in the partner's share of liabilities as a distribution of money to the partner.

> liabilities, shall be considered as a *contribution of money by such partner to the partnership*. [Emphasis added.]

Pursuant to § 722, Dennis' adjusted basis in his partnership interest (outside basis) will be increased by the amount of money he is deemed to have contributed to the partnership. The increase in basis is significant for a number of reasons. For example, his increased basis should enable Dennis to deduct his distributive share of the depreciation deductions generated by the apartment building without being limited by § 704(d). In addition, the increase in Dennis's outside basis will allow him to receive greater distributions of cash from the partnership without gain recognition[3] and make it less likely that § 732(a)(2) will limit him with respect to the basis he would take in any property (other than money) he receives from the partnership in a nonliquidating distribution. (See Chapter 14 addressing partnership distributions.)

In the above example, the amount of money Dennis will be deemed to have contributed to the partnership pursuant to § 752(a), and the corresponding increase in his outside basis under § 722, depend on Dennis's "share" of the $600,000 of liability the partnership incurred in acquiring the apartment building. The Code provides no guidance as to how Dennis's share of the liability will be calculated. The regulations do. Chapter 3 introduced the liability sharing rules of § 752 and the regulations thereunder, noting that different sharing rules are applicable depending on whether the liability is deemed to be recourse or nonrecourse. A review of Chapter 3 will be helpful as you begin your study of this chapter, which will explore in detail the § 752 liability sharing rules.

A. History

Prior to the promulgation of the current regulations, the regulations governing the allocation of partnership liabilities provided:

> **Partner's share of partnership liabilities.** A partner's share of partnership liabilities shall be determined in accordance with his ratio for sharing losses under the partnership agreement. In the case of a limited partnership, a limited partner's share of partnership liabilities shall not exceed the difference between his actual contribution credited to him by the partnership and the total contribution that he is obligated to make under the limited partnership agreement. However, where none of the partners have any personal liability (as in the case of a mortgage on real estate acquired by the partnership without the assumption by the partnership or any of the partners of any liability on the mortgage), then all partners, including limited partners, shall be considered as sharing such liability under § 752(c) in the same proportion as they share the profits.[4]

---

[3] Pursuant to § 731(a)(1), a partner will recognize gain to the extent the partner receives a distribution of money in excess of "the adjusted basis of such partner's interest in the partnership immediately before the distribution."

[4] Reg. § 1.752-1(e) [before the 1984 amendments to the regulations].

Thus, pursuant to the prior regulations, partners shared recourse liabilities in the same ratio as they shared partnership losses; partners shared nonrecourse liabilities in the same ratio as they shared partnership profits.

While these sharing rules seemed simple, they generated considerable controversy and were inadequate to address the broad array of commercial practices and partnership arrangements with respect to liabilities. For example in *Raphan v. United States*, 3 Cl. Ct. 457 (1983), *rev'd*, 759 F.2d 879 (Fed. Cir. 1985), the court concluded that a general partner's guarantee of an otherwise nonrecourse liability of a limited partnership did not require the general partner to be treated as personally liable for the liability, i.e., despite the partner's guarantee, the liability would be treated as nonrecourse. As a result, the limited partners in *Raphan* were entitled to a share of the liability that, in turn, increased their outside basis, thereby enabling them to deduct more partnership losses without being limited by § 704(d). The Claims Court's *Raphan* decision raised the specter of new tax shelter arrangements and drew quick congressional action.

In the Tax Reform Act of 1984, Congress specifically provided that *Raphan* was not to be followed in applying § 752 and the regulations thereunder. Congress further directed Treasury to revise and update the § 752 regulations to take account of commercial practices and arrangements such as liability assumptions, guarantees, indemnity arrangements, etc.[5] In addition, the legislative history of the Tax Reform Act of 1984 directed that revised regulations should ensure that, except in the case of bona fide nonrecourse liability, partners receiving basis increases associated with partnership liabilities actually bear the economic risk of loss with respect to those liabilities.[6] At the same time, Congress indicated that it did not expect regulations to make major changes in the way bona fide nonrecourse liabilities were shared. Nonetheless, it suggested the regulations could provide more certainty regarding the proper allocation of nonrecourse liabilities.

As will become evident, the current regulations, largely finalized in 1991, address the congressional concern regarding *Raphan* by employing an economic risk of loss analysis to determine: (1) the characterization of a partnership liability as a recourse liability and (2) the amount, if any, of each partner's share of partnership recourse liabilities.

With regard to bona fide nonrecourse liabilities, the current regulations continue to provide, as a general rule, that those liabilities will be allocated among the partners on the basis of the partners' share of partnership profits. However, to provide greater accuracy in allocating nonrecourse liabilities and to coordinate the nonrecourse liability sharing rules with the rules related to the allocation of nonrecourse deductions (see Chapter 11) and § 704(c) rules (see Chapter 10), the current regulations provide that a partner's share of those liabilities will equal the sum of:

1. the partner's share of "partnership minimum gain" (discussed in Chapter 11);

---

[5] H.R. Rep. No. 98-861, 98th Cong. 2d Sess. 869 (1984).
[6] H.R. Rep. No. 98-861, 98th Cong. 2d Sess. 869 (1984).

2. any "§ 704(c) gain" that would be allocated to a partner if the partnership disposed of all of its property subject to nonrecourse liability in a taxable transaction for no consideration other than the full satisfaction of such liabilities; and

3. the partner's share of any remaining nonrecourse liabilities (i.e., "excess nonrecourse liabilities") in accordance with the partner's share of partnership profits.

As discussed *infra*, the current regulations also provide greater guidance and flexibility with regard to the application of the general rule that nonrecourse liabilities are allocated based on profit share.

In promulgating the current § 752 liability-sharing regulations, Congress sought to coordinate these regulations with the § 704(b) regulations previously promulgated. As noted by Treasury in proposing the current § 752 regulations:

> The coordination of [the regulations under §§ 752 and 704(b)] reflects the fact that one of the principal purposes for including partnership liabilities in the bases of the partner's interest in the partnership is to support deductions that will be claimed by the partners for the items attributable to those liabilities. The allocation of partnership liabilities among the partners serves to equalize the partnership's basis in its assets (inside basis) with the partners' bases in their partnership interests (outside basis). The provision of additional basis to a partner for the partner's partnership interest will permit the partner to receive distributions of the proceeds of partnership liabilities without recognizing gain under § 731, and to take deductions attributable to partnership liabilities without limitation under § 704(d). By equalizing inside and outside basis, § 752 simulates the tax consequences that the partners would realize if they owned undivided interests in the partners' assets, thereby treating the partnership as an aggregate of its partners. Of course, this goal can only be achieved if the partners that are allocated the deductions attributable to a partnership liability are allocated the basis for that liability. [T.D. 8237, 1989-1 C.B. 180.]

B. Definition of Liability

Before considering the different rules related to the allocation of recourse and nonrecourse liabilities, we must first determine what obligations will be treated as "liabilities" for purposes of § 752(a) and the regulations interpreting and applying that provision. According to the regulations, the term "liability," for purposes of Reg. § 1.752-1(a)(4), includes obligations only if, when, and to the extent that incurring the obligation:[7]

1. *Creates or increases the basis of any of the obligor's assets (including cash).*[8] Thus, in the example above where Dennis' partnership purchases an apartment building using $600,000 borrowed from a third-party lender, the obligation to the third party is a § 752(a) "liability" as it creates a

---

[7] Reg. § 1.752-1(a)(4)(i).

[8] This is the most common type of § 752(a) liability.

partnership basis in the apartment building.[9] As a result, Dennis and the other partners are entitled to an increase in their outside basis to the extent of their share of the liability.

2. *Gives rise to an immediate deduction to the obligor.* For example, if an accrual method partnership accrues interest expense at the close of the taxable year, the accrued but unpaid interest would constitute a "liability" for purposes of § 752(a). As a result, to the extent of their share of that liability, the partners would increase their outside basis.[10]

3. *Gives rise to an expense that is not deductible in computing the obligor's taxable income and is not properly chargeable to capital.* For example, as discussed in Chapter 6, fees paid or incurred to promote the sale of partnership interests (i.e., syndication fees) are not deductible in computing the taxable income of a partnership nor are they chargeable to a capital account. They therefore constitute a "liability" within the meaning of § 752(a) and will thus result in an increase in the aggregate outside basis of the partners.[11]

C. Allocation of Recourse Liabilities

Regulation § 1.752-1(a)(1) defines a recourse liability as follows:

> **Recourse liability defined.** A partnership liability is a recourse liability to the extent that any partner or related person bears the economic risk of loss for that liability under § 1.752-2.

The above definition of recourse liability reflects an effort to respond to Congress's mandate to address the Claims Court's decision in *Raphan*. In determining whether any person bears the economic risk of loss for a liability, the regulations identify a range of obligations that must be taken into account, including contractual obligations outside the partnership agreement, e.g., guarantees, as well as state law obligations. Read Reg. § 1.752-2(b)(3) carefully. For example, a liability that on its face appears to be nonrecourse will be characterized as a recourse liability for purposes of § 752 where a partner, as in *Raphan*, personally guarantees payment of the liability in the event of a

---

[9] The $600,000 loan, combined with the $300,000 of cash contributed by the partners, results in the partnership having a $900,000 basis in the apartment building. § 1012.

[10] At the same time, each partner would be entitled to deduct that partner's distributive share of the deduction allowed the partnership. Thus, the total outside bases of the partners would not change. By contrast, if a cash method partnership accrued interest expense at the end of the year, the accrual of that expense would not give rise to an immediate deduction because a cash method taxpayer may only claim a deduction for amounts actually paid. Likewise, the accrued interest expense would not create or increase the basis of any partnership asset. Therefore, the accrued interest expense would not constitute a "liability" within the meaning of § 752(a) and would not give rise to any increase in the outside bases of the partners.

[11] Of course, when the partnership pays the fees, § 705(a)(2)(B) will cause a reduction of the partners' aggregate outside basis in the same amount.

partnership default.[12] Similarly, were a partner to pledge property as security for an otherwise nonrecourse liability or contribute property to the partnership solely for the purpose of securing that liability, Reg. § 1.752-2(h)(1) and (2) specifically provide the partner will, to that extent, be deemed to bear the economic risk of loss with respect to that liability. To that extent, the loan will be treated as a recourse liability for § 752 purposes.

Regulation § 1.752-2(a) provides the following rule for allocating recourse liabilities:

> **Partner's share of recourse liabilities.** A partner's share of recourse partnership liability equals the portion of that liability, if any, for which the partner or related person bears the economic risk of loss.

Determining a partner's share of recourse liability by reference to the risk of loss a partner bears parallels the requirement in Reg. § 1.704-1(b)(2)(ii) that "[I]n the event there is an economic benefit or economic burden that corresponds to an allocation, the partner to whom the allocation is made must receive such economic benefit or bear such economic burden." Pursuant to this economic effect test of Reg. § 1.704-1(b)(2)(ii), a partner must bear the burden of depreciation to the extent the partner is allocated depreciation deductions allowed the partnership. Similarly, to the extent a partner bears the economic risk of loss associated with a recourse liability, the partner is deemed to have contributed money to the partnership. As a result, the partner's outside basis is increased. §§ 722 and 752(a) and Reg. § 1.752-2(a).

The regulations provide a complex method for determining the extent, if any, to which a partner bears the economic risk of loss. According to the regulations, a partner bears the economic risk of loss for a partnership liability to the extent that, if the partnership "constructively liquidated," the partner or a person "related" to the partner would be obligated to make a payment to any person and would not be entitled to reimbursement.[13] According to the regulations, in a "constructive liquidation," all of the following events are deemed to occur simultaneously:

(i) all of the partnership's liabilities become payable in full;

(ii) except for property contributed to secure a partnership liability, all partnership property, including cash, becomes worthless;[14]

(iii) the partnership disposes of all of its property in a fully taxable transaction for no consideration (*except for relief from nonrecourse debt*);[15]

---

[12] *See*, however, Reg. § 1.752-2(d)(2).

[13] Reg. § 1.752-2(b)(1).

[14] As noted *supra*, a partner may contribute property to a partnership solely for the purpose of securing a partnership liability. Reg. § 1.752-2(h)(2). Reg. § 1.752-2(b)(1)(ii) makes clear that property so contributed will not be deemed worthless for purposes of the constructive liquidation analysis.

[15] Regulation § 1.752-2(b)(2) specifically addresses the computation of gain or loss on the constructive liquidation. Note that, if the constructive liquidation involves items of § 704(c) property or property that

(iv) all items of income, gain, loss, or deduction are allocated among the partners; and

(v) the partnership liquidates.

Consider the following example:

Example 1: Dennis, Peggy, and Michael form a general partnership to which each contributes $100,000 of cash. As a result, each of the partners will have a $100,000 capital account. The partners have agreed to share the profits and losses in proportion to their capital accounts. Thus, Dennis, Peggy, and Michael will each have a one-third share of the partnership's profits and losses. Assume the partnership agreement provides: (1) the partnership will determine and maintain the partners' capital accounts in accordance with the rules of Reg. § 1.704-1(b)(2)(iv), (2) liquidating distributions to the partners will be made in accord with their positive capital accounts, and (3) partners must restore any deficit in their capital accounts. In other words, the partnership agreement satisfies the "economic test" of § 704(b) as developed in the regulations.

Assume the partnership purchases an apartment complex on leased land from an unrelated person for $900,000, using the $300,000 of cash the partners contributed and borrowing the other $600,000 from an unrelated third-party lender. The $600,000 loan is secured by the apartment building. The loan represents a general obligation of the partnership, i.e., no partner has been relieved from personal liability with regard to the loan. Other than the partners' deficit restoration obligation on liquidation of the partnership, no other contractual or statutory payment obligations exist among the partners, the partnership and the lender. As established in the analysis below, the $600,000 loan constitutes a recourse liability because one or more partners bears the economic risk of loss with regard to the loan. How will the $600,000 recourse liability be allocated for § 752 purposes?

Analysis: Because Dennis, Peggy, and Michael have agreed to share partnership profits and losses in proportion to their capital accounts (and thus, given our facts, will share profits and losses equally), we could reasonably assume they share equally the economic risk of loss with regard to the $600,000 liability.[16] Thus, each partner would be allocated a $200,000 share of that liability. If that assumption is correct, the outside basis of each partner will be increased by $200,000, resulting in a $300,000 basis for each partner. Note, the liability has no impact on the capital accounts of the partners. Reg. § 1.704-1(c).

Applying the regulation formula discussed above, our assumption regarding the allocation of the recourse liability would be confirmed. If the apartment building became worthless and the partnership disposed of it for

---

has been subject to revaluation under Reg. § 1.704-1(b)(4)(i), loss is computed with reference to the book value of those properties.

[16] That result is also reinforced by the fact that they are general partners and, as such, would have joint and several liability under state law with respect to the loan. See Uniform Partnership Act (1997) §§ 306(a) and 401(b).

no consideration, the partnership would recognize a book loss of $900,000.[17] If that loss were allocated among the three partners equally, consistent with their distributive shares of losses, each partner would be allocated a $300,000 book loss. That allocation would create a deficit of $200,000 in each partner's capital account, i.e., $100,000 beginning capital account less the $300,000 of book loss allocated to each partner. As required by their partnership agreement, the partners would each be required to contribute $200,000 to the partnership, thus enabling the partnership to satisfy the partnership's $600,000 liability. (*Regulation § 1.752-2(b)(6) assumes each of the partners will make this required contribution irrespective of his or her actual net worth.*[18]) Each partner bears the risk of loss with regard to the $600,000 liability to the extent of $200,000.[19] Pursuant to § 752, therefore, each partner will be deemed to have contributed $200,000 to the partnership and, as assumed above, each partner's outside basis will be increased to $300,000.

It is worth noting that, if the partnership continues to own and manage the apartment building throughout the building's class life as determined under § 168, the partnership will be allowed, in the aggregate, depreciation deductions amounting to $900,000. Consistent with their agreement, the partners would each have a $300,000 distributive share of the $900,000 in depreciation deductions. Disregarding any other items of income, gain, loss, or deduction, each partner's $300,000 outside basis as calculated above is sufficient to enable the partner to deduct the partner's $300,000 share of depreciation deductions without being limited by § 704(d). As noted above, that is a result Treasury sought to achieve in promulgating the current regulations.

Consider the following variation on Example 1:

Example 2: Assume the facts of Example 1 except that, in forming the partnership, Dennis contributed $150,000 of cash, Peggy contributed $100,000 of cash, and Michael contributed $50,000 of cash. Dennis, Peggy and Michael will each have a capital account equal to the amount of cash each contributed to the partnership. Reg. § 1.704-1(b)(2)(iv)(b)(1). The partners agree to share profits and losses in proportion to their capital accounts. Thus, Dennis will have a 50% or one-half interest in the profits and losses, Peggy will have a 33.33% or one-third interest and Michael will have a 16.67% or one-sixth interest. Under these circumstances, how will the $600,000 recourse loan be allocated for § 752 purposes?

Analysis: Again, because the partners have agreed to share profits and losses in the same proportion as their capital accounts, we might reason-

---

[17] The partnership would also recognize a tax loss of $900,000, i.e., amount realized of $0 less the partnership's $900,000 adjusted basis in the apartment building equals a $900,000 loss

[18] This deemed satisfaction of a partner's obligation is disregarded if the facts indicate a plan to circumvent the obligation.

[19] Thus, the $600,000 loan is a recourse liability because one or more partners bears the economic risk of loss for the liability.

ably assume the partners would share the recourse liability in that same proportion. Thus, Dennis would be allocated a one-half share of the $600,000 liability, or $300,000; Peggy would be allocated a one-third share, or $200,000; and Michael would be allocated a one-sixth share, or $100,000.

As in Example 1, the constructive liquidation analysis would confirm our assumption. Again, assuming the apartment building became worthless and was disposed of for no consideration, the partnership would have a $900,000 book loss. That loss would be divided consistent with the partners' loss sharing arrangement, i.e., the book loss would be allocated one-half or $450,000 to Dennis, one-third or $300,000 to Peggy and one-sixth or $150,000 to Michael. As a result of these allocations, each partner would have a deficit capital account as follows: Dennis — a $300,000 deficit; Peggy — a $200,000 deficit; and Michael — a $100,000 deficit. Each partner would be required to contribute cash to the partnership to restore his or her capital account deficit and the amounts contributed would be paid to the lender to satisfy the $600,000 recourse loan. Thus, just as we assumed, Dennis, Peggy, and Michael will each share the economic risk of loss with regard to the recourse loan in proportion to their distributive share of partnership losses. As in Example 1, disregarding any other items of income, gain, loss, or deduction, the increased basis of each partner will enable that partner to deduct his or her share of partnership depreciation with respect to the apartment building without being limited by § 704(d).

Given the accuracy of our assumption in both Examples 1 and 2 above, can we simply forego the use of the constructive liquidation analysis of the regulations and conclude that, in every case, the recourse liability will be allocated consistent with the partner's share of profits and losses? The answer is "No." Consider the following example.

Example 3: Assume the same facts as in Example 1 above, except that the partnership agreement specially allocates the profits and losses as follows: 50% of the profits and losses to Dennis, 35% to Peggy and 15% to Michael. *Assume these special allocations satisfy the requirements of the substantial economic effect test of § 704(b) and the regulations thereunder.* If, as in Examples 1 and 2, we simply determined the economic risk of loss with regard to the liability based on the partners' distributive share of losses, each partner's share of the recourse liability would be as follows: Dennis with a 50% share of partnership losses would be allocated 50% of the liability or $300,000; Peggy would be allocated 35% or $210,000 of the liability and Michael would be allocated 15% or $90,000 of the liability. Would those results be confirmed by application of the constructive liquidation analysis? The answer is "No." If, pursuant to the constructive liquidation envisioned by the regulations, we assume the apartment building is worthless and is disposed of in a taxable transaction for no consideration, the partnership will recognize a $900,000 book loss. Consistent with the special allocations in the partnership agreement, the $900,000 loss would be allocated as follows: one-half or $450,000 to Dennis; 35% or $315,000 to Peggy, and 15% or $135,000 to Michael. The capital accounts of the three partners before and after the hypothetical disposition would be as follows (See Reg. § 1.704-1(b)(2)(iv)(b)(7) :

	Capital Account before Disposition	Capital Account after Disposition
Dennis	$100,000	($350,000) (i.e., $100,000 - $450,000 loss)
Peggy	$100,000	($215,000) (i.e., $100,000 - $315,000 loss)
Michael	$100,000	($ 35,000) (i.e., $100,000 - $135,000 loss)

On the constructive liquidation, Dennis, Peggy, and Michael will have to restore the deficit in their capital accounts. Thus, the three partners will be required to make the following payments: Dennis — a $350,000 payment; Peggy — a $215,000 payment; and Michael — a $35,000 payment. Thus, the three partners bear the economic risk of loss with respect to (and thus have the following shares of) the $600,000 recourse debt in the following amounts: Dennis — $350,000; Peggy — $215,000; and Michael — $35,000. Note how different those allocations are to the allocations we assumed when we simply used the loss sharing arrangement of the partners. The allocation of the recourse debt will result in the partners having increased outside bases as follows: Dennis — $450,000; Peggy — $315,000 and Michael — $135,000. Note that, given the increased basis, each partner will be in a position to deduct his or her aggregate share of the $900,000 in depreciation deductions that the partnership will ultimately be allowed if it owns the apartment building for its class life. For example: Peggy, who has a 35% share of profits and losses, would be allocated 35% or $315,000 of the $900,000 in total depreciation deductions the partnership was allowed. Disregarding any other items of income, gain, loss, or deduction, her increased outside basis of $315,000 enables her to utilize the full $315,000 in deductions without being limited by § 704(d).

Example 3 illustrates well the interrelationship between the recourse liability sharing regulations and the substantial economic effect regulations under § 704(b).[20] If, as in Example 3, the special allocations meet the substantial economic effect test of § 704(b), the partners should be allocated a share of the recourse liability resulting in an increase in basis enabling them to utilize those deductions or losses specially allocated to them, without being limited by § 704(d).

In each of the above examples, the deficit restoration obligation in the partnership agreement resulted in a partner's obligation to make a payment upon the constructive liquidation of the partnership. The regulations recognize that, apart from the partnership agreement, the obligation of a partner to make a payment to any person when a constructive liquidation occurs may be the result of

---

[20] Note: The recourse liability sharing regulations were developed years after the § 704(b) regulations had been promulgated. The recourse liability-sharing regulations were deliberately linked with the § 704(b) regulations to ensure accurate measurement of each partner's share, if any, of the economic risk associated with recourse liabilities.

state statutes or side agreements executed between or among the partners and a lender. Re-read Reg. § 1.752-2(b)(3), detailing the obligations recognized for purposes of the constructive liquidation rule. Consider the following examples.

Example 4: Assume the facts of Example 1, except the partnership agreement was silent with respect to any obligation to restore deficits in the partners' capital accounts.

Analysis: Regulation § 1.752-2(b)(3)(iii) notes that, among the obligations taken into account in determining whether a partner has a payment obligation in the case of a constructive liquidation, are obligations "imposed by state law, including the governing state partnership statute." As general partners, state partnership laws would impose on Dennis, Peggy, and Michael the obligation to repay the loan. See Uniform Partnership Act (1997) §§ 306(a) and 401(b). Because they are equal general partners, they would each be required to contribute an additional $200,000 to satisfy the $600,000 liability. Thus, the results would be identical to those reached in Example 1.

Example 5: Assume the facts of Example 1, except the partnership is a limited partnership with Dennis being the general partner. Assume that, while the partnership agreement requires Dennis to restore any deficit he may have in his capital account upon liquidation, no such requirement exists with respect to Peggy and Michael, the limited partners. Rather, with respect to them, the partnership agreement contains provisions satisfying the "alternate test for economic effect."[21] Assume Peggy and Michael have no obligation to make any additional contributions to the partnership.

Analysis: Pursuant to the partnership agreement, upon a constructive liquidation, the $900,000 book loss recognized by the partnership on the taxable disposition of the apartment building for no consideration would normally be allocated equally, i.e., $300,000 of the loss would be allocated to each of the three partners. Considering, however, that neither Peggy nor Michael has a capital account deficit restoration obligation but, instead, are subject to the alternative test for economic effect, they cannot be allocated loss in excess of their capital accounts. Thus, they will each be allocated $100,000 of the $900,000 loss. The $700,000 balance of the book loss would therefore be allocated to Dennis and would create a $600,000 deficit in his capital account. Dennis has the obligation to restore that deficit and would, as a result, have to make a payment of $600,000 to satisfy the liability. Dennis thus bears the entire economic risk of loss with regard to the $600,000 recourse liability and will be allocated the entire amount. As a result, his outside basis will be increased from $100,000 to $700,000. The result in this example should not be surprising. Except to the extent specifically provided in the partnership agreement, a limited partner has no obligation to contribute additional money or property to a partnership and is thus has limited exposure to loss. By contrast, a general partner in a

---

[21] Reg. § 1.704-1(b)(2)(ii)(d), discussed in Chapter 9.

limited partnership is generally liable under state law for the partnership's recourse liabilities and thus bears the economic risk of loss.[22]

Example 6: Assume the facts of Example 1 except Dennis personally guarantees the $600,000 loan. How will the $600,000 liability be allocated? What difference would it make if, instead of guaranteeing the loan, Dennis agreed to indemnify Peggy and Michael should they incur any loss in excess of the $100,000 that each contributed to the partnership?

Analysis: Applying the constructive liquidation analysis, each of the partners, in either the guarantee or the indemnification situation, would be allocated $300,000 of the $900,000 book loss and, as a result, would have a $200,000 capital account deficit. Each partner would thus be required to contribute an additional $200,000 that would be used to satisfy the loan.

Pursuant to the guarantee, Dennis would be responsible for the entire loan if Peggy and Michael failed to make the required $200,000 contribution to restore their capital account deficits. As noted above, for purposes of determining who bears the economic risk of loss with regard to a recourse liability, Reg. § 1.752-2(b)(6), however, assumes that partners (or related persons) who have payment obligations will actually perform those obligations. Given that assumption, Peggy and Michael are each assumed to make the $200,000 contribution necessary to restore his or her capital account deficit. Thus, Dennis will not be at risk for more than $200,000 of the recourse liability and the results will be the same as those in Example 1, i.e., the three partners will be allocated equal shares of the recourse liability.

With regard to the indemnification agreement, however, the results would be different. Pursuant to that agreement, if Peggy and Michael were each required to pay $200,000 to the partnership to restore their capital account deficits, Dennis would be required to pay each of them $200,000. Thus, Dennis would ultimately bear the entire economic risk of loss with regard to the $600,000 recourse liability. The $600,000 liability is therefore allocated to Dennis, thereby increasing his outside basis to $700,000.

Based on the foregoing examples, we can conclude that:

1. When partners agree to share profits and losses in proportion to their capital accounts, and there are no other statutory or contractual payment obligations existing between or among the partners, the partnership, and the lender, the recourse liability will be allocated in proportion to the loss sharing arrangement of the partners. Under these specific circumstances, we can forego the use of the constructive liquidation analysis of the regulations. (Examples 1 and 2).

2. When the partners have agreed to special allocations of losses, the

---

[22] Again, note that, disregarding all other items of income, gain, loss, and deduction, the partnership would be allowed aggregate depreciation deductions with regard to the apartment building of $900,000. Peggy and Michael could not be allocated more than $100,000 each of those depreciation deductions, and Dennis would be allocated the remaining $700,000. His $700,000 outside basis will enable him to use those deductions without being limited by § 704(d).

constructive liquidation analysis of the regulations must be utilized to ensure accurate allocation of recourse liabilities. (Example 3).

3. The existence of statutory or contractual payment obligations existing between or among the partners, the partnership and the lender is not only relevant in determining the status of a liability as either a recourse or nonrecourse liability, but also plays a significant role in determining who bears the economic risk of loss with respect to a liability. (Examples 4–6).

D. Allocation of Nonrecourse Liabilities

If, after applying the economic risk of loss analysis of Reg. § 1.752-2, no partner bears the economic risk of loss with regard to a liability, that liability is a nonrecourse liability for purposes of § 752 and the regulations thereunder.

> **Regulation § 1.752-1(a)(2). Nonrecourse liability defined.**
>
> A partnership liability is a nonrecourse liability to the extent that no partner or related person bears the economic risk of loss for that liability under § 1.752-2.

As noted above, nonrecourse liabilities have historically been allocated among the partners in the same ratio as the partners' profit sharing ratio. Theoretically, this rule reflects the fact that a partnership will only pay its nonrecourse debt to the extent the partnership generates profits. The current regulations, promulgated in response to the congressional directive in the Tax Reform Act of 1984, continue to employ that general rule for allocating nonrecourse liabilities. The regulations, however, further refine the analysis used in allocating nonrecourse liabilities. In an effort to provide greater certainty regarding the application of § 752 to nonrecourse debt and reflect more accurately the manner in which the partners have agreed to share the profits used to discharge nonrecourse liabilities, the regulations created a three-tier structure to be used in allocating nonrecourse liabilities.

Pursuant to this three-tier analysis, a partner's share of the nonrecourse liabilities of a partnership equals the *sum* of the amounts, if any, allocated to the partner in each of the three tiers. Reg. § 1.752-3(a). The three tiers are as follows:

Tier 1: This tier includes "the partner's share of "partnership minimum gain" determined in accordance with the rules of § 704(b) and the regulations thereunder." Reg. § 1.752-3(a)(1).[23] As exemplified in *Commissioner v. Tufts* and discussed in detail in Chapter 11, "partnership minimum gain" (or "*Tufts* gain") is the gain a partnership is required to recognize if the partnership disposes of property in a taxable transaction for no consideration other than relief from the nonrecourse liability encumbering the property. As discussed in Chapter 11, Reg. § 1.704-2(g)(1) provides that a partner's share of partnership minimum gain is the "sum of nonrecourse

---

[23] Rev. Rul. 95-41, 1995-1 C.B. 132.

deductions allocated to that partner and distributions made to that partner of proceeds of a nonrecourse liability allocable to an increase in partnership minimum income." Review Chapter 11.

Tier 2: This tier includes "the amount of any taxable gain that would be allocated to the partner under § 704 (c) . . . if the partnership disposed of (in a taxable transaction) all partnership property subject to one or more nonrecourse liabilities of the partnership in full satisfaction of the liabilities and for no other consideration." Reg. § 1.752-3(a)(2). This gain is often referred to as the "minimum § 704(c) gain." Example 2 below illustrates the application of Tier 2.

Tier 3: This tier includes "the partner's share of the excess nonrecourse liabilities (those not allocated under Reg. § 1.752-3 (a)(1) and (a)(2)) of the partnership as determined in accordance with the partner's share of partnership profits. The partner's interest in partnership profits is determined by taking into account all facts and circumstances relating to the economic arrangement of the partners. The partnership agreement may specify the partners' interests in partnership profits for purposes of allocating excess nonrecourse liabilities, provided the interests so specified are reasonably consistent with allocations (that have substantial economic effect under the § 704 (b) regulations) of some other significant item of partnership income or gain. Alternatively, excess nonrecourse liabilities may be allocated among the partners in accordance with the manner in which it is reasonably expected that the deductions attributable to those nonrecourse liabilities will be allocated." Reg. § 1.752-3(a)(3). Examples 1, 2, and 3 below illustrate the application of Tier 3.

Consider the following examples examining the allocation of a nonrecourse liability pursuant to the three-tier structure described above.

Example 1: On January 1, Year 1, Maureen contributes $25,000 and Brent contributes $75,000 in cash to form the MB Limited Liability Company (hereinafter the LLC) which will be taxed as a partnership. The LLC uses the $100,000 contributed by Maureen and Brent together with $900,000 the LLC borrows on a nonrecourse basis from an unrelated party to purchase a commercial building on leased land. The nonrecourse liability is secured by the commercial building. No payments are due on the nonrecourse liability for the first 10 years. The LLC's operating agreement satisfies the alternative test for economic effect (Reg. § 1.704-1(b)(ii)(d)) and contains a minimum gain chargeback provision that complies with Reg. § 1.704-2(f).[24] Without going into detail, assume that, while initially all items of LLC income, gain, loss and deduction (with the exception of nonrecourse deductions) will be allocated 75% to Brent and 25% to Maureen, they will, upon the happening of certain events (expected to occur), subsequently shift to an equal allocation of those items. The nonrecourse deductions, however, will always be allocated 70% to Brent and 30% to Maureen. Assume the allocation of nonrecourse deductions satisfies the safe harbor

---

[24] Chapter 11 discusses in detail "minimum gain chargeback" provisions.

requirements of Reg. § 1.704-2(e) and that the other allocations noted above in the LLC agreement will be deemed to have substantial economic effect.[25] The LLC will depreciate the commercial building on a straight-line basis over ten years at the rate of 10%, or $100,000 per year. Assume, in each of the first ten years, the LLC's operating expenses (other than depreciation) will equal the LLC's operating income thus leaving the LLC with a $100,000 loss each year (all allocable to the depreciation deductions). How will the $900,000 of nonrecourse liability be allocated in Years 1 and 2?

Analysis: In Year 1, the LLC will be entitled to $100,000 in depreciation,[26] thereby reducing its basis in the commercial building to $900,000. Consistent with the LLC agreement, the Year 1 depreciation deduction will be allocated $75,000 to Brent and $25,000 to Maureen. Is there any "partnership minimum gain" as a result of the Year 1 depreciation deductions? The answer is "No." As noted above and as discussed in detail in Chapter 11, the LLC would only have "partnership minimum gain" if it sold the commercial building for no consideration other than the full satisfaction of the $900,000 nonrecourse liability encumbering it. If that occurred, the LLC's amount realized of $900,000 would be completely offset by the $900,000 adjusted basis it has in the commercial building. As a result, the LLC has no "partnership minimum gain" at the end of Year 1.

Because there is no partnership minimum gain in Year 1, none of the $900,000 of nonrecourse liability will be allocated pursuant to Tier 1. Likewise, because the LLC has no § 704(c) property, none of the liability will be allocated pursuant to Tier 2. As a result, all $900,000 of the nonrecourse liability will be allocated under Tier 3, i.e., in accord with each partner's interest in partnership profits. Given the different allocations of LLC tax items provided in the facts of this Example, there are a variety of ways in which the LLC could allocate the excess nonrecourse liabilities pursuant to Tier 3. For simplicity sake and to illustrate certain points regarding the nonrecourse allocation rules, we will assume the LLC agreement provides that the excess nonrecourse liabilities will be allocated 75% to Brent and 25% to Maureen during the first ten years. In Year 1, therefore, Brent will be allocated $675,000 of the nonrecourse liability and Maureen will be allocated $225,000 of the liability. In turn, their outside bases would be increased by those respective amounts just as though each had contributed an additional amount of money to the partnership.[27]

---

[25] Review Chapters 9 and 11.

[26] Disregard the application of any depreciation conventions, e.g., the mid-month convention of § 168(d)(4)(B).

[27] In Year 1, the $100,000 depreciation deduction would be allocated 75% (or $75,000) to Brent and 25% (or $25,000) to Maureen thereby reducing the capital account of each to $0. (Brent's initial capital account was $75,000 and Maureen's initial capital account was $25,000. Reg. § 1.704-1(b)(2)(iv)(b)(1).) While Brent's initial outside basis was $75,000 and Maureen's initial outside basis was $25,000, the allocation of $675,000 of the nonrecourse liability to Brent and $225,000 of that liability to Maureen would have increased their outside basis to $750,000 and $250,000 respectively. Each partner's outside basis would be decreased by the depreciation allocated to each in Year 1. Thus, Brent's outside basis would be decreased to $675,000 and Maureen's outside basis would be decreased to $225,000.

In Year 2, the LLC will again be allowed a $100,000 depreciation deduction thereby reducing the adjusted basis in the commercial building to $800,000. Were the LLC at the end of Year 2 to sell the commercial building for no consideration other than the satisfaction of the $900,000 nonrecourse debt, it would recognize $100,000 of gain. That gain thus constitutes "partnership minimum gain" or "Tufts gain." As discussed in Chapter 11, because there has been a net increase of $100,000 in "partnership minimum gain" in Year 2, all $100,000 of the depreciation deduction allowed the partnership will be treated as a "nonrecourse deduction." Reg. § 1.704-2(c). [In other words, the partnership's $100,000 deduction for depreciation in Year 2 is directly related to the $900,000 nonrecourse debt, unlike the depreciation in Year 1, which was directly related to the contributions Brent and Maureen made when they formed the LLC.] Consistent with the LLC operating agreement, the Year 2 depreciation deduction being a nonrecourse deduction will be allocated 70% or $70,000 to Brent and 30% or $30,000 to Maureen. (As noted in the facts for this Example, the allocation of nonrecourse deductions provided by the LLC agreement satisfies the safe harbor of Reg. § 1.704-2(e).) This allocation will result in a $70,000 deficit in Brent's capital account and a $30,000 deficit in Maureen's capital account. Having been allocated $70,000 of nonrecourse deductions, Brent's share of the "partnership minimum gain" is $70,000. Similarly, Maureen's share of the "partnership minimum gain" will equal $30,000, reflecting the allocation to her of $30,000 of the nonrecourse deduction in Year 2. Pursuant to Reg. § 1.704-2(g)(1) and as discussed in Chapter 11, in light of the existence of the minimum gain chargeback provision in the LLC operating agreement, each partner's share of the "partnership minimum gain" will be "added to the limited dollar amount, if any, of the deficit balance in the partner's capital account that the partner is obligated to restore." As a result, the alternative test for economic effect (Reg. § 1.704-1(b)(ii)(d)) is not violated.

In the allocation of the $900,000 nonrecourse liability at the end of Year 2, Tier 1 will now require that $70,000 of that liability be allocated to Brent and $30,000 to Maureen to reflect their respective shares of partnership minimum gain. Once again, none of the $900,000 of nonrecourse liability will be allocated pursuant to Tier 2 as there is no § 704(c) property. After application of Tiers 1 and 2, the remaining (or excess) $800,000 of the nonrecourse liability will be allocated pursuant to Tier 3. Again, given the assumption above that the Tier 3 excess nonrecourse liabilities will be allocated 75% to Brent and 25% to Maureen, Brent would be allocated $600,000 of the excess nonrecourse liabilities and Maureen $200,000.

While, as noted above, in Year 1, Brent had a $675,000 share of the nonrecourse liability and Maureen and a $225,000 share, by the end of Year 2 Brent's share of that liability had been decreased to $670,000 and Maureen's share had been increased to $230,000. The $5,000 decrease in Brent's share is treated under § 752(b) as a distribution of cash to Brent which reduces his outside basis by that amount; the $5,000 increase in Maureen's share of the nonrecourse liability is treated under § 752(a) as an additional cash contribution by her which increases her outside basis by that amount. What should be apparent from the Year 2 analysis is that, given the special allocation of the LLC's nonrecourse deductions, in each of the next eight years, Brent's share of the nonrecourse deductions will continue to decrease at the rate of $5,000 per year while Maureen's share will increase at that same rate. At the end of the 10-year period, Brent's share of the nonrecourse liability will have been reduced to $630,000 and Maureen's share will have increased to $270,000. Note that Maureen's continually increasing share of the nonrecourse liability ensures she will have adequate outside basis necessary to deduct her share of the LLC's nonrecourse deductions (consisting of depreciation deductions) without being limited by § 704(d).

As the prior paragraph has suggested, if the Tier 3 allocation is made strictly on the 75%/25% basis assumed above, a recalculation of the overall allocation of the nonrecourse liability must be made annually during the 10-year depreciation period for the commercial building encumbered by that liability. As suggested above, the regulations, however, afford considerable flexibility with regard to Tier 3 allocations. Read Reg. § 1.752-3(a)(3) carefully. Note that, pursuant to that regulation, "excess nonrecourse liabilities may be allocated among the partners in accordance with the manner in which it is reasonably expected that the deductions attributable to those nonrecourse liabilities will be allocated." Considering that Brent will ultimately be allocated 70% or $630,000 of the $900,000 in nonrecourse deductions resulting from the depreciation of the commercial building in Years 2 through 10, the partners in Year 2 could simply allocate the excess $800,000 of nonrecourse liabilities 70% or $560,000 to Brent and 30% or $240,000 to Maureen. In the aggregate, Brent would thus have a $630,000 share of the nonrecourse liability (i.e., $70,000 from Tier 1 and $560,000 from Tier 2) and Maureen would have a $270,000 share (i.e., $30,000 from Tier 1 and $240,000 from Tier 2).

Example 2: In Year 1, Clare and Bob form a general partnership in which each has a 50% interest in profits and losses. For her partnership interest, Clare contributes a tract of raw land with a fair market value of $500,000 and an adjusted basis of $200,000. (There is thus $300,000 of built-in gain with respect to the land).[28] The land is encumbered by a $300,000 nonrecourse liability that requires no payments for the next five years. Bob contributes $200,000 of cash. How will the $300,000 of nonrecourse liability be shared in Years 1 and 2? In answering this question, assume that the partners utilize the Traditional Method for allocating items with respect to § 704(c) property. (See Chapter 10.)

Analysis: Regulation § 1.704-2(d)(3) provides that, if partnership property encumbered by nonrecourse liabilities is reflected on the partnership books at a value that differs from the property's adjusted tax basis, partnership minimum gain is determined with reference to the contributed property's book value rather than its adjusted basis. Applying that rule, it is clear that

---

[28] Reg. § 1.704-3(a)(3)(ii). *See* Chapter 10 for a detailed discussion of property with "built-in" gain or loss.

because the book value of the property contributed by Clare ($500,000)[29] is greater than the $300,000 of nonrecourse liability, there is no partnership minimum gain immediately after the contribution.[30] Because land is not depreciable, the book value of the land will continue to be greater than the outstanding nonrecourse liability and thus there will never be any partnership minimum gain. There are therefore no Tier 1 allocations with respect to the nonrecourse liability encumbering the land contributed by Clare.

Because the land is § 704(c) property, i.e., at the time Clare contributed the land it had a book value that differed from its adjusted basis,[31] we must consider the possibility that Tier 2 will apply to allocate some of the nonrecourse liability. Under Tier 2, a partner will be allocated an amount of the nonrecourse liability equal to the taxable gain that would be allocated to that partner under § 704(c) were the partnership to dispose of its property subject to nonrecourse liabilities in a taxable transaction for no consideration other than the full satisfaction of the nonrecourse liabilities. In our example, were such taxable disposition to occur with respect to the land contributed by Clare, the partnership would recognize $100,000 of gain, i.e., amount realized of $300,000 (the amount of the nonrecourse liability) less the land's $200,000 adjusted basis. (This $100,000 of gain is commonly referred to as "minimum § 704(c) gain" because it is the amount of gain that would be recognized on a taxable disposition even if the property were to have become worthless.) Because § 704(c) and the regulations thereunder would allocate that gain entirely to Clare,[32] $100,000 of the $300,000 of nonrecourse liability will be allocated to Clare under Tier 2.

The excess nonrecourse liability (i.e., the amount the liability unallocated after applying both Tier 1 and Tier 2) — in this case $200,000 — will be allocated in Tier 3 pursuant to the partners' interest in partnership profits. Because the partners share partnership profits equally, we could allocate the excess $200,000 of nonrecourse liability equally between Clare and Bob. Thus, in the aggregate Clare will have a $200,000 share of the nonrecourse liability and Bob will have a $100,000 share. Because Clare's share of liabilities has decreased from $300,000 to $200,000, she will be deemed under § 752(b) to have received a $100,000 distribution of cash from the partnership. She will not recognize any gain under § 731(a) because her outside basis of $200,000 in her partnership interest is greater than the

---

[29] Reg. § 1.704-1(b)(2)(iv)(d)(1).

[30] If the land were disposed of in a taxable transaction for no consideration other than the satisfaction of the $300,000 of the nonrecourse indebtedness, there would be no partnership minimum gain because we would use the $500,000 book value instead of the land's $200,000 adjusted basis in calculating any gain. In other words, there could not be partnership minimum gain unless the nonrecourse indebtedness exceeded $500,000.

[31] *See* Reg. § 1.704-3(a)(3)(i). § 704(c) property and allocations associated with § 704(c) property are discussed in detail in Chapter 10.

[32] Reg. § 1.704-3(b)(1). Pursuant to this regulation, Clare would be allocated the first $300,000 of the gain recognized by the partnership on a taxable disposition of the land.

deemed cash distribution.[33] Pursuant to § 733, her outside basis will be reduced to $100,000 as a result of the deemed cash distribution. Bob will have increased his share of partnership liabilities by $100,000 and, therefore, pursuant to § 752(a), he will be deemed to have contributed $100,000 of additional cash to the partnership. His outside basis will therefore be increased to $300,000.

The results in Year 2 will be identical to the results in Year 1. Review Revenue Ruling 95-41, included in the materials, for a more complex application of the § 752 regulations to § 704(c) property subject to nonrecourse liabilities.[34]

Example 3: Patrick and Laura each contribute $200,000 in cash to form a general partnership in which they are equal partners. The partnership uses the $400,000 of cash contributed by Patrick and Laura to purchase land that the partnership will use for its commercial sod business. Ten years later, when the land has increased in value to $1,000,000 but still has an adjusted basis of $400,000, the partnership borrows from an unrelated person $300,000 on a nonrecourse basis, giving the land as security for the loan. How will the $300,000 nonrecourse loan be allocated?

Analysis: No part of the $300,000 nonrecourse liability will be allocated pursuant to Tier 1 as there will be no partnership minimum gain because the $400,000 adjusted basis of the land exceeds the nonrecourse liability. Because the land is not § 704(c) property, Tier 2 has no application. As a result, the entire liability will be allocated pursuant to Tier 3. Again, in general the liability would be allocated in accordance with the partners' share of partnership profits. In this case, Patrick and Laura share profits

---

[33] Note how the Tier 2 allocation rules operate to ensure that the contributing partner will not recognize gain on the contribution of property encumbered by nonrecourse liabilities in excess of that partner's adjusted basis in the property.

[34] Tier 2 also applies in the context of a revaluation of property. For example, assume that A and B are equal partners in a general partnership that owns one asset — land with a book value of $30,000 and a fair market value of $100,000. The partnership had purchased the land with the cash that A and B contributed when they formed the partnership. The partnership has an adjusted basis in the land of $30,000. Assume C joins the partnership and contributes $50,000 cash for her one-third partnership share. Pursuant to Reg. § 1.704-1(b)(2)(iv)(f), the partnership elects to revalue (book-up) the land on its books to reflect its $100,000 fair market value. Subsequently, the partnership borrows $60,000 from an unrelated party on a nonrecourse basis, using the land as security. As a result of the revaluation, a book/tax disparity has been created. Section 704(c) principles are applied when a revaluation creates differences between the book value and adjusted tax basis of property. Reg. § 1.704-3(a)(6). Thus, A and B are accountable for the $70,000 of built-in gain with respect to the land. As noted above, pursuant to Reg. § 1.704-2(d)(3), the determination of partnership minimum gain must be made with reference to the book value of the property rather than the property's adjusted basis. Thus, as in Example 2 above, there would be no partnership minimum gain because the land's book value of $100,000 exceeds the nonrecourse liability. Therefore, none of the $60,000 of nonrecourse liability would be allocated pursuant to the Tier 1 analysis. The Tier 2 analysis, however, applies in the case of a revaluation of property. Reg. 1.752-3(a)(2). If the land were disposed of in a taxable transaction in which the only consideration received was the relief the nonrecourse liability to which the land is subject, there would be gain of $30,000 (i.e., $60,000 amount realized less $30,000 adjusted basis). Pursuant to § 704(c), this gain would be allocable in equal shares to A and B. As a result, under Tier 2, A and B would each be allocated $30,000 of the $60,000 nonrecourse liability. None of the liability would be allocable to C.

equally. As a result, the $300,000 nonrecourse liability would be allocated equally between Patrick and Laura. Thus, each would been deemed to have contributed $150,000 of additional cash to the partnership and, pursuant to § 722, the outside basis of each would be increased by $150,000.

Again, considerable flexibility is provided with respect to Tier 3 allocations. For example, if their partnership agreement made special allocations of partnership deductions and losses and those special allocations satisfied the substantial economic effect test of § 704(b), the partnership agreement could specify the partners' interest in partnership profits for purposes of allocating the nonrecourse liability so long as the interests so specified were reasonably consistent with the special allocations.

Revenue Ruling 95-41
1995-1C.B. 132

Facts:

A and *B* form a partnership, *PRS*, and agree that each will be allocated a 50 percent share of all partnership items. *A* contributes depreciable property subject to a nonrecourse liability of $6,000, with an adjusted tax basis of $4,000 and a fair market value of $10,000. *B* contributes $4,000 cash.

Analysis:

Upon *A*'s contribution of the depreciable property to *PRS*, there is $6,000 of § 704(c) built-in gain (the excess of the book value of the property ($10,000) over *A*'s adjusted tax basis in the property at the time of contribution ($4,000)). As a result of the contribution, *A*'s individual liabilities decreased by $6,000 (the amount of the nonrecourse liability which *PRS* is treated as having assumed). *A*'s share of the partnership's nonrecourse liabilities is determined under § 1.752-3.

(1) First Tier Allocations:

Under § 1.752-3(a)(1), a partner's share of the nonrecourse liabilities of *PRS* includes the partner's share of partnership minimum gain determined in accordance with the rules of § 704(b) and the regulations thereunder. § 1.704-2(d)(1) provides that partnership minimum gain is determined by computing, for each partnership nonrecourse liability, any gain the partnership would realize if it disposed of the property subject to that liability for no consideration other than full satisfaction of the liability, and then aggregating the separately computed gains. Pursuant to § 1.704-2(d)(3), partnership minimum gain is determined with reference to the contributed property's book value rather than its adjusted tax basis.

In contrast, § 704(c) requires that allocations take into account the difference between the contributed property's adjusted tax basis and its fair market value. Thus, because partnership minimum gain is computed using the contributed property's book value rather than its tax basis, allocations of nonrecourse liabilities under § 1.752-3(a)(1) are not affected by § 704(c). Moreover, because the book value of the property at the time of contribution ($10,000) exceeds the amount of the nonrecourse liability ($6,000), there is no partnership minimum gain immediately after the contribution, and neither A nor B receive an allocation of nonrecourse liabilities under § 1.752-3(a)(1) immediately after the contribution.

(2) Second Tier Allocations:

Under § 1.752-3(a)(2), a partner's share of the nonrecourse liabilities of the partnership includes the amount of taxable gain that would be allocated to the contributing partner under § 704 (c) if the partnership, in a taxable transaction, disposed of the contributed property in full satisfaction of the nonrecourse liability and for no other consideration. If PRS sold the contributed property in full satisfaction of the liability and for no other consideration, PRS would recognize a taxable gain of $2,000 on the sale ($6,000 amount of the nonrecourse liability less $4,000 adjusted tax basis of the property). Under § 704(c) and § 1.704-3(b)(1), all of this taxable gain would be allocated to A. The hypothetical sale also would result in a book loss of $4,000 to PRS (excess of $10,000 book value of property over $6,000 amount of the nonrecourse liability). Under the terms of the partnership agreement, this book loss would be allocated equally between A and B. Because B would receive a $2,000 book loss but no corresponding tax loss, the hypothetical sale would result in a $2,000 disparity between B's book and tax allocations.

If PRS used the traditional method of making § 704 (c) allocations described in § 1.704-3(b), A would be allocated a total of $2,000 of taxable gain from the hypothetical sale of the contributed property. Therefore, A would be allocated $2,000 of nonrecourse liabilities under § 1.752-3(a)(2) immediately after the contribution.

If PRS adopted the remedial allocation method described in § 1.704-3(d), PRS would be required to make a remedial allocation of $2,000 of tax loss to B in connection with the hypothetical sale to eliminate the $2,000 disparity between B's book and tax allocations. PRS also would be required to make an offsetting remedial allocation of tax gain to A of $2,000. Thus, A would be allocated a total of $4,000 of tax gain ($2,000 actual gain plus the $2,000 allocation of remedial gain) from the hypothetical sale of the contributed property. Therefore, if the partnership adopted the remedial allocation method, A would be allocated $4,000 of nonrecourse liabilities under § 1.752-3(a)(2) immediately after the contribution.

If PRS used the traditional method with curative allocations described in § 1.704-3(c), PRS would be permitted to make reasonable curative allocations to reduce or eliminate the difference between the book and tax allocations to B that resulted from the hypothetical sale. However, PRS's ability to make curative allocations would depend on the existence of other partnership items and could not be determined solely from the hypothetical sale of the contributed property. Because any potential curative allocations could not be determined solely from the hypothetical sale of the contributed property, curative allocations are not taken into account in allocating nonrecourse liabilities under § 1.752-3(a)(2). Therefore, if PRS used the traditional method with curative allocations, A would be allocated $2,000 of nonrecourse liabilities under § 1.752-3 (a)(2) immediately after the contribution.

(3) Third Tier Allocations:

Following the allocation under § 1.752-3(a)(2), *PRS* has excess nonrecourse liabilities that must be allocated between *A* and *B*. § 1.752-3(a)(3) provides several alternatives for allocating excess nonrecourse liabilities.

(a) First, *PRS* may choose to allocate excess nonrecourse liabilities in accordance with the partners' shares of partnership profits. The partners' interests in partnership profits are determined by taking into account all the facts and circumstances relating to the economic arrangement of the partners. The partners' agreement to share the profits of the partnership equally is one fact to be considered in making this determination. Another fact to be considered is a partner's share of § 704 (c) built-in gain to the extent that the gain was not taken into account in making an allocation of nonrecourse liabilities under § 1.752-3(a)(2). This built-in gain is one factor because, under the principles of § 704(c), this excess built-in gain, if recognized, will be allocated to *A*. *A*'s share of § 704(c) built-in gain that is not taken into account in making allocations under § 1.752-3(a)(2) is, therefore, one factor, but not the only factor, to be considered in determining *A*'s interest in partnership profits.

The amount of the § 704(c) built-in gain that is not considered in making allocations under § 1.752-3(a)(2) must be given an appropriate weight in light of all other items of partnership profit. For example, if it is reasonable to expect that *PRS* will have items of partnership profit over the life of the partnership that will be allocated to *B*, *PRS* may not allocate all of the excess nonrecourse liabilities to *A*. Rather, the remaining nonrecourse liabilities must be allocated between *A* and *B* in proportion to their interests in total partnership profits.

(b) Second, the *PRS* partnership agreement may specify the partners' interest in partnership profits for purposes of allocating excess nonrecourse liabilities, provided that the interests specified are reasonably consistent with allocations (that have substantial economic effect under the § 704(b) regulations) of some other significant item of partnership income or gain. The partnership agreement provides that each partner will be allocated a 50 percent share of all partnership items. Assuming that such allocations have substantial economic effect, *PRS* can choose to allocate the excess nonrecourse liabilities 50 percent to each partner. § 704(c) allocations, however, do not have substantial economic effect under the § 704(b) regulations. See § 1.704-1(b)(2)(iv)(d). Accordingly, under this alternative, § 704(c) allocations cannot be used as a basis for allocating excess nonrecourse liabilities.

(c) Finally, *PRS* may choose to allocate the excess nonrecourse liabilities in accordance with the manner in which it is reasonably expected that the deductions attributable to the excess nonrecourse liabilities will be allocated. Because *A* and *B* have agreed to allocate all partnership items 50 percent to each partner, *A* and *B* each will be entitled to allocations of book depreciation of $5,000 over the life of the contributed property. The contributed property, however, has an adjusted tax basis of $4,000 and, regardless of the method used by the partnership under § 704(c), the entire $4,000 of tax depreciation over the life of the contributed property must be allocated to B. Therefore, *PRS* must allocate all of the excess nonrecourse liabilities to *B* if it chooses to allocate the excess nonrecourse liabilities in accordance with the manner that the deductions attributable to the excess nonrecourse liabilities will be allocated.

HOLDINGS

(1) Allocations of nonrecourse liabilities under § 1.752-3(a)(1) are not affected by § 704(c).

(2) Allocations of nonrecourse liabilities under § 1.752-3(a)(2) take into account remedial allocations of gain that would be made to the contributing partner under § 1.704-3(d). Allocations of nonrecourse liabilities under § 1.752-3(a)(2) do not take into account curative allocations under § 1.704-3(c).

(3) Allocations of nonrecourse liabilities under § 1.752-3(a)(3) are affected by § 704(c) in the following manner:

    (a) If the partnership determines the partners' interests in partnership profits based on all of the facts and circumstances relating to the economic arrangement of the partners, § 704(c) built-in gain that was not taken into account under § 1.752-3(a)(2) is one factor, but not the only factor, to be considered under § 1.752-3(a)(3).

    (b) If the partnership chooses to allocate excess nonrecourse liabilities in a manner reasonably consistent with allocations (that have substantial economic effect under the § 704(b) regulations) of some other significant item of partnership income or gain, § 704(c) does not affect the allocation of nonrecourse liabilities under § 1.752-3(a)(3) because § 704(c) allocations do not have substantial economic effect.

    (c) If the partnership chooses to allocate excess nonrecourse liabilities in accordance with the manner in which it is reasonably expected that the deductions attributable to the nonrecourse liabilities will be allocated, the partnership must take into account the allocations required by § 704(c) in determining the manner in which the deductions attributable to the nonrecourse liabilities will be allocated.

Chapter 13

TRANSACTIONS BETWEEN PARTNERS AND PARTNERSHIPS

I. PROBLEMS

1. Alex, a cash method taxpayer, is a lawyer engaged as a solo practitioner in a general practice. In addition, Alex is a partner in a four-person general partnership engaged in a real estate management business. As an equal partner, Alex has a 25% distributive share of the income, deductions, and credits of the partnership. The partnership retains Alex to represent it in a housing discrimination action. In the current year, Alex's fees for this representation amount to $40,000. The partnership computes its taxable income on a calendar-year basis, using the accrual method of accounting. Assume that, disregarding the $40,000 in fees owing to Alex, the partnership during the current year has ordinary income of $150,000, long-term capital gain of $60,000, and $50,000 in ordinary expenses (e.g., rent, utilities, and supplies).

    (a) What is the amount and character of the income Alex must report for the current year as a result of partnership operations and the representation arrangements described above? In answering this question, assume the partnership pays Alex the $40,000 in legal fees during the current year.

    (b) How would your answer to (a) change in the following alternative situations:

    (i) the partnership does not pay Alex the $40,000 until the following year.

    (ii) the partnership's ordinary income for the year was $30,000 instead of $150,000.

    (iii) the $40,000 in fees were for negotiating and drafting an agreement to purchase a large office building in midtown Manhattan.

    (iv) rather than paying Alex $40,000 in legal fees, the partnership paid Alex $40,000 in annual rent for space Alex has leased the partnership in an office building he owns and uses in his law practice. Assume the rent represents the fair market rental value of the leased space.

2. Casey, a cash-method taxpayer, is a partner in a two-person general partnership engaged in the sale of dental supplies. Casey, as an equal

partner, has a 50% distributive share of the income, gain, loss, deductions and credits of the partnership. The partnership has agreed to pay Casey a fixed salary of $60,000 annually to manage the day-to-day business of the partnership. Assume, in the current year, the partnership has ordinary income of $80,000 and long-term capital gain of 20,000. Assume also that the partnership computes its taxable income on a calendar-year basis, using the accrual method of accounting.

(a) What is the amount and character of the income (or loss) Casey, a calendar-year taxpayer, must report for the current year in each of the following alternative situations as a result of partnership operations and the salary arrangement he has with the partnership?

(i) The partnership pays Casey the $60,000 salary during the current year.

(ii) The partnership does not pay Casey the $60,000 salary until the following year.

(iii) The partnership's ordinary income for the year was $30,000 instead of $80,000.

(iv) The partnership has no ordinary income for the year but has only the $20,000 of long-term capital gain.

(v) The partnership agreed to pay Casey 50% of its income before taking into account any guaranteed payments but not less than $60,000.

(vi) The partnership must capitalize the amount it agreed to pay Casey and does not make the payment to Casey until the following year.

(b) How would your answer to part (a)(i) change if the partnership's salary arrangement with Casey provided that Casey would receive a salary equal to 20% of the partnership's taxable income for the year? (Hint: Casey's salary is thus determined with reference to the partnership's income.)

Assignment for Chapter 13:

Complete the problems

Read: Internal Revenue Code: §§ 707(a)(1), (c), 267(a)(2) and (e)(1)–(4)
Treasury Regulations: §§ 1.707-1(a), (c); Prop. Reg. § 1.707-1(c) Ex. 2.
Materials: Overview
Revenue Ruling 81-301
Revenue Ruling 69-180

II. VOCABULARY

guaranteed payment
minimum amount guaranteed payments
fixed amount guaranteed payments

III. OBJECTIVES

1. To identify situations when a partner is acting in her capacity as a partner.
2. To identify situations when a partner is acting in a nonpartner capacity.
3. To distinguish a distributive share from a guaranteed payment.
4. To explain the tax consequences to a partner and a partnership of payments made by a partnership to a partner who is not acting in her capacity as a partner.
5. To explain the circumstances under which payments to a partner will be deemed determined without reference to partnership income.
6. To explain the tax consequence to a partner of a guaranteed payment.
7. To determine the amount and character of income a partner will have when a partnership agrees to pay a partner a minimum amount determined without reference to partnership income for services the partner will perform in her capacity as a partner.
8. To compare and contrast the tax consequences of distributive shares, § 707(a)(1) payments and § 707(c) guaranteed payments.

IV. OVERVIEW

As previously discussed, Subchapter K reflects both aggregate and entity approaches to the tax treatment of partners and partnerships. Recall that, pursuant to the aggregate approach, a partnership is merely an "aggregation of the activities of its partners"[1] each of whom has an undivided interest in each of the partnership's assets. As a result, each partner takes into account her distributive share (income, gain, loss, deduction) of every partnership transaction. By contrast, the entity approach treats the partnership as an entity separate from its partners just as a Subchapter C corporation is treated as an entity separate from its shareholders. Under the entity approach, a partner would be treated as having an undivided interest in the entity, i.e., the partnership itself, and not in each of the partnership assets.

The tension in Subchapter K between the aggregate and entity approaches is particularly apparent when one considers transactions between a partner and her partnership. Partners interact with their partnership in a variety of ways. For example, a partner may render services to her partnership in her capacity as a partner, e.g., she assists in the management of the day-to-day operations of the partnership. By contrast, the partner may be engaged in a business or profession apart from her partnership. Because of the partner's business or professional expertise, the partnership may hire the partner to perform specialized work. For example, a lawyer engaged in private law practice may also own an interest in a real estate partnership that may hire the lawyer to represent the partnership in a land transaction. Instead of the provision of services, other partner/partnership transactions may involve property, e.g., a partner may lend money to a partnership or lease or sell property to a partnership. In each of these situations, the tax

---

[1] Pratt v. Commissioner, 550 F.2d 1023, 1026 (1977).

consequences of any compensation, interest, rent, or purchase price paid by the partnership to the partner will differ depending on whether the partnership is treated as a separate entity or merely as an aggregate of partners.

This chapter will address the tension between the aggregate and entity approaches to the tax treatment of partners and partnerships and the application of those approaches in the context of compensation arrangements in partner/partnership transactions. In that regard, the chapter will discuss the development and application of § 707 enacted as part of the Internal Revenue Code of 1954.

A. Tax Treatment of Partner/Partnership Transactions Prior to the Internal Revenue Code of 1954

Prior to the Internal Revenue Code of 1954, in the absence of any statutory guidance, the courts split on the issue of whether a partnership should be treated for tax purposes as an entity separate from its partners and, in turn, whether the partners could act as nonpartners or outsiders in their dealings with their partnerships. Prior to the enactment of § 707 in 1954 (discussed *infra*), some courts — albeit a minority — concluded a partner could interact with her partnership as an outsider;[2] the majority of courts, however adopted the aggregate approach, concluding that, for tax purposes, a partner could not deal with her partnership as an outsider. The following quote from the Board of Tax Appeal's decision in *Lloyd v. Commissioner*, 15 B.T.A. 82, 87 (1929) (regarding the proper tax treatment of a "salary" paid to partnership managers) embodies this aggregate approach and reflects the rationale for that approach as developed in the early case law:

> It is well settled that partners are not entitled to a salary or compensation for services rendered to the partnership in the absence of an agreement, express or implied, the reason being that the partnership relation imposes upon each member of the firm the obligation to devote his time and abilities to the affairs of the firm. . . . An agreement between partners to pay salaries from profits is nothing more than the determination of a basis for dividing such profits. *A partner devoting his time and energies to the business of the firm is in fact working for himself and can not be considered as an employee of the firm in the sense that he is in the service of another.* It follows, therefore, that he cannot be paid a salary by the firm out of earnings in the sense of compensation for services rendered to an employer. In effect *any* allowances drawn by a partner from partnership assets are payments which he makes to himself and *no man can be his own employer or employee. A partner receiving a salary is merely transferring money from one to another of his own pockets.* . . . [I]t being concluded that payments of compensation to partners are but a means for dividing the partnership profits, *it must necessarily follow that such payments are not proper deductions from income in computing the partnership net income.* [emphasis added]

As the foregoing quote suggests, courts utilizing an aggregate approach, in effect, ignored the existence of the partnership when a partner dealt with her

---

[2] Wegener v. Commissioner, 119 F.2d 49 (5th Cir. 1941), *cert. denied*, 314 U.S. 643 (1941).

partnership. Under this approach, a partner performing services for her partnership was viewed as working for herself and thus could not be considered an employee. Consequently, any compensation paid to the partner was treated as a distributive share of partnership income and would not be deductible by the partnership.

Considerable uncertainty was created by the differing positions of the courts regarding whether a partnership should be treated for tax purposes as a separate entity or merely an aggregate of its partners.[3] Substantial computational problems were created by the latter approach when a payment to a partner for services exceeded partnership income. The following example, based loosely on *Lloyd v. Commissioner*, illustrates the computational difficulties created by the aggregate approach.

> **Example:** In Year 1, Jackson and Will each contribute $100,000 to form the JW Partnership, a cash method, general partnership in which all of the profits and losses are shared equally. Jackson's and Will's initial capital accounts are thus each $100,000. While both Jackson and Will plan to be engaged in the day-to-day operation of the partnership business, Jackson has agreed to manage the business and, as manager, will devote a considerably larger amount of time each week than Will to the business. To compensate Jackson for the additional responsibilities he has assumed, the partnership will pay him a salary of $50,000 per year. No salary will be paid to Will. Consistent with that compensation arrangement, the partnership paid $50,000 to Jackson in Year 1. Assume that, disregarding the $50,000 paid to Jackson, the partnership had either:
>
> (a) $100,000 of partnership income in Year 1; or
>
> (b) $30,000 of partnership income in Year 1.
>
> **Analysis:** Under the aggregate approach articulated in *Lloyd v. Commissioner*, Jackson would not be considered an employee of the JW Partnership. Consistent with *Lloyd*, the partners' agreement regarding the $50,000 "salary" to be paid to Jackson would merely represent an agreement regarding the division of the JW Partnership's income. If the partnership profits were sufficient, any payment made pursuant to the agreement would be considered part of Jackson's distributive share of partnership profits. Thus, if the JW Partnership has $100,000 of income in year 1 (as in alternative (a) above), the application of the aggregate approach of *Lloyd* would be simple. Jackson would be treated as having a $75,000 distributive share of the partnership's income (i.e., $50,000 of salary plus a 50% interest or $25,000 in the remaining $50,000 of partnership income.) The character of that income would, of course, depend on the character of the income to the partnership. § 702. If all of the partnership income were ordinary, Jackson's would have $75,000 of ordinary income. By contrast, if all of the partnership income were long-term capital gain, Jackson would have $75,000 of long-term capital gain.

---

[3] Compare *Wegener v. Commissioner* and *Lloyd v. Commissioner*, noted above.

Application of the aggregate approach becomes considerably more complicated in alternative (b) where the partnership profits are only $30,000 and are thus insufficient to cover Jackson's $50,000 salary. While, pursuant to a *Lloyd* analysis, all $30,000 of the partnership profits would be allocated to Jackson as a distributive share, a question is obviously raised as to the source of the remaining $20,000 Jackson received for his services. *Lloyd v. Commissioner* answered that question indicating that, to the extent partnership profits were insufficient to cover the amounts paid to a partner as compensation for services rendered, the compensation would be deemed paid from each partner's capital account. Thus, $20,000 of the payments received by Jackson would come from Jackson's and Will's capital accounts. Because Jackson and Will are equal partners, each of their capital accounts would be charged with $10,000 of Jackson's salary. To the extent that $10,000 of his salary came from his own capital account, Jackson would have had no income — but, instead, just a return of his investment. Pursuant to *Lloyd*, the $10,000 that came from Will's capital account would constitute income to Jackson and would presumably be deductible by Will under § 162 (because Will would be treated as paying $10,000 of compensation to Jackson for the management services he rendered). Jackson would thus have a total of $40,000 of income.[4]

Consistent with the above analysis, the $30,000 of partnership income allocated to Jackson as a distributive share would have the same character as that income had to the partnership; the $10,000 of Jackson's salary that came from Will's capital account would presumably be ordinary income to Jackson.[5] If, for example, the $30,000 of partnership income for Year 1 were all short-term capital gain, Jackson would thus have $30,000 of short-term capital gain and $10,000 of ordinary income. Jackson could thus have a combination of capital gain and ordinary income as a result of the services he rendered the partnership. This simple example suggests the cumbersome calculations and analysis that would be required were the JW Partnership to have many more partners.

If, by contrast, the JW Partnership were to be treated as a separate entity, the analysis would be considerably simplified. The "salary" the JW Partnership agreed to pay Jackson for the extra services he rendered would be treated as equivalent to a payment made to an outsider or nonpartner. In both alternatives (a) and (b), Jackson would have $50,000 of ordinary income and the partnership (assuming the salary paid to Jackson did not constitute a capital expenditure) would be entitled to a $50,000 deduction. See § 162(a). The partnership, as a result, would have taxable income of $50,000 in alternative (a) (i.e., $100,000 less the $50,000 salary) and, a $20,000 tax loss in alternative (b). Jackson and Will would each have

---

[4] Note that, in either alternative (a) or (b), the partnership would not be entitled to a deduction for the compensation paid to Jackson.

[5] With regard to the $10,000 paid to Jackson from Will's capital account, the requirements for capital gain treatment are not present, i.e., there has been no sale or exchange of a capital asset.

a 50% share of the $50,000 of taxable income in alternative (a) or the $20,000 taxable loss of the partnership in alternative (b).

Congress characterized the application of the aggregate approach in a situation such as that presented in our example as "unrealistic and unnecessarily complicated" and, in the legislative history of the Internal Revenue Code of 1954, indicated its intent to treat partnerships as entities in the case of certain transactions between partners and their partnerships.[6]

B. Tax Treatment of Partner/Partnership Transactions: § 707(a)(1) and (c)

As part of the Act creating the Internal Revenue Code of 1954, Congress enacted § 707(a) and (c) to address the uncertainties and complexities noted above with respect to partner/partnership transactions. As one court aptly noted, § 707 "carves out an exception to the general plan of treating of partnerships as "aggregations."[7] In other words, in certain situations § 707 treats partnerships for tax purposes as entities separate from their partners. Nonetheless, the aggregate approach continues to figure prominently in determining the tax consequences of partner/partnership transactions. Read § 707(a) and (c) carefully.

---

§ 707. Transactions Between Partners and Partnerships

(a) **Partner not acting in capacity as partner.**

(1) **In general.** If a partner engages in a transaction with a partnership other than in his capacity as a member of such partnership, the transaction shall, except as otherwise provided in this section, be considered as occurring between the partnership and one who is not a partner.

(c) **Guaranteed payments.** To the extent determined without regard to the income of the partnership, payments to a partner for services or the use of capital shall be considered as made to one who is not a member of the partnership, but only for the purpose of section 61(a) (relating to gross income) and, subject to section 263, for purposes of section 162(a) (relating to trade or business expenses).

Given § 707(a)(1), one could divide partner/partnership transactions into two broad categories, i.e., (1) transactions in which the partner acts in a nonpartner capacity and (2) transactions in which the partner is acting in her capacity as a partner. Given § 707(c), the second category could, in turn, be divided into two subcategories, i.e., (a) transactions in which a partner acts in her capacity as a partner and the amounts paid or to be paid to her for services or the use of capital are determined without regard to partnership income (i.e., so-called "guaranteed

---

[6] *See* S. Rep. No. 1622, 83rd Cong., 2d Sess.92 (1954).

[7] Pratt v. Commissioner, 550 F.2d 1023, 1026 (1977).

payments") and (b) transactions in which a partner interacts with a partnership in her capacity as a partner and payments to her for services or use of capital are determined with reference to partnership income. The following chart provides an overview of the tax treatment of each of these categories and subcategories of partner/partnership transactions:

Category 1: Partner/Partnership Transactions: Partner Acts in a Nonpartner Capacity

§ 707(a)(1) generally provides that these transactions will be considered as being between a partnership and an outsider or nonpartner. Section 707(a)(1) thus treats the partnership as an entity separate from its partners. In addition to addressing payments made by a partnership to a partner for services rendered, § 707(a)(1) addresses other partner/partnership transactions, including loans of money or property, sales and purchases of property, and the rendering of services by the partnership to the partner.[8]

Category 2: Partner/Partnerships Transactions: Partner Acts in Capacity as Partner

(a) Transactions involving the partnership's payment to a partner for services rendered or for the use of capital when the payment is determined without regard to partnership income. As discussed in greater detail below, § 707(c) provides that payments of this nature will be deemed paid to a nonpartner but only for purposes of §§ 61 and 162. For all other purposes, the payments will be treated in the same manner as a distributive share of partnership profits.[9] Thus, § 707(c) reflects both the aggregate and entity approaches to the tax treatment of partners and partnerships.

(b) Transactions involving partnership payments to a partner for services rendered or for the use of capital when the payments are determined with reference to the partnership's income. The aggregate approach prevails here and these payments will be treated as a distributive share of partnership profits governed by the rules of §§ 702, 704(b), and 731 and taxed accordingly. *See* discussion in Chapter 7.

1. When Does a Partner Act in Her Capacity as a Partner?

As the above categorization of partner/partnership transactions indicates, a threshold issue in determining the tax consequences of these transactions is whether a partner is acting in her capacity as a partner. Section 707(a)(1) applies only if a partner is not acting in her capacity as a partner while § 707(c) applies only if a partner is acting in her capacity as a partner. So when does a partner act in her partner capacity? The Code is silent on this issue and the regulations offer little

---

[8] Reg. § 1.707-1(a).

[9] Thus, for example, the timing of the inclusion of a guaranteed payment (discussed *infra*) in a partner's gross income will be the same as that for the partner's distributive share.

guidance, noting with respect to "a partner not acting in capacity as a partner" that, "in all cases, the substance of the transaction will govern rather than its form."[10] In the quote from *Lloyd v. Commissioner* above, the court stated that "the partnership relation imposes upon each member of the firm the obligation to devote his time and abilities to the affairs of the firm." While *Lloyd* was decided long before the enactment of § 707, that statement remains true today. To the extent a partner is engaged in activities for which the partnership was created in the first place or activities that enable the partnership to function, e.g., broad management services provided on a daily or continuous basis, the partner should be treated as acting in her capacity as a partner.

In the leading case of *Pratt v. Commissioner*,[11] for example, two limited partnerships were created to develop, own, and manage two shopping centers. Under the partnership agreements, the general partners were entitled to receive a "salary" for managing the shopping centers based on a percentage of the gross rentals from the shopping centers. The Tax Court concluded that, in providing the management services, the partners were acting in their capacity as partners.[12] "They were performing basic duties of the partnership or business pursuant to the partnership agreement." The Fifth Circuit, affirming the Tax Court on this point, noted:[13]

> It is perfectly clear that the contract creating the partnership, which provided for the percentage payments to the general partners for their management efforts was made with them *qua* partners. Furthermore, it is equally clear that the duties to be performed were activities for which the partnership was created in the first place, *i.e.*, the management of the shopping centers. . . . Congress determined that, in order for the partnership to deal with one of its partners as an "outsider," the transaction dealt with must be something outside the scope of the partnership. If, on the other hand, the activities constituting the "transaction" were activities which the partnership itself was engaged in, compensation for such

---

[10] Reg. § 1.707-1(a). That regulation provides one example of a transaction in which the partner will not be deemed to act in her capacity as a partner, i.e., a situation in which the partner allows the partnership to use the partner's separately owned property "to obtain credit or to secure firm creditors by guaranty, pledge, or other agreement."

[11] 64 T.C. 203, *aff'd in part and rev'd in part*, 550 F.2d 1023 (5th Cir. 1977).

[12] This conclusion of the Tax Court negated the taxpayer's argument that the payments to them were governed for tax purposes by § 707(a)(1) and were therefore deductible by the partnership as ordinary and necessary business expenses. The Tax Court also held that the payments to the partners were not guaranteed payments under § 707(c) because the payments were computed based on a percentage of gross rentals. Thus, the payments were not "determined without regard to the income of the partnership."

[13] 550 F.2d at 1026. The Fifth Circuit also noted: "It is . . . unimportant that the parties stipulated that the management fees were reasonable in amount or that a like amount would have had to be paid to a third party for these services if they were not paid to the partners themselves. It is not disputed that if these amounts had been paid to non-partners they would have been deductible as ordinary and necessary business expenses under § 162. This fact, however, has no bearing on the question whether, since they were paid to partners, they were paid for 'transaction[s] with a partnership other than in his capacity as a member of such partnership.' Similarly, the fact that the partners intended the fees to be expenses of the partnership cannot modify the limitations placed in the statute." *Id.* at 1027.

transaction must be treated merely as a rearrangement between the partners of their distributive shares in the partnership income.

By contrast, consider a partner engaged in a business, separate and apart from the partnership, whereby the partner provides technical or professional services to others, e.g., legal services, investment services, or information technology services. If the partnership contracts with that partner to provide the same kind of services to the partnership, the partner is likely not acting in her partner capacity and consequently any compensation paid to her for those services will be neither a distributive share of partnership income nor a § 707(c) guaranteed payment. Instead, the compensation would be treated under § 707(a)(1) as payment to an "outsider." Revenue Ruling 81-301, included in the materials, provides a good example of a partner, who in providing services to the partnership, is deemed not to be acting in her capacity as a partner.

Let us now consider in greater detail each of the three types of partner/partnership transactions noted above, particularly those governed by § 707(a)(1) and (c).

2. Transactions Engaged in by a Partner in a Nonpartner Capacity — § 707(a)(1)

As noted above, a partner providing services or capital in a nonpartner capacity will be treated as an outsider to the partnership. As a result, the timing and character of any income received by the partner will be determined as though the partner were a stranger to the partnership. From its standpoint, a partnership would, *subject to § 263*, expect to deduct amounts paid to such a partner. Consider the following fact pattern:

> Benjamin, a lawyer, maintains a solo practice in Spokane, Washington. Benjamin, a cash method taxpayer, is also a partner in a general partnership that owns and manages a number of large apartment complexes in the Spokane area. The partnership was recently sued as a result of a personal injury sustained by a tenant. The partnership retained Benjamin to represent it in the suit. Pursuant to the retainer agreement, the partnership agreed to pay Benjamin at the rate of $200 per hour for his legal services. That hourly rate is the same rate Benjamin charges his other clients. During the current year, Benjamin devoted 50 hours to the matter, which is expected to go to trial during the next year. Although, at the end of the current year, Benjamin billed the partnership for $10,000 (i.e., 50 hours x $200 per hour), the partnership has not yet paid Benjamin.

In view of the discussion above, it should be clear that Benjamin, in providing the legal services, is not acting in his capacity as a partner. Pursuant to § 707(a)(1) and Reg. § 1.707-1(a), Benjamin will generally be treated as an "outsider." As a result, the $10,000 will not be considered a distributive share of partnership income, nor will it be deemed a guaranteed payment under § 707(c). Because he is a cash method taxpayer, Benjamin will include the compensation for his services when he has actual or constructive receipt of that compensation. The character of that income will be ordinary. Reg. § 1.707-1(c).

The partnership will be entitled to a deduction for the compensation it pays to Benjamin. The timing of the deduction will depend on whether the partnership uses the cash or accrual method of accounting. If the partnership uses the cash method, it will be entitled to a deduction in the year it actually pays Benjamin for his services. Reg. § 1.461-1(a)(1). If the partnership uses the accrual method, it would normally claim the deduction when all events have occurred that fix the partnership's liability to pay Benjamin, the amount owing can be determined with reasonable accuracy and economic performance has occurred. Reg. § 1.461-1(a)(2). Thus, one would expect the partnership, were it using the accrual method, to claim a deduction for the $10,000 in the year Benjamin provided the legal services even though the partnership has yet to pay Benjamin. That would have been the result prior to the 1984 act that amended § 267 to provide a partnership and its partners are related persons for purposes of applying the deduction and income matching rule of § 267(a)(2). Read § 267(a)(2) and (e)(1)–(4) carefully. Section 267(a)(2) and (e) create an exception to the general rule that a partner/partnership transaction will be treated as one between the partnership and a nonpartner or outsider when the partner is not acting in her partner capacity. Applying those provisions, if the partnership uses the accrual method of accounting, it will not be allowed a deduction for the amount owed Benjamin until the amount is includible in Benjamin's income.

Scope of § 707(a)(1). In addition to service situations such as that above, § 707(a)(1) may also apply to partner/partnership sales, exchanges, leases, or loans when the partner is not acting in her capacity as a partner. Reg. § 1.707-1(a). Stating what perhaps should be apparent, Reg. § 1.707-1(a) provides that § 707(a)(1), however, is not applicable to *contributions* of money or property by a partner to a partnership or *distributions* of money or property by a partnership to a partner. Rather, contributions to, or any distributions from, partnerships are governed by other provisions of the Code, e.g., §§ 721 and 731 which generally provide for nonrecognition of gain or loss. Thus, when a partner contributes appreciated real estate to a partnership in exchange for a partnership interest, the nonrecognition rule of § 721 applies.[14]

3. Guaranteed Payments

a. Tax consequences of guaranteed payments.

Section 707(c) addresses the tax consequences of so-called "guaranteed payments," i.e., partnership payments, determined without reference to partnership income, for services rendered or for the use of capital made to a partner *acting in her capacity as a partner*. A guaranteed payment, like a § 707(a)(1) payment, will be treated as made to an outsider *but only for the purpose of §§ 61(a) and (subject to the § 263 capital expenditure rules) 162(a)*. For purposes of timing, a guaranteed payment will be treated as a distributive share of

---

[14] Note, however, that Reg. § 1.731-1(c)(3) provides that, where property is contributed to a partnership and within a short period of time a distribution of other property is made to that partner or where the contributed property is distributed to another partner, the distribution may not be treated as a distribution governed by § 731. Rather, the contribution/distribution arrangement may be treated as an exchange of property if the arrangement was intended to effectuate an exchange of property between two more partners or between a partner and the partnership.

profits. In this regard, the regulations specifically provide:[15]

> [A] partner must include such payments as ordinary income for his taxable year within or with which ends the partnership taxable year in which the partnership deducted such payments as paid or accrued under its method of accounting. See § 706(a) and paragraph (a) of § 1.706-1.[16]

Note that the regulation, in addition to addressing the timing of the inclusion of guaranteed payments in a partner's gross income, also characterizes *all* guaranteed payments as "ordinary income." Reg. § 1.707-1(c). That characterization is appropriate considering that guaranteed payments represent compensation for services or for the use of property. Compensation for services rendered or as payment for the use of property always constitutes ordinary income. Thus, guaranteed payments are regarded as a partner's distributive share of ordinary income and are included in the gross income of the partner; the guaranteed payments are, subject to § 263, deductible by the partnership from its ordinary income as a business expense.

b. Payment.

Although § 707(c) and the regulations thereunder use the word "payment," the absence of an actual payment does not negate the application of § 707(c) or the treatment of compensation as a "guaranteed payment." As noted in *Gaines v. Commissioner*, T.C. Memo 1982-731, "Despite the use of the word 'payment' in both § 707(c) and the regulations thereunder, it is clear that no actual payment need be made; if the partnership deducts the amount under its method of accounting, the 'recipient' partner must include the amount in income in the appropriate year."

c. "Determined without reference to the income of the partnership."

Does the phrase "determined without reference to the income of the partnership" encompass payments that are made with reference to the *gross income* of the partnership? The answer to that question is not entirely clear. In *Pratt*, however, the Tax Court concluded "salaries" paid to general partners for managing the partnership's shopping centers were not guaranteed payments governed by § 707(c) "because they were computed as a percentage of gross rental

---

[15] Reg. § 1.707-1(c). Note that in *Miller v. Commissioner*, 52 T.C. 752, 762 (1969), the court stated that the words "but only" in § 707(c) were added to § 707(c) "to provide that guaranteed payments are to be included in income at the same time as a partner's distributive share — not at the time when compensation would ordinarily be included in income [an apparent reference to the recipient partner's method of accounting]. This is the only example in the legislative history of the need for the 'but only' words."

[16] Note that the regulation indicates that § 706 is the statutory authority for the timing of the inclusion of guaranteed payments. Read § 706(a) and note its reference to § 707(c) payments. The legislative history of § 706(a) indicates that the reference to § 707(c) was intended "to make clear that payments made to a partner for services or for the use of capital are includible in his income at the same time as his distributive share of partnership income for the partnership year when the payments are made or accrued . . . " S. Rept. No. 1622, to accompany H.R. 8300 (Pub. L. No. 591), 83rd Cong., 2d Sess 385 (1954).

income received by the partnership." (See footnote 12.) According to the court, the gross rental income was "income" of the partnerships and, thus, the statutory test for a guaranteed payment that it be 'determined without regard to the income of the partnership' was not satisfied."

d. Capitalization of guaranteed payment.

What are the tax consequences to a partner entitled to a guaranteed payment for providing services or for the use of capital if the partnership must capitalize that payment? Consider the following hypothetical roughly based on the facts of *Gaines v. Commissioner*, T.C. Memo 1982-731:

> **Facts:** Evan and Connor, both cash method taxpayers, form a general partnership that elects to use the accrual method of accounting. Evan and Connor each has a 50% share of the profits and losses of the partnership. Evan, *in his capacity as a partner*, performs certain services for the partnership in the current year, and the partnership agrees to pay him $25,000 for those services. That amount was determined without reference to the partnership's income. Disregarding the $25,000 owed to Evan, the partnership has $60,000 of taxable income in the current year. Assuming the amount payable to Evan must be capitalized and is not paid by the partnership until the following year, how much income would Evan have to report in the current year?

> **Analysis:** The $25,000 salary to be paid to Evan is clearly a guaranteed payment. Because the partnership must capitalize the $25,000 owed to Evan, the partnership's taxable income of $60,000 remains unchanged. The $60,000 of taxable income will be allocated in equal shares of $30,000 to Evan and Connor. Thus, these partners will each report $30,000 of income. A question then arises as to the tax consequences in the current year of the capitalized guaranteed payment. As noted above, Reg. § 1.707-1(c) provides that a partner must include a guaranteed payment in the year the partnership "*deducted such payment as paid or accrued under its method of accounting.* The *Gaines* court, addressing a comparable situation, concluded the partner in that case had to include the guaranteed payment in the year the partnership capitalized the payment. The court reasoned as follows:

>> In *Cagle v. Commissioner*, 63 T.C. 86 (1974), *aff'd*, 539 F. 2d 409 (5th Cir. 1976), we held that includability and deductibility of guaranteed payments are two separate questions, and specifically that guaranteed payments are not automatically deductible simply by reason of their being included in the recipient's income. In *Cagle*, we stated:

>>> We think that all Congress meant was that guaranteed payments should be included in the recipient partner's income in the partnership taxable year ending with or within which the partner's taxable year ends and in which the tax accounting treatment of the transaction is determined at the partnership level.

We believe our statement in *Cagle* is an accurate description of the congressional intent. We have found nothing in the statutory language, regulations, or legislative history to indicate that includability in the recipient partner's income was intended to be dependent upon deductibility at the partnership level.

Petitioners seem to argue that there is a patent unfairness in taxing them on nonexistent income [referring to the guaranteed payment], namely income that they have neither received nor benefited from (e.g., through a tax deduction at the partnership level). Their argument has a superficial appeal to it, but on closer analysis must fail. Except for certain very limited purposes, guaranteed payments are treated as part of the partner's distributive share of partnership income and loss. Sec. 1.707-1(c), Income Tax Regs. For timing purposes, guaranteed payments are treated the same as distributive income and loss. Sec. 706(a); sec. 1.706-1(a) and sec. 1.707-1(c), Income Tax Regs. A partner's distributive share of partnership income is includable in his taxable income for any partnership year ending within or with the partner's taxable year. Sec. 706(a). As is the case with a partner's ordinary distributive share of partnership income and loss, any unfairness in taxing a partner on guaranteed payments that he neither receives nor benefits from results from the conduit theory of partnerships, and is a consequence of the taxpayer's choice to do the business in the partnership form. [In a footnote, the court acknowledged that, "as part of a partner's distributive share of profit and loss, the guaranteed payments included in his income increase the partner's basis in his partnership interest. § 705(a)(1) and (2)."] We find no justification in the statute, regulations, or legislative history to permit these petitioners to recognize their income pro rata as deductions are allowed to the partnership. See also *Pratt v. Commissioner,* 64 T.C. 203, 213 (1975), *affd. on this ground,* 550 F. 2d 1023 (5th Cir. 1977).

e. Application of § 707(c) to a fixed amount guaranteed payment.

There are two types of guaranteed payments: fixed amount guaranteed payments and so-called "minimum amount guaranteed payments," i.e., guaranteed payments resulting from arrangements whereby, taking into consideration the partner's distributive share, a partner is assured of receiving a minimum amount and may receive an even greater amount. This latter type of guaranteed payment is discussed *infra.*

The application of § 707(c) to a fixed amount guaranteed payment is best demonstrated using an example. Return to the example regarding the partnership formed by Jackson and Will (the JW Partnership) at the beginning of this Overview. Applying § 707(c), the $50,000 annual "salary" to be paid to Jackson for his managerial services is a classic "guaranteed payment" within the meaning of § 707(c), i.e., the amount to be paid Jackson was determined without reference to the JW Partnership's income and was for services rendered by Jackson in his capacity as a partner. Moreover, it is a fixed amount guaranteed payment, i.e., Jackson is entitled to a specified dollar amount that does not vary. Applying § 707(c), the $50,000 salary would be includible in gross income by Jackson and would be deductible by the partnership. § 61(a)(1) and § 162. Thus, if, disregarding the $50,000 payment to Jackson, the partnership had only $30,000 of income, all of it ordinary, the partnership would have a $20,000 ordinary loss when, pursuant to § 707(c), it was allowed a $50,000 § 162 deduction for the amount paid to Jackson.[17]

When the dust settled, Jackson would have $50,000 of ordinary income under § 61(a) and Jackson and Will, as equal partners, would each have a $10,000 share of the partnership's $20,000 tax loss.[18] As provided by Reg. § 1.707-1(c), Jackson would be required to include the $50,000 of ordinary income in his gross income for the year in which the partnership deducted the payment "as paid or accrued under its method of accounting." Thus, for example, if the partnership were an accrual method taxpayer, Jackson would have to include the $50,000 in his gross income for the year in which the partnership accrued the salary expense, even though he was a cash method taxpayer and the partnership did not pay him the $50,000 salary until the following year. See Reg. § 1.707-1(c)(1) Examples 1 and 3.

By contrast, if the JW Partnership's $30,000 of income in this example were all long-term capital gain, Reg. § 1.707-1(c) Ex. 4 indicates that, "since the items of partnership income or loss must be segregated under § 702(a)," the JW Partnership would be treated as having $30,000 of long- term capital gain and an ordinary loss of $50,000. In addition to having $50,000 of ordinary income as a result of the guaranteed payment, Jackson would be allocated $15,000 of the partnership's long-term capital gain and $25,000 of the partnership's ordinary loss.

f. Application of § 707(c) to "minimum amount guaranteed payments."

Assume, in the JW Partnership example above, the partnership agreement provided that Jackson, instead of being entitled to a "salary" of $50,000, was to receive 50% of the partnership income as determined before taking into account any guaranteed amount. In no case, however, was Jackson to receive less than $70,000. Assuming the income of the partnership were $100,000 determined before taking into account any guaranteed payment, does any part of the $70,000 to be received by Jackson constitute a guaranteed payment? Review Reg. § 1.707-1(c) Ex. 2. Applying that regulation to the facts of our example, the answer would be "Yes." Jackson's distributive share of the $100,000 of partnership income would be $50,000; the other $20,000 Jackson is to receive would constitute a guaranteed payment.[19] The $20,000 guaranteed payment would be deductible by the partnership pursuant to § 162. Thus, the partnership would have $80,000 of net

---

[17] Note that, because § 707(c) and the regulations interpreting that provision already provide for the matching of income and deductions, § 267(a)(2) is not applicable. § 267(e)(4).

[18] Section 707(c) thus negates the complex analysis utilized by the decision in *Lloyd v. Commissioner* and reaches precisely the result that was reached in the analysis of the JW Partnership example above when a pure entity approach was applied.

[19] If, instead, the partnership had $200,000 of income, Jackson's distributive share would be $100,000

income to be divided between the partners pursuant to their distributive shares, i.e., $50,000 to Jackson and $30,000 to Will.[20]

What result if the $100,000 of partnership income consisted of $60,000 of ordinary income and $40,000 of long-term capital gain? Again, the guaranteed payment, under Reg. § 1.707-1(c) Ex. 2, equals $20,000, all of which constitutes ordinary income. The regulation, however, fails to address how the remaining ordinary income and long-term capital gain would be allocated to the partners under circumstances such as these. Revenue Ruling 69-180, included in the materials, does. Pursuant to that ruling, after taking into account the $20,000 guaranteed payment, the partnership would have ordinary income of $40,000 (i.e., $60,000 less $20,000 guaranteed payment). The taxable income of the partnership would thus be $80,000 (i.e., $40,000 of ordinary income plus $40,000 of long-term capital gain). As determined above, Jackson's distributive share of the taxable income is $50,000. Consequently, according to Revenue Ruling 69-180, the effective profit-sharing ratio for the year is as follows: Jackson — 50,000/80,000 or five-eighths; and Will — 30,000/80,000 or three-eighths. Thus, Jackson's *distributive share* of the partnership's remaining $40,000 of ordinary income will be five-eighths of $40,000, or $25,000. Likewise, his distributive share of the partnership's $40,000 of long-term capital gain will be five-eighths of $40,000, or $25,000. Thus, in the current year, Jackson will recognize the following amounts:

$20,000 of ordinary income (the guaranteed payment);

a $25,000 distributive share of the partnership's ordinary income (after taking the guaranteed payment into account); and

a $25,000 distributive share of the partnership's long-term capital gain.[21]

---

and, according to Reg. § 1.707-1(c) Ex. 2, no part of the $100,000 would constitute a guaranteed payment.

[20] In July 2015, the Treasury and the Service issued proposed regulations providing guidance regarding transactions involving disguised payments for services under § 707(a)(2)(A). These proposed regulations are addressed in Chapter 18. The proposed regulations, however, require changes to the existing regulations under § 707(c), specifically Reg. § 1.707-1(c) Ex. 2, discussed above. The proposed regulations change the example to read as follows:

Example 2. Partner C in the CD partnership is to receive 30 percent of partnership income, but not less than $10,000. The income of the partnership is $60,000, and C is entitled to $18,000 (30 percent of $60,000). Of this amount, $10,000 is a guaranteed payment to C. The $10,000 guaranteed payment reduces the partnership's net income to $50,000, of which C receives $8,000 as C's distributive share.

As demonstrated by the proposed example, the effect of this change is to treat the *entire* minimum amount payment as a § 707(c) guaranteed payment, regardless of the amount. Thus, in the Jackson example above, the full $70,000 minimum amount would be a guaranteed payment even though Jackson's 50% distributive share would have produced an income allocation of $50,000. The $70,000 would constitute ordinary income to Jackson and would be deductible by the partnership. As a result of the $70,000 deduction, the partnership would have $30,000 of net income. Pursuant to the partnership agreement, Jackson apparently would not be entitled to any of the $30,000 in net income. Under the proposed regulations, if, as in footnote 19, the partnership had income of $200,000 and Jackson's 50% interest entitled him to $100,000, $70,000 of that amount would constitute a guaranteed payment. As a result, the partnership's net income would be reduced to $130,000, of which $30,000 would be Jackson's distributive share. The change made by the proposed regulations is not effective until final regulations are promulgated.

[21] Noting that Revenue Ruling 69-180 is inconsistent with the proposed regulations briefly discussed in footnote 20, Treasury and the Service have indicated they will revise this ruling when the proposed

g. Transfer of partnership property other than cash in satisfaction of a guaranteed payment.

A partnership may transfer property other than cash in satisfaction of a guaranteed payment. In Revenue Ruling 2007-40,[22] the Service considered the tax consequences of a partnership's transfer of Blackacre (FMV of $800x and Adjusted Basis of $500x) to a partner in satisfaction of a guaranteed payment. The ruling addressed whether the nonrecognition rule of § 731(b) applied to negate gain to the partnership on this transfer. The Service concluded it did not. The Service reasoned as follows:

> A taxpayer that conveys appreciated or depreciated property in satisfaction of an obligation, or in exchange for the performance of services, recognizes gain or loss equal to the difference between the basis in the distributed property and the property's fair market value. *See, e.g., International Freighting Corp., Inc. v. Commissioner,* 135 F.2d 310 (2d Cir. 1943), *United States v. General Shoe Corp.,* 282 F.2d 9 (6th Cir. 1960).
>
> A transfer of partnership property in satisfaction of a partnership's obligation to make a guaranteed payment under § 707(c) is a sale or exchange under § 1001. Because the transfer is a sale or exchange under § 1001, it is not a distribution within the meaning of § 731. Accordingly, the nonrecognition rule in § 731(b) does not apply to the transfer. [As a result, the partnership would be required to recognize $300x gain on the transfer.]

4. Distributive Share — Partner Acting in Her Capacity as Partner and Payments Determined with Reference to Partnership Income

Neither § 707(a)(1) or (c) applies if a special allocation of partnership income is made to a partner who, acting in her partner capacity, renders services or provides property to the partnership for its use. (Note the payment is not a § 707(a) payment because the partner is acting in her partner capacity. The payment is not a § 707(c) guaranteed payment because it is determined with reference to partnership income.) Assuming it satisfies the substantial economic effect test, this special allocation of income will be treated as a distributive share of partnership income and taxed accordingly. As discussed in Chapter 7, the character of any distributive share of partnership income depends on the items of income determined at the partnership level. Thus, for example, if all of the income of a partnership for the year is long-term capital gain, that will be the character of a partner's distributive share of that income. See § 702. Contrast this characterization rule to that with respect to

---

regulations are issued in final form. Consider the example above where partnership income consisted of $60,000 of ordinary income and $40,000 of long-term capital gain, and Jackson was guaranteed no less than $70,000. Under the proposed regulations, the entire $70,000 minimum payment to Jackson would constitute a guaranteed payment, the partnership would have $10,000 of ordinary loss (i.e., $60,000 of ordinary income less the $70,000 deduction for guaranteed payment) and $40,000 of long-term capital gain. Again, Jackson would have $70,000 of ordinary income. Pursuant to the partnership agreement, Jackson would apparently not be entitled to any of the $40,000 long-term capital gain or any of the $10,000 ordinary loss.

[22] 2007-1 C.B. 1426.

§ 707(a)(1) or (c) payments. Pursuant to § 706(a), a partner must include her distributive share of partnership income or loss for the partner's taxable year in which or with which the taxable year of the partnership ends. Because a partnership receives no deduction for a partner's distributive share of income, we do not need to concern ourselves with the capitalization rules of § 263 as we would with regard to either a § 707(a)(1) payment or a § 707(c) guaranteed payment.

D. Conclusion

As discussed above, amounts paid or to be paid to a partner for services rendered to a partnership or for the use of property provided the partnership will be treated in one of three ways:[23]

1. As a payment made to a nonpartner. § 707(a)(1).
2. As a "guaranteed payment" under § 707(c).
3. As a distributive share. §§ 702, 704, and 706(a).

The character of the payments, the timing of inclusion and deductions with respect to the payments, and application of the § 263 capitalization rules to the payments are all implicated depending on which of the three treatments above the payments are accorded.

Revenue Ruling 81-301
1981-2 C.B. 144

ISSUE:

Is an allocation based on a percentage of gross income paid to an advisor general partner subject to § 707 (a) of the Internal Revenue Code, under the circumstances described below?

FACTS

ABC is a partnership formed in accordance with the Uniform Limited Partnership Act of a state and is registered with the Securities and Exchange Commission as an open-end diversified management company pursuant to the Investment Company Act of 1940, as amended. Under the partnership agreement, ABC's assets must consist only of municipal bonds, certain readily-marketable temporary investments, and cash. The agreement provides for two classes of general partners: (1) "director general partners" (directors) who are individuals and (2) one "adviser general partner" (adviser) that is a corporate investment adviser registered as such in accordance with the Investment Advisers Act of 1940, 15 U.S.C.A., § 80b-5 (1971).

Under the partnership agreement, the directors are compensated and have

---

[23] The amounts paid or to be paid could also constitute a so-called "disguised payment" that § 707(a)(2) would recharacterize as a payment made to a nonpartner, thus making the payment subject to the rules of § 707(a)(1). Section 707(a)(2) is discussed in detail in Chapter 18.

complete and exclusive control over the management, conduct, and operation of ABC's activities. The directors are authorized to appoint agents and employees to perform duties on behalf of ABC and these agents may be, but need not be, general partners. Under the partnership agreement, the adviser has no rights, powers, or authority as a general partner, except that subject to the supervision of the directors, the adviser is authorized to manage the investment and reinvestment of ABC's assets. The adviser is responsible for payment of any expenses incurred in the performance of its investment advisory duties, including those for office space facilities, equipment and any of its personnel used to service and administer ABC's investments. The adviser is not personally liable to the other partners for any losses incurred in the investment and reinvestment of ABC's assets.

The nature of the adviser's services are substantially the same as those it renders as an independent contractor or agent for persons other than ABC and, under the agreement, the adviser is not precluded from engaging in such transactions with others.

Each general partner, including the adviser general partner, is required to contribute sufficient cash to ABC to acquire at least a one percent interest in the partnership. The agreement requires an allocation of 10 percent of ABC's daily gross income to the adviser. After reduction by the compensation allocable to the directors and the adviser, ABC's items of income, gain, loss, deduction, and credit are divided according to the percentage interests held by each partner.

The adviser's right to 10 percent of ABC's daily gross income for managing ABC's investment must be approved at least annually by a majority vote of the directors or a majority vote of all the partnership interests. Furthermore, the directors may remove the adviser as investment manager at any time on 60 days written notice to the adviser. The adviser can terminate its investment manager status by giving 60 days written notice to the directors. The agreement provides that the adviser will no longer be a general partner after removal or withdrawal as investment manager, but will continue to participate as a limited partner in the income, gains, losses, deductions, and credits attributable to the percentage interest that it holds.

LAW AND ANALYSIS

§ 61 (a) (1) of the Code provides that, except as otherwise provided by law, gross income means all income from whatever source derived including compensation for services, including fees, commissions, and similar items.

§ 702 (a) of the Code provides that in determining the income tax of a partner, each partner must take into account separately such partner's distributive share of the partnership's items of income, gain, loss, deduction, or credit.

§ 707 (a) of the Code provides that if a partner engages in a transaction with a partnership other than as a member of such partnership, the transaction shall, except as otherwise provided in § 707, be considered as occurring between the partnership and one who is not a partner.

§ 1.707-1 (a) of the Income Tax Regulations provides that a partner who engages in a transaction with a partnership other than in the capacity as a partner shall be treated as if not a member of the partnership with respect to such transaction. Such transactions include the rendering of services by the partner to the partnership. In all cases, the substance of the transaction will govern rather than its form.

§ 707 (c) of the Code provides that to the extent determined without regard to the income of the partnership, payments to a partner for services shall be considered as made to one who is not a member of the partnership, but only for purposes of § 61 (a) and, subject to § 263, for purposes of § 162 (a).

Although the adviser is identified in the agreement as an "adviser general partner," the adviser provides similar services to others as part of its regular trade or business, and its management of the investment and reinvestment of ABC's assets is supervised by the directors. Also it can be relieved of its duties and right to compensation at any time (with 60 days' notice) by a majority vote of the directors. Further, the adviser pays its own expenses and is not personally liable to the other partners for any losses incurred in the investment and reinvestment of ABC's assets. The services performed by the adviser are, in substance, not performed in the capacity of a general partner but are performed in the capacity of a person who is not a partner.

The 10 percent daily gross income allocation paid to the adviser is paid to the adviser in its capacity other than as a partner. Therefore, the gross income allocation is not a part of the adviser's distributive share of partnership income under § 702 (a) of the Code or a guaranteed payment under § 707 (c).

HOLDING

The 10 percent daily gross income allocation paid to the adviser is subject to § 707 (a) of the Code and taxable to the adviser under § 61 as compensation for services rendered. The amount paid is deductible by the partnership under § 162, subject to the provisions of § 265.

Revenue Ruling 69-180
1969-1 C.B. 183

Advice has been requested as to the proper method for computing the partners' distributive shares of the partnership's ordinary income and capital gains under the circumstances described below.

F and G are partners in FG, a two-man partnership. The partnership agreement provides that F is to receive 30 percent of the partnership income as determined before taking into account any guaranteed amount, but not less than 100x dollars. The agreement also provides that any guaranteed amount will be treated as an expense item of the partnership in any year in which F's percentage of profits is less than the guaranteed amount. The partnership agreement makes no provision for sharing capital gains.

For the taxable year in question the partnership income before taking into account any guaranteed amount, is 200x dollars, and consists of 120x dollars of ordinary income and 80x dollars of capital gains.

Section 707(c) of the Internal Revenue Code of 1954 provides that, to the extent determined without regard to the income of the partnership, payments to a partner for services or the use of capital shall be considered as made to one who is not a member of the partnership, but only for the purpose of § 61(a) (relating to gross income) and § 162(a) of the Code (relating to trade or business expenses). § 1.707-1(c) of the Income Tax Regulations provides that for purposes of § 61(a) of the Code guaranteed payments are regarded as a partner's distributive share of ordinary income. Thus, a guaranteed payment is includable in gross income of the recipient as ordinary income, and is deductible by the partnership from its ordinary income as a business expense.

For Federal income tax purposes, F's guaranteed payment, as defined under § 707(c) of the Code is 40x dollars, 100x dollars (minimum guarantee) less 60x dollars distributive share (30 percent of partnership income of 200x dollars). See Example 2 of § 1.707-1(c) of the regulations and Revenue Ruling 66-95, C.B. 1966-1, 169.

For Federal income tax purposes, the taxable income of the partnership amounts to 160x dollars (80x dollars of ordinary income and 80x dollars of capital gains).

§ 704(b) of the Code and § 1.704-1(b)(1) of the regulations provide that if the partnership agreement does not specifically provide for the manner of sharing a particular item or class of items of income, gain, loss, deduction, or credit of the partnership, a partner's distributive share of any such item shall be determined in accordance with the manner provided in the partnership agreement for the division of the general profits or losses (that is, the taxable income or loss of the partnership as described in § 702(a)(9) of the Code). In applying this rule, the manner in which the net profit or loss (computed after excluding any item subject to a recognized special allocation) is actually credited on the partnership books to the accounts of the partners will generally determine each partner's share of taxable income or loss as described in § 702(a)(9) of the Code. Thus, F and G share the capital gains in the same ratio in which they share the general profits from business operations.

The partnership income for the taxable year, after deduction of the guaranteed payment, is 160x dollars. Of this amount, F's distributive share, as determined above under the partnership agreement is 60x dollars. Therefore, G's distributive share is 100x dollars. Hence, the effective profit sharing ratio for the year in question is 6/16 for F and 10/16 for G. Thus, as provided by § 704(b) of the Code, the partnership capital gains as well as the partnership ordinary income are to be shared in the ratio of 6/16 for F and 10/16 for G.

	F	G	Total
Ordinary income	30x dollars	50x dollars	80x dollars
Guaranteed payment	<u>40x dollars</u>		<u>40x dollars</u>
Total ordinary income	**70x dollars**	**50x dollars**	**120x dollars**
Capital gain	<u>30x dollars</u>	<u>50x dollars</u>	<u>80x dollars</u>
Total	100x dollars	100x dollars	200x dollars

AUTHORS' NOTE

Review Overview footnotes 20 and 21 above. Note that the Treasury and the Service intend to revise Revenue Ruling 69-180 to be consistent with proposed regulations addressing disguised payments for services and amending Reg. § 1.707-1(c) Ex. 2 to treat the "entire minimum [guaranteed] amount . . . as a guaranteed payment under section 707(c) regardless of the amount of the income allocation." *See* REG-115452-14, F.R. Vol. 80, No. 141, p. 43655 (July 23, 2015).

Chapter 14

PARTNERSHIP DISTRIBUTIONS

PART A:
Partnership Distributions — General Rules

I. PROBLEMS

1. Assume Jonathan is an equal partner in a three-person partnership and has held his partnership interest for 10 years. Jonathan's outside basis is $100,000 and he has a capital account of $250,000. With regard to each of the following alternative nonliquidating distributions, determine: (1) whether Jonathan will recognize any gain, (2) what basis Jonathan will have in each distributed asset, (3) the character of any gain or loss Jonathan will have upon a subsequent sale of the asset, (4) the impact of the distribution on Jonathan's outside basis, and (5) the impact of the distribution on Jonathan's capital account. In answering the questions, assume each of the non-cash assets distributed was purchased and held long-term by the partnership. In each situation presented, assume the distribution is pro rata, i.e., the partnership distributes to each of the three partners assets of the same character and value as those distributed to Jonathan.

   (a) The partnership distributes to Jonathan Inventory #1 with a fair market value of $25,000 and an adjusted basis of $5,000, and a tract of land held by the partnership for investment with a fair market value of $100,000 and an adjusted basis of $60,000.

   (b) The partnership distributes $110,000 in cash to Jonathan.

   (c) The partnership distributes to Jonathan Accounts Receivable with a fair market value of $25,000 and an adjusted basis of zero and Capital Asset A with a fair market value of $100,000 and an adjusted basis of $120,000.

   (d) Same as (c), except the partnership also distributes to Jonathan Capital Asset B with a fair market value of $75,000 and an adjusted basis of $50,000.

   (e) The partnership distributes to Jonathan cash of $30,000, Inventory #2 with a fair market value of $20,000 and an adjusted basis of $50,000 and Inventory #3 with a fair market value of $30,000 and an adjusted basis of $80,000.

2. Russell and Julie are equal partners in a calendar-year general partnership that has been in existence for 20 years. Russell has a $100,000 outside basis

in his partnership interest while Julie's outside basis is $200,000. Russell and Julie each have a $150,000 capital account. The partnership liquidates and distributes the following assets to Russell and Julie:

To Russell:

Asset	A/B	FMV
Cash	$75,000	$75,000
Inventory #1	$20,000	$15,000
Accounts Receivable	$0	$60,000

To Julie:

Asset	A/B	FMV
Inventory #2	$50,000	$75,000
Capital Asset #1	$30,000	$50,000
Capital Asset #2	$20,000	$25,000

How much gain or loss, if any, must Russell and Julie recognize on the liquidation? What basis will Russell and Julie take in each of the assets they receive?

3. Finn and Avon are equal partners in a general partnership. This year, Finn and Avon each receive a tract of raw land in a nonliquidating distribution from the partnership. The land in both cases is property the partnership purchased and has held for investment and the liabilities (noted below) encumbering the land represent the balance owing on loans incurred by the partnership in purchasing the tracts of land. The land Finn received (Tract #1) has a fair market value of $200,000 and is encumbered by a recourse liability in the amount of $50,000, which Finn assumes. The partnership has an adjusted basis in Tract #1 of $100,000. The land Avon received (Tract #2) has a far market value of $230,000 and is encumbered by a recourse liability in the amount of $80,000, which Avon assumes. The partnership has an adjusted basis in Tract #2 of $250,000. Prior to the distribution, Finn's outside basis in the partnership was $125,000 and Avon's outside basis was $90,000. What basis will Finn and Avon take in the tract of land each receives and what will their outside bases be following the distribution?

Assignment for Part A of Chapter 14:

Complete the Problems

Read: Internal Revenue Code: §§ 721, 724, 731, 732, 733, 735, 741, 752(a) and (b), 7703(a)(43). Skim §§ 704(c)(1)(B), 737, 751(b)–(d).
Treasury Regulations: §§ 1.704-1(b)(2)(iv)(b), (e); 1.731-1; 1.732-1(a)-(c); 1.741-1(a); and 1.752-1(f).

Materials: Overview
Revenue Ruling 79-205
Revenue Ruling 94-4

II. VOCABULARY

nonliquidating distributions
liquidating distributions
unrealized receivables
inventory

III. OBJECTIVES

1. To recall that a partnership will generally not recognize either gain or loss on the distribution of its assets.

2. To explain when gain will be recognized by a distributee partner under § 731 as a result of liquidating or nonliquidating distributions.

3. To recall that, as a general rule, no loss will be recognized by a partner as a result of a nonliquidating distribution.

4. To explain the circumstances under which a distributee partner may recognize loss on the complete liquidation of a partnership.

5. To determine the character of any gain or loss recognized on liquidating or nonliquidating distributions.

6. To determine the bases of assets distributed to partners in a nonliquidating distribution.

7. To determine the bases of assets distributed to partners on the liquidation of a partnership.

8. To explain when a distributee partner may take a basis in distributed assets greater than the basis the partnership had in the assets.

9. To determine the character of assets received by partners in a nonliquidating distribution or on the liquidation of a partnership.

10. To explain the tax consequences to partners who assume liabilities encumbering property distributed to them by the partnership.

IV. OVERVIEW

In Chapter 2, we introduced the nonrecognition regime of Subchapter K, noting that, as a general rule, neither gain nor loss will be recognized by a partnership or its partners on the contribution of property to the partnership or on the distribution of property by a partnership to its partners. Instead, as is typical with nonrecognition rules, the unrecognized gain or loss is preserved through the basis mechanism. Thus, from a tax perspective, moving property into and out of partnerships is generally painless.

Since 1954, however, Congress on a number of occasions has amended the provisions of Subchapter K, adding a number of anti-abuse provisions to prevent distributions from (a) shifting income, gain and loss between and among partners and (b) converting ordinary income into capital gain.[1] Notwithstanding these

---

[1] E.g., §§ 704(c)(1)(B) and (2), 737, and 751.

provisions, however, nonrecognition of gain or loss remains the general rule insofar as distributions from partnerships are concerned.

This chapter is the first of a series of chapters addressing various Code provisions related to distributions. Distributions can be divided into two categories, (1) "nonliquidating distributions"[2] and (2) "liquidating distributions." In turn, liquidating distributions can be divided into two subcategories: (a) distributions that liquidate the entire partnership and (b) distributions that liquidate only the interest of a partner (a "retiring" partner) rather than liquidating the interests of all partners. *This chapter addresses only nonliquidating distributions and distributions that liquidate the entire partnership. Chapter 17 will address the special tax treatment provided for liquidating distributions made to a "retiring" partner in a continuing partnership.*[3] More specifically, this chapter will address a range of issues associated with nonliquidating distributions and distributions that liquidate the entire partnership, including: (1) the nonrecognition of gain except with respect to certain cash distributions; (2) the nonrecognition of loss on nonliquidating distributions and the recognition of loss on liquidating distributions; (3) the basis of property distributed; (4) adjustments to the distributee's outside basis in the context of nonliquidating distributions; (5) the effect of distribution of encumbered assets; and (6) the character of gain or loss on disposition of distributed property. Subsequent chapters will address matters such as the special basis adjustment rules associated with distributions,[4] and the tax consequences of so-called "disproportionate distributions."[5]

---

[2] The Code and Regulations generally distinguish between "distributions in liquidation of a partner's interest in the partnership" and "distributions other than in liquidation of a partner's interest." See, e.g., §§ 731(a)(2), 732(a) and (b) and 733. For simplicity's sake, we adopt in this casebook the terms "liquidating distributions" and "nonliquidating distributions," although we recognize that "nonliquidating distributions" are often referred to as either "current distributions." or "operating distributions." Thus, the term "nonliquidating distributions" in this casebook refers to distributions that do not liquidate a partner's entire interest in the partnership; the term "liquidating distributions" refers to distributions that liquidate the partner's interest or the entire partnership.

[3] Section 736 provides special rules for determining the tax consequences of liquidating distributions to a "retiring" partner and will be the focus of Chapter 17. As is indicated in that chapter, § 736 is generally inapplicable to the liquidation of the entire partnership. It, however, can apply to a two-person partnership where one partner's interest is being liquidated over time.

[4] Chapter 15 addresses § 734, which provides for adjustments to the bases of partnership assets under certain circumstances.

[5] Chapter 16 addresses § 751(b), which applies to so-called "disproportionate distributions," treating such distributions in part as sales or exchanges and in part as distributions. Chapter 15 addresses § 751(b) in detail. *To ensure that this chapter focuses on only the basics, we will assume all distributions are made pro rata among the partners, i.e., when a partnership distributes property, it will distribute the same kind of property (inventory, capital asset, etc.) to each partner in proportion to that partner's interest in the partnership. In so doing, we will avoid the application of § 751(b).*

A. Nonliquidating Distributions

1. The Nonrecognition Rule of § 731

Consistent with congressional intent to allow partners to move property into and out of partnerships without triggering recognition of gain or loss except in limited situations, § 731 provides in relevant part as follows:

---

§ 731. Extent of Recognition of Gain or Loss on Distribution

(a) Partners. In the case of a distribution by a partnership to a partner

(1) gain shall not be recognized to such partner, except to the extent that any money distributed exceeds the adjusted basis of such partner's interest in the partnership immediately before the distribution, and

(2) loss shall not be recognized to such partner, except . . . upon a distribution in liquidation . . .

Any gain . . . recognized under this subsection shall be considered as gain or loss from the sale or exchange of the partnership interest of the distributee partner.

(b) No gain or loss shall be recognized to a partnership on a distribution to a partner of property, including money.

For our purposes in this chapter, § 731(a) and (b) make three critical points regarding nonliquidating distributions[6]:

1. A nonliquidating distribution will result in recognition of gain by a distributee partner only in one instance, that is, where cash is distributed in excess of a partner's outside basis; a nonliquidating distribution of property other than cash will not result in gain recognition regardless of the distributee's outside basis.[7]

---

[6] To prevent game playing, some nonliquidating distributions are recharacterized by the Code and regulations as sales or exchanges that, in turn, can result in the recognition of gain or loss by partners or a partnership. *See, e.g.,* §§ 704(c)(1)(B), 737, and 751(b). These recharacterization provisions will be discussed in later chapters.

[7] Even if the property distributed is § 1245 or § 1250 property, §§ 1245(b)(3) and 1250(d)(3) provide specific exceptions for distributions subject to § 731. In effect, the § 1245 or § 1250 taint will continue to attach to the distributed property. *See* §§ 1245(b)(6)(A) and 1250(d)(6)(A). For example, if a partnership distributed to a partner business equipment with a fair market value of $50,000 and an adjusted basis of $10,000, none of the § 1245 gain inherent in the equipment would be recognized on the distribution and the property would continue to be § 1245 property in the partner's hands. If the equipment continued to be depreciable in the distributee/partner's hands, § 168(i)(7) would require the partner to continue depreciating the property using the same method and time period for depreciation as used by the partnership, i.e., the distributee/partner would stand in the partnership's shoes when it came to the continued depreciation of the property.

2. A nonliquidating distribution will never result in loss recognition by a distributee partner because, by definition, a nonliquidating distribution doesn't terminate a partner's interest and, as a result, a determination cannot be made regarding whether the distributee has actually sustained a loss on her investment in the partnership.[8]

3. A nonliquidating distribution will never result in gain or loss recognition to the partnership.[9]

The operation of the three § 731 nonrecognition rules above is best illustrated by means of a simple example.

Example 1: Assume an LLC (taxed as a partnership) in the business of buying and selling real estate distributes two undeveloped residential lots to its only members, Max and Justin, who each receive one lot. Each lot has a fair market value of $50,000, was purchased six years ago by the LLC, has an adjusted basis of $10,000, and has been held by the LLC for sale to customers as part of its inventory of residential properties.[10] Although Max and Justin have equal interests in the LLC and, during the lifetime of the LLC, have reported equal shares of income, gain, deduction, and loss, their outside bases differ because of the adjusted basis each had in the assets they contributed to the LLC. Thus, assume that immediately prior to the distribution in question, Max had an outside basis of $25,000 and Justin had an outside basis of $125,000. Max and Justin intend to hold for investment purposes the lots distributed to them. Assume also that, prior to the distribution of the lots, the fair market value of each partner's LLC interest was $100,000. Thus, there was $75,000 of gain inherent in Max's one-half interest in the LLC ($100,000 FMV of interest less Max's 25,000 outside basis) and $25,000 of loss inherent in Justin's one-half interest in the LLC (Justin's outside basis of $125,000 less the $100,000 FMV of his interest).

Analysis: Outside basis represents a partner's unrecovered cost in his interest in a partnership. Absent § 731, it would appear the receipt of the lot would result in the recognition of gain by Max because the value of the lot exceeds Max's outside basis or unrecovered cost. By contrast, Justin's outside basis exceeds the value of the lot he receives, raising a question as to whether Justin should recognize some part of the loss inherent in his partnership interest. At the same time, one might also question whether the transfer of the lots by the LLC would result in the LLC's recognition of the gain inherent in the distributed lots. Section 731, however, negates recognition of any gain or loss by the LLC or its members. Max will recognize no gain on the receipt of the lot because, under § 731(a)(1), gain can only be triggered if cash is distributed. Justin will not recognize any loss because § 731(a)(2) provides for loss recognition only on the liquidation

---

[8] Note how, with respect to loss recognition, § 731(a)(2) is limited to *liquidating distributions*.

[9] While § 731 will not trigger gain or loss at the partnership level, other provisions, e.g., § 751(b), may result in gain or loss recognition.

[10] Had the lots been contributed by one of the members, we would have to worry about provisions, e.g. §§ 704(c)(1)(B) and 737, which will be addressed in later chapters of this casebook.

of a partner's interest.[11] Section 731(b) likewise makes clear that the partnership will recognize no gain on the distribution of the lots to Max and Justin.[12]

2. Related Rules Applicable to Nonliquidating Distributions

In the above example, having applied § 731 and determined that no gain or loss is recognized by the parties on the distribution of the lots, you should be asking yourself a number of questions regarding the consequences to Max and Justin: (a) What basis will they take in the lot each receives? (b) How will the distribution affect their outside bases? (c) How will their capital accounts be affected by the distribution? (d) What holding period will they have in the lot each receives? (e) Will the fact that they intend to hold the lots as investment property mean that any gain or loss on a subsequent sale of the lots will constitute capital gain? Let's examine each of these questions and the relevant Code provisions that guide our resolution of the questions.

a. Basis of Distributed Property — The General Rule of § 732.

As noted above, unrecognized gain and loss is preserved through the basis mechanism. In the above example, $40,000 of gain inhered in each lot, i.e., each lot had a fair market value of $50,000 and an adjusted basis to the LLC of $10,000. That $40,000 of gain can be preserved by simply giving Max and Justin the same bases in the lots as the LLC's adjusted bases in those lots. In other words, with respect to the lot each receives, Max and Justin should "stand in the LLC's shoes." Section 732(a) addresses the basis of distributed property and confirms that Max and Justin will generally take the same basis as that of the LLC, i.e., they will have a *transferred basis*[13] in the residential lots they receive. Section 732 provides in relevant part:

---

[11] In other words, as is generally the case, loss is only recognized when there is a closed transaction. Here, Justin continues to have an interest in the LLC after the distribution and thus it would be premature to conclude that he has suffered any tax loss on his investment in the LLC. Furthermore, even if the liquidation requirement of § 731(a)(2) were satisfied, no loss would be recognized by Justin because he has received property other than the property described in § 731(a)(2)(A) and (B).

[12] Section 731 reflects the aggregate approach to the tax treatment of partnerships discussed earlier in this casebook. In effect, the nonrecognition rule of § 731 treats Max and Justin as the owners of whatever property is held by the LLC. Thus, when the LLC distributes the lots, it is just as though Max and Justin are giving themselves their own property. Obviously, under those circumstances, no gain or loss should be recognized. As a result of the distribution, the fair market value of Max's and Justin's respective interests in the LLC will be reduced from $100,000 to $50,000. Of course, the post-distribution value of each LLC interest, plus the FMV of each residential lot equals $100,000, i.e., the same value each member had immediately before the distribution.

[13] § 7703(a)(43).

> ### § 732. Basis of Distributed Property Other Than Money
>
> (a) Distributions other than in liquidation of a partner's interest. —
>
> (1) **General rule.** — The basis of property (other than money) distributed by a partnership to a partner other than in liquidation of the partner's interest shall, except as provided in paragraph (2), be its adjusted basis to the partnership immediately before such distribution.
>
> (2) **Limitation.** — The basis to the distributee partner of property to which paragraph (1) is applicable shall not exceed the adjusted basis of such partner's interest in the partnership reduced by any money distributed in the same transaction.

Note, however, the limitation of § 732(a)(2). This provision recognizes that, in effect, § 732(a)(1)[14] allocates part or all of a partner's outside basis to the property received by the partner thereby preserving, insofar as possible, the unrecognized gain or loss inherent in the property when held by the partnership. In other words, a partner's outside basis is divided between the property the partner receives in the distribution and the partner's continuing interest in the partnership. Thus, the maximum basis allocable to property received in a distribution is necessarily the amount of the distributee partner's outside basis. To allocate any more basis to the distributed property would create a negative outside basis. Section 732(a)(2) and § 733 (discussed below) assure that will not happen. Because cash always has a basis equal to its face amount, § 732(a)(2) provides that a partner's outside basis must first be allocated to any cash received in a distribution before any of the partner's outside basis is allocated to other property distributed.

In the example above, Max and Justin each received a lot with an adjusted basis to the partnership that was less than Max's or Justin's outside basis. Thus, the limitation under § 732(a)(2) would not come into play. Rather, under § 732(a)(1), Max and Justin would take a $10,000 basis in the residential lot each received, thus preserving the $40,000 of gain inherent in each lot.

What would the result be if Max's outside basis at the time of the distribution were only $7,500? Under that circumstance, § 732(a)(2) would limit Max to a $7,500 basis in the residential lot. To give Max the same basis the partnership had in the lot, i.e., a $10,000 basis, would necessitate creating a negative $2,500 outside basis for Max or, absent that, to give Max $2,500 of basis at no cost. If basis refers to unrecovered cost, a negative basis makes no sense. Likewise, giving Max "free" basis makes no sense. "Wait a second," you protest. If Max takes only a $7,500 basis in the distributed lot, what happens to the remaining $2,500 basis the LLC had in the lot? It "disappears"! Thus, while only $40,000 of gain inhered in the lot when held by the partnership, $42,500 of gain inheres in the lot as a result of its distribution to Max. It appears that $2,500 of "extra" gain has been created. As you

---

[14] Section 733 also reflects this allocation of basis.

will study in the next chapter, if the partnership has made a § 754 election, § 734(b) will restore to a partnership any basis that "disappeared" as a result of a distribution, thus offsetting the "extra" gain that appears to be otherwise created.

b. Impact on Distributee's Outside Basis — § 733.

Implicit in § 732(a) is the idea that part (and sometimes all) of the distributee partner's outside basis is allocated to the distributed property. As a corollary, the distributee's outside basis must be decreased by the amount of basis allocated to money or other property the distributee receives. Section 733 so provides.

---

§ 733. Basis of Distributee Partner's Interest

In the case of a distribution by a partnership to a partner other than in liquidation of a partner's interest, the adjusted basis to such partner of his interest in the partnership shall be reduced (but not below zero) by —

(1) the amount of any money distributed to such partner, and

(2) the amount of the basis to such partner of distributed property other than money, as determined under section 732.

With respect to § 733, a number of points should be noted. First, § 733 only applies to nonliquidating distributions. [Why is it not applicable to distributions that liquidate a partner's interest?] Second, by providing that a nonliquidating distribution cannot reduce a partner's outside basis below zero, § 733 affirms that a distribution cannot create a negative outside basis. [As noted above, § 732(a)(2) plays an important role in this regard as it limits the basis that can be accorded distributed property to the amount of a partner's outside basis.] Third, in the case of distributions of property other than money, the reduction in outside basis mandated by § 733 requires that one first compute the basis accorded by § 732 to that distributed property. Finally, consistent with the understanding that money always has a basis equal to the face amount of the money, outside basis is reduced dollar-for-dollar by any cash distribution.

In our example, "when the dust settles" after the LLC's distribution of the lots, Max and Justin each take a § 732(a)(1) basis of $10,000 in the lot distributed to him. As a result, Max's outside basis is reduced to $15,000 and Justin's to $115,000 pursuant to § 733. In the aggregate, Max holds property worth $100,000 (i.e., an LLC interest worth $50,000 and a lot worth $50,000) with an adjusted basis of $25,000 (i.e., $15,000 outside basis and $10,000 basis in the lot). In the aggregate, Justin holds property worth $100,000 (i.e., an LLC interest worth $50,000 and a lot worth $50,000) with an adjusted basis of $125,000 (i.e., $115,000 outside basis and $10,000 basis in the lot). In sum, as a result of the application of §§ 731, 732, and 733, Max's and Justin's outside bases have been allocated between their LLC interest and the lot each received, and the gain or loss inherent in their LLC interests prior to the distribution of the lots has been preserved in the two assets each now holds.

c. Impact on Capital Accounts — Reg. § 1.704-1(b)(2)(iv)(b)(5).

Regulation § 1.704-1(b)(2)(iv)(b)(5) requires a distributee partner's capital account to be reduced by "the fair market value of property distributed to him by the partnership (net of liabilities that such partner is considered to assume or take subject to.)" To satisfy this requirement, Reg. § 1.704-1(b)(2)(iv)(e) provides:

> [T]he capital accounts of the partners first must be adjusted to reflect the manner in which the unrealized income, gain, loss, and deduction inherent in such property (that has not been reflected in the capital accounts previously) would be allocated among the partners if there were a taxable disposition of such property for the fair market value of such property . . .

Pursuant to this regulation, to determine the impact of the distribution of the lots on the capital accounts of Max and Justin, we would first adjust their capital accounts to reflect the manner in which the gain that inhered in the lots would be allocated to Max and Justin were the LLC to sell the lots for their fair market value. Were that the case, they would recognize $80,000 in gain [$100,000 (aggregate amount realized on the sale of the two lots) less $20,000 (aggregate basis of the lots)]. The $80,000 of gain would be allocated in equal shares to Max and Justin increasing their capital accounts by $40,000 each. Reg. § 1.704-1(b)(2)(iv)(b)(3). In turn, under Reg. § 1.704-1(b)(2)(iv)(b)(5) above, Max's and Justin's capital accounts would each be reduced by $50,000, i.e., the fair market value of the residential lot each received in the distribution.

d. Holding Period of Distributed Property — §§ 735 and 1223.

Consistent with the concept that a distributee partner stands in the shoes of the partnership, a partnership's holding period in distributed property is generally tacked to that of the distributee partner's holding period in the distributed property. §§ 735(b) and 1223(2). Thus, given the fact that the LLC in the example above had a long-term holding period in the two lots it distributed, Max and Justin would have a long-term holding period in the lot each received.

e. Character of Gain or Loss on Subsequent Sale of Distributed Property — § 735.

Assume Max sold the lot for $60,000 a year after receiving it from the LLC. As noted in the facts, Max held the lot for investment purposes. Given that Max had a $10,000 basis and a long-term holding period in the lot, one might assume the $50,000 gain Max recognized on the sale would be characterized under § 1222 as long-term capital gain. Note, however, that, if the LLC, instead of distributing the lot to Max, had sold it for $60,000, the LLC, which held the lot as inventory, would have $50,000 of ordinary income.

Can the ordinary income taint associated with the lot when held by the LLC be negated by the distribution of the lot to Max? That question should remind you of a similar question addressed in Chapter 2, i.e., whether the character of the gain or loss associated with property could be changed by contributing the property to a partnership. As you learned in Chapter 2, § 724 generally prevents a character shift when property is *contributed to* a partnership. For example, if one contributes accounts receivable to a partnership, any gain or loss resulting from the partnership's subsequent disposition of the accounts receivables will be treated as ordinary. Reread § 724 to see how it preserves the character of unrealized receivables, inventory, and capital loss property *contributed to* a partnership. Not surprisingly, Congress has enacted a similar provision — § 735 — to address the character of gain or loss resulting from the sale or other taxable disposition of property *distributed by* a partnership. Much like § 724, the purpose of § 735 is to prevent a character shift. Section 735, however, focuses on distributions of property from partnerships rather than on contributions to such entities. Consider the following excerpt from § 735:

---

§ 735. Character of Gain or Loss on Disposition of Distributed Property

(a) **Sale or exchange of certain distributed property.** —

(1) **Unrealized receivables.** — Gain or loss on the disposition by a distributee partner of unrealized receivables (as defined in § 751(c)) distributed by a partnership, shall be considered as ordinary income or as ordinary loss, as the case may be.

(2) **Inventory items.** — Gain or loss on the sale or exchange by a distributee partner of inventory items (as defined in § 751(d)) distributed by a partnership shall, if sold or exchanged within 5 years from the date of the distribution, be considered as ordinary income or as ordinary loss, as the case may be.

(b) **Holding period for distributed property.** — In determining the period for which a partner has held property received in a distribution from a partnership (other than for purposes of subsection (a)(2)), there shall be included the holding period of the partnership, as determined under § 1223, with respect to such property.

(c) **Special rules.** —

(2) **Substituted basis property.** —

(A) **In general.** — If any property described in subsection (a) is disposed of in a nonrecognition transaction, the tax treatment which applies to such property under such subsection shall also apply to any substituted basis property resulting from such transaction . . .

Note that § 735 applies only to unrealized receivables and inventory distributed by a partnership. But for § 735, Max could have converted what otherwise would have been ordinary income into long-term capital gain. With the enactment of § 735,

Congress prevented that result. Thus, Max will have $50,000 of ordinary income when he sells the lot.

Like § 724, § 735 imposes a five-year time limit on its application to inventory.[15] Thus, if Max were to sell the residential lot five years and one day after it was distributed to him, he could claim long-term capital gain treatment on any gain recognized. In other words, the ordinary income taint disappears. Congress was apparently satisfied that no tax abuse occurs if a partner receiving a distribution of inventory is willing to hold it long enough, i.e., at least five years.

Assume that, one year after they received the lots from the LLC, Max and Justin entered into a like-kind exchange whereby Max transferred his lot to Justin and Justin transferred his lot to Max. Six months later Max sold the lot he had received from Justin and recognized $50,000 of gain. Under those circumstances, could Max claim long-term capital gain treatment on the sale of the lot? The answer is "No." Review § 735(c)(2)(A). Obviously, Congress recognized that, without a provision addressing like-kind exchanges, taxpayers could easily thwart the congressional effort to prevent the conversion of ordinary income into capital gain.

While imposing the five-year limit on inventory, § 735 imposes no time limitation on its application to unrealized receivables[16] (e.g., accounts receivable) distributed by a partnership. Thus, any gain or loss recognized by a distributee partner on the disposition of any unrealized receivable distributed to him by the partnership will be characterized as ordinary.

f. Recognition of Gain on Distributions of Money[17] — §§ 731 and 741.

Having addressed the consequences of a simple nonliquidating distribution of property other than cash, let's now consider the consequences of cash distributions. Begin by recalling that, given the pass-through nature of partnerships, tax is imposed only at the partner level. See Chapter 7. Assume, for example, the LLC in which Max and Justin are members earned $10,000 of income in Year 1. Under § 701, the LLC would not be taxed on that income but, instead, under § 702, Max and Justin would each report and be taxed on their $5,000 distributive share of that income even though the LLC did not distribute any of that income to them. To prevent Max and Justin from being taxed again on that income when it is subsequently distributed, § 705 would increase Max's and Justin's outside bases by $5,000 each to reflect the income each had reported. When the LLC subsequently distributed $5,000 in cash to both Max and Justin, neither would have any gain, as each would have at least $5,000 of outside basis to offset the distribution. In other words, the $5,000 distribution each received would not exceed their outside basis and, consequently, no gain would be recognized under § 731(a)(1). To generalize, *if*

---

[15] Skim § 751(d) for the definition of "inventory." Note that "inventory," as defined, encompasses more than just property held for sale to customers in the ordinary course of a trade or business.

[16] Skim § 751(c), which defines "unrealized receivables." For our purposes at this point, it is sufficient to think of "unrealized receivables" as accounts receivable.

[17] Section 731(c) treats money as including "marketable securities." See the discussion in Part B of this chapter regarding the special treatment of distributions of marketable securities.

a partner receives a cash distribution equal to her share of undistributed profits for which she was previously taxed, no gain will be recognized on the distribution.

But what happens if a partner receives cash in an amount greater than her share of undistributed income for which the partner was previously taxed? Then we have to worry about the possibility of gain recognition. Consider the following example:

> **Example 2:** Assume the facts of Example 1 above except that, instead of distributing residential lots worth $50,000 each to Max and Justin, the LLC distributed $50,000 in cash to each of the members.

Regardless of a member's outside basis, a nonliquidating distribution of *property other than cash* will not cause the recognition of the gain inherent in a member's LLC interest because the gain can be preserved in the basis accorded the distributed property by § 732. The same is not true of a money distribution. As previously noted, money always has a basis equal to its face amount, i.e., $50,000 of cash has a $50,000 basis.[18] If Max and Justin each receive a nonliquidating distribution of $50,000 in cash, Justin can use $50,000 of his $125,000 outside basis to offset the $50,000 distribution (in effect allocating $50,000 of his outside basis to the cash distribution); Max cannot do the same because he has only $25,000 of outside basis. To the extent Max receives cash in excess of his outside basis — that is, he receives more money than he has unrecovered cost — § 731(a)(1) requires Max to report gain. In this example, Max must thus report $25,000 of gain. According to § 731(a), that gain will be considered as gain or loss from the sale or exchange of Max's LLC interest. Is Max's LLC interest a capital asset resulting in the gain being characterized as long-term capital gain?[19] § 741 answers that question affirmatively.

---

§ 741. Recognition and Character of Gain or Loss on Sale or Exchange

In the case of a sale or exchange of an interest in a partnership, gain or loss shall be recognized to the transferor partner. Such gain or loss shall be considered as gain or loss from the sale or exchange of a capital asset, except as otherwise provided in § 751 (relating to unrealized receivables and inventory items).

Thus, Max will have $25,000 in long-term capital gain.[20] By forcing Max to recognize gain under these circumstances, § 731 prevents what would otherwise be

---

[18] Read § 732(a) carefully and note that: (1) implicit in this section is the notion that money has a basis equal to its face amount — § 732(a)(1) addresses only the basis of property other than money — and (2) if money and other property are distributed to a partner, the maximum amount of outside basis available to be allocated to the other property is a partner's outside basis less any money distributed in the same transaction.

[19] We are assuming Max held his LLC interest for a number of years prior to the distribution.

[20] Section 751, referenced in § 741, will be studied in Chapter 16 and is not applicable in this situation.

a negative outside basis — that is, if we reduce Max's $25,000 outside basis by the $50,000 in cash distributed, Max would have a negative $25,000 outside basis. As noted above, a negative outside basis makes little sense. Congress prevents that result by requiring gain recognition. Given § 731(a)(1), it is just as though Max's outside basis of $25,000 is adjusted upward by the $25,000 of gain he recognized (a tax cost basis adjustment) and then Max's outside basis is adjusted downward for the distribution to him of the $50,000 in cash. Max's receipt of a $50,000 cash distribution thus results in Max completely recovering his basis, leaving him with a basis of zero. Of course, we don't have to go through all of those steps because § 733 simply directs Max to reduce his outside basis *(but not below zero)* by the amount of cash distributed to him.

Some of the questions considered with respect to distributions of property other than cash are irrelevant to distributions of cash. Thus, for example, we need not worry about the basis of cash or the application of § 735 on a subsequent disposition of cash. We do, however, have to consider the impact of a cash distribution on the member's capital accounts. Not surprisingly, the rule in this regard is straightforward. Regulation § 1.704-1(b)(2)(iv)(b)(4) requires the capital accounts of Max and Justin be reduced by $50,000 each, i.e., the amount of cash distributed to them. Of course, this is appropriate as they have each recovered $50,000 of their equity in the LLC.

3. Distributions of Encumbered Assets — § 752

As discussed in detail in Chapter 12, § 752 (a) treats an increase in a partner's share of liabilities resulting from the partner's assumption of a partnership liability as a contribution of money to the partnership. As a corollary, § 752(b) treats a decrease in a partner's share of the liabilities of a partnership as a distribution of cash to the partner. Let's consider how these rules of § 752 are applied when encumbered properties are distributed by a partnership to a partner.

> **Example 3:** Assume in Example 1 above the LLC had borrowed money to purchase the lots it ultimately distributed to Max and Justin. At the time of the distribution, the balance owing on the purchase money mortgage encumbering each lot was $5,000. Assume Max and Justin agreed to assume the $5,000 mortgage encumbering the lot each received. What are the consequences of the distribution under §§ 731, 732, 733, and 752? Assume Max's and Justin's outside bases, as indicated in Example 1, reflect their share of the purchase money mortgages encumbering the lots.[21]
>
> **Analysis:** Max and Justin are each assuming $5,000 of the LLC's liability and will therefore be treated under § 752(a) as contributing $5,000 in cash to the LLC. Simultaneously, however, they are each being relieved of their share of the mortgages encumbering the lots. As a result, each will be treated under § 752(b) as receiving a distribution of $5,000 in cash. Regulation § 1.752-1(f) allows a netting of the increase and the decrease in

---

[21] Recall that, when the LLC borrowed the money to acquire the lots, Max and Justin, as equal LLC members, would each have been treated as contributing additional cash to the LLC. As a result, each would have increased his outside basis. §§ 752(a) and 722.

liabilities experienced by the members. This netting results in a wash. Thus, neither Max nor Justin is treated as contributing money to or receiving any money from the partnership. Consequently, there is no increase or decrease in Max's or Justin's outside basis.

As in the Analysis of Example 1, Max and Justin will each take a $10,000 basis in the lot distributed to him,[22] and will each reduce his outside basis by $10,000.[23] As discussed above, their capital accounts will first each be increased by $40,000, i.e., their share of the gain inherent in the two lots distributed.[24] Each of their capital accounts will then be reduced by $45,000, i.e., the fair market value of the lot each received net of the $5,000 liability encumbering the lot.[25]

Example 4: Assume the facts of Example 3 except the lot received by Max had a fair market value of $70,000, an adjusted basis of $30,000, and was encumbered by a $25,000 purchase money mortgage the LLC incurred in purchasing the lot. Max assumed the $25,000 mortgage just as Justin assumed the $5,000 mortgage encumbering the $50,000 lot he received. Thus, the net value of the distribution Max and Justin each received was $45,000. What are the consequences to Max and Justin under §§ 731, 732, 733, and 752?

Analysis: This example is similar to Rev. Rul. 79-205, included in the materials. Prior to the distribution of the lots, the LLC owed a total of $30,000 on the two lots. Max and Justin each had a $15,000 share of that liability. As a result of the distribution, Max and Justin each experienced a $15,000 decrease in their share of LLC liability. At the same time, Max, having assumed the mortgage encumbering the lot distributed to him, experienced a $25,000 increase in his share of the LLC's liabilities while Justin experienced a $5,000 increase in his share of those liabilities as a result of assuming the mortgage encumbering the lot distributed to him. When we net the increases and decreases, Max has a net increase in liabilities of $10,000 while Justin has a net decrease in liabilities of $10,000.

As a result of the net increase in his share of LLC liabilities, Max is treated as making a cash contribution of $10,000 to the LLC. § 752(a). Max's $25,000 outside basis will therefore be increased to $35,000. § 722. When Max receives the lot, he will take a § 732(a)(1) basis in the lot of $10,000 and his outside basis will be reduced under § 733 to $25,000. As in Example 3, Max's capital account will be reduced by $45,000.

By contrast, the net decrease in Justin's share of LLC liabilities results in Justin constructively receiving a $10,000 distribution of cash from the LLC.[26] Because Justin's outside basis is greater than $10,000 — in this example

---

[22] § 732(a)(1).

[23] § 733.

[24] Reg. § 1.704-1(b)(2)(iv)(e).

[25] Reg. § 1.704-1(b)(2)(iv)(b)(5).

[26] § 752(b); Reg. § 1.752-1(f).

it is $125,000, no gain will be recognized by Justin on this constructive distribution of cash.[27] Justin will take a $10,000 basis in the lot he receives and, pursuant to § 733, his outside basis will be reduced by $20,000 (the $10,000 deemed cash distribution plus the $10,000 basis he takes in the lot) to $105,000. As in Example 3, Justin's capital account will be reduced by $45,000.

4. The § 732(a)(2) Limitation and the § 732(c) Allocation of Outside Basis Among Distributed Property

As noted above, a distributee's outside basis sets the limit for the aggregate amount of basis allocable to property, including money, distributed to that person. In so doing, § 732(a)(2) prevents a distribution from creating a negative outside basis; § 733 reaffirms this prohibition on negative basis by explicitly stating that the outside basis cannot be reduced below zero by a distribution of cash or other property. In applying § 732(a)(2), we must first reduce the distributee partner's outside basis by the amount of any money distributed to that partner.[28] The remaining outside basis is then allocated to any other property the partner received in the distribution.[29]

> **Example 5:** Assume that, as part of the same distribution in Example 1 above, the LLC also distributed $20,000 in cash to both Max and Justin. What basis would Max and Justin take in the residential lot each received as part of the distribution? What will their outside bases in the LLC be following the distribution?
>
> **Analysis:** Under § 732(a)(2), $20,000 of Max's outside basis of $25,000 would first be allocated to the cash Max received, thus leaving Max with only $5,000 of remaining outside basis. As a general rule, Max would take the same basis in the lot the LLC had, i.e., $10,000, but because Max's remaining outside basis is only $5,000, Max will take only a $5,000 basis in the lot.[30] [Note that pursuant to § 732(c)(1), discussed below, any basis remaining after a distributee partner's outside basis is reduced by any cash distributed is allocated to inventory and unrealized receivables before it is allocated to other property. Of course, in this example, other than the cash the only property that is distributed is the residential lot, which is inventory.] Applying § 733, Max's outside basis of $25,000 would be reduced to $0 by the combination of the $20,000 of cash received and the $5,000 basis allocated to the residential lot.

---

[27] § 731(a)(1).

[28] This ordering is advantageous as it enables the partner to utilize the maximum amount of outside basis to offset cash distributions, thereby reducing or negating gain recognition.

[29] When § 732(a)(2) applies to limit the basis a distributee partner takes in property received in a distribution, the partner's outside basis will necessarily become zero because the entire outside basis will have been allocated to the distributed properties.

[30] Again, this is an example of "disappearing basis," i.e., $5,000 of the partnership's $10,000 basis seems to disappear because Max will only take a $5,000 basis in the lot. As will be discussed in Chapter 15, if the LLC had a § 754 election in effect, the "disappearing" basis could be reallocated to other property held by the LLC.

Unlike Max, Justin has enough outside basis to negate application of § 732(a)(2). $20,000 of Justin's outside basis of $125,000 will first be allocated to the $20,000 of cash he received and, under § 732(a)(1), $10,000 of his remaining outside basis would be allocated to the residential lot, i.e., he would take the same basis in the residential lot as the LLC had in that lot. Under § 733, Justin's outside basis would be reduced to $95,000 as a result of the distribution of the cash and the lot.

When the § 732(a)(2) limitation applies and more than one noncash item of property is distributed to a partner, Congress allocates among the noncash properties the partner's outside basis reduced by any money distributed in the same transaction. Specifically, § 732(c)(1) requires the remaining outside basis to be allocated first to the ordinary income assets, i.e., inventory and unrealized receivables, distributed to a partner before any outside basis is allocated to other noncash assets. Through this ordering rule, Congress seeks to ensure that any ordinary income (or loss) inherent in the property when held by the partnership will be preserved in the hands of the distributee partner. Consider the following excerpt from § 732(c):

---

§ 732. Basis of Distributed Property Other Than Money

(c) Allocation of basis. —

(1) In general. — The basis of distributed properties to which subsection (a)(2) . . . is applicable shall be allocated —

(A) (i) first to any unrealized receivables (as defined in § 751(c)) and inventory items (as defined in § 751(d)) in an amount equal to the adjusted basis of each such property to the partnership, and

(ii) if the basis to be allocated is less than the sum of the adjusted bases of such properties to the partnership, then, to the extent any decrease is required in order to have the adjusted bases of such properties equal the basis to be allocated, in the manner provided in paragraph (3), and

(B) to the extent of any basis remaining after the allocation under subparagraph (A), to other distributed properties —

(i) first by assigning to each such other property such other property's adjusted basis to the partnership, and

(ii) then, to the extent any increase or decrease in basis is required in order to have the adjusted bases of such other distributed properties equal such remaining basis, in the manner provided in paragraph (2) or (3), whichever is appropriate.

(3) Method of allocating decrease. — Any decrease required under paragraph (1)(A) or (1)(B) shall be allocated—

(A) first to properties with unrealized depreciation in proportion to their respective amounts of unrealized depreciation before such decrease (but only to the extent of each property's unrealized depreciation), and

(B) then, to the extent such decrease is not allocated under subparagraph (A), in proportion to their respective adjusted bases (as adjusted under subparagraph (A)).

Consider the following example demonstrating the application of this special basis allocation provision.

Example 6: Assume a general partnership has two equal partners: Zola, who has an outside basis of $50,000, and Cormick, who has an outside basis of $30,000. On May 1 of this year, the partnership makes a nonliquidating distribution to each of the partners as follows:

	Asset	A/B	FMV
To Zola:	Inventory #1	$20,000	$30,000
	Inventory #2	$10,000	$15,000
	Capital Asset #1	$25,000	$45,000
To Cormick:	Inventory #3	$30,000	$30,000
	Inventory #4	$20,000	$15,000
	Capital Asset #2	$10,000	$45,000

Assume the partnership had purchased Capital Asset #1 and Capital Asset #2 five years ago. Zola and Cormick intend to hold as investments each asset distributed to them. What basis will Zola and Cormick take in each asset and what will their outside bases be in their partnership interests after the distribution?

Analysis: With respect to Zola, § 732(c)(1)(A)(i) will require that Zola's $50,000 outside basis be allocated first to any inventory or unrealized receivables Zola received. Here, she received two items of inventory. Thus, she will allocate her outside basis to Inventory #1 and #2 in an amount equal to the basis the partnership had in each of those inventory items. Zola will take a $20,000 basis in Inventory #1 and a $10,000 basis in Inventory #2. She has now allocated $30,000 of her $50,000 basis. Initially, § 732(c)(1)(B)(i) will require Zola to allocate to Capital Asset #1 an amount of basis equal to the partnership's adjusted basis in that asset, i.e., $25,000. Zola, however, has only $20,000 of remaining outside basis available to allocate to Capital Asset #1. Zola will, therefore, take a $20,000 adjusted basis in Capital Asset #1.[31] Applying § 733, Zola's outside basis will be

---

[31] Technically, the § 732(c) analysis would be as follows: (1) under § 732(c)(1)(B)(i), we would initially allocate a basis of $25,000 to Capital Asset #1; (2) because a decrease of $5,000 in the basis of Capital Asset #1 is required to ensure its adjusted basis does not exceed Zola's remaining outside basis of

reduced to $0.[32] (Note that, if the partnership had only a $15,000 basis in Capital Asset #1, Zola would have taken a $15,000 basis in Capital Asset #1 and, under § 733 would have a remaining outside basis of $5,000.

With respect to Cormick, § 732(c)(1)(A)(i) will initially allocate a basis to Inventory #3 and Inventory #4 in the amount of the adjusted basis the partnership had in each of those items. Thus, Inventory # 3 will be allocated an adjusted basis of $30,000 and Inventory #4 an adjusted basis of $20,000. Obviously, the combined basis allocations of $50,000 exceed by $20,000 Cormick's outside basis of $30,000, thereby necessitating a reduction in the initial adjusted basis of those two items of inventory pursuant to § 732(c)(1)(A)(ii). This latter provision directs us to allocate the $20,000 reduction between the two inventory items as provided in § 732(c)(3). Under § 732(c)(3)(A), $5,000 of the $20,000 decrease will first be allocated to Inventory #4 because it has "unrealized depreciation" in that amount.[33] This adjustment results in Inventory #4 now having a $15,000 basis. According to § 732(c)(3)(B), the remaining $15,000 basis decrease must be allocated between Inventory #3 and Inventory #4 "in proportion to their respective adjusted bases (as adjusted under subparagraph (A))." Inventory #3 has an adjusted basis of $30,000 and Inventory #4 has an adjusted basis (as noted above) of $15,000. In the aggregate, these two assets have an adjusted basis of $45,000. Because two-thirds (2/3) of the total adjusted

---

$20,000, § 732(c)(1)(B)(ii) directs us to § 732(c)(3) to allocate the $5,000 decrease. In this example, because there is only one asset, i.e., Capital Asset #1, to which the $5,000 decrease can be allocated, the adjusted basis of Capital Asset #1 will be reduced by $5,000 from $25,000 to $20,000. § 732(c)(3)(B). While this multi-step approach of § 732(c)(1)(B) is necessary where we are dealing with the allocation of remaining basis between or among a number of other distributed properties, there is no reason to go through all of these steps in a case like this when there is only one asset to which § 732(c)(1)(B) applies.

[32] Students may find it helpful to consider how § 732(c)(1) preserves the amount of income inherent in Inventory #1 and #2 at the expense of Capital Asset #1. Zola's outside basis was first allocated to the inventory items in an amount equal to the basis the partnership had in those items. As a result, in the hands of Zola, Inventory #1 continues to have $10,000 of gain inherent in it; Inventory #2 continues to have $5,000 of gain inherent in it. Pursuant to § 735, discussed above, if Zola sells these inventory items within five years of the distribution, any gain or loss would be ordinary, just as it would have been were the partnership to have sold those inventory items. The fact that Zola, unlike the partnership, held the distributed inventory items for investment purposes and not as inventory makes no difference. Congress has thus effectively preserved the amount and character of income associated with the distributed inventory. By contrast, because of the limitation of § 732(a)(2) and the operation of § 732(c), Capital Asset #1 will have only a $20,000 adjusted basis in Zola's hands as compared to the $25,000 adjusted basis it had in the hands of the partnership. Thus, in Zola's hands there is $25,000 of gain inherent in Capital Asset #1 rather than the $20,000 of gain that inhered in that asset when held by the partnership. This basis reduction resulting $5,000 of "extra" gain will be addressed in the next chapter.

[33] "Unrealized depreciation" is the amount by which the adjusted basis of the asset exceeds the asset's fair market value. Here, Inventory #4 has a fair market value of $15,000 and an adjusted basis of $20,000. Unlike Inventory #4, Inventory #3 has no "unrealized depreciation." By allocating the decrease in basis first to items having "unrealized depreciation," Congress apparently saw a benefit to the federal fisc of eliminating, to the extent possible, any built-in loss. Because taxpayers can pick and choose when to sell assets, one would expect a taxpayer to sell an asset with built-in loss before selling an asset with built-in gain. If the taxpayer had a choice, the taxpayer would therefore prefer to allocate a basis decrease to assets with gain and not to assets with loss. Taxpayer would then sell the loss assets first and defer the sale of gain assets as long as possible. To some extent, § 732(c)(3)(A) negates that technique.

basis is attributable to Inventory #3, 2/3 or $10,000 of the remaining decrease must be allocated to Inventory #3 and 1/3 or $5,000 allocated to Inventory #1. When this frenzy of adjustments is complete, Inventory #3 will have an adjusted basis of $20,000, and Inventory #4 will have an adjusted basis of $10,000. Cormick will have no remaining outside basis to allocate. As a result, he will take a zero basis in Capital Asset #2. Applying § 733, Cormick's basis in his partnership interest will be reduced to zero.[34]

Examples 5 and 6 highlight a number of important points regarding *nonliquidating* distributions:

1. If § 732(a)(2) does not apply, a distributee partner will *always* take a transferred basis in each distributed asset, i.e., will take the same basis the partnership had in the distributed asset.

2. The basis allocated to an item of property other than cash will never exceed the partnership's basis in that property regardless of whether § 732(a)(2) applies.

3. If § 732(a)(2) applies, at a minimum, the amount of *gain* that inhered in inventory and unrealized receivables when held by the partnership will be preserved by giving the distributee partner, insofar as possible, the same basis as the partnership's basis in those assets.

4. If § 732(a)(2) applies, at a minimum, the amount of gain that inhered in other assets when held by the partnership will be preserved, but the same is not true for any loss that inhered in the asset.

B. Liquidating Distributions

Note: As indicated at the outset of this Overview, liquidating distributions can be divided into two subcategories: distributions that liquidate the entire partnership and distributions that liquidate only the interest of a "retiring" partner. The latter type of liquidating distribution is addressed in Chapter 17. Only liquidating distributions that liquidate the entire partnership will be discussed in this part of the chapter.

If a partnership voluntarily discontinues its business and liquidates, the tax consequences of the liquidating distributions made to partners are similar in many respects to the tax consequences of nonliquidating distributions discussed above. Thus, the consequences of liquidating distributions are generally as follows:[35]

(a) gain is recognized by a distributee partner only if the cash, if any, distributed exceeds the partner's outside basis;

(b) each partner, to the extent possible, takes the same basis in the assets as the partnership had;

---

[34] Evaluating the results to Cormick, it is worthwhile noting all of the partnership's gain that inhered in Inventory #3 was preserved while the loss that inhered in Inventory #4 has been eliminated.

[35] As with the discussion of the general rules applicable to nonliquidating distributions, our discussion of the general rules applicable to distributions in liquidation of the entire partnership ignore the potential applicability of § 751(b), discussed in Chapter 16, and other special anti-abuse provisions applicable to distributions.

(c) the character of assets received by a partner is generally the same as the character the assets had at the partnership level, thereby preventing the conversion of ordinary income into capital gain; and

(d) no gain or loss is recognized by the liquidating partnership.

Under limited circumstances, liquidating distributions, unlike nonliquidating distributions, can result in the recognition of loss by a distributee partner or an increase in the basis of assets distributed. On liquidating distributions, the possibility of loss recognition or an increase in basis is necessitated by the fact that liquidation terminates the partners' interests in the entity, thus requiring a full accounting for each partner's outside basis. To account for a partner's entire outside basis, the Code allocates that basis to the assets distributed to the partner and/or permits the partner to recover some or all of that basis through a loss deduction. In that regard, §§ 732(b) and (c) and 731(a)(2) are the operative provisions.

---

§ 732(b). Distributions in Liquidation

The basis of property (other than money) distributed by a partnership to a partner in liquidation of the partner's interest shall be an amount equal to the adjusted basis of such partner's interest in the partnership reduced by any money distributed in the same transaction.

---

1. Recognition of Loss

Study the following language from § 731(a)(2) allowing for the recognition of loss under limited circumstances on the liquidation of a partner's interest.

---

§ 731. Extent of Recognition of Gain or Loss on Distribution.

(a) **Partners.** — In the case of a distribution by a partnership to a partner —

(2) loss shall not be recognized to such partner, *except that upon a distribution in liquidation of a partner's interest in a partnership where no property other than that described in subparagraph (A) or (B) is distributed to such partner,* loss shall be recognized to the extent of the excess of the adjusted basis of such partner's interest in the partnership over the sum of —

(A) any money distributed, and

(B) the basis to the distributee, as determined under § 732, of any unrealized receivables (as defined in § 751(c)) and inventory (as defined in § 751(d)).

Any gain or loss recognized under this subsection shall be considered as gain or loss from the sale or exchange of the partnership

> interest of the distributee partner. [Emphasis added.]

Because a complete liquidation of a partnership constitutes a closed transaction for all partners, recognition of loss is appropriate if a partner's outside basis cannot be entirely accounted for as required by § 732(b) by allocating it to distributed assets. Thus, if a partner upon liquidation of the partnership, receives a distribution consisting solely of cash, the partner will recognize loss to the extent the partner's outside basis was greater than the amount of cash distributed.

Example 1: Jackie, Sara, and Suzanne each own a one-third interest in the ABC Partnership. Jackie's adjusted basis (outside basis) in her partnership interest is $100,000. Assume Jackie and the other two partners each receives $60,000 in cash and no other property upon the complete liquidation of the partnership. Pursuant to § 732(b), Jackie's outside basis will first be reduced by the $60,000 cash distribution, thus leaving a remaining outside basis of $40,000. Because there are no other distributed assets to which this $40,000 can be allocated, § 731(a)(2) provides that Jackie will recognize a $40,000 loss that will be treated as a loss from the sale or exchange of her partnership interest.[36]

On a liquidation of a partnership, the potential for loss recognition exists not only when cash is the sole asset distributed to a partner; loss can also be triggered if only unrealized receivables or inventory are distributed to a partner in liquidation of her interest.[37] As discussed above, Congress, seeking to preserve the ordinary income or loss inherent in unrealized receivables (as defined in § 751(c)) and inventory (as defined in § 751(d)), has limited the amount of outside basis that can be allocated to those items to the amount of the partnership's adjusted basis in those items.[38] § 732(c)(1)(A). Cash distributions, of course, will absorb an amount of a partner's outside basis equal to the amount of the cash distributed — no more and no less. Thus, if a distributee partner receives a liquidating distribution consisting only of cash, unrealized receivables, and/or inventory, there is only a limited amount of outside basis that can be allocated to those items. If the distributee's outside basis is greater, the distributee could account for this excess outside basis only by recognizing a loss; that is precisely the circumstance under which § 731(a)(2) (reprinted above) will allow loss recognition. By contrast, if the distributee were to receive one or more of the three types of property listed above — that is, cash, unrealized receivables, and inventory — and other property as well, no loss would be recognized because it would be possible to allocate the outside basis in excess of that allocated to the cash, unrealized receivables, and/or inventory to the other

---

[36] If, instead, Jackie and each of the other partners had received $150,000 in cash as liquidating distributions, Jackie would have recognized a gain of $50,000 just as she would have had the distribution been a nonliquidating distribution of $150,000.

[37] Loss can be recognized if the partner receives a liquidating distribution comprised only of some combination of cash, unrealized receivables, and inventory.

[38] As noted above, to the extent that a partner's remaining basis is less than the aggregate adjusted basis of the unrealized receivables and inventory distributed to a partner, § 732(c)(1)(A)(ii) provides for the allocation of any decrease "required in order to have the adjusted basis of such properties equal the basis to be allocated." *See* Example 6 above addressing the application to Cormick of the "decrease" rule of § 732(c)(3) to unrealized receivables and inventory.

property, even if it meant giving the other property a basis greater than its fair market value. Thus, Congress has limited the circumstances under which a loss can be recognized under § 731(a)(2) on a liquidation.

> **Example 2:** In Example 1 above, assume Jackie and the other two partners each received cash of $60,000, accounts receivable with a fair market value of $30,000 and an adjusted basis of $0, and inventory with a fair market value of $40,000 and an adjusted basis of $20,000. After first reducing Jackie's outside basis by the $60,000 of cash distributed to her, the remaining $40,000 of outside basis would be allocated pursuant to § 732(c)(1)(A)(ii) as follows: $0 to the accounts receivable distributed to Jackie and $20,000 to the inventory distributed to Jackie. As there are no other assets to which the remaining $20,000 of Jackie's basis may be allocated, Jackie will recognize a $20,000 loss (thus accounting for her remaining outside basis) pursuant to § 731(a)(2). The loss will be treated as a loss from the sale or exchange of Jackie's partnership interest. § 731(a)(flush language). Section 741 will characterize the loss as capital loss.

2. Potential Increase or Decrease in Basis of Assets (Other than Unrealized Receivables and Inventory) Distributed in Liquidation of the Partners' Interests

As noted above, the partners' entire outside bases must be accounted for when a partnership is liquidated. If assets other than cash, unrealized receivables, and/or inventory are received by a distributee partner in liquidation of the partner's interest, no loss will be recognized. Instead, the partner's outside basis, reduced for any cash distributed, will be allocated among the other assets received by the partner. As indicated, a partner's remaining outside basis will first be allocated to unrealized receivables and inventory in an amount equal to the partnership's adjusted basis in each of those assets. Any excess outside basis will then be allocated to other assets in the manner discussed above. If, however, the excess outside basis (i.e., the basis remaining after reduction for cash distributed and the basis allocated to unrealized receivables and inventory) is greater than the aggregate adjusted basis of the partnership in the other assets distributed to the partner, an increase in the basis of those other assets[39] will be necessitated to ensure the partner's outside basis is accounted for in full. As a corollary to this rule, if the excess outside basis is less than the aggregate adjusted basis of the partnership in the other assets, a decrease in the basis of those other assets will be necessitated. Study the following excerpt from § 732(c) providing the rules for allocating a partner's outside basis to other assets:

---

[39] Consistent with the congressional purpose to preserve ordinary income and ordinary loss, the basis the distributee partner takes in unrealized receivables and inventory is not increased.

> **§ 732. Basis of distributed property other than money**
>
> **(c) Allocation of basis. —**
>
> (1) In General. – The basis of distributed properties to which subsection (a)(2) <u>or (b)</u> is applicable shall be allocated —
>
> **(A)** *[The Code provides here for the allocation of outside basis to unrealized receivables and inventory received by the partner. See discussion above.]*
>
> **(B)** to the extent of any basis remaining after the allocation under subparagraph (A), to other distributed properties —
>
>   **(i)** first by assigning to each such other property such other property's adjusted basis to the partnership, and
>
>   **(ii)** then, to the extent any increase or decrease in basis is required in order to have the adjusted bases of such other distributed properties equal such remaining basis, in the manner provided in paragraph (2) or (3), whichever is appropriate.
>
> (2) Method of Allocating Increase. Any increase required under paragraph (1)(B) shall be allocated among the properties —
>
> **(A)** first to properties with unrealized appreciation in proportion to their respective amounts of unrealized appreciation before such increase (but only to the extent of each property's unrealized appreciation), and
>
> **(B)** then, to the extent such increase is not allocated under subparagraph (A), in proportion to their respective fair market values.
>
> (3) Method of Allocating Decrease. *[See discussion in Part A of this Chapter]*.

Consider the following examples demonstrating the increase and decrease rules of § 732(c) in the context of distributions liquidating the entire partnership.

Example 3: Assume Laura has a $190,000 adjusted basis in her partnership interest. Her capital account has a fair market value of $180,000. Upon liquidation of the partnership, Laura and each of the other partners receive the following property:

Assets	A/B	FMV
Cash	$15,000	$15,000
Accounts Receivable	$0	$30,000
Inventory	$15,000	$45,000
Capital Asset #1	$50,000	$60,000
Capital Asset #2	$40,000	$30,000
Total:	**$120,000**	**$180,000**

Analysis: Laura has not received cash in excess of basis and thus she will not recognize any gain on the liquidating distribution. § 731(a)(1). Instead, Laura has a loss built into her partnership interest. For reasons discussed above, Laura will not recognize any loss on the liquidating distribution. Her $190,000 basis will first be reduced by the $15,000 of cash distributed to her. Pursuant to § 732(c)(1)(A), $15,000 of Laura's basis will then be allocated to the inventory she receives and $0 basis will be allocated to the accounts receivable.

After taking into account the cash, inventory, and accounts receivable Laura has received, her remaining basis of $160,000 will be allocated to Capital Assets #1 and #2 in an amount equal to the basis the partnership had in each of those assets. § 732(c)(1)(B)(i). Thus, $50,000 of Laura's remaining $160,000 outside basis will be allocated to Capital Asset #1 and $40,000 to Capital Asset #2, leaving $70,000 of outside basis to be allocated. As a result, the basis of Capital Assets #1 and #2 must be increased.

Pursuant to § 732(c)(2)(A), the $70,000 of increase will first be allocated to Capital Asset #1 in the amount of the unrealized appreciation inhering in that asset, i.e., $10,000. There is no unrealized appreciation in Capital Asset #2. Section 732(c)(2)(B) requires the remaining $60,000 of outside basis be allocated in proportion to the respective fair market values of Capital Assets #1 and #2. Capital Asset #1 would be allocated 2/3 of the $60,000 increase or $40,000; Laura's adjusted basis in Capital Asset #1 (with a FMV of $60,000) will thus be $100,000. Capital Asset #2 (with a FMV of $30,000) will be allocated the other 1/3 of the increase or $20,000; Laura's adjusted basis in Capital Asset #2 will thus be $60,000.

Example 4: Assume the facts of Example 3, except that Laura's outside basis instead of being $190,000 was $70,000. After allocating $30,000 of the outside basis to the cash, inventory, and accounts receivable, Laura's remaining outside basis would be only $40,000. Pursuant to § 732(c)(1)(B)(i), Capital Assets #1 and #2 would be allocated a basis equal to the adjusted basis the partnership had in each of those assets. Thus, Capital Asset #1 would be allocated $50,000 of basis, and Capital Asset #2 would be allocated $40,000 of basis. The problem, of course, is that there is only $40,000 remaining basis to be allocated. As a result, a decrease of $50,000 in basis is required. Pursuant to § 732(c)(3)(A), $10,000 of that decrease is allocated to Capital Asset #2 to take into account the unrealized depreciation inhering in that asset. As a result, the adjusted basis of Capital Account #2 is reduced to $30,000. The remaining $40,000 of decrease is then allocated between Capital Assets #1 and #2 in proportion to their respective adjusted basis (taking into account the allocation required by § 732(c)(3)(A)). Thus, 5/8 of the remaining decrease of $40,000 or $25,000 will be allocated to Capital Asset #1, resulting in an adjusted basis of $25,000 for that asset; 3/8 of the remaining decrease of $40,000 or $15,000 will be allocated to Capital Asset #2, resulting in an adjusted basis of $15,000 for that asset.

Note the difference between the increase and decrease allocation rules — §§ 732(c)(2)(B) and 732(c)(3)(B). Section 732(c)(2)(B) provides that any increase in basis remaining after applying § 732(c)(2)(A) be allocated based on the respective fair market value of the other assets, while § 732(c)(3)(B) provides that any decrease in basis remaining after applying § 732(c)(3)(A) be allocated based on the respective adjusted basis of the other assets. Regarding decreases, Congress opted for allocation in proportion to adjusted basis rather than fair market value as in the case of increases, because a *decrease* based on fair market values might result in the decrease being allocated to an asset in an amount greater than the asset's adjusted basis, a result that would produce a negative basis.

C. Other Provisions Related to Liquidating Distributions

In addition to the nonrecognition rule of § 731 and the basis rules of § 732, part A of this Overview addressed a range of provisions that are equally applicable to both liquidating and nonliquidating distributions. Thus, the special holding period rules of §§ 735 and 1223 apply to liquidating distributions as do the characterization rules of § 735. Section 731(a) treats any recognized gain or loss resulting from a liquidating distribution as a sale or exchange of a partnership interest. In turn, § 741 generally treats gains and losses from the sale or exchange of partnership interests as sales or exchanges of capital assets. Liquidating distributions of encumbered assets trigger results under § 752 comparable to those with respect to nonliquidating distributions of encumbered assets as discussed above. In Chapter 16, you will study § 751(b), addressing so-called "disproportionate distributions" and treating distributions (both liquidating and nonliquidating) in part as sales or exchanges and in part as distributions subject to the §§ 731 and 732 rules discussed in this chapter.

Revenue Ruling 79-205
1979-2 C.B. 255

ISSUES

When a partnership makes a non-liquidating distribution of property, (1) is a partner permitted to offset the increase in the partner's liabilities against the decrease in the partner's liabilities in determining the extent of recognition of gain or loss? and (2) is partnership basis adjusted before or after the property distribution?

FACTS

A and B are general partners in M, a general partnership, which was formed for the purposes of owning and operating shopping centers.

On December 31, 1977, M made nonliquidating distributions in a single transaction of a portion of its property to A and B. A and B are equal partners in M. M, A and B are calendar year taxpayers. No assets of the type described in § 751 (a) of the Internal Revenue Code of 1954 were distributed by M to either A or B.

Immediately prior to the distribution A had an adjusted basis for A's interest in M of $1,000x$ dollars, and B had an adjusted basis for B's interest in M of $1,500x$ dollars. The property distributed to A had an adjusted basis to M of $2,000x$ dollars, and was subject to liabilities of $1,600x$ dollars. The property distributed to B had an adjusted basis to M of $3,200x$ dollars and was subject to liabilities of $2,800x$ dollars. A's individual liabilities increased by $1,600x$ dollars by reason of the distribution to A. B's individual liabilities increased by $2,800x$ dollars by reason of the distribution to B. A's share and B's share of the liabilities of M each decreased by $2,200x$ dollars (½ of $1,600x$ + ½ of $2,800x$ dollars) by reason of the distributions. The basis and fair market value of the properties distributed were greater than the liabilities to which they were subject.

LAW

Section 705 (a) of the Code provides, in part, that the adjusted basis of a partner's interest in a partnership shall be the basis of such interest determined under section 722 decreased (but not below zero) by partnership distributions as provided in section 733.

Section 722 of the Code provides, in part, that the basis of a partnership interest acquired by a contribution of money shall be the amount of such money.

Section 731 (a) (1) of the Code provides that in the case of a distribution by a partnership to a partner gain shall not be recognized to such partner, except to the extent that any money distributed exceeds the adjusted basis of such partner's interest in the partnership immediately before the distribution.

Section 732 (a) (1) of the Code provides that the basis of property (other than money) distributed by a partnership to a partner other than in liquidation of the partner's interest shall, except as provided in section 732 (a) (2), be its adjusted basis to the partnership immediately before such distribution.

Section 732 (a) (2) of the Code provides that the basis to the distributee partner of property to which section 732 (a) (1) is applicable shall not exceed the adjusted basis of such partner's interest in the partnership reduced by any money distributed in the same transaction.

Section 733 of the Code provides that in the case of a distribution by a partnership to a partner other than in liquidation of a partner's interest, the adjusted basis to such partner of the interest in the partnership shall be reduced (but not below zero) by the amount of any money distributed to such partner and the amount of the basis to such partner of distributed property other than money, as determined under section 732.

Section 752 (a) of the Code provides that any increase in a partner's share of the liabilities of a partnership, or any increase in a partner's individual liabilities by reason of the assumption by such partner of partnership liabilities, shall be considered as a contribution of money by such partner to the partnership.

Section 752 (b) of the Code provides that any decrease in a partner's share of the liabilities of a partnership, or any decrease in a partner's individual liabilities by reason of the assumption by the partnership of such individual liabilities, shall be considered as a distribution of money to the partner by the partnership.

Section 752 (c) of the Code provides that for purposes of section 752 a liability to which property is subject shall, to the extent of the fair market value of such property, be considered as a liability of the owner of the property.

ANALYSIS & HOLDING

In general, partnership distributions are taxable under section 731(a)(1) of the Code only to the extent that the amount of money distributed exceeds the distributee partner's basis for the partner's partnership interest. This rule reflects the Congressional intent to limit narrowly the area in which gain or loss is recognized upon a distribution so as to remove deterrents to property being moved in and out of partnerships as business reasons dictate. See S. Rep. No. 1622, 83rd Cong., 2nd Sess., page 96 (1954). Here, since partner liabilities are both increasing and decreasing in the same transaction offsetting the increases and decreases tends to limit recognition of gain, thereby giving effect to the Congressional intent. Consequently, in a distribution of encumbered property, the resulting liability adjustments will be treated as occurring simultaneously, rather than occurring in a particular order. Therefore, on a distribution of encumbered property, the amount of money considered distributed to a partner for purposes of section 731(a)(1) is the amount (if any) by which the decrease in the partner's share of the liabilities of the partnership under section 752(b) exceeds the increase in the partner's individual liabilities under section 752(a). The amount of money considered contributed by a partner for purposes of section 722 is the amount (if any) by which the increase in the partner's individual liabilities under section 752(a) exceeds the decrease in the partner's share of the liabilities of the partnership under section 752(b). The increase in the partner's individual liabilities occurs by reason of the assumption by the partner of partnership liabilities, or by reason of a distribution of property subject to a liability, to the extent of the fair market value of such property. Because the distribution was part of a single transaction, the two properties are treated as having been distributed simultaneously to A and B. Therefore, all resulting liability adjustments relating to the distribution of the two properties will be treated as occurring simultaneously, rather than occurring in a particular order.

TREATMENT OF PARTNER A

A will be deemed to have received a net distribution of $600x$ dollars in money, that is, the amount by which the amount of money considered distributed to A ($2,200x$

dollars) exceeds the amount of money considered contributed by A ($1{,}600x$ dollars). Because $600x$ dollars does not exceed A's basis for A's interest in M immediately before the distribution ($1{,}000x$ dollars), no gain is recognized to A.

Under section 732(a) of the Code, the basis to A of the property distributed to A is the lesser of (i) the adjusted basis of the property to the partnership ($2{,}000x$ dollars), or (ii) the adjusted basis of A's partnership interest ($1{,}000x$ dollars) reduced by the amount of money deemed distributed to A ($600x$ dollars). Therefore, the basis of the property in A's hands is $400x$ dollars. Under section 733, the adjusted basis of A's partnership interest ($1{,}000x$ dollars) is reduced by the amount of money deemed distributed to A ($600x$ dollars) and by the basis to A of the distributed property ($400x$ dollars). The adjusted basis of A's partnership interest is therefore reduced to zero.

TREATMENT OF PARTNER B

B will be deemed to have made a net contribution of $600x$ dollars, that is, the amount by which the amount of money considered contributed by B ($2{,}800x$ dollars) exceeds the amount of money considered distributed to B ($2{,}200x$ dollars). In applying sections 732(a) and 733 of the Code to B, the adjustment to B's basis in B's partnership interest attributable to the liability adjustments resulting from the distributions will be treated as occurring first, and the distribution of property to B as occurring second. By so doing, B's basis for the distributed property is increased and B's basis in B's partnership interest is decreased. This allocation gives greater effect to the general rule of section 732(a)(1), which provides for the partner to have the same basis in distributed property as the partnership had for that property. Therefore, the first step is that B's basis for B's partnership interest ($1{,}500x$ dollars) is increased under sections 722 and 705(a) by the amount of the net contribution deemed made by B ($600x$ dollars), and is equal to $2{,}100x$ dollars. Next, under section 732(a) of the Code, the basis to B of the property distributed to B is the lesser of (i) the adjusted basis of the property to the partnership ($3{,}200x$ dollars), or (ii) the adjusted basis of B's partnership interest ($2{,}100x$ dollars) reduced by the amount of money deemed distributed to B (zero). Therefore, the basis of the property in B's hands is $2{,}100x$ dollars. Under section 733, the adjusted basis of B's partnership interest ($2{,}100x$ dollars) is reduced by the amount of money deemed distributed to B (zero) and by the basis to B of the distributed property ($2{,}100x$ dollars). The adjusted basis of B's partnership interest is therefore zero.

Revenue Ruling 94-4
1994-1 C.B. 196

ISSUE

If a deemed distribution of money under 752(b) of the Internal Revenue Code occurs as a result of a decrease in a partner's share of the liabilities of a partnership, is the deemed distribution taken into account at the time of the distribution or at the end of the partnership taxable year?

LAW

Under 752 (b), a decrease in a partner's share of partnership liabilities is considered a distribution of money to the partner by the partnership. The partner will recognize gain under 731(a)(1) if the distribution of money exceeds the adjusted basis of the partner's interest immediately before the distribution.

Section 1.731-1(a)(1)(ii) of the Income Tax Regulations provides that for purposes of 731 and 705, advances or drawings of money or property against a partner's distributive share of income are treated as current distributions made on the last day of the partnership taxable year with respect to that partner.

Rev. Rul. 92-97, 1992-2 C.B. 124, treats a deemed distribution of money to a partner resulting from a cancellation of debt as an advance or drawing under 1.731-1(a)(1)(ii) against that partner's distributive share of cancellation of indebtedness income.

HOLDING

A deemed distribution of money under 752 (b) resulting from a decrease in a partner's share of the liabilities of a partnership is treated as an advance or drawing of money under 1.731-1(a)(1)(ii) to the extent of the partner's distributive share of income for the partnership taxable year. An amount treated as an advance or drawing of money is taken into account at the end of the partnership taxable year. A deemed distribution of money resulting from a cancellation of debt may qualify for advance or drawing treatment under this revenue ruling and under Rev. Rul. 92-97.

PART B:
Distribution of Marketable Securities

I. PROBLEMS

1. Anne is an equal one-quarter partner in the four-person ABCD Partnership, which provides business consulting services and advice to its clients. Anne has held her partnership interest for five years. At the beginning of this year, ABCD purchases Hi-Tech stock for $10,000, and six months later, when the stock is still worth $10,000, distributes it to Anne in a nonliquidating distribution. ABCD also distributes $10,000 in cash to each of the other partners. Assume the Hi-Tech stock is ABCD's only marketable security. What are the tax consequences to Anne if her outside basis at the end of the year is $6,000?

2. Assume the facts of Problem 1, except that (1) the value of the stock at the time of distribution is $40,000, (2) Anne's outside basis is $20,000, (3) the partnership distributes $40,000 in cash to each of the other partners, and (4) the distributions are liquidating distributions. What are the tax consequences to Anne?

3. Assume the facts of Problem 2, except the distribution is a nonliquidating distribution. What are the tax consequences to Anne?

4. Assume the facts of Problem 2, except ABCD also owns three other marketable securities, Yesterday stock (value $10,000; adjusted basis $30,000), Today stock (value $30,000; adjusted basis $20,000), and Tomorrow stock (value $50,000; adjusted basis $30,000). What are the tax consequences to Anne, assuming the partnership liquidates only Anne's interest and cash is the only other asset of the partnership?

5. Assume the facts of Problem 4, except ABCD distributes both the Hi-Tech stock and the Tomorrow stock to Anne.

Assignment for Part B of Chapter 14:

Complete the Problems.

Read: Internal Revenue Code: §§ 731(c)(1), (2)((A), (3)(A), (3)(B), (4), (5), (6); § 741; 1092(d)(1).
Treasury Regulations: § 1.731-2(a), (b)(1), (2), (c)(2), (g), (j) Exs. 1, 2, 5.
Materials: Overview

II. VOCABULARY

marketable securities
actively traded financial instruments
share of net gain

III. OBJECTIVES

1. To recall the definition of a marketable security.

2. To recall that a distribution of a marketable security is generally treated as a distribution of money.

3. To recall that there are exceptions for distributions of marketable securities contributed by the distributee partner and for marketable securities that were not marketable securities when acquired by the partnership.

4. To recall that the amount of the distribution treated as a distribution of money is reduced by the distributee's share of net gain.

5. To determine the distributee's share of net gain.

6. Upon a distribution of marketable securities, to determine the gain recognized by the distributee, the adjusted basis of the securities in the hands of the distributee, and the adjusted basis of the distributee's interest in the partnership.

IV. OVERVIEW

Section 731(c) provides that a distribution of marketable securities to a partner shall ordinarily be treated as a distribution of cash. As a result, under § 731(a)(1), a distribution of marketable securities will generate gain to the distributee partner to the extent the distribution exceeds the partner's adjusted basis in her partnership interest.

---

§ 731. Extent of Recognition of Gain or Loss on Distribution

(c) Treatment of marketable securities.

(1) In general. For purposes of *subsection (a)(1)* and section 737

(A) the term "money" includes marketable securities, and

(B) such securities shall be taken into account at their fair market value as of the date of the distribution.

[**Authors' Note:** Section 737 is discussed in Chapter 19]

Assume, for example, that Paula, a one-third partner in the NOP Partnership, has an outside basis of $30 in her partnership interest and would like to receive a $50 cash distribution in order to invest in marketable securities. If NOP simply distributes cash of $50 to Paula, she will have the funds she needs to invest in marketable securities, but at the price of a tax gain of $20 under § 731(a)(1). Suppose, instead, that NOP uses the $50 of cash to acquire the marketable securities Paula wants and then distributes them to Paula. In the absence of § 731(c), distribution of the securities generates no gain to Paula; she would take them with a basis of $30 (pursuant to § 732(a)(1) and (2)), preserving built-in gain of $20 for the future, but incurring no current gain. In effect, prior to the enactment of § 731(c), the distribution rules of Subchapter K discussed previously in this Overview made it possible for a partner to receive a distribution of marketable securities without recognition of gain, even though the marketable securities were essentially the equivalent of cash and had a value greater than the distributee partner's outside basis. Form thus trumped substance. In 1984 Congress enacted § 731(c), restricting this technique by treating the distribution of marketable securities as cash for § 731 purposes. As a result, in the foregoing example, Paula would recognize gain of $20 on the distribution of the $50 in marketable securities from NOP, just as would have occurred on the distribution of $50 in cash.

Marketable securities include actively traded financial instruments — stocks and other equity interests, debt instruments, options, forward or futures contracts, notional principal contracts, and derivatives — as well as certain actively traded foreign currencies. § 731(c)(2)(A), (C). (A marketable security is actively traded if it is actively traded under § 1092(d)(1); see Reg. § 1.731-2(c)(2). Certain financial interests and instruments are also treated as marketable securities under § 731(c)(2)(B)). For § 731(c) purposes, the securities are valued as of the date of the distribution. § 731(c)(1)(B).

Section 731(c)(3)(B) provides an important limitation[40] on the amount of the distribution treated as money, a limitation enabling a partner "to receive a distribution of marketable securities without recognizing the gain that is attributable to *his share* of the partnership's net appreciation with respect to securities of the type distributed."[41] In the foregoing example, the NOP Partnership purchased the marketable securities and immediately distributed them to Paula. Suppose, however, that NOP had purchased the securities for $20 some time ago, and they had since appreciated in value to $50. Assume the securities in question were the partnership's only marketable securities. To the extent of the reduction in the distributee partner's share of partnership unrealized gain in marketable securities, the deemed cash distribution is also reduced. In this case, the reduction is $10: Paula's one-third share of NOP's unrealized gain of $30 (value of $50, basis of $20) in marketable securities was $10 before the distribution, and was $0 afterwards (because NOP no longer had any marketable securities). § 731(c)(3)(B). Accordingly, the deemed cash distribution here is $50, less $10, for a total of $40, and Paula's § 731(a)(1) gain is only $10, not $20. (The statutory formulation compares the change in the partner's before and after share of net gain in marketable securities of the "same class and issuer" as the distributed security; the regulations extend this to provide that all of the partnership's marketable securities are deemed to be of the same class and issuer. § 731(c)(3)(B); Reg. § 1.731-2(b)(1).)

> ### § 731(c)(3)(B). Limitation on Gain Recognized.
>
> In the case of a distribution of marketable securities to a partner, the amount taken into account under [§ 731(c)(1)] shall be reduced (but not

---

[40] Section 731(c)(3)(A) provides a number of other exceptions noted below that are beyond the scope of this chapter.

[41] H. Rep. No. 826(I), 103rd Cong., 2d Sess. (1994). (Emphasis added.)

> below zero) by the *excess* (if any) of—
>
> (i) such partner's distributive share of the net gain which would be recognized if all of the marketable securities of the same class and issuer as the distributed securities held by the partnership were sold (immediately before the transaction to which the distribution relates) by the partnership for fair market value, *over*
>
> (ii) such partner's distributive share of the net gain which is attributable to the marketable securities of the same class and issuer as the distributed securities held by the partnership immediately after the transaction, determined by using the same fair market value as used under clause (i).

Suppose, as an additional example, that NOP held marketable securities A and B. Assume that Marketable Securities A had a value of $100 and a basis of $40, and that Marketable Securities B had a value of $75 and a basis of $30. If NOP distributes Marketable Securities B to Paula, the deemed cash distribution of $75 is reduced by $15 to $60 on account of the decrease in Paula's share of partnership unrecognized net gain. (Paula's one-third share of the partnership's unrecognized net gain in marketable securities before the distribution was a total of $35: $20 on account of Marketable Securities A, $15 on account of Marketable Securities B. After the distribution of B, Paula's share of the partnership's remaining unrecognized net gain is only $20.) Because Paula's outside basis was $20, the distribution of Marketable Securities B resulted in a deemed cash distribution of $60 and a gain of $40 to Paula.

As indicated in the preceding example, when a distribution of marketable securities generates gain under § 731(c), the basis of the securities in the hands of the distributee partner is the normal § 732 basis, increased by the gain recognized on the distribution. § 731(c)(4)(A). If multiple marketable securities are distributed, the basis increase due to the § 731(c) gain is allocated in proportion to their unrealized appreciation before the distribution. § 731(c)(4)(B).

> ### § 731(c)(4). Basis of Securities Distributed
>
> (A) In general. The basis of marketable securities with respect to which gain is recognized by reason of this subsection shall be—
>
> (i) their basis determined under section 732, *increased by*
>
> (ii) the amount of such gain.
>
> (B) Allocation of basis increase. Any increase in basis attributable to the gain described in subparagraph (A)(ii) shall be allocated to marketable securities in proportion to their respective amounts of unrealized appreciation before such increase.

Return to our initial example, where Paula's outside basis was $30, and where the NOP Partnership purchased marketable securities for $50 and then immediately distributed them to Paula (when their value was also $50): Under the rules of § 732(a)(2), the securities would normally have a basis in Paula's hands of $30. (The partnership's basis in the securities was $50, and while Paula would ordinarily take that basis herself under § 732(a)(1), the limitation of § 732(a)(2) prevails.) As a result, however, of the gain recognition of $20 under § 731(c), Paula's basis in the securities is stepped up to $50. The basis step-up leaves Paula in the same position she would have been in if NOP had distributed $50 cash to Paula — resulting in § 731(a)(1) gain of $20 — and Paula had then purchased the marketable securities for $50. Finally, note that, pursuant to § 731(c)(5), the distributee partner's outside basis is reduced to zero under the normal rules of §§ 733 and 734 "as if no gain were recognized, and no adjustment were made to the basis of property, under this subsection."

Section 731(c)(5). Subsection Disregarded in Determining Basis of Partner's Interest in Partnership and of Basis of Partnership Property

Sections 733. . . . shall be applied as if no gain were recognized, and no adjustment were made to the basis of property, under this subsection.

Certain distributions of marketable securities are excepted from the deemed cash rule, including securities that were contributed to the partnership by the distributee partner; securities that were not marketable securities when acquired by the partnership; and securities distributed by an investment partnership (subject to definitional requirements and limitations). § 731(c)(3)(A), (C).

Chapter 15

INSIDE BASIS ADJUSTMENTS UNDER § 734

I. PROBLEMS

1. Ten years ago, Giovanni, Francesca, and Stefano formed a general partnership in which each has a one-third interest in capital and profits. The partners' only contributions to the partnership have consisted of cash. This year, the partnership distributed $75,000 in cash to Stefano and his interest in the partnership was reduced from one-third to one-fifth. At the time of the distribution, the partnership balance sheet was as follows:

	Partnership Assets			Partners' Capital	
	A/B	FMV		A/B	FMV
Cash	$90,000	$90,000	Giovanni	$60,000	$150,000
Capital Asset #1	$60,000	$210,000	Francesca	$60,000	$150,000
Capital Asset #2	$30,000	$150,000	Stefano	$60,000	$150,000
Total	$180,000	$450,000		$180,000	$450,000

Explain the tax consequences to Stefano and the partnership, assuming the partnership has made a § 754 election.

2. Assume the facts of Problem 1, except that the partnership liquidated Stefano's interest by distributing Capital Asset #2 to him. Explain the tax consequences to Stefano and the partnership, again assuming the partnership has made a § 754 election.

3. Larry, Olivia, Shane, and Eloise are equal partners in a general partnership. The partners' only contributions to the partnership have consisted of cash. This year, the partnership paid Larry $80,000 in cash in complete liquidation of his interest. Immediately prior to the liquidation of Larry's interest, the partnership's balance sheet was as follows:

	Partnership Assets			Partners' Capital	
	A/B	FMV		A/B	FMV
Cash	$100,000	$100,000	Larry	$120,000	$80,000
Inventory A	$60,000	$80,000	Olivia	$120,000	$80,000
Inventory B	$80,000	$60,000	Shane	$120,000	$80,000
Capital Asset	$240,000	$80,000	Eloise	$120,000	$80,000
Total	$480,000	$320,000		$480,000	$320,000

(a) Assuming the partnership has made a § 754 election, what are the tax consequences to Larry and the partnership on the liquidation of

Larry's partnership interest?[1]

(b) How would your answer to (a) change if, instead of distributing cash to Larry in liquidation of his interest, the partnership distributed the Capital Asset to Larry?

Assignment for Chapter 15:

Complete the Problems

Read: Internal Revenue Code: §§ 731(a), 732(a) and (b), 734(a)–(d), 741, 754, 755
Treasury Regulations: §§ 1.734-1; 1.754-1(a), (b)(1), (3), (c); 1.755-1(a)(1), (3), (c). Prop. Reg. § 1.734-1(a)(1), (2)(i), (b)(2)(i), (ii) Ex. 3.
Materials: Overview

II. VOCABULARY

basis adjustment
substantial basis reduction rule
§ 754 election

III. OBJECTIVES

1. To recall that, with respect to a partnership distribution of property to a partner, absent a § 754 election or a substantial basis reduction, no adjustment may be made to the partnership's basis in its undistributed assets.

2. To identify the circumstances in which an adjustment is required to be made to a partnership's basis in its undistributed assets as a result of the distribution of property to a partner.

3. To determine the amount of any basis adjustment required under § 734(b) or (d) as a result of the distribution of property to a partner.

4. To recall that any basis adjustment required under § 734(b) or (d) as a result of the distribution of property to a partner must be allocated to the partnership's undistributed property of the same character as the property distributed to a partner.

5. To apply § 755 to determine how any basis adjustment required by § 734(b) or (d) will be allocated among the partnership's undistributed assets.

6. To recall that if, following a distribution, a partnership does not have any remaining property of the same character as the property distributed, any basis adjustment required by § 734(b) or (d) must be held in abeyance until

---

[1] As will be discussed in Chapter 17, pursuant to § 736(b), the tax consequences of this liquidating distribution would be determined under the general distribution rules of §§ 731, 732, and 741. Section 751(b), addressing so-called "disproportionate distributions," is not applicable in a situation such as presented in this problem where there is no "§ 751 property." (Inventory A and B do not qualify as "substantially appreciated inventory" within the meaning of § 751(b) and therefore are not "§ 751 property." See discussion in Chapter 16.)

the partnership acquires property of the same character as the property distributed.

IV. OVERVIEW

Most of the time, when a partnership makes a distribution to a partner, nothing dramatic happens. Of course, as discussed in Chapter 14, a distributee partner's capital account is decreased by the amount of money and the fair market value of other property distributed, and the partner's outside basis is likewise decreased by the amount of money or the adjusted basis of any other property distributed. Most of the time, no gain or loss is recognized by the partner on the distribution, and the distributed property has the same adjusted basis in the hands of the partner as it did in the hands of the partnership. But not always! This chapter addresses those "not-always" situations and the special basis adjustment rule of § 734(b) applicable in these situations if the partnership has made a § 754 election.

At the outset, let us clarify that this chapter addresses only the distributions governed by the recognized gain or loss rules of § 731(a) and by the distributed-property basis rules of § 732(a) and (b) discussed in detail in Chapter 14. Recall that, in some circumstances, a purported distribution might be a guaranteed payment or other payment treated as occurring in a nonpartner capacity under § 707(a) or (c). See Chapter 13. Chapters yet to come will consider other special statutory rules regarding distributions, including § 751(b) (providing that, where a partnership holds so-called "hot assets," the distribution may be treated in part as a sale or exchange between the partner and the partnership — see Chapter 16) and §§ 704(c)(1)(B), 707(a)(2), or 737 (which treat certain distribution as disguised sales — see Chapters 18 and 19). The distributions addressed in this chapter will not engage these other statutory rules.

A. Basis Disparities Created by Certain Partnership Distributions

Basis disparities are created (1) by the recognition of gain or loss to a partner, pursuant to § 731, on a partnership's distribution of property to that partner and (2) by the increase of basis or loss of basis with respect to assets distributed to a partner. Section 734(b) is designed to address these basis disparities. Consider the following examples:

Example 1 — Recognition of Gain on Distribution: Assume Amy, Ben, Carol, and Dan are equal partners in the ABCD Partnership they formed many years ago. The partnership assets and the partners' capital accounts are as follows:

	Partnership Assets			Partners' Capital	
	A/B	FMV		A/B	FMV
Cash	$500	$500	Amy	$300	$500
Inventory A	$200	$100	Ben	$300	$500
Inventory B	$100	$200	Carol	$300	$500
Capital Asset A	$200	$700	Dan	$300	$500
Capital Asset B	$200	$500			
Total	$1,200	$2,000		$1,200	$2,000

Assume ABCD makes a liquidating distribution of $500 to Amy.[2] As discussed in Chapter 14, gain is recognized on cash distributions, whether liquidating or nonliquidating, in excess of outside basis. Pursuant to § 731(a)(1)[3] Amy recognizes gain of $200 on the liquidation of her partnership interest. This gain is long-term capital gain. § 741. Following the liquidation of Amy's interest, the partnership's balance sheet would be as follows:

	Partnership Assets			Partners' Capital	
	A/B	FMV		A/B	FMV
Inventory A	$200	$100	Ben	$300	$500
Inventory B	$100	$200	Carol	$300	$500
Capital Asset A	$200	$700	Dan	$300	$500
Capital Asset B	$200	$500			
Total	$700	$1,500		$900	$1,500

Note that a $200 disparity has arisen between the partnership's aggregate inside basis and the partners' aggregate outside bases, a disparity caused by Amy's recognition of $200 of gain. Prior to the cash distribution to Amy, a sale by ABCD of all its assets would have generated net income of $800, allocated $200 each to the four partners.[4] After the cash distribution to Amy, the same net appreciation, i.e., $800, remains in the partnership assets. As a result, a sale of assets would generate net gain of $267 (instead of $200) allocable to each of the three remaining partners.[5] Thus, at least temporarily, those partners would be overtaxed.[6] This distortion, however,

---

[2] Note that the inventory is not, in the aggregate, "substantially appreciated" within the meaning of § 751(b)(3) and, consequently, the items of inventory do not constitute so-called "§ 751 property" or "hot assets." As a result, distributions from the ABCD Partnership will not be recharacterized under the special rules of § 751(b) as involving in part a deemed sale or exchange. We will study § 751(b) in detail in Chapter 16.

[3] Technically, § 736 applies when a partner like Amy "retires" from the partnership. Section 736 is addressed in detail in Chapter 17. Suffice it to say that, on the facts presented, § 736(b) would direct us to apply the general rules of § 731 to the distribution liquidating Amy's partnership, and, as a result, Amy will recognize $200 of gain. § 731(a)(1).

[4] Ignore ordinary income and capital gain distinctions for the moment.

[5] There would be $800 of gain recognized on the hypothetical sale. This gain would be allocated in equal shares of $267 to each of the three remaining partners.

[6] As noted, the net gain lurking in the partnership assets was only $800, but the total gain taxed to

will be resolved when the partnership is completely liquidated: the allocation of $267 net gain to each of the three remaining partners increases their outside basis to $567 each; the $500 distribution each would receive[7] were the partnership to liquidate immediately following the sale results in a $67 capital loss to each partner. §§ 731(a)(2) and 741. That this resolution must await liquidation of the partnership is obviously unappealing, as is the fact that the deductibility of the $67 capital loss could be limited by the capital loss limitation rules of § 1211(b).

Example 2 — Recognition of Loss on Distribution: Assume the facts of Example 1, except Amy (and each of the other three partners) had an outside basis of $600 instead of $300, and Capital Asset A had a basis of $1,400 instead of $200. As discussed in Chapter 14, recognition of loss can occur only on a liquidating distribution consisting solely of cash, unrealized receivables, and/or inventory. § 731(a)(2). In this example, the liquidating distribution of $500 in cash to Amy would result in a recognized loss of $100, i.e., Amy's outside basis of $600 exceeds the liquidating payment of $500 by $100.

As a result of the liquidation of Amy's interest, the partnership's balance sheet would be as follows:

	Partnership Assets			**Partners' Capital**	
	A/B	FMV		A/B	FMV
Inventory A	$200	$100	Ben	$600	$500
Inventory B	$100	$200	Carol	$600	$500
Capital Asset A	$1,400	$700	Dan	$600	$500
Capital Asset B	$200	$500			
Total	$1,900	$1,500		$1,800	$1,500

As in Example 1, following the distribution, the balance sheet no longer balances, i.e., the aggregate of the partners' outside bases is less than the aggregate basis the partnership has in its assets. Prior to the cash distribution to Amy, a sale of all partnership assets would have resulted in a net loss of $400, allocated $100 to each partner. After the cash distribution to Amy, the same $400 net loss continues to lurk in partnership assets and $133 of that loss would be allocable to each of the three remaining partners were the partnership to sell all of its assets. Thus, $400 in net losses has turned into $500 of net losses (the $100 loss recognized by Amy on the cash distribution and the $400 net loss ultimately allocable to the remaining three partners)! Again, a sale of partnership assets followed by liquidation of the partnership would restore order, i.e., the $400 net loss recognized on the sale would be allocated $133 to each partner, thus reducing their outside basis from $600 to $467. The

---

the four partners would be $1,000: $200 to Amy and $267 each to the remaining three partners. Thus, there is $200 of "extra" gain.

[7] Each of the three remaining partners has a $500 capital account and thus is entitled to receive a liquidating distribution of $500.

subsequent liquidating distribution of $500 to each partner would result in the recognition of $33 gain by each partner. From a tax angle, the partners would benefit if (1) the partnership sold the assets enabling the partners to take advantage of the "extra" loss ($33 per partner) and (2) delayed as long as possible the liquidation of the partnership so as to avoid triggering the recognition of the offsetting gain of $33 to each partner.

Example (3) — Basis Decrease on Property Distribution: Assume the facts of Example 1, except ABCD makes a liquidating distribution to Amy consisting of $300 in cash and Inventory B. Because the cash distribution does not exceed Amy's outside basis, Amy recognizes no gain; her outside basis is reduced to zero by the distribution. §§ 731(a)(1) and 733. Accordingly, Amy takes a basis of zero in Inventory B. § 732(b). Note that Amy thus has $200 of built-in gain in Inventory B, which fully accounts for the $200 of built-in gain in her partnership interest before the liquidating distribution. But consider the situation for the remaining partners after the distribution to Amy:

	Partnership Assets			Partners' Capital	
	A/B	FMV		A/B	FMV
Cash	$200	$200	Ben	$300	$500
Inventory A	$200	$100	Carol	$300	$500
Capital Asset A	$200	$700	Dan	$300	$500
Capital Asset B	$200	$500			
Total	$800	$1,500		$900	$1,500

Once again, a basis disparity appears. The basis of Inventory B decreased by $100 as a result of its distribution to Amy. A sale of the remaining partnership assets would generate net gain of $700, allocated $233 each to the remaining partners.[8] But prior to the liquidating distribution to Amy, each partner's built-in gain was only $200, an aggregate total net gain of $800. As a result of the distribution, each partner has a $233 share of the gain inherent in the partnership assets — a $33 increase per partner. The distribution of Inventory B to Amy, in effect, creates $100 of "extra" gain, i.e., there is an aggregate total net gain of $900 ($200 built-in gain for Amy and $233 each for the other three partners). Each partner's $33 increase in gain will be offset by a loss of $33 on liquidation of the partnership. (The $233 gain each partner would recognize on the hypothetical sale of partnership assets will increase each partner's outside basis to $533; a subsequent $500 liquidating distribution to each partner would produce a loss of $33.) Again, as in Example 1, the timing is undesirable, and the capital loss on liquidation may not be immediately deductible due to § 1211 limitations.

Example 4: Basis Increase on Property Distributions: Assume the facts of Example 1, except that, instead of cash, the partnership distributes Capital Asset B to Amy in liquidation of her interest. Because Amy's

---

[8] Again, we ignore capital and ordinary distinctions.

outside basis is $300, her basis in Capital Asset B will be $300 on the liquidating distribution. § 732(b). Note that the basis of the property has thus increased by $100, from $200 in the hands of the partnership to $300 in Amy's hands. Amy's built-in gain of $200 on her partnership interest is thus preserved in the basis she takes in Capital Asset B. But consider the situation for the remaining partners:

	Partnership Assets			**Partners' Capital**	
	A/B	FMV		A/B	FMV
Cash	$500	$500	Ben	$300	$500
Inventory A	$200	$100	Carol	$300	$500
Inventory B	$100	$200	Dan	$300	$500
Capital Asset A	$200	$700			
Total	$1,000	$1,500		$900	$1,500

The distribution creates a basis disparity favorable to the remaining partners. Were the partnership to sell the remaining assets, it would recognize a net gain of $500 allocable in equal shares (of $167) to the three remaining partners. Total net partnership gain of $800 before the distribution to Amy has been reduced to $700 as a result of the distribution — Amy's built-in gain of $200 in Capital Asset B and the net gain of $500 in the remaining assets. $100 of gain has seemingly disappeared! Again, as in the prior examples, all is evened out on liquidation. A sale of partnership assets, followed by an immediate liquidation of the partnership, would result in each partner's outside basis being increased from $300 to $467, i.e., $300 initial basis plus the $167 of gain allocable to each partner on the sale of the assets. Each partner would then recognize $33 of gain on the receipt of the $500 cash distribution each would receive on the liquidation of the partnership. § 731(a)(1). The aggregate gain of $100 recognized by the partners on the liquidating distribution would thus account for the $100 of gain that seemingly disappeared as a result of the distribution to Amy. Delaying the timing of the gain recognition until liquidation is, of course, favorable to the remaining partners.

All of the foregoing examples involved distributions that liquidated a partner's interest. As discussed in Chapter 14, distortions similar to those illustrated in the above examples, however, can also occur as a result of nonliquidating distributions. *See* §§ 731(a)(1) (recognition of gain) and 732(a)(2) (limitation on the basis of distributed property).[9]

B. The § 754 Election and the § 734(b) Adjustment

In each of the foregoing examples, the distribution to Amy created a disparity between the remaining partners' aggregate outside basis and the aggregate inside basis of the remaining partnership property. The disparities arose because, pursuant to § 734(a), no adjustment could be made to the basis of partnership

---

[9] Losses, of course, can only be recognized on liquidating distributions. § 731(a)(2).

property unless the election authorized by § 754 was in effect.[10] These disparities, in turn, created distortions ("extra" partnership gain or loss) that were resolved only on the liquidation of the partnership.

---

§ 734. Adjustment to Basis of Undistributed Partnership Property Where Section 754 Election or Substantial Basis Reduction

(a) General Rule. The basis of partnership property shall not be adjusted as the result of a distribution of property to a partner unless the election, provided in section 754 (relating to optional adjustment to basis of partnership property), is in effect with respect to such partnership or unless there is a substantial basis reduction with respect to such distribution.

Had the ABCD Partnership made a § 754 election, § 734(b) would have required an adjustment to the basis of partnership property that would eliminate the basis disparity in the examples above and thus avoid the creation of the "extra" partnership gain or loss noted in those examples.

A partnership makes a § 754 election in a written statement filed with its partnership return. Reg. § 1.755-1(b). The election applies to all distributions made in the election year and subsequent years. Reg. § 1.755-1(a). It can be revoked with the approval of the Internal Revenue Service for "sufficient reason" — such as a change in the nature of the partnership business or the character of its assets, or the frequency of partnership distributions, but not primarily to avoid reductions in the basis of partnership assets. Reg. § 1.755-1(c)(1).

If a § 754 election is in effect, § 734(b) and the regulations thereunder provide a series of steps that must be followed in making the required inside basis adjustments necessary to address the basis disparities created by partnership distributions.

Step 1: Determine the Amount of the Basis Adjustment Required by § 734(b)

---

§ 734(b). Method of Adjustment

In the case of a distribution of property to a partner by a partnership with respect to which the election provided in section 754 is in effect or with respect to which there is a substantial basis reduction, the partnership shall —

(1) increase the adjusted basis of partnership property by —

---

[10] Even if a § 754 election were not in effect, however, an adjustment to the basis of undistributed partnership properties would be mandated if there is a "substantial basis reduction" with respect to a distribution of property to a partner. § 734(a). This special rule is discussed *infra*.

> (A) the amount of any gain recognized to the distributee partner with respect to such distribution under section 731(a)(1), and
>
> (B) in the case of distributed property to which section 732(a)(2) or (b) applies, the excess of the adjusted basis of the distributed property to the partnership immediately before the distribution . . . over the basis of the distributed property to the distributee, as determined under section 732, or
>
> (2) decrease the adjusted basis of partnership property by —
>
> (A) the amount of any loss recognized to the distributee partner with respect to such distribution under section 731(a)(2), and
>
> (B) in the case of distributed property to which section 732(b) applies, the excess of the basis of the distributed property to the distributee, as determined under section 732, over the adjusted basis of the distributed property to the partnership immediately before such distribution . . .

The § 734(b) adjustment will be an increase in the basis of partnership property when (1) the distribution (whether a liquidating or nonliquidating distribution) creates recognized gain, or (2) the distribution (whether a liquidating or nonliquidating distribution) results in a decrease in the basis of property as it moves from the partnership to the distributee partner. The amount of the § 734(b) increase equals the amount of the recognized gain or the amount of the decrease in basis in the distributed property. Thus, in Example (1), the distribution of $500 cash to Amy resulted in gain of $200 under § 731(a). With a § 754 election in effect, the partnership would increase the basis of remaining partnership property by $200, eliminating the "extra" $200 gain created by the distribution. Similarly, in Example (3), there was a decrease in the basis of Inventory B from $100 when held by the partnership to zero when held by Amy. With a § 754 election in effect, the partnership would increase the basis of remaining partnership property by $100, eliminating the "extra" $100 of built-in gain created by the distribution.

The § 734(b) adjustment will be a decrease in the basis of partnership property when (1) a liquidating distribution creates § 732 recognized loss, or (2) a liquidating or nonliquidating distribution results in an increase in the basis of property as it moves from the hands of the partnership to those of the distributee partner. The amount of the decrease will equal the recognized loss or the amount of the increase in the basis of the distributed property. Thus, in Example (2) above, when Amy recognized loss of $100 on the liquidating distribution of cash, application of § 734(b) would result in a decrease of $100 in the basis of remaining partnership property, eliminating the "extra" $100 of loss created by the distribution. Similarly, in Example (4) above, where the distribution of Capital Asset B increased its basis from $200 when held by the partnership to $300 when received by Amy, a § 754 election would require a decrease of $100 in the basis of remaining partnership property, thus accounting for the $100 gain that seemingly disappeared as a result of the liquidating distribution to Amy.

Because a § 754 election can thus be helpful to the remaining partners when it eliminates the "extra" gain created by a distribution, there is an incentive to make the § 754 election in those circumstances. But once made, the election can work in the other direction as well and eliminate the extra built-in loss or the disappearance of gain created on other distributions. And, as the regulations remind us, avoiding the "stepping down [of] the basis of partnership assets upon a . . . distribution" is not a sufficient reason to revoke a § 754 election. Reg. § 1.755-1(c)(1).

Having determined the total increase or decrease in partnership basis required by § 734(b), the next step is to allocate the basis adjustment between or among the remaining partnership assets.

Step 2: Allocate the § 734(b) Adjustment to Property of the Same Class

---

§ 755. Rules for Allocation of Basis.

(a) General Rule. Any increase or decrease in the adjusted basis of partnership property under section 734(b) . . . shall, except as provided in subsection (b), be allocated

(1) in a manner which has the effect of reducing the difference between the fair market value and the adjusted basis of partnership properties, or

(2) in any other manner permitted by regulations prescribed by the Secretary.

(b) Special Rule. In applying the allocation rules provided in subsection (a), increases or decreases in the adjusted basis of partnership property arising from a distribution of, or a transfer of an interest attributable to, property consisting of

(1) capital assets and property described in section 1231(b), or

(2) any other property of the partnership

shall be allocated to partnership property of a like character except that the basis of any such partnership property shall not be reduced below zero . . .

The § 734(b) adjustment must be allocated to property of the same class as the distributed property. § 755(b). For this purpose, there are two classes of property: (1) capital assets and property described in § 1231(b) (for convenience, capital assets) and (2) all other property (for convenience, ordinary income property). *Id.* Thus, if the § 734(b) adjustment is occasioned by a basis shift in a capital asset, the adjustment must be made to the partnership's remaining capital assets; if the basis adjustment is occasioned by a basis shift in ordinary income property, the adjustment must be made to the partnership's remaining ordinary income property. Suppose the adjustment is occasioned by a recognized gain — necessarily, capital gain — under §§ 731(a)(1) and 741, or by a recognized loss — necessarily, capital loss — on liquidation under §§ 731(a)(2) and 741. The § 734(b) adjustment must be made to remaining capital assets of the partnership.

Step 3: Prorate the § 734(b) Adjustment within a Class Based on Appreciation/Value or Depreciation/Basis

Having determined the total amount of the § 734(b) basis increase or decrease (Step 1) and the class of property to which it must be applied (Step 2), the § 734(b) adjustment must be allocated within that class in accordance with § 755 and the regulations thereunder. The general rule, under § 755(a)(1), is to make the adjustment in such a way as to reduce the difference between the value and the basis of the property being adjusted. But further guidance is needed and is supplied by the § 755 regulations as follows:

> In the case of a basis increase, the increase must be prorated among the appreciated properties of the appropriate class in proportion to their relative amounts of unrealized appreciation, but only to the extent of the unrealized appreciation. Any remaining increase under § 734(b) must be allocated among all properties in the class in proportion to their value. Reg. § 1.755-1(c)(2)(i).

> In the case of a decrease, the decrease must be prorated among properties in the appropriate class in proportion to their relative amounts of unrealized depreciation, but only to the extent of the unrealized depreciation. Any remaining decrease must be allocated among all properties in the class based upon their adjusted bases (as adjusted under the preceding sentence). Reg. § 1.755-1(c)(2)(ii). However, where the amount of a decrease exceeds its basis, the basis can be reduced to zero, but not below zero. Reg. § 1.755-1(c)(3).[11]

C. Application of § 734(b) to Examples (1)–(4) in Part A

Assume the ABCD Partnership had in effect a § 754 election at the time of the distributions set forth in Examples (1)–(4) above. Given that election, let us now revisit those examples to illustrate the application of the steps outlined above for adjusting the partnership's inside basis.

> **Example (1):** In this example, Amy recognized a gain of $200 on the cash distribution of $500. With a § 754 election in effect, the § 734(b) adjustment is an increase of $200. § 734(b)(1)(A). It must be applied to capital assets in proportion to the relative amounts of unrealized appreciation in the two capital assets held by the ABCD Partnership. § 755 and Reg. § 1.755-1(c)(1)(ii) and (2)(i). Before the distribution, the partnership assets and capital accounts were as follows:

---

[11] Note that no allocation of a basis decrease in partnership property is to be made to the stock of a corporate partner. § 755(c).

	Partnership Assets			Partners' Capital	
	A/B	FMV		A/B	FMV
Cash	$500	$500	Amy	$300	$500
Inventory A	$200	$100	Ben	$300	$500
Inventory B	$100	$200	Carol	$300	$500
Capital Asset A	$200	$700	Dan	$300	$500
Capital Asset B	$200	$500			
Total	$1,200	$2,000		$1,200	$2,000

The appreciation in Capital Asset A is $500; the appreciation in Capital Asset B is $300. Capital Asset A will thus receive 5/8, or $125, of the $200 adjustment, increasing its basis to $325. The remaining 3/8, or $75, of the $200 adjustment will be applied to Capital Asset B, increasing its basis to $275. The partnership assets with the § 734(b) adjustment and the capital accounts will be as follows:

	Partnership Assets			Partners' Capital	
	A/B	FMV		A/B	FMV
Inventory A	$200	$100	Ben	$300	$500
Inventory B	$100	$200	Carol	$300	$500
Capital Asset A	$325	$700	Dan	$300	$500
Capital Asset B	$275	$500			
Total	$900	$1,500		$900	$1,500

The "extra" $200 of built-in gain that resulted from the distribution when no § 754 election was in effect (see the analysis of Example 1 in Part A) has been eliminated.

Example (2): In this example, each partner's outside basis was $600 instead of $300, and the basis of Capital Asset A was $1,400 instead of $200. The liquidating cash distribution of $500 thus resulted in a recognized loss of $100 to Amy. The partnership assets and capital accounts before the distribution were as follows:

	Partnership Assets			Partners' Capital	
	A/B	FMV		A/B	FMV
Cash	$500	$500	Amy	$600	$500
Inventory A	$200	$100	Ben	$600	$500
Inventory B	$100	$200	Carol	$600	$500
Capital Asset A	$1,400	$700	Dan	$600	$500
Capital Asset B	$200	$500			
Total	$2,400	$2,000		$2,400	$2,000

The liquidating distribution of $500 resulted in Amy recognizing a capital loss of $100. §§ 731(a)(2) and 741. The § 734(b) adjustment is therefore a decrease of $100 which must be applied to capital assets based on relative amounts of unrealized depreciation. §§ 734(b)(2)(A) and 755(b). In this case, only Capital Asset A is depreciated, so the entire decrease is applied to that asset. Reg. § 1.755-1(c)(2)(ii). After the liquidation of Amy's interest and given the § 734(b) adjustment, the partnership balance sheet will be:

	Partnership Assets			Partners' Capital	
	A/B	FMV		A/B	FMV
Inventory A	$200	$100	Ben	$600	$500
Inventory B	$100	$200	Carol	$600	$500
Capital Asset A	$1,300	$700	Dan	$600	$500
Capital Asset B	$200	$500			
Total	$1,800	$1,500		$1,800	$1,500

The "extra" loss of $100 noted in the analysis of Example 2 in Part A is thus eliminated.

Example 3: In this example, Amy received $300 cash and Inventory B in a liquidating distribution. Before the distribution, the partnership assets and capital accounts were as follows:

	Partnership Assets			Partners' Capital	
	A/B	FMV		A/B	FMV
Cash	$500	$500	Amy	$300	$500
Inventory A	$200	$100	Ben	$300	$500
Inventory B	$100	$200	Carol	$300	$500
Capital Asset A	$200	$700	Dan	$300	$500
Capital Asset B	$200	$500			
Total	$1,200	$2,000		$1,200	$2,000

The cash distribution reduced Amy's outside basis to zero. Inventory B then took a basis of zero in Amy's hands, a reduction of $100 from its basis in the hands of the partnership. With a § 754 election in place, there is a § 734(b) basis increase of $100 that must be applied to the same class of property as Inventory B. Thus, the $100 basis increase must be applied to ordinary income property, with the increase amount first being allocated to ordinary income property based upon relative amounts of unrealized appreciation, and, second, to ordinary income property based upon relative values. Here, there is no appreciated ordinary income property. The only remaining ordinary income property, Inventory A, is depreciated, not appreciated. Nonetheless, in these circumstances, the $100 basis increase must be applied to Inventory A. Following the distribution and the § 734(b) adjustment, the partnership balance sheet will be as follows:

	Partnership Assets			Partners' Capital	
	A/B	FMV		A/B	FMV
Cash	$200	$200	Ben	$300	$500
Inventory A	$300	$100	Carol	$300	$500
Capital Asset A	$200	$700	Dan	$300	$500
Capital Asset B	$200	$500			
Total	**$900**	**$1,500**		**$900**	**$1,500**

Note that, prior to the distribution, the $100 built-in loss on Inventory A was balanced by the $100 built-in gain on Inventory B. The distribution left Amy with built-in gain of $200 in Inventory B (value of $200, basis of zero in her hands). With the § 734(b) adjustment, there is now a built-in loss of $200 in Inventory A in the hands of the partnership. Ordinary income has thus been shifted to Amy, with offsetting ordinary loss to the remaining partners.[12]

Example 4: In this example, Amy received Capital Asset B in a liquidating distribution. Before the distribution, the partnership assets and capital accounts were as follows:

	Partnership Assets			Partners' Capital	
	A/B	FMV		A/B	FMV
Cash	$500	$500	Amy	$500	$300
Inventory A	$200	$100	Ben	$300	$500
Inventory B	$100	$200	Carol	$300	$500
Capital Asset A	$200	$700	Dan	$300	$500
Capital Asset B	$200	$500			
Total	**$1,200**	**$2,000**		**$1,200**	**$2,000**

As a result of the distribution, the basis of Capital Asset B increased from $200 in the hands of the partnership to $300 in Amy's hands. With a § 754 election in effect, the § 734(b) adjustment is a decrease of $100, which must be applied to property of like class based, first, upon relative amounts of unrealized depreciation and, second, to property of like class based upon relative adjusted basis (following the adjustment based upon amounts of depreciation). There is no capital asset with unrealized depreciation. The only remaining capital asset, Capital Asset A, is appreciated. Nonetheless, the $100 basis decrease is applied to this property. (Note that the decrease here does not impermissibly reduce basis below zero.) After the distribution and § 734(b) adjustment, the partnership balance sheet will be as follows:

---

[12] As indicated in footnote 2, Because the inventory in the aggregate was not "substantially appreciated" within the meaning of § 751(b)(3), the disproportionate distribution of inventory to Amy would not trigger the special recharacterization rules of § 751(b) that are discussed in detail in Chapter 16.

	Partnership Assets			**Partners' Capital**	
	A/B	FMV		A/B	FMV
Cash	$500	$500	Ben	$300	$500
Inventory A	$200	$100	Carol	$300	$500
Inventory B	$100	$200	Dan	$300	$500
Capital Asset A	$100	$700			
Total	$900	$1,500		$900	$1,500

In this example, the predistribution appreciation of $800 in Capital Assets A and B has been preserved: Amy holds capital Asset B with a value of $500 and basis of $300, accounting for $200 of the appreciation; the partnership holds capital Asset A with unrealized appreciation of $600 following the § 734(b) adjustment.

D. Additional Examples of § 734(b) Adjustments

The following examples illustrate the application of §§ 734(b) and 755 in more complex situations than presented in Examples (1)–(4) above. Assume a § 754 election is in effect in all of the following examples.

Example 5. Assume the RST Partnership must make a § 734(b) basis increase of $500 on account of the distribution of Inventory A to Ron that resulted in a $500 decrease in the basis of Inventory A.[13] The partnership's remaining assets are:

	Partnership Assets	
	A/B	FMV
Inventory B	$400	$1,000
Inventory C	$600	$800
Inventory D	$1,800	$1,000
Capital Asset A	$1,800	$2,000
Total	$3,300	$4,800

In allocating the $500 § 734(b) adjustment, we must first allocate the adjustment to property of like class — here, the inventory items. Next, we allocate the basis increase to items within that class based upon relative amounts of unrealized appreciation. The appreciated inventory items are Inventory B and Inventory C. The total appreciation in the two items is $800, of which 75% ($600 of $800) is attributable to Inventory B and 25% ($200 of $800) is attributable Inventory C. The adjustment to Inventory B is $375 (75% of the $500 adjustment) and the adjustment to Inventory C is $125 (25% of the $500 adjustment). The bases of the assets are now as follows:

---

[13] We will assume that § 751(b), which recharacterizes certain distributions as in part sales or exchanges between a partner and a partnership and in part as a distribution, does not apply to this distribution. Section 751(b) is discussed in detail in Chapter 16.

	Partnership Assets	
	A/B	FMV
Inventory B	$775	$1,000
Inventory C	$725	$800
Inventory D	$1,800	$1,000
Capital Asset A	$500	$2,000
Total	**$3,800**	**$4,800**

Example 6: Assume the same facts as Example (5) — that is, a distribution to Ron of Inventory A, requiring a § 734(b) basis increase of $500 — except the remaining partnership assets do not include Inventory B.[14] As in Example (5), the $500 basis increase required by § 734(b) is first allocated to appreciated inventory — now only Inventory C. But the increase in basis allocated under this step cannot exceed $200, the amount of the unrealized appreciation inherent in Inventory C. The $300 of remaining basis increase must be allocated to like class property — Inventory C and Inventory D — based upon their relative fair market values, $800 and $1,000, respectively. Inventory C's share of the $300 increase under this step is approximately $133; Inventory D's share of the $300 increase under this step is approximately $167. (These dollar amounts reflect Inventory C's $800 share — about 44.4% — of the combined value of $1,800, and Inventory D's $1,000 share — about 55.6% — of the combined value of $1,800. As a result, 44.4% of the remaining $300 of basis increase, or $133, will be allocated to Inventory C and 55.6% of the remaining $300 basis increase, or $167, will be allocated to Inventory D.) Therefore, the $500 § 734(b) basis adjustment is allocated as follows: $333 to Inventory C and $167 to Inventory D. The following table reflects the partnership assets and bases taking into account the § 734(b) adjustments:

	Partnership Assets	
	A/B	FMV
Inventory C	$933	$800
Inventory D	$1,967	$1,000
Capital Asset A	$500	$2,000
Total	**$3,400**	**$3,800**

Example (7). Assume the same facts as Example (5) — that is, a distribution to Ron of Inventory A, requiring a § 734(b) basis increase of $500 — except the only remaining partnership asset is Capital Asset A. Again, the $500 basis increase must be allocated to the same class of property as Inventory A, i.e., ordinary income property. The partnership, however, has no assets of that class. Under these circumstances, the adjustment is suspended until the partnership acquires property of that

---

[14] Again, assume that § 751(b) did not apply to the distribution.

class. At that time, the § 734(b) increase of $500 may be applied to such property. *See* Reg. § 1.755-1(c)(4).

Example (8): Assume the same facts as Example (5) — that is, a distribution of Inventory A to Ron — except the § 734(b) adjustment to be made on account of the distribution is a $500 decrease to ordinary income property. Recall that Inventory B and C are appreciated; the only depreciated inventory is Inventory D, so the entire $500 decrease is made to its basis.

Suppose, however, that the § 734(b) adjustment was a $1,000 decrease to ordinary income property. Again, the only depreciated inventory is Inventory D. The amount of its unrealized depreciation is $800 (value $1,000, basis $1,800), so the first $800 of the decrease is applied to Inventory D. The remainder of the decrease, $200, must be allocated in proportion to the adjusted bases of property of like class, as determined after the first step of the adjustment (the $800 reduction in the basis of Inventory D). The adjusted bases of Inventory B, Inventory C, and Inventory D (including the $800 decrease) are $400, $600, and $1,000, respectively. Allotting the remaining $200 decrease proportionately results in decreases of $40 to Inventory B, $60 to Inventory C, and $100 to Inventory D. (Inventory D's total decrease is thus $900.) Following the basis adjustments, the partnership's assets and their bases are as follows:

	Partnership Assets	
	A/B	FMV
Inventory B	$360	$1,000
Inventory C	$540	$800
Inventory D	$900	$1,000
Capital Asset A	$500	$2,000
Total	**$2,300**	**$4,800**

E. The Mandatory Basis Adjustment of § 734(d): The Substantial Basis Reduction Rule

To this point, basis adjustments to remaining partnership property following a distribution to a partner have taken place only when a § 754 election was in place. Historically, without that election, no adjustment to basis could be made as a result of a liquidating or nonliquidating distribution. This part of the chapter discusses a relatively recent exception to this rule: a mandatory basis adjustment that is made regardless of whether a § 754 election is in effect.

Recall from Examples (1)–(4) in Part A of this chapter that the consequences of a distribution — recognized gain, recognized loss, basis change to distributed property — can be favorable or unfavorable to the remaining partners. In some circumstances (see Examples (1) and (3)), the distribution creates "extra" gain causing the remaining partners to be "overtaxed" on a sale of partnership property. A § 754 election eliminates the "extra" gain. In other circumstances (see Examples (2) and (4)), however, the distribution creates "extra" loss or the disappearance of gain, causing the remaining partners to be "undertaxed" on a sale of partnership property, and a § 754 election is to be avoided.

Enter the substantial basis reduction rule of § 734(d). In 2004, Congress amended § 732(b) to provide that a basis adjustment is required not only when a § 754 election is in effect, but also when there is "a substantial basis reduction." Under § 734(d), this occurs when the sum of (1) the recognized loss, if any, on a liquidating distribution and (2) the basis reduction, if any, on distributed property exceeds $250,000.[15] The 2004 amendments were intended to counter partnership distributions that brought about undertaxation of the remaining partners by creating large losses. Consider the following example:

Example The LMN Partnership has three assets. The partnership balance sheet is as follows:

	Partnership Assets			Partners' Capital	
	A/B	FMV		A/B	FMV
Capital Asset A	$200,000	$600,000	Larry	$500,000	$600,000
Capital Asset B	$500,000	$600,000	Mary	$500,000	$600,000
Capital Asset C	$800,000	$600,000	Nancy	$500,000	$600,000
Total	$1,500,000	$1,800,000		$1,500,000	$1,800,000

As reflected by the above balance sheet, there is, in the aggregate, $300,000 of appreciation inherent in the partnership assets. Each of the three equal partners has a one-third (or $100,000) share of that appreciation.

Assume the partnership makes a liquidating distribution to Larry of Capital Asset A, which will have a basis in his hands of $500,000 under § 732(b). Without a § 754 election and disregarding § 734(d), the balance sheet following the distribution would be as follows:

	Partnership Assets			Partners' Capital	
	A/B	FMV		A/B	FMV
Capital Asset B	$500,000	$600,000	Mary	$500,000	$600,000
Capital Asset C	$800,000	$600,000	Nancy	$500,000	$600,000
Total	$1,300,000	$1,200,000		$1,000,000	$1,200,000

Larry's $100,000 share of the net partnership appreciation is preserved: Capital Asset A has a value of $600,000 and a basis of $500,000 in his hands. But Mary's and Nancy's shares of net gain have disappeared, from $100,000 net appreciation each, to $50,000 net depreciation each. (Capital Assets B and C have an aggregate value of $1,200,000 and aggregate basis of $1,300,000.)[16] Even if a § 754 election is not in effect, there is a substantial basis reduction because the excess of Capital Asset A's basis in

---

[15] The substantial basis reduction rules do not apply to "securitization partnerships," a term defined in § 743(f), in part, as any partnership the sole business activity of which is to issue securities that provide for a fixed principal amount. We will not consider these partnerships in this chapter.

[16] Note that, had LMN distributed Capital Asset C to Larry instead of Capital Asset A, Mary and

Larry's hands ($500,000) over its basis in the hands of the partnership ($200,000) is more than $250,000. It is $300,000. Accordingly, § 734(d) mandates that the basis of Capital Asset B and the basis of Capital Asset C be decreased by a total of $300,000. The decrease is based, first, upon their relative amounts of unrealized depreciation. Capital Asset C is the only depreciated capital asset (depreciated by $200,000) so the first $200,000 of decrease is applied to Capital Asset C, reducing its basis to $600,000. The remaining decrease of $100,000 is then allocated based upon the relative bases of Capital Asset B ($500,000) and Capital Asset C ($600,000, as adjusted). Capital Asset B will reduce its basis by about $45,000, and Capital Asset C will further reduce its basis by about $55,000. (Capital Asset B's basis of $500,000 is approximately 45% of the aggregate basis of $1,100,000; Capital Asset C's basis of $600,000 is approximately 55% of the aggregate basis of $1,100,000.) The total basis decrease for Capital Asset C is thus $200,000 plus $55,000, or $255,000. The partnership balance sheet after the distribution of Capital Asset A and the mandatory adjustments to Capital Assets B and C is as follows:

	Partnership Assets			**Partners' Capital**	
	A/B	FMV		A/B	FMV
Capital Asset B	$455,000	$600,000	Mary	$500,000	$600,000
Capital Asset C	$545,000	$600,000	Nancy	$500,000	$600,000
Total	$1,000,000	$1,200,000		$1,000,000	$1,200,000

F. The Partnership Anti-Abuse Rules

Chapter 21 discusses partnership anti-abuse rules established by regulation at the end of 1994. At the time Treasury promulgated the anti-abuse rules, there was considerable concern that partnership rules were being exploited in ways inconsistent with the overall aim of Subchapter K. One of the concerns expressed in example form was the use of partnerships to duplicate losses through the *absence* of a § 754 election. See Reg. § 1.701-2(d) Ex. 8. The 2004 statutory amendments creating the substantial basis reduction provisions — that operate even in the absence of a § 754 election — have presumably gone a long way to alleviate the Service's concern with duplication of losses through distributions of partnership property. The statutory amendments suggest, in general, a willingness to tolerate loss creations not exceeding $250,000. Even then, of course, the Service could use the anti-abuse rules to attack a particular distribution as being so egregious as not to be consistent with the intent of Subchapter K; but it will likely be unusual now for the Service to challenge distributions on account of the absence of a § 754 election.

Nancy's share of net partnership appreciation would have been *greater* after the distribution than it was before.

Chapter 16

DISPROPORTIONATE DISTRIBUTIONS: § 751(b)

I. PROBLEMS

Fifteen years ago, Abigail, Brian, and Clare formed the ABC Partnership, a general partnership. Each of the three partners has an equal one-third interest in the partnership. On January 1, 2016, the partnership has the following balance sheet: [Assume none of the partnership's assets is § 704(c) property and all assets have been held by the partnership for more than one year.]

	Partnership Assets			Partners' Capital	
	A/B	FMV		A/B	FMV
Cash	$290,000	$290,000	Abigail	$220,000	$400,000
Inventory	$150,000	$450,000	Brian	$220,000	$400,000
Capital Asset #1	$45,000	$225,000	Clare	$220,000	$400,000
Capital Asset #2	$95,000	$75,000			
Capital Asset #3	$80,000	$160,000			
Total	**$660,000**	**$1,200,000**		**$660,000**	**$1,200,000**

(a) Applying the current § 751(b) regulations, explain the tax consequences to Brian and the partnership of the following alternative distributions in liquidation of Brian's partnership interest. Unless otherwise provided, assume the partnership has not made a § 754 election.

    (i) $150,000 of inventory, Capital Asset #1 and $25,000 in cash.

    (ii) $250,000 in cash and $150,000 of inventory.

    (iii) Capital Asset #3 and $240,000 of cash. Assume a § 754 election was in effect.

    (iv) Same as (iii) except that the partners agree that Brian received $150,000 of the cash for relinquishing his interest in the partnership inventory.

b. Explain the tax consequences to Brian and the partnership of the following alternative nonliquidating distributions made to Brian:

    (i) The partnership distributed $125,000 in cash and $75,000 in inventory to Brian and Brian's interest in the partnership was reduced from one-third to one-fifth.

    (ii) The partnership distributed $200,000 in cash to Brian and Brian's interest in the partnership was reduced from one-third to one-fifth.

Assignment for Chapter 16:

Complete the Problems

Read: Internal Revenue Code: §§ 731(a), (b), and (d), 732(a) and (b), 741, 751(b)–(d)
Treasury Regulations: § 1.751-1(b)(1)-(4)(i), (c)(1) and (2), (d), (e), (g) Exs. 2 and 3. Skim Prop. Reg. § 1.751-1(b)(1)–(3), (f), (g) Exs. 1, 2, and 4.
Materials: Overview
Revenue Ruling 84-102

II. VOCABULARY

unrealized receivables
substantially appreciated inventory
§ 751 property (or hot assets)
other property (or cold assets)
deemed distribution
deemed sale or exchange

III. OBJECTIVES

1. To recall the purpose of § 751(b).
2. To identify distributions that are disproportionate within the meaning of § 751(b).
3. To describe the deemed distribution and deemed sale or exchange presumed to occur in a transaction governed by § 751(b).
4. To determine the tax consequences to both the distributee partner and the partnership of distributions to which § 751(b) applies.
5. To evaluate the efficacy of § 751(b) in achieving the congressional purpose of that provision.

IV. OVERVIEW

Section 751(b), the focus of this chapter, is often overlooked as partners and partnerships address the tax consequences of liquidating and nonliquidating distributions. The provision is both complex and flawed. Despite many calls for its repeal, § 751(b) remains a part of the Subchapter K landscape. As discussed in the final part of this chapter, however, Treasury recently issued proposed regulations designed to simplify the application of § 751(b) and ensure that the provision better achieves its purpose. A basic understanding of § 751(b) and the existing regulations interpreting and applying that provision, however, remains essential for those advising partners and partnerships. That understanding will also place in focus the significance of the proposed regulations.

A. The Purpose of § 751(b)

Section 751(b) characterizes certain distributions as involving, in part, a sale or exchange. Congress enacted the provision in 1954 to prevent partners from using their partnerships to convert ordinary income into capital gain by shifting ordinary income among the partners.[1] Let us begin our examination of § 751(b) using an example to analyze the tax implications of a simple liquidating distribution, *initially assuming that § 751(b) doesn't exist*. Given this assumption, our analysis will illustrate the congressional purpose in enacting the provision. We will then apply § 751(b) to the distribution in the example and evaluate how effectively § 751(b) achieves its purpose.

> **Example 1:** In Year 1, Fred, Monica, and Judson each contributed $150 in cash to form a general partnership in which they have equal interests. *(Assume that all numbers used in this example and its analysis below are in thousands.)* For simplicity's sake, assume that, during its existence, the partnership has consistently distributed all income as it is earned. In Year 10 the partnership liquidated Fred's partnership interest by paying Fred $120 in cash.[2] The partnership had the following balance sheet immediately prior to the liquidation of Fred's interests.[3]
>
> | | Partnership Assets | | | Partners' Capital[4] | |
> |---|---|---|---|---|---|
> | | A/B | FMV | | A/B | FMV |
> | Cash | $150 | $150 | Fred | $150 | $120 |
> | Inventory | $60 | $90 | Monica | $150 | $120 |
> | Capital Asset | $240 | $120 | Judson | $150 | $120 |
> | **Total** | **$450** | **$360** | | **$450** | **$360** |

If § 751(b) did not exist, we would look to § 731(a) and (b) to determine the amount of gain or loss, if any, to be recognized by Fred and the partnership on the

---

[1] *See* H.R. Rep. No. 1337, at 70 (1954).

[2] As noted in Chapter 14, liquidating distributions can be divided into two subcategories, i.e., distributions that liquidate the entire partnership and distributions that liquidate the interest of a "retiring" partner. Example 1 presents the latter subcategory of liquidating distributions. As will be discussed in detail in Chapter 17, § 736 is applicable to such distributions. As you will learn in that chapter, § 736(a), *in limited circumstances*, treats part of the liquidating payment as a distributive share or guaranteed payment. If § 736(a) is inapplicable, however, the liquidating payment to a retiring partner will, pursuant to § 736(b), be treated under the general distribution rules you have studied in Chapter 14, i.e., §§ 731, 732, and 741. Example 1 does not implicate § 736(a) and thus we will simply apply the general distribution rules previously examined. As will be discussed *infra*, however, § 751(b) will impact the analysis of the tax consequences to the "retiring" partner and the partnership.

[3] Note that the balance sheet reflects the fair market value of the partnership's assets and the partners' capital accounts at the time of the liquidation of Fred's interest.

[4] Regulation § 1.704-1(b)(2)(iv)(f) allows a partnership, on the occurrence of certain events, e.g., a liquidation of a partner's interest, to increase (book-up) or decrease (book-down) the capital accounts of the partners to reflect the revaluation of partnership property. We will assume the partnership elected to adjust its capital accounts to reflect a revaluation of its property pursuant to this regulation. Thus, the FMV figure shown with respect to each partner's interest on the balance sheets in this chapter constitutes the partner's capital account based upon the revaluation.

liquidating distribution.[5] As reflected in the above balance sheet, immediately before the liquidation of his interest, Fred has a loss of $30 inherent in his partnership interest (FMV of $120, adjusted basis of $150). Will any of that $30 loss be recognized when Fred receives a liquidating distribution of $120? As you studied in Chapter 14, § 731(a)(2) provides for the possibility of loss recognition on the liquidation of a partner's interest to the extent a partner receives only money, unrealized receivables and/or inventory on the liquidation of his interest. Here, Fred receives only cash. Because the cash received by Fred is less than Fred's outside basis, Fred would recognize a $30 loss on the liquidation of his partnership interest. § 731(a)(2). Section 731(a) provides that Fred's loss will be considered a loss from the *sale or exchange* of his partnership interest. In addition, § 741 provides that Fred's loss will be treated as a loss from the sale or exchange of a capital asset *except as provided by § 751*[6] (again, we are disregarding § 751 at this point). Fred would thus recognize a $30 capital loss on the liquidation of his partnership interest. Because he held his partnership interest for more than 12 months, Fred's loss would be a long-term capital loss. The partnership will not recognize any gain or loss on the liquidating distribution. § 731(b).

Pursuant to the aggregate approach to the taxation of partners and partnerships, Fred, as an equal partner in the three-person partnership, would be deemed to have a one-third interest in each of the partnership's assets, i.e., the cash, inventory, and capital asset. Thus, from a tax standpoint, Fred has a one-third share or $10 of the $30 of ordinary income inherent in the partnership's inventory and a $40 share of the $120 of the loss inherent in its capital asset. Instead of receiving a liquidating distribution consisting of one-third of each of each of the partnership's assets, however, Fred received only cash. In effect, Fred has given up his interest in both the Inventory and the Capital Asset in exchange for more cash. As noted in the analysis above, were we to disregard § 751(b), the only tax consequence to Fred on the liquidating distribution is the recognition of a $30 long-term capital loss. Fred has thus converted what should have been a $10 share of ordinary income and a $40 share of long-term capital loss into $30 of long-term capital loss. Following the liquidation of Fred's interest, the partnership's balance sheet would be as follows:

	Partnership Assets			**Partners' Capital**	
	A/B	FMV		A/B	FMV
Cash	$30	$30	Monica	$150	$120
Inventory	$60	$90	Judson	$150	$120
Capital Asset	$240	$120			
Total:	$330	$240		$300	$240

As you look at this balance sheet, it should be apparent that Monica and Judson would each recognize $15 of ordinary income if the partnership subsequently sold the Inventory for $90. Likewise, they each would recognize $60 of long-term capital

---

[5] Review Chapter 14 addressing the basic rules governing distributions. As will be discussed in Chapter 19, there are other provisions, e.g., § 704(c)(1)(B) and § 737, which, under limited circumstances, might also be applicable. Those provisions, however, are not applicable in this example.

[6] Note how § 751 overrides § 741.

loss if the partnership sold the Capital Asset for $120.[7] Contrast these results to the results if Fred had remained in the partnership and the partnership sold both the Inventory and the Capital Asset for their fair market values. In that case, Fred, Monica, and Judson would each have a $10 share of the $30 in ordinary income associated with the Inventory and a $40 share of the $120 loss associated with the Capital Asset. The shifting to Monica and Judson of all the ordinary income inherent in the Inventory suggests the concern that prompted Congress to enact § 751.

B. Application of § 751(b)

Let us now examine the operation of § 751(b) and the current regulations interpreting that provision by applying § 751(b) to the liquidating distribution to Fred in the above example. Study the specific language of § 751(b). (Note how § 751(b) converts part of what appears to be a distribution into a sale or exchange. In doing so, it overrides the nonrecognition rules of § 731 discussed in Chapter 14.)

---

§ 751(b). Certain distributions treated as sales or exchanges.

(1) General rule: to the extent a partner receives in a distribution

(A) partnership property which is —

(i) unrealized receivables, or

(ii) inventory items which have appreciated substantially in value in exchange for all or a part of his interest in other partnership property (including money) or

(B) partnership property (including money) other than property described in subparagraph (A)(i) or (ii) in exchange for all or a part of his interest in partnership property described in subparagraph (A)(i) or (ii), such transaction shall, under regulations prescribed by the Secretary, be considered as a sale or exchange of such property between the distributee and the partnership (as constituted after the distribution).

The Service in Notice 2006-14[8] has provided the following helpful summary of the operation of § 751(b) and the regulations interpreting it:

> The [Code and the regulations] require the identification of two classes of assets: **(1) hot assets** (unrealized receivables as defined in § 751(c) and

---

[7] Note that the above balance sheet doesn't balance. As discussed in detail in Chapter 15, were a § 754 election in effect, the balance sheet would be balanced as a result of the application of §§ 734(b)(2)(A) and 755 and Reg. § 1.755-1(c)(1)(ii). The fact that Monica and Judson each recognize $60 of capital loss instead of $45 of capital loss is due to the absence of a § 754 election — but the shift of all the ordinary income to them would occur even with the § 754 election. It is the character shifting § 751(b) addresses.

[8] 2006-1 C.B. 498. Notice 2006-14 set the stage for the recently proposed § 751(b) regulations. As discussed briefly below, the Service in this Notice requested comments on alternative approaches to § 751(b).

substantially appreciated inventory as defined in § 751(b)(3) and (d)); and **(2) cold assets** (assets other than unrealized receivables and substantially appreciated inventory). In computing the distributee partner's income under § 751(b), the current regulations provide that the distributee partner's share of the partnership's hot assets and cold assets before and after the distribution must be compared. For purposes of this comparison, **each partner's share of the partnership's hot and cold assets is determined by reference to the *gross value of the assets*.** If the distribution results in an exchange of all or a portion of the distributee partner's share of one class of assets (relinquished assets) for assets in the other class (acquired assets), it is necessary to construct a deemed exchange by identifying which relinquished assets are treated as exchanged for which acquired assets. . . . [T]o accomplish the exchange, the distributee partner is treated as (1) receiving the relinquished assets . . . in a nonliquidating distribution and (2) engaging in a taxable exchange [or sale] of those assets for the acquired assets. . . . Both the distributee partner and the other partners may recognize income or loss on the exchange. The distributee partner and the partnership then hold the exchanged assets (or portions thereof) with a cost basis under § 1012. The rest of the actual distribution (that part that is not subject to § 751(b)) is characterized under the general rules for partnership distributions prescribed in §§ 731-736. [Emphasis added.]

As indicated in the Notice, the current regulations use a "gross value approach" as the method for computing each partner's share of partnership "751 property" or "hot assets" and "other property" or "cold assets"[9] to determine whether a distribution reduces a partner's interest in the partnership's § 751 property. Current Reg. § 1.751-1(b) and (g) Exs. 2 and 3 apply an "asset exchange" approach to determine the tax consequences of distributions when § 751(b) applies. The Notice's summary of the operation of § 751(b) and the current regulations thus suggests the following multi-step approach for determining the tax consequences associated with liquidating and nonliquidating distributions subject to § 751(b). We will use this multi-step process in demonstrating the application of § 751(b) to the facts of Example 1 above.

Step 1: Determine whether the Partnership Holds "§ 751 Property"

Section 751(b) is applicable *only* if the partnership has either "unrealized receivables" as defined in § 751(c) or "substantially appreciated inventory items" as defined in § 751(b)(3)(A). *These are assets that generate ordinary income or loss.* In enacting § 751(b), Congress sought to ensure that a *liquidating or nonliquidating*[10] distribution by a partnership holding "unrealized receivables" and/or "substantially appreciated inventory" did not, in effect, convert for any partner what otherwise would have been ordinary income into capital gain. Thus, the first step in the

---

[9] In other words, the current regulations do not determine a partner's interest in § 751 property by reference to the partner's share of the unrealized gain or loss in that property.

[10] Section 751(b) is equally applicable to distributions that liquidate the entire partnership or distributions that liquidate only a "retiring" partner's interest.

§ 751(b) analysis must be a determination of whether any of these items of property are held by the partnership.

The regulations refer to "unrealized receivables" and "substantially appreciated inventory" as "§ 751 property" and, as noted in the Service's summary in Notice 2006-14 above, these items have typically been referred to as "hot assets." Property other than unrealized receivables and substantially appreciated inventory is referred to in the regulations as "other property." In Notice 2006–14, items of "other property" are referred to as "cold assets."[11] (Again, see the above summary of the Service regarding the operation of § 751(b).)

The term "unrealized receivables" is defined in § 751(c) to include not only rights to payments not previously included in income for goods delivered or to be delivered and services rendered or to be rendered, but also § 1245 property to the extent of the amount of gain that would be subject to § 1245 recapture.

"Inventory" is defined in § 751(d) and includes: (1) property described in § 1221(a)(1) (inventory and property held for sale to customers in the ordinary course of a trade or business), (2) property that on sale or exchange would not be either a capital asset or property described in § 1231,[12] and also (3) partnership property *which if held by the distributee partner* would be described in (1) or (2) above. Inventory items are substantially appreciated in value if their fair market value exceeds 120 percent of the partnership's adjusted basis in the inventory items.[13] The terms "inventory items which have appreciated substantially in value" or "substantially appreciated inventory items" refer to the aggregate of all such partnership items. As the regulations note:

> These terms do not refer to specific partnership inventory items or to specific groups of such items. For example, any distribution of inventory items by a partnership the inventory items of which are substantially appreciated in value shall be a distribution of substantially appreciated inventory for the purposes of § 751(b), even though the specific inventory items distributed may not be appreciated in value. Similarly, if the aggregate of partnership inventory items are not substantially appreciated

---

[11] For example, cash and capital assets are "other property" or "cold assets." In this chapter, we will generally use the terms employed by the regulations, i.e., "§ 751 property" to encompass "unrealized receivables" and "substantially appreciated inventory" and "other property" to encompass assets other than "unrealized receivables" and "substantially appreciated inventory."

[12] Reg. § 1.751-1(d)(2)(ii) provides that this category of inventory includes accounts receivable acquired in the ordinary course of business for services or from the sale of stock in trade as do any other unrealized receivables. By including unrealized receivables in inventory, it is possible that inventory in the aggregate will meet the "substantially appreciated" requirement of § 751(b)(3). For example, if a partnership had accounts receivable valued at $100 with a $0 basis and inventory valued at $100 with a $90 basis, the inventory, without the inclusion of the accounts receivable, would not be "substantially appreciated." But with the accounts receivable being treated as inventory, the inventory in the aggregate will have a value of $200 and an adjusted basis of only $90 and, as a result, will be will be "substantially appreciated." Thus, in this example, both the accounts receivable and the inventory will be "hot assets." *Inclusion of unrealized receivables in the inventory, however, will not result in taxation of the unrealized receivables twice.* After you have studied this Overview, you should be able to explain why that is always true.

[13] § 751(b)(3)(A).

in value, a distribution of specific inventory items, the value of which is more than 120 percent of their adjusted basis, will not constitute a distribution of substantially appreciated inventory items.[14]

To prevent a partnership from acquiring inventory immediately prior to a distribution so as to negate the partnership's inventory from being "substantially appreciated" (i.e., to prevent the inventory from satisfying the 120% rule), Congress specifically provided that inventory so acquired will be excluded in determining whether the partnership's inventory is "substantially appreciated." § 751(b)(3)(B).

In Example 1, the partnership holds substantially appreciated inventory (i.e., the Inventory's fair market value of $90 is more than 120% of the partnership's $60 adjusted basis in the Inventory (120% of $60 = $72). See Reg. § 1.751-1(g) Ex. 2(b).

Step 2: Taking into account any continuing interest a distributee partner may have in the partnership, determine whether that partner has received a disproportionate share of either "§ 751 property" (hot assets) or "other property" (cold assets)

As noted in Reg. § 1.751-1(b)(1)(ii), § 751(b) "does not apply to the extent that a distribution consists of the distributee partner's share of § 751 property or his share of other property." To determine whether a partner has received a disproportionate share of § 751 property or of "other property," one must consider not only the assets distributed, but also any continuing share the distributee may have in remaining partnership property.[15] The following table, based on Notice 2006-14 and the specific regulations interpreting and applying § 751(b), will indicate whether there has been a change (an increase or decrease) in the partner's share of "§ 751 property" or "other property." It will also set the stage for determining that part of the distribution which will be characterized by § 751(b) and the regulations as an "exchange" or a "sale." Thus, for example, if the table below indicates that a partner's share of § 751 property had increased, one would expect a corresponding decrease in the partner's share of "other property." *(Taken together, Steps 1 and 2 thus reflect the "gross value" approach of the current regulations as noted in the Notice 2006-14 summary above.)*

---

[14] Reg. § 1.751-1(d)(1).

[15] Reg. § 1.751-1(b)(1)(ii) specifically states that "in determining whether a partner has received only his share of either § 751 property or of other property, his interest in such property remaining in the partnership immediately after a distribution must be taken into account." See also Notice 2006–14, *supra*.

IV. OVERVIEW

Interest in "§ 751 Property" (or "Hot Assets")		**Interest in "Other Property" (or "Cold Assets")**	
FMV of "751 property" received	$___	FMV of "other property" received	$___
Plus		**Plus**	
Share of "§ 751 property" post-distribution	$___	Share of "other property" post-distribution	$___
Less		**Less**	
Share of "§ 751 property" pre-distribution	$___	Share of "other property" pre-distribution	$___
Increase (or decrease) in share of "§ 751 property"	$___	**Increase (or decrease) in share of "other property"**	$___

Using the facts of our example regarding the liquidation of Fred's partnership interest, we would complete the above table as follows:

Interest in "§ 751 Property" (or "Hot Assets")		**Interest in "Other Property" (or "Cold Assets")**	
FMV of "751 property" received	$0	FMV of "other property" received	$120
Plus		**Plus**	
Partner's share of "§ 751 property" post-distribution	$0[16]	Share of "other property" post-distribution	$0[17]
Less		**Less**	
Share of "§ 751 property" pre-distribution	$30	Share of "other property" pre-distribution	$90
Increase (or decrease) in share of "§ 751 property"	($30)	**Increase (or decrease) in share of "other property"**	$30

Thus, Fred has experienced a $30 decrease in his share of "§ 751 property" and has a corresponding $30 increase in his share of "other property." Consequently, the distribution will be treated, in part, as an exchange (or sale) of § 751 property for "other property." Pursuant to Reg. § 1.751-1(b)(1)(iii), the distribution must therefore be divided for the purpose of applying § 751(b). The rules of § 751(b) must first be applied to the part of the distribution treated as a sale or exchange; the general distribution rules of § 731 *et seq.* will then be applied to the part of the distribution not treated as a sale or exchange. Reg. § 1.751-1(b)(1)(iii).

---

[16] Because Fred's partnership interest is being liquidated, he will have no continuing interest in any "§ 751 property" or "other property" the partnership may continue to own.

[17] *Id.*

Step 3: Determine what part of the distribution will be treated as a sale or exchange.

The completed table above makes clear that Fred has received more than his share of "other property." In effect, he has "exchanged" his $30 interest in the substantially appreciated inventory for an additional $30 of "other property" — in this case, cash. Under § 751(b), he is deemed to have sold his interest in the substantially appreciated inventory for $30 of cash. To that extent, the liquidating distribution is not a distribution to which § 731 applies. Fred will be taxed on that "sale." See Reg. § 1.751–1(g) Ex. 2(c).

Step 4. Determine the property the partner is presumed to have received in a distribution and that the partner will relinquish in the deemed sale or exchange.

For purposes of determining the tax consequences to the partner and the partnership of the sale or exchange deemed to occur under § 751(b), it is first necessary to determine the property the partner will be treated as relinquishing in the deemed sale or exchange and the adjusted basis the partner has in that property. Note that Reg. § 1.751-1(g) Ex. 4(c) provides the partners may agree what property or properties will be deemed sold or exchanged. In the absence of such agreement, the distributee partner will be presumed to have sold or exchanged "a proportionate amount of each property in which he relinquished an interest."

As to the distributee partner's adjusted basis in the relinquished property, Reg. § 1.751-1(b)(2) and (3) provide that the partner will have the same adjusted basis "as if the distributee partner had received such property in a current distribution immediately before the actual distribution which is treated wholly or partly as a sale or exchange under § 751(b)." Thus, one should assume the partnership first distributed the relinquished property to the distributee partner. See Reg. § 1.751(g) Ex. 2(d)(1).

In our example, because Fred has given up his interest in the partnership's § 751 property, consisting solely of the Inventory, the identification of the property deemed relinquished is easy. Fred is deemed to have sold $30 of inventory to the partnership. Thus, we first assume a distribution of $30 of the Inventory to Fred. Under § 732, Fred's adjusted basis in the $30 of Inventory will be $20, i.e., one-third of the partnership's adjusted basis of $60 in the inventory it owns.

Consider the partnership balance sheet following this deemed distribution:

	Partnership Assets			Partners' Capital	
	A/B	FMV		A/B	FMV
Cash	$150	$150		$130*	$90**
Inventory	$40	$60	Fred	$150	$120
Capital Asset	$240	$120	Monica	$150	$120
Total	**$430**	**$330**	Judson	$430	$330

* Pursuant to § 733, Fred's partnership basis would be reduced by the $20 adjusted basis he would take in the $30 of inventory deemed distributed to him.

** Fred's capital account (FMV) would be reduced by the fair market value of the inventory distributed to him. Reg. § 1.704-1(b)(2)(iv)(5).

Step 5: Determine the tax consequences to the distributee partner and the partnership on the deemed sale or exchange of the property presumed to have been distributed to that partner.

Having identified the property deemed distributed to the distributee partner and the adjusted basis of that property, § 751(b) and the regulations then assume the distributee partner enters into a deemed exchange or sale of that property with the partnership. The deemed sale or exchange has tax consequences to both the distributee partner and the partnership, i.e., potential gain or loss recognized, as well as basis and capital account implications. See Reg. § 1.751-1(g) Ex. 1(d) and (e). *(Taken together, Steps 3, 4 and 5 thus reflect the "asset exchange approach" of the current regulations referenced by the summary in Notice 2006-14 above.)*

Let's consider those tax consequences again using the facts of our example and focusing first on the tax implications for Fred. Because the only property Fred actually received in the distribution was $120 in cash, he will be deemed to have received that $30 of cash as a result of the sale of the $30 of Inventory deemed distributed to him in Step 4 above. Because his adjusted basis in that Inventory was $20, Fred will have $10 of ordinary income. Reg. § 1.751-1(b)(2) (last sentence).

By contrast, the partnership will be treated as purchasing from Fred $30 of the Inventory for $30 of cash. Because this is a cash purchase, there obviously would be no gain or loss to the partnership. Note, however, that Reg. §§ 1.751-1(b)(2)(ii) and (3)(ii) provide that, were there to be income, gain, or loss triggered to the partnership as a result of a deemed sale or exchange, the income, gain, or loss "would be allocated only to partners *other than the distributee* and [would be] separately taken into account [by those partners] under § 702(a)(8)." (Emphasis added.) Pursuant to § 1012, the partnership will take a $30 basis in the $30 of Inventory deemed to be purchased from Fred. In the aggregate, therefore, the partnership's basis in the Inventory will be $70, i.e., the $40 noted in the prior balance sheet plus the $30 basis in the Inventory deemed purchased from Fred.

Consider the partnership balance sheet after the deemed sale:

	Partnership Assets			**Partners' Capital**	
	A/B	FMV		A/B	FMV
Cash	$120	$120	Fred	$130	$90
Inventory	$70	$90	Monica	$150	$120
Capital Asset	$240	$120	Judson	$150	$120
Total	$430	$330		$430	$330

Step 6. Determine the tax consequences of that part of the distribution treated under § 731 *et seq.*

Having addressed that part of the distribution treated under § 751(b) as a sale or an exchange, we next consider the remainder of the distribution that is treated under § 731 and related distribution provisions. In our example, this part of the liquidating distribution involves the transfer of $90 in cash to Fred.[18] As noted above, under § 731(a)(2), Fred will recognize loss to the extent his outside basis is greater than the cash distributed. Here, Fred's outside basis as shown on the balance sheet (included as part of the discussion in Step 5) is $130. Fred will therefore have a $40 recognized loss. That loss will be characterized under § 741 as a long-term capital loss. § 741. When the $40 long-term capital loss is combined with the $10 of ordinary income Fred was required to recognize as part of the deemed sale above, Fred has a net loss of $30. This makes sense since Fred had a $30 loss built into his partnership interest immediately prior to the liquidation of that interest. See Reg. § 1.751–1(g) Ex. 1(e)(2).

Consider the partnership balance sheet following the liquidation:

	Partnership Assets			Partners' Capital	
	A/B	FMV		A/B	FMV
Cash	$30	$30			
Inventory	$70	$90	Monica	$150	$120
Capital Asset	$240	$120	Judson	$150	$120
Total	**$340**	**$240**		**$300**[19]	**$240**

Note that the balance sheet does not balance. Were the partnership to sell all of its remaining assets, it would recognize a net $100 loss ($20 of ordinary income on the sale of the Inventory and $120 long-term capital loss on the sale of the Capital Asset) that would be allocable to Monica and Judson. Considering that, prior to the distribution to Fred, only $30 of loss inhered in Monica's and Judson's partnership interests (for a total of $60,000 of loss), it seems odd that they should now each have a $50 share of the partnership's $100 of net loss. It appears that $40 of "extra" loss has been created. As discussed in detail in Chapter 15, this "extra" loss is a function of § 734(a) that generally prevents the adjustment of the partnership's basis in its undistributed assets following a distribution to a partner unless a § 754 election is in effect. Of course, as noted in Chapter 15, this $40 of "extra" loss will ultimately be offset by $40 of gain when the partnership liquidates.[20] Were a § 754 election in effect, however, the basis disparity reflected in the above balance sheet would be negated. The basis of the Capital Asset would be adjusted downward to reflect the $40 loss Fred recognized on the distribution. § 734(b)(2)(A) and Reg.

---

[18] The other $30,000 of the $120,000 distribution to Fred was, of course, treated as acquired in a sale as noted in the analysis of Steps 4 and 5 above.

[19] *See* footnote 7 above.

[20] Monica's and Judson's outside basis would each be reduced to $100 as a result of the allocation to them of $50 of net loss each when the partnership sold its remaining assets. Subsequently, when both Monica and Judson received $120 in liquidation of their partnership interests, they would each recognize $20 of gain. Thus, the $40 of "extra" loss noted above has been offset by a total of $40 of gain recognized on the complete liquidation of the partnership.

§ 1.755-1(c)(1)(ii). Review Chapter 15. As a result of the § 734(b) adjustment, a sale by the partnership of its remaining assets would result in total net loss of $60 ($20 of ordinary income on the Inventory's sale and $80 long-term capital loss on the Capital Asset's sale.) The problem of "extra" loss is thus resolved.

Having considered the application of § 751(b) and the current regulations in the context of a liquidating distribution, let us now consider their application to a nonliquidating distribution. Again, we will use the six-step analysis utilized above in determining the tax implications to the partner and the partnership of a nonliquidating distribution that results in a reduction, but not the liquidation, of the distributee partner's interest in the partnership. Consider the following example:

> **Example 2:** A general partnership was formed 10 years ago by Quinn, Austin, and Abbey, who each have an equal one-third interest in the partnership. On January 1, 2016, the partnership has the following balance sheet. None of the assets shown on the balance sheet is § 704(c) property, and each of the assets has been held by the partnership for more than one year. Assume the balance sheet has been restated to reflect fair market values. See Reg. § 1.704-1(b)(2)(iv)(f). *(Assume all numbers in this Example and the analysis below are in thousands.)*

	Partnership Assets			**Partners' Capital**	
	A/B	FMV		A/B	FMV
Cash	$250	$250	Abbey	$200	$400
Inventory	$150	$450	Austin	$200	$400
Capital Asset #1	$150	$300	Quinn	$200	$400
Capital Asset #2	$50	$200			
Total	$600	$1,200		$600	$1,200

> On January 2, 2016, Abbey received Capital Asset #2 in a nonliquidating distribution. Given this distribution, the partners agree that Abbey will have only a one-fifth interest in partnership capital and profits. Using the six steps discussed previously, let us consider the tax consequences to Abbey and the partnership.

Step 1: Determine whether the partnership holds "§ 751 property"

Again, in this example there is substantially appreciated inventory, i.e., the Inventory's fair market value is greater than 120% of its adjusted basis. Thus, the partnership has § 751 property and, as a result, § 751(b) will be applicable to the distribution if the distribution, in light of her remaining interest in the partnership, alters Abbey's interest in § 751 property and "other property."

Step 2: Taking into account any continuing interest a distributee partner may have in the partnership, determine whether that partner has received a disproportionate share of either § 751 property (hot assets) or "other property" (cold assets)

The same table utilized in the liquidating distribution example reveals that Abbey has received a disproportionate share of "other property" as follows:

Interest in "§ 751 Property" (or "Hot Assets")		Interest in "Other Property" (or "Cold Assets")	
FMV of "751 property" received	$0	FMV of "other property" received	$200
Plus		**Plus**	
Share of "§ 751 property" post-distribution	$90	Share of "other property" post-distribution	$110
Less		**Less**	
Share of "§ 751 property" pre-distribution	($150)	Share of "other property" pre-distribution	($250)
Increase (or decrease) in share of "§ 751 property"	($60)	Increase (or decrease) in share of "other property"	$60

Abbey's share of "other property" has thus increased by $60 while her share of § 751 property has been reduced by the same amount. Section 751(b) is therefore applicable.

Step 3: Determine what part of the distribution will be treated as a sale or exchange.

As the table reflects, Abbey has exchanged $60 of her interest in the partnership Inventory for an additional $60 interest in "other property." Thus, $60 of the nonliquidating distribution of Capital Asset #2 will be considered under § 751(b) as having been received as a result of an exchange wherein Abbey exchanged $60 of Inventory for a $60 share of Capital Asset #2.

Step 4. Assume a distribution to the partner of the property the partner will be deemed to have sold or have relinquished in a deemed exchange.

As discussed Example 2, this step requires a deemed distribution to the partner of the property to be relinquished in the exchange. The partner's adjusted basis in this property will be the basis the partner would have taken under § 732 had the property actually been distributed to the partner. If $60 of the partnership's Inventory had been distributed to Abbey, she would take the same basis in the Inventory as the partnership had. Given the facts presented above, Abbey would thus take a $20 basis in the Inventory deemed distributed to her. (There is a 3:1 ratio between the Inventory's fair market value and its adjusted basis. Therefore, the adjusted basis of $60 of Inventory is $20.)

Following the deemed distribution, the partnership balance sheet would be as follows:

	Partnership Assets				Partners' Capital	
	A/B	FMV			A/B	FMV
Cash	$250	$250	Abbey		$180*	$340**
Inventory	$130	$390	Austin		$200	$400
Capital Asset #1	$150	$300	Quinn		$200	$400
Capital Asset #2	$50	$200				
Total	**$580**	**$1,140**			**$580**	**$1,140**

* Pursuant to § 733, Abbey's partnership basis would be reduced by the adjusted basis she would have in the $60 of inventory deemed distributed to her.

** Abbey's capital account (FMV) would be reduced by the fair market value of the Inventory deemed distributed to her. Reg. § 1.751–1(b)(2)(iv)(5).

Step 5: Determine the tax consequences to the distributee partner and the partnership on the deemed sale or exchange of the property presumed to have been distributed to that partner.

Abbey is exchanging $60 of Inventory with a $20 basis for a $60 share of Capital Asset #2. Abbey would recognize $40 of gain on this taxable exchange (i.e., amount realized $60 less adjusted basis of 20). The $40 of gain on the exchange will be ordinary income as the Inventory is not a capital asset. § 1221(a)(1). Abbey will take a fair market value basis in the $60 share of Capital Asset #2 she receives in the deemed exchange. *Philadelphia Park Amusement Co. v. United States*, 126 F. Supp. 184 (Ct. Cl. 1954).

The partnership is exchanging $60 of Capital Asset #2 for $60 of Inventory. The partnership has a basis in the $60 share of Capital Asset #2 of $15 (i.e., 60/$200 x $50 = $15). The partnership thus recognizes $45 of gain on the exchange. As previously discussed, the $45 of gain is allocated to the other partners, i.e., to Austin and Quinn. Reg. § 1.751–1(b(3)(ii). They will thus each report $22.50 of gain thereby increasing their outside basis. The partnership will take a $60 basis in the Inventory it receives in the exchange. § 1012. The total adjusted basis of the partnership's Inventory will therefore be $190 (i.e., $130 adjusted basis after the deemed distribution of Inventory to Abbey in Step 4 plus the $60 basis of the Inventory received by the partnership in the deemed exchange).

The partnership balance sheet following this deemed exchange will be as follows:

	Partnership Assets				Partners' Capital	
	A/B	FMV			A/B	FMV
Cash	$250	$250	Abbey		$180	$340
Inventory	$190	$450	Austin		$222.50	$400
Capital Asset #1	$150	$300	Quinn		$222.50	$400
Capital Asset #2	$35	$140				
Total	**$625**	**$1,140**			**$625**	**$1,140**

Step 6. Determine the tax consequences of that part of the distribution treated under § 731 *et seq*.

Having addressed the treatment of $60 of Capital Asset #2 deemed to have been received by Abbey in an exchange, we now turn to the remaining $140 share of Capital Asset #2 Abbey received. This amount of Capital Asset #2 is treated under § 731 and related provisions. As noted in the balance sheet in Step 5 above, the partnership has a $35 adjusted basis in the $140 remaining share of Capital Asset #2. Pursuant to § 731(a)(1), no gain is recognized to Abbey on her receipt of this share of Capital Asset #2. Abbey will take a $35 basis in this share of that asset. § 732(a)(1). In the aggregate, therefore, Abbey will have a basis in Capital Asset #2 equal to $95 (i.e., $60 as a result of the exchange plus $35 as a result of the distribution).

Following the distribution, the balance sheet of the partnership will be as follows:[21]

	Partnership Assets			**Partners' Capital**	
	A/B	FMV		A/B	FMV
Cash	$250	$250	Abbey	$145*	$200**
Inventory	$190	$450	Austin	$222.50	$400
Capital Asset #1	$150	$300	Quinn	$222.50	$400
Total	**$590**	**$1,000**		**$590**	**$1,000**

*Abbey's outside basis in the partnership is reduced by the adjusted basis she takes in the $140 share of Capital Asset #2 that was distributed to her. § 733.
**Abbey's capital account likewise must be reduced by the $140 share of Capital Asset #2 distributed to her. Reg. § 1.704–1(b)(2)(iv)(5).

C. Limitations and Exceptions

As the above example illustrated, § 751(b) divides partnership property into two categories, i.e., "§ 751 property" and "other property." Section 751(b) only applies to distributions wherein a partner gives up an interest in one of these two categories for a greater interest in the other category. Thus, § 751(b) is inapplicable to the extent a distribution consists of the distributee partner's share of "§ 751 property" or the partner's share of "other property."[22] The regulations also make clear that § 751(b) is inapplicable "to current drawings or to advances against the partner's distributive share, or to a distribution which is, in fact, a gift

---

[21] In Example 2, unlike Example 1, the balance sheet balances following the distribution. Thus, even if a § 754 election were in effect, there would be no adjustment to basis required by § 734(b) as Abbey recognized neither gain nor loss on the distribution of $140 of Capital Asset #2 (see Step 6 above), and took the same basis the partnership had in that $140 portion of Capital Asset #2. There is likewise no adjustment to basis required by the § 734(d), the "substantial basis reduction" rule discussed in Chapter 15.

[22] Reg. § 1.751-1(b)(1)(ii).

or payment for services or for the use of capital."[23]

If a distribution consists only of property the distributee partner contributed to the partnership, § 751(b) does not apply.[24] As discussed in the next chapter, § 751(b) also does not apply to payments made to a retiring partner or a deceased partner to the extent those payments constitute either a distributive share of partnership income or guaranteed payments under § 736(a) which is discussed in Chapter 17.[25] Section 751(b), however, will apply to § 736(b) payments, i.e., payments made to a retiring partner for that partner's partnership interest, to the extent that they involve an exchange of substantially appreciated inventory items for "other property."[26]

D. § 751(b) — An Imperfect Remedy

As discussed above, § 751(b) is intended to negate the shifting of ordinary income to other partners, i.e., to alter the partners' interests in "§ 751 property" — i.e., unrealized receivables or substantially appreciated inventory. By lumping all unrealized receivables and all substantially appreciated inventory into the same class, however, § 751(b) and the current regulations in some circumstances enable the very shifting of ordinary income Congress and Treasury sought to negate.

Example 3: Assume Amy, Brent, and Clare years ago each contributed $150 in cash to form the ABC Partnership, a cash method partnership in which each of the partners has an equal one-third interest. *(Assume all numbers in this example are in thousands.)* Assume the partnership has the following balance sheet:

	Partnership Assets			Partners' Capital	
	A/B	FMV		A/B	FMV
Cash	$150	$150	Amy	$140	$170
Inventory	$270	$270	Brent	$140	$170
Accounts Receivable	$0	$90	Clare	$140	$170
Total	**$420**	**$510**		**$420**	**$510**

Assume this year the partnership made a nonliquidating distribution of $30 of Inventory to Amy, $30 of Inventory to Brent and $30 of the Accounts Receivable to Clare. Following the distribution, the partners will remain equal partners. Have any of the partners received a disproportionate distribution that would trigger the application of § 751(b)?

Analysis: With regard to **Step 1** in our multi-step analysis, it should be clear that the partnership has § 751 property, i.e., it has unrealized receivables and substantially appreciated inventory. Note, the inventory is

---

[23] *Id.*
[24] Reg. § 1.751-1(b)(4)(i).
[25] Reg. § 1.751-1(b)(4)(ii).
[26] *Id.*

substantially appreciated because it includes the accounts receivable. Reg. § 1.751-1(d)(2)(ii). Turning to **Step 2**, the § 751(b) table will be as follows with respect to each of the three partners:

Interest in "§ 751 Property" (or "Hot Assets")		**Interest in "Other Property" (or "Cold Assets")**	
FMV of "751 property" received	$30	FMV of "other property" received	$0
Plus		**Plus**	
Share of "§ 751 property" post-distribution	$90	Share of "other property" post-distribution	$50
Less		**Less**	
Share of "§ 751 property" pre-distribution	$120	Share of "other property" pre-distribution	$50
Increase (or decrease) in share of "§ 751 property"	$0	**Increase (or decrease) in share of "other property"**	$0

Thus, there has not been a disproportionate distribution, i.e., no partner has given up any interest in § 751 property for a larger share of "other property" or vice versa. Section 751(b) therefore doesn't apply. Applying §§ 731(a) and 732(a), none of the partners will recognize any gain or loss and Clare will have a $0 basis in the $30 of accounts receivable, while Amy and Brent will each have a $30 basis in the $30 of inventory they received. Amy and Brent will therefore have $0 of ordinary income when they sell their share of inventory for $30, while Clare will have $30 of ordinary income when she collects the $30 of accounts receivable. Thus, the distribution effectively shifted ordinary income to Clare.

As Example 3 illustrates, the "gross value approach" for determining a partner's interest in § 751 property allows distributions (such as those to Amy, Brent, and Clare) to reduce a partner's share of the unrealized gain in the partnership's § 751 property without triggering the application of § 751(b) (as was the case with the distribution of the $30 of Inventory to Amy and Brent). Similarly, Revenue Ruling 84-102, included in the materials, provides that deemed distributions of cash pursuant to § 752(b), resulting from a change in the allocation of partnership indebtedness when a new partner is added, may result in the original partners' share of the gross value of the partnership's assets changing, even though those partners' share of the unrealized gain inherent in § 751 property does not necessarily change.

E. The Proposed § 751(b) Regulations

Notice 2006-14 (cited above) notes: "The current regulations under § 751(b) were published in 1956 and have not been amended to reflect significant changes in Subchapter K and in the operations of contemporary partnerships. Moreover, the current § 751(b) regulations have been widely criticized as being extraordinarily complex and burdensome and as not achieving the objectives of the statute." (See example and discussion in Part D of this Overview.) Notice 2006-14 asked for comments on: (1) replacing the gross value approach to determining a partner's interest in § 751 property[27] with a "hypothetical sale" approach (discussed below); and (2) replacing the asset exchange approach[28] with a "hot asset sale" approach (discussed below).

Having received numerous comments in response to its request in Notice 2006-14, Treasury issued proposed regulations in 2014 to replace the current § 751(b) regulations. The preamble to the proposed regulations notes that the proposed regulations adopt the "hypothetical sale" approach highlighted in Notice 2006-14 "as the method by which the partners must measure their respective interests in § 751 property for the purpose of determining whether a distribution reduces a partner's interest in the partnership's § 751 property."[29] *See* Prop. Reg. § 1.751-1(b)(2)(ii). The preamble explains the "hypothetical sale" approach as follows:

> Under the hypothetical sale approach, a partner's interest in § 751 property is determined by reference to the amount of ordinary income that would be allocated to the partner if the partnership disposed of all of its property for fair market value immediately before the distribution. More specifically, the hypothetical sale approach applies section 704(c) principles in comparing: (1) the amount of ordinary income that each partner would recognize if the partnership sold all of its property for fair market value immediately before the distribution, with (2) the amount of ordinary income each partner would recognize if the partnership sold all of its property (and the distributee partners sold the distributed assets) for fair market value immediately after the distribution. If the distribution reduces the amount of ordinary income (or increases the amount of ordinary loss) from section 751 property that would be allocated to, or recognized by, a partner (thus reducing that partner's interest in the partnership's section 751 property), the distribution triggers section 751(b).[30] [Under the proposed regulations, a distribution that reduces a partner's interest in the partnership's § 751 property is referred to as a "section 751(b) distribution."]

Specifically, employing the hypothetical sale approach, the proposed regulations require a distributee partner to determine her "net section 751 unrealized gain or loss" both before and after a distribution. Prop. Reg. § 1.751-1(b)(2)(ii). In turn, those before-and-after figures are used to calculate the distributee partner's "section 751(b) amount," if any. Section 751(b) only applies to a distribution that gives rise to a "section 751(b) amount." Prop. Reg. § 1.751-1(b)(2)(ii).

---

[27] *See* Steps 1 and 2 above of the current regulation's multi-step approach for determining the tax consequences of distributions subject to § 751(b).

[28] *See* Steps 3, 4, and 5 above of the current regulation's multi-step approach for determining the tax consequences of distributions subject to § 751(b).

[29] REG-151416-06, 2014-2 C.B. 870.

[30] The Preamble to the proposed regulations notes that "commentators [responding to the request of Notice 2006-14] agreed that, when compared against the gross value approach, the hypothetical sale approach is more consistent with Congress's intent in enacting § 751(b), easier to apply, and reduces the likelihood that § 751(b) would unnecessarily accelerate ordinary income." REG-151416-06, 2014-2 C.B. 870.

The hypothetical sale approach noted above relies on § 704(c) principles[31] to preserve a partner's share of unrealized gain or loss in § 751 property. As a result, the regulations mandate that a partnership maintaining its capital accounts in accord with Reg. § 1.704-1(b)(2)(iv)[32] revalue its assets immediately prior to the distribution in accordance with Reg. § 1.704-1(b)(2)(iv)(f) if the partnership, following the distribution of money or property (other than a *de minimis* amount) to a partner for an interest in the partnership, owns § 751 property. Prop. Reg. § 1.751-1(b)(2)(iv).[33]

As noted above, the current regulations employ an "asset exchange approach" in determining the tax consequences of the part of a distribution to which § 751(b) applies. (See Steps 3, 4, and 5 in the multi-step approach of the current regulations.) Notice 2006-14 requested comments on replacing that approach with the so-called "hot asset sale approach." Pursuant to the "hot asset sale approach," the partnership is deemed "to distribute the relinquished § 751 property to the partner whose interest in the partnership's § 751 property is reduced, and then deems the partner to sell the relinquished § 751 property back to the partnership immediately before the actual distribution."[34] The preamble to the proposed regulations notes:

> While most commentators agreed that the hot asset sale approach is an improvement over the existing regulations' asset exchange approach, commentators were able to identify situations in which the hot asset sale approach fails to achieve the correct result or causes undesirable results under other Code provisions. [Other commentators] advocated adopting, in lieu of the hot asset sale approach, . . . a "deemed gain" approach in which a "section 751(b) distribution" results in: (1) the partnership recognizing ordinary income in the aggregate amount of each partner's reduction in the partner's interest in § 751 property, (2) the partnership allocating ordinary income to the partner or partners whose interest in § 751 property was reduced by the distribution, and (3) the partnership making appropriate basis adjustments to its assets to reflect its ordinary income recognition. One variation of the deemed gain approach would require capital gain recognition in certain cases.

---

[31] *See* Chapter 10, addressing in detail § 704(c)(1)(A) regarding the tax consequences of contributed property with built-in gain or loss.

[32] *See* Chapter 9, addressing special allocations.

[33] Although the rules contained in Prop. Reg. § 1.751-1(b)(2) addressing the distributions to which § 751(b) applies (including the rules discussed above regarding the use of the "hypothetical sale" approach and the revaluation of partnership assets) only apply to distributions on or after the rules are adopted as final regulations, Prop. Reg. § 1.751-1(f) provides a partnership and its partners may apply these rules "for purposes of determining a partner's interest in the partnership's section 751 property on or after November 3, 2014." As a condition of doing so, however, the proposed regulations require the partnership and its partners to apply Prop. Reg. § 1.751-1(a)(2) (determination of the gain or loss on the sale or exchange of a partnership interest — see Chapter 20 Part A) and Prop. Reg. § 1.751-1(b)(4) (general principles and anti-abuse rules) "for all partnership sales, exchanges, and distributions, including any distributions the partnership makes after a termination of the partnership under section 708(b)(1)(B) — see Chapter 20 Part D.

[34] REG-151416-06, 2014-2 C.B. 870.

The IRS and the Treasury Department determined that a deemed gain approach produces an appropriate outcome in the greatest number of circumstances out of the approaches under consideration, and that the hot asset sale approach also produced an appropriate outcome in most circumstances. However, no one approach produced an appropriate outcome in all circumstances. *Therefore, these proposed regulations withdraw the asset exchange approach of the current regulations, but do not require the use of a particular approach for determining the tax consequences of a "section 751(b) distribution."* Instead, these proposed regulations provide that if, under the hypothetical sale approach, a distribution reduces a partner's interest in the partnership's § 751 property, giving rise to a "section 751(b) amount," then the partnership must use a reasonable approach that is consistent with the purpose of § 751(b) to determine the tax consequences of the reduction. [Emphasis added.]

See Prop. Reg. § 1.751-1(b)(3)(i) addressing the determination of tax consequences of "section 751(b) distributions using a reasonable approach."[35] Note that Prop. Reg. § 1.751-1(b)(3)(iii) requires the partnership and partners to make appropriate adjustments to the partners' outside basis, the basis of § 751 property and other property consistent with whatever "reasonable approach" was utilized so as to reflect any ordinary income or capital gain recognized. Section 704(c) amounts must be adjusted accordingly.

The proposed regulations provide a series of examples illustrating the application of the various rules set forth in those regulations. *See* Prop. Reg. § 1.751-1(g). The following example from the proposed regulations[36] illustrates the basic rules noted above:

Example: (i) A, B, and C each contribute $120 to partnership ABC in exchange for a one-third interest. A, B, and C each share in the profits and losses of ABC in accordance with their one-third interest. ABC purchases land for $100 in Year 1. At the end of Year 3, when ABC holds $260 in cash and land with a value of $100 and has generated $90 in zero-basis unrealized receivables, ABC distributes $150 cash to C in complete liquidation of C's interest. ABC has a § 754 election in effect. To determine if the distribution is a distribution to which section 751(b) applies, ABC must apply the test set forth in Prop. Reg. § 1.751-1(b)(2) addressing the hypothetical sale approach.

(ii)(A) Pursuant to Prop. Reg. § 1.751-1(b)(2)(iv), ABC revalues its assets and its partners' capital accounts are increased under Reg. § 1.704-1(b)(2)(iv)(f) to reflect each partner's share of the unrealized gain in the partnership's assets. Before the distribution, ABC's balance sheet is as follows:

---

[35] The provisions of Prop. Reg. § 1.751-1(b)(3) only apply after they are finalized by Treasury. Prop. Reg. § 1.751-1(f).

[36] Prop. Reg. § 1.751-1(g) Ex. 3. We have slightly modified the example to highlight more clearly the provisions of the proposed regulations being applied and to note other chapters in this casebook that address specific points made in the example.

	Partnership Assets			Partners' Capital	
	Tax	Book		Tax	Book
Cash	$260	$260	A	$120	$150
Unrealized Receivables	$0	$90	B	$120	$150
Real Property	$100	$100	C	$120	$150
Total	**$360**	**$450**		**$360**	**$450**

(B) If ABC disposed of all of its assets in exchange for cash in amounts equal to the fair market values of these assets immediately before the distribution, A, B, and C would each be allocated $30 of net income from ABC's § 751 property. Accordingly, A, B, and C's "net section 751 unrealized gain" immediately before the distribution is $30 each under Prop. Reg. § 1.751-1(b)(2)(ii).

(iii)(A) Because ABC has elected under § 754, and because [C] recognizes $30 gain on the distribution of cash [i.e., cash received of $150 and outside basis of $120], the basis of the real property is increased to $130 under section 734(b). [See Chapter 15.] After the distribution (but before taking into account any consequences under this section), ABC's balance sheet would be as follows:

	Partnership Assets			Partners' Capital	
	Tax	Book		Tax	Book
Cash	$110	$110	A	$120	$150
Unrealized Receivables	$0	$90	B	$120	$150
Real Property	$130	$100	C	$0	$0
Total	**$240**	**$300**		**$240**	**$300**

(B) Because C is no longer a partner in ABC, C would not be allocated any net income from ABC's section 751 property immediately after the distribution. Also, C did not receive any § 751 property in the distribution. Accordingly, C's "net section 751 unrealized gain" immediately after the distribution is $0 under Prop. Reg. § 1.751-1(b)(2)(iii).

(iv) Because C's "net section 751 unrealized gain" is greater immediately before the distribution than immediately after the distribution, § 751(b) applies to the distribution. Under Prop. Reg. § 1.751-1(b)(2)(i), C has a "section 751(b) amount" equal to $30, the amount by which C's share of pre-distribution net section 751 unrealized gain ($30) exceeds C's share of post-distribution net section 751 unrealized gain ($0). Accordingly, Prop. Reg. § 1.751-1(b)(3)(i) requires C to recognize $30 of ordinary income using a reasonable approach consistent with the purpose of this section. ABC considers two approaches, the first of which is described in paragraphs (v) and (vi) of this example, and the second of which is described in paragraphs (vii) and (viii) of this example.

(v) **The "Deemed Gain Approach"** — Assume ABC adopts an approach under which, immediately before the "section 751(b) distribution," C is deemed to recognize $30 of ordinary income. To reflect C's recognition of

$30 of ordinary income, C increases its basis in its ABC partnership interest by $30, and the partnership increases its basis in the unrealized receivable by the $30 of income recognized by C, immediately before the distribution. Provided the partnership applies the approach consistently for all "section 751(b) distributions," ABC's adopted approach is reasonable. After taking into account the tax consequences of the "section 751(b) distribution" immediately prior to the cash distribution, ABC's modified balance sheet is as follows:

	Partnership Assets			Partners' Capital	
	Tax	Book		Tax	Book
Cash	$260	$260	A	$120	$150
Unrealized Receivables	$30	$90	B	$120	$150
Real Property	$100	$100	C	$150	$150
Total	$390	$450		$390	$450

(vi) After determining the tax consequences of the § 751(b) distribution, the rules of §§ 731 through 736 apply. [Section 736 is discussed in Chapter 17.] Accordingly, C recognizes no gain or loss under section 731(a) upon the distribution. Because C recognizes no gain on the distribution, the basis of the partnership real property is not adjusted. After the distribution, ABC's balance sheet is as follows:

	Partnership Assets			Partners' Capital	
	Tax	Book		Tax	Book
Cash	$110	$110	A	$120	$150
Unrealized Receivables	$30	$90	B	$120	$150
Real Property	$100	$100	C	$0	$0
Total	$240	$300		$240	$300

(vii) **The "Hot Asset Sale Approach"** — Assume alternatively that ABC adopts an approach under which, immediately before the "section 751(b) distribution," C is deemed to —

(A) Receive a distribution of ABC's unrealized receivables with a fair market value of $30 and a tax basis of $0;

(B) Sell the unrealized receivable to ABC in exchange for $30, recognizing $30 of ordinary income; and

(C) Contribute the $30 to ABC.

Provided the partnership applies this approach consistently for all "section 751(b) distributions," ABC's adopted approach is reasonable. After taking into account the tax consequences of the section 751(b) distribution immediately prior to the cash distribution, ABC's modified balance sheet is the same as the balance sheet shown in paragraph (v) of this example.

(viii) After determining the tax consequences of the "section 751(b) distribution," the rules of §§ 731 through 736 apply. The tax consequences under the rules of §§ 731 through 736 are the same tax consequences described in paragraph (vi) of this example.

Revenue Ruling 84-102
1984-2 C.B. 119

ISSUE:

What are the consequences to the partners under § 751(b) of the Internal Revenue Code when a new partner joins the partnership under the circumstances described below?

FACTS:

A, B, and C were equal partners in partnership P. At the time of the transaction described below, the value of each partner's interest was $25x$ dollars. D acquired a 25 percent interest in P by contributing $25x$ dollars to P. Prior to D's contribution, the liabilities of P totaled $100x$ dollars, and each partner's share of the liabilities was approximately $33.3x$ dollars. In addition, the unrealized receivables of P (as defined in § 751 (c) of the Code) were $40x$ dollars, and each partner's share of the unrealized receivables was approximately $13.3x$ dollars. After the contribution by D, each partner's share of the liabilities of P was $25x$ dollars; A, B, and C's share of P's liabilities each decreased by approximately $8.3x$ dollars. Furthermore, each partner's share of P's unrealized receivables was $10x$ dollars; A, B, and C's share of the unrealized receivables each decreased by approximately $3.3x$ dollars.

LAW AND ANALYSIS:

Section 721 (a) of the Internal Revenue Code provides that no gain or loss shall be recognized to a partnership or to any of its partners in the case of a contribution of property to the partnership in exchange for an interest in the partnership.

Section 722 of the Code provides that the basis of an interest in a partnership acquired by a contribution of property, including money, to the partnership shall be the amount of such money and the adjusted basis of such property to the contributing partner.

Section 752 (a) of the Code provides that any increase in a partner's share of the liabilities of a partnership shall be considered as a contribution of money by such partner to the partnership.

Section 752 (b) of the Code provides that any decrease in a partner's share of the liabilities of a partnership shall be considered as a distribution of money to the partner by the partnership.

Pursuant to §§ 733 and 731 (a)(1) of the Code, a distribution of money by a partnership to a partner, results in a reduction of the partner's basis in the partnership interest and, to the extent the distribution exceeds basis, capital gain to the partner. However, § 731 (c) provides that § 731 shall not apply to the extent otherwise provided by § 751. See also §§ 1.731-1 (a) (1) and 1.751-1 (b) of the Income Tax Regulations.

Section 751(b)(1)(B) of the Code provides that, to the extent a partner receives a distribution of partnership property (including money) other than property described in § 751(a)(1) or (2) in exchange for all or part of the partner's interest in partnership property described in § 751(a)(1) or (2), such transaction shall be considered a sale or exchange of such property between the distributee partner and the partnership. Section 751(a)(1) of the Code refers to the "unrealized receivables" of a partnership as defined in § 751 (c) of the Code.

In the instant case, A, B, and C are each treated as having received a cash distribution from P of $8.3x$ dollars in accordance with § 752(b) of the Code. Of this amount, $3.3x$ dollars is treated under § 731(c) and 751(b)(1)(B) as being received by each partner in exchange for the interest in unrealized receivables given up. The remaining $5x$ dollars is treated in accordance with § 731(a) of the Code.

Although D has a $10x$ dollar interest in the unrealized receivables of P upon becoming a partner, § 751(b) of the Code has no application with respect to D. There is no actual or deemed distribution of property from P to D as required by § 751(b). Further, D has an "increased" interest in the unrealized receivables of P as a result of becoming a partner. Any distribution of property (other than property described in § 751(a)(1) or (2)) from P to D would have to result in a decreased interest in the unrealized receivables for § 751(b)(1)(B) to apply.

HOLDING:

The tax consequences to D of becoming a partner are determined under §§ 721, 722 and 752(a) of the Code. D is treated as having contributed 50x dollars, the actual contribution of $25x$ dollars plus the deemed contribution of $25x$ dollars under § 752(a), in exchange for the partnership interest. D's basis in the partnership interest is $50x$ dollars in accordance with § 722 of the Code. Section 751(b) does not apply to new partner D because there is no actual or deemed distribution of property from P to D.

Partners A, B, and C are each treated as having received a distribution of $8.3x$ dollars under § 752 (b) of the Code. Of this amount, $3.3x$ dollars is treated under § 751(b)(1)(B) as being received by each partner in exchange for the interest in unrealized receivables given up.

Chapter 17

DISTRIBUTIONS TERMINATING A RETIRING PARTNER'S INTEREST

I. PROBLEMS

Western Connection, a calendar-year general partnership in which capital is a material income-producing factor, has been in existence for 20 years. Maureen, Patrick, and Katie, the three general partners, each owns a one-third interest in the capital and profits of the partnership. Maureen will retire this year from the partnership business, and her partnership interest will be liquidated. Given Maureen's retirement, the partnership elected to revalue its property and, in turn, to restate the capital accounts of its partners, to reflect fair market values. (See Reg. § 1.704-1(b)(2)(iv)(f).) As a result of the revaluation, the partnership, which has never made a § 754 election, has the following balance sheet:

	Partnership Assets			Partners' Capital	
	A/B	FMV		A/B	FMV
Cash	$180,000	$180,000	Maureen	$100,000	$150,000
Acc'ts Receivable	$0	$90,000	Patrick	$100,000	$150,000
Capital Asset #1	$60,000	$30,000	Katie	$100,000	$150,000
Capital Asset #2	$60,000	$90,000			
Goodwill	$0	$60,000			
Total	$300,000	$450,000		$300,000	$450,000

In each of the following alternative liquidation scenarios, explain the tax consequences to Maureen and to the partnership. In each alternative, assume the partnership agreement was silent with regard to any payment for goodwill. Construct the balance sheet of the partnership immediately following Maureen's retirement.

(a) In complete liquidation of Maureen's interest, the partnership will pay Maureen $90,000 in cash and will distribute to her $30,000 of the accounts receivable and Capital Asset #1.

(b) In complete liquidation of Maureen's interest, the partnership will pay Maureen $150,000 in cash. What difference, if any, would it make if the partnership made a § 754 election?

(c) In complete liquidation of Maureen's interest, the partnership will pay Maureen $160,000 in cash. Assume the $10,000 excess amount over Maureen's capital account is in the nature of mutual insurance and is not attributable to her interest in partnership assets.

(d) Same as (a) except the partnership is a service partnership in which capital is not a material income-producing factor and the partnership agreement provides for a payment with respect to goodwill.

(e) Same as (b) except the partnership is a service partnership in which capital is not a material income-producing factor.

(f) Same as (e) except the partnership will pay Maureen $50,000 in cash immediately and $50,000 in cash in each of the next two years. What flexibility would Maureen have with respect to reporting any income, gain, or loss on the liquidation?

Assignment for Chapter 17:

Complete the Problems

Read: Internal Revenue Code: §§ 731(a), (b), and (d); 736; 751(b)–(d)
Treasury Regulations: § 1.736-1

    Materials: Overview
                      Commissioner v. Jackson Investment Company

II. VOCABULARY

retiring partner
mutual insurance
Section 736(a) payments
Section 736(b) payments
unstated goodwill
stated goodwill
material income-producing factor

III. OBJECTIVES

1. To determine whether a partnership is one in which capital is a material income-producing factor.

2. To categorize liquidating distribution as § 736(a) or § 736(b) payments.

3. To explain the tax consequences to the retiring partner and the partnership of a payment categorized as a § 736(a) payment.

4. To explain the tax consequences to the retiring partner and the partnership of a payment categorized as a § 736(b) payment.

5. To explain the tax consequences to a retiring partner and a partnership where liquidation payments are made in installments over a number of years and the liquidation payments consist of both § 736(a) payments and § 736(b) payments.

6. To determine the amount and character of gain or loss a retiring partner must recognize each year where the total § 736(b) payments are a fixed sum and the liquidating payments are to be made over more than one year.

7. To recall that payments made to a partner for unrealized receivables, if classified as § 736(a) payments, are only § 736(a) payments to the extent the payments *exceed the partner's share of the partnership's basis in the unrealized receivables.*

8. To recall that payments made to a partner for unstated goodwill, if classified as § 736(a) payments, are only § 736(a) payments to the extent the payments *exceed the partner's share of partnership basis in the unstated goodwill.*

IV. OVERVIEW

Liquidating payments to a "retiring partner"[1] may represent several items. For example, they could represent in part the fair market value of a partner's interest in the assets of the partnership (including inventory), a partner's interest in the partnership's unrealized receivables, including fees billed and unbilled, and/or a partner's interest in partnership goodwill. Some part of liquidating payments could also be attributable to an "arrangement in the nature of mutual insurance among the partners."[2] Prior to 1954, there was no statutory guidance related to the tax treatment of "payments" made by a partnership to a "retiring" partner. As a result, it was not surprising that judicial treatment of liquidating payments to a retiring partner was inconsistent.

To simplify the law and provide greater certainty to retiring partners and their partnerships, Congress in 1954 enacted § 736. Section 736, however, merely classifies the liquidating payments received by the retiring partner. Once § 736 has classified the payments, other sections of Subchapter K (addressed in previous chapters) apply to determine the tax consequences of the payments to the retiring partner and the partnership.

Section 736 applies only to payments made by the partnership to a retiring partner and does not apply to transactions between partners, e.g., the purchase of a partner's interest by another partner.[3] Furthermore, it is important to note the term "payment" as used in § 736(a) should not be interpreted as limiting § 736 to situations in which the retiring partner receives solely cash payments, although that will often be the case. Because the partnership itself is not liquidating,[4] but rather will continue to carry on its profit-seeking activities, the distribution of assets other

---

[1] The term "retiring partner" will be used throughout this chapter to refer to a living partner whose interest is liquidated by the partnership. It will also refer to a successor of a deceased partner.

[2] H.R. Rep. No. 1337, 83rd Cong., 2d Sess. 71–72 (1954); Reg. § 1.736-1(a)(2). Mutual insurance represents amounts paid to a retiring partner for something other than that partner's interest in the tangible or intangible property of a partnership. For example, if upon the death of a partner, the partnership agreement provided that the partnership would pay the estate of the deceased partner an amount greater than the fair market value of the deceased partner's interest in the partnership, we could think of that arrangement as one representing mutual insurance.

[3] Reg. § 1.736-1(a)(1)(i). Section 736 is also inapplicable "if the estate or other successor in interest of a deceased partner continues as a partner in its own right under local law." *Id. See* Chapter 20 Part C addressing the death of a partner.

[4] *See* Chapter 14 for a discussion of the tax consequences associated with the complete liquidation of a partnership.

than cash to a retiring partner may not be feasible. Given the necessity of maintaining sufficient cash on-hand, partnerships, rather than making a lump sum payment of cash to a retiring partner, will often arrange to make the liquidating payments over time. As discussed below, liquidation payments made in installments raise a host of questions that are addressed in the regulations interpreting and applying § 736.

A. Section 736 Classification

Section 736 classifies payments to a retiring partner by assigning the payments to one of two categories: § 736(b) payments or § 736(a) payments. In general, § 736(b) payments are payments made in exchange for the retiring partner's interest in partnership property (except payments in the nature of mutual insurance and, in some cases, payments for unrealized receivables and goodwill), while § 736(a) payments are all other payments received by the retiring partner. Reg. § 1.736-1(a)(2). Section 736(b) payments are treated for tax purposes as distributions subject to the general distribution rules, including §§ 731, 732, 741, and 751(b) previously studied. By contrast, § 736(a) payments are treated as either a partner's distributive share or as guaranteed payments.

As discussed below, historically, payments for a retiring partner's interest in a partnership's "unrealized receivables" as defined in § 751(c) [see discussion of § 751(c) in Chapter 16] and payments for so-called "unstated goodwill" (i.e., goodwill when the partnership agreement does not provide for payments with respect to goodwill) were, in all cases, treated as § 736(a) payments, i.e., they were not treated as payments for the retiring partner's interest in partnership property. In 1993, Congress significantly amended the rules related to the tax treatment of retiring partners. For purposes of the § 736 classification rules *only*, the 1993 amendments also limited the meaning of "unrealized receivables," to those items originally treated as "unrealized receivables" when Congress initially enacted the term, i.e., "unbilled amounts and accounts receivable." See H.R. Rep. No. 103-11, at 344–345, 103rd Cong., Sess. 1 (1993). (Read § 751(c) carefully and note the exception for § 736.) In addition, as a result of the congressional amendments to § 736 in 1993, payments for a partner's interest in a partnership's "unrealized receivables" (as defined for purposes of § 736) and "unstated goodwill" will now commonly be classified as § 736(b) payments.

B. Tax Significance of § 736 Classification of Payments to a Retiring Partner

As noted at the outset, once liquidating payments have been classified by § 736, other provisions previously addressed in this casebook apply to determine the tax treatment of both the retiring partner and the partnership. The different tax treatment afforded § 736(a) and § 736(b) payments is significant. In that regard, consider the following points:

1. Section 736(a) Payments — Guaranteed Payments

If a payment is classified as a § 736(a) payment and is determined without regard to the income of the partnership, it is treated as a guaranteed payment under § 707(c).[5] As provided in the regulations, the retiring partner will have ordinary income under § 61(a) and the partnership will be allowed a § 162 deduction with respect to the payment.[6] The deduction, of course, reduces the amount of income (or increases the loss) to be allocated to the remaining partners. The ability of the partnership to deduct § 736(a) payments immediately, rather than capitalize them as part of the partnership's liquidation of a retiring partner's interest can be of particular importance in the negotiations regarding the liquidation.

2. Section 736(a) payments — Distributive Share

If a payment is a § 736(a) payment and is determined by reference to the income of the partnership, it is treated as a distributive share.[7] Pursuant to § 702, the retiring partner will be required to account for that share in computing her taxable income. As discussed in Chapter 7, the character of a partner's distributive share of income is determined by the character of the income of the partnership. To the extent a § 736(a) payment is characterized as a distributive share of partnership income, the distributive shares of the other partners will be reduced. Thus, in effect, the distributive share treatment of § 736(a) payments enables the partnership to deduct those payments, thus producing results comparable to that of § 736(a) payments treated as guaranteed payments.[8] In sum, the classification of a payment to a retiring partner as a § 736(a) payment has obvious advantages to a partnership, not the least of which is the possibility of a deduction or its equivalent rather than capitalization of the payment.

3. Section 736(b) Payments — Distributions

If the payment is classified as a § 736(b) payment, the payment will be treated in the same manner as a distribution in complete liquidation under the rules of §§ 731, 732, 741, and, where applicable, 751(b).[9] Generally, these rules provide for nonrecognition of gain or loss by the distributee partner except in limited circumstances.[10] Likewise, the partnership will generally recognize no gain or loss on a liquidating

---

[5] § 736(a)(2); Reg. § 1.736-1(a)(3)(ii). Guaranteed payments are discussed in detail in Chapter 13.

[6] Reg. § 1.736-1(a)(4). Note that the regulation specifically states that the partnership will be allowed a deduction under § 162 for the guaranteed payment. Unlike § 707(c), the regulation makes no mention of capitalization pursuant to § 263. Thus, given the specific language of the regulation, even though a payment for a partner's interest in "unrealized receivables" would normally constitute a capital expenditure, the partnership will be allowed an immediate deduction for the guaranteed payment. This result highlights one of the conceptual difficulties associated with § 736.

[7] § 736(a)(1); Reg. § 1.736-1(a)(3)(i).

[8] Reg. § 1.736-1(a)(4).

[9] Reg. § 1.736-1(a)(2).

[10] For example, as discussed in Chapter 14, § 731(a)(1) provides for gain recognition when the cash received exceeds the partner's outside basis, and § 731(a)(2) provides for loss in the case of liquidations, but only if the liquidating distribution is limited to certain types of property. When applicable, § 751(b) requires recognition of gain or loss in the case of certain disproportionate distributions. *See* Chapter 16.

distribution.[11] Assume, for example, in liquidation of his interest, a retiring partner receives from the partnership a cash payment classified as a § 736(b) payment. Disregarding any application of § 751(b) and assuming the partner had held the partnership interest for many years, the partner would recognize gain to the extent that the cash payment exceeded the partner's outside basis.[12] The partner would recognize loss to the extent the payment were less than the partner's outside basis.[13] Pursuant to § 741, the partner's gain or loss would be characterized as a long-term capital gain or a long-term capital loss. By contrast, were the partner to receive § 736(b) payments consisting of cash as well as other property, the deemed distribution would require not only application of the gain and loss recognition rules of § 731, but also application of the basis allocation rules of § 732. Chapter 14 discusses in detail the § 732 basis allocation rules.

4. Application of § 751(b)

As noted above, § 751(b) is applicable with respect to § 736(b) payments, but does not apply to § 736(a) payments.[14] As discussed in Chapter 16 addressing § 751(b), "unrealized receivables" as defined in § 751(c), together with substantially appreciated inventory, constitute "§ 751 property" or "hot assets." Section 751(b) is triggered when a partnership holds "§ 751 property" and there is a disproportionate distribution — whether a liquidating or nonliquidating distribution. As discussed below, payments for a retiring partner's interest in unrealized receivables will sometimes be classified as § 736(a) payments. In those instances, the exemption of § 736(a) payments from the application of § 751(b) will generally result in "substantially appreciated inventory" being the only "§ 751 property" one must consider when applying § 751(b) to § 736(b) payments.[15]

5. Section 736(b) payments — Impact on Partnership

Unlike § 736(a) payments, § 736(b) payments are not deductible by the partnership. Furthermore, because § 736(b) payments are treated as distributions, § 734(a) will, as a general rule, deny the partnership any adjustment to the bases it has in its assets. As discussed in Chapter 15, however, under certain circumstances § 734 allows (or mandates) adjustments to the basis of partnership property.[16] Specifically, § 734(a) mandates a reduction in a partnership's inside basis if there is a

---

[11] § 731(a)(2). In certain cases, however, § 751(b) may apply and create a recognition event.

[12] § 731(a)(1).

[13] § 731(a)(2).

[14] Reg. §§ 1.736-1(a)(2) and 1.751-1(b)(4)(ii).

[15] § 751(b)(2)(B); Reg. § 1.736-1(b)(4). In Chapter 16, detailing the rationale for and the application of § 751(b), we utilized a table to determine whether there has been a change (an increase or decrease) in the partner's share of "hot assets" or "§ 751 property." As required by Reg. § 1.751-1(b)(1)(ii), that table compared a partner's interest in "§ 751 property" and "other property" both before and after the distribution. To the extent payments for a partner's share of a partnership's "unrealized receivables," as defined for purposes of § 736, are classified as § 736(a) payments and are therefore exempt from § 751(b), those unrealized receivables will not be taken into account in either the before or after calculations in the table.

[16] Adjustments to basis will, of course, affect the amount of depreciation deductions a partnership may be allowed with regard to depreciable property.

"substantial basis reduction" as defined in § 734(d). More important, if a § 754 election is in effect and a retiring partner recognizes gain pursuant to § 731(a)(1) as a result of the receipt of § 736(b) payments, § 734(b)(1)(A) increases a partnership's bases in undistributed capital assets or § 1231 assets. Conversely, § 734(b)(2)(A) decreases a partnership's bases in undistributed capital assets or § 1231 property if, pursuant to § 731(a)(2), the partnership recognizes a loss on a liquidating distribution. Section 734(a)(2) and § 734(b)(2) also require adjustments (either an increase or a decrease) to a partnership's basis in an asset to the extent a disparity exists between the adjusted basis a retiring partner takes in an asset received in a liquidating distribution and the basis the partnership had in that asset. To the extent § 751(b) applies to § 736(b) payments, e.g., the partnership has substantially appreciated inventory and makes liquidating payments solely in cash to the retiring partner, the operations of § 751(b) may result in the partnership increasing its basis in the inventory deemed purchased from the retiring partner. Review Chapter 16.

C. The 1993 Amendments to § 736 and § 751(c)

Prior to the 1993 amendments to § 736, payments to a retiring partner for that partner's interest in the partnership's unrealized receivables as defined in § 751(c) and payments for "unstated goodwill" were not treated as payments in exchange for an interest in partnership property. As a result, such payments constituted § 736(a) payments regardless of the nature of the partnership or the status of a partner as a general or limited partner.[17]

---

§ 736(b). Payments for Interest in Partnership.

. . . .

(2) Special rules. — For purposes of this subsection, payments in exchange for an interest in partnership property shall not include amounts paid for —

(A) unrealized receivables of the partnership (as defined in § 751(c)) or

(B) goodwill of the partnership, except to the extent that the partnership agreement provides for a payment with respect to goodwill.

---

[17] Although § 736(b)(2) is silent on the matter, the regulations both prior to and subsequent to the 1993 amendments to § 736 limit the amount of the payments for unrealized receivables and unstated goodwill deemed to constitute § 736(a) payments. Specifically, Reg. § 1.736–1(b)(2) and (3) provide that: (a) payments made to a partner for unrealized receivables are only § 736(a) payments to the extent the payments *exceed the partner's share of the partnership's basis in the unrealized receivables*; and (b) payments made to a partner for unstated goodwill are likewise only § 736(a) payments to the extent the payments *exceed the partner's share of partnership basis in the unstated goodwill*. Thus, to the extent of the partner's share of partnership basis, if any, payments for unrealized receivables and unstated goodwill will be considered § 736(b) payments and treated as distributions.

A deduction is generally not allowed for the costs incurred in acquiring the unrealized receivables (e.g., accounts receivable) or the goodwill of a going concern. Rather, such costs constitute capital expenditures. As discussed above, by classifying payments to a retiring partner for "unrealized receivables" and "unstated goodwill" as § 736(a) payments characterized either as a distributive share or guaranteed payment, § 736 enabled partnerships to deduct (or achieve the equivalent of a deduction for) those payments. As Congress noted in the legislative history to the 1993 amendments to § 736:[18]

> By treating a payment for unstated goodwill and unrealized receivables as a guaranteed payment or distributive share, present law in effect permits a deduction for an amount that would otherwise constitute a capital expenditure. The treatment does not measure partnership income properly. It also threatens to erode the rule requiring capitalization of such payments generally.

The opportunity afforded partnerships by § 736 to deduct rather than capitalize payments to a retiring partner for unrealized receivables and unstated goodwill resulted in considerable tax planning focused on maximizing the combined tax savings for both the retiring and continuing partners. Planning with regard to goodwill tended to take center stage in accomplishing overall tax savings.[19] See *Commissioner v. Jackson Investment Company* included in the materials.

Congress in 1993 enacted § 736(b)(3) to address its concern regarding deductions (or the equivalent of deductions) for payments that constitute capital expenditures.

---

§ 736(b). Payments for interest in partnership

. . . .

. . . .

(3) Limitation on application of paragraph (2). Paragraph (2) shall apply only if —

(A) capital is not a material income-producing factor for the partnership, and

(B) the retiring or deceased partner was a general partner in the partnership.

---

[18] H.R. Rep. No. 103-11, at 344, 103rd Cong., 1st Sess. (1993).

[19] Were the partnership agreement to provide payments to retiring partners for goodwill, § 736(b) would apply to those payments. Prior to the enactment of § 197 in 1993, goodwill was not depreciable. As a result, even if a § 754 election were in effect and resulted in an inside basis adjustment to partnership goodwill under § 734(b), the partnership would not be allowed to recover that basis by way of depreciation deductions. Thus, from the partnership's standpoint, it was typically preferable if no provision was made in the partnership agreement with respect to payment for goodwill. As a result, a payment for unstated goodwill would be classified as a § 736(a) payment that commonly would be a guaranteed payment deductible by the partnership.

As a result of § 736(b)(3), liquidating payments to a retiring partner for unrealized receivables and unstated goodwill will be treated as made in exchange for the partner's interest in partnership property and thus be § 736(b) payments *unless the payments are made to a general partner in a partnership in which capital is not a material income-producing factor*. Thus, for example, payments to a limited partner for unrealized receivables or unstated goodwill will not be § 736(a) payments regardless of whether capital is a material income-producing factor for the partnership.

The legislative history of the 1993 amendments to § 736 provided the following guidance regarding whether capital is a material income-producing factor:

> The determination of whether capital is a material income-producing factor [will] be made under principles of present and prior law.[20] For purposes of this provision, capital is not a material income-producing factor where substantially all the gross income of the business consists of fees, commissions, or other compensation for personal services performed by an individual. The practice of his or her profession by a doctor, dentist, lawyer, architect, or accountant will not, as such, be treated as a trade or business in which capital is a material income-producing factor even though the practitioner may have a substantial capital investment in professional equipment or in the physical plant constituting the office from which such individual conducts his or her practice so long as such capital investment is merely incidental to such professional practice.[21]

In 1993, Congress also amended § 751(c) (defining "unrealized receivables) for purposes of that provision's application to § 736. As noted above, a reading of § 751(c) reflects that the term "unrealized receivables" encompasses not only traditional receivables such as a cash method taxpayer's accounts receivable for services rendered or to be rendered or accounts receivable for goods delivered or to be delivered, but also for depreciation recapture amounts, etc. Thus, for example, prior to the 1993 amendments, any § 1245 gain inherent in partnership assets constituted an unrealized receivable. Payments to a retiring partner for that partner's share of any § 1245 gain inherent in partnership property were treated as § 736(a) payments. In turn, the partnership was allowed a deduction (or the equivalent of a deduction) for these payments. The 1993 amendment to § 751(c) changed that result by eliminating depreciation recapture as a § 751(c) unrealized receivable for purposes of § 736. As noted by Congress in the legislative history to the 1993 Act:

> When originally enacted, the term "unrealized receivables" was limited to unbilled amounts and accounts receivable. The tax deferral resulting from immediate deduction of amounts paid for these items is relatively short because payment is usually received in the near future. Such deferral is considerably longer, however, with respect to the deduction of other items now included in the expanded definition of unrealized receivables, such as depreciation recapture on business assets, which are slow to give rise to

---

[20] See Reg. § 1.704-1(e)(1)(iv).

[21] Note 18, *supra*, at 345.

ordinary income. . . . The bill . . . repeals the special treatment of payments made for unrealized receivables (other than unbilled amounts and accounts receivable) for all partners. Such amounts [will now] be treated as made in exchange for the partner's interest in partnership property. Thus, for example, a payment for depreciation recapture [will] be treated as made in exchange for an interest in partnership property, and not as a distributive share or guaranteed payment that could give rise to a deduction or its equivalent.[22]

Pursuant to § 751(c) as amended in 1993, for § 736 purposes, § 1245 or § 1250 depreciation recapture of amounts inherent in partnership assets will not be treated as unrealized receivables and thus can never be classified as § 736(a) payments. Rather, such payments will be characterized as payments for partnership property and classified as § 736(b) payments. Because § 736(b) payments are governed by the general distribution rules, including § 751(b), depreciation recapture under § 1245 or § 1250 will, notwithstanding the 1993 amendments to § 736, be treated as "§ 751 property" or a "hot asset."

D. Application of § 736 under Current Law

Following the 1993 amendments to § 736 discussed above, *all liquidating payments* made by a partnership to a retiring partner will be classified as § 736(b) payments except for:

1. payments for unrealized receivables and unstated goodwill made to a retiring *general partner* in a partnership *in which capital is not a material income-producing factor* for the partnership; and
2. payments in the nature of mutual insurance.

As a corollary, § 736(a) will only come into play in two situations:

1. when, among the payments made by a partnership to a retiring partner, there are payments in the nature of mutual insurance; or
2. when the retiring partner is a general partner in a partnership in which capital is not a material income-producing factor and the partnership makes payments to that partner for unrealized receivables[23] or unstated goodwill.

Let us now consider some examples demonstrating the application of § 736 in situations where all payments to a retiring partner are made at the same time. We will consider the special rules related to liquidation payments made in installments over a multi-year period *infra*.

Example 1. Assume Patrick is a general partner in a three-person general partnership in which *capital is a material income-producing factor*. Patrick has a one-third interest in the capital and profits of the partnership

---

[22] Note 18, *supra*, at 344–45.

[23] Note that an in-kind distribution of accounts receivable to a retiring partner would not be governed by § 736(a) even if that distribution were to a general partner in a partnership for which capital was not a material income-producing factor.

which uses the cash method of accounting. He has held his interest in the partnership for many years. Assume, at the time of Patrick's retirement from the partnership, the partnership balance sheet and the partners' capital accounts were as follows:[24]

	Partnerships Assets			Liabilities and Partners' Capital	
	A/B	FMV		A/B	FMV
Cash	$150,000	$150,000	Liability		$30,000
Accounts Receivable	$0[25]	$60,000	Patrick	$80,000	$140,000
Land	$90,000	$180,000	Katie	$80,000	$140,000
Goodwill	$0[26]	$60,000	Quinn	$80,000	$140,000
Total	**$240,000**	**$450,000**		**$240,000**	**$450,000**

Assume the land is encumbered by a $30,000 nonrecourse liability. In liquidation of Patrick's interest in the partnership, the partnership pays to Patrick $140,000 in cash and Patrick is relieved of his $10,000 share of the nonrecourse liability. (Thus, Patrick has received a total of $150,000.) The partnership agreement is silent regarding any payment for goodwill.

Analysis:

a. Tax Results Prior to the 1993 Amendments to § 736: Prior to the 1993 amendments, the total payments to Patrick of $150,000 (i.e., $140,000 in cash plus relief from $10,000 share of nonrecourse liability) would have been divided between § 736(b) payments, i.e., the payment for Patrick's interest in partnership assets other than the accounts receivable and unstated goodwill, and § 736(a) payments, i.e., the payment for Patrick's share of the partnership's accounts receivable and unstated goodwill. Thus, because Patrick was a one-third partner, the § 736(b) payments would have consisted of $50,000 for Patrick's share of partnership cash and $60,000 for his interest in the land (which includes his $10,000 share of the liability) for total § 736(b) payments of $110,000. Note that because the partnership agreement did not provide for payment with respect to goodwill, there is unstated goodwill the payment for which will be treated as a § 736(a) payment.[27] Thus, Patrick's total § 736(a) payments would have been $40,000, i.e., $20,000 for unstated goodwill and $20,000 for Patrick's share of the partnership's accounts receivable.

Pursuant to § 736(b), the $110,000 Patrick received for his share of the partnership's cash and land would be treated as a distribution. Section

---

[24] Assume the partnership, in view of Patrick's retirement, elected to revalue its property and, in turn, the capital accounts of its partners to reflect fair market values. *See* Reg. § 1.704-1(b)(2)(iv)(f).

[25] Because the partnership is a cash method partnership, it has yet to include the accounts receivable in income. As a result, the partnership has a zero basis in the accounts receivable.

[26] The goodwill has no basis as it is goodwill created by the partnership rather than acquired goodwill.

[27] Technically, the goodwill would be measured today using the residual method mandated by § 1060.

751(b) would not be applicable because the payment for the accounts receivable is not a § 736(b) payment and therefore is not taken into account in the distribution analysis under § 736(b). As a result, there is no "§ 751 property" (or "hot assets") that would trigger application of § 751(b). Applying the normal distribution rules, Patrick will recognize $30,000 of gain pursuant to § 731(a)(1). This gain will be treated under § 741 as a long-term capital gain. If the partnership has made a § 754 election, it will be entitled to increase its basis in its capital assets and § 1231 assets by $30,000 under § 755.[28] Thus, if a § 754 election is in effect, the partnership's adjusted basis in the land will be increased from $90,000 to $120,000.

Pursuant to § 736(a), the $40,000 Patrick receives for his share of unrealized receivables and unstated goodwill will be treated as a guaranteed payment because the amount is determined without regard to partnership income. Reg. § 1.736–1(a)(3)(ii). As a guaranteed payment, the $40,000 will constitute ordinary income to Patrick and be currently deductible by the partnership.[29] (Note how the pre-1993 law enabled the partnership to deduct currently an amount (the acquisition cost of Patrick's interest in unrealized receivables and goodwill) that under general tax principles should have been capitalized.)

b. Tax Results Following the 1993 Amendments to § 736. Because capital is a material income-producing factor in the partnership, § 736(b)(3) is applicable and, as a result, the payments for both the accounts receivable and goodwill will be treated as § 736(b) payments. Section 736(a) will thus have no application to the liquidation of Patrick's interest. Unlike the pre-1993 amendment results, the analysis under § 736(b) will now include application of § 751(b). The accounts receivable constitute "§ 751 property" or "hot assets" and thus the distribution will be bifurcated. A part of the distribution will be treated as a sale or exchange of property between the partnership and Patrick; the remainder of the distribution will be treated under the normal distribution rules — § 731 *et seq.*

Having studied the multi-step § 751(b) analysis in Chapter 16, it should be obvious that under § 751(b) Patrick will be deemed to have received a distribution of $20,000 of the zero-basis accounts receivable (i.e., his share of the accounts receivable) and then be deemed to have sold those receivables to the partnership for $20,000 in cash. (See Steps 2–4 of the 6-step § 751(b) analysis discussed in Chapter 16.) Thus, the deemed distribution/deemed sale will account for $20,000 of the liquidating distribution. As a result of the § 751(b) analysis, Patrick will have $20,000 of ordinary income and the partnership will take a $20,000 basis in the accounts receivable it is deemed to have purchased from Patrick. (See Step 5 of the 6-step § 751 analysis.) The remaining $130,000 of the $150,000 liquidating distribution received by Patrick will be treated under the normal distribution rules, i.e., § 731 *et seq.* (See Step 6 of the 6-step

---

[28] § 734(b)(1)(A); Reg. § 1.755-1(c)(1). See Chapter 15.

[29] § 707(c); Reg. § 1.707-1(c).

§ 751(b) analysis.) As a result, pursuant to § 731(a)(1), Patrick will recognize $50,000 of gain (i.e., $130,000 less Patrick's $80,000 adjusted basis in his partnership interest). The $50,000 of gain will be characterized under § 741 as long-term capital gain.

Again, if the partnership has a § 754 election in effect, the partnership will be entitled to increase its inside basis in its capital assets and § 1231 assets by $50,000.[30] Pursuant to § 755, this $50,000 increase will be allocated between the land and goodwill in proportion to their respective amounts of unrealized appreciation before such increase.[31] Here the land has $90,000 of unrealized appreciation and the goodwill has $60,000 of unrealized appreciation. Therefore, 60%, or $30,000, of the $50,000 basis adjustment will be allocated to the land and the remaining 40%, or $20,000, will be allocated to the goodwill. Thus, the partnership's basis in its land will be increased from $90,000 to $120,000 while the partnership's basis in the goodwill will be increased from $0 to $20,000. Pursuant to § 197, the partnership will presumably be entitled to amortize over a 15-year period its $20,000 basis in the goodwill. Contrast these results with the pre-1993 results.

Example 2: Assume the facts of Example 1 except that the partnership is a service partnership and capital is not a material income-producing factor.

Analysis: Because Patrick is a general partner in a service partnership in which capital is not a material income-producing factor, § 736(b)(2) will be applicable. Thus, the $20,000 payment for Patrick's interest in the accounts receivable and the $20,000 payment for unstated goodwill constitute § 736(a) payments. The tax results will be identical to those noted in Example 1 with respect to liquidating distributions prior to the effective date of the 1993 amendments:

(a) The $40,000 in § 736(a) payments will be guaranteed payments treated as ordinary income to Patrick and currently deductible by the partnership.

(b) The remaining $110,000 of liquidating payments will be § 736(b) payments and will result in $30,000 of long-term capital gain pursuant to § 731(a)(1)(A) and § 741.

(c) If the partnership has a § 754 election in effect, the partnership will increase its basis in the land to reflect the $30,000 of gain recognized by Patrick.

Example 3: Assume the facts of Example 2 except that Patrick is a limited partner.

Analysis: Because Patrick is a limited partner, § 736(b)(2) is inapplicable.[32] All of the payments to Patrick will be treated as § 736(b) payments, just as

---

[30] § 734(b)(1)(A).

[31] Reg. § 1.755-1(c)(2). See Chapter 15.

[32] § 736(b)(3).

they are in the analysis of Example 1, which takes into account the 1993 amendments to § 736. Thus, even though the partnership is a service partnership in which capital is not a material income-producing factor, the payments for accounts receivable and unstated goodwill will be classified as § 736(b) payments.

Example 4: Assume the facts of Example 2 except that, instead of a partnership, the entity is a limited liability company (LLC) taxed as a partnership and Patrick holds a membership interest in the LLC.

Analysis: Section 736(b)(3) specifically provides that unrealized receivables and unstated goodwill constitute § 736(a) payments only if the payee is a *general partner* in a partnership in which capital is not a material income-producing factor. Is a member of a limited liability company a general partner for purposes of § 736? While that specific question has yet to be answered definitively, the courts have held that, at least for purposes of the passive loss rules of § 469, a member of an LLC is not a limited partner and thus for § 469 purposes is treated as a general partner would be treated.[33] If Patrick, as a member of the LLC, is treated as a general partner, the tax consequences to Patrick and the partnership are the same as those discussed in Example 2 *supra*. If, by contrast, Patrick is not treated as a general partner, the consequences are those discussed in Example 3 *supra*.

E. Liquidating a Partner's Interest by a Series of Distributions

As noted above, it is not uncommon for a partnership to make liquidating payments to a retiring partner in installments over a number of years. This often occurs where the liquidating payments are to be made in cash and the partnership has insufficient funds to make a lump-sum liquidating payment. The regulations specifically provide that, in the case of the liquidation of a retiring partner's interest through a series of distributions, the partner's interest is not considered liquidated until the final distribution has been made.[34]

The liquidation of a retiring partner's interest through a series of distributions (installments) raises a number of questions. If installment payments represent both (a) payments for a retiring partner's interest in partnership property, i.e., § 736(b) payments, and (b) either guaranteed payments or distributive shares under § 736(a), how should these installment payments be allocated over the years between § 736(a) and § 736(b)? With regard to § 736(b) payments, when will gain or loss, if any, be recognized? How are contingent payments allocated? May the partnership agreement specify the allocation of payments? These and other questions are specifically addressed by Reg. § 1.736-1(b)(5) and (6), discussed below. As will become apparent, the regulations provide partners considerable flexibility with regard to installment payments.

---

[33] Garnnet v. Commissioner, 132 T.C. 368 (2009); Thompson v. Commissioner, 87 Fed. Cl. 728 (2009); Newell v. Commissioner, T.C. Memo 2010-23.

[34] Reg. § 1.761-1(d).

If the total amount to be received by the retiring partner is fixed and payable over a specific number of years and represents a mix of § 736(a) and § 736(b) payments, the amount of § 736(b) payments deemed made each year is determined by multiplying the total payments the retiring partner is *entitled to receive* (not the total amount actually received) that year by a fraction. The numerator of that fraction is the total of all § 736(b) payments the retiring partner will receive over time; and the denominator is the aggregate of all the § 736(a) and (b) payments the retiring partner will receive over time.[35] If, in a given year, a retiring partner were to receive payments totaling less than the § 736(b) payment amount for that year (determined by using the formula noted above), the entire amount actually received by the retiring partner is treated as a § 736(b) payment, and the deficiency is added to the portion of the subsequent year's payments that are deemed to be § 736(b) payments.[36]

If the total payments to be received by a retiring partner are not fixed, payments actually received by the retiring partner are treated first as being in exchange for that partner's interest in partnership property under § 736(b) to the extent of the value of that interest.[37] Any payments thereafter are treated as § 736(a) payments.[38]

Notwithstanding the above rules, if the retiring partner and the remaining partners agree, any method may be used to allocate the annual payments to the retiring partner between § 736(b) and § 736(a) payments so long as the total amount allocated to § 736(b) payments does not exceed the retiring partner's share of the fair market value of partnership property at the time of the partner's retirement.[39]

With regard to amounts treated as § 736(b) payments, any gain or loss to be recognized will be determined pursuant to § 731 unless, of course, § 751(b) is applicable, in which case both §§ 731 and 751(b) will be applicable in determining gain or loss to be recognized by the retiring partner. Assuming § 751(b) does not apply, and liquidating payments are made solely in cash, a retiring partner receiving payments would first recover her basis in her partnership interest before recognizing any gain. Loss would be recognized only after the taxpayer had received all payments and the amount of loss could be determined. Thus, in effect, the recognition of both gain and loss is deferred.

Assuming § 751(b) does not apply, if the total § 736(b) payments to be received is a fixed sum and the payments are solely in cash, the retiring partner may elect to allocate any gain or loss recognized among the various payments received during the payout period. This allocation is made by allocating a portion of the retiring partner's outside basis to each § 736(b) payment. The portion of the outside basis allocable to a given payment is determined by multiplying the retiring partner's outside basis by a fraction, the numerator of which is the amount of the § 736(b)

---

[35] Reg. § 1.736-1(b)(5)(i).

[36] *Id.*

[37] Reg. § 1.736-1(b)(5)(ii).

[38] *Id.*

[39] Reg. § 1.736-1(b)(5)(iii).

payment and the denominator of which is the total amount of § 736(b) payments to be received.[40] The election to allocate gain and loss is made in the tax year the retiring partner receives his first § 736(b) payment.[41]

Consider the following examples demonstrating the application of the above rules:

Example 1: Charlotte is retiring from a three-person service general partnership in which capital is not a material income-producing factor. Charlotte, who has held her interest as a general partner for many years, has a one-third interest in the capital and profits of the partnership. At the time of her retirement on July 1, Year 1, the partnership, which uses the cash method of accounting, had the following balance sheet:

	Partnership Assets			**Partnership Capital**	
	A/B	FMV		A/B	FMV
Cash	$150,000	$150,000	Dan	$80,000	$150,000
Accounts Receivable	$0	$120,000	Charlotte	$80,000	$150,000
Land	$90,000	$150,000	Will	$80,000	$150,000
Goodwill	$0	$30,000			
Total	$240,000	$450,000		$240,000	$450,000

The partnership has agreed to pay Charlotte $150,000 in cash for her partnership interest as follows: $30,000 in Year 1 and $30,000 in each of the following four years. Because the partnership agreement makes no provision for the payment for goodwill, the goodwill is characterized as "unstated goodwill." On July 1, Year 1, the partnership pays Charlotte $30,000 in cash as required by the liquidation agreement. Assume Charlotte and the partnership made no agreement regarding the portion of each payment constituting a § 736(b) payment and the portion constituting a § 736(a) payment.

Analysis: The $150,000 in payments to Charlotte must first be classified. Because Charlotte is a general partner and capital is not a material income-producing factor in the partnership, the amount paid Charlotte for her share of accounts receivable and for unstated goodwill will be classified as § 736(a) payments. § 736(b)(2) and (3). The payments for Charlotte's interest in partnership cash and land will be classified as § 736(b) payments. The § 736(b) payments will total $100,000, i.e., Charlotte's share of the cash is $50,000 and her share of the land has a fair market value of $50,000. The remaining $50,000 of payments to be received by Charlotte are § 736(a) payments, consisting of $30,000 for Charlotte's share of the accounts receivable and $20,000 for her share of unstated goodwill. Because the § 736(a) payments are determined without reference to income of the partnership, they are treated as guaranteed payments.

---

[40] Reg. § 1.736-1(b)(6).

[41] *Id.*

Pursuant to the regulation rules discussed above, the $30,000 payment received by Charlotte on July 1, Year 1 must be allocated between the § 736(b) payment for the year and the § 736(a) payment. The § 736(b) amount will be determined by multiplying the $30,000 payment by a fraction, the numerator of which will be $100,000 (the total § 736(b) payments to be received) and the denominator of which will be $150,000 (the aggregate of all of the § 736(a) and (b) payments to be received by Charlotte over time). As a result, the Year 1 $30,000 payment and the $30,000 payment made in each of the subsequent four years will be treated as consisting of $20,000 of § 736(b) payment and $10,000 of § 736(a) payment. See Reg. § 1.736–1(b)(5)(i).

The $10,000 § 736(a) payment each year will be treated as a guaranteed payment under § 707(c) because it is determined without regard to partnership income. Reg. § 1.736-1(a)(3)(ii). As a guaranteed payment, the $10,000 payment would be characterized as ordinary income to Charlotte and would be deductible by the partnership. § 707(c) and Reg. § 1.707-1(c).

With regard to the § 736(b) payment of $20,000, Charlotte would not recognize any gain in Year 1 as she has ample outside basis. After the Year 1 payment, Charlotte's outside basis would be reduced from $80,000 to $60,000 and would ultimately be reduced to $0 after the Year 4 payment.[42] In Year 5, the $20,000 § 736(b) payment would trigger recognition of $20,000 of gain. The gain would be characterized as long-term capital gain.[43] Thus, gain recognition has been deferred until the last payment.

With regard to the $20,000 of gain she ultimately will recognize as a result of the § 736(b) payments, Charlotte has the option of spreading that gain over the five § 736(b) payments she will receive. Reg. § 1.736–1(b)(6). She will do this, as indicated above, by allocating a portion of her $80,000 outside basis to each of the § 736(b) payments. The portion of her outside basis allocated to each $20,000 payment will be $16,000, determined by multiplying her total adjusted basis of $80,000 by a fraction, the numerator of which will be $20,000 (the amount of each § 736(b) payment) and the denominator will be $100,000 (the total of the five § 736(b) payments she will receive). Thus, Charlotte will recognize $4,000 of long-term capital gain upon receipt of each of the five annual $20,000 § 736(b) payments. Were Charlotte's adjusted basis in her partnership interest to be greater than $100,000 so that Charlotte would ultimately recognize a loss under § 731(a)(2), she could likewise elect to recognize some of the loss with each § 736(b) payment, rather than waiting until she had received all of the § 736(b) payments.

Example 2: Assume the same facts as Example 1. In Year 2, the partnership experienced unexpected losses and could only pay Charlotte

---

[42] § 733.

[43] §§ 731 and 741.

$15,000 in cash rather than the $30,000 agreed upon. The partnership agreed it would subsequently make up the deficiency in the Year 2 payment.

Analysis: As discussed in Example 1, the Year 2 $30,000 payment, if made, would have consisted of a $20,000 § 736(b) payment and a $10,000 § 736(a) payment. If, under circumstances such as those presented in this Example, the amount actually received by a retiring partner is less than the § 736(b) payment, the regulations provide the entire payment received will be deemed a § 736(b) payment and any deficiency will be added to the following year's § 736(b) payment. Reg. § 1.736–1(b)(5)(i). Thus, the entire $15,000 payment received by Charlotte in Year 2 will be treated as a § 736(b) payment and, as a result, no part of the payment will constitute a § 736(a) payment. If we assume in Year 3 the partnership pays Charlotte not only the $30,000 it was required to pay her for that year but also an additional $15,000 to make up for the Year 2 deficiency, Charlotte in Year 3 will be deemed to have received a $25,000 § 736(b) payment (i.e., $20,000 as in Example 1 plus an additional $5,000 to make up for the deficiency in the § 736(b) payment in Year 2). The remainder of the $45,000 in payment received by Charlotte in Year 3 will constitute a guaranteed payment under § 736(a). Thus, Charlotte will have a $20,000 guaranteed payment in Year 3.

Example 3: Assume the facts of Example 1, except the partnership, instead of paying Charlotte a fixed sum for her partnership interest, will pay Charlotte a percentage of the partnership's annual income for five years. Pursuant to this arrangement, the partnership paid Charlotte $35,000 in Year 1.

Analysis: As discussed above, the regulations provide that, under these circumstances, all payments must first be treated as § 736(b) payments to the extent of the value of the retiring partner's interest in partnership property.[44] Here, the fair market value of Charlotte's interest in partnership property (all property of the partnership other than accounts receivable and unstated goodwill) is $100,000. Thus, the entire $35,000 will constitute a § 736(b) payment. Because Charlotte's outside basis is $80,000 she will have no gain in Year 1. [Note that, because the total of the § 736(b) payments to be received by Charlotte is not a fixed sum, the election discussed above regarding the spreading of gain associated with § 736(b) payments is not available to Charlotte.[45]] Once Charlotte has received payments under this arrangement totaling $100,000, all additional payments will be § 736(a) payments. Because any additional payments depend on the income of the partnership, the additional payments will be treated as distributive shares of partnership income and will have the same character as the partnership's income.

---

[44] Reg. § 1.736-1(b)(5)(ii).

[45] Reg. § 1.736-1(b)(6).

Example 4: Assume the facts of Example 1, except the partnership is one in which capital is a material income-producing factor.

Analysis: Under these circumstances, the amounts paid to Charlotte for her interest in partnership accounts receivable and unstated goodwill will not be classified as § 736(a) payments. Instead, as discussed above, all payments will be classified as § 736(b) payments and treated under the distribution rules including §§ 731 and 751(b). Because accounts receivable constitute "§ 751 property" or "hot assets," § 751(b) will be applicable because Charlotte is receiving only cash from the partnership. Charlotte's share of the accounts receivable amount to $40,000. Considering the liquidating distributions as a whole and applying the § 751(b) analysis discussed in Chapter 16, Charlotte will be deemed to have received a distribution of $40,000 of accounts receivable with a zero basis and, in turn, will be deemed to have sold the accounts receivable back to the partnership for $40,000. On the deemed distribution of the $40,000 of accounts receivable, Charlotte would have taken a zero basis[46] and will thus recognize $40,000 of ordinary income when she is deemed to have sold the accounts receivable back to the partnership for $40,000 in cash. Consequently, $40,000 of the total of $150,000 in § 736(b) payments she is receiving will constitute ordinary income; the other $110,000 will be nontaxable return of basis ($80,000) and long-term capital gain ($30,000).[47] The regulations provide no guidance regarding a method for taking the § 751(b) ordinary income into account, when a retiring partner receives liquidating payments in installments. Given the broad flexibility noted above that the regulations accord a retiring partner with regard to the recognition of gain or loss on liquidating payments received in installments, we believe the service should allow a retiring partner, like Charlotte in this example, to allocate the § 751(b) ordinary income element proportionately over the payout period. Thus, because the $40,000 ordinary income element constitutes 4/15 of the total liquidating payments of $150,000 to be received by Charlotte, we believe 4/15 of each annual $30,000 payment, or $8,000, should constitute ordinary income; the remaining $22,000 of each annual payment should be characterized proportionately as well, i.e., as a nontaxable return of basis ($16,000) and as long-term capital gain ($6,000).

F. Conclusion

As enacted in 1954, § 736 was intended to simplify the taxation of payments in liquidation. While it accomplished that purpose to some extent, it also created confusion and set the stage for a level of planning Congress ultimately deemed inappropriate. In 1993, Congress amended § 736 to eliminate major difficulties it identified with regard to that provision. By significantly limiting the applicability of § 736(a), the 1993 amendments simplified matters considerably. As this Overview indicates, however, § 736 continues to be complicated. In reflecting on § 736, you

---

[46] § 732.

[47] §§ 731 and 741.

should question whether it makes sense for § 736 to continue to exist in the Code. Would it be better to treat all liquidating payments under the general distribution rules, including § 751(b)? Under any circumstance, further guidance regarding the application of § 751(b) to installment payments would be welcome.

COMMISSIONER v. JACKSON INVESTMENT COMPANY
346 F.2d 187 (9th Cir. 1965)

BARNES, J.,

. . . The question presented for our consideration involves the construction of § 736 of the Internal Revenue Code of 1954. That section, drafted as part of a series of provisions intended to clarify and simplify the tax laws with respect to partnerships, provides as follows: . . .

The intended purpose of this provision was to permit the participants themselves to determine whether the retiring partner or the remaining partners would bear the tax burdens for payments in liquidation of a retiring partner's interest. Thus, under the general approach of subsection (a), the tax burden is borne by the retiring partner — he recognizes the payments as taxable income, and the remaining partners are allowed a commensurate deduction from partnership income. Under subsection (b), the general rule conceives an approach of nonrecognition of ordinary income to the retiring partner, but places the tax burden on the partnership by denying a deduction from income for the payments. This latter subsection, however, adopts a special rule — (b)(2)(B) — in an express effort to assist the participants to decide *inter sese* upon the allocation of the tax burden. This special rule lies at the heart of the present controversy. Under this rule, payments for the good will of the partnership are deductible by the partnership (and hence recognizable as ordinary income to the retiring partner) "except to the extent that the partnership agreement provides for a payment with respect to good will." If the partnership agreement provides for a payment with respect to good will, the tax burden is allocated to the partnership — no deduction is allowed and the retiring partner need not recognize the payments as ordinary income. In the present case, petitioner contends that this exception under § 736(b)(2)(B) applies, and thus the deductions taken by the partnership should be disallowed. We must determine, therefore, whether the parties intended to place the tax burden on the partnership by expressly incorporating into the partnership agreement a provision for payment to the retiring partner with respect to good will.

It is undisputed that the original Partnership Agreement did not contain a provision for partnership good will or a payment therefor upon the withdrawal of a partner. On May 7, 1956, however, the three partners executed an instrument entitled "Amendment of Limited Partnership Agreement of George W. Carter Co." This instrument provided for Ethel Carter's retirement, and bound the partnership to compensate Ethel in the amount of $60,000.00 in consideration for her withdrawal. After the necessary adjustment of the figures, it was determined that $19,650.00 of the amount was in return for Ethel's "15% Interest in the fair market value of all the net assets of the partnership." The other $40,350.00, the amount in controversy here, was referred to as "a guaranteed payment, or a payment for good will." The $40,350.00 was paid by the partnership in three annual parts, and deductions were made for good will expense in the partnership net income for each of the years. It is these deductions that petitioner challenges.

The decision of the Tax Court (six judges dissenting), concluded that the document entitled "Amendment of Limited Partnership Agreement of George W. Carter Co." was not a part of the partnership agreement, and therefore, the exception of § 736(b)(2)(B) was not applicable. As a result, the court held that the amounts in question were legitimate deductions from the partnership income under the terms of § 736(a)(2). The court founded its conclusion on the fact that the "Amendment" was solely designed to effect a withdrawal of one of the partners; it was not at all concerned with any continued role for Ethel in the partnership affairs.

We cannot agree with the interpretation of the majority of the Tax Court. We find this view unduly interferes with the clear objective of the statute, i.e., to permit and enable the partners to allocate the tax burdens as they choose, and with a minimum of uncertainty and difficulty. If a partnership agreement such as the one involved here, had no provision regarding the withdrawal of a partner, and the partners negotiated to compensate the retiring partner with payments that could be treated by the recipient at capital gain rates, the statutory scheme should not be read to frustrate the parties' efforts. An amendment to the partnership agreement which incorporates the plan of withdrawal and which designates the amount payable as being in consideration for the partnership good will seems clearly to be an attempt to utilize § 736(b)(2)(B), affording capital gain rates to the retiring partner but precluding an expense deduction for the partnership. Simply because the subject matter of the amendment deals only with the liquidation of one partner's interest, we should not thwart whatever may be the clear intent of the parties by holding the amendment is not part of the partnership agreement. The Internal Revenue Code of 1954 expressly touches upon modifications of partnership agreements, and it gives no support to the thesis that an amendment dealing with the withdrawal of a partner cannot be considered a part of the partnership agreement. § 761(c) provides:

> Partnership Agreement. — For purposes of this subchapter, a partnership agreement includes any modifications of the partnership agreement made prior to, or at, the time prescribed by law for the filing of the partnership return for the taxable year (not including extensions) which are agreed to by all the partners, or which are adopted in such other manner as may be provided by the partnership agreement.

We hold, therefore, in harmony with the intent of the parties to the partnership, that the "Amendment of Limited Partnership Agreement of George W. Carter Co." was a modification of the partnership agreement within the meaning of § 761(c). As such, the requirement of a provision in the partnership agreement as specified in § 736(b)(2)(B) is satisfied.

There remains, however, an additional requirement to call into operation § 736(b)(2)(B), viz., that the provision for payment in the partnership agreement be with respect to good will. As noted above, the payment of the $40,350.00 was inartistically described in the Amendment as a "guaranteed payment, or a payment for good will." The "guaranteed payment" terminology seems to expressly incorporate § 736(a)(2), which would permit an expense deduction to the partnership, while recognizing the payments as ordinary income to the retiring partner. The "good will" language, on the other hand, would appear directed to § 736(b)(2)(B), which results in the opposite tax consequences. In resolving this conflict, we feel the most helpful guide is to pay deference to what we may determine was the revealed intent of the parties. An examination of the entire amendment leads us to conclude that, notwithstanding the use of the words "guaranteed payment," the parties intended to invoke § 736(b)(2)(B), not § 736(a)(2). The Amendment expressly states the following (which we find impossible to harmonize with the majority opinion of the Tax Court or the arguments advanced by respondents in their brief):

> It is recognized by all the parties hereto that the prior agreements among the partners do not provide for any payment to any partner in respect to good will in the event of the retirement or withdrawal of a partner, but George W. Carter Company will nevertheless make a payment to Ethel M. Carter in respect to good will as herein provided in consideration of her entering into this agreement and her consent to retire from the partnership upon the terms herein expressed.

The meaning of this language as well as the words chosen to express it leads to the conclusion that the $40,350.00 was to be a payment "in respect to good will," with the parties intending to be governed by the tax consequences of § 736(b)(2)(B). The concluding paragraph of Judge Raum's dissenting opinion in the Tax Court, joined in by five other judges, expresses in our judgment sound reasoning, and we incorporate it here as a summary statement of our viewpoint:

> To fail to give effect to the plain language thus used by the parties is, I think, to defeat the very purpose of the pertinent partnership provisions of the statute, namely, to permit the partners themselves to fix their tax liabilities *inter sese*. Although the May 7, 1956, agreement may be inartistically drawn, and indeed may even contain some internal inconsistencies, the plain and obvious import of its provisions in respect of the present problem was to amend the partnership agreement so as to provide specifically for a goodwill payment. This is the kind of thing that § 736(b)(2)(B) dealt with when it allowed the partners to fix the tax consequences of goodwill payments to a withdrawing partner. And this is what the partners clearly attempted to do here, however crude may have been their effort. I would give further effect to that effort, and would not add further complications to an already overcomplicated statute.

The decision of the Tax Court is reversed and the matter is remanded to that court for further proceedings consistent with this opinion.

Chapter 18

DISGUISED PAYMENTS FOR SERVICES AND DISGUISED SALES OF PROPERTY

I. PROBLEMS

1. Amy, Ben, and Carly are equal partners in the ABC partnership, formed to construct and operate an office building. The partnership enters an agreement with Carly, an architect, to provide architectural services in connection with its construction of the office building. Carly will waive the fee of $500,000 she would normally charge for this type of project. Under the agreement, for each of the first two years, Carly will receive a special allocation of $250,000 from partnership net income. The building has been pre-leased and will generate $1,000,000 of rental income per year for the first five years. Does the special allocation constitute a disguised payment for services?

2. Would the answer to Problem 1 change if the building was not pre-leased?

3. Would the answer to Problem 2 change if the special allocation was 25% of gross income for each of the first two years, and Carly's partnership interest was to be liquidated upon making the second payment to her?

4. On January 1, Year 4, Rose contributes Greenacre, a tract of raw land worth $200,000 with an adjusted basis of $120,000, to the QRST partnership in exchange for an interest in the partnership. The partnership, which has cash of $300,000, plans to construct a $200,000 office building on Greenacre. On the same day as the transfer of Greenacre, Rose receives a distribution of $100,000 of cash from the partnership. What are the tax consequences of the distribution?

5. Assume the facts of Problem 4, except the $100,000 distribution took place on July 1, Year 6. What are the tax consequences of the distribution?

6. Assume the facts of Problem 5, except further assume another partner made a cash contribution of $100,000 in Year 4 that was used to purchase two-year government securities. Would the answer change if the planned office building cost $500,000 instead of $200,000, and the partnership took out a short-term construction loan during Year 5 to complete the construction?

7. Assume the facts of Problem 4, except Rose's contribution of Greenacre was subject to a recourse mortgage of $100,000, which Rose had incurred on January 1, Year 1, to pay her gambling debts. Rose received a one-quarter interest in the partnership in return for her contribution.

There was no cash distribution to her. What are the tax consequences from Rose's contribution of Greenacre?

8. Assume the facts of Problem 7, except Rose had incurred the mortgage on January 1, Year 3. What are the tax consequences from Rose's contribution of Greenacre?

9. Would the answer to Problem 8 change if: (1) the $100,000 mortgage incurred on January 1, Year 3, had been incurred to install drainage pipelines on Greenacre; (2) Greenacre was worth $225,000, instead of $200,000, at the time of contribution; and (3) the partnership, in addition to taking Greenacre subject to the $100,000 mortgage, also distributed $25,000 in cash to Rose?

Assignment for Chapter 18:

Complete the Problems

Read: Internal Revenue Code: § 707(a)(2). Skim: §§ 704(b); 707(a)(1); 707(c).
Treasury Regulations: §§ 1.707-3(a)(1), (2), 4, (b)(1), (2), (c)(1), (2), (d), (f) Ex. 1; 1.707-4(a)(1), (2), (b)(1), (d); 1.707-5(a)(1), (2)(i)&(ii), (3), (6)(i)&(ii), (7)(i)&(ii), (b)(1), (f) Exs. 2, 5, 6, 10; 1.707-7(a).
Proposed Regulations: Prop. Reg. § 1.707-2(b)(2), (c), (d).

Materials: Overview

II. VOCABULARY

disguised payment
disguised sale
entrepreneurial risk
simultaneous transfer
qualified liability
net equity percentage
debt-financed distribution
operating cash flow distribution

III. OBJECTIVES

1. To recall that payment by a partnership to a partner may be treated as a distributive share, a guaranteed payment, or a payment in its capacity as other than a partner.

2. To determine the character, timing, and potential capitalization applicable to a payment by a partnership to a partner.

3. To recall and apply the factors involved in determining whether a payment to a partner is properly characterized as a payment in her capacity as other than a partner.

4. To recall and apply the test for determining when transfers between a partnership and a partner will be treated as a sale.

5. To identify the facts and circumstances that may tend to prove the existence of a sale.
6. To recall the rebuttable presumptions for transfers made more than two years apart and for transfers made within two years.
7. To determine whether a liability is a qualified liability.
8. To determine a partner's share of recourse and nonrecourse liabilities for purposes of the disguised sales rules.
9. To determine whether and to what extent a partnership's assumption of a qualified or nonqualified liability may constitute consideration for a sale.
10. To recall that a reasonable guaranteed payment for capital, a reasonable preferred return, and an operating cash flow distribution are not treated as part of a sale of property.

IV. OVERVIEW

Basic structural aspects of Subchapter K — the single level of taxation, the flexibility to make special allocations of partnership items, the generally tax-free nature of contributions and distributions — can encourage efforts to disguise, as nontaxable transfers, payments that might be "properly characterized," to use the words of § 707(a)(2)(A) and (B), as payments for services or as consideration for sales or exchanges. This chapter examines § 707(a)(2) and its regulations, the statutory and administrative responses to these disguised arrangements.

A. Disguised Payments for Services

We turn first to § 707(a)(2)(A) and "disguised" payments for services. Some background may be helpful. Recall the different tax consequences of payments and allocations made under § 704(b), § 707(a)(1), and § 707(c): Payments for services under § 707(a)(1) and § 707(c) generate ordinary income to the service-provider, whereas the character of allocations of tax items to a partner under § 704(b) is determined at the partnership level. A further difference relates to the timing of income: Under § 706(a) income inclusion turns on the partnership's tax year for allocations or payments made under § 704(b) or § 707(c), whereas the partner's method of accounting controls timing for § 707(a)(1) payments.

As discussed in Chapter 13, § 707(a)(1) announces a general rule applicable to a partner engaged in a transaction with her partnership in a nonpartner capacity: The partner will, for purposes of that transaction, be treated as a nonpartner or outsider. For example, if a partner provides services to her partnership in a nonpartner capacity, the tax consequences of that transaction should be those a nonpartner would have.[1] In contrast, if a partner is providing services to the partnership in her capacity as a partner, the tax consequences will be governed by

---

[1] Under § 267(e)(1)-(4), however, a partnership and its partners are related persons for purposes of applying the deduction and income matching rule of § 267(a)(2), thus creating an exception to the general rule that a partner/partnership transaction will be treated as a transaction between the partnership and a nonpartner when the partner is not acting in her capacity as a partner.

the distributive share rules of § 704(b), where the allocation to the partner for services is based upon partnership income, and by the guaranteed payment rules of § 707(c), where the payment for services is not based upon partnership income. Suppose the services a partner is providing to the partnership — and is being paid for — are capital in nature. For example, assume a partner is a lawyer whom the partnership hires to provide legal services incident to the partnership's acquisition of real estate. If the payment for the legal services is properly characterized as being made to the partner for services she provided in a nonpartner capacity, the payment must be capitalized; if the payment, however, takes the form of a special allocation under § 704(b) as if the partner were acting in her capacity as a partner, the other partners effectively enjoy the same result as a currently deductible payment would have provided.

---

§ 707(a)(2)(A). Treatment of Certain Services and Transfers of Property

If—

(i) a partner performs services for a partnership or transfers property to a partnership,

(ii) there is a related direct or indirect allocation and distribution to such partner, and

(iii) the performance of such services (or such transfer) and the allocation and distribution, when viewed together, are properly characterized as a transaction occurring between the partnership and a partner acting other than in his capacity as a member of the partnership,
such allocation and distribution shall be treated as a transaction described in paragraph (1) [that is, as a transaction occurring between the partnership and one who is not a partner].

As initially enacted in 1954, § 707(a) consisted in its entirety of what is now § 707(a)(1). Section 707(a)(2)(A) was added in 1984 to strengthen the Service's efforts to prevent partnerships from being "used to effectively circumvent the requirement to capitalize certain expenses . . . by making allocations of income and corresponding distributions in place of direct payments for property or services." S. Rep. 98-169, p. 225, 98th Cong. 2d Sess (1984).[2] The legislative history to § 707(a)(2)(A) provides an instructive example of the problem that provision sought to resolve.[3] Assume A, who contributes cash for one of four 25% interests in the

---

[2] Although § 707(a)(2)(A) includes property transfers within its scope, it is clear that its focus is really upon the performance of services in a nonpartner capacity. A property transfer in exchange for an allocation or distribution is unlikely to take place where the property has been properly valued and reflected in capital accounts at fair market value on contribution. See, for example, S. Rep. 98-169 at p. 228. Accordingly, this discussion of § 707(a)(2)(A) will be limited to its application to the performance of services in exchange for an allocation or distribution.

[3] This example from the legislative history is now Ex. 1 of the proposed regulations to § 707(a)(2)(A), discussed below. See Prop. Reg. § 1.707-2(d) Ex. 1.

ABCD Partnership, is an architect who provides architectural services in connection with a building constructed by the partnership. The building is expected to generate gross income of at least $100,000 per year indefinitely. Instead of receiving his normal fee of $40,000 for his architectural services, A receives, in addition to his 25% share of partnership rental income, a special allocation of $20,000 of partnership gross income for each of the first two years after the building is leased up. The partnership is expected to have enough cash available to make this distribution. If this arrangement is respected, the partnership has effectively deducted the cost of A's architectural services instead of capitalizing them in the cost basis of the building. Assuming for purposes of illustration that the partnership's gross income and net income are $100,000 per year, the special allocation under § 704(b) would result in the ABCD partners each reporting only $20,000 of income from operations (one-quarter of $80,000 — i.e., $100,000 less the $20,000 annual special allocation to A). If the arrangement is recast as a payment to A under § 707(a)(1) for services not in his capacity as a partner, then A still has $20,000 of income in each of the first two years (the timing of which is based upon A's method of accounting) but, because the payments to A must be capitalized, the partnership's income to be split among the partners for the first two years is $100,000 instead of $80,000, and the share reported by each partner would be $25,000 (less whatever depreciation deduction was attributable to capitalizing the $40,000 fee to A) instead of $20,000.

With respect to services, § 707(a)(2)(A) provides that, if (1) a partner performs services for a partnership for which there is a related allocation and distribution to the partner and (2) the services and the allocation and distribution are together "properly characterized" as a transaction between the partnership and one who is not a partner (i.e., a partner not acting in his capacity as a partner), the allocation and distribution will be treated as a § 707(a)(1) transaction between the partnership and one who is not a partner. As noted, in enacting § 707(a)(2)(A), Congress determined that payments for services having "the substantial economic effect of direct payments for such . . . services under the facts and circumstances of the case" should be treated as such rather than as allocations of income under § 704. See S. Rep. 98-169 at p. 226.

Proposed regulations issued in 2015 under § 707(a)(2)(A) draw heavily upon the legislative history of the provision. To begin with, the proposed regulations note that whether an allocation and distribution constitute payment for services in a nonpartner capacity depends on all the facts and circumstances. Prop. Reg. § 1.707-2(c)(1). In this regard, the proposed regulations provide a non-exclusive list of six factors that may be taken into account. The proposed regulations explicitly state "the most important factor is significant entrepreneurial risk," and "an arrangement that lacks significant entrepreneurial risk constitutes a payment for services." By contrast, "an arrangement that has significant entrepreneurial risk will generally not constitute a payment for services unless other factors establish otherwise." Prop. Reg. § 1.707-2(c).

Given the centrality of significant entrepreneurial risk to this classification of payments, the proposed regulations expand upon the topic, noting that the determination of its presence or not "is based upon the service provider's entrepreneurial risk relative to the overall entrepreneurial risk of the partnership." In addition, the proposed regulations provide five facts and circumstances that create a rebuttable presumption that an arrangement lacks substantial entrepreneurial risk:

(1) a capped allocation of partnership income that is reasonably expected to apply;

(2) an allocation of a reasonably certain share of income to the service-provider;

(3) an allocation of gross income;

(4) an allocation that is predominantly fixed in amount, reasonably determinable under the circumstances, or designed to assure sufficient net profits are highly likely to be available; and

(5) an arrangement under which the service-provider gives a non-binding waiver of payment for future services or non-timely notification of such a waiver.

Prop. Reg. § 1.707-2(c)(1)(i)–(v).

While the presence of significant entrepreneurial risk ordinarily results in a determination that the arrangement does not constitute payment for services, other factors may establish that it does. The proposed regulations list five secondary factors that may outweigh, on a facts and circumstances test, the primary factor of significant entrepreneurial risk and lead to a conclusion that the arrangement constitutes payment for services:

(1) Transitory Nature of Interest: An interest held by the service-provider that is transitory or one of short duration;

(2) Time Frame of Allocation and Distribution: an allocation and distribution to the service-provider that has a time frame comparable to that in which a non-partner would receive payment;

(3) Purpose to Obtain Tax Benefits: becoming a partner primarily to obtain tax benefits not available otherwise;

(4) Relative Value of Interest: the small value of the service-provider's interest relative to the allocation and distribution in question; and

(5) Differing Allocations or Distributions: different allocations for different services, provided by one person or related persons, with significantly varying levels of entrepreneurial risk.

Prop. Reg. § 1.707-2(c)(2)–(6).

Recall the example above, drawn from legislative history and now Ex. 1 of the proposed regulations. The example concludes that the payment of $20,000 per year to A, the architect, should be treated as a disguised payment for services under § 707(a)(1) rather than as a distributive share. The example notes, first, the allocation to A is capped in amount and the cap is reasonably expected to apply; and, second, the allocation is made out of gross income. These are two of the facts and circumstances indicating an arrangement lacks significant entrepreneurial risk. Given these facts and circumstances, the example finds a presumption arises that the arrangement lacks significant entrepreneurial risk; it further finds there are no additional facts and circumstances to the contrary; and it therefore concludes the arrangement lacks significant entrepreneurial risk. Because the presence of significant entrepreneurial risk is a *sine qua non* for finding an arrangement is not a payment for services, the lack of significant entrepreneurial risk means the arrangement constitutes payment for services.

Other examples in the proposed regulations follow a similar approach. An arrangement is examined for facts and circumstances that point toward, or away from, the presence of significant entrepreneurial risk. If significant entrepreneurial risk is found to be lacking, the examination is over, and the arrangement constitutes payment for services. If significant entrepreneurial risk is found to be present, however, the examination continues to determine whether "other factors," such as the five secondary factors in the proposed regulations noted above, overcome, or do not overcome, the finding of significant entrepreneurial risk.

Even allocations and distributions that are contingent in amount, though ordinarily indicative of distributive share treatment, may sometimes be properly characterized as a fee when the services to be performed are those the partner has performed or could perform for third parties and the compensation arrangement is substantially similar to the compensation arrangement there would normally be with a third party. See Ex. 2 of the proposed regulations where a special allocation will be paid to a broker-partner effecting trades for the partnership without charging the normal brokerage commission. Although the allocation may appear to be contingent and not substantially fixed in amount, it is computed in a manner approximating the foregone commissions, is allocated from gross income and is reasonably determinable under the facts and circumstances. The example concludes that the allocation lacks significant entrepreneurial risk and is a disguised payment for services.

Finally, the proposed regulations note that: (1) the time to determine the proper characterization of an arrangement is when it is entered into or modified; (2) an arrangement treated as payment for services under § 707(a)(2)(A) is treated as payment for services for all purposes of the Internal Revenue Code; and (3) "when appropriate, the partnership must capitalize these amounts" and "treat the arrangement as a payment to a non-partner in determining the remaining partners' shares of taxable income or loss." Prop. Reg. § 1.707-2(b)(2)(i.).

B. Disguised Sales

Section 707(a)(2)(B) provides that a transfer of money or other property from a partner to a partnership, and a related transfer of money or other property from the partnership to the partner, will be treated as made in a nonpartner capacity if, when viewed together, they are "properly characterized" as a sale or exchange of property — i.e., as a "disguised sale." The problem the statute addresses can be illustrated by an example. Assume Andy owns Blackacre with a value of $20 and a basis of $10. If Andy sells a half-interest in Blackacre to Bonnie for $10, and they thereupon contribute their half-interests in Blackacre to the AB Partnership for equal partnership interests, Andy will wind up with the partnership interest, plus $10 in cash and a tax gain of $5 from the sale of the Blackacre half interest to Bonnie. If the arrangement instead is that Andy contributes Blackacre to the partnership, Bonnie contributes $10 to the partnership, and the AB partnership then distributes the $10 of cash to Andy, his recognized gain will be zero (his outside basis of $10 from the contribution of Blackacre is sufficient to absorb the cash distribution), but economically Andy is in the same place: he holds the half-interest in the partnership and cash of $10.

---

§ 707(a)(2)(B). Treatment of Certain Property Transfers

If—

(i) there is a direct or indirect transfer of money or other property by a partner to a partnership,

(ii) there is a related direct or indirect transfer of money or other property by the partnership to such partner (or another partner), and

(iii) the transfers described in clauses (i) and (ii), when viewed together, are properly characterized as a sale or exchange of property, such transfers shall be treated either as a transaction described in paragraph (1) [that is, as a transaction occurring between the partnership and one who is not a partner] or as a transaction between 2 or more partners acting other than in their capacity as members of the partnership.

Section 707(a)(2)(B) was intended to address transactions such as these — and much more complicated ones as well — and determine whether they were "properly characterized" as sales between a partnership and a partner acting in a nonpartner capacity. But a counter-problem is readily apparent: the statute could potentially treat as a disguised sale any contribution of property that was followed, perhaps years later, by the sort of perfectly ordinary distribution routinely made by partnerships to partners. In other words, how should the phrase "properly characterized" be fleshed out administratively to capture the contribution and distribution that are in fact a disguised sale, but not the ordinary contribution and ordinary distribution that are not? One answer is to carve out certain categories of distributions that will not be treated as disguised sales; these categories, created by the regulations and subject to special rules — guaranteed payments, operating cash flow distributions, and others — are noted below. Another answer is to develop a general test for distinguishing disguised sales from non-sale contributions and distributions, and that is what we turn to now.

1. Definition of Disguised Sale

The regulations provide that a transfer of property (but not money) by a partner to a partnership, and a transfer of money or other consideration (including liability relief) by the partnership to the partner constitute a sale, in whole or in part, only if, "based on all the facts and circumstances, (i) the transfer of money or other consideration would not have been made but for the transfer of property; and (ii) in cases in which the transfers are not made simultaneously, the subsequent transfer is not dependent on the entrepreneurial risks of partnership operations." Reg.

§ 1.707-3(b)(1). Stated differently, in cases of simultaneous transfers, the only question is whether, based on all the facts and circumstances, the transfer by partnership to partner would have been made but for the partner's transfer of property to the partnership. If the answer is "No," the transfer constitutes a sale. In cases of nonsimultaneous transfers, a disguised sale is not present — even if the partnership's transfer would not have been made but for the partner's transfer — if the partnership's transfer to the partner is dependent on the "entrepreneurial risks of partnership operations." In effect, the partner's willingness to subject her receipt of the money or other consideration to entrepreneurial risk will prevent characterization of the transfer as a disguised sale.

The regulations provide a nonexclusive list of 10 facts and circumstances that point to a sale, among them: (1) the timing and amount of the partnership's transfer is reasonably certain at the time of the partner's transfer; (2) the partner has a legally enforceable right to the transfer from the partnership; (3) the partner's right to the money or other consideration is secured; (4) the partnership holds liquid assets, beyond the reasonable needs of the business, to be available for the transfer; and (5) partnership distributions or allocations are designed to exchange the benefits and burdens of ownership of the property. Reg. § 1.707-3(b)(2).

2. Two-Year Presumption

In addition, of particular significance, the regulations create a two-year rebuttable presumption for distinguishing transfers that are disguised sales from those that are not. If the partner-to-partnership and partnership-to-partner transfers are made within a two-year period, the transfers are presumed to be a sale unless the facts and circumstances clearly establish they do not in fact constitute a sale. Reg. § 1.707-3(c)(1). Conversely, if the transfers are more than two years apart, they are presumed not to constitute a sale unless the facts and circumstances clearly establish the contrary. Reg. § 1.707-3(d).

3. Tax Consequences of a Sale

Assume Mary, a one-third partner in the MNO Partnership, contributes Greenacre (value of $1,000, adjusted basis of $200) to the partnership and simultaneously receives $1,000 in cash as a distribution from the partnership. Further assume that, based on all the facts and circumstances, the cash distribution would not have been made but for the transfer of Greenacre. The transfer will accordingly be treated as a disguised sale under Reg. § 1.707-3(b)(1)(i). Mary will realize and recognize gain of $800 ($1,000 amount realized less basis of $200). The MNO Partnership will be treated as having purchased Greenacre for $1,000, which will be the partnership's basis in the property.

Suppose, alternatively, the simultaneous cash distribution by MNO to Mary was only $600 instead of $1,000, but that the distribution would not have been made were it not for the transfer of Greenacre. The transfer would now be treated as in part a sale (of $600 worth of Greenacre) and in part a contribution (of the remaining $400 worth of Greenacre). Because the sale portion is 60% of the total value, that portion will be attributed 60% of the adjusted basis, or $120. Mary's gain on the sale portion will thus be $480. She will be treated as contributing $400 worth of Greenacre, with a basis of $80 (40% of the total basis of $200). The MNO Partnership will have a cost basis of $600 in the purchased portion of Greenacre and a transferred basis of $80 in the contributed portion, for a total basis of $680. See Reg. § 1.707-3(f) Ex. 1.

If the transfer and distribution are not simultaneous, and the transfer is held to constitute a sale, it is typically necessary to determine the interest component of the transaction. For example, assume, as before, that Mary transfers Greenacre to the partnership and one year later receives a distribution of $1,100. The transfer will be treated as a disguised sale only if, under all the facts and circumstances, (1) the distribution of money would not have been made but for the transfer of Greenacre and (2) the distribution was not dependent on the entrepreneurial risks of partnership operations. Reg. § 1.707-3(b)(1). Note that, because the transfers take place within a two-year period, there would be a rebuttable presumption that they constituted a sale. Reg. § 1.707-3(c)(1). All the facts and circumstances, including the 10 factors listed in Reg. § 1.707-3(b)(2), would need to be considered. If the conclusion were that the transfer of Greenacre constituted a sale, then, according to the regulations, it must be treated as a sale for all purposes of the Code, including the installment sales provisions of § 453 and the interest-imputation rules of §§ 483 and 1274. Reg. § 1.707-3(a)(2). If we assume that, under the applicable provisions, $100 is treated as interest (more specifically, as original issue discount taxable as interest), then Mary will recognize $100 of interest income and will have gain on the sale of $800. (The amount realized would be $1,000 because $100 of the $1,100 distribution is characterized as interest. The adjusted basis of Greenacre was $200.)

The statutory provisions and mathematical calculations necessary to determine the periodic amounts of original issue discount under §§ 483 and 1274, and thus the timing of income inclusion to Mary and interest deductions to the partnership, are outside the scope of this chapter. The inclusion of this example here is intended simply to point out that interest imputation and installment sale treatment must be taken into account on a nonsimultaneous disguised sale. The calculations and complications are enhanced if the disguised sale transfer and distribution are separated by more than a year (although the two-year presumption would usually provide an upper limit); or if there is more than one distribution treated as consideration for the transferred property; or if the transfer constitutes a sale only in part and is in part a contribution.

4. Liabilities

The presence of liabilities complicates matters as well. Suppose David, a one-quarter partner in the ABCD Partnership, contributes Brownacre to the partnership. Assume Brownacre has a value of $1,000, an adjusted basis of $500, and a recourse mortgage of $400 encumbering the property. ABCD takes Brownacre subject to the mortgage. As a result of the contribution to a partnership in which he has only a one-quarter partnership interest, David's liabilities have decreased from $400 before the contribution to $100 afterward. Does this liability shift of $300 in David's favor constitute in part a disguised sale of Brownacre? If so, routine contributions of encumbered property would frequently result in disguised sale treatment, causing disruption of partnership formations and operations.

The regulations address this problem by dividing liabilities into "qualified liabilities" and "liabilities other than qualified liabilities" ("nonqualified liabilities"). In general terms, a partnership's assumption of a qualified liability on a contribution of encumbered property (or the partnership's taking contributed property subject to a qualified liability) is not in and of itself treated as consideration for the contribution, i.e., not treated as a disguised sale. With respect to the assumption of, or taking subject to, nonqualified liabilities, however, a disguised sale may well be present. See Reg. § 1.707-5(a)(1), (5).

As a preliminary matter, note how partners' shares of recourse liabilities and nonrecourse liabilities are determined for purposes of the disguised sale rules. A partner's share of a recourse liability is determined under the usual rules of § 752 and its regulations, which focus on the partner's economic risk of loss. Reg. § 1.707-5(a)(2)(i). With respect to nonrecourse liabilities, however, the usual rules of § 752 and its regulations are not applied. Instead, a partner's share of nonrecourse liabilities is determined solely in accordance with the partner's share of partnership profits. Reg. § 1.707-5(a)(2)(ii). (The partner's share of partnership minimum gain or § 704(c) gain is not taken into account.)

According to Reg. § 1.707-5(a)(6)(ii), qualified liabilities consist of the following:

(1) Liabilities incurred by the contributing partner more than two years before the transfer that have encumbered the property throughout that period;

(2) Liabilities incurred within two years of the transfer, but not incurred "in anticipation of the transfer;"

(3) Liabilities allocable to capital expenditures with respect to the property; and

(4) Liabilities incurred in the ordinary course of business, but only if all of that business' assets are transferred (other than assets not material to a continuation of business).

In addition, if a qualified liability is a recourse liability, it cannot exceed the fair market value of the transferred property, reduced by other liabilities senior in priority that either encumber the property or are described in (3) or (4) above. Reg. § 1.707-5(a)(6)(i).

Liabilities incurred within two years of transfer — other than those that come within the capital expenditure or ordinary course of business categories, (3) and (4) above — are presumed to be incurred "in anticipation of the transfer," and thus classified as nonqualified liabilities, unless the facts and circumstances clearly establish that they were not so incurred. Reg. § 1.707-5(a)(7)(i). Liabilities claimed to come within the not-incurred-in-anticipation category must be disclosed to the Internal Revenue Service. Reg. § 1.707-5(a)(7)(ii).

A partnership's assumption of, or taking subject to, a nonqualified liability is treated as consideration on a sale to the partner to the extent the liability exceeds the partner's share of the liability immediately after the assumption. Reg. § 1.707-5(a)(1). For example, if the amount of a nonqualified liability is $100,000, and the partner's share of it immediately after the assumption by the partnership is $25,000, the consideration to the partner is $75,000. (For purposes of determining the reduction in a partner's share of a liability immediately after the assumption, subsequent reductions in the share of the liability are to be taken into account if such subsequent reductions are anticipated and are part of a plan that has a principal purpose of minimizing the extent to which the assumption is treated as a sale. Reg. § 1.707-5(a)(3).)

By way of a more complete example, assume Mary transfers Whiteacre to the MNOP Partnership, in which she is a one-quarter partner. Whiteacre has a value of $450,000, an adjusted basis of $200,000, and is subject to a recourse indebtedness of $300,000. One week before the transfer and in anticipation of it, Mary borrowed the $300,000 for purposes unconnected to Whiteacre or the partnership. MNOP assumes the $300,000 liability. The liability is a nonqualified liability. The reduction in Mary's share of the liability is $225,000 ($300,000 less $75,000, her share of the liability after the assumption as a one-quarter partner). As a result, Mary is treated as having sold $225,000 of Whiteacre for $225,000 of liability relief. Because $225,000 is half the value of Whiteacre, the sale of that half will be attributed half of the adjusted basis of Whiteacre, or $100,000. Mary thus has a gain of $125,000 (amount realized of $225,000 less adjusted basis of $100,000) on the partnership's assumption of the liability. See Reg. § 1.707-5(f) Ex 2. Mary is treated as selling half of Whiteacre to the partnership and as contributing the remaining half.

By contrast, the partnership's assumption of, or taking subject to, a qualified liability does not constitute consideration for a transfer of encumbered property by a partner — at least where the transfer does not otherwise constitute a sale. But consider the possibility that a transfer of encumbered property may be treated as a sale independently of the partnership's assumption of a qualified liability. Suppose, for example, that the partnership not only assumes a qualified liability but also transfers cash to the partner as consideration for the transfer of the property. In these circumstances, the assumption of the qualified liability may be treated as partial consideration for the transfer. See Reg. § 1.707-5(a)(5).

Assume, for example, that Kathy transfers Redacre to the KLM Partnership. Redacre has a value of $165,000, an adjusted basis of $75,000, and is transferred subject to a $75,000 recourse liability incurred more than two years ago that has been secured by Redacre since then. Assume Kathy's share of the liability after its assumption by the partnership is $25,000. The liability is a qualified liability because it was incurred more than two years ago, and its assumption by the partnership is not treated as part of a sale. But now, further assume the partnership transferred $30,000 in cash to Kathy upon the transfer of Redacre and the assumption of the $75,000 liability, and that the $30,000 cash is treated as consideration for the transfer. The regulations provide that, in such circumstances, the assumption of the qualified liability is treated as consideration to the extent of the lesser of:

(1) the consideration that would be treated as transferred to the partner if this were not a qualified liability — here, that amount is $50,000, which is the excess of the $75,000 qualified liability over Kathy's $25,000 share of the liability after the transfer; or

(2) the amount obtained by multiplying the qualified liability (here, $75,000) by the partner's "net equity percentage" with respect to the property (here,

that percentage is one-third, determined as follows: The net equity percentage is the result obtained by dividing the aggregate amounts treated as consideration on the transfer — here, $30,000 of cash — by the equity in the property transferred — here, $90,000, the excess of the $165,000 value over the $75,000 encumbrance). Accordingly, multiplying the $75,000 qualified liability by the one-third net equity percentage results in a product of $25,000. Reg. § 1.707-5(a)(5)(ii).

Putting it all together, the assumption of the qualified liability of $75,000 is treated as consideration to the extent of $25,000 (the lesser of $50,000 in (1) above and $25,000 in (2) above). But Kathy also received $30,000 in cash — that is what forced us into these calculations regarding the qualified liability! Thus, her total consideration is $55,000. Kathy is thus treated as selling $55,000 worth of Redacre for cash and liability relief. Because $55,000 is one-third of the total value of $165,000, the sale carries out $25,000 of basis, one-third of the total basis of $75,000. Kathy's gain is $30,000, the difference between the amount realized of $55,000 and the basis of $25,000. (This example is drawn from Reg. § 1.707-5(f) Exs. 5 and 6.)

5. Debt-Financed Distribution

We consider briefly one other type of liability treated as consideration for a transfer. Suppose the property transferred to the partnership is unencumbered. But subsequent to the transfer, the partnership incurs a liability, and within 90 days thereafter it makes a cash distribution to the contributing partner. This so-called debt-financed distribution may be treated as consideration for the sale, in part, of the transferred property. The debt-financed consideration rule requires that: (1) the partner transfers property to a partnership; (2) the partnership incurs a liability; (3) all or a portion of the proceeds of the liability are allocable to a transfer of consideration to the partner; and (4) the transfer to the partner occurs within 90 days of incurring the liability. In these circumstances, the transfer to the partner is taken into account to the extent the amount of the transfer exceeds the partner's share of the liability. The amount of the transfer taken into account may then be treated, subject to the other rules of Reg. § 1.707-5, as consideration for a sale, in part, of the contributed property. See Reg. § 1.707-5(b), -5(f) Ex 10.

6. Guaranteed Payments and Preferred Returns; Cash Flow Distributions; Reimbursement for Preformation Expenses; Partnership-to-Partner Sales

The bulk of the discussion to this point in this section of the chapter has involved general rules for distinguishing ordinary contributions and distributions from disguised sales of property. We now turn briefly to note certain special categories of distributions that will not be treated as disguised sales.

The regulations provide that a guaranteed payment for capital made to a partner is not treated as part of a sale of property. Reg. § 1.707-4(a)(1). The reason is obvious: if the payment is in fact a payment for the use of a partner's capital, it is *ipso facto* not payment for a sale of property. The characterization of the payment is not controlling. If the payment is determined without regard to the income of the partnership (as is required by the definition of a guaranteed payment per § 707(c)) and is reasonable in amount, it is presumed to be a guaranteed payment for capital unless the facts and circumstances clearly establish that it is part of a sale. Reg. § 1.707-4(a)(1). Similarly, a preferred return — that is, a preferential distribution of cash flow to a partner on account of capital contributed, matched by allocation of partnership income and gain to the extent available — that is characterized as a preferential return and is reasonable in amount is presumed not to be part of a sale of property by the partner unless the facts and circumstances clearly establish the contrary. Reg. § 1.707-4(a)(2). As to what constitutes a "reasonable amount" for a guaranteed payment or a preferred return, see Reg. § 1.707-4(a)(3)(ii).

As noted earlier in this chapter, if a transfer of property by a partner and a transfer of money or other property by a partnership occur within a two-year period, the transfers are presumed to constitute a sale unless the facts and circumstances clearly establish that they do not constitute a sale. Reg. § 1.707-3(c). Notwithstanding this presumption, "operating cash flow distributions" are presumed not to be part of a sale of property unless the facts and circumstances clearly establish the contrary. Reg. § 1.707-4(b)(1). In general terms, distributions to a partner will be treated as operating cash flow distributions to the extent they do not exceed the partner's share of partnership net cash flow from operations (and are not presumed to be guaranteed payments for capital, are not reasonable preferred returns, and are not characterized as distributions to a partner in a nonpartner capacity). The regulations provide a safe harbor for such distributions. Reg. § 1.707-4(b)(2)(ii). They also allow operating cash flow distributions (as well as guaranteed payments for capital and preferred returns that are not presumed to be part of a sale of property) to be retained for distribution in a later year without losing the benefit of this presumption. Reg. § 1.707-4(c).

The regulations also provide that transfers to a partner will not be treated as a sale to the extent that the transfer reimburses the partner for certain preformation expenditures — specifically, for those capital expenditures incurred, during the two-year period prior to the partner's transfer of property to the partnership, either on account of partnership organization and syndication costs or on account of property contributed by the partner to the partnership. In the latter instance, however, such reimbursements cannot exceed 20% of the value of the contributed property, except when the value of the contributed property does not exceed 120% of the property's basis. Reg. § 1.707-4(d).

Finally, we note only in passing that rules similar to those that apply on disguised sales of property by a partner to the partnership are to be applied in determining whether a transfer of property by the partnership to a partner should be treated as a sale in whole or in part to the partner. Reg. § 1.707-6(a).

Chapter 19

DISTRIBUTIONS OF § 704(c) PROPERTY AND DISTRIBUTIONS OF PROPERTY TO THE CONTRIBUTING PARTNER

I. PROBLEMS

1. Jennifer, Karen, and Larry are equal members of the JKL Partnership. Earlier this year (Year 1), Karen and Larry each contributed $1,000 in cash to the partnership, and Jennifer contributed Greenacre, a nondepreciable capital asset, to the partnership. At the time of the contribution, Greenacre had a value of $1,000 and an adjusted basis of $300. In Year 4, when Greenacre was worth $5,000, JKL distributed it to Karen in complete liquidation of her interest in the partnership. What are the tax consequences of the distribution? What impact, if any, does the distribution have on the adjusted bases of partnership interests and the distributed property? (Assume in this and in each problem that follows that § 751(b) is inapplicable.)

2. How does the answer to Problem 1 change if Greenacre is worth $500 at the time of the distribution?

3. How does the answer to Problem 1 change if the distribution to Karen takes place in Year 10?

4. Assume the facts of Problem 1 except that instead of contributing $1,000 in cash in Year 1, Karen purchased Brownacre (a nondepreciable capital asset) for $1,000 and promptly contributed it to the partnership in Year 1 when it was still worth $1,000. Assume further in Year 4, there was no distribution of Greenacre or any other distribution to Karen, but Brownacre was distributed to Jennifer in a nonliquidating distribution. At the time of the distribution, Brownacre was worth $2,500, and Jennifer's adjusted basis in her partnership interest was $1,500. What are the tax consequences of the distribution of Brownacre? What impact, if any, does the distribution have on the adjusted bases of partnership interests and of the contributed and distributed property?

5. Assume the facts of Problem 4, except that Jennifer's adjusted basis in her partnership interest at the time of the distribution of Brownacre was $2,000.

6. Assume the distribution to Jennifer in Problem 5 consisted not only of Brownacre, but also of $500 of cash.

7. Assume the facts of Problem 4, except Karen had purchased Brownacre for $500 several years before, and it was worth $1,000 when she contributed it to the partnership.

8. Assume the facts of Problem 4, except that in Year 4 there were two nonliquidating distributions at the same time: (1) Greenacre, with a value of $2,500 (rather than $5,000) and an adjusted basis of $300, was distributed to Karen; and (2) Brownacre, with a value of $2,500 and an adjusted basis of $1,000, was distributed to Jennifer.

Assignment for Chapter 19:

Complete the Problems

Read: Internal Revenue Code: §§ 704(c); 737.
        Treasury Regulations: §§ 1.704-3(a)(3); 1.704-4(a)(2), (5) Exs. 1, 2, and 3, (d)(2), (3), (4); (e)(1), (2); 1.737-1(b)(1); (c)(2)(iv); (e) Exs. 1, 2, & 3; 1.737-3(a), (b), (c), (e) Exs. 1, 2, and 3.
        Materials: Overview

II. VOCABULARY

mixing bowl transactions
precontribution gain
precontribution loss
net precontribution gain
excess distribution
eligible property

III. OBJECTIVES

1. To determine the gain or loss, if any, recognized on the distribution of contributed property to a noncontributing partner.

2. To determine the book and tax gain or loss on the distribution of contributed depreciable property to a noncontributing partner.

3. Where gain or loss is recognized on the distribution of contributed property, to determine the adjustments to the outside basis of the contributing partner and the adjustments to the inside basis of the contributed property.

4. To recall that § 737 does not apply to a transaction subject to § 707(a)(2)(B).

5. To determine the net precontribution gain and the excess distribution gain, if any, on the distribution of property subject to § 737.

6. To recall the lesser-of rule with respect to net precontribution gain and excess distribution gain.

7. Where gain is recognized under § 737, to determine the adjustments to the outside basis of the contributing partner and the inside basis of the contributed property.

8. Where § 704(c)(1)(B) and § 737 both apply to a transaction, to recall that § 704(c)(1)(B) is applied first.

9. Where § 704(c)(1)(B) and § 737 both apply to a transaction, to determine the gain recognized under each provision.

IV. OVERVIEW

A. Mixing Bowl Transactions

This chapter addresses the congressional and administrative responses under § 704(c)(1)(B) and § 737 to so-called "mixing bowl transactions." These are transactions under which a partnership, having received appreciated or depreciated property from one partner, distributes the same property to a different partner, or transactions under which a partnership, having received appreciated property from one partner, distributes a different property to that same partner. We address each type of transaction in turn.

B. Distributions of § 704(c) Property

As discussed in Chapter 10, when a partner contributes appreciated or depreciated property to a partnership,[1] § 704(c)(1) requires that partnership gain or loss recognized in a subsequent taxable disposition of the property be allocated to the contributing partner to the extent of the property's "built-in gain" or "built-in loss."[2] Thus, for example, assume Alex, a one-third partner in the ABC Partnership, contributes Blackacre to ABC when Blackacre has a value of $100 and an adjusted basis of $70. Blackacre is thus § 704(c) property with $30 of built-in gain. If ABC later sells Blackacre for $130, realizing and recognizing a gain of $60, the first $30 of the gain must be allocated to Alex under § 704(c)(1)(A). The remaining $30 of the gain will be allocated $10 to Alex and $20 to the other partners in accordance with their partnership agreement. Section 704(c)(1)(A) thus prevents Alex from shifting the precontribution (built-in) gain of $30 on Blackacre to the other partners.

Suppose, however, that instead of selling Blackacre, ABC distributes it to Barbara, one of the other ABC partners, who subsequently sells the property for $130. Because ABC recognizes no gain on the distribution (§ 731(b)), and because Barbara would typically take Blackacre with a carryover basis of $70 from the partnership (§ 732(a)(1)), the precontribution or built-in gain of $30 would effectively be shifted to Barbara on her subsequent sale. In essence, distributing property with built-in gain to a non-contributing partner provides an opportunity to shift that gain away from the contributing partner in violation of the underlying policy of § 704(c). Section 704(c)(1)(B) blocks this gain-shifting by requiring the contributing partner to recognize the built-in gain if the contributed property is

---

[1] This property is characterized as "§ 704(c) property" and is defined as property the book value of which, at the time of contribution, differs from the contributing partner's adjusted basis in the property. Reg. § 1.704-3(a)(3)(i). In other words, it is property with so-called "built-in gain" or "built-in loss."

[2] "Built-in gain" and "built-in loss" are specially defined in Reg. § 1.704-3(a)(3)(ii).

distributed to a non-contributing partner within seven years of its contribution. By its terms, however, § 704(c)(1)(B) does not apply to a distribution of contributed property to the contributing partner; the provision applies only if the contributed property is distributed to another partner. Thus, in the above example, assuming the distribution of Blackacre to Barbara occurs within seven years of its contribution by Alex, Alex would be required to recognize gain of $30 on the distribution.

---

§ 704(c). Contributed Property

(1) General — Under regulations prescribed by the Secretary —

(B) if any property [contributed by a partner to a partnership] is distributed (directly or indirectly) by the partnership (other than to the contributing partner) within 7 years of being contributed —

(i) the contributing partner shall be treated as recognizing gain or loss (as the case may be) from the sale of such property in an amount equal to the gain or loss which would have been allocated to such partner under [§ 704(c)(1)(A)] if the property had been sold at its fair market value at the time of the distribution,

(ii) the character of such gain or loss shall be determined by reference to the character of the gain or loss which would have resulted if such property had been sold by the partnership to the distributee, and

(iii) appropriate adjustments shall be made to the adjusted basis of the contributing partner's interest in the partnership and to the adjusted basis of the property distributed to reflect any gain or loss recognized under this subparagraph.

The statutory language provides specifically that the contributing partner shall be treated as recognizing gain or loss on the distribution in the amount that would have been allocated to the contributing partner if the property had been sold at its fair market value at the time of distribution. § 704(c)(1)(B)(i). Thus, if Blackacre, contributed with a value of $100 and a basis of $70, had declined in value to $90 at the time of distribution, Alex would recognize gain of only $20 on the distribution to Barbara (assuming the distribution occurred within seven years of the contribution).

Note that § 704(c)(1)(B) also applies to contributed property (§ 704(c) property) with precontribution or built-in loss. If Blackacre had a value of $50 and basis of $70 upon contribution by Alex, and if it were distributed within seven years to Barbara when its value remained $50, Alex would recognize a loss of $20, the built-in loss, upon its distribution. If, instead, Blackacre's value were $40 on distribution, Alex's loss would again be $20, the amount that would have been allocated to him had the property been sold at fair market value of $40 at the time of distribution. The remaining $10 of loss would be allocated as provided by the partnership agreement.

Section 704(c)(1)(B) provides for two additional consequences upon recognition of gain or loss to the contributing partner. First, the character of the gain or loss recognized shall be determined as if the property had been sold by the partnership to the distributee. § 704(c)(1)(B)(ii). Second, correlative adjustments are made to the contributing partner's outside basis and also to the adjusted basis of the distributed property. § 704(c)(1)(B)(iii). Thus, in the foregoing examples, where Alex recognizes varying amounts of gain or loss on the distribution to Barbara, Alex's basis in his partnership interest will be increased (or decreased) by the gain (or loss) recognized on the distribution. Reg. § 1.704-4(e)(1). Similarly, ABC's adjusted basis in Blackacre will be increased (or decreased) by the gain (or loss) Alex recognizes. Reg. § 1.704-4(e)(2). In the opening example, where Blackacre has a value of $100 and a basis of $70 on contribution, and a value of $130 on distribution to Barbara: Alex recognizes a gain of $30 and increases his outside basis by $30. ABC's adjusted basis in Blackacre similarly increases by $30, so its basis on distribution to Barbara is $100. Under § 732(a)(1), this will ordinarily be the basis Barbara takes in Blackacre, and thus in her hands the property has $30 of gain inherent in it (value $130, basis $100).

To this point, we have not considered the impact of the ceiling rule under § 704(c).[3] To return to our example, Alex contributes Blackacre with a value of $100 and a basis of $70. Assume Blackacre has declined in value to $90 at the time of its distribution to Barbara. Economically, the partnership has sustained a book loss of $10, but for tax purposes the partnership would have recognized a gain of $20 had it sold the property to Barbara. If the partnership uses the traditional method of making § 704(c) allocations,[4] Alex must recognize a gain of $20 on the distribution. Despite the book loss, under the traditional method with the ceiling rule, there is no tax loss to allocate. If, however, the partnership is using the remedial method of making § 704(c) allocations, then in the example just given, Alex would be allocated an additional tax gain of $6.67. (Recall that there was a book loss of $10. Had the property been sold, the other partners, owners of the remaining two-thirds of the partnership, would have been allocated an aggregate tax loss of $6.67 for their share of the $10 book loss, and Alex would be imputed an offsetting remedial allocation of $6.67 of income, increasing his total gain to $26.67 — i.e., $20 from the remaining precontribution gain and the additional $6.67 under the remedial method. Reg. § 1.704-4(a)(5) Ex 3.) The regulations do not indicate how Alex's gain on distribution would be computed under the traditional method with curative allocations, but presumably it would compute the gain to Alex on distribution to be consistent with the gain that would have been allocated to Alex on a sale.

For gain purposes, § 704(c)(1)(B) applies not only to the contributing partner but to that partner's successor as well. See § 704(c)(3); Reg. § 1.704-4(d)(2). A built-in loss, however, may be taken into account only by the contributing partner. § 704(c)(1)(C)(i). The built-in loss cannot be transferred, and, in the event of the death of the contributing partner, the loss is lost. Moreover, consistent with the

---

[3] Chapter 10 provides a detailed discussion of the ceiling rule and its consequences. Review Chapter 10 carefully.

[4] *See* Chapter 10 for a full discussion of the traditional method, the traditional method with curative allocations, and the remedial method for allocating tax items with respect to § 704(c) property.

non-transferability of the loss, the Code provides that, for purposes of determining allocations to other partners with respect to such contributed loss property, the property's basis must be treated as equal to the property's value at the time of contribution. § 704(c)(1)(C)(ii).

There are a number of statutory and regulatory exceptions to § 704(c)(1)(B). Thus, under § 704(c)(2) there is an exception for certain like-kind distributions: If ABC, having distributed Blackacre to Barbara, distributes like-kind property Whiteacre to Alex on a timely basis, Alex may not be required to recognize gain on the distribution of Blackacre. To come within the exception for like-kind distributions: (1) the distributed properties (here Blackacre and Whiteacre) must be like-kind; and (2) the distribution to the contributing partner (here the distribution of Whiteacre to Alex) must occur on the earlier of 180 days after the distribution of the contributed property (here, the distribution of Blackacre to Barbara) or the due date, with extensions, of the contributing partner's tax return (here, Alex's tax return) for the year the contributed property was distributed (here, the year Blackacre was distributed to Barbara). If the requirements are met, the gain or loss otherwise recognized on the distribution of the contributed property is reduced by the built-in gain or loss of the like-kind property distributed to the contributing partner. For example, recall that Blackacre was contributed by Alex with a value of $100 and a basis of $70, and was distributed to Barbara within seven years when its value was $130. Assume Whiteacre is distributed to Alex on a timely basis with a value of $50 and an adjusted basis to Alex under § 732(a)(1) of $40. Although Alex would normally recognize gain of $30 on the distribution of Blackacre to Barbara under § 704(c)(1)(B), the like-kind distribution of Whiteacre to Alex, with built-in gain of $10 in Alex's hands, reduces the § 704(c)(1)(B) gain Alex recognizes to $20. Reg. § 1.704-4(d)(3), (4) Ex. Nonrecognition treatment to that extent reflects that the disposition would have been a like-kind exchange outside the partnership.

The regulations also provide exceptions to the operation of § 704(c)(1)(B) in case of: (1) property contributed before October 1, 1989; (2) distributions of contributed property occurring in certain liquidations of partnerships; (3) deemed distributions in § 708(b)(1)(B) terminations of partnerships; (4) complete transfers to another partnership of all assets and liabilities of the transferor partnership; and (5) incorporation of a partnership. Reg. § 1.704-4(c)(1)–(5). Consistent with the purposes behind the enactment of § 704(c)(1)(B), the provision does not apply to the extent the disguised sales rules of § 707(a)(2)(B) apply. Reg. § 1.704-4(a)(2). The regulations also contain an anti-abuse rule permitting the Commissioner to recast a transaction that has as a principal purpose the achievement of a tax result that is inconsistent with § 704(c)(1)(B). Reg. § 1.704-4(f)(1).

C. Distributions to the Partner Who Contributed § 704(c) Property

As discussed in Chapter 10, § 704(c)(1)(A) requires that, on the taxable disposition of § 704(c) property, any gain or loss recognized that is attributable to the property's "built-in gain" or "built-in loss" must be allocated to the contributing partner. Section 704(c)(1)(B), discussed above, supports this policy against shifting tax gain or loss by imposing a similar recognition rule on a distribution of contributed property to another partner within seven years of contribution.

But suppose the contributed property is not sold or distributed. Suppose, instead, the contributing partner receives a distribution of other property from the partnership. The disguised sale rule of § 707(a)(2)(B), discussed at length in Chapter 18, provides in part that, if there is a transfer of property by a partner to a partnership, and a related transfer of other property by the partnership to the partner, and if the two transfers together are properly characterized as a sale or exchange, the transfers may be so characterized for tax purposes. But § 707(a)(2)(B) is an uncertain tool, with its proper-characterization standard in the statute and a rebuttable two-year presumption in the regulations. Section 737 more directly addresses the potential income-shifting on a distribution to the contributing partner of property other than the contributed property.

---

§ 737. Recognition of Precontribution Gain in the Case of Certain Distributions to Contributing Partner.

(a) General Rule. In the case of any distribution by a partnership to a partner, such partner shall be treated as recognizing gain in an amount equal to the lesser of —

(1) the excess (if any) of (A) the fair market value of property (other than money) received in the distribution over (B) the adjusted basis of such partner's interest in the partnership immediately before the distribution reduced (but not below zero) by the amount of money received in the distribution, or

(2) the net precontribution gain of the partner.

Gain recognized under the preceding sentence shall be in addition to any gain recognized under section 731. The character of such gain shall be determined by reference to the proportionate character of the net precontribution gain.

(b) Net Precontribution Gain. For purpose of this section, the term "net precontribution gain" means the net gain (if any) which would have been recognized by the distributee partner under section 704(c)(1)(B) if all property which

(1) had been contributed to the partnership by the distributee partner within 7 years of the distribution, and

(2) is held by such partnership immediately before the distribution,

had been distributed by such partnership to another partner.

The basic rule of § 737 is that gain is recognized on the distribution of other property to a partner within seven years of the partner's contribution of § 704(c) property. Note that, unlike § 704(c)(1)(B), which applies to both gains and losses, § 737 applies only to gains. Specifically, § 737 provides that, on a distribution to a partner, the partner recognizes gain equal to the lesser of two amounts: (1) The "net precontribution gain" of the partner, defined as the net gain that would have been recognized by the partner under § 704(c)(1)(B) if all property contributed by the partner within the seven years before the distribution, and held by the partnership immediately before the distribution, had been distributed to another partner; or (2) the excess (if any) of the value of property (other than money) received in the distribution, over the partner's adjusted basis in her partnership interest, reduced (but not below zero) by money received in the distribution. This latter gain is referred to in the regulations as the "excess distribution" gain. Reg. § 1.737-1(b)(1).

For example, assume Alex contributes Blackacre (nondepreciable property) to the ABC Partnership at a time when its value is $100 and its basis is $70. Blackacre is thus § 704(c) property. Assume ABC distributes Whiteacre to Alex more than two years later (thus creating the presumption that the contribution and distribution are not a § 707(a)(2)(B) sale), but still within seven years of Alex's contribution of Blackacre (thus coming within the § 737 time frame). If Blackacre is the only § 704(c) property Alex has contributed to ABC, and if ABC continues to hold Blackacre, Alex's "net precontribution gain" on the distribution of Whiteacre is $30 — that is, if Blackacre were distributed to another partner, Alex would have recognized gain of $30 on the distribution pursuant to § 704(c)(1)(B). In order to apply the "lesser of" test of § 737(a), it is necessary to also know the "excess distribution" gain — that is, the difference between the value of Whiteacre, the property received in the distribution, and Alex's basis in his partnership interest immediately before the distribution. Assume the value of Whiteacre is $100 and that Alex's basis in his partnership interest is $60. The "excess distribution" gain is thus $40 (Whiteacre value of $100 less Alex's outside basis of $60). Because the lesser of the net precontribution gain ($30) and the excess distribution gain ($40) is $30, Alex would recognize gain of $30 on the distribution of Whiteacre to him by the partnership. Suppose, however, that Alex's basis in his partnership interest had been $80 instead of $60. In that case, the excess distribution gain would have been $20 (the $100 value of Whiteacre less the outside basis of $80), which is less than the net precontribution gain of $30. Under the lesser-of rule, Alex would recognize a gain of $20 on the distribution of Whiteacre.

Note that, in determining the amount of gain under § 737, any money distributed is specially treated. (For purposes of § 737, marketable securities are treated as money. § 731(c)(1). Also see Chapter 14.) Section 737(a)(1) provides that, in determining the value of the distribution, money that is part of the distribution is disregarded. In determining the partner's outside basis, the basis is reduced (but not below zero) by any money distributed.[5] Thus, to build on a prior example, assume that, in addition to distributing Whiteacre (value of $100), ABC distributed cash of $20 to Alex. Because the excess distribution test excludes money from the value of the property distributed, the amount of the distribution remains $100. But in calculating Alex's basis in his partnership interest, the predistribution basis — here, in our initial example, $60 — is reduced to $40 by the cash distribution of $20.

---

[5] The reason for ignoring the cash in computing the amount of the distribution, but reducing predistribution basis by the cash distributed, is to leave to § 731(a)(1) the determination of whether the cash distributed results in the recognition of gain — the cash portion of the distribution thus generates gain only to the extent it exceeds the partner's predistribution basis.

Thus, the excess distribution gain becomes $100 minus $40, or $60. Recall that the net contribution gain is $30, so that, under the lesser-of rule of § 737, Alex recognizes gain of $30 on the distribution of Whiteacre and $20 in cash. But suppose, instead, Alex's basis in his partnership interest were $80 and the cash distribution were $5. Now the excess distribution gain is $25. (The $25 figure is arrived at by taking the value of Whiteacre, $100, and reducing it by $75; the $75 reduction is arrived at by taking the predistribution basis of $80 and reducing it by the cash distribution of $5.) Because the excess distribution gain of $25 is less than the net precontribution gain of $30, Alex would recognize gain of $25 under the lesser-of rule on the distribution of Whiteacre and $5 cash.

Collateral basis consequences from the § 737 distribution include: (1) an increase in the adjusted basis of the partner's interest in the partnership by the amount of any § 737(a) gain recognized; and (2) basis adjustments to the § 704(c) property held by the partnership to reflect the gain recognized under § 737(a). § 737(c)(1) and (2). Specifically, the distributee partner's outside basis is increased by the gain recognized under § 737, but the increase is ignored in determining the excess distribution gain under § 737(a)(1) and is also ignored in determining gain recognized under § 731(a) if money was distributed in the same distribution. Reg. § 1.737-3(a). Thus, to return to the initial facts of the example in this section: Alex contributed Blackacre (value of $100, adjusted basis of $70) to the ABC Partnership, and, within seven years, received Whiteacre (value of $100) in a distribution from ABC at a time when Alex's outside basis was $60. Based on these facts, Alex's § 737 gain was $30, and as a result of this gain, Alex's adjusted basis in his partnership interest is increased from $60 to $90.

Alex's adjusted basis in Whiteacre, the distributed property, is determined under § 732(a) or (b), whichever is applicable, and for this purpose the outside basis increase noted above is taken into account. Reg. § 1.737-3(b)(1). For example, assuming the applicability of the nonliquidating rules of § 732(a), Alex would take a transferred basis in Whiteacre equal to the partnership's adjusted basis in Whiteacre, but not in excess of Alex's outside basis of $90. § 732(a)(2). Alex's outside basis would be reduced accordingly, but not below zero.

Finally, the partnership's inside basis in the contributed property, Blackacre, is adjusted as set forth in Reg. § 1.737-3(c). These rules, in general, increase the inside basis of "eligible property" by the gain recognized under § 737 - in our example, by $30. ("Eligible property" is property that (i) entered into the calculation of net precontribution gain; (ii) has a value in excess of its basis; (iii) is of the same character as the § 737 gain; and (iv) was not distributed previously or in the same distribution that produced the § 737 gain. Reg. § 1.737-3(c)(2).) The rules for making the adjustment can sometimes become complex, but the contributed property will often constitute eligible property. In this case, if we make what appears to be the reasonable assumption that Blackacre is eligible property, and the further assumption that it is the only eligible property held by ABC, the adjustment is straightforward: the adjusted basis of Blackacre is increased from $70, the adjusted basis given in our example, to $100. See Reg § 1.737-3(e) Ex. 3.

There are a number of exceptions to the application of § 737. To the extent distributed property includes property contributed by the distributee partner, such property is not taken into account in determining either the net precontribution gain or the value of the property distributed for purposes of calculating the excess distribution gain. (This rule, however, does not apply where the distributed property consists of an interest in an entity, to the extent the value of the interest is attributable to property contributed to the entity after the contribution of the interest to the partnership. § 737(d)(1).) Finally, § 737 does not apply to the extent § 751(b) applies to the distribution. § 737(d)(2).

The regulations also provide exceptions similar to those under § 704(c)(1)(B). Section 737 does not apply to terminations under § 708(b)(1)(B); to complete transfers to another partnership; to certain divisive transactions; or to incorporation of a partnership. Reg. § 1.737-2(a), (b), (c). There is also an anti-abuse rule that can be applied to recast the transaction for federal tax purposes "if a principal purpose of a transaction is to achieve a tax result that is inconsistent with the purpose of section 737." Reg. § 1.737-4(a).

D. Application of §§ 704(c)(1)(B) and 737 to the Same Transaction

Section 704(c)(1)(B) and § 737 can apply to the same distribution. Drawing upon an example in the regulations, assume Alex contributed both Blackacre (value $100, adjusted basis $70) and Greenacre (value $200, adjusted basis $150) to ABC and that Barbara contributed Whiteacre (value $300, adjusted basis $300) to ABC. More than two years later, but within seven years of Alex's contributions, ABC distributes Blackacre (value now $350) to Barbara and distributes Whiteacre (value now $350) to Alex. Assume Alex's basis in his partnership interest is $220 at the time of the distributions. Under § 704(c)(1)(B) Alex recognizes the precontribution built-in gain of $30 on the distribution of Blackacre to Barbara. But § 737 is also applicable to Alex because of the distribution of Whiteacre to him.

In these circumstances, the regulations provide that § 704(c)(1)(B) is applied before the application of § 737. See Reg. § 1.737-3(e) Ex. 2. Thus, as noted, Alex recognizes gain of $30 under § 704(c)(1)(B). For § 737 purposes, this gain needs to be taken into account. Accordingly, Alex's net precontribution gain of $80 ($30 on account of Blackacre; $50 on account of Greenacre) is reduced to $50 on account of the § 704(c)(1)(B) gain of $30. Reg. § 1.737-1(c)(2)(iv). But the lesser-of test also requires the calculation of Alex's excess distribution gain, the excess of (A) the value of the property distributed: here Whiteacre worth $350, over (B) Alex's outside basis: here, $250, because the recognized § 704(c)(1)(B) gain of $30 increased the outside basis from $220 to $250. Thus, because Alex's net precontribution gain is $50, and his excess distribution gain is $100 ($350 value of distributed Whiteacre, less Alex's adjusted basis of $250), he recognizes gain of $50 on the receipt of Whiteacre under the lesser-of rule of § 737(a). *See* Reg. § 1.737-1(e) Ex 3.

In this example, note that one person, Alex, was subject to the application of both § 704(c)(1)(B) and § 737 on the distribution of two properties. But the distribution of a single property can trigger § 704(c)(1)(B) for one person and § 737 for another. For example, assume that Alex and Barbara had each contributed appreciated property to the partnership. The subsequent distribution of one of properties to the noncontributing partner could trigger the application of § 704(c)(1)(B) to the contributing partner and the application of § 737 to the distributee partner. In the example above, both Alex and Barbara contributed property to the ABC partnership, but the property Barbara contributed had a value equal to its basis and therefore was not § 704(c) property. Thus, § 704(c)(1)(B) did not apply to Barbara on the later distribution of that property to Alex.

Chapter 20

TRANSFERS OF PARTNERSHIP INTERESTS

PART A:
SALE OR EXCHANGE OF A PARTNERSHIP INTEREST

I. PROBLEMS

1. Fifteen years ago, Patrick, Cathy, and Daniel formed a calendar-year, general partnership in which each has an equal one-third interest. Assume each of the partners contributed $200,000 in cash in creating the partnership. On January 1, 2016, Cathy sold her partnership interest to Maureen for $400,000. At the time of the sale, the partnership had the following balance sheet: [Assume the partnership has held the Capital Assets for more than one year.]

	Partnership Assets			**Partners' Capital**	
	A/B	FMV		A/B	FMV
Cash	$180,000	$180,000	Cathy	$200,000	$400,000
Inventory	$225,000	$450,000	Patrick	$200,000	$400,000
Capital Asset #1	$75,000	$360,000	Daniel	$200,000	$400,000
Capital Asset #2	$120,000	$210,000			
Total	$600,000	$1,200,000		$600,000	$1,200,000

(a) Explain the tax consequences to Cathy of the sale.

(b) How would your answer to (a) change, if at all, if Capital Asset #2 was a collectible within the meaning of § 408(m) (without regard to paragraph (3) thereof)?

(c) Assuming the partnership had not made a § 754 election, how much gain or loss, if any, must Maureen report if the partnership, immediately following Maureen's purchase of Cathy's interest, sells Capital Asset #1 for $360,000? What will Maureen's outside basis and capital account be following the sale?

(d) How would your answers to (c) change if a § 754 election were in effect when Maureen purchased Cathy's partnership interest?

(e) How would your answer to (a) and (d) change if, upon the formation of the partnership, Cathy, instead of contributing $200,000 cash to the partnership, had contributed $50,000 of cash and Capital Asset #2 with a fair market value of $150,000 (and an adjusted basis of

437

$120,000)?

(f) Assuming no § 754 election were in effect when Maureen purchased Cathy's partnership interest, explain a circumstance under which a § 732(d) election by Maureen would be beneficial.

2. Fred, Monica, and Judson each have a one-third interest in the capital, profits, and losses of a calendar-year, general partnership that uses the cash method of accounting. In Year 1, Fred and Monica each contributed $120,000 of cash, while Judson contributed a tract of land (Land #1) with a fair market value of $120,000 and an adjusted basis of $90,000. The partnership subsequently purchased a second tract of land (Land #2) for $225,000 and held it subject to a nonrecourse liability in the amount of $75,000. A poor investment, Land #2 has steadily decreased in value. Assume in Year 5 Judson sells his interest in the partnership to Maria, an unrelated party, for $200,000. Maria pays Judson $175,000 in cash and takes his interest subject to his $25,000 share of the partnership's nonrecourse liability. The partnership at the time of the sale had the following balance sheet:

	Partnership Assets			Liabilities and Partners' Capital	
	A/B	FMV		A/B	FMV
			Liability		$75,000
Cash	$150,000	$150,000	Fred	$175,000*	$175,000
Inventory	$30,000	$60,000	Monica	$175,000*	$175,000
Accounts Receivable	$0	$90,000	Judson	$145,000*	$175,000
Land #1	$90,000	$180,000			
Land #2	$225,000	$120,000			
Total	$495,000	$600,000		$495,000	$600,000

* The outside basis of each partner reflects the partner's one-third share of the $75,000 liability encumbering Land #2.

(a) Explain the tax consequences to Judson on the sale of his partnership interest.

(b) Assuming the partnership has made a § 754 election, explain the tax consequences to Maria when the partnership subsequently sells Land #2 for $120,000 and collects the full $90,000 of the accounts receivable.

Assignment for Part A of Chapter 20:

Complete the Problems

Read: Internal Revenue Code: §§ 1(h)(5)(B), 732(d), 741, 742, 743(a)–(d), 751(a), (c), (d), 755(a) and (b).
Treasury Regulations: §§ 1.1(h)-1(b), (c), (f) Exs. 1, 2 and 5, 1.732-1(d), 1.741-1(a), (b), (d), (e) and (f), 1.742-1, 1.743-1(a)–(e) and (g)(1), 1.751-1(a), (c)(1)–(4)(i), (iii), (iv), (d), (e), (g) Ex. 1, 1.755-1(a)(1), (3) and (4)(i)(A), (b)(1)–(3); Prop. Reg. § 1.751-1(a)(1) and (2). Skim Prop. Reg. § 743-1.

Materials: Overview
            Ledoux v. Commissioner

II. VOCABULARY

§ 751 property
hot assets
inventory
unrealized receivables
partnership's previously taxed capital
§ 754 election
§ 732(d) election
capital gain look-through rules
substantial built-in loss

III. OBJECTIVES

1. To explain the tax consequences to a partner on the sale of her partnership interest.

2. To explain the application of the capital gain look-through rules on the sale or exchange of a partnership interest.

3. To recall that there is generally no adjustment to the partnership's inside basis on the sale of a partnership interest.

4. To determine the outside basis of the transferee partner.

5. To explain in general the tax consequences to the transferee partner if no § 754 election is in effect.

6. To calculate a transferee partner's interest in a partnership's previously taxed capital.

7. To determine the adjustments to the partnership's inside basis on the sale of a partnership interest if a § 754 election is in effect.

8. To recall that the basis adjustments provided by § 743(b) constitute an adjustment to the basis of partnership property with respect to the transferee partner only.

9. To explain the significance to a transferee of an election under § 732(d).

IV. OVERVIEW

The sale or exchange of a partnership interest has significant tax consequences for both the transferor and the transferee. This chapter will explore those tax consequences. The tax treatment of sales and exchanges of partnership interests is much more complex than one might initially imagine. That complexity is a function of congressional efforts to prevent the conversions of ordinary income into capital gain, to ensure appropriate application of allocations required by § 704(c), and to set the stage for the possibility of a special basis election by transferees.

A. Tax Consequences to the Transferor Partner

We will use the following fact pattern, referred to as the "Basic Facts," with some variations in explaining the tax consequences to both the transferor partner and the transferee:

Basic Facts: Ten years ago, Abbey, Clare, and Evan each contributed $210,000 in cash to form a calendar-year general partnership — hereinafter the ACE Partnership or ACE. The three partners each had an equal one-third interest in the partnership. On January 1 of the current year,[1] Abbey sold her partnership interest to Austin, an unrelated person, for $400,000. At the time, no § 754 election was in effect, and the ACE Partnership had the following balance sheet:

	Partnership Assets[2]			Partners' Capital	
	A/B	FMV		A/B	FMV
Cash	$240,000	$240,000	Abbey	$210,000	$400,000
Inventory	$150,000	$450,000	Clare	$210,000	$400,000
Capital Asset #1[3]	$90,000	$300,000	Evan	$210,000	$400,000
Capital Asset #2[4]	$150,000	$210,000			
Total	$630,000	$1,200,000		$630,000	$1,200,000

As previously discussed, Subchapter K reflects both the entity and aggregate approaches to the taxation of partners and partnerships. Let us begin our analysis of the tax consequences to Abbey of a sale assuming Subchapter K utilized either a pure entity or aggregate approach.

1. The Entity vs. Aggregate Approach to Partnership Taxation

a. Entity approach.

If the tax consequences of a sale of a partnership interest were governed by a pure entity approach, Abbey's sale or her partnership interest would be comparable to the sale by an investor of stock in a corporation, i.e., the sale of her partnership interest would simply be treated as a sale of a capital asset with no regard paid to the actual assets held by the ACE Partnership. Pursuant to § 1001,

---

[1] Section 706(c)(2) and Reg. § 1.706-1(c)(2) provide that a partnership's tax year will close with respect to a partner who sells or exchanges her entire interest in a partnership. Under those circumstances, the selling partner must include in her taxable income her distributive share of items described in § 702(a) and any guaranteed payments under § 707(c) for her partnership taxable year ending with a sale. Thus, were Abbey to have sold her interest after the partnership had generated income, gain, or loss for the year, Abbey would have to take into account her distributive share of those items. *See* discussion *infra* addressing the determination of the varying interests of partners during the year.

[2] Assume the book value of each of the partnership assets initially was the same as the adjusted basis of the asset. Thus, the partnership has no § 704(c) property.

[3] Assume Capital Asset #1 is unimproved land that has been held by the partnership for more than one year.

[4] Assume Capital Asset #2 is unimproved land that has been held by the partnership for 11 months.

Abbey's gain on the sale would be $190,000 (i.e., amount realized of $400,000 less adjusted basis of $210,000 = $190,000). As suggested above, Abbey would treat her partnership interest as a capital asset much as she would treat as capital assets any corporate stock she acquired for investment purposes. On the sale of her interest in ACE, Abbey would thus have $190,000 of long-term capital gain.

b. Aggregate approach.

By contrast, if the tax consequences of a sale of a partnership interest were governed by a pure aggregate approach, Abbey would be treated as having sold an undivided one-third interest in (i.e., her share of) each of ACE's assets. Under this approach, Abbey's tax consequences would be as follows:

Cash: Abbey's one-third share of the partnership cash would be $80,000.

Partnership inventory: On the sale of her undivided one-third interest in the partnership inventory (with a fair market value of $150,000 and an adjusted basis of $50,000), Abbey would realize and recognize $100,000 of *ordinary income*.

Capital Asset #1: On the sale of her undivided one-third interest in Capital Asset #1 (with a fair market value of 100,000 and an adjusted basis of $30,000), Abbey would realize and recognize *$70,000 long-term capital gain*.

Capital Asset #2: On the sale of her one-third interest in Capital Asset #2 (with a fair market value of $70,000 and an adjusted basis of $50,000), Abbey would realize and recognize a $20,000 *short-term capital gain*.

As the above analysis indicates, the difference between a pure entity and a pure aggregate approach is significant. Although both approaches produce the same aggregate amount of income, i.e., $190,000, reflecting the total gain inherent in Abbey's partnership interest, the character of that income is significantly different depending on the approach taken. Congress was concerned that the pure entity approach would enable a partner like Abbey to convert ordinary income into capital gain. At the same time, it recognized that a pure aggregate approach would require a cumbersome process of allocating the purchase price among every asset held by the partnership and calculating gain and loss with regard to each asset. Seeking to prevent the conversion of ordinary income into capital gain and yet negate the burden an asset-by-asset approach would entail, Congress chose to treat the sale of a partnership interest in a manner reflecting both the entity and aggregate approaches. Thus, while § 741 generally provides that gain or loss recognized on the sale or exchange of an interest in a partnership will be considered "as gain or loss from a capital asset" (thus reflecting an entity approach), § 741 qualifies this rule, making it subject to the special rules of § 751 related to "unrealized receivables and inventory items" (thus reflecting an aggregate approach). With regard to sales or exchanges of partnership interests, § 751(a) is the operative provision and, as will be demonstrated below, serves to prevent the conversion of ordinary income to capital gain.

2. Application of Section 751(a): General Rules

> § 751. Unrealized Receivables and Inventory Items
>
> (a) **Sale or exchange of interest in partnership.** The amount of any money, or the fair market value of any property, received by a transferor partner in exchange for all or a part of his interest in the partnership attributable to —
>
> (1) unrealized receivables of the partnership, or
>
> (2) inventory items of the partnership, shall be considered as an amount realized from the sale or exchange of property other than a capital asset.

As the provision clearly indicates, § 751(a) is applicable on the sale or exchange of a partnership interest only if the partnership holds "unrealized receivables" and/or "inventory."[5] These assets are referred to in the regulations as "section 751 property" [hereinafter referred to as "§ 751 property"] and, in the tax literature, as "hot assets."[6] These two terms encompass ordinary income items and are specially defined in § 751. Read § 751(c) and (d) carefully. Note that, pursuant to § 751(c), the term "unrealized receivables" is defined to include rights to payments *not previously included in income* for goods delivered or to be delivered and services rendered or to be rendered.[7] For example, trade accounts receivable of a cash method taxpayer are unrealized receivables. (Trade accounts receivable of an accrual method taxpayer, however, are not unrealized receivables as they have already been included in income.) Indicative of the congressional effort to prevent ordinary income from being converted into capital gain, § 751(c) also includes as "unrealized receivables" § 1245 and § 1250 property *to the extent of the amount of gain that would be subject to § 1245 or § 1250 recapture* were the property sold by the partnership. For example, assume a partnership owns a piece of equipment that, if sold by the partnership for its fair market value, would trigger $60,000 of

---

[5] Prior to changes effective in 1997, § 751(a) (addressing the sale or exchange of partnership interests) and § 751(b) (addressing distributions that alter a partner's interest in ordinary income property — see Chapter 16) both required inventory to be "substantially appreciated" before it would trigger application of those provisions. § 751(b) still imposes the "substantially appreciated" requirement on inventory, while § 751(a) does not.

[6] As discussed in Chapter 16, "§ 751 property" or "hot assets" have a slightly different meaning in § 751(b), i.e., only "unrealized receivables" and "substantially appreciated inventory" constitute § 751 property for § 751(b) purposes whereas "unrealized receivables" and "inventory" constitute § 751 property for § 751(a) purposes.

[7] Reg. § 1.751-1(c) amplifies this part of the definition of "unrealized receivables," indicating that rights to payments for goods and services "must have arisen under contracts or agreements *in existence at the time of the sale or distribution*, although the partnership may not be able to enforce payment until a later time." (Emphasis added.) Thus, the fact that a partnership will enter into future contracts to provide goods or services does not give rise to an "unrealized receivable." Regulation § 1.751-1(c) also includes as unrealized receivables any "rights to payment for work or goods begun but incomplete at the time of the sale or distribution."

gain, $40,000 of which would be characterized under § 1245(a)(1) as ordinary income. Pursuant to § 751(c), the potential § 1245(a)(1) gain of $40,000 inherent in the equipment would constitute an "unrealized receivable."[8]

The term "inventory" like the term "unrealized receivables" encompasses a range of ordinary income assets. "Inventory" is defined in § 751(d) to include: (1) property described in § 1221(a)(1) (e.g., inventory and property held for sale to customers in the ordinary course of a trade or business), (2) property which on sale or exchange would not be either a capital asset or property described in § 1231,[9] and also (3) partnership property *that, if held by the distributee partner,* would be described in (1) or (2) above.[10]

If § 751(a) is applicable, the partnership sale or exchange is, in effect, divided into two parts: (1) the part of the total amount realized that is attributable to the transferor partner's share of unrealized receivables and inventory is treated as an amount realized from the sale or exchange of property other than a capital asset; and (2) the remainder of the total amount realized is treated as realized from the sale or exchange of a capital asset under § 741.[11]

In applying § 751(a), the regulations[12] effectively provide a three-step process:

Step 1. Calculate the total capital gain or loss the transferor partner would realize absent § 751(a). Thus, one would simply apply the § 1001 formula to compute the transferor partner's gain or loss on the sale or exchange.[13] Abbey would thus realize $190,000 of gain on the sale of her partnership interest, i.e., amount realized of $400,000 less her adjusted basis of $210,000.

Step 2. Determine the amount of income or loss that would be allocated[14] to the transferor partner with respect to the partnership's unrealized receivables and inventory if the partnership, immediately prior to the

---

[8] Any remaining gain would not be an unrealized receivable.

[9] Reg. § 1.751-1(d)(2)(ii) provides that this category of inventory includes accounts receivable acquired in the ordinary course of business for services or from the sale of stock in trade and to any other unrealized receivables. The overlap created by the inclusion of unrealized receivables in inventory was purposeful. As noted in footnote 5 above, prior to 1997, both § 751(a) and 751(b) required special treatment of inventory only if the inventory were "substantially appreciated." As discussed in Chapter 16, by including unrealized receivables in inventory, there was a greater likelihood of inventory being "substantially appreciated." In 1997, Congress eliminated the "substantial appreciation" requirement for inventory with respect to § 751(a), while retaining it for § 751(b). Thus, the overlap noted above has no significance in the context of the sale or exchange of a partnership interest.

[10] Note the strong aggregate flavor of part (3) of the inventory definition.

[11] Reg. § 1.751-1(a).

[12] Reg. § 1.751-1(a)(2).

[13] Pursuant to § 752(d), to the extent the transferee assumes or takes subject to the transferor partner's share of liabilities, that amount of liabilities will be included in the transferor partner's amount realized on the transaction.

[14] Note that, in allocating the income or loss, one must take into account the application of § 704(c) (allocations associated with contributed property, discussed in Chapter 10) Reg. § 1.751–1(a)(2). Proposed regulations also require one to take into acccount § 743 (as it relates to basis adjustments pursuant to Reg. § 1.743-1(j)(3)). Prop. Reg. § 1.751-1(a)(2).

partner's sale of her partnership interest, sold for cash all of its assets at their fair market value.[15] That amount of gain or loss will be characterized as ordinary. With regard to our fact pattern, had the ACE Partnership sold its inventory immediately prior to Abbey's sale, it would have realized $300,000 of gain. Abbey's share of that gain would be $100,000 and would be characterized as ordinary income.

Step 3. Subtract from the total capital gain or loss calculated in Step 1 the amount of income or loss calculated in Step 2. The resulting amount of gain or loss will be treated as the transferor partner's capital gain or loss. Applying this step to Abbey's sale of her interest in ACE, Abbey would have $90,000 of long-term capital gain, i.e., Step 1 of $190,000 less Step 2 amount of $100,000 equals $90,000.

Note that, even though the partnership had held Capital Asset #2 for less than a year, Abbey nonetheless is entitled to long-term capital gain because she has held her partnership interest for more than one year. This result suggests an entity flavor to the operation of § 751(a).

3. Special Look-through Rules with Respect to Capital Gain

What difference, if any, would it make if, in the Basic Facts at the outset of this Overview, Capital Asset #1 were real property with unrecaptured § 1250 gain of $60,000 and Capital Asset #2 were a collectible within the meaning of § 408(m) (without regard to § 408(m)(3))? Unrecaptured § 1250 gain and collectibles gain are subject to higher maximum tax rates than other long-term capital gain. In view of the different maximum capital gain rates, you should not be surprised that Congress and Treasury require any long-term capital gain (resulting from Step 3 above) allocable to the sale of a partner's share of collectibles or property with unrecaptured § 1250 gain be taxed at the rates applicable to those categories of long-term capital gain. To ensure that result, § 1(h)(5) and Reg. § 1.1(h)-1(b) and (c) use the same look-through approach utilized for § 751(a) purposes. Applying those provisions to our example, Abbey's share of the $60,000 of unrecaptured 1250 gain on the hypothetical sale of Capital Asset #1 is $20,000 and her share of the gain on the hypothetical sale of Capital Asset #2 is $20,000. Thus, Abbey's overall $90,000 of long-term capital gain will be comprised of:

$20,000 of unrecaptured § 1250 gain subject to a maximum capital gain rate of 25%;

$20,000 of collectibles gain subject to a maximum capital gain rate of $28%; and

$50,000 of residual long-term capital gain rate generally taxed at a maximum capital gain rate of 20%.

---

[15] Thus, the partners cannot allocate the purchase price to specific assets. Furthermore, the fair market value of assets must take into account § 7701(g), providing that assets encumbered by nonrecourse indebtedness will be deemed to have a fair market value not less than that of nonrecourse indebtedness. Reg. § 1.751-1(a)(2) and Prop. Reg. § 1.751-1(a)(2) (October 2014).

B. Tax Consequences to the Transferee

1. In General

On the sale or exchange of a partnership interest, the transferee will take a § 1012 cost basis in the partnership interest acquired. Otherwise, the transferee will generally stand in the shoes of the transferor partner. Thus, as a result, the transferee will have:

(1) the same share of the partnership's inside basis the transferor partner had at the time of the sale or exchange[16];

(2) the same distributive share of partnership profits and losses attributable to the interest acquired; and

(3) the same capital account the transferor partner had in the transferred interest.[17]

Pursuant to § 743(a), the inside basis of the partnership (i.e., the partnership's basis in its assets) remains the same for all purposes on the sale or exchange of a partnership interest *unless the partnership has made a § 754 election* (see *infra*).[18] Thus, although, pursuant to the aggregate approach, a purchaser of a partnership interest can be considered to have purchased an undivided interest in each of the partnership's assets,[19] no adjustment is allowed to the partnership's bases in its assets unless a § 754 election is in effect.[20] (Note the strong entity flavor of § 743(a).)

Given the Basic Facts above, Austin, having paid $400,000 for the partnership interest purchased from Abbey, will have a $400,000 basis in that interest. § 1012. His distributive share, his share of the partnership's inside basis, and his capital account will be the same as Abbey's. Because a § 754 election was not in effect, the partnership's bases in its assets will remain the same. Thus, immediately after Abbey's sale of her interest to Austin, the partnership's balance sheet will be as follows:

---

[16] This assumes the partnership has not made a § 754 election and does not have a "substantial built-in loss" within the meaning of § 743(d)(1) immediately after the transfer. Also note that § 704(c)(1)(C) will limit a transferee's share of basis with respect to § 704(c) property contributed by the transferor partner and having a built-in loss. Prop. Reg. § 1.704-3(f)(3)(iii)(A).

[17] Reg. § 1.704-1(b)(2)(iv)(l).

[18] Even absent an election under § 754, however, the basis of partnership property must be adjusted if, at the time of the transfer, the partnership has a "substantial built-in loss." § 743(b). Pursuant to § 743(d), a partnership will have a substantial built-in loss if the partnership's adjusted basis in its assets exceeds by more than $250,000 the fair market value of its property. This "substantial-built-in-loss rule" prevents a transferee partner from benefiting significantly from the failure of the partnership to make a § 754 election, i.e., but for this rule, a transferee could deduct losses to which the transferee is not entitled.

[19] Considering the balance sheet of the partnership at the time Austin purchased Abbey's one-third interest, it is reasonable to conclude that the $400,000 purchase price was calculated as follows: $80,000 for a one-third share of the partnership cash; $150,000 for a one-third share of the inventory; $100,000 for a one-third share of Capital Asset #1; and $70,000 for a one-third share of Capital Asset #2.

[20] *See*, however, footnote 18.

	Partnership Assets			Partners' Capital	
	A/B	FMV		A/B	FMV
Cash	$240,000	$240,000	Austin	$400,000	$400,000
Inventory	$150,000	$450,000	Clare	$210,000	$400,000
Capital Asset #1	$90,000	$300,000	Evan	$210,000	$400,000
Capital Asset #2	$150,000	$210,000			
Totals	**$630,000**	**$1,200,000**		**$820,000**	**$1,200,000**

Note the aggregate inside basis of the partnership does not match the aggregate outside basis of the partners. There is a $190,000 difference. That difference results from the failure to adjust the partnership's inside basis when Austin purchased Abbey's interest.

The failure to adjust the partnership's inside basis on the sale or exchange of a partnership interest almost invariably results in some unexpected tax consequences to the transferee. Consider, for example, the impact on Austin of the sale by the ACE Partnership of all of its Inventory for its fair market value of $450,000. The partnership would realize $300,000 of ordinary gain, which would be allocated to the partners based on their distributive shares. Because Austin has a one-third distributive share in the profits and losses of the ACE Partnership, he will be allocated $100,000 of the $300,000 of ordinary income the partnership realized on the sale of the Inventory.

From Austin's standpoint, the allocation to him of $100,000 of ordinary income seems inequitable because he, in effect, paid $150,000 for a one-third share of the $450,000 of Inventory and, thus, should have no income when the Inventory is sold for $450,000.[21] Nonetheless, absent a § 754 election, Austin must report $100,000 of ordinary income. As a result, pursuant to § 705(a)(1)(A), Austin's outside basis would be increased by $100,000 to reflect the income he had to report. A loss of $100,000 would then inhere in Austin's partnership interest (i.e., FMV of partnership interest $400,000 and outside basis of $ 500,000). Ultimately, on a sale of his interest or on the liquidation of the partnership, Austin would recognize a $100,000 loss, thus offsetting the $100,000 of income he had to recognize when the Inventory was sold. That eventuality, however, provides little solace to Austin. Not only will the offsetting loss be delayed until there is a disposition or liquidation of Austin's interest, there will also be a disparity in character because the $100,000 loss will likely be a *capital loss*[22] whereas Austin was required to report $100,000 of *ordinary income* on the sale of the Inventory. In addition, were Austin to die before the partnership was liquidated, the loss inhering in his partnership interest would disappear because § 1014 would step down the basis of his partnership interest to $400,000.

---

[21] Of course, were the partnership's basis in the Inventory greater than the fair market value of the inventory, Austin could reap a tax benefit (i.e., a loss deduction) as a result of the no-adjustment-to-basis rule of § 743(a). Notwithstanding the lack of a § 754 election, however, if the partnership had a "substantial built-in loss" immediately after the transfer, § 743(b) would force an adjustment to the inside basis of the partnership.

[22] § 741.

2. § 754 and the Basis Adjustment under § 743

a. The § 754 Election.

On the sale or exchange of a partnership interest, Congress has provided a method for adjusting the inside basis of the partnership *for the benefit of the transferee* thereby alleviating the distortions of timing and character Austin would experience in our hypothetical. § 743(b). The basis adjustment rules of § 743(b), however, only apply if a partnership makes an election under § 754 or, if the partnership has a substantial built-in loss immediately after the transfer. If a partnership makes a § 754 election, two optional basis adjustment provisions become applicable — § 734(b) in the case of a distribution of property (discussed in Chapter 15) and § 743(b) in the case of a transfer of a partnership interest. Once made, the § 754 election applies to all distributions of property by the partnership and to all transfers of partnership during the taxable year for which the election becomes effective and for all subsequent taxable years. The election can be revoked subject to certain limitations.[23]

To make the § 754 election, the partnership must provide a statement setting forth the name and address of the partnership, a declaration that the partnership elects under § 754, and a signature by any one of the partners. The statement making the election must be filed with the partnership return for the taxable year during which the distribution or transfer occurs. It must be filed not later than the time for filing the partnership tax return for that year.[24]

b. The § 743(b) adjustments to basis.

Pursuant to § 743(b), on a sale or exchange of a partnership interest, a partnership that has made a § 754 election[25] will adjust the basis of partnership property *with respect to the transferee partner only*. The effect of § 743(b) is to provide the transferee partner a cost basis in each partnership asset. With that understanding, let us consider the specifics of this provision and the regulations interpreting it.

Section 743(b) provides the following formulas for determining the *aggregate* amount of basis adjustments to partnership assets if a § 754 election is in effect:

> The *aggregate amount of increase* in the adjusted basis of the partnership property equals "the excess of the basis to the transferee partner of his interest in the partnership over his proportionate share of the adjusted basis of the partnership property."

> The *aggregate amount of decrease* in the adjusted basis of the partnership property equals "the excess of the transferee partner's proportionate share of the adjusted basis of the partnership property over the basis of his interest in the partnership."

---

[23] Reg. § 1.754-1(c).

[24] Reg. § 1.754-1(b)(1).

[25] As noted previously, even if a § 754 election has not been made, the § 743(b) basis adjustments must be made if a partnership has a "substantial built-in loss immediately after [a] transfer."

Section 743(b) directs that a partner's proportionate share of the adjusted basis of partnership property be determined in accordance with the partner's interest in partnership capital. In addition, it requires that, because the transferee partner stands in the shoes of the transferor partner, any gain or loss allocable to the transferor partner as a result of the application of § 704(c) (dealing with contributed property) be taken into account. The regulations create a complex formula to accommodate the statutory requirement that § 704(c) be applied in determining a transferee partner's share of the partnership's adjusted basis in its assets.

Let us now assume the ACE Partnership had a § 754 election in effect when Abbey sold her interest to Austin. In a situation such as that presented by our Basic Facts where the partnership holds no § 704(c) property, one could readily determine the transferee partner's share of the partnership's adjusted basis without recourse to the regulation formula. Thus, in our example, because Austin owns a one-third equal interest in the ACE Partnership, he would have a $200,000 share of the partnership's aggregate adjusted basis of $600,000. In turn, applying the § 743(b) formula for basis adjustment, Austin would be entitled to a total basis adjustment of $190,000 (i.e., his outside basis of $400,000 less his proportionate share ($210,000) of the partnership's adjusted basis in its assets). Let us now consider the regulation formula for determining a transferee's share of the partnership's adjusted basis.

For purposes of determining a transferee's share of the partnership's adjusted basis in its assets, the regulations assume a hypothetical transaction in which all the partnership's assets are sold for cash immediately after the transfer.[26] In view of that hypothetical sale, a transferee's share of the partnership's aggregate adjusted basis in its assets will be equal "to the sum of the transferee's interest as a partner in the partnership's previously taxed capital, plus the transferee's share of partnership liabilities."[27] A partner's interest in the partnership's "previously taxed capital" is equal to:

> *the cash the transferee would receive if the partnership liquidated immediately after the hypothetical sale of its assets*
>
> *Plus*
>
> *any tax loss (including any remedial allocation under Reg. § 1.704-3(d)) allocable to the transferee from the hypothetical sale*
>
> *Less*
>
> *any tax gain (including any remedial allocation under Reg. § 1.704-3(d)) allocable to the transferee from the hypothetical sale.*[28]

---

[26] Reg. § 1.743-1(d)(2).

[27] Reg. § 1.743-1(d)(1).

[28] The formula for computing a partner's share of a partnership's "previously taxed capital" may seem odd, but there is logic to it. The formula is reminiscent of that used in computing the basis a taxpayer has in an installment note. Section 453B(b) provides that the taxpayer's basis in an installment note is the difference between the face amount of the note and the amount of income that would be triggered

Applying this formula to Austin's situation in our example, Austin's share of cash were the ACE Partnership to have liquidated immediately following the hypothetical sale of its assets would be $400,000, (i.e., the hypothetical sale of all the partnership assets for their fair market value would produce total cash of $1,200,000 as shown on the balance sheet above and Austin's share of that amount would be one-third or $400,000). The partnership would have realized a net gain of $570,000 on the hypothetical sale (i.e., $1,200,000 amount realized less aggregate basis of $630,000). Austin's one-third share of that gain would be $190,000. Subtracting the $190,000 of gain from Austin's $400,000 share of the cash would result in Austin having a $210,000 share of the partnership's previously taxed capital. We would then add Austin's share of any partnership liabilities to the $210,000 to arrive at Austin's share of the partnership's adjusted basis in its assets. The ACE Partnership has no liabilities in our example and therefore Austin's share of the partnership's adjusted basis is $210,000 — exactly the same figure we arrived at previously. As a result, under § 743(b), Austin's basis adjustment would be $190,000 (i.e., Austin's outside basis of $400,000 less his $210,000 share of the partnership's adjusted basis).[29]

c. § 755 — Allocation of § 743(b) Adjustments.

Austin's $190,000 § 743(b) basis adjustment must be allocated among the partnership's assets. § 755 will govern the allocation of the basis adjustment.[30] Read § 755 carefully. Section 755(a)(1) requires the adjustment to be allocated "in a manner which has the effect of reducing the difference between the fair market value and the adjusted basis of partnership properties." In addition, it directs that, to the extent the adjustment is a function of either (1) capital assets or § 1231(b) property or (2) other property, the adjustment must be allocated to property of "like character." (An allocation, however, cannot reduce the basis of partnership property below zero.) § 755(b).

The regulations elaborate on these rules and provide a three-step process for the allocation of the § 743(b) adjustment. First, the value of each partnership asset must be determined. Second, the § 743(b) basis adjustment must be allocated between two classes of property — capital gain property (defined to include both capital assets and § 1231(b) property) and ordinary income property (all property other than capital assets and § 1231(b) property). Third, the portion of the basis

---

if the note were paid in full. That same approach is used in determining a transferee's share of the partnership's "previously taxed capital." Thus, according to Reg. § 1.743–1(d)(1), if a partnership would have net gain on the hypothetical sale of its assets, a transferee's share of the partnership's "previously taxed capital" would equal the cash the transferee would receive in a liquidation following the hypothetical sale less the transferee's share of gain (taking into account § 704(c)) from the hypothetical sale. If a partnership would have a net loss on the hypothetical sale of its assets (because its aggregate adjusted basis was greater than the amount that would be realized on the sale), a transferee's share of the partnership's "previously taxed capital" would equal the cash the transferee would receive in a liquidation following the hypothetical sale plus the transferee's share of loss (taking into account § 704(c)) from the hypothetical sale.

[29] Note that Austin's basis adjustment exactly equals the amount of gain Abbey had to report and assures that his share of inside basis exactly equals his outside basis. This, of course, make sense as it prevents double taxation of the gain inherent in Abbey's partnership interest.

[30] § 743(c).

adjustment allocated to each class is allocated to each item within that class.[31] With regard to the second step, the regulations provide that the portion of the overall adjustment allocated to the class of assets consisting of ordinary income property will equal the amount of income, gain, or loss allocable to the transferee if all of the ordinary income property were sold immediately after the transfer; the balance of the overall adjustment will generally be allocated to the class of assets consisting of capital assets and § 1231(b) property. Reg. § 1.755-1(b)(2)(i). Likewise, with regard to the third step, the regulations provide that, in general, the adjustment allocated to each asset within the class will equal the amount of income, gain, or loss allocable to the transferee partner if that asset were sold for cash immediately after the transfer. Reg. § 1.755-1(b)(3). (The regulation, however, employs a detailed formula for arriving at this general result.) The regulations also provide that the portion of the basis adjustment allocated to one of the classes can be an increase while the portion allocated to the other class can be a decrease. Reg. § 1.755-1(b)(1)(i). In other words, the § 743(b) basis adjustment is a *net adjustment* to be allocated between the two classes. Similarly, adjustments within a class can be a combination of increases to some assets and decreases to other assets consistent with the § 755 requirement that the allocations have the effect of reducing the difference between the fair market value of assets and the assets' adjusted basis. Reg. § 1.755-1(b)(1)(i). As a result of this three-step process, the transferee will generally have a cost basis in each of the partnership assets.

Applying § 755 and the regulations to Austin, we would first determine the amount of income, gain, or loss allocable to the ordinary income property of the ACE Partnership. In this case, the Inventory is the only such property. If the Inventory were sold for $450,000 of cash, the Ace Partnership would realize $300,000 of ordinary income. As an equal one-third partner, Austin would be allocated $100,000 of that ordinary income. Thus, that amount of the $190,000 total basis adjustment is allocated to the Inventory. The remaining $90,000 of the overall basis adjustment is allocated to the class of assets consisting of Capital Assets #1 and #2. This $90,000 adjustment must then be allocated between these two capital assets. If Capital Asset #1 were sold for $300,000, the partnership would realize $210,000 of long-term capital gain. Austin's share of that gain would be $70,000. Thus, $70,000 of the $90,000 basis adjustment will be allocated to Capital Asset #1. If the partnership sold Capital Asset #2 for its fair market value of $210,000, the partnership would realize $60,000 of short-term capital gain. Austin's share of that gain would be $20,000. Therefore, $20,000 of the $90,000 basis adjustment allocated to the capital asset class will be allocated to Capital Asset #2. Again, these basis adjustments are for the benefit of Austin only.

As a result of the § 743(b) basis adjustments, were the Ace Partnership to sell any of its assets immediately after Abbey's transfer of her interest to Austin, Austin would have no gain or loss. For example, if the partnership sold all of its inventory for $450,000, Austin's one-third share of the amount realized would be $150,000 and his adjusted basis in his interest in the Inventory would also be $150,000, i.e., a combination of his $50,000 share of the partnership's $150,000 basis in the Inventory plus the $100,000 § 743(b) basis adjustment. Austin would

---

[31] Reg. § 1.755-1(a)(1).

therefore recognize no gain on the sale of the Inventory.

d. The Section 743(b) Adjustment to Basis when a Partnership Holds Section 704(c) Property.

As noted above, the complex formula provided by the § 743 regulations for determining the amount of the § 743(b) adjustment to inside basis is designed to account for the operation of § 704(c). Consider the following variation on the Basic Facts at the outset of this Overview. Assume that, while Clare and Evan each contributed $210,000 in cash in forming the partnership, Abbey, instead of contributing cash, contributed Capital Asset #1, which at the time of contribution had a fair market value of $210,000 and an adjusted basis of $90,000. Assume Capital Asset #1 subsequently appreciated and had a fair market value of $300,000 at the time Abbey sold her partnership interest to Austin. Assume the sale price was $360,000 and that the partnership's balance sheet at the time Abbey sold her partnership interest was as follows and that the partnership had a § 754 election in effect:

	Partnership Assets			Partners' Capital		
	A/B	FMV		A/B	Book	FMV
Cash	$120,000	$120,000	Abbey	$90,000	$210,000	$360,000
Inventory	$150,000	$450,000	Clare	$210,000	$210,000	$360,000
Capital Asset #1[32]	$90,000	$300,000	Evan	$210,000	$210,000	$360,000
Capital Asset #2[33]	$150,000	$210,000				
Total	$510,000	$1,080,000		$510,000	$630,000	$1,080,000

As a result of the sale, Abbey would recognize $270,000 of gain. Pursuant to § 751(a) and the analysis in the previous example, Abbey would have $100,000 of ordinary income and $170,000 of long-term capital gain.

With respect to Austin, if a § 754 election were in effect, the following analysis would follow with respect to the computation of the § 743 adjustment. Capital Asset #1 would be § 704(c) property with $120,000 of built-in gain at the time Abbey contributed it. On the hypothetical sale by the partnership of its assets following Austin's purchase of Abbey's interest, the partnership would recognize aggregate gain of $570,000 just as before. Of that gain, $210,000 would result from the hypothetical sale of Capital Asset #1. Under § 704(c) principles, $120,000 of the $210,000 gain would be allocable to Austin (who now stands in Abbey's shoes) and the $90,000 balance would be allocable in equal shares to all three partners (i.e., $30,000 each). Thus, Austin would have $150,000 of gain as the result of the hypothetical sale of Capital Asset #1. That amount of gain, when combined with Austin's $100,000 share of gain from the hypothetical sale of the partnership's

---

[32] Assume again Capital Asset #1 is unimproved land that has been held by the partnership for more than one year.

[33] Assume again Capital Asset #2 is unimproved land that has been held by the partnership for 11 months.

inventory and $20,000 share of the gain from the hypothetical sale of Capital Asset #2, would result in a total of $270,000 gain being allocated to Austin. Thus, Austin's share of the partnership's previously taxed capital would be $90,000 ($360,000 cash deemed received on the hypothetical liquidation less $270,000 of gain allocable to Austin on the hypothetical sale). Again, there are no partnership liabilities. Thus, Austin's share of the partnership's adjusted basis in its assets would be $90,000. His § 743(b) adjustment would be $270,000 (i.e., Austin's outside basis of $360,000 less his $90,000 share of the partnership's adjusted basis).

In allocating the $270,000 adjustment to the inside basis of partnership property for the benefit of Austin, the same analysis utilized above applies. Thus, pursuant to § 755, $100,000 of the adjustment would be applied to the basis of the partnership inventory, $150,000 of the adjustment would be applied to the basis of Capital Asset #1 and $20,000 to the basis of Capital Asset #2. As a result, if the partnership's assets were sold for their fair market value immediately following Austin's purchase of Abbey's partnership interest, Austin would have no gain or loss.

e. The Section 743 Adjustment to Basis when Liabilities Encumber Partnership Property.

Return to the Basic Facts at the outset of this Overview but now assume Abbey, Clare, and Evan each contributed only $190,000 in cash in forming the partnership. Assume also that, immediately following its formation, the partnership purchased Capital Asset #2 for $150,000, using $90,000 of its own cash and borrowing the other $60,000 of the purchase price on a nonrecourse basis from a local lender. The nonrecourse liability is secured by a mortgage on Capital Asset #2. Assume that at the time Abbey sold her interest, the partnership still owed the lender $60,000 on Capital Asset #2. Taking the $60,000 liability into account, assume the partnership had the following balance sheet at the time Abbey sold her interest:

	Partnership Assets			Liabilities and Partners' Capital	
	A/B	FMV		A/B	FMV
Cash	$240,000	$240,000	Liability		$60,000
Inventory	$150,000	$450,000	Abbey	$210,000*	$380,000
Capital Asset #1	$90,000	$300,000	Clare	$210,000*	$380,000
Capital Asset #2	$150,000	$210,000	Evan	$210,000*	$380,000
Total	$630,000	$1,200,000		$630,000	$1,200,000

* Note that, consistent with § 752(a) (discussed in Chapter 11), Abbey, Clare, and Evan will each have a one-third share of the $60,000 liability which, in turn, will increase their outside basis from $190,000 (the cash each contributed) to $210,000 as shown on the balance sheet.

Assume Abbey sells her interest to Austin for $400,000. Austin pays Abbey $380,000 in cash and assumes Abbey's $20,000 share of the nonrecourse liability encumbering Capital Asset #2. Abbey's amount realized is again $400,000, i.e., $380,000 cash plus the liability relief of $20,000. Her gain is therefore $190,000, $100,000 of which will be characterized as ordinary income pursuant to § 751(a) with the remaining $90,000 treated as long-term capital gain. See analysis of § 751(a) above.

If a § 754 election is in effect, Austin will be entitled to the benefit of a § 743(b) adjustment to the inside basis of the partnership assets. Pursuant to § 743(b), the amount of the adjustment will be the difference between Austin's outside basis (here, $400,000 pursuant to § 1012) and his share of the partnership inside basis. Reg. § 1.743-1(d) provides the formula for determining Austin's share of the partnership's adjusted basis, i.e., the "sum of the transferee's interest as a partner in the partnership's previously taxed capital, plus the transferee's share of partnership liabilities." Applying the formula noted above for the determination of a transferee partner's interest in the partnership previously taxed capital, Austin's interest in the partnership's previously taxed capital is $190,000 computed as follows: $380,000 (the cash Austin would receive if the partnership liquidated immediately after the hypothetical sale of its assets) plus $0 (any tax loss allocable to Austin from the hypothetical sale) less $190,000 (Austin's one-third share of the $570,000 of gain that would be realized by the partnership on the hypothetical sale). To this figure of $190,000, we then add Austin's share of the partnership's $60,000 liability, i.e., $20,000. Austin's § 743(b) adjustment is therefore $190,000 ($400,000, less $210,000), which will be allocable under § 755 in the same manner as in the example at the outset of this Overview.

3. Special Basis to Transferee — § 732(d)

Because once made, a § 754 election applies to all subsequent distributions and transfers of partnership interests and, given that it can result in a downward adjustment of basis that would not otherwise be mandated, a partnership may be reluctant to make a § 754 election. If a partnership has not made a § 754 election, a transferee[34] receiving a distribution of partnership property within two years after a transfer may elect to treat, as the partnership's adjusted basis in such distributed property, the adjusted basis the partnership would have had if a § 743(b) adjustment were in effect. § 732(d) and Reg. § 1.732-1(d)(1)(iii).

---

§ 732(d). Special Partnership Basis to Transferee

For purposes of subsections (a), (b), and (c), a partner who acquired all or a part of his interest by a transfer with respect to which the election provided in section 754 is not in effect, and to whom a distribution of property (other than money) is made with respect to the transferred interest within 2 years after such transfer, may elect, under regulations prescribed by the Secretary, to treat as the adjusted partnership basis of such property the adjusted basis such property would have if the adjustment provided in section 743 (b) were in effect with respect to the partnership property. The Secretary may by regulations require the application of this subsection in the case of a distribution to a transferee

---

[34] A transfer for purposes of § 732(d) occurs upon a sale or exchange of a partnership interest or upon the death of a partner. Reg. § 1.732-1(d)(1)(i).

> partner, whether or not made within 2 years after the transfer, if at the time of the transfer the fair market value of the partnership property (other than money) exceeded 110 percent of its adjusted basis to the partnership.

Thus, for example, assume the Basic Facts at the outset of this Overview. In addition, assume that Ace Partnership, which has never made a § 754 election, distributed to Austin, Clare, and Evan one-third of the Inventory each (i.e., $150,000 of the $450,000 of Inventory) within two years of Austin's purchase of Abbey's partnership interest. If Austin makes an election under § 732(d), the amount of his share of partnership basis that is attributable to the Inventory (i.e., one-third of $150,000 or $50,000) will be increased by $100,000 (the same increase noted above when a § 754 election was in effect). Thus, Austin will have a $150,000 basis in $150,000 of Inventory. Were Austin to immediately sell the Inventory of for $150,000, he would have no gain or loss.[35] (By contrast, Clare and Evan would simply take a $50,000 basis in the share of Inventory each of them received. § 732(a)(1).)

The § 732(d) basis adjustment applies *only for purposes of distributions* to the transferee. It does not apply for purposes of determining partnership depreciation or a partnership's gain or loss on disposition of its property.[36]

The transferee must make the § 732(d) election[37] on her tax return (1) for the year of distribution if the distributed property in the hands of the transferee is depreciable or amortizable; or (2) for any taxable year no later than the first taxable year in which the basis of any of the distributed property (other than that noted in (1) above) is pertinent in determining her income tax. Reg. § 1.732-1(d)(2).

Note that, under § 732(d) and Reg. § 1.732-1(d)(4), the basis adjustment may be mandatory, even if the distribution does not occur within two years of the transferee's acquisition of her partnership interest, if the fair market value of the property exceeded 110 percent of its adjusted basis to the partnership and certain other requirements are met. Furthermore, some distributions to a transferee may trigger application of § 751(b).

C. Conclusion

As discussed in detail above, the tax consequences of a sale or exchange of a partnership interest are complex and reflect both aggregate and entity notions of partnerships. Section 751(a) operates to bifurcate the sale or exchange and thereby prevent the transferor partner from converting ordinary income into capital gain. In determining the amount of ordinary income (or loss) and capital gain (or loss) a transferor partner must recognize on a sale or exchange, § 704(c) must be taken into account. While the transferee partner will take a fair market value outside

---

[35] *See* Reg. § 1.732-1(d)(1)(vi) Ex.

[36] Reg. § 1.732-1(d)(1)(iv) and (vi) Ex.

[37] Reg. § 1.732-1(d)(3) provides the requirements for the schedule a transferee must submit with her tax return in making the § 732(d) election.

basis in the acquired partnership interest, the transferee partner will otherwise generally stand in the shoes of the transferor partner, assuming (a) the transferor/partner's share of inside basis (except where a the partnership has a "substantial built-in loss immediately after the transfer), (b) the transferor partner's distributive share of partnership income and loss, and (c) the transferor partner's capital account. Absent a § 754 election (or a situation involving a partnership with a substantial built-in loss immediately after a transfer of a partnership interest), a transferee partner is subject to a range of distortions discussed above. If, however, a § 754 election has been made by the partnership (or if the partnership has a substantial built-in loss), the partnership's inside basis will be adjusted pursuant to § 743 with respect to the transferee partner only, thereby eliminating these distortions by generally providing the transferee partner with a fair market value basis in each of the partnership's assets.

LEDOUX v. COMMISSIONER
77 T.C. 293 (1981), *aff'd per curiam*, 695 F.2d 1320 (11th Cir. 1983)

STERETT, JUDGE:

[T]he sole issue . . . for our decision is whether any portion of the amount received by petitioner John W. Ledoux pursuant to an agreement for the sale of a partnership interest was attributable to an unrealized receivable of the partnership and thus was required to be characterized as ordinary income under section 751, I.R.C. 1954.

FINDINGS OF FACT:

[The petitioner had a 25% interest in the Collins-Ledoux partnership that had as its stated purpose the "carrying on of the business of managing and operating a greyhound dog racing plant in Seminole County, Florida." The partnership had a contract with the Sanford-Orlando Kennel Club, Inc. "to manage and operate the Greyhound Racing Track, owned by the Sanford-Orlando Kennel Club, Inc.," for a period of 20 years commencing on October 1, 1955. The dog track management contract was subsequently extended on two different occasions conditioned on improvements being made to the dog track and certain additional annual payments being made. Ed.]

Petitioner John W. Ledoux was a manager of the operations of the racetrack for the Collins-Ledoux partnership. Petitioner received compensation for his services in the form of salary, which was charged as an expense of the track operation. Along with his salary, petitioner received a share of the net profits of the Collins-Ledoux partnership. Petitioner's duties included, among other things, the directing of promotional, advertising, and development activities on behalf of the Collins-Ledoux partnership.

In addition, during this period the partnership made improvements to the corporation's property. Virtually every building was replaced except for the main grandstand, which was remodeled extensively. The Collins-Ledoux partnership also acquired property adjacent to the corporation's dog track property for additional parking, paddocks, and kennels, all of which were used in connection with the operation of the dog track. The partnership invested $56,114.56 in equipment for operation of the racetrack, $64,000.71 in improvements to the clubhouse on the corporation's property, $180,327.27 for other new buildings on the corporation's property, and $51,774.93 for kennels on adjacent land owned by the partnership.

The partnership's actions with respect to operation and management of the dog track were eminently successful. During the period from 1955 to 1972, the gross income from track operations increased from $3.6 million to $23.6 million, and the net income to the Collins-Ledoux partnership increased from $72,000 to over $550,000. The increases in gross and net income were attributable to the work of the partnership, including petitioner, and to the general economic growth in the Central Florida area. Accordingly, the fair value of the right to operate the greyhound racetrack in Seminole County, Fla., pursuant to the racing permit held by the corporation and pursuant to the dog track agreement, increased significantly during the period from 1955 to 1972.

After the 1972 racing season two of the partners, Jerry Collins and Jack Collins, decided to purchase petitioner's 25-percent partnership interest. They agreed to allow Ledoux to propose a fair selling price for his interest. Ledoux set a price based on a price-earnings multiple of 5 times his share of the partnership's 1972 earnings. This resulted in a total value for his 25-percent interest of $800,000. There was no valuation or appraisal of specific assets at the time, and the sales price included his interest in all of the assets of the partnership.

At the request of Jerry Collins, petitioner drafted a "Memorandum Agreement," which reflected the arm's-length agreement of the parties. The memorandum was submitted to Jerry Collins and his attorney, and after slight revision, was executed by the parties to the sale on July 19, 1972. It stated, in part, that the "Seller agrees to sell his complete interest in the partnership of Collins, Collins, and Ledoux and to give up all rights, benefits, and obligations of the various agreements involved." It also stated that "In the determination of the purchase price set forth in this agreement, the parties acknowledge no consideration has been given to any item of goodwill."

At the closing, there was no discussion about values of, or allocation to, any specific assets. In fact, no part of the sales price was allocated to any specific partnership asset. At the time of the sale, the partnership assets consisted of an escrow deposit; certain prepaid expenses; a stock investment in Sanford-Seminole Development Co.; investment in land, buildings, and equipment; improvements on the corporation's property used in connection with the operation of the dog track; and rights arising out of the dog track agreement.

On his 1972 Federal income tax return, petitioner properly elected to report the gain from the sale of his partnership interest under the installment method as prescribed in section 453. Petitioner calculated the total gain on such sale to be as follows:

Sales price	$ 800,000.00
Basis in partnership interest	62,658.70
Total gain on sale	737,341.30

During 1972, 1973, and 1974, petitioner received payments in accordance with the October 17, 1972, agreement of sale. In each of those years, he characterized the reported gain, calculated pursuant to the installment sales method, as capital gain.

After consummation of the sale of petitioner's interest in the Collins-Ledoux partnership, the remaining partners continued to operate the dog track under the agreement of July 9, 1955, as amended.

Respondent, in his notice of deficiency, did not disagree with petitioner's calculation of the total gain. However, he determined that $575,392.50 of the gain was related to petitioner's interest in the dog track agreement and should be subject to ordinary income treatment pursuant to section 751.

OPINION

The sole issue presented is whether a portion of the amount received by petitioner on the sale of his 25-percent partnership interest is taxable as ordinary income and not as capital gain. More specifically, we must decide whether any portion of the sales price is attributable to "unrealized receivables" of the partnership.

Generally, gain or loss on the sale or exchange of a partnership interest is treated as capital gain or loss. Sec. 741.

Petitioner contends that the dog track agreement gave the Collins-Ledoux partnership the right to manage and operate the dog track. According to petitioner, the agreement did not give the partnership any contractual rights to receive future payments and did not impose any obligation on the partnership to perform services. Rather, the agreement merely gave the partnership the right to occupy and use all of the corporation's properties (including the racetrack facilities and the racing permit) in operating its dog track business; if the partnership exercised such right, it would be obligated to make annual payments to the corporation based upon specified percentages of the annual mutuel handle. Thus, because the dog track agreement was in the nature of a leasehold agreement rather than an employment contract, it did not create the type of "unrealized receivables" referred to in section 751.

Respondent, on the other hand, contends that the partnership operated the racetrack for the corporation and was paid a portion of the profits for its efforts. As such, the agreement was in the nature of a management employment contract. When petitioner sold his partnership interest to the Collinses in 1972, the main right that he sold was a contract right to receive income in the future for yet-to-be-rendered personal services. This, respondent asserts, is supported by the fact that petitioner determined the sales price for his partnership interest by capitalizing his 1972 annual income (approximately $ 160,000) by a factor of 5. Therefore, respondent contends that the portion of the gain realized by petitioner that is attributable to the management contract should be characterized as an amount received for unrealized receivables of the partnership. Consequently, such gain should be characterized as ordinary income under section 751.

The legislative history is not wholly clear with respect to the types of assets that Congress intended to place under the umbrella of "unrealized receivables." The House report states: "The term 'unrealized receivables or fees' is used to apply to any rights to income which have not been included in gross income under the method of accounting employed by the partnership. The provision is applicable mainly to cash basis partnerships which have acquired a contractual or other legal right to income for goods or services" Essentially the same language appears in the report of the Senate committee. S. Rept. 1622, 83d Cong., 2d Sess. 98 (1954).

In addition, the regulations elaborate on the meaning of "unrealized receivables" as used in section 751. Section 1.751-1(c), Income Tax Regs., provides:

> Sec. 1.751-1(c) *Unrealized receivables*. (1) The term "unrealized receivables", * * * means any rights (contractual or otherwise) to payment for —
>
> (i) Goods delivered or to be delivered (to the extent that such payment would be treated as received for property other than a capital asset), or
>
> (ii) Services rendered or to be rendered, to the extent that income arising from such rights to payment was not previously includible in income under the method of accounting employed by the partnership. Such rights must have arisen under contracts or agreements in existence at the time of sale or distribution, although the partnership may not be able to enforce payment until a later time. For example, the term includes trade accounts receivable of a cash method taxpayer, and rights to payment for work or goods begun but incomplete at the time of the sale or distribution.
>
> (3) In determining the amount of the sale price attributable to such unrealized receivables, or their value in a distribution treated as a sale or exchange, any arm's length agreement between the buyer and the seller, or between the partnership and the distributee partner, will generally establish the amount or value. In the absence of such an agreement, full account shall be taken not only of the estimated cost of completing performance of the contract or agreement, but also of the time between the sale or distribution and the time of payment.

The language of the legislative history and the regulations indicates that the term "unrealized receivables" includes any contractual or other right to payment for goods delivered or to be delivered or services rendered or to be rendered. Therefore, an analysis of the nature of the rights under the dog track agreement, in the context of the aforementioned legal framework, becomes appropriate. A number of cases have dealt with the meaning of "unrealized receivables" and thereby have helped to define the scope of the term. Courts that have considered the term "unrealized receivables" generally have said that it should be given a broad interpretation. Cf. *Corn Products Co. v. Commissioner*, 350 U.S. 46, 52 (1955) (the term "capital asset" is to be construed narrowly, but exclusions from the definition thereof are to be broadly and liberally construed). For instance, in *Logan v. Commissioner*, 51 T.C. 482, 486 (1968), we held that a partnership's right in quantum meruit to payment for work in progress constituted an unrealized receivable even though there was no express agreement between the partnership and its clients requiring payment.

In *Roth v. Commissioner*, 321 F.2d 607 (9th Cir. 1963), aff'g 38 T.C. 171 (1962), the Ninth Circuit dealt with the sale of an interest in a partnership which produced a movie and then gave a 10-year distribution right to Paramount Pictures Corp. in return for a percentage of the gross receipts. The selling partner claimed that his right to a portion of the payments expected under the partnership's contract with Paramount did not constitute an unrealized receivable. The court rejected this view, however, reasoning that Congress "meant to exclude from capital gains treatment any receipts which would have been treated as ordinary income to the partner if no transfer of the partnership interest had occurred." 321 F.2d at 611. Therefore, the partnership's right to payments under the distribution contract was in the nature of an unrealized receivable.

A third example of the broad interpretation given to the term "unrealized receivable" is *United States v. Eidson*, 310 F.2d 111 (5th Cir. 1962), rev'g an unreported opinion (W.D. Tex. 1961). The court there considered the nature of a management contract which was similar to the one at issue in the instant case. The case arose in the context of a sale by a partnership of all of its rights to operate and manage a mutual insurance company. The selling partnership received $170,000 for the rights it held under the management contract, and the Government asserted that the total amount should be treated as ordinary income. The Court of Appeals agreed with the Government's view on the ground that what was being assigned was not a capital asset whose value had accrued over a period of years; rather, the right to operate the company and receive profits therefrom during the remaining life of the contract was the real subject of the assignment. 310 F.2d at 116. The Fifth Circuit found the Supreme Court's holding in *Commissioner v. P. G. Lake, Inc.*, 356 U.S. 260 (1958), to be conclusive:

> The substance of what was assigned was the right to receive future income. The substance of what was received was the present value of income which the recipient would otherwise obtain in the future. In short, consideration was paid for the right to receive future income, not for an increase in the value of the income-producing property.

In *United States v. Woolsey*, 326 F.2d 287 (5th Cir. 1963), rev'g 208 F. Supp. 325 (S.D. Tex. 1962), the Fifth Circuit again faced a situation similar to the one that we face herein. The Fifth Circuit considered whether proceeds received by taxpayers on the sale of their partnership interests were to be treated as ordinary income or capital gain. There, the court was faced with the sale of interests in a partnership which held, as one of its assets, a 25-year contract to manage a mutual insurance company. As in the instant case, the contract gave the partners the right to render services for the term of the contract and to earn ordinary income in the future. In holding that the partnership's management contract constituted an unrealized receivable, the court stated:

When we look at the underlying right assigned in this case, we cannot escape the conclusion that so much of the consideration which relates to the right to earn ordinary income in the future under the "management contract," taxable to the assignee as ordinary income, is likewise taxable to the assignor as ordinary income although such income must be earned. Section 751 has defined "unrealized receivables" to include any rights, contractual or otherwise, to ordinary income from "services rendered, *or to be rendered*," (emphasis added) to the extent that the same were not previously includable in income by the partnership, with the result that capital gains rates cannot be applied to the rights to income under the facts of this case, which would constitute ordinary income had the same been received in due course by the partnership. * * * It is our conclusion that such portion of the consideration received by the taxpayers in this case as properly should be allocated to the present value of their right to earn ordinary income in the future under the "management contract" is subject to taxation as ordinary income.

Petitioner attempts to distinguish *United States v. Woolsey, supra,* and *United States v. Eidson, supra,* from the instant case by arguing that those cases involved a sale or termination of contracts to manage mutual insurance companies in Texas and that the management contracts therein were in the nature of employment agreements. After closely scrutinizing the facts in those cases, we conclude that petitioner's position has no merit. The fact that the *Woolsey* case involved sale of 100 percent of the partnership interests, as opposed to a sale of only a 25-percent partnership interest herein, is of no consequence. In addition, the fact that *Eidson* involved the surrender of the partnership's contract right to manage the insurance company, as opposed to the continued partnership operation in the instant case, also is not a material factual distinction.

The dog track agreement at issue in the instant case is similar to the management contract considered by the Fifth Circuit in *Woolsey*. Each gives the respective partnership the right to operate a business for a period of years and to earn ordinary income in return for payments of specified amounts to the corporation that holds the State charter. Therefore, based on our analysis of the statutory language, the legislative history, and the regulations and relevant case law, we are compelled to find that the dog track agreement gave the petitioner an interest that amounted to an "unrealized receivable" within the meaning of section 751(c).

Petitioner further contends that the dog track agreement does not represent an unrealized receivable because it does not require or obligate the partnership to perform personal services in the future. The agreement only gives, the argument continues, the Collins-Ledoux partnership the right to engage in a business.

We find this argument to be unpersuasive. The words of section 751(c), providing that the term "unrealized receivable" includes the right to payment for "services rendered, or to be rendered," do not preclude that section's application to a situation where, as here, the performance of services is not required by the agreement. As the Fifth Circuit said in *United States v. Eidson, supra*:

The fact that * * * income would not be received by the [partnership] unless they performed the services which the contract required of them, that is, actively managed the affairs of the insurance company in a manner that would produce a profit after all of the necessary expenditures, does not, it seems clear, affect the nature of this payment. It affects only the amount. That is, the fact that the taxpayers would have to spend their time and energies in performing services for which the compensation would be received merely affects the price at which they would be willing to assign or transfer the contract.

Consequently, a portion of the consideration received by Ledoux on the sale of his partnership interest is subject to taxation as ordinary income.

Having established that the dog track agreement qualifies as an unrealized receivable, we next consider whether all or only part of petitioner's gain in excess of the amount attributable to his share of tangible partnership assets should be treated as ordinary income. Petitioner argues that this excess gain was attributable to goodwill or the value of a going concern.

With respect to goodwill, we note that petitioner's attorney drafted, and petitioner signed, the agreement for sale of partnership interest, dated October 17, 1972, which contains the following statement in paragraph 7:

> 7. In the determination of the purchase price set forth in this agreement, the parties acknowledge no consideration has been given to any item of goodwill.

The meaning of the words "no consideration" is not entirely free from doubt. They could mean that no thought was given to an allocation of any of the sales price to goodwill, or they could indicate that the parties agreed that no part of the purchase price was allocated to goodwill. The testimony of the attorney who prepared the document indicates, however, that he did consider the implications of the sale of goodwill and even did research on the subject. He testified that he believed, albeit incorrectly, that, if goodwill were part of the purchase price, his client would not be entitled to capital gains treatment.

Petitioner attempts to justify this misstatement of the tax implications of an allocation to goodwill not by asserting mistake, but by pointing out that his attorney "is not a tax lawyer but is primarily involved with commercial law and real estate." We find as a fact that petitioner agreed at arm's length with the purchasers of his partnership interest that no part of the purchase price should be attributable to goodwill. The Tax Court long has adhered to the view that, absent "strong proof," a taxpayer cannot challenge an express allocation in an arm's-length sales contract to which he had agreed. . . . In *Spector v. Commissioner*, 641 F.2d 376 (5th Cir. 1981), revg. 71 T.C. 1017 (1979), the Fifth Circuit, to which an appeal in this case will lie, appeared to step away from its prior adherence to the "strong proof" standard and move toward the stricter standard enunciated in *Commissioner v. Danielson*, 378 F.2d 771, 775 (3d Cir. 1967), remanding 44 T.C. 549 (1965), cert. denied 389 U.S. 858 (1967). However, in this case, we need not measure the length of the step since we hold that petitioner has failed to introduce sufficient evidence to satisfy even the more lenient "strong proof" standard.

We next turn to petitioner's contention that part or all of the purchase price received in excess of the value of tangible assets is attributable to value of a going concern. In *VGS Corp. v. Commissioner*, 68 T.C. 563 (1977), we stated that —

> Going-concern value is, in essence, the additional element of value which attaches to property by reason of its existence as an integral part of a going concern. * * * [The] ability of a business to continue to function and generate income without interruption as a consequence of the change in ownership, is a vital part of the value of a going concern. * * * [68 T.C. at 591–592; citations omitted.]

However, in the instant case, the ability of the dog racing track to continue to function after the sale of Ledoux's partnership interest was due to the remaining partners' retention of rights to operate under the dog track agreement. Without such agreement, there would have been no continuing right to operate a business and no right to continue to earn income. Thus, the amount paid in excess of the value of Ledoux's share of the tangible assets was not for the intangible value of the business as a going concern but rather for Ledoux's rights under the dog track agreement.

Finally, we turn to petitioner's claim that a determination of the value of rights arising from the dog track agreement has never been made and no evidence of the value of such rights was submitted in this case. We note that the $ 800,000 purchase price was proposed by petitioner and was accepted by Jack Collins and Jerry Collins in an arm's-length agreement of sale evidenced in the memorandum of agreement of July 19, 1972, and the agreement for sale of partnership interest of October 17, 1972. In addition, the October 17, 1972, sales agreement, written by petitioner's attorney, provided in paragraph 1 that the "Seller [Ledoux] sells to buyer [Jerry Collins and Jack Collins] all of his interest in [the partnership] * * * including but not limited to, *the seller's right to income* and to acquire the capital stock of The Sanford-Orlando Kennel Club, Inc." (Emphasis added.) Section 1.751-1(c)(3), Income Tax Regs., provides that an arm's-length agreement between the buyer and the seller generally will establish the value attributable to unrealized receivables.

Based on the provision in the agreement that no part of the consideration was attributable to goodwill, it is clear to us that the parties were aware that they could, if they so desired, have provided that no part of the consideration was attributable to the dog track agreement. No such provision was made. Furthermore, the agreement clearly stated that one of the assets purchased was Ledoux's rights to future income. Considering that petitioner calculated the purchase price by capitalizing future earnings expected under the dog track agreement, we conclude that the portion of Ledoux's gain in excess of the amount attributable to tangible assets was attributable to an unrealized receivable as reflected by the dog track agreement.

Decision will be entered for the respondent.

PART B:
THE VARYING INTERESTS RULE

I. PROBLEMS

JKL is a cash method calendar year partnership, consisting of equal partners A, B, C, and D. Over the course of Year 1, JKL earned a total of $120,000 of ordinary income, incurred $74,000 of ordinary deductions, earned $60,000 of capital gains, and sustained $30,000 of capital losses. During the first three months of the year (January 1 through March 31), JKL earned $60,000 of ordinary income, incurred $24,000 of ordinary deductions, earned $40,000 of capital gains, and sustained $5,000 of capital losses. During the next six months (April 1 through September 30), JKL earned $90,000 of ordinary income, incurred $39,000 of ordinary deductions, earned $20,000 of capital gains, and sustained $10,000 of capital losses. In the last three months of the year (October 1 through December 31), JKL earned $50,000 of ordinary income, incurred $11,000 of ordinary deductions, and sustained $15,000 of capital losses. None of the partnership items is an extraordinary item. Assume capital is a material income-producing factor for JKL. Assume that JKL uses the monthly convention and does not perform optional regular monthly or semi-monthly closings. On April 1, A sells her partnership interest to new partner E. On September 24, B sells half his partnership interest to new partner F.

(a) If JKL uses the proration method with respect to the April 1 sale and the interim closing method with respect to the September 24 sale, what are A's and B's distributive shares of partnership items for the year?

(b) Would the answer to Problem 1 change if JKL uses the interim closing method with respect to the April 1 sale and the proration method with respect to the September 24 sale?

(c) If, on February 5, JKL sustains a $40,000 capital loss that constitutes an extraordinary item, how would that capital loss be allocated? Assume the small item exception does not apply.

(d) If, on September 30, JKL makes a payment for the use of property that is attributable to the period from January 1 through August 31, how would that expense be allocated? Assume the de minimis exception for allocable cash basis items does not apply.

Assignment for Part B, Chapter 20:

Complete the Problems.

Read: Internal Revenue Code: § 706(d)(1), (2).
Treasury Regulations: § 1.706-4. Prop. Reg. § 1.706-2.
Materials: Overview

II. VOCABULARY

varying interests rule
variation date
interim closing method
proration method
segment
proration period
calendar-day, monthly, and semi-monthly conventions
contemporaneous partners
extraordinary item
small item exception
allocable cash basis item
de minimis exception for allocable cash basis items

III. OBJECTIVES

1. To determine the variation dates and deemed variation dates.
2. To determine the segments in a partnership's taxable year.
3. To determine the proration periods in a partnership's taxable year.
4. To apply the interim closing method.
5. To apply the proration method.
6. To determine the allocation of partnership items in accordance with a partner's varying interests in the partnership.
7. To identify and allocate extraordinary items.
8. To identify allocable cash basis items and allocate appropriate portions to each day in the period to which they are attributable.

IV. OVERVIEW

A partner's interest in a partnership may change during the course of the partnership's tax year. For example, as in Part A of this chapter, the interest may change because of the sale or exchange of a partnership interest: the purchaser becomes a member of the partnership, or perhaps increases her pre-existing interest in the partnership; the seller is no longer a member of the partnership, or perhaps simply decreases his interest in the partnership. But a change in a partner's interest during the course of the year may occur for other reasons as well: a new partner can make a contribution and become a member of the partnership, diluting the interests of the pre-existing partners; or an existing partner can make an additional contribution (or receive a distribution) that thereby increases (or thereby decreases) his interest in the partnership relative to the other partners. How should partnership income, gain, losses, deductions and credits — i.e., partnership items — be allocated among the partners where the interests of one or more have them has changed — i.e., have varied — over the course of the year? Do the partners, by amending the partnership agreement, have the flexibility to allocate partnership items for the year in whatever manner they wish, regardless of the variations in interests that have occurred? Indeed, taken to an extreme, may a calendar year partnership allocate, for example, a full year's losses or deductions to a partner who joined the partnership on December 31? As you have undoubtedly already guessed, the answer to these latter questions is "No."

A. Varying Interests: The General Rule

> **§ 706(d). Determination of Distributive Share When Partner's Interest Changes**
>
> (1) **In General** — Except as provided in paragraphs (2) and (3), if during any taxable year of the partnership there is a change in any partner's interest in the partnership, each partner's distributive share of any item of income, gain, loss, deduction, or credit of the partnership for such taxable year shall be determined by the use of any method prescribed by the Secretary by regulations which takes into account the varying interests of the partners in the partnership during such taxable year.

Under the general rule of § 706(d)(1), whenever there is a change in any partner's interest in the partnership during the partnership's taxable year, each partner's distributive share of partnership items must be determined by a prescribed method "which takes into account the varying interests of the partners in the partnership during such taxable year." As indicated above, the variation can occur for many different reasons, and the operation of the varying interests rule does not depend on whether it occurred by reason of a sale of all or part of a partner's interest or otherwise. Nonetheless, let us assume that partner A, one of three equal partners in ABC, a calendar year partnership, sells his interest to D on June 30, and that there are no further variations in interests for the remainder of the year. The general rule of § 706(d)(1) requires the distributive shares of partnership items allocated to A and D take into account that A was a one-third partner for the first six months of the year, and that D was a one-third partner for the remainder of the year.

B. Allocating Distributive Shares

When a partner's interest in a partnership varies during the partnership's tax year, the partner's distributive share of partnership items must generally be determined under either the "*interim closing method*," under which there is an interim closing of the partnership's books and an allocation of partnership items based on the interests of the partners at the time of the interim closing; or the "*proration method*," under which the partnership items are prorated over the period to which the proration applies. The interim closing method is the "default method"; the proration method can be used only if the partners, through the partnership agreement, so choose. Otherwise, the interim closing method is used. Reg. § 1.706-4(a)(3)(iii). Note that so-called "extraordinary items," discussed *infra*, may not be prorated. Reg. § 1.706-4(e)(1).

Assume, for example, that A, a partner in ABCDE, a calendar year partnership, all of whose partners have equal interests, sells her interest to F on August 25. Assume there are no other variations in interests during the year and assume ABCDE has no extraordinary items. Under the interim closing method, there is an interim closing of the partnership books on August 25, and A's distributive share of partnership items is determined based upon that closing. In contrast, if the partners agree to use of the proration method, then A's distributive share would be determined by prorating through August 25 the partnership items for the full year.

Use of the interim closing method creates a "segment." Reg. § 1.706-4(a)(4)(vi). If there are multiple interim closings during the year, then multiple segments are created, each one beginning immediately after the previous interim closing and ending at the time of the next interim closing. If there are no interim closings during the year, the partnership has only one segment — i.e., a segment that consists of the entire tax year of the partnership, beginning on the first day of the year and ending on the last day of the year. (Note there may be no interim closings during the year because there have been no variations in any partner's interest during the year; even if there have been variations in partners' interests, the partners may have elected to use the proration method with respect to all the variations, in which case there would similarly be no interim closings during the year.)

Let's return to ABCDE and A's sale of her interest in the partnership to F on August 25. The sale to F creates a change in A's interest in the partnership — and a change in F's as well. Under the interim closing method, the first segment of the year would begin on January 1 and end on the close of the day on August 25. The second segment would begin on August 26 and end on the close of the day on December 31. If the partners chose the proration method, there would be just the one segment: January 1 through December 31.

"Proration periods" are the portions of a segment created by a variation in a partner's interest, with respect to which the partners choose to apply the proration method. Reg. § 1.706-4(a)(3)(viii). In the immediately preceding example, if the only variation in interests occurred on the August 25 sale, and the partners chose the proration method, the segment and also the proration period would be the entire tax year of the partnership.

There may, of course, be multiple sales of partnership interests during the year, each creating a variation in interests and each, potentially at least, but not necessarily, creating a segment. Returning again to ABCDE, assume as before that A sells her interest in the partnership to F on August 25, and, in addition, assume B sells his interest to G on October 29. If the interim closing method applies with respect to both sales, three segments have been created: January 1 to August 25; August 26 to October 29; and October 30 to December 31. If the proration method is used for both sales — i.e., for both variations — there is only one segment, January 1 to December 31. May the partnership, however, elect the proration method with respect to one variation, but not the other? The answer is "Yes." Reg. § 1.706-4(a)(3)(iii). (The same regulation, however, indicates that future published guidance may place restrictions on the use of different methods. We will assume that no such restrictions apply to the ABCDE partnership.) If the proration method is agreed upon with respect to the August 25 sale, but not the October 29 sale, the first segment runs from January 1 to October 29; the second segment runs from October 30 to December 31. The interim closing on October 29 determines the amount of partnership items allocable to the first segment of the partnership year, January 1 to October 29. The remaining partnership items for the year will be those partnership items allocable to the second segment, the period from October 30 to December 31.

The first proration period within the first segment extends from January 1 to August 25, when the first variation within the first segment occurs. The second proration period within the first segment extends from August 26 to October 29, when the second variation occurs. Reg. § 1.706-4(a)(3)(viii). Under our assumptions regarding the two sales, the second variation results in an interim closing of the books on October 29. ABCDE will accordingly prorate, over the period January 1 to October 29, its partnership items for that period as determined pursuant to the interim closing on October 29. Because A is a 20% partner from January 1 to August 25, A is allocated 20% of each item for the first proration period; and B, C, D, and E are also each allocated 20% of each item for that first period. During the second proration period, from August 26 to October 29, partners B, C, D, E, and F are each 20% partners, and each will be allocated 20% of each partnership item for that second proration period. For the second segment, the period from October 30–December 31, partners C, D, E, F, and G had 20% interests, so each will be allocated 20% of each partnership item for the second segment.

In the foregoing example, the dates of the sales — the variation dates — were the dates on which the sales actually occurred, August 25 and October 29. The regulations, however, authorize the partnerships to select conventions under which variations are deemed to occur on dates other than the ones on which they actually occurred. Pursuant to Reg. § 1.706-4(c)(1), partnerships are generally permitted to choose from three conventions: (1) Under the *calendar-day convention*, the variation is deemed to occur at the end of the calendar day on which it occurs; (2) Under the *semi-monthly convention*, if a variation occurs on the first through the fifteenth day of a month, it is deemed to occur on the last day of the preceding month; if the variation occurs on the sixteenth through the last day of a month, it is deemed to occur at the end of the fifteenth day of the month; and (3) Under the *monthly convention*, if a variation occurs on the first through the fifteenth day of the month, it is deemed to occur on the last day of the preceding month; if the variation occurs on the sixteenth through the last day of the month, it is deemed to occur at the end of the last day of the month. Recall in our example that the sales occurred on August 25 and October 29. Under the semi-monthly convention, each sale would be deemed to occur at the end of the fifteenth day of the month. Under the monthly convention, each sale would be deemed to have occurred at the end of the last day of the month.

Under the regulations, partnership generally can use the calendar-day convention for each variation. For all variations for which the partnership uses the interim closing method, however, it may, by agreement of the partners, use the semi-monthly or monthly convention instead of the calendar-day convention. Thus, a partnership cannot use the semi-monthly or monthly convention when it uses the proration method. Instead, it must use the calendar-day convention. A partnership using the semi-monthly or monthly convention with the interim closing method must use the same convention for all variations to which the interim closing method applies. Reg. § 1.706-4(c)(3)(i). Finally, by agreement of the partners, and as an optional matter, a partnership may perform regular monthly or semi-monthly interim closings of its books, even though no variation occurs. Reg. § 1.706-4(d)(1).

C. Exceptions to the Varying Interest Allocation Rules

The regulations provide two exceptions to the varying interest allocation rules described above. First, there is an exception for "permissible changes among contemporaneous partners." Reg. § 1.706-4(b)(1). Under this exception, the varying interest rule does not apply to changes in the allocations of partnership items "among contemporaneous partners for the entire partnership year (or any contemporaneous partners for a segment if the item is entirely attributable to a segment)" so long as the variation in the interest is not attributable to contributions (or distributions) of money or property and the allocations satisfy § 704(b). Thus, contemporaneous partners can vary allocations among themselves through amendments to the partnership agreement as long as the allocations satisfy § 704(b) and are not attributable to capital contributions or distributions.

Under a second exception to the varying interest allocation rules described above, there is a "safe harbor for partnerships for which capital is not a material income-producing factor." Reg. § 1.706-4(b)(2). Under this safe harbor, service partnerships are permitted to take account of varying interests during the year by using "any reasonable method" to determine a partner's share of partnership items, provided the allocations satisfy § 704(b).

D. Extraordinary Items

The regulations create a special category of partnership items called "extraordinary items," which generally are not eligible for proration and which must be allocated "among the partners in proportion to their interests in the partnership item at the time of day the extraordinary item occurred," regardless of allocation method or convention otherwise used. Reg. § 1.706-4(e)(1). An extraordinary item is an exception to the use of conventions. It is also an exception to the proration method, and it generally cannot be allocated under that method across the segment in which it occurs.

There are 11 classes of extraordinary items created by the regulations. Reg. § 1.706-4(e)(2)(i)–(xi). Included among the 11 classes are: (1) Any item from the disposition (other than in the ordinary course of business) of a capital asset; (2) Any item from the disposition (other than in the ordinary course of business) of property used in the taxpayer's trade or business within the meaning of § 1231(b), regardless of holding period; (3) Any item from the settlement of a tort or similar third-party liability or payment of a judgment; and (4) Any item which, if ratably allocated, would result in a substantial distortion of income for any return in which it is included.

Nonetheless, the regulations carve out a "small item exception" from the general definition of extraordinary items. Under the small item exception, a partnership may treat what would otherwise be an extraordinary item as other than an extraordinary item, provided the total of all items in the particular class of extraordinary items (for example, the capital asset class noted above) is less than 5% of partnership gross income or gross expenses and losses, and the total of all extraordinary items from all classes of extraordinary items amounting to less than 5% of gross income or expenses and losses does not exceed $10,000,000. Reg. § 1.706-4(e)(3). This small item exception makes it possible to have what would otherwise be extraordinary items treated instead under the normal allocation methods and conventions.

E. The Ten-Step Allocation Process

The regulations direct partnerships to follow a 10-step process in determining the allocation of partnership items subject to the varying interest rule, and they illustrate this process with an example we will also use:

Facts: Assume PRS is a calendar-year partnership with three equal partners, A, B, and C. Partner A sells half of its interest (i.e., one-sixth of the partnership) to D on April 16, which date becomes the first variation date. Partner B sells half of its interest (i.e., again, one-sixth of the partnership) to E on August 6, which becomes the second variation date. The partnership has no extraordinary items. The partnership is not a service partnership and thus must use the interim closing method or proration method; it cannot use "any reasonable method," as service partnerships may. The partners agree to use the proration method for the April 16 variation, but do not agree to the proration method for the August 6 variation, which therefore must use the interim closing method (the "default method"). Because the proration method applies to the April 16 variation, the partnership must use the calendar-day convention. Because the interim closing method applies to the August 6 variation, the partnership may use the monthly or semi-monthly convention if it wishes — assume it applies the semi-monthly convention.

Finally, assume PRS has partnership items for the year as follows: $75,000 of ordinary income, $33,000 of ordinary deductions, $12,000 of capital gains in the ordinary course of business, and $9,000 of capital losses in the ordinary course of business. Within the year, for the period January 1–July 31, PRS has $60,000 of ordinary income, $24,000 of ordinary deductions, $12,000 of capital gains in the ordinary course of business, and $6,000 of capital losses in the ordinary course of business. For the period August 1–December 31, PRS has $15,000 of ordinary income, $9,000 of ordinary deductions, and $3,000 of capital losses in the ordinary course of business.

The Analysis under the 10-Step Process: The 10 steps are as follows.

1. Determine whether there are exceptions to the varying interests that apply. In this case, no exceptions apply: (1) PRS is not a service partnership; and (2) neither of the year's variations is the result of a change in allocations among contemporaneous partners.

2. Determine whether there are any extraordinary items. The facts state that there are none.

3. Determine the methods that apply to each variation. Here, the proration method applies to the first variation; the interim closing method applies to the second.

4. Determine the deemed date of each variation under the selected convention. Under the proration method, the calendar-day convention applies to the April 16 variation; the deemed date of the variation is thus the end of the day on April 16. PRS has selected the application of the semi-monthly convention to the August 6 variation. Under that convention, the deemed date of the variation is the end of the day on July 31, the last day of the preceding month.

5. Determine whether the partnership elects to perform the optional regular monthly or semi-monthly interim closings. Here, PRS does not so elect, so the only interim closing in this case occurs on the deemed variation date of July 31.

6. Determine the segments for the year. Here the first segment is from January 1 to July 31. The second segment is from August 1 to December 31.

7. Determine the items allocable to each segment. Here, the items allocable to the January 1 to July 31 segment are $60,000 of ordinary income; $24,000 of ordinary deductions; $12,000 of capital gains; and $6,000 of capital losses. The items allocable to the August 1 to December 31 segment are $15,000 of ordinary income; $9,000 of ordinary deductions; and $3,000 of capital losses.

8. Determine the proration periods. Here, the first proration period begins January 1 and ends on the end of the day April 16, when the first variation takes place. The second proration period begins April 17 and ends on the end of the day July 31, which is the end of the first segment.

9. Prorate the partnership items among the proration periods. Here, each proration period has an equal number of days, 106. Accordingly, 50% of each item from the first segment is allocated to each proration period. Therefore, $30,000 of ordinary income, $12,000 of ordinary deductions, $6,000 of capital gains, and $3,000 of capital losses are allocated to each of the two proration periods.

10. Determine each partner's share of partnership items in each segment and proration period. Here, during the first proration period (January 1 to April 16), each of the three partners A, B, and C, are allocated one-third of the ordinary income ($10,000 each), ordinary deductions ($4,000 each), capital gains ($2,000 each), and capital losses ($1,000 each). During the second proration period (April 17 to July 31), partners A and D have one-sixth interests, and partners B and C have one-third interests. Accordingly, A and D are allocated one-sixth of the ordinary income ($5,000 each), ordinary deductions ($2,000 each), capital gains ($1,000 each), and capital losses ($500 each). Partners B and C are allocated one-third of the ordinary income ($10,000 each), ordinary deductions ($4,000 each), capital gains ($2,000 each), and capital losses ($1,000 each). For the second segment (August 1 to December 31), partners A, B, D, and E have

one-sixth interests, and partner C has a one-third interest. The partnership items allocable to the second segment are $15,000 of ordinary income, $9,000 of ordinary deductions, and $3,000 of capital losses. Accordingly, the one-sixth interests of A, B, D, and E result in allocations of ordinary income ($2,500 each), ordinary deductions ($1,500 each), and capital losses ($500 each). One-third partner C is allocated ordinary income ($5,000), ordinary deductions ($3,000), and capital losses ($1,000).

For the full year, A's allocations are $17,500 of ordinary income, $7,500 of ordinary deductions, $3,000 of capital gains, and $2,000 of capital losses. B's allocations are $22,500 of ordinary income, $9,500 of ordinary deductions, $4,000 of capital gains, and $2,500 of capital losses. C's allocations are $25,000 of ordinary income, $11,000 of ordinary deductions, $4,000 of capital gains, and $3,000 of capital losses. D's allocations are $7,500 of ordinary income, $3,500 of ordinary deductions, $1,000 of capital gains, and $1,000 of capital losses. E's allocations are $2,500 of ordinary income, $1,500 of ordinary deductions, and $500 of capital losses.

F. Allocable Cash Basis Items

Section 706(d)(2)(A) provides special allocation rules for "allocable cash basis items," including interest, taxes, payments for the use of property or services,[38] and other items specified in regulations. § 706(d)(2)(B).[39] Proposed regulations add to the list deductions previously deferred under § 267(a)(2) and any deduction, loss, income, or gain item "that accrues over time and that would, if not allocated as an allocable cash basis item, result in the significant misstatement of a partner's income." Prop. Reg. § 1.706-2(a)(2)(iv), (v).

In determining a partner's distributive share of any allocable cash basis item, an "appropriate portion" of the item must be assigned to each day in the period to which it is attributable, and the portion so assigned must be allocated among the partners in proportion to their interests in the partnership at the close of each day. § 706(d)(2)(A). The particular concern this rule addresses is that, without the rule, partnerships "might attempt to avoid the retroactive allocation rules by using the cash method, . . . deferring payment of deductible items until near the close of the partnership's taxable year . . . [and then using] the interim closing method" to accomplish, in substance, a retroactive allocation to a partner newly admitted at the time the deferred payment is made. H.R. Rep. No. 98-432, at 1212–1213 (1984).

Assume, for example, that a $12,000 interest expense is paid by the PRS partnership, a cash method calendar-year partnership, on December 1 of Year 1 (a non-leap year). Assume the interest expense is attributable to every day in the partnership's taxable year, and further assume the de minimis exception discussed below does not apply. If A, B, and C are equal one-third partners in PRS, and A sells her interest in PRS to D on July 1, Year 1, then A is a partner in PRS for 181 days of Year 1, and is entitled under § 706(d)(2)(A) to 181/365 of her otherwise

---

[38] The proposed regulations exclude deductions for the transfer of partnership interests in connection with the performance of services. Prop. Reg. § 1.706-2(a)(2)(iii).

[39] There is also a special rule for items attributable to interests in lower tier partnerships, a rule beyond the scope of this chapter. § 706(d)(3).

allocable share of the interest expense. Partner D is entitled to 184/365 of his otherwise allocable share of the interest expense. Accordingly, partners B and C are each entitled to allocations of $4,000 of the $12,000 interest expense, A is entitled to a $1,983.56 allocation ($4,000 x 181/365), and D is entitled to a $2,016.44 allocation ($4,000 x 184/365). See Prop. Reg. § 1.706-2(b) Ex. 1, from which this example is drawn.

Special allocation rules apply to any portion of an allocable cash basis item attributable to a period not within the taxable year of payment. If any portion is attributable to a period after the close of the taxable year of payment, that portion will be assigned to the last day of the taxable year. § 706(d)(2)(C)(ii). Conversely, if any portion is attributable to a period before the beginning of the taxable year, it is assigned to the first day of the taxable year and allocated among persons who are partners in the partnership during the period to which the payment is attributable, in accordance with their varying interests over the period. Any amount so allocated to a person who is not a partner on the first day of the taxable year shall be capitalized and allocated among partnership properties under the principles of § 755. § 706(d)(2)(C)(i), (D). Assume, for example, that A, B, and C are equal partners in cash method calendar-year partnership PRS, and that A sells her interest to D on December 31, Year 1. Further assume PRS makes a $6,000 payment in November, Year 2, for the use of property attributable to all of Year 1 and all of Year 2. Assume the de minimis exception discussed below does not apply, and that the $6,000 payment must be allocated under the foregoing rules of § 706(d)(2). Under the rules, half of the $6,000 payment, made in Year 2, is allocable to Year 1. The $3,000 portion allocable to Year 1 must therefore be assigned to the first day of Year 2 to partners A, B, and C, the partners during Year 1. Because A is not a partner in Year 2, however, her $1,000 share of the $3,000 expense must be capitalized and treated as a § 743(b) adjustment for D's benefit, allocable among PRS assets under § 755 principles. *See* Prop. Reg. § 1.706-2(b) Ex. 2, from which this example is drawn. Partners B and C are each allocated $1,000 shares of the $3,000 expense allocable to Year 1. (Of the $6,000 payment, $3,000 is allocable to Year 2 and is allocated equally, in $1,000 amounts, to partners B, C, and D, the Year 2 partners.)

The De Minimis Exception. The proposed regulations for allocable cash basis items create a de minimis exception. Under that exception, any allocable cash basis item will not be subject to the allocable cash basis rules of § 706(d)(2) if: (1) the total amount of any particular class of allocable cash basis items is less than 5% of partnership income and of expenses and losses, and (2) the total amount of allocable cash basis items amounting to less than 5% of partnership income and of expenses and losses does not exceed $10,000,000. Prop. Reg. § 1.706-(2)(c).

PART C:
THE DEATH OF A PARTNER

I. PROBLEMS

1. Maureen is a one-quarter partner in the JKLM partnership. JKLM and its partners all use the cash method and the calendar year. JKLM earns $7,000 in January and $1,000 per month per month the remaining months of the year. Maureen dies on July 1 of the current year. How much income will Maureen's executor report on her final return?

2. Doris is a one-quarter partner in the ABCD partnership, a services partnership, which uses the cash method and the calendar year, as do all the partners. The balance sheet of the partnership is as follows at Doris's death on January 1:

	Partnership Assets			Liabilities and Partners' Capital	
	A/B	FMV		A/B	FMV
			Liabilities		$100
Cash	$280	$280	Ann	$220	$400
Accounts Receivable	$0	$260	Bill	$220	$400
Equipment	$220	$420	Charles	$220	$400
Capital Asset	$340	$480	Doris	$220	$400
Installment Obligation	$40	$60			
Goodwill	$0	$200			
Total	$880	$1,700		$880	$1,700

ABCD has not made a § 754 election. The difference between the adjusted basis and the value of the equipment is § 1245 gain. The installment obligation represents the partnership's sale of a capital asset.

   (a) Assume Doris' partnership interest is sold by her estate to the remaining partners for $425 under a pre-existing buy-sell agreement. Partnership goodwill is unstated. The remaining partners pay the estate $400 in cash and assume Doris' $25 share of the partnership's liability. What are the tax consequences to Doris' estate?

   (b) Assume the facts of (a), except Doris' estate does not sell the interest to the remaining partners, but instead, under a pre-existing buy-sell agreement, receives a liquidating distribution of $400 in cash, and the remaining partners assume Doris' $25 share of the partnership's liability. What are the tax consequences to the estate?

   (c) Does the answer to (b) change if the goodwill is stated rather than unstated?

   (d) Assume Doris' daughter Diana succeeds to her interest and there is no sale or liquidation of the interest. Does it matter to Diana if a § 754 election is in effect?

Assignment for Part C, Chapter 20:

Complete the Problems

Read: Internal Revenue Code: §§ 443(a)(2); 691(a)(1), (a)(4), (c); 704(c)(1)(C); 706(c)(1),(c)(2)(A); 736(a), (b); 751(c); 753; 1014(a)(1), (b)(1), (b)(6), (c); Skim §§ 743(b), (d); 751(b); 754.
Treasury Regulations: §§ 1.691(a)-(1)(b); 1.691(a)-2(b) Exs. 1 and 5, 1.691(a)-3(a); 1.742-1; 1.753-1. Skim §§ 1.743-1(b); 1.755-1(b)(4)(I).

Materials: Overview

II. VOCABULARY

decedent's final return
interim closing of partnership books
proration of distributive share
statutory income in respect of decedent (IRD)
judicially created income in respect of a decedent (IRD)
date of death basis
successor in interest
buy-sell agreement
installment receivables
stated and unstated goodwill
§ 743(b) adjustment

III. OBJECTIVES

1. To recall the partnership year closes with respect to a partner upon the death of that partner.

2. To determine the distributive share of partnership items for a deceased partner in the year of death.

3. To determine the adjusted basis of a partnership interest acquired from a decedent.

4. To determine amounts of items of income included on the decedent's final return.

5. To determine the partnership items and payments that constitute income in respect of a decedent.

6. To determine the tax consequences of a liquidating distribution to a decedent's successor in interest and the tax consequences of the successor's sale or retention of the deceased partner's partnership interest.

IV. OVERVIEW

This part focuses on selected tax issues arising out of the death of a partner.

A. Closing of Partnership Taxable Year

Under § 706(c)(2)(A), the partnership's taxable year closes with respect to a partner upon the death of that partner. The closing of the tax year with respect to the deceased partner means the partner's distributive share of partnership items of income and loss through the date of death will be reported on the decedent's final return. Prior to the enactment of § 706(c)(2)(A) in 1998, the partnership tax year did not close with respect to the partner upon death. As a result, the decedent's share of partnership income and loss for the entire partnership year was typically reported on the fiduciary's (executor's) 1041 return for the first tax year after the decedent's death. By way of illustration of the difference, assume Mary, a partner in the MNO Partnership, dies on December 1, and the taxable year is the calendar year for both Mary and the partnership. (As discussed in Chapter 6, pursuant to § 706(b)(1), it will indeed be the norm for most partners and partnerships to report on the calendar year.) Under prior law, Mary's share of income and loss for the entire year would wind up being reported on her fiduciary's (executor's) 1041 return for her estate for the period December 1 through December 31 (assuming the estate adopted the calendar year as well).[40] Under current § 706(c)(2)(A), however, Mary's distributive share for January 1 through November 30 would be reported on her final tax return. Her estate would report the distributive share for the period December 1 through December 31 on the fiduciary's (executor's) 1041 return. The determination of the distributive shares for the periods involved would be determined by an interim closing of the books or, if the partners all agreed, by a reasonable proration of the shares, as discussed in Part B above dealing with the varying interests of partners during a partnership taxable year. *See* Reg. § 1.706-1(c)(2)(ii).

B. Basis, Income in Respect of a Decedent, and their Interaction

Chapter 17 discussed the central role of § 736(a) and § 736(b) in determining the tax consequences on the liquidation of a partner's interest through retirement. Section 736 often has a similar role to play on the death of a partner, but we will begin instead with special rules relating to determination of basis and to income in respect of a decedent (IRD).

On the death of a partner, the basis of the partner's partnership interest will step-up (or step-down) to its fair market value on the partner's date of death (or alternate valuation date) under the usual rules of § 1014(a)(1). (See § 1014(f) imposing a basis consistency rule.) But § 1014(c) excepts from step-up "property which constitutes a right to receive an item of income in respect of a decedent under section 691." Such property, in other words, retains its pre-date-of-death basis. What property constitutes IRD? Section 691 does not define the term. Instead, it directs that "all items of gross income in respect of a decedent which are

---

[40] The pre-1998 treatment avoided income-bunching of more than 12 months' income on the decedent's final return where the decedent and the partnership had different taxable years, a concern that tended to become moot because a partnership generally must adopt the tax year of its majority partner or all its principal partners. § 706(b)(1)(B).

not properly includible" in the decedent's income as of the date of death, shall be included upon receipt in the income of the decedent's estate or other successor. § 691(a)(1). Thus, it is the decedent's successor in interest who will be taxed on the IRD on receipt.

The regulations suggest, as two important examples of items of IRD, salary earned but unpaid as of decedent's death, and the gain on property sold before death when payment had not been received before death. Reg. § 1.691(a)-2(b) Exs. 1 and 5. The reason for the denial of basis step-up is obvious: if the unpaid salary or unpaid sales proceeds received a basis step-up to fair market value, the salary and the gain on the sale would go entirely untaxed on account of an accounting method — the cash method — postponing recognition of income until receipt, in contrast to the accrual method taxing the salary upon earning and the sales income upon consummation of the sale. Thus, the salary and the gain on the sale, not being reportable as of decedent's death, will not receive a step-up in basis and, therefore, will be taxed to decedent's estate or other successor upon receipt.[41]

In the context of a partnership, a common type of IRD for a cash method partnership will be accounts receivable for partnership services rendered, but unpaid, as of decedent's death. Assume, for example, Donald is a partner with a one-third partner in BCD, a law partnership, and that at Donald's death the partnership assets consist of cash of $60; zero-basis accounts receivable of $90 (with a value of $90); and land worth $150 (with an adjusted basis of $75). The value of Donald's partnership interest is thus $100 (based on $300 in partnership assets with Donald as a one-third partner). Assume Donald's basis in his partnership interest is $45.

If the basis of Donald's interest were stepped-up at his death to its fair market value of $100, Donald's successor might not be taxed either on the partnership's collection of the receivables or the hypothetical sale of the land at its date of death value. Specifically, if there were a basis step-up to $100, and if a § 754 election were in place, Donald's successor would have the benefit of an inside basis adjustment for the receivables and the land, eliminating income for the successor on partnership collection or sale. With a basis step-up, but without the § 754 election, there would not be an inside basis adjustment, and Donald's successor would be allocated a one-third share of the income on collection of the receivables and recognition of the gain inherent in the land, but an offsetting loss — albeit different in timing and perhaps in character — would be built into the basis of the partnership interest. But, as noted, § 1014(c) denies a basis step-up to IRD items and, with the classification of the receivables (but not the appreciated land) as IRD, the successor's basis in the interest would instead be $70, allowing a basis step-up

---

[41] Items of IRD are included in the gross estate of the decedent where they may contribute to estate tax liability if the decedent's taxable estate is of sufficiently great value. If the items of IRD had been received during the decedent's lifetime, they would have been taxable, and that tax liability would have reduced decedent's estate. Accordingly, as a rough effort to provide some adjustment for the added estate tax liability, § 691(c) authorizes an income tax deduction for the successors who include the IRD items in income. The method of computing the income tax deduction for those entitled to it is set forth in § 691(c)(2). Of course, because of the large unified credit (see § 2010), the typical estate incurs no estate tax liability, and in such cases there is no § 691(c) deduction.

to be allocated to the appreciated land, but not to the receivables. See Reg. § 1.755-1(b)(4)(i).

By way of elaboration on this example, suppose the land were subject to a mortgage of $30. The basis of the partnership interest, upon Donald's death, would now be $80, an increase of $10 on account of Donald's share of the partnership's liabilities. (This is consistent with the basic partnership principle that provides basis to partners for their share of partnership liabilities.) Thus, the basis of a partnership interest on the death of a partner can be summarized as the fair market value of the interest under § 1014, increased by the decedent's share of partnership liabilities, and reduced by items of IRD attributable to the decedent. Reg. § 1.742-1.

Let's see how we get to this summary through the provisions of subchapter K. What is IRD in the partnership context? Section 753 states that the amount includible in the gross income of the successor to a deceased partner under § 736(a) shall be considered IRD. Recall that § 736 applies to liquidating distributions and that, from the interplay of § 736(a) and (b) discussed in Chapter 17, § 736(a) payments, made to a general partner in a partnership where capital is not a material income-producing factor, include unrealized receivables as defined in § 751(c) and unstated goodwill. The accounts receivable in our example constitute unrealized receivables, and thus, when a liquidating distribution of $100 is made by the partnership, the $30 of § 736(a) payments are accordingly IRD and enjoy no basis step-up. Donald's successor in interest will be taxed on $30 of ordinary income on the liquidating payment of $100.

At the risk of further complication, note that § 751(b), which treats disproportionate distributions of unrealized receivables and substantially appreciated inventory as sales or exchanges, can apply to distributions to a deceased partner's successor in interest, but only to the extent those distributions are governed by § 736(b). Distributions governed by § 736(a) are explicitly not subject to § 751(b). See § 751(b)(2)(B); Reg. § 1.751-1(b)(4). In our example, $30 of the $100 liquidating distribution is treated as ordinary income under § 736(a). Section 751(b) does not apply to this portion of the payment. The remainder of the payment, $70, is a § 736(b) payment. Although § 736(b) distributions are potentially subject to § 751(b), because none of the remaining property — cash and land — constitutes § 751 property, § 751(b) is inapplicable. But because the property treated as distributed, Donald's portion of the appreciated land, enjoys a basis step-up to fair market value under § 1014(a), there is no further gain to Donald's successor on the deemed exchange of his share of the appreciated land for cash.

Beyond the statutory IRD of § 753, there is also so-called judicially created IRD, where case law has broadened IRD beyond § 736(a) payments to include partnership rights to certain income that would be IRD if held by an individual. Assume the decedent's successor in interest succeeds to the partnership interest itself and does not receive payments in liquidation of the decedent's interest. Because § 753 states that § 736(a) payments are IRD, does that mean in the partnership context that only § 736(a) payments are IRD? Does the absence of payments in liquidation mean that a § 1014 basis step-up extends, for example, to the deceased partner's interest in partnership receivables as well as other partnership property? *See Woodhall v. Commissioner*, 454 F.2d 226 (9th Cir. 1972) and *Quick's Trust v. Commissioner*, 444 F.2d 90 (8th Cir. 1971), denying a basis step-up for the deceased partner's share of the partnership's zero-basis receivables under § 743(b) when a § 754 election is in effect. Should the approach of *Woodhall* and *Quick's Trust* be applied to other partnership items that would be IRD if held by an individual, such as payments due on an installment sales contract? See § 691(a)(4).

Recall that the land in our example has a value of $150 and a basis of $75. Suppose instead of land the asset was depreciable equipment, where the $75 difference between value and basis represented $75 of § 1245 depreciation recapture. Would the depreciation recapture be an unrealized receivable under § 751(c)? As we saw in Chapter 17, the answer is "No." For purposes of § 736, unrealized receivables under § 751(c) do not include depreciation recapture. Accordingly, the basis step-up of § 1014 would extend to Donald's interest in the depreciable equipment in this example, provide his successor with a fair market value basis in that interest, and eliminate gain on a liquidating payment for that interest — just as if Donald died owning a one-third interest in the equipment outside the partnership.

Consider next the presence of goodwill among the partnership assets. Recall that payments for goodwill in liquidation of a retiring general partner's interest in the partnership in which capital is not a material income-producing factor may fall (1) within § 736(a) if the goodwill is unstated, or (2) within § 736(b) if the goodwill is stated. We saw in the retirement context that payments for stated goodwill provided capital gain to the retiring partner, but with no deduction or distributive share reduction to the continuing partners; in contrast, payments for unstated goodwill provided ordinary income to the retiring partner, but also a deduction or distributive share reduction to the continuing partners. Note how the stakes change in the context of death of a partner. If the payments in liquidation include payments for stated goodwill — a § 736(b) payment — the goodwill is not IRD, the decedent's successor will enjoy a § 1014 basis step-up with respect to the goodwill, and payments on account of the goodwill will thus be tax-free. However, if the goodwill is unstated, and is thus, as a result, a § 736(a) payment and IRD under § 753, payment for the goodwill is taxable to the successor (and deductible to the partnership).

C. Inside Basis Adjustments

To be explicit about a matter alluded to previously: Under § 743(b), discussed in Part A, the death of a partner results in a transfer of the deceased partner's interest in the partnership. Accordingly, if a § 754 election is in effect — or if the partnership has a substantial built-in loss within the meaning of § 743(d) — the basis of partnership property is adjusted as set forth within § 743(b) — but none of that adjustment may be allocated to items of IRD. Reg. § 1.755-1(b)(4)(i). If a § 754 election is not in effect, step-up in outside basis to fair market value occurs nonetheless, but not for items of IRD, and inside basis adjustments to partnership property that would occur with a § 754 election in effect do not occur.

PART D:
TERMINATION OF A PARTNERSHIP

I. PROBLEMS

1. Ron, Sue, and Tom are partners in the RST Partnership. Ron holds a 50% interest in capital and profits; his partnership interest has a book value and fair market value of $100,000, and an outside basis of $40,000. Sue and Tom each hold 25% interests in RST; each of their interests has a book value and fair market value of $50,000, and an outside basis of $20,000. The partnership's assets consist of $150,000 in cash and of Blackacre, a capital asset with a value of $50,000 and an adjusted basis of $10,000. Determine whether there is a termination of the RST Partnership in any of the following alternative circumstances:

   (a) Upon Ron's withdrawal from the partnership and receipt of a $100,000 liquidating distribution on March 1, Year 1;

   (b) Upon Ron's and Sue's withdrawals from the partnership, and their receipt of liquidating distributions of $100,000 and $50,000, respectively, on March 1, Year 1;

   (c) Upon Paula's contribution of $300,000 on April 1, Year 1, in return for a 60% interest in partnership capital and profits, and proportionate reductions in the interests of Ron (from 50% to 20%) and Sue and Tom (both from 25% to 10%);

   (d) Upon Sue's sale of her 25% interest to Don for $50,000 on March 1, Year 1, and Tom's sale of his 25% interest to Ron for $50,000 on December 1, Year 1;

   (e) Upon Sue's sale of her 25% interest to Don for $50,000 on March 1, Year 1, and Don's sale of the interest to Ron for $50,000 on December 1, Year 1; or

   (f) Upon Ron's gift of his 50% interest to his daughter Lisa on March 1, Year 1.

2. For any terminations in Problem 1, what are the tax consequences to the partnership and the partners?

Assignment for Part D, Chapter 20:

Complete the problems.

Read: Internal Revenue Code: § 708(a), (b)(1).
Treasury Regulations: §§ 1.708-1(b)(1), (2), (3), (4); 1.736-1(a)(6).
Materials: Overview

II. VOCABULARY

termination of partnership
cessation of business

III. OBJECTIVES

1. To recall that a partnership terminates when no part of its business continues to be carried on by a partner.

2. To recall that a partnership terminates when there is a sale or exchange of at least 50% of partnership capital and profits within a 12-month period.

3. To know the partnership tax year closes with respect to all partners upon termination.

4. To determine the consequences under §§ 731 and 732 of a termination of the partnership on account of cessation of business.

5. To determine the consequences of a termination of a partnership upon the sale or exchange of at least 50% of its capital and profits interests within a 12-month period.

IV. OVERVIEW

---

§ 708. Continuation of a Partnership.

(a) **General Rule** — For purposes of this subchapter, an existing partnership shall be considered as continuing if it is not terminated.

(b) **Termination**

(1) General rule — For purposes of subsection (a), a partnership shall be considered as terminated only if—

(A) no part of any business, financial operation, or venture of the partnership continues to be carried on by any of its partners in a partnership, or

(B) within a 12-month period there is a sale or exchange of 50 percent or more of the total interest in partnership capital and profits.

Under § 708, an existing partnership is deemed to continue until terminated. § 708(a). And termination occurs only if (1) "no part of any business, financial operations or venture of the partnership continues to be carried on by any of its partners in a partnership" (§ 708(b)(1)(A)); or (2) "within a 12-month period there is a sale or exchange of 50 percent or more of the total interest in partnership capital and profits" (§ 708(b)(1)(B)). The § 708 regulations provide significant detail on whether and when termination occurs under these two statutory standards.

A. Cessation of Business

The regulations emphasize the statutory requirement that termination occurs only when "no part" of a partnership business continues to be carried on by any partner. Thus, when all the partners in a partnership agree to dissolve the partnership, the partnership does not terminate until "all remaining assets, consisting only of cash, are distributed to the partners." Reg. § 1.708-1(b)(1). Similarly, if one partner in a two-person partnership retires or dies, and the retiring partner or the deceased partner's successor is to receive payments in liquidation of the partnership interest, the partnership is not terminated until the entire interest of the retiring partner or deceased partner has been liquidated; the partnership is a continuing one until the last liquidation payment has been made. Reg. §§ 1.708-1(b)(1)(ii); 1.736-1(a)(6). In effect, a complete cessation of partnership activities seems to be required for termination under § 708(b)(1)(A). Of course, some events may immediately terminate the partnership under this standard. For example, when two of the three members of a three-person partnership sell their partnership interests to the third partner on the same day — in the example in the regulations, two 20-percent partners sell their interests to the 60-percent partner — the partnership is terminated on the day of the sale because there is only one member left, and one member is not enough to make a partnership. Or, as the regulation states, "Since the business is no longer carried on by any of its partners in a partnership," termination occurs on the day of the sales. Reg. § 1.708-1(b)(1).

B. Termination Consequences Under § 708(b)(1)(A)

Under § 706(c)(1), the taxable year of the partnership closes upon termination with respect to all partners. Reg. § 1.708-1(b)(3). The tax consequences to the partners on liquidation of their interests on termination of the partnership are principally governed by § 731, discussed in Chapter 14.

C. Sale or Exchange of 50-Percent of Interests within 12 Months

The second occasion for termination of a partnership is the sale or exchange of at least 50% of the interests in partnership capital and profits within a 12-month period. Thus, if A sells his 50% interest in the AB Partnership to C, the partnership terminates. If W and X, each holding 25% interests in the WXYZ Partnership, sell their interests within a 12-month period, the partnership terminates. Again, the regulations provide considerable helpful detail on the statutory test. For example, sales or exchanges to other members of the partnership count towards the 50% mark, but dispositions by gift or bequest or inheritance, or liquidation of a partner's interest, do not count as a "sale or exchange," the statutory requirement. Reg. § 1.708-1(b)(2). The same regulation states that the 50% level must be reached, within 12 months, with respect to both capital and profits interests. But the same interest cannot be counted twice for purposes of the 50% 12-month test: thus, if A sells his 30% interest to X, and X within 12 months sells the 30% interest to Y, there have not been sales of 60% of partnership interests within 12 months, only 30%. Reg. § 1.708-1(b)(2).

D. Consequences of Termination under § 708(b)(1)(B)

As a result of termination, the taxable year of the terminated partnership closes for all partners. Under the 50%/12-month test, the date of termination is the date of the sale or exchange that, by itself, or that, in conjunction with sales or exchanges within the previous 12 months, reaches the 50%/12-month mark. Reg. § 1.708-1(b)(3)(ii). Under prior regulations, termination under this test resulted in a deemed distribution to partners of the assets and liabilities of the terminated partnership, followed by a deemed contribution of those assets and liabilities to the new partnership, an approach that could cause tax gain and loss to the partners on the deemed distribution of assets and liabilities. Under current regulations, however, the analysis is different: the terminated partnership is deemed to distribute all its assets and liabilities to the new partnership in return for interests in the new partnership. The terminated partnership then immediately is deemed to transfer to the partners the interests in the new partnership in exchange for their interests in the terminated partnership. Reg. § 1.708-1(b)(4). The approach taken by the current regulations essentially ensures there will be no tax consequences to the partners of the terminated partnership beyond the closing of the partnership's taxable year. Collateral aspects of the current regulations are that the capital accounts of the partners in the terminated partnership carry over to the new partnership as do the book value and tax basis of partnership properties. In effect, the deemed contribution and liquidation of the terminated partnership are disregarded. Reg. § 1.708-1(b)(4) Ex. (ii).[42]

---

[42] Two other features of the approach taken by the regulations relate to matters studied in other chapters: (1) § 704(c) property is not created by the termination; the new partnership's § 704(c) property is limited to § 704(c) property existing in the terminated partnership, and § 704(c)(1)(B) gain and § 737 gain are not triggered by the deemed distribution. (2) If the terminated partnership had a § 754 election in effect, or makes a § 754 election on its final return following termination, it will apply to the incoming purchasing partner and produce inside basis adjustments under §§ 743 and 755. *See* Reg. § 1.708-1(b)(5).

NOTE ON MERGERS AND DIVISIONS OF PARTNERSHIPS

This note reviews the basic rules regarding partnership mergers and divisions.

1. Continuing Partnerships: The More-Than-50% Test

Under the general rule of § 708(a), a partnership is considered as continuing if it is not terminated. Under the special rules of § 708(b)(2), where two or more partnerships merge or consolidate, the resulting partnership is considered the continuation of any merging or consolidating partnership whose partners own more than 50% of the capital and profits interests of the resulting partnership. § 708(b)(2)(A). Similarly, when a partnership divides into two or more partnerships, any resulting partnership, the members of which own more than 50% of the capital and profits interests of the prior partnership, is considered a continuation of the prior partnership.

---

§ 708(b)(2). Special Rules —

(A) Merger or consolidation — In the case of the merger or consolidation of two or more partnerships, the resulting partnership shall, for purposes of this section, be considered the continuation of any merging or consolidating partnership whose members own an interest of more than 50 percent in the capital and profits of the resulting partnership.

(B) Division of a partnership — In the case of a division of a partnership into two or more partnerships, the resulting partnerships (other than any resulting partnership the members of which had an interest of 50 percent or less in the capital and profits of the prior partnership) shall, for purposes of this section, be considered a continuation of the prior partnership.

---

2. Merger or Consolidation

Assume A and B each own 50% of the AB Partnership, and C and D each own 50% of the CD Partnership. If the two partnerships merge and form the ABCD Partnership, in which A and B each own a 30% interest, and C and D each own 20% interests, the resulting ABCD Partnership is a continuation of the AB Partnership, and the CD Partnership is deemed terminated as of the date of the merger. Reg. § 1.708-1(c)(5) Ex. 1. If none of the merging or consolidating partnerships had members who satisfied the more-than-50% test (as would be the case if A, B, C, and D each owned 25% of ABCD), then both the AB Partnership and the CD Partnership would be deemed terminated as of the date of the merger. Conversely, assume two or more of the merging or consolidating partnerships satisfy the more-than-50% test. For example, assume the merging partnerships are the AB Partnership, in which A owns a 40% interest and B owns a 60% interest, and the BC Partnership, in which B owns a 60% interest and C owns a 40% interest. Assume the resulting partnership is the ABC partnership. In this case, both merging partnerships, thanks to B's 60% interest in both, satisfy the more-than-50% test. In these circumstances, "unless the Commissioner permits otherwise," the resulting partnership shall be considered the continuation "solely of that partnership which is credited with the contribution of assets having the greatest fair market value (net of liabilities) to the resulting partnership." The other partnerships shall be considered terminated. Reg. § 1.708-1(c)(5) Ex. 2. The resulting partnership retains the employer identification number (EIN) of the continuing partnership and files a return for the tax year of that partnership. Reg. § 1.708-1(c)(2).

3. Carrying Out the Merger: Assets-Over or Assets-Up

Mergers and consolidations are ordinarily effected by the "assets-over" form. That is, in a merger or consolidation, the terminated partnerships will ordinarily contribute their assets over to the resulting partnership in exchange for interests in the resulting partnership; these interests are then distributed to partners of the terminated partnerships in liquidation. Reg. § 1.708-1(c)(3)(i).

Alternatively, a merger or consolidation can be effected by the "assets-up" form. Under that form, assets and liabilities are typically deemed distributed to the partners by the terminating partnerships in a merger or consolidation in liquidation of their interests, and the recipient partners are then deemed to contribute those assets and liabilities in return for interests in the resulting or recipient partnerships. Reg. § 1.708-1(c)(3)(ii). The assets-up form will be respected for tax purposes, with tax consequences flowing from that form, if the merger or consolidation follows the steps for that form. Unless the steps for the assets-up form are followed, the merger or consolidation will be deemed to have undertaken the assets-over form. Reg. § 1.708-1(c)(3)(i).[43]

In determining the tax consequences of mergers and divisions, the tax consequences will follow the form of the merger or division — that is, assets-over in the usual case, but assets-up when that form is adopted — and the tax results may vary based upon the form chosen. For example, the adjusted basis of partnership assets in the resulting partnership may differ based on whether the assets are viewed as having been contributed by the terminated partnership to the resulting partnership (assets-over) or as having been contributed by the partners themselves following the liquidation of their interests in the terminated partnership (assets-up). In the latter case, the basis of the property received by the partners in liquidation of their interests would be determined under the rules of § 732(b), and thus the contribution of those assets to the resulting partnership may result in a different inside basis than would occur under the assets-over form. Furthermore, §§ 704(c)(1)(B) and 737 (the "mixing bowl" provisions) also apply differently under the different forms of merger or consolidation. Neither of these two provisions apply to a transfer by a partnership of all its assets and liabilities to another partnership pursuant to the

---

[43] Under the so-called "interests-over" form, the partners are deemed to contribute their partnership interests to the resulting partnership and receive interests in the resulting partnership in return. The resulting partnership then liquidates the terminating partnership. The interests-over form is not a permitted form, so tax consequences from the use of that form will be determined under the assets-over form. See, for example, Reg. § 1.708-1(c)(5) Ex. 4, where an interests-over transaction was deemed for federal tax purposes to follow the assets-over form.

assets-over form. Reg. §§ 1.704-4(c)(4), 1.737-2(b)(1). In contrast, § 704(c)(1)(B) gain or § 737 gain may be triggered under the assets-up form.[44]

Note that tax consequences may include increases or decreases in partners' liabilities under § 752. Potential gain recognition on account of liability relief in a merger or consolidation is determined by netting liability increases and decreases. See Reg. § 1.752-1(f) and Reg. § 1.752-1(g), Ex. 2, where B's share of liabilities before the merger ($630 in one merging partnership, $20 in the other) was netted with B's share of liabilities after the merger ($250 in the resulting partnership) for a $400 net decrease in liabilities, treated as a $400 distribution to B.

Under a special rule in the regulations, a sale of all or a part of a partner's interest in the terminated partnership to the resulting partnership will, in fact, be treated as a sale if the merger agreement so specifies, including the amount paid, and the selling partner consents to treat the transaction as a sale under § 741. Reg. § 1.708-1(c)(4).

Finally, note that, if a merger or consolidation is part of a "larger series of transactions," the substance of which is inconsistent with the form of the merger or consolidation, the form may be disregarded and the series of transactions recast in accordance with their substance. Reg. § 1.708-1(c)(6).

4. Divisions

Assume the ABCD Partnership is owned by A (40%), B (20%), C (20%) and D (20%). On a division into the AB Partnership and the CD Partnership, both AB and CD are resulting partnerships because each results from the division of Partnership ABCD and each has at least two partners who were partners in ABCD, the prior partnership. Reg. § 1.708-1(d)(4)(iv). Based upon the more-than-50%-test, however, only the AB Partnership will be considered a continuation of ABCD; the CD Partnership will be considered a new partnership formed on the date of the division. Reg. § 1.708-1(d)(5) Ex 1. If none of the resulting partnerships had satisfied the more-than-50% test — if, for example, ABCD had been owned 25% each by its four partners — none of the resulting partnerships is considered a continuation of the prior partnership, and the prior partnership is considered terminated. Reg. § 1.708-1(d)(1). The resulting partnerships would then all be considered new partnerships formed on the date of the division.

Suppose that more than one of the resulting partnerships satisfy the more-than-50% test. For example, assume B is a 60% owner of the ABC partnership, which divides into the AB Partnership and the BC Partnership. In this case, both AB and BC are continuations of the ABC Partnership. Only one of the continuing partnerships, however, is considered to be the "divided partnership;" it is only the divided partnership that files a return for the taxable year of the ABC Partnership and retains its employer identification number. Any other resulting partnership,

---

[44] Although no gain results from the merger itself under §§ 704(c)(1)(B) and 737, later distributions can bring about such gain. Moreover, the Service, in a ruling subsequently revoked, took the position that a new seven-year period for § 704(c) property began with the merger. Proposed regulations not finalized would apply the position taken by the revoked ruling. Rev. Rul. 2004-43, 2004-1 C.B. 842, revoked by Rev. Rul. 2005-10, 2005-1 C.B. 492. *See* Prop. Reg. §§ 1.704-3(a)(9), 1.704-4(c)(4), 1.737-2(b).

both those that are regarded as continuing and those regarded as new, file separate returns for the tax year beginning after the day of the division and obtain new employer identification numbers. Reg. § 1.708-1(d)(2). The rules for determining the divided partnership are as follows: First, the divided partnership must be a continuing partnership; second, if the resulting partnership that, in form, transferred the assets and liabilities is a continuing partnership, it is the divided partnership; third, if no form for the division was followed, or, if the partnership that in form transferred assets and liabilities is not a continuing partnership, then (where two or more resulting partnerships satisfy the more-than-50% test), the continuing resulting partnership with assets having the greatest fair market value (net of liabilities) is treated as the divided partnership. Reg. § 1.708-1(d)(4)(i).

The regulations provide the following example: The ABCD Partnership is owned by A (40%), B (40%), C (10%), and D (10%). ABCD owns property X (value $500), property Y (value $300) and property Z (value $200). ABCD divides into three partnerships: (1) newly formed AB1 Partnership, to which property X is contributed, with interests in AB1 distributed to equal partners A and B; (2) AB2 Partnership, formerly titled the ABCD Partnership, which continues to hold property Y. (C and D cease to be partners in ABCD and are not partners in what has become the AB2 Partnership.); and (3) newly formed CD Partnership, to which property Z is contributed, with interests in CD distributed to equal partners C and D. Note that both AB1 and AB2 satisfy the more-than-50% test and are thus continuing partners of the ABCD Partnership. The CD Partnership is considered a new partnership formed the day after the division. Because resulting partnership AB2 in form transferred the assets and liabilities of ABCD in connection with the division, and because AB2 is a continuing partnership, it is the "divided partnership" that files a return for the tax year of prior partnership ABCD and retains its employer identification number. Reg. § 1.708-1(d)(5) Ex. 4.

5. Carrying Out the Division: Assets-Over or Assets-Up

As was the case with respect to mergers and consolidations, divisions are ordinarily effected by the assets-over form — that is, the assets and liabilities are typically treated as being contributed by the prior partnership to one or more recipient partnerships in exchange for interests in the recipient partnerships, with the prior partnership then distributing those interests to its partners in liquidation of their interests in the prior partnership. Reg. § 1.708-1(d)(3)(i). Where the division takes the assets-over form, the tax consequences follow that form.

Again, as was the case with mergers, a division can be effected by the assets-up form, under which assets and liabilities are typically deemed distributed to the partners by the prior partnership in liquidation of their interests, and the recipient partners are then deemed to contribute those assets and liabilities in return for interests in the resulting or recipient partnerships. Reg. § 1.708-1(d)(3)(ii). The assets-up form will be respected for tax purposes, with tax consequences flowing from that form, if the division follows the steps for that form; if not, the division will be treated as following the assets-over form. Reg. § 1.708-1(d)(3)(I).

Resulting partnerships that are continuing partnerships are bound by elections made by the prior partnerships. Reg. § 1.708-1(d)(2)(ii). As is true of mergers, if the substance of a larger series of transactions is inconsistent with the form of a division, the form may be disregarded and the transaction recast in accordance with the substance. Reg. § 1.708-1(d)(6).

Chapter 21

THE ANTI-ABUSE REGULATIONS

I. PROBLEMS

1. Larry is a limited partner in the GL Limited Partnership. The general partner is General Corporation, which has a 1% interest in GL. Larry has a 99% interest and is particularly interested in the limited liability he has through GL, as well as the single level of tax. May the arrangement be recast under the anti-abuse regulations?

2. Nancy, a high-bracket individual, and ABC Corporation, which has a large net operating loss, form the NA Partnership. NA purchases a building for business operations, with the purchase financed largely through nonrecourse indebtedness. The depreciation deductions attributable to the building are allocated entirely to Nancy. Is the transaction likely to be inconsistent with the intent of Subchapter K?

3. Mary acquires an interest as a limited partner in the XY Partnership by a contribution of $100,000. Several years later, when Mary's capital account and adjusted basis in her partnership interest are $100,000, Mary's interest in XY is liquidated by a distribution to her of land worth $100,000, which has an adjusted basis to XY of $10,000. XY does not have a § 754 election in place. Should it make such an election? Will the transaction be recast if it does not?

4. Carefully review Ex. 7 of Reg. § 1.701-2(d). What were the tax benefits sought by the PRS Partnership, what were the arrangements designed to bring them about, and what factors led to the conclusion that the transaction could be recast?

Assignment for Chapter 21:

Complete the Problems.

Read: Internal Revenue Code: § 701.
Treasury Regulations: § 1.701-2(a), (b), (c), (d) Exs. 1, 6, 7 & 9. Skim Reg. § 1.701–2(e), (f) Ex. 1, (h), (i).
Materials: Overview

II. VOCABULARY

anti-abuse rules
intent of Subchapter K
clearly contemplated results

recasting a transaction for federal tax purposes
general anti-abuse rule
abuse of entity rule

III. OBJECTIVES

1. To recall three requirements implicit in the intent of Subchapter K.
2. To recall the clear reflection of income requirement may be treated as satisfied by a transaction producing results that do not clearly reflect income when the ultimate tax results are clearly contemplated by the transaction.
3. To recall the general anti-abuse rule under which a transaction can be recast if a principal purpose of the transaction is to reduce substantially the present value of the partners' aggregate tax liability in a manner inconsistent with the intent of Subchapter K.
4. To apply the non-exclusive list of factors that may be considered in a facts and circumstances analysis in determining whether such a principal purpose exists.
5. To describe the scope of the power of the Commissioner to recast a transaction.
6. To recall the abuse of entity rule under which a partnership may be treated as an aggregate of its partners.
7. To recall the anti-abuse rules apply only to income taxes.
8. To recall other statutory and nonstatutory authorities and principles, in addition to the anti-abuse rules, may be asserted to challenge transactions.

IV. OVERVIEW

Regulation § 1.701-2, proposed in 1994 and finalized with significant changes in 1995, established two general partnership anti-abuse rules. The regulation was born out of a concern at the time that partnerships had been designed, and were continuing to be designed, with an ever-increasing degree of sophistication and complexity so as to achieve tax results that not only were unintended by Congress, but were difficult for the Internal Revenue Service to combat through the existing statutes and regulations of Subchapter K. The anti-abuse regulation has been controversial, particularly when first proposed, but even after being significantly modified and finalized. One may ask whether the regulation is unnecessarily broad and vague and whether pre-existing statutes and doctrines — specific anti-abuse rules within Subchapter K itself and its regulations, judicial doctrines such as substance over form and business purpose — were not sufficient to deal with perceived abuses of the partnership tax structure. The recent codification of the economic substance doctrine in § 7701(o), along with the dearth of case law applying the general anti-abuse rules, continue to raise questions about the role of the regulation that contains these general rules.

According to Reg. § 1.701-2(a), "Subchapter K is intended to permit taxpayers to conduct joint business (including investment) activities through a flexible economic arrangement without incurring an entity level tax." The regulation goes on to say that three requirements are "implicit in the intent of Subchapter K": first, the partnership be bona fide and each transaction or series of related transactions have a "substantial business purpose;" second, the form of each transaction satisfy "substance over form principles;" and third, the tax consequences of partnership operations and transactions "accurately reflect the partner's economic agreement and clearly reflect the partner's income (collectively, proper reflection of income)." The regulation acknowledges, however, that the application of some provisions of Subchapter K and its regulations may, in some circumstances, for administrative convenience or other policy reasons, "produce tax results that do not properly reflect income." Accordingly, the third requirement, the clear reflection of income requirement, will be treated as satisfied with respect to a transaction, provided that (1) the first two requirements are satisfied and (2) the application of the provision in question to the transaction under examination, and the ultimate tax results that flow from the transaction, are "clearly contemplated" by that provision.

The General Anti-Abuse Rule. The general anti-abuse rule provides that "if a partnership is formed or availed of in connection with a transaction a principal purpose of which is to reduce substantially the present value of the partners' aggregate federal tax liability in a manner inconsistent with the intent of Subchapter K, the Commissioner can recast the transaction for federal tax purposes as appropriate to achieve tax results that are consistent with the intent of Subchapter K." Reg. § 1.701-2(b). Under this authority, the regulation provides that the partnership itself can be disregarded and its assets and activities be treated as those of the partners; purported partners can be treated as not being partners; methods of accounting can be adjusted; partnership items can be reallocated; and "claimed tax treatment [may] otherwise be adjusted or modified."

Whether the requisite "principal purpose" exists to reduce aggregate federal tax liability in a manner inconsistent with the intent of Subchapter K is based upon all the facts and circumstances, including, most significantly, "a comparison of the principal business purpose for a transaction and the claimed tax benefits resulting from the transaction." Reg. § 1.701-2(a). Listed factors, described as "illustrative only," and thus not necessarily determinative of the outcome by their presence or absence, include the following: (1) whether the partners' aggregate federal tax liability is "substantially less" than would have been the case had the partners owned the assets and conducted the activities outside the partnership format; (2) whether the aggregate federal tax liability from purportedly separate transactions is "substantially less" than would have been the case with a single integrated transaction; (3) whether a partner necessary for the tax result has a nominal interest in the partnership, is protected substantially from risk, or has little participation in partnership profits other than a return in the nature of a preferred return on capital; (4) whether substantially all the partners are related; (5) whether literal compliance with allocation rules nonetheless produces results inconsistent with § 704(b), as may be the case with special allocations to partners legally or effectively tax-exempt; (6) whether property nominally contributed is substantially retained by the contributing partner in terms of the benefits and burdens of ownership; and (7) whether ownership benefits and burdens of property are in fact substantially shifted to the distributee partner before or after the actual distribution of the property.

The scope and application of the general anti-abuse rule are illuminated to some extent by a number of examples, which the taxpayer is nonetheless warned "do not delineate the boundaries of either permissible or impermissible types of transactions." Reg. § 1.701-2(d). In one example, a corporate general partner with a 1% partnership interest and an individual limited partner with a 99% interest have chosen the limited partnership form in order to provide the individual with limited liability without subjecting income to an entity-level tax. The Commissioner is not allowed to recast this transaction because permitting taxpayers to conduct their business activities so as to avoid an entity-level tax is within the intent of Subchapter K, and the individual's retention indirectly, through his 99% partnership interest of substantially all the burdens and benefits of ownership of property contributed to the partnership, is consistent with this intent. Reg. § 1.701-2(d) Ex.1. Similarly, other examples find the use of the partnership format to avoid the Subchapter S shareholder requirements, or to avoid a more restrictive foreign tax credit limitation, or to avoid the gain recognition that would occur under §§ 351(e) and 357(c) with the corporate form are each consistent with the intent of Subchapter K. Reg. § 1.701-2(d) Exs. 2–4.

As noted earlier, the anti-abuse regulation recognized that there are provisions of Subchapter K and the regulations thereunder that, for reasons of administrative convenience or otherwise, can produce tax results that do not properly reflect income. Two of the most common are the regulations allocating nonrecourse deductions with respect to which no partner bears the economic burden or risk of loss, and the regulation conclusively presuming that the basis of property is equal to its value and that depreciation deductions are always matched by a decline in the value of the asset. See Reg. §§ 1.704-2(b); 1.704-1(b)(2)(iii)(c). The anti-abuse regulation provides that the clear reflection of income requirement will be treated as satisfied if the ultimate tax results arising out of the application of such a provision to the transaction in question were "clearly contemplated" by the provision. Thus, where nonrecourse debt was validly allocated to the partner under Reg. §§ 1.704-2(e) and 1.752-3, and where the allocation of depreciation deductions has substantial economic effect because of the "value-equals-basis" safe harbor of the regulations, the special allocations were consistent with the intent of Subchapter K. Reg. § 1.701-2(d) Ex. 6. By way of contrast, a transaction making use of a temporary partner with a nominal interest was found, based on all the facts and circumstances, to have been formed and availed of with a principal purpose of reducing aggregate tax liability in a manner inconsistent with Subchapter K, leaving the Commissioner free to recast the transaction as appropriate. Reg. § 1.701-2(d) Ex. 7.

Abuse of Entity Rule. In addition to the general anti-abuse rule, the regulation provides an abuse of entity rule under which the Commissioner may treat a partnership as an aggregate of its partners to carry out the purpose of any provision of the Code or regulations — except when a provision of the Code or regulations prescribes treatment of the partnership as an entity, and that treatment and the ultimate tax results are clearly contemplated by the provision. Reg. § 1.701-2(e).

This special anti-abuse rule reflected concern with the use of the partnership format with corporate partners in a manner that avoids corporate level limitations that would apply to corporations outside the partnership format. Note, however, that the abuse of entity rule does not require a tax avoidance purpose. Thus, examples show that aggregate treatment of a partnership is appropriate to carry out, in one case, the purpose of the § 163(e)(5) limitation on corporate-level interest deductions and, in another, the purpose of the § 1059 limitation on the benefits of the dividends-received deduction. Reg. § 1.701-2(f) Exs. 1 & 2.

Availability of Other Anti-Abuse Provisions and Doctrines. The anti-abuse regulation by its own terms indicates that it is not an exclusive remedy for perceived abuse, stating that the Commissioner may "continue to assert and rely upon applicable nonstatutory principles and other statutes and regulatory authorities to challenge transactions." The anti-abuse regulation, it concludes, "does not limit the applicability of those principles and authorities." Reg. § 1.701-2(h). Finally, by its terms, the regulation is limited to Subtitle A — the income tax — of the Code and does not extend, for example, to estate and gift taxes. Reg. § 1.701-2(i).

TABLE OF CASES

[References are to pages]

B

Basye; United States v., 410 U.S. 441 (1973) . . 105
Bogardus v. Commissioner, 302 U.S. 34 (1937). .79
Boynton v. Commissioner, 72 T.C. 1147 (1979) . 155

C

Campbell v. Commissioner, 943 F.2d 815 (8th Cir. 1991) 66
Campbell v. Commissioner, T.C. Memo 1990-162.66
Comm'r v. Culbertson, 337 U.S. 733 (1949) . . . 189
Commissioner v. (see name of defendant)
Corn Prods. Refining Co. v. Comm'r, 350 U.S. 46 (1955). 458
Crane v. Commissioner, 331 U.S. 1 (1947). . 39; 49; 233; 249; 251; 257; 262

D

Danielson; Commissioner v., 378 F.2d 771 (3d Cir. 1967) 461
Davis; United States v., 370 U.S. 65 (1962). .60; 80
Demirjian v. Commissioner, 54 T.C. 1691 (1970). 105
Demirjian v. Commissioner, 457 F.2d 1 (3d Cir. 1972) 105
Diamond v. Commissioner, 492 F.2d 286 (7th Cir. 1974) 72
Duberstein; Commissioner v., 363 U.S. 278 (1960). 79

E

Eidson; United States v., 310 F.2d 111 (5th Cir. 1962). 459, 460

G

Gaines v. Commissioner, T.C. Memo 1982-731 . 296, 297
Garnett v. Comm'r, 132 T.C. 368 (2009) . . 146; 402
General Shoe Corp.; United States v., 282 F.2d 9 (6th Cir. 1960). 301

H

Hale, T.C. Memo 1965-274 (1965). 75

I

International Freighting Corp., Inc. v. Commissioner, 135 F.2d 310 (2d Cir. 1943) 301

J

Jackson Inv. Co.; Commissioner v., 346 F.2d 187 (9th Cir. 1965). 408

Jacobson; Commissioner v., 336 U.S. 28 (1949) . 254

K

Kenan v. Commissioner, 114 F.2d 217 (2d Cir. 1940). 60; 80
Kenroy, Inc. v. Commissioner, T.C. Memo 1984-232 (1984). 58
Kirby Lumber Co; United States v., 284 U.S. 1 (1931). 254
Kresser v. Commissioner, 54 T.C. 1621 (1970). .154

L

Lakeland Grocery Co. v. Commissioner, 36 B.T.A. 289 (1937). 254
Ledoux v. Commissioner, 77 T.C. 293 (1981) . . 455
Ledoux v. Commissioner of IRS, 695 F.2d 1320 (11th Cir. 1983). 455
Lloyd v. Commissioner, 15 B.T.A. 82 (1929). . 288
Logan v. Commissioner, 51 T.C. 482 (1968) . . . 459

M

Mark IV Pictures v. Commissioner, 969 F.2d 669 (8th Cir. 1992). 66
Mark IV Pictures, Inc. v. Commissioner, T.C. Memo 1990-571 66
McDougal v. Commissioner, 62 T.C. 720 (1974) . 69; 77
Meinerz v. Commissioner, T.C. Memo 1983-191. 141
Millar v. Commissioner, 577 F.2d 212 (CA3) . . 250
Miller v. Commissioner, 52 T.C. 752 (1969) . . . 296

N

Newell v. Comm'r, T.C. Memo 2010-23 (2010). 146; 402

O

Orrisch v. Commissioner, 55 T.C. 395 (1970) . . 154; 179

P

P. G. Lake, Inc; Commissioner v., 356 U.S. 260 (1958). 459
Peracchi v. Commissioner, 143 F.3d 487 (1998). .46

[References are to pages]

Philadelphia Park Amusement Co. v. United States, 126 F. Supp. 184 (Ct. Cl. 1954) 377
Pratt v. Commissioner, 64 T.C. 203 293
Pratt v. Commissioner, 550 F.2d 1023 (1977) . . .287; 291; 293

Q

Quick's Trust v. Commissioner, 444 F.2d 90 (8th Cir. 1971) 478

R

Raphan v. United States, 3 Cl. Ct. 457 (1983) . . .264
Raphan v. United States, 759 F.2d 879 (Fed. Cir. 1985) 264
Roth v. Commissioner, 38 T.C. 171 (1962). . . .459
Roth v. Commissioner, 321 F.2d 607 (9th Cir. 1963) 459

S

Schulman v. Commissioner, 93 T.C. 623 (1989). .58
Sennett v. Commissioner, 80 T.C. 825 (1983) . . 142
Sennett v. Commissioner, 752 F.2d 428 (9th Cir. 1985) 142
South Texas Lumber Co.; Commissioner v., 333 U.S. 496 (1948). 256
Spector v. Commissioner, 71 T.C. 1017 (1979). .461
Spector v. Commissioner, 641 F.2d 376 (5th Cir. 1981) 461
St. John v. United States, 1983 U.S. Dist. LEXIS 11635 (Nov. 16, 1983). 66
Stranahan's Estate v. Commissioner, 472 F.2d 867 (6th Cir. 1973). 65

T

Thompson v. United States, 87 Fed. Cl. 728 (2009). 402
Tufts v. Commissioner, 70 T.C. 756 (1978). . . .250
Tufts v. Commissioner, 651 F.2d 1058 (1981) . . 251
Tufts; Commissioner v., 456 U.S. 960 (1982) . . 251
Tufts; Commissioner v., 461 U.S. 300 (1982).39, 40; 49; 51; 249; 262

U

United States v. (see name of defendant)

V

Vestal v. United States, 498 F.2d 487 (8th Cir. 1974). 66
VGS Corp. v. Commissioner, 68 T.C. 563 (1977). 462

W

Wegener v. Commissioner, 119 F.2d 49 (5th Cir. 1941). 288
Woodhall v. Commissioner, 454 F.2d 226 (9th Cir. 1972). 478
Woodsam Associates, Inc. v. Commissioner, 198 F.2d 357 (2d Cir. 1952). 238; 255
Woolsey v. United States, 208 F. Supp. 325 (S.D. Tex. 1962). 459
Woolsey; United States v., 326 F.2d 287 (5th Cir. 1963). 459, 460

TABLE OF STATUTES

[References are to sections and footnotes]

BOOKS

Title

Federal Taxation of Partnerships and Partners, W. McKee, W. Nelson & R. Whitmire (1977) . 33; 34
IRS Partnership Audit Technique Guide (Rev. December 2007) 247
WILLIS ON PARTNERSHIP TAXATION (1971) 75

CODE OF FEDERAL REGULATIONS (C.F.R.)

Title 26

1.752-1(c) 256
1.1001-2(b) 254

DEFICIT REDUCTION ACT OF 1984

generally 196

FEDERAL REGISTER

61 F.R. 66584-66593 (December 18, 1996) . . 14; 15
REG-115452-14, F.R. Vol. 80, No. 141 (July 23, 2015) 306
REG-151416-06, 2014-2 C.B. 870 . . . . . . 381; 382

HOUSE REPORTS

Report

H.R. 8300 (Pub. L. No. 591) 296
H.R. 9662 . . . . 75; 76
H. Rep. No. 826(I), 103rd Con., 2d Sess. (1994) . 339
H.R. Rep. No. 1337, 83 Cong. 2nd Sess. (1954) . . 1; 4; 256; 365; 391
H.R. Rep. No. 98-432 (1984) 471
H.R. Rep. No. 98-681, 98th Cong. 2d Sess. 869 (1984) 264
H.R. Rep. No. 103-11, 103rd Cong. Sess. 1 (1993) 392; 396
H.R. Rep. No. 99-841 (Conf. Rep.), 99th Cong., 2d Sess., II-318-19 (1986), 1986-3 (Vol. 4) C.B. 319 112

INTERNAL REVENUE ACT OF 1954

generally 1; 2; 4; 20

INTERNAL REVENUE ACT OF 1986

generally 111; 112

INTERNAL REVENUE CODE (I.R.C.)

Section

1(h) 26
1(h)(1) 7
1(h)(1)(C) 7
1(h)(1)(D) 7
1(h)(5) 444
1(h)(5)(B) 438
1(h)(11) 7; 122
1(h)(11)(B) 115
11 . . . . 6; 7; 23
61 . . . . 58; 60; 73; 74; 292; 304
61(a) 295; 299; 304; 305; 393
61(a)(1) 299; 303
61(a)(7) 6; 8
61(a)(12) 185
61(a)(13) 84; 91; 100; 106; 116; 117; 126; 152
63(c)(6)(D) 116; 124
83 . 55; 58; 59; 60; 63; 65; 66; 67; 68; 69; 70; 71; 84
83(a) 59; 62; 64; 99
83(a)-(c) 56
83(b) 64; 67; 70; 71
83(b)(1) 64
83(c)(1) 60
83(c)(2) 60; 64
83(h) 56; 59; 60; 62; 64; 65; 69; 98
108 . . . . 187; 254
108(a) 184
108(e)(2) 53
151 . . . . 123; 124
155 81
162 . . 59; 60; 62; 102; 290; 292; 293; 299; 304; 393
162(a) 290; 295; 304; 305
162(a)(1) 81
163(e)(5) 493
164(a) 123
165 113
165(b) 40; 136; 137; 143
165(c)(1) 21

TABLE OF STATUTES

[References are to sections and footnotes]

INTERNAL REVENUE CODE (I.R.C.) —Cont.

Section	
165(c)(2)	23
166(b)	136
167	24; 28
168	28; 234; 269
168(b)	40
168(d)(4)(B)	276
168(i)(7)	22; 194; 222; 223; 311
170	124
170(b)	120
170(c)	122
170(c)(4)	129
172	123; 124
181	2
182	2
183	2
184	2
186	2
187	2
188	2
189	2
190	2
191	2
197	396; 401
211 et seq	123; 124
243	8
263	294; 295; 296; 302; 304; 393
263(a)	89
263(a)(1)	129
265	304
267	295
267(a)(2)	286; 295; 299; 413; 471
267(e)	295
267(e)(1)-(4)	286; 295; 413
267(e)(4)	299
301(d)	8
311(b)	8
311(b)(1)	8
316	6; 8
331(a)	9
331(b)	9
334(a)	9
351	5; 25; 26; 29; 32; 33; 34; 35; 36; 47
351(a)	5; 25; 57
351(d)	25
351(d)(1)	57
351(e)	47; 492

INTERNAL REVENUE CODE (I.R.C.) —Cont.

Section	
357(b)	44
357(c)	53; 492
357(c)(3)(A)	53
358(a)(1)	23
362(a)	23
368(c)	5
408(m)	437; 444
408(m)(3)	444
442	112
443(a)(2)	474
444	112; 113
444(a)	104
444(b)(1)	104; 112
444(b)(2)	112
444(b)(3)	104
444(b)(4)(c)	104
453	25; 456
453B	25
453(b)	25
453B(a)	25
453B(b)	448
453(c)	25
453(d)	105
465	136; 137; 143; 144; 145; 146
465(a)(1)	143
465(a)(1)(A)	143
465(a)(2)	144
465(b)	144
465(b)(4)	144
465(b)(6)(B)	144
465(b)(6)(C)	144
465(b)(6)(D)	144
465(d)	143
469	136; 137; 143; 145; 146; 402
469(a)(1)(A)	145
469(b)	145
469(c)(1)	145
469(c)(2)	145; 146
469(c)(7)	146
469(e)(1)	146
469(g)(1)	145; 147
469(g)(2)	147
469(h)(1)	145
469(h)(2)	146
469(i)	146
469(j)(6)	147

INTERNAL REVENUE CODE (I.R.C.)
—Cont.

Section

483 420
501(c)(3) 115; 120
611 123
651 105
652 105
661 105
662 105
691 475
691(a)(1) 474; 476
691(a)(4) 474; 478
691(c) 474; 476
691(c)(2) 476
701 . . . 2; 5; 23; 104; 105; 116; 117; 131; 318; 489
701-777 1
702 . 2; 100; 106; 107; 116; 121-122; 126; 131; 179; 289; 292; 301; 302; 318; 393
702-704 6
702(a) . 115; 117; 121-122; 123; 124; 126; 152; 299; 303; 304; 440
702(a)(1) 123; 139
702(a)(1)-(7) 122; 123; 124; 156
702(a)(2) 125; 137; 139
702(a)(3) 123; 125; 137; 139
702(a)(4) 123; 124; 125; 129; 137
702(a)(6) 124
702(a)(7) 139
702(a)(8) . . 123; 124; 125; 135; 137; 139; 152; 156; 373
702(a)(9) 153; 305
702(b) 105; 121; 122
703 . . . . 105; 116; 123; 124; 131; 221; 222
703(a) 105; 123; 124; 127
703(a)(1) 121; 123
703(a)(2) 124
703(a)(2)(A) 124
703(a)(2)(B) 124
703(a)(2)(C) 124; 129
703(a)(2)(D) 124
703(a)(2)(E) 124
703(a)(2)(F) 124
703(b) 105; 106; 117
704 . . . . 117; 131; 158; 222; 302; 415

INTERNAL REVENUE CODE (I.R.C.)
—Cont.

Section

704(a) 6; 100; 106; 116; 118; 152; 153; 180
704(b) . . 6; 105; 116; 131; 151; 153; 154; 155; 156; 167; 175; 177; 179; 180; 183; 185; 191; 201; 226; 234; 259; 265; 268; 270; 271; 274; 275; 281; 283; 284; 292; 305; 412; 413; 414; 468; 491
704(b)(1) 118; 119; 155
704(b)(2) . . 118; 119; 154; 155; 156; 163; 178; 179
704(c) . 18; 38; 39; 49; 51; 53; 68; 80; 185; 195; 196; 197; 201; 202; 203; 204; 207; 208; 209; 210; 215; 221; 224; 226; 227; 261; 264; 265; 267; 275; 276; 277; 278; 279; 280; 281; 282; 283; 284; 363; 375; 381; 382; 383; 421; 426; 427; 428; 429; 430; 431; 432; 433; 435; 439; 440; 443; 445; 448; 449; 451; 454; 482
704(c)(1) 196; 198; 199; 200; 427
704(c)(1)(A) . 23; 25; 28; 38; 51; 53; 63; 84; 92; 93; 95; 99; 118; 119; 131; 141; 151; 153; 193; 195; 196; 200; 201; 202; 203; 204; 206; 208; 215; 261; 382; 427; 428; 430
704(c)(1)(B) . . 8; 201; 308; 309; 311; 312; 345; 366; 427; 428; 429; 430; 431; 432; 434; 435; 482; 484; 485
704(c)(1)(B)(i) 428
704(c)(1)(B)(ii) 429
704(c)(1)(B)(iii) 429
704(c)(1)(C) . . . 195; 204; 210; 211; 220; 221; 222; 223; 224; 445; 474
704(c)(1)(C)(i) 429
704(c)(1)(C)(ii) 430
704(c)(2) 196; 197; 198; 199; 200; 309; 430
704(c)(3) 53; 429
704(d) . . 53; 126; 135; 136-137; 138; 139; 140; 142; 143; 144; 145; 146; 162; 213; 234; 242; 256; 257; 261; 263; 264; 265; 269; 270; 271; 273; 278
704(e) 189; 190
704(e)(1) 190; 191
704(e)(2) 190; 191
704(f)(3)(ii)(C) 222
704(f)(3)(ii)(D) 222
705 . 38; 91; 116; 126; 127; 130; 131; 139; 195; 220; 223; 318; 336
705(a) 127; 333; 335
705(a)(1) 53; 95; 100; 137; 298

TABLE OF STATUTES

[References are to sections and footnotes]

INTERNAL REVENUE CODE (I.R.C.)
—Cont.

Section

705(a)(1)(A) . . 5; 23; 127; 128; 138; 198; 205; 206; 446
705(a)(1)(B). 127; 128
705(a)(2) . . 6; 53; 98; 114; 128; 137; 138; 140; 298
705(a)(2)(A). 128; 160; 232; 233
705(a)(2)(B). 128; 129; 130; 236; 239; 266
705(b)(2)(B). 89
705(c)(2)(A). 23
706. . . . . 105; 296
706(a) . 104; 106; 107; 111; 116; 296; 298; 302; 413
706(b). 104; 108-109; 116
706(b)(1). 2; 109; 110; 475
706(b)(1)(B). 109; 112; 475
706(b)(1)(B)(ii). 110
706(b)(1)(B)(iii). 110; 111
706(b)(1)(C). 109; 110; 111
706(b)(3). 109
706(b)(4). 109
706(c). 140
706(c)(1) 474; 481
706(c)(2) 440
706(c)(2)(A) 474; 475
706(d). 140; 465
706(d)(1). 463; 465
706(d)(2). .472
706(d)(2)(A) 471
706(d)(2)(B) 471
706(d)(2)(C)(i) 472
706(d)(2)(C)(ii). 472
706(d)(2)(D) 472
706(d)(3). .471
707. . . . . .288; 291; 293; 303
707(a). 291; 301; 302; 303; 304; 345; 414
707(a)(1) . . 286; 287; 291; 292; 293; 294; 295; 301; 302; 412; 413; 414; 415; 416
707(a)(2). 302; 345; 412; 413
707(a)(2)(A). 300; 413; 414; 415; 417
707(a)(2)(B) . 44; 413; 417; 418; 426; 430; 431; 432
707(c). . .62; 69; 80; 286; 287; 291; 292; 293; 294; 295; 296; 298; 299; 300; 301; 302; 304; 305; 306; 345; 393; 400; 405; 412; 413; 414; 423; 440
708. 480
708(a). 479; 480; 483
708(b)(1). .479
708(b)(1)(A). 480; 481
708(b)(1)(B). 382; 430; 434; 480; 482

INTERNAL REVENUE CODE (I.R.C.)
—Cont.

Section

708(b)(2). .483
708(b)(2)(A). 80; 483
709. . . . . .104; 113; 114
709(a). .113; 114
709(b). 113
709(b)(1). 113; 114
709(b)(2). .113
709(b)(3). .114
721. . .5; 18; 20; 21; 22; 23; 24; 25; 26; 29; 30; 32; 33; 34; 35; 36; 38; 41; 48; 50; 56; 57; 58; 60; 61; 66; 68; 69; 73; 74; 75; 79; 84; 87; 88; 102; 196; 204; 206; 215; 295; 308; 387
721-723. 195
721(a). 20; 30; 32; 33; 386
721(b). 21; 23; 47
721(b)(1). 74
722 . .18; 20; 21; 22; 23; 24; 27; 29; 38; 41; 45; 48; 50; 52; 53; 60; 61; 62; 64; 84; 87; 88; 90; 102; 126; 127; 138; 196; 197; 204; 215; 233; 242; 261; 263; 267; 281; 320; 321; 333; 334; 335; 386; 387
723 . . 18; 22-23; 24; 27; 29; 38; 45; 47; 48; 50; 51; 53; 60; 61; 62; 79; 80; 81; 84; 87; 88; 102; 196; 197; 204; 215; 217; 261
724 . . . . 18; 28; 308; 317; 318
724(c) 29
731.41; 42; 44; 46; 47; 48; 50; 52; 94; 96; 198; 205; 265; 292; 295; 301; 308; 309; 311; 312; 313; 315; 318; 320; 321; 327; 332; 336; 338; 339; 344; 345; 346; 365; 367; 374; 378; 387; 392; 393; 394; 403; 405; 407; 431; 480; 481
731-736. . . . . .368; 385; 386
731(a). . .42; 46; 52; 126; 279; 311; 319; 329; 332; 344; 345; 351; 364; 365; 366; 380; 385; 387; 390; 433
731(a)(1) . . 8; 9; 23; 38; 43; 44; 46; 47; 50; 52; 53; 94; 96; 101; 126; 128; 160; 198; 200; 207; 232; 263; 312; 318; 319; 320; 322; 331; 333; 334; 336; 338; 339; 341; 346; 348; 349; 351; 352; 378; 386; 393; 394; 395; 400; 401; 432
731(a)(1)(4). 401
731(a)(2). . .8; 9; 94; 126; 129; 198; 200; 207; 310; 312; 313; 327-328; 329; 347; 349; 352; 354; 366; 374; 393; 394; 395; 405
731(a)(2)(A). 313
731(a)(2)(B) 313
731(b) . . 8; 301; 311; 313; 364; 365; 366; 390; 427

INTERNAL REVENUE CODE (I.R.C.)
—Cont.

Section

731(c). 318; 338; 339; 340; 341; 387
731(c)(1). 337; 339; 432
731(c)(1)(B) 339
731(c)(2)(A) 337; 339
731(c)(2)(B) 339
731(c)(2)(C) 339
731(c)(3)(A). 337; 339; 341
731(c)(3)(B). 337; 339-340
731(c)(3)(C) 341
731(c)(4) 337; 340
731(c)(4)(A) 340
731(c)(4)(B) 340
731(c)(5) 337; 341
731(c)(6) 337
731(d). 364; 390
731 et seq 371; 374; 378; 400
732 . . 308; 313; 314; 319; 320; 321; 323; 327; 332; 334; 340; 344; 351; 365; 372; 376; 392; 393; 394; 407; 480
732(a). 310; 313; 315; 319; 335; 344; 345; 364; 380; 433
732(a)(1). 8; 314; 315; 319; 321; 323; 333; 335; 338; 341; 378; 427; 429; 430; 454
732(a)(2) . . 263; 314; 315; 322; 323; 325; 326; 333; 338; 341; 349; 351; 433
732(b) . . 9; 310; 327; 328; 344; 345; 348; 349; 351; 360; 364; 484
732(c). 9; 322; 323-324; 325; 327; 329; 330
732(c)(1). 322; 323; 325
732(c)(1)(A) 328; 331
732(c)(1)(A)(i) 324; 325
732(c)(1)(A)(ii). 325; 328; 329
732(c)(1)(B) 325
732(c)(1)(B)(i) 324; 331
732(c)(1)(B)(ii). 325
732(c)(2)(A) 331; 332
732(c)(2)(B). 331; 332
732(c)(3) 325; 328
732(c)(3)(A). 325; 331; 332
732(c)(3)(B). 325; 332
732(d). 438; 439; 453; 454
733 . . 38; 41; 45; 46; 50; 52; 94; 96; 101; 116; 127; 128; 233; 280; 308; 310; 314; 315; 320; 321; 322; 323; 324; 325; 326; 333; 335; 341; 348; 373; 377; 378; 386; 405
734. . . . . .310; 341; 350; 394
734(a) 349; 350; 374; 394

INTERNAL REVENUE CODE (I.R.C.)
—Cont.

Section

734(a)(2) 395
734(a)-(d) 344
734(b) . 315; 344; 345; 350-351; 352; 353; 354; 355; 356; 357; 358; 359; 375; 378; 384; 396
734(b)(1)(A). 353; 395; 400; 401
734(b)(2) 395
734(b)(2)(A). 354; 367; 374; 395
734(d). 344; 359; 360; 361; 378; 395
735 . . . . 308; 316; 317; 318; 320; 325; 332
735(a). .317
735(b). 316; 317
735(c). .317
735(c)(2)(A) 318
736 . . 310; 346; 385; 390; 391; 392; 394; 395; 396; 397; 398; 399; 402; 407; 408; 475; 477; 478
736(a). 365; 379; 390; 391; 392; 393; 394; 395; 396; 397; 398; 399; 400; 401; 402; 403; 404; 406; 407; 474; 475; 477; 478
736(a)(1). 393
736(a)(2) 409; 410
736(b). 344; 346; 365; 379; 390; 392; 393; 394; 395; 396; 397; 398; 399; 400; 401; 402; 403; 404; 405; 406; 407; 474; 475; 477; 478
736(b)(2) 395; 401; 404
736(b)(2)(B). 408; 409; 410
736(b)(3) 396; 397; 400; 401; 402; 404
737. 8; 308; 309; 311; 312; 338; 345; 366; 426; 427; 431; 432; 433; 434; 435; 482; 484; 485
737(a) 431; 432; 433
737(a)(1) 432; 433
737(b). .431
737(c)(1) 433
737(c)(2) 433
737(d)(1) 434
737(d)(2) 434
741 . . 26; 46; 64; 73; 127; 198; 207; 308; 318; 319; 329; 332; 337; 344; 346; 347; 352; 354; 364; 365; 366; 374; 392; 393; 394; 400; 401; 405; 407; 438; 441; 443; 446; 457; 485
742. 438
743 . . . . 443; 447; 451; 452; 455; 482
743(a). 445; 446
743(a)-(d). 438
743(b). 142; 221; 439; 445; 446; 447; 448; 449; 450; 451; 452; 453; 474; 478
743(c). .449
743(d). 445; 474; 478

TABLE OF STATUTES

[References are to sections and footnotes]

INTERNAL REVENUE CODE (I.R.C.) —Cont.

Section

743(d)(1) 445
743(f) 360
751 . . 224; 309; 319; 344; 346; 364; 366; 367; 368; 369; 370; 371; 372; 375; 376; 378; 379; 380; 381; 382; 383; 384; 387; 394; 398; 400; 407; 439; 441; 442; 455; 457; 458; 460
751(a) . 333; 438; 441; 442; 443; 444; 451; 452; 453; 454
751(a)(1) 387
751(a)(2) 317; 387
751(b) . 8; 9; 310; 311; 312; 326; 332; 344; 345; 346; 356; 357; 358; 363; 364; 365; 367; 368; 369; 370; 371; 372; 373; 374; 375; 376; 378; 379; 380; 381; 382; 383; 384; 385; 386; 387; 392; 393; 394; 395; 400; 401; 403; 407; 408; 425; 434; 442; 443; 454; 474; 477
751(b)(1)(B) 387
751(b)(2)(B) 394; 477
751(b)(3) 346; 356; 368; 369
751(b)(3)(A) 368; 369
751(b)(3)(B) 370
751(b)-(d) 308; 364; 390
751(c) . 29; 317; 318; 323; 327; 328; 367; 368; 369; 386; 387; 392; 394; 395; 397; 398; 438; 442; 443; 460; 474; 477; 478
751(d) . 317; 318; 323; 327; 328; 368; 369; 438; 442; 443
751(d)(1)(B) 387
752 . 41; 42; 43; 44; 45; 49; 50; 51; 52; 53; 138; 144; 230; 237; 238; 255; 261; 262; 263; 264; 265; 266; 267; 268; 269; 274; 280; 320; 321; 332; 334; 421; 485
752(a) . . 41; 42; 48; 52; 84; 90; 138; 230; 233; 242; 256; 257; 262-263; 265; 266; 267; 277; 280; 308; 320; 321; 334; 386; 387; 452
752(a)-(c) 38
752(b) . 41; 42; 43; 44; 46; 47; 48; 52; 96; 230; 233; 256; 257; 262; 277; 279; 308; 320; 321; 334; 335; 336; 380; 386; 387
752(c) 255; 256; 257; 263; 334
752(d) 251; 256; 257; 443
753 . . . . 474; 477; 478
754 . . . 47; 315; 322; 343; 344; 345; 349; 350; 351; 352; 353; 354; 355; 356; 357; 359; 360; 361; 363; 367; 374; 378; 384; 389; 395; 396; 400; 401; 437; 438; 439; 440; 445; 446; 447; 448; 451; 454; 455; 473; 474; 476; 478; 482; 489

INTERNAL REVENUE CODE (I.R.C.) —Cont.

Section

755 . . 344; 352; 353; 357; 367; 400; 401; 449; 450; 452; 453; 472; 482
755(a) 352; 438
755(a)(1) 353; 449
755(b) 352; 354; 438; 449
755(c) 353
761(a) 2
761(b) 189; 190; 191
761(c) 153; 155; 186; 409
761(f) 14
770 75
901 . . . . 122; 123
1001 . . . . 19; 24; 205; 251; 301; 440
1001(a) 40; 251
1001(b) 252; 254; 255
1001(c) 19
1012 . . . 39; 89; 197; 205; 253; 262; 266; 368; 373; 377; 445; 453
1014 . . . . 141; 199; 200; 251; 446; 477; 478
1014(a) 477
1014(a)(1) 474; 475
1014(b)(1) 474
1014(b)(6) 474
1014(c) 474; 475; 476
1014(f) 475
1015 141
1016(a)(1) 23
1016(a)(2) 222
1016(a)(2)(A) 81
1031 20
1031(b) 41
1031(d) 20; 40; 41
1033 . . . . 105; 106
1059 493
1060 399
1092(d)(1) 337; 339
1201 7
1211 348
1211(b) 120; 121; 347
1212 . . . . 121; 142
1221 26
1221(1) 26
1221(a)(1) 369; 377; 443
1222 316

INTERNAL REVENUE CODE (I.R.C.)
—Cont.

Section

1222(3)..................................26
1223..................26; 316; 317; 332
1223(1)..........18; 26; 27; 46; 48; 198; 199
1223(2)..18; 26; 27; 28; 45; 141; 142; 197; 216; 316
1223(9)...............................142
1231....24; 26; 27; 28; 61; 92; 115; 120; 121; 122;
123; 125; 127; 128; 130; 135; 137; 138; 139;
140; 198; 216; 369; 395; 400; 401; 443
1231(a)...............................78; 81
1231(a)(1).............................28; 121
1231(a)(4)(C).........................120; 121
1231(b)........24; 28; 81; 352; 449; 450; 468
1245....17; 18; 24; 25; 61; 83; 115; 311; 369; 397;
398; 442; 473; 478
1245(a)................................24; 61
1245(a)(1)............................24; 25; 443
1245(a)(2)(A)............................25
1245(a)(3)...............................25
1245(a)(3)(A)............................24
1245(b)(3).........................18; 24; 311
1245(b)(6)(A)...........................311
1250..................25; 311; 398; 442; 444
1250(d)(3)............................25; 311
1250(d)(6)(A)...........................311
1274...................................420
1361(b)(1)...............................5
1361(b)(2)...............................5
1363(a)..................................6
1366(a)..................................6
1366(c)..................................6
1366(d)(1)...............................6
1367(a)(1)(A)............................6
1367(a)(1)(B)............................6
1367(a)(2)(B)............................6
1367(a)(2)(C)............................6
1368(b)..................................8
1371..................................9; 29
1371(a)...............................5; 8
1374..................................6; 105
1375..................................6; 105
2010...................................476
7519...................................112
7701....................................14
7701(a)(2)...........................2; 10; 14
7701(a)(3)............................10; 14

INTERNAL REVENUE CODE (I.R.C.)
—Cont.

Section

7701(a)(43)............................141
7701(g)................................444
7701(o)................................490
7703....................................15
7703(a)(43).........................308; 313
7704....................................14
7704(b)..............................66; 67
Subchapter C......3; 5; 6; 8; 9; 13; 53; 57; 120
Subchapter C, Supplement F...............2
Subchapter J..........................105
Subchapter K..1; 2; 4; 5; 6; 8; 9; 19; 23; 27; 29; 41;
44; 85; 94; 102; 104; 105; 107; 118; 125; 126;
129; 131; 152; 191; 196; 287; 309; 339; 361;
364; 380; 391; 413; 440; 477; 489; 490; 491; 492
Subchapter S....................3; 5; 6; 9; 105
Subtitle A................................2

INVESTMENT ADVISERS ACT OF 1940

Section

80b-5 (1971)...........................302

INVESTMENT COMPANY ACT OF 1940

generally..............................302

I.R.S. FORMS

Number

1065 (Schedule K-1)............116; 124; 132
8832...................................16

I.R.S. NOTICES

Notice

1995-1 C.B. 297, Notice 95-14............13
2005-43, 2005-1 C.B. 1221.............67; 71
2006-14, 2006-1 C.B. 498..367; 369; 370; 373; 380;
381; 382

LAW REVIEW/LAW JOURNAL ARTICLES

The Diamond Case, Cowan, 27 Tax Law Review
161 (1972)...........................73; 75
Note, 82 Colum. L Rev., 1526............253

LAW REVIEW/LAW JOURNAL ARTICLES—Cont.

Tax Shelters, Nonrecourse Debt, and the Crane *Case,* Bittker, 33 Tax L. Rev 277 (1978)... .253; 255

MISCELLANEOUS PUBLICATIONS

Conf. Rep. 98-861, P.L. 98-369, 98th Cong. 2d Sess. 53
Hearings on Advisory Group Recommendations on Subchapters C, J, and K of the Internal Revenue Code before the House Comm. on Ways and Means, 86th Cong., 1st Sess. 53 (1959)..... 76
Internal Revenue Service Statistics of Income Bulletin (Fall 2015)................... 4
Joint Committee on Taxation, General Explanation of the Tax Reform Act of 1976, H.R. 10612, 94th Con., P.L. 94-445 (1976)............ 157
Staff of the Joint Committee on Taxation, *General Explanation of the Tax Reform Act of 1976,* 94th Cong. 2d Sess., 1976-3 vol. 2 C.B. 47..... 143

NATIONAL HOUSING ACT
Section
221(b)......................... .255
221(d)(4)....................... .255

REVENUE PROCEDURES
Rev. Proc.
72-51, 1972-2 C.B. 832 .... 108; 112
74-33, 1974-2 C.B. 489 108
93-27, 1993-2 C.B. 343 .... 58; 66; 67; 71
2001-43, 2001-2 C.B. 191 .... 66; 67; 71
2006-46, 2006-2 C.B. 859.............. 111
2015-53, 2015-44 I.R.B. 615............. 7

REVENUE RULINGS
Rev. Rul.
60-182, 1960-1 C.B. 264.............. .108
64-56, 1964-1 C.B. 133............... .35
64-56, 1964-1 (Part 1) C.B. 133......... 34
66-7, 1966-1 C.B. 188............ .27; 197
66-95, 1966-1 C.B. 169.............. 305
69-180, 1969-1 C.B. 183 ..... 286; 300; 304-306
70-45, 1970-1 C.B. 17............... .34
71-564, 1971-2 C.B. 179.............. 34
74-175, 1974-1 C.B. 52.............. 142
76-111, 1976-1 C.B. 214.............. .254

REVENUE RULINGS
Rev. Rul.
79-205, 1979-2 C.B. 255 ..... 308; 321; 332-335
79-288, 1979-2 C.B. 139............... 34
81-301........................ .286; 294
81-301, 1981-2 C.B. 144........... .302-304
84-102, 1984-2 C.B. 119 ..... 364; 380; 386-387
85-32, 1985-1 C.B. 186............... 114
87-57, 1987-2 C.B. 117............... 112
87-111, 1987-2 C.B. 160............. .113
88-76, 1988-2 C.B. 360.............. 4; 13
91-31, 1991-1 C.B. 19............... .185
92-97, 1992-2 C.B. 124.............. 336
94-4, 1994-1 C.B. 196............308; 335-336
95-41, 1995-1 C.B. 132 ... 261; 274; 280; 281-284
99-43, 1999-2 C.B. 506....... 151; 157; 183-188
2004-43, 2004-1 C.B. 842............ .485
2005-10, 2005-1 C.B. 492............ .485
2007-40, 2007-1 C.B. 1426............ 301

SENATE REPORTS
Report
S. Rep. No. 98-169, 98th Cong. 2d Sess. (1984)..................... 414; 415
S. Rep. No. 781, 82nd Cong., 1st Sess., 1951-2 C.B. 458........................ .190
S. Rep. No. 1622, 83d Cong., 2d Sess. (1954). .154; 256; 291; 296; 334; 458

TAX DETERMINATIONS T.D.
6175, 1956-1 C.B. 211............... .257
8237, 1989-1 C.B. 180............... .265

TAX REFORM ACT OF 1976
generally.............. 154; 155; 156; 163

TAX REFORM ACT OF 1984
generally 28; 202; 264; 274

TAX REFORM ACT OF 1986
generally...................... 108

TREASURY REGULATIONS
Regulation
1.1(h)-1(b)................... 438; 444
1.1(h)-1(c)................... .438; 444
1.1(h)-1(f), Ex. 1.................. .438

TREASURY REGULATIONS—Cont.
Regulation

1.1(h)-1(f), Ex. 2	438
1.1(h)-1(f), Ex. 5	438
1.61-2(d)(2)	21
1.61-2(d)(2)(i)	23; 91
1.83-1(a)	64
1.83-3(b)	63; 66
1.83-3(e)	56; 59
1.83-6(b)	56
1.83-6(c)	69
1.162-7(b)(2)	81
1.167(a)-2	28
1.167(g)-1	40; 81
1.351-1(c)	47
1.441-1(c)(2)	112
1.453-9(c)(2)	18; 25
1.461-1(a)(1)	295
1.461-1(a)(2)	295
1.469-4	146
1.691(a)-1(b)	474
1.691(a)-2(b), Ex. 1	474; 476
1.691(a)-2(b), Ex. 5	474; 476
1.691(a)-3(a)	474
1.701-1	116
1.701-2	490
1.701-2(a)	489; 491
1.701-2(b)	489; 491
1.701-2(c)	489
1.701-2(d)	492
1.701-2(d), Ex. 1	489; 492
1.701-2(d), Ex. 6	489; 492
1.701-2(d), Ex. 7	489; 492
1.701-2(d), Ex. 8	361
1.701-2(d), Ex. 9	489
1.701-2(d), Exs. 2-4	492
1.701-2(e)	489; 492
1.701-2(f), Ex. 1	489; 493
1.701-2(f), Ex. 2	493
1.701-2(h)	489; 493
1.701-2(i)	489; 493
1.702-1(a)(1)-(5)	116
1.702-1(a)(7)	116
1.702-1(a)(8)	116; 122
1.702-1(a)(8)(i)	124
1.702-1(a)(8)(ii)	122
1.702-1(a)(9)	116
1.702-1(b)	116
1.702-1(c)(1)	116

TREASURY REGULATIONS—Cont.
Regulation

1.702-2	116; 124
1.703-1	116
1.703-1(a)(1)(i)	124
1.704-1	234
1.704-1(b)	235
1.704-1(b)(1)	141; 305
1.704-1(b)(1)(iii)	191; 227
1.704-1(b)(1)(iv)	227
1.704-1(b)(1)(iv)-(vi)	195
1.704-1(b)(2)	154; 180; 181; 186
1.704-1(b)(2)(i)	185
1.704-1(b)(2)(ii)	185; 267
1.704-1(b)(2)(ii)(a)	151; 157
1.704-1(b)(2)(ii)(b)	150; 151; 158; 194; 225; 232; 233; 235; 248; 259; 260
1.704-1(b)(2)(ii)(b)(1)	226
1.704-1(b)(2)(ii)(b)(3)	149
1.704-1(b)(2)(ii)(c)	151; 164
1.704-1(b)(2)(ii)(d)	150; 151; 163; 164; 232; 235; 248; 272
1.704-1(b)(2)(ii)(g)	151; 158
1.704-1(b)(2)(ii)(i)	151; 166
1.704-1(b)(2)(iii)	149; 183; 185
1.704-1(b)(2)(iii)(a)	151; 167; 172; 185; 187
1.704-1(b)(2)(iii)(b)	151; 168; 185; 187
1.704-1(b)(2)(iii)(b)(2)	167
1.704-1(b)(2)(iii)(c)	151; 170; 186; 187; 492
1.704-1(b)(2)(iii)(c)(2)	187
1.704-1(b)(2)(iv)	89; 130; 149; 158; 163; 176; 187; 229; 268; 382
1.704-1(b)(2)(iv)(1)	445
1.704-1(b)(2)(iv)(3)	100; 168
1.704-1(b)(2)(iv)(5)	373; 378
1.704-1(b)(2)(iv)(a)	116
1.704-1(b)(2)(iv)(a)-(d)(3)	230
1.704-1(b)(2)(iv)(b)	84; 88-89; 116; 131; 135; 151; 195; 232; 308
1.704-1(b)(2)(iv)(b)(1)	87; 127; 159; 196; 197; 225; 242; 269; 276
1.704-1(b)(2)(iv)(b)(2)	87; 197; 224
1.704-1(b)(2)(iv)(b)(3)	91; 131; 140; 316
1.704-1(b)(2)(iv)(b)(4)	94; 101; 166; 320
1.704-1(b)(2)(iv)(b)(5)	316; 321
1.704-1(b)(2)(iv)(b)(6)	140
1.704-1(b)(2)(iv)(b)(7)	91; 131; 140; 160; 271
1.704-1(b)(2)(iv)(c)	89-90
1.704-1(b)(2)(iv)(d)	283

TABLE OF STATUTES

[References are to sections and footnotes]

TREASURY REGULATIONS—Cont.
Regulation
1.704-1(b)(2)(iv)(d)(1) 195; 196; 197; 279
1.704-1(b)(2)(iv)(d)(2) 151; 164
1.704-1(b)(2)(iv)(d)(3) 93; 96; 153; 195; 206
1.704-1(b)(2)(iv)(e) 308; 316; 321
1.704-1(b)(2)(iv)(e)(1) 224
1.704-1(b)(2)(iv)(f) . . . 86; 140; 159; 187; 194; 195;
   224; 225; 226; 280; 365; 375; 382; 383; 389; 399
1.704-1(b)(2)(iv)(f)(1)-(4) 225
1.704-1(b)(2)(iv)(f)(2) 225
1.704-1(b)(2)(iv)(f)(5) 224
1.704-1(b)(2)(iv)(f)(5)(i) 87; 224
1.704-1(b)(2)(iv)(f)(5)(iii) 87; 99
1.704-1(b)(2)(iv)(g) 185; 195
1.704-1(b)(2)(iv)(g)(3) 91; 151; 160; 203; 208
1.704-1(b)(2)(iv)(h)(1) 195
1.704-1(b)(2)(iv)(i) 184; 185
1.704-1(b)(3) 176; 185; 187; 232; 234; 235
1.704-1(b)(3)(i) 116; 118; 151
1.704-1(b)(3)(ii) 116; 118; 151
1.704-1(b)(3)(iii) 151; 171; 177; 178
1.704-1(b)(4)(i) 68; 185; 226; 268
1.704-1(b)(4)(vi) 187
1.704-1(b)(5), Ex. 1(i) 163
1.704-1(b)(5), Ex. 1(xi) 172
1.704-1(b)(5), Ex. 2 171
1.704-1(b)(5), Ex. 3 171
1.704-1(b)(5), Ex. 4(ii) 166
1.704-1(b)(5), Ex. 5 173
1.704-1(b)(5), Ex. 5(ii) 175
1.704-1(b)(5), Ex. 6 169
1.704-1(b)(5), Ex. 7 171
1.704-1(b)(5), Ex. 14(i) 226
1.704-1(b)(5), Ex. 14(iv) 226; 227
1.704-1(b)(5), Exs. 1-7 151
1.704-1(b)(ii)(d) 260; 275; 277
1.704-1(c) 84; 268
1.704-1(c)(2) 196; 197; 199
1.704-1(d) 135
1.704-1(d)(1) 84; 137
1.704-1(d)(2) 136; 137; 138; 139
1.704-1(d)(4), Ex. 1 138
1.704-1(d)(4), Ex. 2 138
1.704-1(d)(4), Ex. 3 139
1.704-1(e) 84
1.704-1(e)(1)(iv) 190; 397
1.704-1(e)(2) 190
1.704-1(e)(3) 191

TREASURY REGULATIONS—Cont.
Regulation
1.704-1(f) 84
1.704-1(h)(1) 84
1.704-2 . . . . 156; 234; 240
1.704-2(b) 230; 234; 492
1.704-2(b)(1) 234; 236
1.704-2(b)(2) 236; 237; 238; 240; 243; 246
1.704-2(c) 230; 239; 241; 244; 277
1.704-2(d)(1) 230; 238; 281
1.704-2(d)(3) 278; 280; 281
1.704-2(e) . . 230; 231; 234; 235; 240; 249; 261; 276;
                                                277; 492
1.704-2(e)(2) 230; 231; 246
1.704-2(f) 260; 275
1.704-2(f)(1) 230; 246; 248
1.704-2(f)(2) 246
1.704-2(f)(2)-(4) 246
1.704-2(f)(3) 230; 246
1.704-2(f)(6) 230
1.704-2(g)(1) 230; 241; 245; 274; 277
1.704-2(g)(2) 230; 245; 247
1.704-2(g)(3) 238
1.704-2(h) 230
1.704-2(h)(1)-(3) 241
1.704-2(j)(1) 230
1.704-2(j)(1)(ii) 239
1.704-2(j)(1)(iii) 239
1.704-2(j)(2) 230
1.704-2(m), Ex. 1(3)(i) 230
1.704-2(m), Ex. 1(ii) 248; 249
1.704-2(m), Ex. 1(i)-(iv) 230
1.704-3 153
1.704-3(a) 226
1.704-3(a)(1) 202; 224
1.704-3(a)(1)-(6) 195
1.704-3(a)(2) 202; 203
1.704-3(a)(3) 426
1.704-3(a)(3)(i) 202; 279; 427
1.704-3(a)(3)(ii) 202; 204; 215; 278; 427
1.704-3(a)(6) 226; 280
1.704-3(a)(6)(i) 226
1.704-3(b) 195; 282
1.704-3(b)(1) 203; 204; 208; 279; 282
1.704-3(b)(2), Ex. 1 . . . . 204; 208
1.704-3(b)(2), Ex. 1(ii) 203; 210
1.704-3(b)(2), Ex. 1(iii) 204; 211
1.704-3(b)(2), Ex. 1(iv) 210
1.704-3(c) 282

TABLE OF STATUTES

[References are to sections and footnotes]

TREASURY REGULATIONS—Cont.
Regulation

1.704-3(c)(1)	212; 214
1.704-3(c)(1)-(4), Ex. 1	195
1.704-3(c)(1)-(4), Ex. 2	195
1.704-3(c)(1)(iii)	214
1.704-3(c)(4), Ex. 2	212
1.704-3(d)	282; 284; 448
1.704-3(d)(1)	215
1.704-3(d)(1)-(7), Ex. 1	195
1.704-3(d)(1)-(7), Ex. 2	195
1.704-3(d)(2)	194; 217; 218
1.704-3(d)(3)	216
1.704-3(d)(4)	215
1.704-3(d)(5)	215
1.704-3(d)(7), Ex. 1	217
1.704-3(d)(7), Ex. 2	215
1.704-3(e)(1)	195
1.704-3(e)(1)(i)	224
1.704-3(e)(1)(ii)	224
1.704-3(e)(2)	195; 202
1.704-4(a)(2)	426; 430
1.704-4(a)(5), Ex. 1	426
1.704-4(a)(5), Ex. 2	426
1.704-4(a)(5), Ex. 3	426; 429
1.704-4(c)(1)-(5)	430
1.704-4(c)(4)	485
1.704-4(d)(2)	426; 429
1.704-4(d)(3)	426; 430
1.704-4(d)(4)	426; 430
1.704-4(e)(1)	426; 429
1.704-4(e)(2)	426; 429
1.704-4(f)(1)	430
1.705-1(a)	116
1.705-1(a)(1)	127
1.705-1(a)(3)	128
1.706-1	296
1.706-1(a)	104; 298
1.706-1(b)(1)-(4)	104
1.706-1(b)(3)	110; 111
1.706-1(c)(2)	440
1.706-1(c)(2)(ii)	475
1.706-4	463
1.706-4(a)(3)(iii)	465; 466
1.706-4(a)(3)(viii)	466; 467
1.706-4(a)(4)(vi)	466
1.706-4(b)(1)	468
1.706-4(b)(2)	468
1.706-4(c)(1)	467

TREASURY REGULATIONS—Cont.
Regulation

1.706-4(c)(3)(i)	468
1.706-4(d)(1)	468
1.706-4(e)(1)	465; 468
1.706-4(e)(2)(i)-(xi)	468
1.706-4(e)(3)	469
1.707-1(a)	286; 292; 293; 294; 295; 303
1.707-1(c)	286; 294; 296; 297; 298; 299; 305; 400; 405
1.707-1(c)(1), Ex. 1	299
1.707-1(c)(1), Ex. 3	299
1.707-1(c), Ex. 1	80
1.707-1(c), Ex. 2	299; 300; 305; 306
1.707-1(c), Ex. 4	299
1.707-3(a)(1)	412
1.707-3(a)(2)	412; 420
1.707-3(a)(4)	412
1.707-3(b)(1)	412; 419; 420
1.707-3(b)(1)(i)	419
1.707-3(b)(2)	412; 419; 420
1.707-3(c)	424
1.707-3(c)(1)	412; 419; 420
1.707-3(c)(2)	412
1.707-3(d)	412; 419
1.707-3(f), Ex. 1	412; 420
1.707-4(a)(1)	412; 423; 424
1.707-4(a)(2)	412; 424
1.707-4(a)(3)(ii)	424
1.707-4(b)(1)	412; 424
1.707-4(b)(2)(ii)	424
1.707-4(c)	424
1.707-4(d)	412; 424
1.707-5	423
1.707-5(a)(1)	412; 421
1.707-5(a)(2)(i)	412; 421
1.707-5(a)(2)(ii)	412; 421
1.707-5(a)(3)	412; 422
1.707-5(a)(5)	421; 422
1.707-5(a)(5)(ii)	423
1.707-5(a)(6)(i)	412; 421
1.707-5(a)(6)(ii)	412; 421
1.707-5(a)(7)(i)	412; 421
1.707-5(a)(7)(ii)	412; 421
1.707-5(b)	423
1.707-5(b)(1)	412
1.707-5(f), Ex. 2	412; 422
1.707-5(f), Ex. 5	412; 423
1.707-5(f), Ex. 6	412; 423

TABLE OF STATUTES

[References are to sections and footnotes]

TREASURY REGULATIONS—Cont.
Regulation

Regulation	Reference
1.707-5(f), Ex. 10	.412; 423
1.707-6(a)	.424
1.707-7(a)	.412
1.708-1(b)(1)	.479; 481
1.708-1(b)(1)(ii)	.481
1.708-1(b)(2)	.479; 481
1.708-1(b)(3)	.479; 481
1.708-1(b)(3)(ii)	.482
1.708-1(b)(4)	.479; 482
1.708-1(b)(4), Ex. (ii)	.482
1.708-1(b)(5)	.482
1.708-1(c)(2)	.484
1.708-1(c)(3)(i)	.484
1.708-1(c)(3)(ii)	.484
1.708-1(c)(4)	.485
1.708-1(c)(5), Ex. 1	.483
1.708-1(c)(5), Ex. 2	.484
1.708-1(c)(5), Ex. 4	.484
1.708-1(c)(6)	.485
1.708-1(d)(1)	.485
1.708-1(d)(2)	.486
1.708-1(d)(2)(ii)	.486
1.708-1(d)(3)(i)	.486
1.708-1(d)(3)(I)	.486
1.708-1(d)(3)(ii)	.486
1.708-1(d)(4)(i)	.486
1.708-1(d)(4)(iv)	.485
1.708-1(d)(5), Ex. 1	.485
1.708-1(d)(5), Ex. 4	.486
1.708-1(d)(6)	.487
1.709-1(b)(1)	.104
1.709-1(b)(2)	.113
1.709-2(a)	.114
1.709-2(a)-(c)	.104
1.709-2(b)	.114
1.709-2(c)	.113
1.721-1	.57-58; 74; 75
1.721-1(1)(b)	.73
1.721-1(a)	.18; 25
1.721-1(b)	.75; 76
1.721-1(b)(1)	.25; 32; 56; 57; 73; 80
1.721-1(b)(2)	.56; 62; 81
1.722-1	.18; 38; 44; 45; 56
1.723-1	.18
1.731-1	.308
1.731-1(a)(1)	.387
1.731-1(a)(1)(ii)	.336

TREASURY REGULATIONS—Cont.
Regulation

Regulation	Reference
1.731-1(c)(3)	.295
1.731-2(a)	.337
1.731-2(b)(1)	.337; 339
1.731-2(b)(2)	.337
1.731-2(c)(2)	.337; 339
1.731-2(g)	.337
1.731-2(j), Ex. 1	.337
1.731-2(j), Ex. 2	.337
1.731-2(j), Ex. 5	.337
1.732-1(a)-(c)	.308
1.732-1(d)	.438
1.732-1(d)(1)(i)	.453
1.732-1(d)(1)(iii)	.453
1.732-1(d)(1)(iv)	.454
1.732-1(d)(1)(vi), Ex	.454
1.732-1(d)(2)	.454
1.732-1(d)(3)	.454
1.732-1(d)(4)	.454
1.734-1	.344
1.736-1	.390
1.736-1(a)(1)(i)	.391
1.736-1(a)(2)	.392; 393; 394
1.736-1(a)(3)(i)	.393
1.736-1(a)(3)(ii)	.393; 400; 405
1.736-1(a)(4)	.393
1.736-1(a)(6)	.479; 481
1.736-1(b)(2)	.395
1.736-1(b)(3)	.395
1.736-1(b)(4)	.394
1.736-1(b)(5)	.402
1.736-1(b)(5)(i)	.403; 405; 406
1.736-1(b)(5)(ii)	.403; 406
1.736-1(b)(5)(iii)	.403
1.736-1(b)(6)	.402; 404; 405; 406
1.737-1(b)(1)	.426; 432
1.737-1(c)(2)(iv)	.426; 434
1.737-1(e), Ex. 1	.426
1.737-1(e), Ex. 2	.426
1.737-1(e), Ex. 3	.426; 434
1.737-2(a)	.434
1.737-2(b)	.434
1.737-2(b)(1)	.485
1.737-2(c)	.434
1.737-3(a)	.426; 433
1.737-3(b)	.426
1.737-3(b)(1)	.433
1.737-3(c)	.426; 433

TABLE OF STATUTES

[References are to sections and footnotes]

TREASURY REGULATIONS—Cont.
Regulation

1.737-3(c)(2)	433
1.737-3(e), Ex. 1	426
1.737-3(e), Ex. 2	426; 434
1.737-3(e), Ex. 3	426; 433
1.737-4(a)	434
1.741-1(a)	308; 438
1.741-1(b)	438
1.741-1(d)	438
1.741-1(e)	438
1.741-1(f)	438
1.742-1	438; 474; 477
1.743-1(a)-(e)	438
1.743-1(b)	474
1.743-1(d)	453-454
1.743-1(d)(1)	448; 449
1.743-1(d)(2)	448
1.743-1(g)(1)	438
1.743-1(j)(3)	443
1.751-1(a)	438; 443
1.751-1(a)(2)	443; 444
1.751-1(b)	368; 387
1.751-1(b)(1)-(4)(i)	364
1.751-1(b)(1)(ii)	370; 378; 394
1.751-1(b)(1)(iii)	371
1.751-1(b)(2)	372; 373
1.751-1(b)(2)(ii)	373
1.751-1(b)(2)(iv)(5)	377
1.751-1(b)(3)	372
1.751-1(b)(3)(ii)	373; 377
1.751-1(b)(4)	477
1.751-1(b)(4)(i)	379
1.751-1(b)(4)(ii)	379; 394
1.751-1(c)	442; 458
1.751-1(c)(1)	364
1.751-1(c)(1)-(4)(i)	438
1.751-1(c)(1)(iii)	438
1.751-1(c)(1)(iv)	438
1.751-1(c)(2)	364
1.751-1(c)(3)	462
1.751-1(d)	364; 438
1.751-1(d)(1)	370
1.751-1(d)(2)(ii)	369; 380; 443
1.751-1(e)	364; 438
1.751-1(g), Ex. 1	438
1.751-1(g), Ex. 1(d)	373
1.751-1(g), Ex. 1(e)(2)	374
1.751-1(g), Ex. 2	364; 368

TREASURY REGULATIONS—Cont.
Regulation

1.751-1(g), Ex. 2(b)	370
1.751-1(g), Ex. 2(c)	372
1.751-1(g), Ex. 2(d)(1)	372
1.751-1(g), Ex. 3	364; 368
1.751-1(g), Ex. 4(c)	372
1.752-1	261
1.752-1(a)(1)	38; 43; 90; 266
1.752-1(a)(2)	38; 49; 274
1.752-1(a)(4)	265
1.752-1(a)(4)(i)	265
1.752-1(b)	38
1.752-1(c)	38; 256
1.752-1(d)	256
1.752-1(d)(1)	38
1.752-1(e)	38; 41; 263
1.752-1(f)	38; 43; 308; 320; 321; 485
1.752-1(g), Ex. 1	38; 43
1.752-1(g), Ex. 2	485
1.752-2	266; 274
1.752-2(a)	38; 43; 261; 267
1.752-2(b)	38; 261
1.752-2(b)(1)	43; 90; 267
1.752-2(b)(1)(ii)	267
1.752-2(b)(2)	267
1.752-2(b)(3)	266; 272
1.752-2(b)(3)(i)	90
1.752-2(b)(3)(iii)	43; 272
1.752-2(b)(6)	43; 269; 273
1.752-2(d)(2)	267
1.752-2(f), Exs. 1-4	261
1.752-2(h)	261
1.752-2(h)(1)	267
1.752-2(h)(2)	267
1.752-3	281; 492
1.752-3(a)	38; 242; 244; 260; 261; 274
1.752-3(a)(1)	274; 275; 281; 282; 284
1.752-3(a)(2)	49; 275; 280; 282; 283; 284
1.752-3(a)(3)	49; 50; 275; 278; 283; 284
1.752-3(c), Ex. 1	261
1.752-3(c), Ex. 2	261
1.753-1	474
1.754-1(a)	344
1.754-1(b)(1)	344; 447
1.754-1(b)(3)	344
1.754-1(c)	344; 447
1.755-1(a)	350
1.755-1(a)(1)	344; 438; 450

TREASURY REGULATIONS—Cont.
Regulation

Regulation	Reference
1.755-1(a)(3)	344; 438
1.755-1(a)(4)(i)(A)	438
1.755-1(b)	350
1.755-1(b)(1)-(3)	438
1.755-1(b)(1)(i)	450
1.755-1(b)(2)(i)	450
1.755-1(b)(3)	450
1.755-1(b)(4)(i)	477; 478
1.755-1(b)(4)(I)	474
1.755-1(c)	344
1.755-1(c)(1)	350; 352; 400
1.755-1(c)(1)(ii)	353; 367; 375
1.755-1(c)(2)	401
1.755-1(c)(2)(i)	353
1.755-1(c)(2)(ii)	353; 355
1.755-1(c)(3)	353
1.755-1(c)(4)	359
1.761-1(a)	2
1.761-1(b)	2
1.761-1(c)	153
1.761-1(d)	402
1.1001-1(a)	19
1.1001-2(a)	38; 40
1.1001-2(a)(1)	51; 234
1.1001-2(a)(4)(i)	234
1.1001-2(b)	254
1.1223-3	27
1.1223-3(b)(1)	18
1.1223-3(f), Ex. 1	27; 197
1.1245-6(a)	24
15a.453-1(b)(2)(iv)	44
15a.453-1(b)(3)(i)	44
301.7701-1(a)(1)	14
301.7701-1(a)(2)	14
301.7701-1(a)(4)	14
301.7701-1(b)	15
301.7701-1(b)(2)	15; 16
301.7701-2(a)	15
301.7701-2(b)	15
301.7701-2(b)(1)	15; 16
301.7701-2(b)(2)	15
301.7701-2(b)(3)	16
301.7701-2(b)(3)-(8)	15
301.7701-2(b)(4)	16
301.7701-2(b)(5)	16
301.7701-2(b)(6)	16
301.7701-2(b)(7)	16

TREASURY REGULATIONS—Cont.
Regulation

Regulation	Reference
301.7701-2(b)(8)	16
301.7701-2(c)(1)	2
301.7701-3	15
301.7701-3(a)	15; 16; 68
301.7701-3(b)	15
301.7701-3(c)(1)(iii)	15
301.7701-3(c)(2)(i)	15
301.7701-3(f)(2)	68
301.7701-4	15

Proposed Regulations

Regulation	Reference
1.83-3(e)	56
1.83-3(l)	56; 67; 84; 98; 99
1.83-3(l)(1)	67
1.83-3(l)(1)(ii)	67
1.83-3(l)(1)(iii)	67
1.168-4(d)(5)	22
1.465-66	144
1.465-66(b)	145
1.469-5(a)(3)	146
1.704-1(b)(2)(iv)(f)	84; 224
1.704-3(a)(9)	485
1.704-3(f)(1)-(3)(ii)	195
1.704-3(f)(1)(i)	221
1.704-3(f)(1)(ii)	221
1.704-3(f)(2)(i)	221
1.704-3(f)(2)(iii)	221
1.704-3(f)(3)(ii)	221
1.704-3(f)(3)(ii)(D)(2)	223
1.704-3(f)(3)(iii)(a)	445
1.704-3(g)	224
1.704-4(c)(4)	485
1.706-2	463
1.706-2(a)(2)(iii)	471
1.706-2(a)(2)(iv)	471
1.706-2(a)(2)(v)	471
1.706-2(b), Ex. 1	472
1.706-2(b), Ex. 2	472
1.706-2(c)	472
1.707-1(c), Ex. 2	286
1.707-2(b)(2)	412
1.707-2(b)(2)(i)	417
1.707-2(c)	412; 415
1.707-2(c)(1)	415
1.707-2(c)(1)(i)-(v)	416
1.707-2(c)(2)-(6)	416
1.707-2(d)	412
1.707-2(d), Ex. 1	414

TABLE OF STATUTES

TS-15

[References are to sections and footnotes]

TREASURY REGULATIONS—Cont.
Regulation

1.721-1(b)	.56; 69; 70; 98
1.721-1(b)(1)	69; 84; 98; 99
1.721-1(b)(2)	.56
1.721-2	.69
1.734-1(a)(1)	.344
1.734-1(a)(2)(i)	.344
1.734-1(b)(2)(i)	.344
1.734-1(b)(2)(ii), Ex. 3	.344
1.737-2(b)	.485
1.743-1	.438
1.751-1(a)(1)	.438
1.751-1(a)(2)	.382; 438; 443; 444
1.751-1(b)(1)-(3)	.364
1.751-1(b)(2)	.382; 383
1.751-1(b)(2)(i)	.384
1.751-1(b)(2)(ii)	.381; 384
1.751-1(b)(2)(iii)	.384
1.751-1(b)(2)(iv)	.382; 383
1.751-1(b)(3)	.383
1.751-1(b)(3)(i)	.383; 384
1.751-1(b)(3)(iii)	.383
1.751-1(b)(4)	.382
1.751-1(f)	.364; 382; 383
1.751-1(g)	.383
1.751-1(g), Ex. 1	.364

TREASURY REGULATIONS—Cont.
Regulation

1.751-1(g), Ex. 2	.364
1.751-1(g), Ex. 3	.383
1.751-1(g), Ex. 4	.364
1.761-1(b)	.56; 64

Temporary Regulations

1.469-2T(d)(6)	.143
1.469-5T(a)	.145
1.469-5T(e)(2)	.146

UNIFORM PARTNERSHIP ACT (1997)
Section

306(a)	.43; 268; 272
401(b)	.268; 272

UNITED STATES CODE (U.S.C.)
Title:

12:1215*l*(b)	.255
12:1215*l*(d)(4)	.255
15:80b-5	.302
26:702	.76
Tit. 26	.2

INDEX

[References are to sections.]

A

ALLOCATIONS
§743 adjustments . . . 20A[IV][B][2][c]
Contributed property (See CONTRIBUTED PROPERTY, subhead: "Generally reasonable" allocation methods)
Income and deductions (See INCOME AND DEDUCTIONS, ALLOCATION OF)
Liabilities, allocation of recourse and nonrecourse (See LIABILITIES, ALLOCATION OF RECOURSE AND NONRECOURSE)
Nonrecourse deductions (See NONRECOURSE DEDUCTIONS, ALLOCATION OF)
Passed-through losses of different character
 . . . 8[IV][C]
Recourse debt, contributed property encumbered by
 . . . 3[IV][B][1]
Varying interests rule (See VARYING INTERESTS RULE)

ANTI-ABUSE REGULATIONS
Generally . . . 21[I]-[IV]

B

BALANCE SHEETS
Generally . . . 5[IV][A]; 5[IV][D]
Impact of partnership operations on . . . 5[IV][B]

C

CAPITAL ACCOUNTS
Generally . . . 5[IV][C]; 5[IV][D]
"Booking-up" and "booking down" of
 . . . 10[IV][F]
Deficit restoration obligations . . . 11[IV][C][7]
Distributions impact on . . . 14A[IV][A][2][c]
Pass-through of income, gain, loss, deduction and credit impact on . . . 7[IV][C]
§704(d) limitation on deduction of passed-through losses . . . 8[IV][D]

CLASSIFICATION OF PARTNERSHIPS
Choice of entities, benefits of
 General partnership . . . 1[B][1]
 Limited liability companies . . . 1[B][1]
 Limited partnership . . . 1[B][1]
 Partnership
  Generally . . . 1[B][2]
  Deductibility of losses . . . 1[B][2][d]
  Equity interests, classes of . . . 1[B][2][a]
  Liquidating distributions . . . 1[B][2][g]
  Nonliquidating distributions, treatment of
   . . . 1[B][2][f]
  Nonrecognition of gain and loss on contributions of property . . . 1[B][2][b]

CLASSIFICATION OF PARTNERSHIPS—Cont.
Choice of entities, benefits of—Cont.
 Partnership—Cont.
  Owners, number and character of
   . . . 1[B][2][a]
  Rates, tax . . . 1[B][2][e]
  Single level of tax . . . 1[B][2][c]
Definitions of partnership and partner . . . 1[A]
Unincorporated business entities
 Check-the-box regulations . . . 1[C][2]
 History . . . 1[C][1]

CONTRIBUTED PROPERTY
Generally . . . 10[IV][G]
"Booking-up" and "booking down" of capital accounts . . . 10[IV][F]
Enactment of §704(c)(1)(A) . . . 10[IV][B]
"Generally reasonable" allocation methods
 Curative allocations with traditional methods
  . . . 10[IV][C][2]
 Remedial allocations method . . . 10[IV][C][3]
 Traditional method
  Generally . . . 10[IV][C][1]
  Depreciable §704(c) property, allocation of deductions of . . . 10[IV][C][1][b]
  Sale of depreciable property, allocation of gain or loss on . . . 10[IV][C][1][c]
  Sale of nondepreciable §704(c) property, allocation of gain or loss on
   . . . 10[IV][C][1][a]
Pre-1984 law . . . 10[IV][A]
Revaluation of property . . . 10[IV][F]
"Small disparities," exception for . . . 10[IV][E]
Special rule when property has built-in loss
 . . . 10[IV][D]

D

DEATH OF PARTNER
Basis and income interaction . . . 20C[IV][B]
Inside basis adjustments . . . 20C[IV][C]
Taxable year, closing of partnership
 . . . 20C[IV][A]

DISGUISED PAYMENTS FOR SERVICES
Generally . . . 18[IV][A]

DISGUISED SALES
Cash flow distributions . . . 18[IV][B][6]
Debt-financed distribution . . . 18[IV][B][5]
Definition . . . 18[IV][B][1]
Guaranteed payments . . . 18[IV][B][6]
Liabilities . . . 18[IV][B][4]
Partnership-to-partner sales . . . 18[IV][B][6]
Preferred returns . . . 18[IV][B][6]
Reimbursement for preformation expenses
 . . . 18[IV][B][6]
Tax consequence . . . 18[IV][B][3]
Two-year presumption . . . 18[IV][B][2]

I-1

DISTRIBUTIONS

Disproportionate distributions under §751(b)
    Application of section . . . 16[IV][B]
    Exceptions . . . 16[IV][C]
    Imperfect remedy . . . 16[IV][D]
    Limitations . . . 16[IV][C]
    Proposed regulations . . . 16[IV][E]
    Purpose of section . . . 16[IV][A]
Liquidating
    Generally . . . 14A[IV][C]
    Basis of assets, potential increase or decrease in . . . 14A[IV][B][2]
    Loss, recognition of . . . 14A[IV][B][1]
Marketable securities . . . 14B[IV][A][1]
Nonliquidating
    Basis of distributed property . . . 14A[IV][A][2][a]
    Character of gain or loss on subsequent sale . . . 14A[IV][A][2][e]
    Encumbered assets . . . 14A[IV][A][3]
    Holding period . . . 14A[IV][A][2][d]
    Impacts
        Capital accounts . . . 14A[IV][A][2][c]
        Distributee's outside basis . . . 14A[IV][A][2][b]
    Limitation . . . 14A[IV][A][4]
    Money, recognition of gain on distributions of . . . 14A[IV][A][2][f]
    Nonrecognition rule of §731 . . . 14A[IV][A][1]
Retiring partner's interests, terminating (See RETIRING PARTNER'S INTEREST, TERMINATING)
§704(c) property
    Contributing partner, distributions to . . . 19[IV][C]
    Distributions of . . . 19[IV][B]
    Mixing bowl transactions . . . 19[IV][A]
    Same transaction, application of §737 to . . . 19[IV][D]

E

ENCUMBERED PROPERTY

Contribution of
    Accounts payable, treatment of . . . 3[IV][E]
    Acquisition of property, debt related to . . . 3[IV][A]
    Distribution of property, debt related to . . . 3[IV][A]
    Future considerations . . . 3[IV][F]
    Nonrecourse liabilities
        Excess of basis . . . 3[IV][D]
        Not in excess of basis . . . 3[IV][C]
    Recourse debt, contributed property encumbered by
        Allocation of recourse liabilities . . . 3[IV][B][1]
        Treatment of nonrecourse liabilities . . . 3[IV][B][2]
Distribution of . . . 14A[IV][A][3]
Transferee in sale or exchange of interest, tax consequences to . . . 20A[IV][B][2][e]

F

FORMATION EXPENSES

Generally . . . 6[IV][B]
Organizational expenses . . . 6[IV][B][1]
Syndication expenses . . . 6[IV][B][2]

G

GUARANTEED PAYMENTS

Disguised sales . . . 18[IV][B][6]
Retiring partner's interest, tax significance of terminating . . . 17[IV][B][1]
Tax treatment of transactions between partners and partnerships (See TAX TREATMENT OF TRANSACTIONS BETWEEN PARTNERS AND PARTNERSHIPS, subhead: Guaranteed payments)

H

HOLDING PERIODS

Distribution . . . 14A[IV][A][2][d]
Nonrecognition of gain or loss . . . 2[IV][F]

I

INCOME AND DEDUCTIONS, ALLOCATION OF

Generally . . . 9[IV][D]
History . . . 9[IV][A]
1976 Reform Act . . . 9[IV][B]
§704(b) regulations
    Partner's-Interest-in-the-Partnership test . . . 9[IV][C][2]
    Substantial Economic Effect test (See subhead: Substantial Economic Effect test)
    Substantiality test (See subhead: Substantiality test)
Substantial Economic Effect test
    Codification of . . . 9[IV][B]
    Economic effect test
        Alternative test . . . 9[IV][C][1][a][ii]
        Economic equivalence test . . . 9[IV][C][1][a][iii]
        Primary test . . . 9[IV][C][1][a][i]
Substantiality test
    After-tax economic consequences, allocations with . . . 9[IV][C][1][b][iii]
    Shifting allocations . . . 9[IV][C][1][b][i]
    Transitory allocations . . . 9[IV][C][1][b][ii]

INSIDE BASIS ADJUSTMENTS

Anti-abuse rules, partnership . . . 15[IV][F]
Death of partner . . . 20C[IV][C]
Disparities created by distributions . . . 15[IV][A]
Mandatory basis adjustment . . . 15[IV][E]
§734(b) adjustment
    Generally . . . 15[IV][B]
    Application to examples . . . 15[IV][C]; 15[IV][D]
§753 election . . . 15[IV][B]

[References are to sections.]

INSIDE BASIS ADJUSTMENTS—Cont.
Substantial basis reduction rule . . . 15[IV][E]

L

LIABILITIES, ALLOCATION OF RECOURSE AND NONRECOURSE
Allocations
    Nonrecourse liabilities . . . 12[IV][D]
    Recourse liabilities . . . 12[IV][C]
Definition of liability . . . 12[IV][B]
History . . . 12[IV][A]

M

MARKETABLE SECURITIES
Distributions . . . 14B[IV][A][1]

N

NONRECOGNITION OF GAIN OR LOSS
Generally . . . 2[IV][A]; 2[IV][H]
Basis
    Inside, partner's . . . 2[IV][B]
    Outside, partner's . . . 2[IV][B]
Character of gain or loss on distribution of contributed property . . . 2[IV][G]
Holding periods . . . 2[IV][F]
Property . . . 2[IV][E]
Scope of nonrecognition under section 721
    Section 721 and section 435B property . . . 2[IV][D][2]
    Section 721 and section 1245 property . . . 2[IV][D][1]
United States v. Stafford . . . 2[IV][H]

NONRECOURSE DEDUCTIONS, ALLOCATION OF
Generally . . . 11[IV][A]
Definitions
    Capital account deficit restoration obligations . . . 11[IV][C][7]
    Decrease in partnership minimum gain . . . 11[IV][C][5]
    Increase in partnership minimum gain . . . 11[IV][C][3]
    Measure of nonrecourse deductions, partnership minimum gain as . . . 11[IV][C][4]
    Net decrease in partnership minimum gain, partner's share of . . . 11[IV][C][8]
    Nonrecourse deductions . . . 11[IV][C][1]
    Partnership minimum gain . . . 11[IV][C][2]
    Partner's share of partnership minimum gain . . . 11[IV][C][6]
Safe harbor rules
    Generally . . . 11[IV][B]
    Minimum gain chargeback requirement . . . 11[IV][D][1]
    Reasonable consistency requirement . . . 11[IV][D][2]

O

OUTSIDE BASIS
Distribution of nonliquidating assets . . . 14A[IV][A][2][b]
Nonrecogntion of gain or loss . . . 2[IV][B]
§704(d) limitation on deduction of passed-through losses . . . 8[IV][A]

P

PASS-THROUGH OF INCOME, GAIN, LOSS, DEDUCTION AND CREDIT
Generally . . . 7[IV][E]
Basis, impact on partner's . . . 7[IV][C]
Capital accounts, impact on . . . 7[IV][C]
Distributive share
    Generally . . . 7[IV][A]
    Accounting for partner's . . . 7[IV][B]
Limitations on deduction of losses (See §704(d) LIMITATION ON DEDUCTION OF PASSED-THROUGH LOSSES)

R

RETIRING PARTNER'S INTEREST, TERMINATING
Generally . . . 17[IV][F]
Current law, application of §736 under . . . 17[IV][D]
1993 amendments to §736 and §751(c) . . . 17[IV][C]
Section 736 classification . . . 17[IV][A]
Series of distributions, liquidating interest by . . . 17[IV][E]
Tax significance
    Application of §751(b) . . . 17[IV][B][4]
    Distributions . . . 17[IV][B][3]
    Distributive share . . . 17[IV][B][2]
    Guaranteed payments . . . 17[IV][B][1]
    Impact on partnership, payments' . . . 17[IV][B][5]

S

SALE OR EXCHANGE OF INTEREST
Generally . . . 20A[IV][C]
Transferee, tax consequences to
    Generally . . . 20A[IV][B][1]
    §754 and basis adjustment under §743
        Adjustments to basis . . . 20A[IV][B][2][b]
        Allocation of §743 adjustments . . . 20A[IV][B][2][c]
        Encumbered property . . . 20A[IV][B][2][e]
        Partnership holding §704(c) property . . . 20A[IV][B][2][d]
        §754 election . . . 20A[IV][B][2][a]
Transferor, tax consequences to
    Generally . . . 20A[IV][A]
    Aggregate approach . . . 20A[IV][A][1][b]

[References are to sections.]

SALE OR EXCHANGE OF INTEREST—Cont.
Transferor, tax consequences to—Cont.
   Application of section 751(a)
     . . . 20A[IV][A][2]
   Capital gain, look-through rules with respect to
     . . . 20A[IV][A][3]
   Entity approach . . . 20A[IV][A][1][a]

SERVICES IN EXCHANGE FOR PARTNERSHIP INTERESTS, CONTRIBUTION OF
Generally . . . 4[IV][D]
Capital interest for services . . . 4[IV][A]
Profits interest for services . . . 4[IV][B]
2005 proposed regulations relating to compensatory transfers . . . 4[IV][C]

§704(d) LIMITATION ON DEDUCTION OF PASSED-THROUGH LOSSES
Adjusted outside basis, determination of
   . . . 8[IV][A]
Allocation among losses of different character
   . . . 8[IV][C]
Beneficiary of carryover of disallowed loss
   . . . 8[IV][E]
Capital accounts, impact on . . . 8[IV][D]
Excess of limitation, treatment of losses in
   . . . 8[IV][B]

T

TAXABLE YEAR
Generally . . . 6[IV][A]; 6[IV][A][2]
Computation purposes, partnership as entity for tax
   . . . 6[IV][A][1]
Income includible by partners, year in which
   . . . 6[IV][A][2]

TAX TREATMENT OF TRANSACTIONS BETWEEN PARTNERS AND PARTNERSHIPS
Generally . . . 13[IV][C]
Capacity as partner, acting in . . . 13[IV][B][1]
Distributive share . . . 13[IV][B][4]
Guaranteed payments
   Capitalization of . . . 13[IV][B][3][d]
   "Determined without reference to income of partnership" . . . 13[IV][B][3][c]
   Fixed amount . . . 13[IV][B][3][e]

TAX TREATMENT OF TRANSACTIONS BETWEEN PARTNERS AND PARTNERSHIPS—Cont.
Guaranteed payments—Cont.
   Minimum amount . . . 13[IV][B][3][f]
   Payment . . . 13[IV][B][3][b]
   Tax consequences of . . . 13[IV][B][3][a]
   Transfer of property other than cash in satisfaction of . . . 13[IV][B][3][g]
Nonpartner capacity, transactions engaged by partner in . . . 13[IV][B][2]
Prior to Internal Revenue Code of 1954, tax treatment . . . 13[IV][A]

TERMINATION OF PARTNERSHIP
Cessation of business . . . 20D[IV][A]
Consequences under §708(b)(1) . . . 20D[IV][B]; 20D[IV][D]
Retiring partner (See RETIRING PARTNER'S INTEREST, TERMINATING)
Sale or exchange of 50-percent of interests within 12 months . . . 20D[IV][C]

TRANSACTIONS BETWEEN PARTNERS AND PARTNERSHIPS
Tax treatment (See TAX TREATMENT OF TRANSACTIONS BETWEEN PARTNERS AND PARTNERSHIPS)

TRANSFERS OF INTERESTS
Death of partner (See DEATH OF PARTNER)
Sale or exchange of partnership interest (See SALE OR EXCHANGE OF INTEREST)
Termination of partnership (See TERMINATION OF PARTNERSHIP)
Varying interests rule (See VARYING INTERESTS RULE)

V

VARYING INTERESTS RULE
Allocation of distributive shares . . . 20B[IV][B]
Cash basis items . . . 20B[IV][F]
Exceptions to rule . . . 20B[IV][C]
Extraordinary items . . . 20B[IV][D]
General rule . . . 20B[IV][A]
Ten-step allocation process . . . 20B[IV][E]